Foreword

This book has been designed to bring together the major elements of environmental law, policy and management for those who need ready access to this wide and diverse subject. It is intended to be a reference book for environmental managers and lawyers and the ever increasing number of professionals who are discovering – sometimes to their surprise – that environmental matters are relevant to their work.

The need for this book arises from the transformation in the status of environmental issues over the last decade. Driven by increasing public concern about pollution, destruction of valuable habitats, etc., two developments have taken place. The first has been the proliferation of legislation. In Europe, the EC has enacted some 300 environmental *Directives* and *Regulations* and a number of the Member States have been in the forefront of legislative innovation.

This is, however, a worldwide phenomenon, not least because some of the most intractable environmental threats can only be tackled effectively on a truly global scale and many environmental and conservation measures are the result of worldwide, collective action.

Similarly where problems are more local – for example, the issue of contaminated land – individual governments are reacting to public concern by enacting strict new laws. The point has been reached in many developed countries where the main focus of law makers is beginning to shift from developing tighter controls to ensuring more effective enforcement and to developing new, usually financial, mechanisms for achieving environmental improvement.

The second development has been outside the legal arena. Increasingly members of the public have sought to influence those whose activities might harm the environment to improve their performance. They have done so directly – by joining one or more of the many campaigning pressure groups – and indirectly by preferring products and services which are (or which claim to be) 'environmentally friendly'.

This second development has had a profound effect on many businesses. Companies have responded in a variety of ways – developing new products and methodologies, emphasising their 'green' credentials in their advertising and imposing environmental standards on their own suppliers.

In some cases legislation has reinforced these developments. The new EC eco-labelling law for consumer products and environmental auditing law for industrial sites are good examples. They have been adopted simply because the practices concerned have become so common that legislation has been considered necessary to ensure that a prescribed level of performance is achieved.

The effect of all these developments has been to bring environmental matters to the forefront of commercial decision making. The company secretary, the marketing manager, the production director, the transportation manager, the personnel director, the finance director, etc. are all affected by environmental issues relevant to their company. Their advisers – bankers, investment and insurance advisers, accountants, lawyers, public relations and advertising consultants, etc. – also need to be abreast of the issues.

The aim of this book is to be a useful source of information for all who need to know about environmental matters. In dealing with the environment, nothing is simple and the complexity of the subject is already reflected in the law, the substance of which has become immensely difficult and sophisticated. This book is not intended to be a compendium in which the industrial or commercial manager can find comprehensive advice on all imaginable problems,

Foreword

but rather as a volume to alert the careful and efficient manager to the nature and scale of the issues which may impact on the day-to-day operation of his plant and ultimately on the balance sheet. It is unusual to find both legal and non-legal aspects dealt with in one volume. We hope that by presenting the subject in this way a clear appreciation of the complexity and breadth of the subject will be provided.

Freshfields
June 1993

Contents

Table of Cases

Table of Cases

Table of Cases

Cases from Other Jurisdictions

Table of UK Statutes

Table of UK Statutes

Table of Statutory Instruments

Table of Statutory Instruments

Table of Statutory Instruments

Table of Statutory Instruments

Table of Statutory Instruments

Table of Statutory Instruments

Table of Statutory Instruments

Table of EC Secondary Legislation and Treaties

Table of EC Secondary Legislation and Treaties

Table of International Conventions

Table of International Conventions

1 Introduction

1.1 AIMS AND OBJECTIVES OF THIS BOOK

This book is designed to serve the needs of the wide variety of people – lawyers, managers or other professionals – who now find that environmental matters have become an important part of their responsibilities.

In particular it is intended for use by:

— lawyers in private practice advising corporate clients; lawyers in local authority employment and other areas of the public sector; and by 'in-house' lawyers in industry and business;

— managers in industry: some with specific environmental responsibilities; others with responsibilities for production, transportation, marketing, finance or personnel – all of whom will have been discovering over just the last few years that developments in environmental law and policy are having a marked impact on the performance of their particular corporate functions;

— professionals who advise industry or who provide services to industry: bankers, investment and insurance advisers, accountants, insolvency practitioners, receivers and administrators, scientific and other technical environmental consultants, public relations and advertising consultants. All these also should now be alert to the impact on their activities of the complex and fast-moving developments in environmental law and policy.

To meet the everyday needs of this diverse variety of persons this book seeks:

— to bring together, in a single volume of reasonably manageable size, the major elements of environmental law and environmental policy; and

— to explain the significance of these matters, and the opportunities they may present, in terms of best practice in environmental management.

1.2 DIVERSITY AND COMPLEXITY

This is an ambitious task. Like the environment itself nothing in environmental law is simple. The subject may, in many respects, be still quite young but it has already acquired a volume and degree of complexity that has made it very much a matter for the specialist.

1.3 The international and EC dimensions

A particular aspect of this complexity (and volume) is the significance of legal and policy developments occurring outside the United Kingdom: at international and at EC level. On any environmental issue a wide variety of different sources of law may need first to be located and then interpreted and applied. These may include treaties, protocols, *EC Regulations* and *Directives*, domestic Acts of Parliament, and statutory instruments: to say nothing of the significance of that vast array of 'quasi-law' contained in ministerial circulars and statements, central Government policy documents, codes of practice and so on.

1.4 Identification of future trends

A further complicating factor is that significant aspects of the law are still in the process of being brought into operation, and so it may be necessary for advice to be given, and for action to be taken, upon both a view as to the law as it currently stands and also of the law as it is expected shortly (or less shortly!) to be.

And this brings us on to a further important matter. Commercial decisions taken today need to be imbued with some vision as to the state and nature of environmental law and policy which may prevail in years to come. In other words managers should seek from their advisers some reasonably informed speculation as regards future operating conditions in terms of the impact of environmental law and policy.

In this matter some image may be discerned in the crystal ball by looking at international policy developments. Treaty requirements, in the course of time, filter down into national legal provisions; and EC Environmental Action programmes periodically foreshadow and set the agenda for European legislation, with subsequent impacts on Member States. Closer to home, several UK Government departments (e.g. DoE, DTI, MAFF), and each of the environmental agencies (e.g. HMIP, the National Rivers Authority) will at any one time be involved in the ongoing process of policy development on environmental matters. A process likely to be marked by the issuing of green papers, draft regulations, draft codes of practice: hinting at the shape of things to come, and also giving some potentially valuable opportunity for constructive input from those most likely to be affected. It is on this mass of documents that attention must focus when a vision of the immediate and longer term future is sought.

1.5 DEVELOPMENT OF ENVIRONMENTAL LAW AND ENVIRONMENTAL MANAGEMENT

The need for this book arises from, and reflects, the transformation in the status of environmental issues over the last decade or so. In this matter, as in so many, the United Kingdom, along with Western Europe generally, is following in the wake of experience in North America. We should be alert to that experience and be anxious to learn lessons from it: many positive, but some more cautionary.

The development in North America during the 1960s of wide-spread public concern about 'the environment' served first of all to put such issues onto the political and the legislative agendas; and then, quite rapidly, onto the corporate management agenda. Laws became stricter, and those stricter laws became more stringently enforced. Penalties and financial liabilities which had formerly been ignored as insignificant in comparison with the scale of corporate activity began to become a matter of commercial concern. In addition, industrial producers soon became aware of the phenomenon of environmental consumerism; and this added to the impetus for companies to address environmental issues as a management priority. A poor corporate image, flowing from a 'dirty' product being produced in a 'dirty' way, might well give away a competitive advantage in the market to a competitor able to foster an image more environmentally benign. And the public was not to be taken as gullible. Public relations exercises might back-fire badly unless the image presented reflected the true position, or at any rate reflected sterling and transparent attempts to make improvements in environmental performance (e.g. by setting ambitious targets for emission reductions, energy efficiency, natural resource utilisation etc.).

What North America experienced in the late 1970s and early 1980s has become a part of the European corporate and legal experience of the late 1980s and the 1990s. The same public concern became manifest following graphically publicised pollution accidents, such as the *Amoco Cadiz* oil spillage and the *Sandoz-Basel* contamination of the Rhine. Concern also grew about more everyday and ongoing industrial and vehicular pollution, resulting in deterioration in air and water quality; and also as regards the impact of development of many kinds (industrial, commercial and residential) on wildlife habitats and other places prized for their landscape or recreational value.

1.6   EC environmental policy

Just as had occurred in North America, this heightening of public concern brought the matter to the political stage. Following in the wake of a UN Conference on the Human Environment in Stockholm in 1972 (the oft-forgotten precursor to the Rio Summit of 1992) the EC Council of Ministers determined to bring environmental issues fully onto the EC agenda. The Council declared that the Community should no longer concern itself exclusively with the attainment within the Community of material wealth; it acknowledged formally that the standard of living of citizens within the Community is dependent upon, and should be measured in relation to, non-material factors as well as material ones. Environmental quality should, therefore, rank as a matter deserving EC attention: both as an objective in its own right, and as a factor to moderate, and balance against, the attainment of other EC objectives.

The EC Council called upon the EC Commission to formulate proposals for a coherent and distinctive EC environmental policy: and the Commission's First Environmental Action Programme followed shortly. Such Programmes usually cover a period of five years, although for the Fifth Action Programme, agreed in 1992, the Commission has not been able to resist the temptation of setting an agenda to the end of the millenium. The Programmes have consisted of general statements of the governing principles which underlie Community law and policy, supported by a description of the kinds of proposals which the Commission proposes should be prepared and brought forward into the Community legislative process.

1.7   EC environmental principles

Some of these general principles are worth mentioning at this early stage: for example, the 'polluter pays' principle; the 'preventive' principle; the 'precautionary' principle. Each of these has had significant effects on the substance of Community law. The 'polluter pays' idea is at the heart of the recent European Commission consultative paper on environmental liability (see 3 ENVIRONMENTAL LITIGATION); the preventive principle is the foundation behind the Community's requirements of Environmental Assessment of major development projects (see 7 ENVIRONMENTAL ASSESSMENT and 21 PLANNING AND THE ENVIRONMENT); and the precautionary approach may explain (and justify) some of the water and air quality standards to be found in EC environmental quality directives (see 4 ATMOSPHERIC POLLUTION and 29 WATER ENVIRONMENT).

In more recent times these traditional principles have been supplemented by the acknowledgement that environmental considerations should be integrated into all aspects of community policy: environmental policy is not something which can be formulated and implemented separately from policy on agriculture, transport, energy etc. Further, the Community has formally recognised that the kind of development to which the Community should aspire is that which is of a 'sustainable' nature. Indeed, the amendments agreed at Maastricht will, when operative, incorporate this approach into its revised statement of the principal goals of Community policy.

1.8   The influence of the European Community

With this clear political mandate to act (the *legal* base for EC environmental action was less assured until the *Single European Act* of 1986), coupled with a groundswell of public support (on what other issues does the general public seem so strongly to support Community policy?), the Commission has been active in bringing forward and securing agreement to what is now a very large number of measures. Practically every chapter of this book testifies to the influence of the Community – air quality standards, atmospheric emissions and the BATNEEC principle (see 4 ATMOSPHERIC POLLUTION and 16 INTEGRATED POLLUTION CONTROL); water quality standards (drinking water, bathing waters, groundwater etc.) (see 29 WATER ENVIRONMENT); provisions relating to waste and hazardous substances (see 5 CONTROL OF DANGEROUS SUBSTANCES and 28 WASTE MANAGEMENT); assessment of environmental impact (see 7 ENVIRONMENTAL ASSESSMENT and 21 PLANNING AND THE ENVIRONMENT); environmental auditing (see 8 ENVIRONMENTAL AUDITS); access to environmental information (see 12 ENVIRON-MENTAL INFORMATION). It is not far from the mark to say that UK Government action on environmental matters consists principally of measures to implement *Directives* agreed at EC level. In some instances such *Directives* may have been strongly supported, perhaps even initiated, by the UK. In other contexts acceptance may have been more grudging; and since 1986, with the introduction of majority voting procedures, measures may not have been unanimously agreed at all.

Two important points should be made in connection with this very substantial EC involvement in environmental law and policy. First, by the time the UK Government begins to draft implementing legislation (Acts or statutory instruments) it may be too late for industry and business to do more than lobby on points of relatively minor detail: the substantial obligations will already have been determined at EC level. This means that it is important for sectors of industry and business to keep a keen watch as regards proposals for Community measures and make constructive proposals, at the appropriate juncture, at EC level. The second point is that it seems to be the case that there is, in the Community legislative process, a readiness to accept and incorporate well presented and well argued suggestions for improvements to legislative proposals. For all the talk of the 'democratic deficit' within the Community there does appear to be a genuine willingness to engage in wide-ranging consultative exercises in order to seek to produce improvements both as to matters of general approach and as to matters of detail.

2   The Players

2.1   The purpose of this chapter is to introduce in outline the more important of the many international, national and local departments, agencies and organisations which play a role in the formation, implementation or enforcement of environmental law in the United Kingdom. At best, it can only be the most cursory of descriptions, as the interactions between the bodies introduced in this chapter can be both multi-faceted and complicated. Furthermore, there are many organs of government, at all levels, which have an incidental or peripheral involvement with environmental issues. Such involvement, in any particular case, may be far from trivial, but, as it does not reflect the principal role of the organisation in question, it is not possible to devote space to it in this chapter. An example of such an organisation is a Sea Fisheries Committee, whose powers to control pollution of waters in a manner which is detrimental to the species of fish for which that committee is responsible under the fisheries legislation may be of real importance in a particular case, but whose main functions concern the management and protection of fishery resources rather than environmental protection for its own sake.

2.2   In addition, it is clearly established Government policy that responsibility for the environment, although centred in the Department of the Environment, is an integral part of the functions of all other Ministries, who are under a duty to ensure that their policies and programmes have due regard for environmental qualities. The Environment White Paper, *This Common Inheritance*, published in 1990, announced a new requirement that each Department should nominate a 'green' Minister who would be responsible for considering the environmental implications of that Department's activities and for overseeing the implementation in the Department of the policies set out in the White Paper. Departments were also encouraged to reflect in their annual reports the actions which they take in the environmental field.

2.3   This chapter will examine the individual roles of the main Government Departments active in environmental matters, of the national agencies and of local government authorities. Reference will also be made to the role of the European Community institutions.

2.4   It is, of course, true that, in many instances, governmental responsibilities abut and complement one another. In some fields, they appear to overlap. In July 1991 the Government announced that it proposes to bring forward legislation to rationalise implementation and enforcement competences by establishing a new Environment Agency. This would bring together HMIP, the NRA and the waste regulation functions of local authorities. In the regulatory field, therefore, areas of overlap between these bodies should be eliminated.

2.5   **GOVERNMENT DEPARTMENTS**

The Department of the Environment (DoE)

The DoE is the Government Department charged with principal responsibility for environmental legislation and policy. Some other Ministries, however, are active in the field of environmental and natural resource management. Prominent among these are the Department of Trade and Industry, the Department of Transport and the Ministry of Agriculture, Fisheries and Food. In Scotland and Wales, environmental matters are dealt with by the Scottish and Welsh Offices respectively.

2.6 The Players

The DoE is primarily responsible for the promotion of new environmental legislation and for overseeing its implementation. The Secretary of State has an important appellate function in the environmental licensing and enforcement processes, as well as being charged with strategic supervision of the Department's programme. He or she is assisted by Ministers of State, whose titles reflect the extent of their portfolios. These include the Minister of State for the Environment and the Countryside and the Minister of State for Local Government and Planning.

Internally, the Department is divided into a number of Directorates. Of these, the most pertinent for the purposes of this book are the following.

2.6 *The Directorate of Environmental Policy and Analysis*

As its title suggests, this Directorate is responsible for the formulation of policy on environmental issues generally. It is perhaps not so widely appreciated as it should be that the DoE has a significant international role to play, as so much of the UK's environmental legislation is driven by external influences, whether emanating from the European Community or from the wider international sphere. It is this Directorate which provides the interface.

In the national dimension, the Directorate includes amongst its functions the compilation and publication of environmental data in the form of statistics.

2.7 *The Directorate of Pollution Control and Wastes*

The responsibilities of this Directorate range from overseeing the law relating to litter to the environmentally sound management of radioactive wastes. Its staff deal, not only with legal and policy issues, but are also obliged to address the technical aspects of waste management, both in the direction of research activities and in the provision of guidance (both to the waste management industry and Waste Regulatory Authorities and to industry and the community at large). The Directorate oversees the functioning of the waste management licensing system.

2.8 *The Water Directorate*

This Directorate oversees all aspects of water quality and supply. The setting of statutory water quality objectives and the achievement of EC standards for water quality are included in its remit. It also includes the Drinking Water Inspectorate. Sub-divisions of the Directorate are concerned with the managing of the discharge consent system under the *Water Resources Act 1991* and land-based marine pollution. This Directorate is also responsible for supervising the activities of the National Rivers Authority.

2.9 *Directorate of Air, Climate and Toxic Substances*

This is another Directorate with a wide-ranging and heterogeneous set of responsibilities. A major part of its activities concerns the management of chemical safety issues, including the regulation of entry into the UK market of newly-developed chemicals through the operation of the chemical notification scheme. It is also the UK focal point for the various international mechanisms for the control of transfrontier movement of substances which are banned or severely restricted in the country of export, operated both by the International Register of Potentially Toxic Chemicals (under the auspices of the United Nations Environment Programme) and by the Organisation for Economic Co-operation and Development. The Directorate is also responsible for overseeing the controls on genetically modified organisms and the control of bio-engineering.

6

The Directorate's remit also covers air pollution and has therefore expanded enormously to reflect recent appreciation of the global scale of atmospheric issues. A Global Atmosphere Division has been created. On the national level, the Directorate is responsible for policy development (including research, this is an increasingly significant task in air pollution matters) and it also has an operational function in that it exercises supervision over control of air pollution by local authorities.

The rapid growth of concern about the global climate as one of the most important and contentious environmental issues on the international level (culminating in the adoption at the 1992 Rio de Janeiro United Nations Conference on Environment and Development of the Framework Convention on Global Climatic Change) has added further to the work of this Directorate, which takes lead responsibility for issues such as combating the greenhouse effect and preventing further degradation of the ozone layer.

2.10   *Planning and Development Control Directorate*

This Directorate exercises the DoE's traditional control over the planning and development control system, not only in formulating planning policy and issuing guidance to local planning authorities, but also in administering the Secretary of State's pivotal role in the working of the planning system, whether in determining appeals, calling in applications which present issues of regional or national importance or otherwise. The Directorate sponsors the Planning Inspectorate (the body which handles most planning appeals, as well as a range of other functions, on behalf of the Department), which has recently become an independent executive agency.

European Community law requires that major projects which are likely to have a significant effect on the environment should be subject to a special procedure to assess their environmental impact. As most (although, in practice, not all) of such projects normally require the grant of planning permission, the environmental assessment system in the UK has been grafted onto the planning process and so falls within the remit of this Directorate.

2.11   *Rural Affairs Directorate*

This Directorate has responsibility for issues such as access to the countryside, National Parks and other areas which are designated for landscape or amenity purposes. It is also responsible for wildlife and habitat conservation (National Nature Reserves, Sites of Special Scientific Interest, Special Protection Areas, etc.) and acts as the focal point for the UK's participation in many international conventions in the conservation field.

2.12   **Ministry of Agriculture, Fisheries and Food (MAFF)**

Environmental factors now play an increasingly large role in agricultural policy, especially since the institution of a range of schemes (usually involving financial incentives) designed to encourage farmers to take land out of production, particularly of cereals, to promote 'extensive' farming and the diversification of the rural economy. Particularly important are the Environmentally Sensitive Areas (ESAs), designated by MAFF under the terms of the *EC Agricultural Structures Regulations 1985* (as amended), to provide support for traditional methods of farming which have regard to and preserve the environmental or landscape characteristics of some two dozen areas ranging from uplands to chalk grasslands. Similarly, the Farm Woodland Grant Scheme has encouraged replanting. Other programmes, including the much-criticised 'set-aside' scheme, have attracted adverse comment both from farmers and from conservation interests. In addition, MAFF sponsors the Agricultural Development Advisory Service (ADAS), which provides farmers with technical assistance and advice on a wide range of problems, including the avoidance, mitigation and control of agricultural pollution, particularly of soil and water, and on soil conservation and protection generally. Financial assistance in the form of grants is also made available to enable farmers to invest in pollution control equipment.

In addition to its major tasks of formulating and administering agricultural and fisheries policy (much of which has direct environmental relevance), MAFF also has functions relating to the control of agro-chemicals, and the licensing of the dumping of waste at sea under the *Food and Environment Protection Act 1985*. MAFF's Pesticides Safety Division is responsible for clearing new pesticides for use.

2.13   Department of Trade and Industry (DTI)

Although the DTI originally had few specific environmental responsibilities, it has become involved in the promotion of initiatives in environmentally-sound technologies, particularly those which involve the reduction or reuse of waste through the Environmental Technology Innovation Scheme (which it co-sponsors with the DoE).

When the Department of Energy was abolished in 1992, the DTI inherited many of its functions. These included the promotion of energy efficiency, the regulation of the UK oil and gas reserves, the oversight of the coal industry, the generation and supply of electricity, the direction of nuclear policy, etc. These functions, many of which have an important bearing on the UK's response to major issues of international environmental concern have moved the DTI to a position rather nearer the centre of the environmental stage than that which it formerly occupied.

The DTI is also the Department responsible for the Government's scientific environmental research carried out at the Warren Spring and other laboratories and centres. In June 1993 the President of the Board of Trade, Michael Heseltine, announced that a National Environmental Technology Centre (NETC) is to be established at Culham and Harwell, following a merger between the Warren Spring Laboratory and AEA Technology.

2.14   Department of Transport (DoT)

The DoT features on the environmental scene principally as the sponsor of the national road-building programme, in which context it is not popularly regarded as displaying an excess of environmental sensitivity. This function is part of the Department's overall direction of transport policy and planning, which covers land, sea and air traffic. The Department has begun to address the environmental aspects of transport, both in terms of energy demand and of pollution.

The Department has special responsibility for marine pollution questions. It is the Ministry which implements international conventions relating to the prevention of or response to marine pollution casualties (such as the MARPOL convention which governs pollution by oil, bulk and packaged chemicals, garbage and sewage from ships). It also deals with the UK's involvement in the affairs of the International Oil Pollution Compensation Fund. Both MARPOL and the IOPC Fund operate under the auspices of the International Maritime Organisation, the headquarters of which are situated in London and the DoT, as the interface with the host Government of the Organisation, has significant influence.

As initiatives such as 'road pricing' designed both to ease town centre congestion and to reduce exhaust emission, came to be more actively considered, the DoT is being drawn increasingly into environmental matters. The general relationship between transport and the environment is of increasing concern, particularly as a result of the Climate Change Convention signed at the Rio Summit.

2.15   NATIONAL AGENCIES WITH ENVIRONMENTAL FUNCTIONS

Her Majesty's Inspectorate of Pollution (HMIP)

HMIP is the central Government inspectorate responsible in England and Wales for six key areas of environmental protection:

(1)   regulation of the potentially most polluting processes through the system of integrated pollution control introduced by *Part I* of the *Environmental Protection Act 1990*;

(2)   regulation under the *Health and Safety at Work etc. Act 1974* of the air emissions from those processes which will, ultimately, fall under the new IPC (see INTEGRATED POLLUTION CONTROL (16)) regime;

(3)   regulation of sites which use, store or dispose of radioactive material under the *Radioactive Substances Act 1960*;

(4)   issuing consent to discharge 'red list' pollutants into sewers under the *Water Industry Act 1991*;

(5)   research on pollution control and radioactive waste disposal;

(6)   provision of expert advice to the Government, other regulators and industry.

HMIP was formed by amalgamating into a single body the four former central Government pollution inspectorates – the Industrial Air Pollution Inspectorate (formerly known as the Alkali Inspectorate) whose function was to regulate the atmospheric discharges from certain installations; the Radiochemical Inspectorate, responsible for regulating radioactive waste; the Hazardous Waste Inspectorate whose role was to advise waste disposal authorities; and the Water Pollution Inspectorate, whose functions transferred to the National Rivers Authority on 1 September 1989.

2.16   In April 1993 HMIP underwent a major internal restructuring. HMIP's new structure has six divisions.

(1)   *Operations Divisions*. This is the Division with prime responsibility for regulating industry. It is organised into seven regions:

Midlands Region (based in Birmingham)

South West Region (based in Bristol)

Wales Region (based in Cardiff)

North East Region (based in Leeds)

North West Region (based in Lancaster)

Anglian Region (based in Bedford and Lincoln)

Southern Region (currently based in London but moving to Fleet).

(2)   *Regulatory Systems Division*. This division exists to develop procedures and standards for regulation, to audit their implementation, provide guidance to the Operations Division and to have executive responsibility for HMIP Quality Assurance.

(3)   *Business Strategy Division.* This division exists to identify and address strategies to enhance HMIP's ability to fulfil its functions, and to provide technical information, in support of the regulatory function.

(4)   *Pollution Policy Division.* This division contributes to the formulation of UK policy to protect the environment.

(5)   *Resources Division.* This division exists to obtain the resources to enable HMIP to discharge its functions and to advise on their allocation and management.

(6)   *Corporate Development and Secretariat.* This division supports the Director and Chief Inspector and Senior Executive in providing the corporate management of HMIP.

2.17   National Rivers Authority (NRA)

The NRA was created by the *Water Act 1989* at the same time as water privatisation. It assumed the responsibility and functions of the former regional water authorities. Like HMIP, the NRA is a national body but is organised regionally to provide a network of integrated river basin management.

The NRA has responsibility under the *Water Resources Act 1991* for granting consents for discharges to water, except where IPC applies. Where levels of effluent are found to exceed consent limits, it has powers to enforce compliance through prosecution if necessary. The NRA also monitors general hydrological matters and maintains a Regional Rivers Advisory Committee for each area based on the old regional water authority regions. It has a wide range of other responsibilities relating to the management of water resources, including flood defence. In an interesting new development the NRA has taken advantage of its ownership of riparian rights and of the river-bed to pursue civil actions against polluters.

2.18   Health and Safety Executive (HSE)

The *Health and Safety at Work etc. Act 1974* provides a legislative framework for the achievement of standards of health and safety at work. The Health and Safety Executive is responsible to the Secretary of State for Employment and to other Secretaries of State for the administration of the *Health and Safety at Work etc. Act 1974*. There is, of course, no rigid separation of the work place from the wider environment and many regulations made under the *Health and Safety at Work etc. Act 1974* have implications for general environmental protection. Among many 'environmental' responsibilities of the HSE are the regulation of activities involving asbestos, of installations handling hazardous substances, of activities which may result in major accidents and of substances which may cause health hazards.

Oversight of the work of the HSE is in the hands of the Health and Safety Commission.

2.19   Royal Commission on Environmental Pollution (RCEP)

The Royal Commission is a permanent body whose members are recognised for their experience and expertise in environmental matters. It produces authoritative reports on topical environmental problems. These reports are often sharply critical and are meticulously researched and documented. Since its creation in 1971 its reports, although merely advisory, have had a profound influence on the direction of Government policy. Influential reports published by the RCEP include Air Pollution Control: An Integrated Approach (1976) which was the harbinger of IPC; Managing Waste: The Duty of Care (1985); and The Release of Genetically Engineered Organisms to the Environment

(1989). The Royal Commission's most recent report, its 17th (May 1993) was on waste incineration. It is currently studying transport and pollution.

2.20   Office of Water Services (OFWAT)

The Director-General of Water Services is the Head of the Office of Water Services established after the privatisation of the water supply industry in 1989 to act as a regulator of the industry in the public interest. Although the Director-General is best-known for his or her function in regulating the prices which the water undertakers can charge customers for supply, he or she also has some environmental functions, such as ensuring that the water undertakers have regard to their general duties as to the environment and nature conservation set out in the *Water Industry Act 1991*.

2.21   Natural Environment Research Council

NERC is the Government's medium for the promotion and co-ordination of research in the environmental sciences and other related disciplines. It is also the principal conduit for public funding of such research.

2.22   Local government

The structure of local government is complex with some areas (Greater London and the six major metropolitan areas) having a single tier of authority and the remainder of the country having two tiers – county (in Scotland regional) councils and district councils. All these bodies have important environmental functions. The structure is currently under further review and it is expected that, as a result, many more single tier (or 'unitary') authorities will come into being.

County councils

There are two main environmental responsibilities given to the county councils. They act as strategic planning authorities for their counties and they are also the planning authorities for mineral operations and for waste management.

Under the new regime of waste management established by the *Environmental Protection Act 1990*, county councils are both Waste Disposal Authorities and Waste Regulation Authorities. Their functions in the former capacity are largely confined to overseeing arrangements for the disposal of waste and the provision of civic amenity tips. As Waste Regulatory Authorities, their role is to compile waste plans for their area and license and inspect waste operations and act as the enforcing authority in cases of non-compliance. Formerly, county councils also operated waste disposal sites themselves, but their powers to do so were curtailed by the *Environmental Protection Act 1990*, which required them to set up new 'arm's length' companies, Local Authority Waste Disposal Companies ('LAWDACs') to operate the former local authority sites.

District councils

District Councils enjoy a wide range of environmental functions, usually discharged by the Environmental Health Department. A major new role for district councils is the regulation of emissions to air from scheduled processes under *Part I* of the *Environmental Protection Act 1990*. That Act also confirmed the position of district councils as the bodies responsible for tackling statutory nuisances, including noise. Perhaps most important of all, district councils are the planning authorities for the overwhelming majority of planning applications and accordingly have the responsibility of judging whether environmental impact assessments are required and, generally of whether new development is to be permitted.

2.23   EUROPEAN COMMUNITY ('EC')

The European Economic Community was established on 1 January 1958 by the *Treaty of Rome* and presently consists of twelve Member States and four central institutions:

—   the Council of Ministers,

—   the Commission,

—   the European Parliament, and

—   the European Court of Justice ('the ECJ').

In addition there is the Economic and Social Committee consisting of representatives of employers, trade unions and consumers and which is consulted on all proposed environmental legislation.

2.24   Although the *Treaty* did not contain any express provisions relating to environmental protection issues, environmental issues have not been ignored. Two *Treaty* provisions were initially used as the legal basis for EC environmental legislation, *Articles 100* and *235*, dealing respectively with the approximation of laws and action to attain the objectives of the EC. However in 1986 the *Single European Act* introduced a separate chapter on the environment into the *Treaty* in *Article 130*, although many environmental measures continue to be made under *Article 100a* which is the basis on which laws are enacted in furtherance of the creation of the 'single market'.

Environmental legislation made under *Article 100a* only requires a 'qualified majority' of votes rather than unanimity and there have been disputes between the EC institutions as to whether this new Article is the correct basis for particular pieces of legislation. In the case of the *Titanium Dioxide Directive*, for example, the Commission brought an action against the Council, arguing that the correct basis for the *Directive* should have been *Article 100a* and not *Article 130s*. The European Court of Justice (ECJ) found in favour of the Commission.

2.25   The *Maastricht Treaty*, if ratified, further builds on these changes by extending the consideration of environmental issues to the preparation of all EC laws, not just those relating to the single market. Hence environmental considerations are set to become key factors when developing future Community policies.

2.26   Additionally, Action Programmes have been formulated, each lasting for five years with the present one (the fifth) covering the period from the end of 1992. These programmes amount to statements of legislative intent and of policy regarding environmental protection. The new Action Programme focuses on those activities which damage the environment and aims to take action before irreversible damage occurs.

2.27   The Commission, which plays a fundamental role in the legislative process – it initiates the legislation – consists of 23 Directorates General (DG), each of which is allocated an area of responsibility. Each DG formulates initial proposals which are later considered by the Commission as a whole. DGXI is the principal environment Directorate. It is divided into Directorates responsible for:

—   nuclear safety;

—   industry and the environment; and

—   maintaining the quality of the environment.

2.28   Legislation of the Community takes one of two principal forms.

(1)   *Regulations* have general application and are 'directly applicable' in all Member States, in other words no national implementing measures are required since a *Regulation* automatically becomes law (in the UK by virtue of *section 2(1)* of the *European Communities Act 1972*).

(2)   *Directives* are binding on Member States as to the results to be achieved within a stated period of time but the actual method of implementation is left to individual Member States – a *Directive* therefore is generally a framework, filled in by each Member State. This latter principle is not always true, some *Directives* do contain detailed standards and provisions.

Thus, whilst *Regulations* are automatically law and enforceable in a Member State, the enforceability of a *Directive* is dependent on further legislative activity by each Member State. Failure to implement a *Directive* at all or in full will mean that the Member State is in breach of its *Treaty* obligations. In such circumstances the ECJ has held that provided the *Directive* is clear, precise and unconditional it will be 'directly effective' in the defaulting Member State from the date it should have been implemented but only in actions brought against the Member State itself or an 'emanation of the State' such as a local authority or public sector undertaking.

2.29   The Commission has a duty to ensure that environmental legislation is correctly adopted by Member States within the time limit laid down and also that, once adopted, the legislation is properly applied. In order to carry out this duty the Commission has the power ultimately to bring a Member State before the ECJ [*Article 169*] and if the action is correctly founded the ECJ will issue a judgment to that effect. The *Maastricht Treaty* (if ratified) will give the ECJ additional power to impose an 'appropriate' unlimited fine. Environmental proceedings which have been brought against the UK Government include those under *Article 169* for alleged failure to implement fully the *Drinking Water Directive* and alleged failure to implement the *Directive on Environmental Assessment in* respect of some road schemes.

2.30   In 1990 the Council of Ministers passed *Regulation 1210/90* setting up the European Environment Agency, responsible for gathering, co-ordinating and disseminating information relating to environmental matters. At least initially, it will not be an enforcement or regulatory body. In November 1993 the Member States finally agreed that the European Environment Agency should be located in Copenhagen. This decision brought *Regulation 1210/90* into force in the Member States.

2.31   SCOTLAND AND NORTHERN IRELAND

In Scotland, the basic pattern of environmental institutions as described above applies (see SCOTLAND (26)). However, there are some differences. Sewage and water supply are currently in the hands of regional councils and river purification boards are responsible for water quality. The Scottish equivalent of HMIP is Her Majesty's Industrial Pollution Inspectorate (HMIPI).

In Northern Ireland (see NORTHERN IRELAND (19)), the differences are more marked primarily as a result of direct rule. The majority of environmental responsibilities reside with the Department of Environment for Northern Ireland and its divisions. The position is explained in some detail in NORTHERN IRELAND (19).

3 Civil Liability and Compensation for Environmental Harm

3.1 INTRODUCTION

This chapter is intended (*a*) to explain the framework within which the law in England and Wales provides rights of compensation to those whose property or health is harmed by environmental hazards or rights to prevent such harm occurring or continuing and (*b*) to highlight some of the principal areas of practice and procedure which arise in bringing or defending environmental cases. In several of the following chapters there is a more detailed treatment of certain areas of the substantive law on which cases of this sort may be based.

The principles relating to civil liability for environmental damage do not constitute a single body of law. They are more a patchwork of rights and duties which have been developed by the courts over many years in the general area of the law of Tort, and specifically in the tort of nuisance. The continuing analysis and re-appraisal by the courts of the basic principles underlying these rights and duties is exemplified in the recent decision of the House of Lords in the case of *Cambridge Water Company v Eastern Counties Leather plc, 9 December 1993*. These Common Law rights and duties have, in turn, been supplemented and modified by legislation. Such legislation may:

(*a*) expressly give a person a special right to be compensated for a certain type of damage (e.g. for damage caused by waste criminally deposited on land – *Control of Pollution Act 1974, s 88* now replaced by *Environmental Protection Act 1990, s 73(6)*), or

(*b*) by inference, create rights to compensation and other remedies for particular categories of person who have been harmed by breaches of specific duties which the statute imposes on others (in the environmental context see *Boyce v Paddington BC [1923] 1 Ch 109*). A breach of statutory duty which creates a civil liability in this way is treated as a tort, like nuisance or negligence (see below), or

(*c*) may clarify, extend or restrict the basic common law rights and liabilities. Examples are the *Congenital Disabilities (Civil Liability) Act 1976* which legislates for children to have rights of action at law in respect of damage to their health caused by pre-natal events and *Nuclear Installations Act 1965, s 12* which displaces any common law liabilities for damage or injury done in breach of duties laid down in that Act.

As well as making awards of damages as compensation, in appropriate cases the civil courts will also grant injunctions ordering a person who is causing environmental harm to cease the activities which are responsible. Injunctions may also be granted to restrain activities which threaten to do such harm. Occasionally injunctions may be 'mandatory', i.e. requiring the party injuncted, not simply to stop the activity complained of, but to take positive remedial action – such as to remove or make safe a source of pollution.

Injunctions are available from both the High Court and local County Courts. They are frequently available at short notice at the very beginning of litigation and on an interim basis, pending full trial of the dispute or some further court application by the defendant prior to trial to have the injunction lifted. Special rules apply to the granting of interim injunctions and these are discussed more fully at 3.19 below.

claims based on common law torts or for breach of statutory duties also fit into a
r legal framework, of which significant features are the following.

3.2 Civil claims and 'remedial liability' and statutory control of nuisances

The legal rights under common law and statute by which private individuals may seek
redress lie alongside:

(i)   the special cost recovery (remedial liability) powers available to the local
authorities and various other environmental agencies as part of their regulatory
functions. These powers typically permit the regulators to clean-up pollution, or
to take unilateral preventative action to combat it, and then to recover their costs
from the party responsible (see the powers of the National Rivers Authority
under *Water Resources Act 1991, s 161* (clean-up of polluted waters and
groundwater) and of Her Majesty's Inspectorate of Pollution under *Environmental Protection Act 1990, s 27* (clean-up in the context of integrated pollution
control)). (Remedial liability is discussed in more detail in 3.20 *et seq.* below) and

(ii)   the powers and duties of the regulatory bodies to prevent or abate environmental
harm other than through the use of injunctions granted by the civil courts (see
above). Examples are the statutory duties of local authorities to abate designated
'statutory nuisances' by means of a notice procedure and magistrates' court
proceedings (*Environmental Protection Act 1990, ss 79–82*). The Health and
Safety Executive has similar, and potentially overlapping, powers (see 3.4 below).

3.3 Civil claims and criminal liability

Control of industrial activity and its potentially harmful effects on the environment lies
with a number of statutory regulators, such as Her Majesty's Inspectorate of Pollution,
the National Rivers Authority and local authorities (see above). Other relevant agencies include the Waste Regulation Authorities and certain Government departments,
such as The Ministry of Agriculture Fisheries and Food. The statutory schemes which
these bodies administer are based largely on the principle of permitting or authorising
relevant activities, with the enforcement of criminal penalties as the ultimate sanction
for operating without the necessary authorisation, or operating in breach of the terms
of an authorisation which has been granted, e.g. an authorisation to carry on a
'prescribed process' under *Environmental Protection Act 1990, s 6* or an authorisation to
dispose of radioactive waste under *Radioactive Substances Act 1993, s 13.*

It is not only the regulators who may bring prosecutions. In certain circumstances
private individuals, associations or action groups may seek to prosecute offences
themselves (see *Prosecution of Offenders Act 1985, s 6*), subject to the overriding power
of the Government law officers to takeover the conduct of such private prosecutions.
Prosecutions initiated by private groups are becoming a feature of the enforcement of
environmental controls. Prosecutions have been brought by the Anglers' Co-operative
Association under the *Control of Pollution Act 1974* including in connection with the
Camelford water pollution incident in 1991. Also in 1991 Greenpeace successfully
prosecuted Albright and Wilson in respect of the company's chemical effluent discharges into the Irish Sea. At the same time Greenpeace embarked on what was ultimately
an unsuccessful legal challenge to the prosecution policy adopted toward the company
by the relevant regulatory body, the National Rivers Authority.

The ability of private individuals, or groups, to enforce the criminal law provides a
person aggrieved by a polluting activity with an additional legal means of bringing
pressure to bear on the person responsible for that activity to cause him to abate it or to
prevent its repetition. To an industrial undertaking the threat of repeated prosecution

and escalating fines and, possibly, the imprisonment of its senior employees may be as effective as the threat of a civil injunction, and more effective than a damages claim.

The activities which have given rise to the criminal prosecution may also have caused loss or damage to private individuals. Securing a criminal conviction may assist such an individual in a subsequent civil action he may bring to recover compensation for that loss or damage. A criminal conviction is not conclusive of any civil liability, but *Civil Evidence Act 1968, s 11* provides that such a conviction is admissible in evidence for the purpose of proving, where it is relevant to an issue in civil proceedings, that the criminal offence was committed. The contents of the information or complaint on which the conviction was based are also admissible. This rule of evidence may be of particular value in claims for damages arising from public nuisance (see 3.12 *et seq.* below), since this form of nuisance is not only a criminal offence but, where a person has suffered particular damage arising from its commission, it is also a civil law tort. Where a conviction for a public nuisance has been obtained a person who has been injured as a result of its commission will often, in practice, need only show his loss, and that that loss was over and beyond that suffered by that section of the public also affected by the nuisance, to succeed also in a civil claim to recover compensation.

The standard of proof in a criminal case is higher than that required in a civil action. Therefore, even in cases where the claimant in civil proceedings is not basing his claim on public nuisance (where, as explained above, the conviction itself may well be determinative of the *entire* question of civil liability) but, for example, he is claiming in private nuisance or negligence, the civil courts will regard the defendant as facing an uphill task in persuading them that a finding made by the criminal court which is relevant to any issue of civil liability which is before them was incorrectly made (see *Stupple v Royal Insurance Co Ltd [1971] 1 QB 50* and *Hunter v Chief Constable of West Midlands [1982] AC 529*).

It should, however, be borne in mind that by no means every conviction for an offence arising out of an environmental incident or polluting activity will assist in a civil claim for damages relating to the same event. Evidence of the conviction is only admissible to the extent that it is 'relevant to any issue in those [civil] proceedings'. Thus, for example, a conviction for breaching limits on permitted discharge levels imposed by a condition in a licence to discharge liquid effluent will itself be of no direct relevance to the central issue of causation in a civil action in the tort of negligence brought by local residents against the convicted licensee, alleging that his plant discharges have led to health problems. The conviction may become relevant if the defendant runs the defence of statutory authority (see 3.17 below). Otherwise, the conviction would assist the residents little in their civil actions.

What may, in practice, assist the claimant more than *Civil Evidence Act, s 11* is the general obligation on each side in civil litigation to show to the other all the documents he has that relate to questions in that litigation, other than those documents which are treated as 'privileged' from such disclosure (see Discovery at 3.26 below). Thus, internal documents which a company responsible for a pollution incident might prepare in anticipation of a prosecution (except to the extent that they are prepared for its lawyers or for the getting up of its defence) may have to be disclosed later to the claimant in civil proceedings. Similarly, the claimant may be able to introduce in evidence at the trial of the civil action written statements of evidence taken by the regulatory authorities as part of an earlier prosecution exercise, if he is able to obtain copies.

3.4 Environmental liability and liabilities in the workplace

Environmental hazards have little respect for geography. A significant release of toxic substances at an industrial plant may do as much harm to the health of the workforce as the resultant discharges may do to the environment and to the population outside the plant. Lax procedures in complying with controls over routine discharges are likely to be reflected in poor health and safety procedures on-site. Workers themselves may be a pathway for environmental contamination and a source of risk to members of the public (see *Hewett v Alf Brown's Transport Ltd [1992] ICR 530* in which the wife of a worker had suffered from lead poisoning through exposure to the dust on her husband's work clothes which she washed for him at home. The Court of Appeal found against the claimant on the facts but recognised the possibility of claims against industrial employers in negligence for not operating on-site occupational safety procedures which would prevent this sort of potential off-site hazard).

Claims brought by employees for occupational health effects will usually be based on the alleged negligence of the company in failing to discharge its common law duty of care to seek to avoid injury to its workforce. There are also separate statutory duties owed by employers to employees under numerous regulations made under *Health and Safety at Work Act 1974, s 15* which may provide an alternative basis for a civil action (see *Health and Safety at Work Act 1974, s 47(2)*). The so-called 'double barrelled' action of simultaneous but alternative claims (*a*) in the common law tort of negligence (see 3.15 below) and (*b*) for breach of statutory duty are a standard feature of occupational health claims (see *Kilgollan v Cooke & Co Ltd [1956] 1 All ER 294*).

The Health and Safety Executive (HSE) also has its own powers of intervention in respect of hazards in the workplace. It can serve improvement and prohibition notices on the industrial undertakings which it regulates if there is an actual or threatened breach of the Health and Safety legislation or, in the case of a prohibition notice, a danger to health either to the workforce or to the public outside the plant. (*Health and Safety at Work Act 1974, ss 21, 22, 33* – see generally Tolley's Health and Safety at Work Handbook 1994, paragraphs 17.7, 17.8, 17.15, 33.20.) Improvement notices can require an undertaking to take remedial action at its own cost e.g. to introduce improved safety procedures or to install new process equipment. A prohibition notice usually takes the form of a direction to cease the offending activity. In certain cases an industrial activity (for example, one which is producing high gaseous or dust emissions) may be subject to action of this sort on the part of the HSE as well as exposing the operator to the exercise of statutory abatement powers by the local authority because it is creating a statutory nuisance in the locality (see above and 3.13 below).

Nor, conversely, do the powers of the environmental agencies stop at the factory gate. As was also mentioned above and is discussed more fully in 3.20 below, Her Majesty's Inspectorate of Pollution have power under *Environmental Protection Act 1990, s 27* which will, in certain cases, permit them to carry out clean-up works on industrial premises where criminal breaches of integrated pollution control have occurred. Waste Regulation Authorities will have similar powers to impose remedial liability in respect of the unlawful depositing of controlled waste. [*Environmental Protection Act 1990, s 59*].

As can be seen, there are overlapping systems of controls provided for by the Health and Safety and the Environmental Protection legislation which empower both the HSE and the environmental agencies to act ultimately in the interests of employees and the general public. Often it will be as effective, and certainly more cost-effective, for a person who considers that his health or property is being damaged by a particular activity to seek the intervention of one or more of these regulatory bodies as it would be for him to take action in the courts to enforce his own civil law rights.

3.5   European Community law

As in many other areas of law and regulation, European Community law continues to play an increasingly influential role. The rights to compensation for environmental harm, and to prevent such harm occurring, established under the common law and domestic statutes cannot be considered in isolation from Community law. It is expressly incorporated into English law under the *European Communities Act 1972* and it takes precedence over other domestic laws whenever the two conflict. (See the decision of the European Court of Justice in the *Algemene Transport* case (*Case 26/62*) and the *Factortame* case *[1991] AC 603*.)

In the environmental field the most important European Community legislation is in the form of *Directives*. The implementation of *Directives* by means of specific domestic legislation (e.g. the *Directive on Basic Safety Standards* (*180/836/Euratom*) which is implemented in the United Kingdom by the *Ionising Radiation Regulations* (*SI 1985 No 1335*)) frequently create new duties and potential liabilities which are enforceable, including between private parties. However, in certain circumstances, the courts in Member States may enforce clearly expressed rights which are contained in *Directives* against those States and their 'emanations' regardless of whether the *Directive* in question has been implemented by that State. This is the so-called principle of 'direct effect'. An 'emanation of state' has been widely defined to include regulatory bodies and nationalised industries (see *Forster & another v British Gas plc (Case 188/89)*). In this way, *Directives* may be used in the domestic courts, including in England, to overcome arguments marshalled in defence of claims run against Governments or Government-controlled bodies that are inconsistent with *Directives*. Following the decision of the European Court of Justice in the *Francovitch* case (*Cases 6/90 and 9/90*) it is possible that they may also be used to claim monetary compensation against such bodies where some loss has resulted directly from the non-implementation or contravention of a *Directive* (see also *Garden Cottage Foods v Milk Marketing Board [1983] 3 WLR 143*).

There has been a large body of *Directives* created during the past 20 years with the specific purpose of protecting the environment. The number continues to increase. The subjects covered by these *Directives* range from drinking water quality to the disposal of toxic waste. Although not yet tested in the English courts, this body of Community legislation is likely to contain a number of specific obligations which do satisfy the test necessary for them to have direct effect and, which are, therefore, capable of being deployed in litigation against governmental bodies and state enterprises as described. The list of *Directives* containing obligations which may have direct effect are regarded as including those *Directives* which specify maximum concentration values for specified substances in, for example, industrial emissions and environmental media. Examples are *Directive 85/513/EEC* dealing with cadmium discharges and *Directive 85/203/EEC* and *Directive 80/779/EEC* covering nitrogen dioxide and sulphur dioxide emissions respectively.

Even in litigation between private parties where the principle of 'direct effect' is inapplicable (*Duke v GEC Reliance [1988] AC 618*) the decision of the House of Lords in *Litster v Firth Dry Dock and Engineering Co Ltd [1990] 1 AC 546* and of the European Court of Justice in the *Marleasing* case (*Case 106/89*) make it clear that both the legislation passed by a Member State to implement a *Directive* and even the wider provisions of that State's domestic law which already cover the area legislated for in the *Directive*, must be interpreted liberally, so as to secure the proper applicability of the *Directive's* provisions. Thus, in any environmental litigation in which obligations imposed by a *Directive* are in issue it is to the *Directive*, rather than to the relevant domestic law, that those advising the litigants should first look in framing the claim and its defence.

In the area of substantive environmental law, it is also from the European Community that we can expect major reform of our system of civil liability. In 1989 a draft Directive was published proposing a strict liability regime for damage done to the environment by waste. After some controversy and subsequent revision in 1991, it has not been proceeded with. However, a broader and similarly radical initiative was launched by the European Commission in March 1993 with the issue for consultation of its Green Paper on *Civil Liability for Environmental Damage*. (See also the UK Government's Response of 8 October 1993 and the House of Lords' Select Committee on the European Communities 3rd Report, 'Remedying Environmental Damage' of 14 December 1993.) One of the key objectives of a Community-wide system of environmental liability would be to assist the operation of the new Single European Market by removing differences in the civil liability regimes operated in Member States which might tend to distort competition. This thinking underlies the Green Paper's proposals.

The Green Paper is not just concerned with damage done by waste but with environmental damage from a broader (and as yet undefined) range of activities. It also suggests possible measures for furthering the long-held European Community environmental principles of (*a*) seeking to prevent damage before it occurs (the 'precautionary principle') and (*b*) where damage does occur, to ensure that 'the polluter pays'. Key proposals include the following.

—   The application of principles of strict liability for damage (which, in contrast to certain of the present common law torts, would not require a claimant to prove 'fault' or a particular state of mind on the part of the person responsible).

—   Obligations to be imposed on the person responsible to pay for the restoration of damage to the environment (which may result in greater costs to the polluter than under the present common law rules for assessing loss and damage in tort).

—   In complex situations where a number of separate polluters may be responsible for the damage or where a particular polluter cannot pay because he is uninsured or insolvent, clean-up and compensation obligations should be funded by joint compensation fund arrangements involving compulsory levies on various industry sectors.

The Green Paper is intended to lead to new European Community legislation. If it does, that legislation can be expected to be in terms which would have a profound effect on the present civil liability system in England and Wales which has been outlined above. It is to be noted that several of the Green Paper's proposals, for example in relation to compensation and clean-up for damage to the environment and the principle of mandatory insurance arrangements, are reflected in the Council of Europe Convention on Civil Liability for Damage Resulting from Activities Dangerous to the Environment which was adopted in March 1993 and which is open for ratification by the European Community itself. [*Article 32(1)*]. The Green Paper expressly contemplates such ratification.

3.6   THE GROUNDS FOR CIVIL LIABILITY AND REMEDIES

As was discussed above, civil liability for environmental harm may result from a breach of statutory duty or may be created by specific provision in domestic legislation, such as *section 73(6)* of the *Environmental Protection Act 1990*. It may also arise from obligations imposed by, or derived from, European Community legislation, in particular the many *Directives* regulating the discharge of substances into the environment. The third and most significant source of liability, however, remains the common law and certain of the individual species of civil wrongs, or 'torts', which have been developed by the courts. The relevant 'environmental torts' are negligence, nuisance, trespass and the so-called 'rule in *Rylands v Fletcher*'. Of these torts only the rule in *Rylands v Fletcher* and certain aspects of the law on nuisance can be described as having been developed specifically to address the consequences of pollution or the other effects on the environment of hazardous substances and activities. The origins of nuisance and trespass, in particular, long pre-date the Industrial Revolution. Also, each tort has a separate lineage and they have all been developed by the courts to a significant extent in isolation from each other. The result is that, in many cases, a claimant may be able to base his legal claims for damage arising from a single event, or series of events, on breaches of more than one of these torts. He may, indeed, argue that there have been breaches of all of them – in the hope of succeeding at least with one. For example, in the leading case of *Halsey v Esso Petroleum Co Ltd [1961] 1 WLR 683* an emission of acidic oil residues from the defendant's plant resulted in a general claim under *Rylands v Fletcher* and specific claims in private nuisance for damage to personal clothing on the claimant's neighbouring property and in public nuisance for damage to his motor car which he had parked on the public highway. Another result, however, is that the types of damage which the claimant will be permitted to recover may differ according to the particular tort on which he has succeeded in establishing liability and, as we shall see later, injunctions are not generally available in respect of all these torts.

The principal constituents of each of these torts is as follows.

3.7   THE TORTS

Nuisance

The various types of nuisance (public, private and statutory – see below) are based on a fundamental duty that each person has not to conduct himself in a manner which unreasonably interferes with the use by others of their land and property, or with the enjoyment of others' public rights. Even the lawful use of one's own land may constitute a private nuisance to a neighbour whose enjoyment of his own property is affected by it, unless that use can be justified by, for example, showing that the interference or damage was the natural result of reasonable use of the land (see the many nineteenth century cases on flooding and de-watering of land resulting from building and mining operations on adjoining properties e.g. *Popplewell v Hodkinson (1869) LR 4 Exch 248*).

Not every land use or other activity which gives rise to 'nuisance' in a colloquial sense will be actionable at law. The types of interference and damage which will provide a ground for legal action have been developed in the case law on private and public nuisance or have been established by relevant statutes, and a potential claimant must have regard to the established categories of nuisance in framing his case. Throughout the relevant case law runs the principle indicated above; that liability in nuisance will not be imposed where the interference complained of arises from the defendant's 'reasonable use' of his own property. This requires the court to strike a balance between the respective interests of claimant and defendant having regard to prevailing standards of reasonable land usage and, in the case of private nuisance, the levels of interference that a neighbouring property owner or occupier can be expected to tolerate (see dicta of Lord Goff in *Cambridge Water Company v Eastern Counties Leather plc, 9 December 1993*) ('the *Cambridge Water Company* case'). It is, however, the case that once an apparent nuisance has been established it is for the defendant to show that the relevant harm or interference arises naturally from a reasonable user of land (*Kraemers v AG for Tasmania [1966] Tas SR 113*).

Although the taking of precautions to prevent damage occurring may be relevant to the question of whether the defendant's use was reasonable (see above), an essential feature of both public and private nuisance is that the exercise of reasonable care, or even the highest standard of care, by the defendant to try to avoid the damage is not necessarily a defence. In this particular sense, nuisance is a 'strict liability' tort (see the *Cambridge Water Company* case). Thus, the employing of diligent, well-qualified management and the installation of expensive state-of-the-art effluent treatment systems will avail a company little if its routine discharges cause foreseeable damage to a neighbouring property (as to the further requirement of foreseeability of damage see 3.11 below). This distinguishes common law nuisance both from the tort of negligence and also from statutory nuisance where the defendant can rely on his investment in staff and high quality plant as part of a 'best practicable means' defence (see 3.13 below).

3.8   *Private nuisance*

A right to sue in private nuisance will in general arise where the consequences of a person's activities (often some particular use of his own land):

(1)   encroach upon the land belonging to another (a claim in private nuisance generally requires the claimant to be the owner or occupier of the land affected; the rights of the other members of his household may thus be restricted (*Malone v Laskey [1907] 2 KB 141*)); or

(2)   cause physical damage to land of another and his other property (including buildings, personal possessions, livestock and plants and trees) which are on that land, or

(3)   unreasonably interfere with another in the 'comfortable and convenient enjoyment of his land'. (*Thompson-Schwab v Costaki [1956] 1 WLR 335*).

3.9   *Private nuisance categories (1) and (2) – discussion*

Category (1) nuisance, encroachment on land, bears certain resemblances to the separate tort of trespass (see below). Both categories (1) and (2), encroachment on land and damage to neighbouring property, are established simply by showing that the relevant encroachment or damage has occurred. Unlike category (3), wider, more subjective considerations such as the situation and character of the land effected (see below) tend not to be of high importance in deciding liability (*St Helens Smelting Co v Tipping (1865) 11 HLC 642*), although the defence of 'reasonable user' (see above) is a principle available in respect of all three categories of private nuisance.

Examples of encroachment generally relate to the physical, and localised, effects of one neighbouring property on another, such as the flow of rainwater from buildings onto neighbouring property or the intrusion of tree branches and roots. Category (1) nuisance thus has limited significance for establishing liability in relation to the effects of industrial activity where the results are generally wider spread.

Category (2) nuisance, damage to property, requires tangible damage to physical property to the land itself or to buildings and goods which are located on it. The prospect, or fear of such damage is not enough to establish liability (*Sedleigh-Denfield v O'Callaghan [1940] AC 880*). Thus, for example, a cattle farmer who was compelled to slaughter his herd because the animals had consumed high levels of toxins which had been deposited on his fields as a result of a malfunction at a neighbouring waste incineration plant would be able to recover in nuisance the cost of the animals, and probably also the profit he could have expected to have made on their sale. On the other hand, a neighbouring farmer who merely took preventive action to move his cattle elsewhere for fear of his land being similarly contaminated, thereby also losing the opportunity to sell them at a particularly good market price, would not be able to recover his loss of profit on that sale, at least under this category of nuisance – or indeed at all, for there are doubts as to whether private nuisance generally permits the recovery of pure economic loss. Examples of cases in which compensation has been awarded, or injunctions granted, in respect of physical damage to property resulting from industrial activity include subsidence and damage to growing crops from toxic emissions (*Manchester Corp v Farnworth [1930] AC 171*).

An actionable nuisance need not, however, comprise an operation or activity on the part of the defendant. A person who ought reasonably to know that some natural hazard on his land may cause damage to neighbouring property is under a duty to take reasonable steps to minimise the risk of known or foreseeable damage. If his failure to do so results in such damage an action may be brought against him in nuisance as well as in negligence (*Leakey v National Trust [1980] 1 All ER 17* – the landslip of a bank onto a neighbouring property).

3.10   *Private nuisance category (3) – discussion*

Category (3) nuisance, unreasonable interference with another in the comfortable and convenient enjoyment of his land, one would expect to be the basis on which a person who had suffered personal injury from pollution or other industrial emissions would usually bring his claim. There are, however, uncertainties on this point as a result of observations made in the House of Lords in the case of *Read v J Lyons & Co Ltd [1947] AC 156* to the effect that personal injury on its own could not be compensated in private nuisance without also there being some negligence on the part of the defendant (see 3.15 Negligence below). A well-advised claimant would, however, always run a claim for personal injury which he had suffered as a category (3) private nuisance as well as in negligence where the facts of the case permitted this to be done. Certainly liability for category (3) nuisance will include compensation for the physical effects on a person himself, and on his well-being, arising directly from occupying a property which is subject to the nuisance. The conventional definition of private nuisance which falls under this category is, 'conduct which gives rise to personal inconvenience and interference with one's enjoyment, one's quiet, one's personal freedom, anything that discomposes or injuriously affects the senses or the nerves' (*St Helens Smelting Co v Tipping* – see above). Thus, a claim may lie for unpleasant odours (*Benjamin v Storr (1874) LRCP 400* and *Bone v Seale [1975] 1 WLR 797*), dust and particulates (*Pwllbach Colliery v Woodman [1915] AC 634* – coaldust); smoke and fumes (*Beardmore v Tredwell (1862) 3 Giff 683* – brickburning); noise (*Gaunt v Fynney (1872) 8 Ch App 8* – factory noise) and vibration (*Hoare v McAlpine [1923] 1 Ch 167* – building works).

As indicated above, the courts, in assessing whether a category (3) nuisance has been committed, will not apply an absolute standard of liability, but will take into account rather more subjective issues such as the circumstances in which the nuisance was created, the personal circumstances and condition of the person claiming to be affected and the situation and character of the land concerned. In particular:

(*a*)   the degree of inconvenience or discomfort suffered must be such as would significantly affect any person who might occupy the plaintiff's land, irrespective of age or state of health. Any abnormal sensitivities or particular medical condition of the people actually living there will not generally be considered (*Bloodworth v Cormack [1949] NZLR 1058*);

(*b*)   the character of the neighbourhood in which the affected land is situated is usually very relevant. Noise emissions from an industrial plant on the outskirts of a quiet rural village may be actionable whereas even higher noise emissions from a similar plant in the centre of a large industrial town may very well not be. The case of *Gillingham Borough Council v Medway (Chatham) Dock Co Ltd [1993] 3 All ER 923* introduced the notion that a grant of planning permission could change the character of a neighbourhood for this purpose. In this case, the defendant dock company, and their tenants, had such permission to operate a small cargo terminal in the former naval dockyards at Chatham. This generated a certain volume of night-time heavy goods traffic which was the source of the complaint and an activity which the local authority, on behalf of local residents, sought to restrict by seeking a High Court injunction using *Local Government Act 1972, s 222* (see below). The action failed because the traffic movements were no greater than those contemplated by the grant of planning permission and the permission itself was found to be a decisive factor in evaluating the character of the neighbourhood. This case was brought in public nuisance but these aspects of the judgment are equally applicable to cases of private nuisance.

3.11   *Private nuisance – general issues*

It is now clear from the unanimous decision of the House of Lords in the *Cambridge Water Company* case that a person will only be liable in private, as well as public, nuisance if the damage in respect of which the claim against him is made is of a type which was reasonably foreseeable at the time that he engaged in the activities from which it resulted. Foreseeability of this sort is certainly a key element in succeeding in a claim in negligence (see 3.15 below). The alternative approach, (which had been adopted by the Court of Appeal in the *Cambridge Water Company* case) was to regard nuisance, or at least certain types of nuisance, as imposing a liability for all damage to which the nuisance had, in the course of events, given rise regardless of any 'fault' (i.e. reasonable foreseeability of the consequences of his activities) on the part of the defendant. The Court of Appeal's judgment (*The Times, 29 December 1992*) had disturbed the conventional view that foreseeability of damage was a prerequisite to liability in private nuisance in all circumstances (see *The Wagon Mound (No 2)* [1967] 1 AC 617). The Court of Appeal had suggested that, in certain circumstances, the law of nuisance might require a degree of foreseeability of harm, and in other cases not. *The Cambridge Water Company* case itself arose from the routine handling of the solvent, perchloroethene ('PCE') on the defendant company's site. There had been regular spillages of the solvent onto the ground. The solvent had, over time, travelled downwards through the permeable layers beneath the site into the underlying aquifer from which the claimant water company abstracted drinking water at a borehole a little over a mile from the site. In 1983 traces of the solvent were detected in local drinking water at average concentration levels higher than the Guide Levels specified in the 1980 *EC Directive relating to the Quality of Water intended for Human Consumption (80/778/EC)* (and higher also than the maximum concentration value for PCE which was subsequently set by the UK Government in 1989 by reference to the World Health Organisation's tentative guideline values). From at least 1985 onwards these legislative developments meant that the aquifer was not a suitable source of drinking water. The water company took its borehole out of commission and invested £1 million in an unsuccessful attempt to clean-up the aquifer. It also sought an injunction and damages from the defendant company. The claim was based on negligence (see 3.15 below), nuisance and the rule in *Rylands v Fletcher* (see 3.16 below). The trial judge found that the practices which had led to the gradual pollution of the aquifer had all but ceased in 1976, although the pollution still continued. He gave judgment against the water company in respect of its claims in negligence and nuisance because the evidence he had heard showed that the defendant company's employees could not reasonably have foreseen in 1976, or at any time before then, that spillages of the sort they had allowed to occur would have led to elevated levels of PCE in the aquifer or that the water company's operations would have been affected in the way they ultimately were. Although the water company only pursued its appeal on the *Rylands v Fletcher* head of claim, the Court of Appeal effectively overturned the trial judge's finding on the nuisance claim. The Court of Appeal regarded the ground water beneath the defendant's land as a 'natural right incident to the ownership of land'. It held that liability in

24

private nuisance for interference with these sorts of rights did not require the damage which ultimately occurred to be foreseeable. The water company thus succeeded in its appeal.

This decision became a source of anxiety to industry and its insurers, particularly since it appeared to be that liability might be imposed in private nuisance for gradual pollution which was retrospective in effect. For example, in the case before the Court, the damage had only manifested itself long after the cause of the pollution had occurred and at a time when technical knowledge was such that appropriate measures had already been put in place to eliminate the cause.

The House of Lords took a different view on this issue. Re-stating the principle in *The Wagon Mound (No 2)* – see above, it held that, although the liability in nuisance was strict (in the sense that liability would be imposed even though a defendant had exercised reasonable care and skill to avoid the harm which had occurred) it did not follow that the defendant should be liable for damage which was not reasonably foreseeable. The spillages on the defendant company's premises which had caused the pollution of the aquifer had ceased a number of years before the various scientific and legislative developments which had caused the claimant water company to attempt its remediation of the aquifer. Accordingly, the damage done to the water company was unforeseeable at the time the relevant spillages occurred and the defendant company could not be held liable in nuisance. The practical implications of this foreseeability requirement in case of long-term operations causing gradual pollution are considered further in the context of negligence in 3.15 below.

Liability in private nuisance generally attaches not only in respect of actions carried out by the defendant himself or his employees. Where property changes hands the new owner or occupier will be liable to his neighbours for allowing an existing source of nuisance to continue if he fails to take reasonable steps to bring it to an end in circumstances where he knows, or should reasonably have known, of the existence of the nuisance (*Sedleigh-Denfield v O'Callaghan [1940] AC 880*). The new occupier may be liable even if the source of the nuisance on his land is not apparent, hence the desirability for reasonable inquiries and site audits before acquiring an existing industrial site. This potential liability is, however, subject to an important qualification relating to historic pollution. In the *Cambridge Water Company* case, the House of Lords was asked to consider whether liability in nuisance should be imposed for continuing off-site pollution resulting from the spillages, several years before, of chemicals onto the defendants' land. As explained above damage had not been foreseen at the time the spillages had taken place but, so it was argued, the defendants could now be held liable for the damage caused by the continuing migration of the chemicals from under its land which was still occurring after such damage had become foreseeable by the defendant. The House of Lords' answer was in the negative. It was held that there was no liability for pollutants which had 'become irretrievably lost in the ground below'. Thus, the House of Lords firmly set its face against 'retrospective liability' in the narrow sense of that term. The case cannot, however, be safely treated by purchasers or lessees of industrial premises as relieving them of legal responsibility for the acts of pollution of their predecessors. Where the source of the pollution has not moved beyond the control of the new owner or occupier of the site and there are steps which can still be taken to remedy or reduce it, then, on the authority of *Sedleigh-Denfield v O'Callaghan* (see above), the failure to take these steps is still sufficient to give rise to a liability in nuisance. Similarly, where a person employs a contractor to carry out works which require special precautions to be taken to avoid a nuisance affecting neighbouring properties he will be responsible for the contractor's deliberate or negligent failure to take those precautions and he may be liable for the nuisance which results (*Alcock v Waite, The Times, 23 December 1991*).

3.12 Civil Liability and Compensation for Environmental Harm

3.12 *Public nuisance*

As indicated above, the common features of private nuisance and public nuisance are the requirement for some damage or annoyance or inconvenience arising from interference with rights which the claimant enjoys and the requirement of foreseeability of the type of damage or inconvenience complained of. In public nuisance, however, it is not necessary for the claimant to show that his ownership or occupation of land has been affected. Also, unlike private nuisance, public nuisance is a criminal offence as well as being a civil tort.

A claim for compensation in the civil courts may be brought by an individual where a public nuisance has been committed and that claimant can show that he has suffered particular damage (which may be pure economic loss (*Harper v Haden [1933] 1 Ch 298*)) which goes over and beyond the general inconvenience and disturbance suffered by other members of the public as a result of the nuisance. To be a public nuisance, the relevant activity and its effect, does not have to be widespread. It is sufficient if a class of citizens who 'come within the sphere or neighbourhood of the operation' of the nuisance are materially affected in terms of reasonable comfort and convenience.

The subjective circumstances which are taken into account in assessing whether a private nuisance in category (3) private nuisance (see above) has been committed will also be relevant to the establishing of a public nuisance. (See the *Gillingham Borough Council* case – above.)

A person who owns or rents a home in a neighbourhood which is affected by industrial pollution may be able to bring legal claims in both public and private nuisance (see *Halsey v Esso Petroleum Co Ltd* – above). There may, however, be other local residents whose only ground for redress is in public nuisance because the ill effects from which they are suffering are not also directly linked to a private interest in land which is being affected. Particular advantages of claims in public nuisance are as follows:

(*a*) recovery for personal injury without necessarily proving negligence on the part of the person responsible, is more clearly established in public than in private nuisance and under the rule in *Rylands v Fletcher* (see 3.10 above and 3.16 below);

(*b*) they permit legal claims to be brought in respect of the harmful effects on land which is not privately owned, e.g. amenity spaces or the seashore. If the claimant can show particular damage greater than that suffered by other members of the public affected, he may have a basis for legal action (*Southport Corporation v Esso Petroleum [1954] 2 QB 182* and *Shoreham by Sea UDC v Dolphin Canadian Proteins Ltd [1972] LGR 261*); and

(*c*) local authorities have special statutory powers under *Local Government Act 1972, s 222* which permit them to seek injunctions in the civil courts to restrain public nuisances. This power is quite separate from the duties and powers of local authorities to abate statutory nuisances (see below). The action is brought in the name of the local authority, but the legal rights which the authority is seeking to enforce and protect are those of the private citizens affected by the nuisance. (See the *Gillingham Borough Council* case – above.)

3.13 *The statutory nuisances*

The rights of private individuals to bring civil claims in respect of public and private nuisances must be distinguished from the power of local authorities in respect of statutory nuisances.

Under *Environmental Protection Act 1990, ss 79–82*, local authorities are empowered to serve abatement notices where they are satisfied that one or more of certain specified 'statutory nuisances' exists, or is likely to occur or recur, within their area. Abatement notices may require the cessation of the nuisance or restrict its occurrence or recurrence or it may require work to be done, or other steps to be taken, by the person responsible for the nuisance to prevent occurrence or recurrence [*section 80(1)*]. Abatement notices are to be served on the person responsible for the nuisance or, where he cannot be found or the nuisance has not yet occurred, on the owner or occupier of the premises from which they have arisen or may arise [*section 80(2)*]. Contravention of an abatement notice, or failure to comply with its terms, is a criminal offence. Where the offence is committed on industrial, trade or business premises, the fine is up to a maximum of £20,000 [*sections 80(4) and (5)*]. In respect of certain of the statutory nuisances, it is a defence to a criminal prosecution to prove that 'best practicable means' were used to prevent, or to counteract the effects of, the nuisance [*sections 80(7),(8)*].

A person served with an abatement notice has a right of appeal to the magistrates' court within 21 days of service of the notice [*section 80(3)*].

There is a further procedure under *section 82* for a 'person aggrieved by the existence of a statutory nuisance' to seek court orders similar to abatement notices, where the local authority has not exercised its own powers.

Section 79 lists the 'statutory nuisances' to which the abatement notice powers and rights of 'persons aggrieved' apply. They are as follows:

(*a*)   premises which are in a state which is prejudicial to health or constitutes a nuisance;

(*b*)   smoke emitted from premises which is prejudicial to health or creates a nuisance;

(*c*)   fumes or gas emitted from premises which are prejudicial to health or create a nuisance;

(*d*)   any dust, steam, smell or other effluvia arising on industrial, trade or business premises which are prejudicial to health or create a nuisance;

(*e*)   any accumulation or deposit which is prejudicial to health or creates a nuisance;

(*f*)   any animal kept in such a place or manner as to be prejudicial to health or to create a nuisance;

(*g*)   noise emitted from premises so as to be prejudicial to health or to create a nuisance; and

(*h*)   any other matter which is made a statutory nuisance by other legislation.

As may be seen, a person whose home is affected by serious pollution has a variety of measures at his disposal to try to bring it to an end, namely:

(i)   bringing his own court action for an injunction to restrain a private nuisance;

(ii)   to persuade the local authority to exercise its powers under *Local Government Act 1972, s 222* to seek an injunction in public nuisance on his behalf and that of his neighbours;

(iii) to encourage the local authority to serve an abatement notice under the *Environmental Protection Act*;

(iv)   to issue his own proceedings in the Magistrates Court for an order under *Environmental Protection Act 1990, s 80* or

(v)   to ask the Health and Safety Executive to investigate and if appropriate, to issue an improvement or prohibition notice (see 3.4 above).

3.14 Civil Liability and Compensation for Environmental Harm

3.14 Trespass

Trespass occurs where there is some unjustifiable intrusion by one person onto land which is owned or occupied by another. There is some overlap with private nuisance, in particular category (1) nuisance, encroachment on land (see above). It is not, however, necessary for the claimant to show that the trespass has caused actual damage for him to be able to establish his claim, unlike in private nuisance.

In principle, actions both for monetary compensation and for injunctions to restrain or remove the source of the trespass, are available.

A severe limitation on the use of the tort of trespass in pollution cases is the requirement that the interference with the land must be of a direct nature. Also, where the interference arises from the exercise of the defendant's rights over his own property (e.g. permitting sewage to flow from his land onto the claimant's land (*Gibbings v Hungerford [1904] 1 Ir R 211*)) the action should be brought in private nuisance and not in trespass. The requirement for directness of effect seems to exclude the possibility of an action in trespass where polluting matter has been deposited on the claimant's property following its discharge into a watercourse and the deposition on the property occurs through the operation of natural forces and after a period of time (*Jones v Llanrwst UDC [1911] 1 Ch 393* and *Southport Corporation v Esso Petroleum Co* – above). Where, however, trespass is of potential use, particularly because it does not require proof of damage to establish liability, is in cases of dumping or 'fly tipping' and in road and rail traffic spillage cases.

3.15 Negligence

The tort of negligence has wide application across the whole range of public and commercial activity – medical and professional services, the building industry, regulatory control, brokerage and agency, the care of the young and the ill and in employment relationships. It is also a basis for civil claims in certain environmental cases, although its use in this area has been more limited than the use of public and private nuisance (see above) and the rule in *Rylands v Fletcher* (see below).

The essence of this tort is breach of a duty of care imposed by the law on one person in his dealings with another which has produced foreseeable damage which is not too 'remote'. The key elements are:

(a) the existence of a situation in which the law requires a person to exercise reasonable care towards another person, or class of persons of which the claimant is a member;

(b) breach by the defendant of that objective standard of care;

(c) establishment of a link between the carelessness and the damage or injury which has resulted, and

(d) the reasonable foreseeability of the carelessness giving rise to the damage or injury which it has caused.

The situations in which a duty to take care to avoid a particular sort of harm is imposed are myriad and the list is not closed.

The standard of care which the law will require will vary from situation to situation, but the underlying theme is that the degree of care to be exercised is that which 'a reasonable man' would have exercised in the relevant situation (*London Graving Dock Co Ltd v Horton [1951] AC 737*). Where an activity requires a special degree of skill or expertise, then the appropriate standard of care is that which one would expect from someone with those skills to exercise in the relevant situation (*Bolam v Friern Hospital*

Management Committee [1957] 1 WLR 582). Thus, for manufacturing concerns and for those handling potentially hazardous substances or waste, the test to be applied is that of reasonable industry standards, bearing in mind that the courts have tended to look to higher, rather than lower, standards where dangerous materials are involved (see *Dominion Natural Gas Co Ltd v Collins [1909] AC 640* and *Read v J Lyons & Co Ltd* above). Indeed the inherent danger of a substance or operation may be so great that the standard of care imposed will be tantamount to an 'insurance against risk' (*Adelaide Chemical Co v Carlyle (1940) 64 CLR 514*) and create a liability which is close to strict liability in the sense that the taking of precautions of even the highest order will not necessarily provide a successful defence.

In the case of a sudden pollution incident, it is clear that establishing a failure to meet industry standards will take a person whose health or property has been affected by the incident a long way towards establishing liability in negligence – a duty of care will undoubtedly be owed by the industrial concern to avoid the damaging effects of accidental pollution on those who live or work near the relevant site and the principal effects of the contamination or other pollution will usually be readily foreseeable and will not be too remote.

The advantages to a potential claimant of an action in negligence are that:

(a)   he does not have to show an interest in land which has been affected (he may, for example, be a visitor to the area at the time of the relevant incident);

(b)   he does not have to demonstrate some particular loss relative to that suffered by other members of the public who may have been affected, as he would have to do in an action in public nuisance;

(c)   it is clearly established that compensation for personal injury is recoverable in negligence, and

(d)   there is a general principle in relation to personal injury resulting from negligence that the defendant must be 'take the claimant as he finds him', so that, if injury of the sort which has occurred was reasonably foreseeable, then the defendant is required to compensate the claimant for the full extent of the injuries which have resulted, even though the degree of them may also be due to some hyper-sensitivity on the claimant's part. (*Bourhill v Young [1943] AC 92* and *Smith v Leech Brain & Co Ltd [1962] 2 QB 405*).

There are, however, certain difficulties in pursuing a claim in negligence, principally:

(a)   the reluctance of the courts to award compensation in negligence for pure economic loss which does not arise directly from some damage to physical property or from injury (see *Nitrigen Eireann Teoranta v Inco Alloys [1992] 1 All ER 854*),

(b)   the unavailability, generally, of injunctions which are based on allegations of negligence (*Miller v Jackson* – see above), and

(c)   the practical and evidential difficulties which a claimant may face in demonstrating that the defendant's conduct which gave rise to the incident which caused his loss did in fact fall below the relevant standard of care. For example, a plant explosion may be due to simple carelessness or it may, in fact, result from an unforeseen and unusual occurrence over which the plant operator could not reasonably be expected to have exercised control. Even with the aid of Discovery of documents (see 3.26 *et seq.* below), it may be difficult for a claimant to show it was indeed carelessness. Similarly, establishing the relevant industry standards below which it is alleged that the defendant fell may be both a costly and complex process.

3.16 Civil Liability and Compensation for Environmental Harm

It is this last difficulty of establishing the relevant industry standards that may cause particular problems in relation to claims arising from gradual pollution which has been occurring over a period of years. As indicated above, questions of whether the defendant has exercised the requisite degree of care and of foreseeability may cause little difficulty for a claimant where his damage or injury has resulted from a sudden incident. However, the damage that might have been foreseeable to a plant manager, exercising reasonable skill and diligence, many years ago when the gradual pollution from his plant was occurring may, in the light of advances in technical knowledge, be substantially less than would be foreseeable by such a manager at the time the claim is brought. The decisions of the trial judge and the House of Lords in the *Cambridge Water Company* case make it clear that in relation to both negligence and nuisance that foreseeability is determined by reference to current conditions and knowledge and not by the retrospective attribution of contemporary knowledge to those responsible at the time the activities giving rise to the harm occurred.

The cases in which negligence has been successfully argued in the environmental context have been largely restricted to those where localised harm has been done by public utilities, such as gas and electricity companies, in failing to exercise special precautions in carrying out their operations (e.g. *North Western Utilities Ltd v London Guarantee and Accident Co Ltd [1936] AC 108*). However a somewhat different application of the law of negligence in the environmental field arises from the case of *Scott-Whitehead v National Coal Board (1987) 53 P&CR 263*. In this case, a local water authority was found liable in negligence for failing to warn farmers whose land bordered two rivers that excess quantities of chloride had entered the water courses from local mine workings and posed a threat to growing crops. Liability for 'failing to warn' is a development which has been mirrored in the area of product liability. It is capable of further development in the environmental field. In preparing emergency procedures for major accidents or spillages which could have an off-site effect, plant operators would be well-advised to establish adequate warning procedures to avoid negligence claims run on this basis.

3.16 The rule in Rylands v Fletcher

This tort was, until the House of Lords' decision in the *Cambridge Water Company* case, conventionally treated by practitioners and commentators as being one of strict liability in the widest sense of that term, requiring neither a breach of a duty of care on the part of the defendant nor foreseeability of damage (see 'Toxic Torts', Pugh and Day (1992), p 112). The purpose of the tort was thought to be one of putting the person who has committed it effectively in the position of insurer for all the damage which naturally arose from its commission.

The origin of the rule is the judgment of Blackburn J and the speech of Lord Cairns in the House of Lords in the eponymous case of *Rylands v Fletcher (1866) LR 1 Ex 265* and *(1868) LR 3 HL 330*. As refined by the House of Lords, the rule provides that a person who, in circumstances which involve a non-natural use of land, 'brings onto his land and collects and keeps there anything likely to do mischief if it escapes is liable for all the damage which is the natural consequence of its escape'. In *Rylands v Fletcher* the thing which escaped from the defendant's land was water which flooded a mine under the neighbouring property which belonged to the claimant. Even though this incident occurred without any fault on the part of the defendant, he was held liable for the damage resulting from the flooding.

Although the tort is potentially beneficial to a claimant, in that he has no need to show any lack of due care on the part of the person responsible, it is only of use in certain factual circumstances, namely those where:

(a)   there is the accumulation or keeping on land of something which is inherently hazardous;

(b)   the accumulation or keeping of the relevant thing is a 'non natural use' of land – a requirement which has been applied on a case by case basis with no consistency and one which is liable to be something of a shifting target as industrial practices develop and the attitudes of society change (see *Musgrove v Pandelis [1919] 2 KB 43* where the keeping of an ordinary car in a garage was considered to be a non-natural use of land and the *Cambridge Water Company* case below);

(c)   the thing has escaped, and

(d)   caused the relevant loss or damage (which is of a type which was reasonably foreseeable – see the discussion of the *Cambridge Water Company* case below).

An action under the rule in *Rylands v Fletcher* lies not just against a person who is keeping a hazard upon his own land, but against anyone who is responsible for the accumulation or keeping of a hazard, even on a third party's land (*North Western Utilities Ltd v London Guarantee and Accident Co [1936] AC 108*). Nor does the claimant have to be an owner or occupier of neighbouring property which itself may be affected by the escape. Although doubted by Lord Macmillan in *Read v J Lyons & Co Ltd* (above), it appears that liability is owed to all persons who suffer damage from that escape (*British Celanese Ltd v AH Hunt (Capacitors) Ltd [1969] 1 WLR 959*).

Again, the uncertainties mentioned in relation to private nuisance with regard to the recovery of damages for personal injury without having to prove negligence on the part of the person responsible apply also to the rule in *Rylands v Fletcher*.

A number of exceptions and defences to the rule in *Rylands v Fletcher* have been developed in the case law. The defence of statutory authority, which also applies to nuisance claims, is considered later. Another exception, specific to the rule in *Rylands v Fletcher*, is that the owner or keeper of the relevant hazard is not liable for an escape which has occurred as a result of the deliberate or intentional (not merely negligent) act of a third party in circumstances where there is no negligence on the part of the defendant in exercising any supervision or control which he may have had over the third party (*Rickards v Lothian [1913] AC 263*). An example of this situation would be where hazardous substances had been released from an industrial plant as a result of malicious damage done to process safety equipment during the course of a break-in at the plant. In such circumstances, the plant owner would very likely fall within the exception and have no liability under the rule in *Rylands v Fletcher* – although there might be a case against him in negligence. The situation may well be different in the case where the release results from the deliberate act of a contractor whom the plant owner has instructed to carry out work on-site. There then will be difficult factual questions as to whether the plant operator should have foreseen, and prevented, this occurrence and whether, in particular, he was negligent in the system of contractor supervision he had put in place.

The rule in *Rylands v Fletcher* is principally directed to damage caused by isolated events although it has been applied to chronic and periodic escapes. The cases in which the rule in *Rylands v Fletcher* has given rise to liability include escapes of water (as in the case of *Rylands v Fletcher* itself); escapes of sewage (*Humphries v Cousins (1877) 2 CPD 239*); fire spreading from one property to another (*Jones v Festiniog Ry (1868) LR 3 QB*); escapes of gas (*Dominion Natural Gas Co v Collins* – see above) and toxic substances (*Dell v Chesham UDC [1921] 3 KB 427*). So far as toxic waste is concerned, there is, as noted at 3.1 above, an express obligation imposed by *Environmental Protection Act 1990, s 73(6)* to pay compensation for any damage caused by waste which is criminally deposited on land. The liability is that of the person who deposited the waste, or knowingly caused or permitted it to be deposited. It should be noted that this statutory liability is imposed without affecting the other Common Law rights and remedies of the statutory claimant. Thus, a person who has suffered damage as a result of a release or spillage of toxic waste may have claims both under the *Environmental Protection Act 1990* and also under the rule in *Rylands v Fletcher*, as well as in nuisance.

There is now some doubt as to whether the rule in *Rylands v Fletcher* will survive long as a useful alternative claim to an action in nuisance following the House of Lords' fundamental re-appraisal of the rule in the *Cambridge Water Company* case. The House of Lords held that the rule in *Rylands v Fletcher* had never been anything other than a sub-species of the tort of nuisance, extending the law of nuisance to cases of isolated escapes from land. It followed that foreseeability of relevant damage was as much a prerequisite of liability under the rule as it was in nuisance (see 3.11 above) – for this reason the claimant water company in the *Cambridge Water Company* case also failed in its *Rylands v Fletcher* claim. The House of Lords expressly rejected the contention that the rule in *Rylands v Fletcher* should be treated as an embryonic tort of strict liability for damage caused by ultra-hazardous operations such as it had become in the United States (see *Restatement of Torts* (2d) Vol 3 (1977) para 519). The House of Lords' view was that a development of this sort required statutory reform. One conclusion to be drawn from the *Cambridge Water Company* case is that a claimant will not, in most pollution cases, derive great additional benefit from running a claim based on the rule in *Rylands v Fletcher* as an alternative to a claim in nuisance, although where the constituent elements of the rule are satisfied, analogies between the case in question and the facts of previous cases decided on the basis of the rule may be helpful in establishing liability. It may be noted that the House of Lords itself did not go so far as to treat the rule in *Rylands v Fletcher* as a dead letter. The House went on to consider whether the defendant company's handling of solvents on its land constituted a 'non-natural use' of land. Its conclusion, which ironically fortifies the application of the rule in this particular respect, was that the storing of substantial quantities of chemicals and the manner in which they were used by the defendant company was a 'classic' non-natural use. The facts that the relevant chemicals were in common use in industry and that the local community derived a public benefit from the operations on the company's site were insufficient to bring the case within the 'natural use' exception to the rule in *Rylands v Fletcher*. This result did not help the claimant water company because of the finding on the requirement of foreseeability (see above) but, notwith-standing the general doubts expressed above, it may assist claimants in future cases in which the relevant foreseeability is established and where the facts fall within the ambit of the rule in *Rylands v Fletcher*.

3.17   The defence of statutory authority

There are various specific defences and limitations on liability available in respect of each of the torts discussed above, but one of the more significant in the context of environmental law is the defence of statutory authority. It is a general defence in tort law, but many of the decided cases have been in the area of nuisance.

Although not to so great an extent as in the period of rapid expansion of the railway system in the middle of the last century, a good deal of major infrastructure develop-ment is still carried out under specific enabling legislation (e.g. the Channel Tunnel and the development of the London Docklands). Similarly, the privatised utilities and a number of longer established undertakings, such as the United Kingdom Atomic Energy Authority, conduct their day to day operations on the basis of detailed rights, powers and duties conferred by Acts of Parliament. Moreover, a large part of industrial activity in the United Kingdom is authorised by statute to the extent that many businesses require licences and authorisations from the environmental agencies and other regulatory bodies to carry on their operations as part of statutory permitting schemes.

The essence of the defence of statutory authority is that, where a person is authorised under legislation to carry on a particular activity or to use land in a particular way, and a nuisance to others will inevitably arise as a result, then the legislation will be treated as having authorised the creation of this nuisance, provided that reasonable precautions are taken to prevent the nuisance occurring (see *Vaughan v Taff Ry (1860) 5 H&N 679, Allen v Gulf Oil Refining Ltd [1981] AC 1001* and *Tate & Lyle v Greater London Council [1983] 2 AC 509*).

The key question is always whether the legislation in question did intend to sanction the particular nuisance which occurred and in each case it is a matter for careful interpretation of that legislation. The cases where the defence has succeeded relate mainly to Acts of Parliament enabling a specific project to be undertaken or creating powers and duties for statutory undertakers to carry out their services or businesses. The authority, where it exists, is not, however, 'transferable'. Buckley J observed in his judgment in the *Gillingham Borough Council* case (see above) that the defendant dock company could not avail itself of any defence that might have been available to the local port authority by virtue of the *Medway Ports Authority Act 1973* even though the port authority had delegated many of its functions to the dock company and effectively operated through it.

The operation of the defence may go beyond the express authorisation of a particular activity by a specific Act of Parliament itself. It may be available to those who carry out that activity by virtue of authorisations or licences granted by regulatory bodies under statute. The policy argument in favour of this view in the environmental context is that a great deal of individual activity creates a measurable degree of interference and intrusion into the lives of others. Where the degree of such an effect is within limits which have been prescribed by a regulatory body, such as Her Majesty's Inspectorate of Pollution (whose principal responsibility is to protect the environment and public health and who will have considered the tolerability of the exposure to the effect which the public will receive in setting those limits) the operator should have the benefit of the defence. Otherwise, he will have to work to dual standards, the one that is set in the authorisation and the other possibly higher, and certainly uncertain, standard arising from the possibility of civil claims in nuisance being brought.

The fear that this extension of the statutory authority defence to permitting systems may lead to too great a degree of immunity for potential polluters is not groundless, but it may not be a serious issue in practice. Relevant authorisations seldom set just quantitive limits on activity. There will typically be an underlying, and overriding, obligation to minimise exposures, such as BATNEEC in integrated pollution control and ALARP in relation to radioactive disposal authorisations.

3.18 THE REMEDIES

Damages

As has been explained above, the proof of some significant damage or harm is an essential ingredient in establishing basic liability in each of the various torts which have been examined, with the exception of trespass. Indeed, the reasonable foreseeability of that harm or damage may also be relevant to the liability issue (in particular in the tort of negligence). As was also observed, these torts differ in the types of damage for which they will allow a person to be compensated (e.g. pure loss of profit or other similar economic loss will not generally be available in a negligence claim and there are questions as to the ability to recover compensation for pure personal injury in private nuisance and under the rule in *Rylands v Fletcher*).

Where liability is established in a particular tort and the type of loss in question is in principle recoverable, the amount or 'measure' of damages that will be awarded as compensation is also assessed by reference to detailed legal principles which have been developed by the courts. For example, where goods are damaged the 'normal measure' of compensation is the amount by which the value of the damaged goods has been reduced – that figure usually being calculated on the basis of relevant repair costs (see *The London Corporation [1935] P 70*). Where the goods are destroyed the amount of compensation is the amount which would have to be paid in the market to buy the same goods (see *The Clyde Navigation Trustees v Bowring [1929] 34 HLC 319*). In each situation the claimant may also look to the defendant to compensate him for certain consequential losses e.g. the loss of income from the damaged or destroyed goods or the simple loss of the use of them (see e.g. *Liesbosch Dredger v SS Edison [1933] AC 449*). In personal injury cases, the claimant will be entitled to recover compensation for his pecuniary damage (e.g. loss of wages, actual and prospective, and medical expenses) as well as for the physical injury itself which will encompass both pain and suffering and any loss of facility or loss of enjoyment of life.

The measure of compensation for damage done to land, where the two important torts are nuisance and trespass, is also the diminution in the value of the land. In certain cases this is based on a 'market value' approach and in other cases by reference to the cost of making good the damage done or abating a relevant nuisance or, indeed, both (see *Bunclark v Hertfordshire CC (1977) 243 EG 381*). Where there is a category (3) private nuisance involving interference with quiet enjoyment, the annoyance, inconvenience and discomfort suffered by the claimant as a result of the nuisance will be compensated in a way analogous to personal injury (see *Bone v Seale* and *Halsey v Esso Petroleum* – above), but, as indicated above, without regard being paid to any abnormal sensitivities on the part of the claimant. Loss of profits and extra expenses incurred as a result of the damage done to land or interference with its use should be recoverable also. There are a number of public nuisance cases where such loss and expense has been recovered (see *Dodd Properties (Kent) v Canterbury City Council [1980] 1 WLR 433*). Thus, by way of example, a smallholder who is successful in a legal action against the operator from whose waste disposal site toxic material has migrated thereby contaminating the claimant's fields and garden should be compensated for the cost of cleaning-up the contamination, the loss of income from the sale of his free-range eggs which he has been unable to sell because they also contain unacceptably high levels of toxins and the expense he has incurred in moving his family to a local guest house for the week during which the clean-up operation was in progress.

In broad terms, damages which are awarded for breaches of tort are intended to do no more than to put the claimant in the position he would have been in had the tort not been committed (*Livingstone v Rawyards Coal Co (1880) 5 App Cas 25*). The principles of assessment outlined above are directed to achieving this result. There are, however, in tort cases, circumstances in which the courts will, award extra, higher, damages which go beyond this principle. These are 'aggravated' damages and 'exemplary' (or 'punitive') damages. The former will be awarded in cases where the relevant tort was committed in such a way that the victim's dignity and pride has been seriously injured. Exemplary damages are limited to two situations. The most important of the two is the circumstance where the person committing the tort did so calculating that he would make a profit for himself that might exceed any level of compensation he would have to pay his victim under the usual damages assessment rules. The object of the award is to ensure that 'the tort does not pay' (*Broome v Cassell & Co Ltd [1971] 2 QB 354*).

Awards of aggravated and exemplary damages are only made in extreme cases and are rare. There is one nuisance case in England in which they have been awarded and this involved a landlord's serious harassment of his tenants. In the environmental field, they were refused in the case of *Halsey v Esso Petroleum Co Ltd* (above) and a claim for them was abandoned at the start of trial in *Merlin v British Nuclear Fuels plc [1990] 3 All ER 711*. Nonetheless, the seeking of aggravated and exemplary damages has recently been a feature of a number of large-scale environmental cases. This development has received a set-back with the judgment of the Court of Appeal in the case of *AB v South West Water Services Ltd [1993] 1 All ER 609*, an action arising out of the Camelford water pollution incident. The claimant's relevant claim was in public nuisance. The argument for exemplary damages was based on an allegation that the defendant water company had deliberately misled consumers as to the health risks of the incident with a view to maintaining its profits. The Court of Appeal held that (*a*) in principle, exemplary damages were not available in public nuisance cases, but only in certain restricted historic categories of tort and (*b*) that, even if the defendant had, as alleged, attempted to cover up a tort its action was intended to limit its damages, which was quite a different thing from committing a tort in the first place with a view to gain. The claim for exemplary damages was struck out. So, too, was the claim for aggravated damages. These had been claimed on the basis of prolonged pain and suffering said to have arisen from the fact that the nuisance was allowed to continue for longer than it should. These were held to be instances of harm which should be compensated for on the normal basis of assessment (see above).

3.19   Injunctions

In certain environmental cases a court injunction may be the only effective remedy. Private individuals can apply for injunctions in respect of claims in private nuisance and trespass, and, in principle, for breaches of the rule in *Rylands v Fletcher*. Injunctions in the tort of negligence seem not to be available (*Miller v Jackson* – see above). Injunctions in respect of public nuisance are either brought directly by the Attorney General or on the initiative of a private individual by means of a 'relator action' in which the Attorney General is formally joined as a Plaintiff. Alternatively, local authorities may seek injunctions in respect of public nuisances under *Local Government Act 1972, s 222* – see 3.12 above.

Injunctions are granted both by the High Court and by county courts. [*Supreme Court Act 1981, s 37(1)*; *County Courts Act 1984, s 38*]. In practice, major environmental injunctions will be sought in the High Court.

Injunctions may be 'prohibitive' (or 'negative') simply requiring the defendant to cease or refrain from the activity complained of (see *Pride of Derby etc. Ltd v British Celanese Ltd [1953] Ch 149* – an injunction restraining the discharge of sewage into a river until such time as an improved treatment plant was installed). They may also be 'mandatory', requiring the defendant to take some positive action, including action which may involve him in expense e.g. to clean-up off-site contamination. In the case of *Morris v Redland Bricks Ltd [1970] AC 652* an injunction was granted requiring the defendant to carry out underpinning work to neighbouring land which had been affected by subsidence from earth and clay extraction.

Injunctions, particularly prohibitory injunctions, may be granted on a *quia timet* basis. This is where no damage has yet occurred but there is a situation where, if the injunction were not granted, there would be a real possibility of it occurring.

Injunctions will be granted in such terms as are appropriate to protect the claimant's legitimate interests. Thus, for example, an injunction may restrict, rather than prohibit outright, the offending activity (see *The Gillingham Borough Council* case (above) where the injunction was not for a total ban on goods vehicle movements, but for a restriction on such movements during night-time hours).

An injunction may be sought in addition to a damages claim. For example, an individual may claim damages for the historic effects of an on-going nuisance and an injunction to restrain its continuation. An injunction is not, however, a remedy which a person is entitled to as of right. It is granted at the discretion of the Court.

Because of the length of time it takes for most legal actions to come to trial, it is open to a claimant to apply for an 'interim' injunction (whether of a prohibitory, mandatory or *quia timet* type) at an earlier stage in the legal proceedings. In urgent cases this may be even before the High Court Writ or County Court Summons has been issued. An application for an interim, or 'interlocutory' injunction will take the form of a short hearing before a judge who will decide the matter on the basis of evidence set out in affidavits. In cases of extreme urgency, injunctions can be granted on an *ex parte* basis i.e. without the defendant or prospective defendant being present before the judge – although the terms of the *ex parte* injunction will usually provide for the defendant to be given notice of the injunction and an opportunity to be heard at an early date to have the injunction varied or set aside. In the most extreme cases, an injunction could be obtained at any time of the day or night, even without affidavit evidence and sometimes by way of oral submissions made on the telephone by counsel to the judge (as in *British Nuclear Fuels plc v Stichting Greenpeace Nederland & Others (1987) unreported*). However, a particular feature of interim injunctions is that, generally, the claimant will be required to give an 'undertaking in damages'. The effect of this is to require the claimant to reimburse the defendant for any loss or expense he may incur as a result of complying with the injunction should the injunction subsequently be set aside or refused at full trial. An exception to the requirement for an undertaking is in cases where a public body is seeking the injunction to prevent a breach of the law that would be harmful to the public, or to a section of the public e.g. an application by a local authority under *Local Government Act 1972, s 222* for an injunction to restrain a public nuisance (*Kirklees BC v Wickes Building Supplies Ltd [1992] 3 All ER 717*).

Special factors are taken into account by the Court in deciding whether to grant an interim injunction. These were laid down in the case of *American Cyanamid Co v Ethicon [1975] AC 396*. They are as follows:

(*a*)   the claimant's action must not be frivolous or vexatious, in other words

(*b*)   he must show that there is a real question to be tried; or

(*c*)   that there is a real prospect that he would succeed in his claim for a permanent injunction at trial;

(*d*)   the claimant must also show that damages are an inadequate remedy for him and that he will be able to meet any cost that might arise out of his undertaking in damages (see above), and

(*e*)   that the 'balance of convenience' is in the claimant's favour i.e. that the damage to the claimant would be greater if the application were refused and he was successful at trial than the damage caused to the defendant if the application were to be allowed and the defendant was successful at trial or that there is some wider public interest in favour of the injunction being granted.

Rather than having an interim injunction made against him, a defendant may prefer to give an undertaking to the Court in terms similar to that of the injunction which is being sought. A prospective claimant will, where time permits, normally seek such an undertaking before starting legal action. The sanction for breaching a Court undertaking is the same as that for breaching an injunction (see below).

Often, the obtaining of an interim injunction will effectively be the end of the matter. Because of the time which it would take for the matter to come to trial (unless a special order were made for trial to be expedited) a defendant who has had to incur substantial expenditure in complying with an interim injunction will have little incentive to take the matter through to full trial, particularly if the activity which is subject to the injunction is not of a long-term nature. A claimant may also apply to transform his interim injunction into a final injunction by seeking summary judgment on the basis that the defendant has no arguable case to his claim. The summary judgment procedure is relatively quick and, again, is based only on affidavit evidence. (See *British Nuclear Fuels plc v Greenpeace (Rainbow Warrior Holdings) Ltd & Others (1983) unreported*).

Disobeying an injunction, both interim and final, is a contempt of court, punishable by fine or imprisonment, or, in the case of a company, sequestration of the company's assets by a court-appointed receiver. Directors of companies against which injunctions have been obtained, or by whom undertakings have been given, may themselves be in contempt if there is any complicity on their part in breach of that injunction or undertaking.

Injunctions have been sought and obtained on both sides of 'the environmental divide'. There are numerous instances of injunctions granted to restrain offensive or intrusive industrial activity (*Crump v Lambert* and *Halsey v Esso Petroleum Co Ltd* – see above). On the other hand, injunctions in nuisance, trespass, and conspiracy to injure business have been obtained by companies against individuals and environmental action groups involved in direct action campaigns against their activities and business interests. (See *British Nuclear Fuels plc v Greenpeace (Rainbow Warrior Holdings) Ltd & Others* and *British Nuclear Fuels plc v Stichting Greenpeace Nederland & Others* (above) and *British Nuclear Fuels plc v Stichting Rubicon & Others (1990) also unreported.)* Sometimes, a company seeking an injunction against a group of people taking direct action against its activities will have difficulty in identifying all the individuals involved or the organisation, if any, on whose behalf they are acting. In such circumstances, the Court may direct that one or more individuals who can be identified should be sued as representative defendants. Such a direction may be made even though those individuals may only be peripherally involved in the action complained of and even though the effect of an injunction against them would be to impose personal liability on them (*Michaels Furriers) Ltd v Askew (1983) 127 SJ 597*).

3.20   Remedial liability

As briefly described at 3.2 above, the environmental agencies have special powers to impose remedial liability on a polluter. In particular, they have the power to carry out clean-up works and to seek recovery of the costs from the person responsible. The statutory provisions under which these agencies may clean-up pollution or carry out work to prevent its occurrence are discussed further in THE PLAYERS (2).

The most significant of these statutory provisions are:

Environmental Protection Act 1990

—   *Section 27*

> —   clean-up in the context of integrated pollution control and local authority air pollution control;

—   *Section 42*

> —   emergency remedial works on licensed waste disposal sites;

—   *Section 59*

> —   removal of unlawfully deposited waste (see also *Control of Pollution Act 1974, s 16*);

—   *Section 61*

    —   powers to remediate sites upon which controlled waste has been deposited (not yet in force).

Water Resources Act 1991

—   *Section 161*

    —   cost of action or works done by the National Rivers Authority to clean-up polluted waters (including ground water) or to prevent such pollution occurring.

Town and Country Planning Act 1990

—   *Section 215*

    —   remediation of the appearance of derelict land.

Several general points may be made about these various provisions:

(*a*)   Although these various statutory provisions have a common theme, there are many significant differences in their detailed wordings. The precise wording used may be critical in establishing liability in any individual case. Similar, but different, technical expressions used include 'caused or knowingly permitted' cf. 'knowingly caused or knowingly permitted', and 'person who is for the time being the owner of land', cf. 'occupier', cf. 'person who caused the statutory nuisance'. These various expressions are not free from uncertainty as to their meaning and scope. For example, the expressions 'owner' and 'occupier' are more layman's descriptions of fact than precise legal concepts known to property law. Similarly, the circumstances in which it may be said that a person may have 'knowingly permitted' something to occur, or a state of affairs to prevail, has uncertain scope. It also remains to be seen to what extent, and in what circumstances, lenders with security interests in land may fall within these various statutory categories. This is a question which also affects the position of receivers and administrators as regards their dealings with insolvent companies and their property.

(*b*)   Factual and legal uncertainties arising out of these provisions have, for the moment at least, given rise to some caution on the part of the environmental agencies. The scheme of things is that they have to undertake the work in question and incur expenses which may be significant before they can seek recovery of their costs. If it should prove, in any particular case, that the agencies are unable to satisfy the precise statutory requirements for cost recovery they may, at the end of the day, be substantially out of pocket. For agencies operating on tight budgets this may be a significant disincentive to embarking on widespread clean-up and preventive operations. This concern of the agencies is reflected in the recently reported proposal of the National Rivers Authority to exercise its private law rights as a riparian owner of stretches of the rivers Doe Lea and Rother to seek a Court declaration that an alleged polluter is liable under the common law to bear the cost of removing dioxin-contaminated sediment from these two rivers. This action is being taken as an alternative to statutory action under *Water Resources Act 1991, s 161*. This *Act* only permits the recovery of 'reasonable' costs for work which the National Rivers Authority must first have undertaken. It appears that the Authority views the incurring of the prospective costs of more than £1 million before seeking to recover them as too great a risk to take. It is hoped to establish the defendant company's civil law liability before starting clean-up. It should, however, be noted that because clean-up is, in certain circumstances, a duty of the environmental agency, an

38

interested party could take proceedings by way of judicial review to enforce the performance of the agency's duty. In other words, it may mean that the option of 'not risking the budget' is not legally open to the agency in question.

(c)   The right of an agency to recover 'reasonable' costs of clean-up presents another potential difficulty, this time for the person on whom the liability is sought to be imposed. It may be that that person could argue that the work which has been done could reasonably have been done more cheaply. However, it does not seem that there is any clear obligation under the relevant legislation to ensure that the cost incurred is proportionate to the environmental benefit produced. Thus, it may be that a large sum of money is spent by an agency to produce a relatively minor environmental improvement – the costs are recoverable in full so long as the work that was actually done could not reasonably have been done for less. The only opportunity to challenge such a demand would be to argue, in judicial review proceedings, that the agency in question had abused its powers in acting in the way it had e.g. by acting unreasonably. This may provide an opportunity for the courts to invoke Continental and European Community Law concepts of 'proportionality'.

3.21   LITIGATING ENVIRONMENTAL CLAIMS

The threat of environmental litigation for industrial concerns has increased greatly in recent times. This is a result not just of the wider powers of the environmental agencies to impose remedial liability but of changes in publication administration and legal procedure that have increased the will and capability of private individuals to bring civil claims against major polluters. Claims concerning property impairment or damage to health arising from pollution will frequently involve many claimants and will be demanding on legal resources and especially expensive to mount, as well as to defend. Recent developments have gone some way toward recognising, if not resolving, these problems for private claimants.

A typical public liability environmental case which industry might face would involve many potential claimants, of differing ages and financial means, but with a number of common ties, specifically, likely residence in the same community or geographical area; the same types of injury or damage (although with differences in degree); the same incident or series of incidents giving rise to their claims and broadly the same causes of action. In a number of respects, this sort of legal case resembles a major negligence claim against a pharmaceutical company or transport 'disaster' litigation. Much of the recent pioneering work in organising and running multi-claimant suits in England has been done in these types of case. The lessons which have been learned there are equally applicable to the environmental field. As scientific research on the biological effects of toxins and carcinogens continues, potential defendants need to be alive to the creativity and proven track record of lawyers experienced in multi-claimant suits in their use of developing scientific evidence.

Particular developments and initiatives are as follows.

3.22   Finding claimants and organising the action

Virtually everyone who lives near to a major manufacturing plant will be aware of the fact – he or she may even be employed there. Not many, however, will be aware of the nature and quantity of pollutants emitted from the plant and virtually no one will have any sensible information with which to associate any health impairment from which he or his family may be suffering with those emissions. There may be suspicions and local gossip but, invariably, it is only when a well-resourced pressure group, or a lawyer with relevant experience, takes an interest that a proper analysis of causation and the formulation of potential claims can be made. It has, for many years, been permissible for solicitors to seek information from other solicitors as to whether the latter have clients who may have suffered particular damage or injury from specific exposures (commonly to pharmaceutical products). This is usually done by notices in professional journals. The purpose of these notices is to try to pool information or to make common cause. English Law Society rules made it difficult for solicitors to hold themselves out to the public as specialists, (for example in pursuing pollution claims) and, effectively, to advertise for prospective clients. However, the relaxation of Law Society Rules has now permitted an approach to the public of this sort, including by way of written advertisement. Whilst the solicitor placing such an advertisement should still take care to avoid the appearance of 'ambulance chasing', this technique can be, and in certain cases has now been, used as part of the first step in drawing together and beginning the co-ordination of a group of potential claimants.

In parallel with this development, there have grown up a number of permanent and *ad hoc* groups, often headed by legal practitioners, to monitor and to co-ordinate, particular types of litigation. Examples in England are the Environmental Law Foundation, a group of lawyers and scientists seeking generally to develop and promote legal remedies for environmental torts and, with particular relevance to the nuclear industry, the Radiation Victims Round Table. None of these UK groups stands comparison with the large and well-resourced US environmental bodies, such as the Sierra Club, but the growth of organisations of this size at a European level is not inconceivable.

Where there are many prospective claimants and a number of law firms acting on their behalf it has become an accepted, indeed a vital, technique for the firms of solicitors to co-operate closely with each other. This may be not only for the sharing of information, but also for the joint preparation and initiation of legal proceedings if there is sufficient common interest between the various claimants to justify it. Steering, or co-ordination, committees of solicitors are established and this may lead to a single law firm being selected as the 'lead solicitor' to appear on the Court record on behalf of all claimants. The benefits to the claimants of this approach are obvious – technical expertise is fully shared and one of the major obstacles to successful pursuits of the actions, namely the limited financial resources of individual claimants, is addressed, even if not surmounted.

Not only is close co-operation of this sort between claimants' solicitors now a conventional approach; it is one which the English Law Society seeks to promote. The Law Society has appointed an Information Co-ordinator who will take responsibility, in appropriate cases, for running a register of solicitors who are representing relevant individuals and will advertise the register in the professional journals. The Law Society will call and sponsor meetings of interested solicitors for them to start the process of co-ordination.

3.23   Funding

Legal Aid

Legal Aid is a government-funded scheme for the provision of financial assistance to individuals who need advice or representation in criminal and civil cases. The scheme provides assistance for persons engaged in civil litigation whether or not they are a claimant or a defendant. The scheme is essentially for private individuals with modest capital and income. The scheme is administered on an area – geographical basis. Aid for civil litigation is given subject to satisfying the two fairly basic criteria of (*a*) financial eligibility and (*b*) reasonable grounds, in the case of a prospective claimant, for bringing the action. Legal Aid may be granted subject to conditions or for up to particular points in the preparation of the case for trial.

Once granted to an individual, Legal Aid can make possible the bringing of very large and difficult technical cases which would have been far beyond the means of the claimant himself; the Legal Aid Board will, and in recent years has, supported major civil claims at a cost of hundreds of thousands of pounds. In these circumstances, the less wealthy claimant, who is financially eligible for Legal Aid, has a greater potential ability to bring litigation than the claimant who has more money but, as a result, no eligibility.

As discussed earlier, the public liability environmental claims which an industrial company may face are likely to be multi-claimant affairs with all claims based on the same incident or series of incidents. In actions of this sort, the Legal Aid Board is likely to take a pro-active role. It may nominate one of its area offices to deal with all relevant applications for Legal Aid (whereas the normal procedure might lead to the involvement of several such offices). Where there are a large number of claimants and several law firms involved who are taking co-ordinated action, as described above, the Legal Aid Board, will in practice, liaise closely with the lawyers' co-ordination committee before the legal action is started. It may play a role in decisions as to how the various claims should be cast and taken forward procedurally.

The provision of Legal Aid in large multi-claimant actions is regarded as an area deserving particular consideration and as subject to its own special policy considerations. The *Civil Legal Aid (General) Regulations* were amended on 1 April 1992 to permit the Legal Aid Board to enter into special contracts with solicitors working on multi-party personal injury actions involving ten or more legally-aided claimants which involve common issues of fact or law arising out of the same cause or event. These new arrangements have particularly in mind litigation arising from a disaster or claims against drug companies (see Legal Aid Handbook 1992, paragraph 16). They are equally applicable to mass personal injury claims arising from pollution or other environmental harm. The purpose of the contracting arrangement is to allow more advantageous terms for payment-on-account for claimants' lawyers, thus encouraging law firms to undertake work of this sort. Contracts may be awarded to law firms, or groups of firms, to undertake work on the 'generic' aspects of the claims (i.e. the major liability issues common to all the claims), with individual claimants free to instruct other firms to undertake the work on their specific claim in co-ordination with the firm or firms handling the generic matters.

A prospective defendant does not have to be notified, either by the Legal Aid Board or by the claimant, that an application is being made for Legal Aid to bring a claim against him. Nor is he entitled to see the papers filed in support of the application. The defendant is usually informed when the Writ or County Court Summons is served on him. Where, however, a person hears of an intended application for Legal Aid to sue him it is open to him to make representations to the Legal Aid Board before it makes its decision, including for example, observations on relevant factual matters concerning the claim that the claimant himself, and therefore, the Legal Aid Board may not know of. Decisions to grant Legal Aid may be challenged by the prospective defendant by way of judicial review. Leave to bring such an application was obtained in the High Court in an environmental case involving several hundred legally-aided claimants in July 1993 (*The People of Docklands' Litigation*).

3.24   *The Fees System*

The ability of lawyers in the United States to charge clients on a 'contingent fee' basis has been a potent force in enabling Americans to pursue large scale environmental cases in the courts. Under the *Courts and Legal Services Act 1990*, English lawyers are now able to accept cases on a 'conditional fee' basis in certain proceedings, including personal injury cases. Although these new fee arrangements do not permit a 'no win, no fee' arrangement they provide for an up-lift in fees if the case is successful. They may improve access to legal representation, particularly to those who are not eligible for Legal Aid. This, combined with the making of costs sharing arrangements between claimants (see below) and the more effective use of Legal Aid funds in multi-claimant actions involving health effects, increases the scope for environmental claims against industry to be brought.

3.25 *The running of group actions*

The 'class action' in the United States is sometimes regarded as a model which should be adopted in this country for large scale litigation, including big pollution claims. The present English Supreme Court Rules of procedure do, however, permit, with the application of judicial ingenuity and an element of co-operation between the claimants and between the claimants and defendant, the creation of a single action, or series of actions, which bear at least a passing resemblance to the classic US 'class action'.

The particular procedural rules and practices facilitating a group action include the following:

(*a*)   the 'representative action' i.e. a *single* plaintiff bringing *one* action; suing in his own name and also as representative for other people who have broadly the same interest in the proceedings;

(*b*)   joint proceedings i.e. the joining of *all* plaintiffs in a *single* action. This is possible where there are common issues for the claimants and common events leading up to the action;

(*c*)   consolidation of proceedings i.e. amalgamation in *one* set of proceedings of *separate* actions which may have been started independently but where the considerations applying to joint proceedings set out above are also present;

(*d*)   the 'test case' or 'lead action'. The Courts have wide powers to stay proceedings. This power, combined with the making of a 'costs sharing order', can be used to encourage a group of claimants to select one or two 'test' or 'lead' actions, rather than running all claims together or in parallel (see *Davies v Eli Lilley & Co* [1987] 1 WLR 1136 and the *HIV Haemophiliac Litigation* (1990));

(*e*)   where there are several sets of different proceedings, the assignment of the cases to a single judge. He can then make appropriate orders in each case and try to achieve a sensible management of the trial, or series of trials. This may include the service of one set of 'master pleadings' dealing with the general allegations and defences and the carrying out by the defendant of a single exercise of Discovery of documents. In May 1991, the Supreme Court Procedure Committee published, for lawyers, the 'Guide for Use in Group Actions'. This publication amounted to the official recognition that, even without further reform, England already has an imperfect, but workable system for organising and running multi-claimants suits.

3.26 *Disclosure of documents in civil litigation (Discovery)*

An understanding of the rules of Discovery is essential for anyone involved in the conduct of environmental civil litigation. The extent of the Discovery obligation and the impact which it may have on the outcome of a case is often not appreciated, particularly in the case of litigants with little previous experience of the adversarial common law system.

The volume of environmental information being generated in recent years, either for reasons of regulatory compliance or (paradoxically) voluntarily by companies keen to establish their 'green credentials' has made it all the more important for companies firstly to understand the potential risk of having to disclose all relevant documents to an adversary and secondly to understand the potential ways of lawfully protecting documents from disclosure.

Discovery is the process by which the parties to a legal action are compelled to disclose to each other the existence of all documents in their possession, custody or power which are relevant to a matter in issue in the action. The documents may subsequently be inspected (subject to claims for privilege which are discussed below) by the party to whom disclosure has been given and copies may be taken. The most relevant documents, and often those which may simply contain prejudicial or embarrassing material, will be read out in open court at the trial.

'Relevance' is very widely interpreted and covers all documents which relate to the questions that separate the parties and which will be resolved in the litigation, regardless of whether the documents help or harm the case of the person making disclosure (*Compagnie Financière du Pacifique v Peruvian Guano Co (1882) 11 QBD 55*). The term 'document' includes all copies of documents (even if identical to the original, but note, particularly, that this will include copies which have added annotations), draft documents, drawings, manuscript notes, notes of meetings, diary entries, video/sound recordings, computer disks and databases.

Documents are in the 'possession custody or power' of a party to litigation if they are either in his physical possession or the possession of his agent or are held by another person but the party has the right to call for their inspection. The obligation to disclose documents may therefore extend to documents held by companies within the same Group.

The obligation to give Discovery is on-going and applies to any further documents coming into existence generally after proceedings are started, right up to the end of the trial.

A party must also disclose the existence of documents which he *used* to have in his possession, custody or power but which he no longer has. When he discloses the existence of these documents he must state, as far as he knows, when he last had the documents and what has become of them.

As soon as litigation is in prospect all parties must preserve all relevant documents which they have or control. This means that there must be an immediate suspension of any routine destruction of documents which could conceivably be relevant and measures must be put in place to ensure the documents are not inadvertently destroyed.

It is important to note, in the environmental context, that in a personal injury case it is open both to the potential claimant and the defendant to apply for pre-action Discovery of documents. [*Supreme Court Act 1981, ss 35, 35*; *County Court Act 1984, s 52*]. Thus, even before proceedings are commenced, a company may find itself faced with a request for disclosure of documents to a *prospective* litigant. The scope of such pre-action Discovery can, in some cases, be quite extensive and involve a potential defendant company in considerable time and expense before the substantive litigation starts. Documents may also be obtained from third parties in personal injury cases. [*Supreme Court Act 1981, ss 34, 35*; *County Court Act 1984, s 53*]. The documents which may be obtained in this way are not restricted to medical or hospital records but could, for example, include logs and working papers produced and held by an engineering company which had been contracted by the defendant to carry out safety or maintenance work on plant which had failed, leading to an accidental release of the substance which is alleged to have caused the claimant's injury. These rules provide the claimant in a health affects case with the considerable benefit of acquiring, at an early stage, a substantial amount of evidence to help him prepare his case.

Although little can be done to protect documents which are required by law (for example, under the *Environmental Protection Act 1990* or the *Water Resources Act 1991* or by special conditions imposed in a discharge permit) to be prepared and held by a company, there are certain steps which can be taken to minimise the extent of documents which may have to be disclosed:

(*a*)   a defendant company's employees should be careful about the manner in which sensitive matters are committed to writing. Where a sensitive issue relating to the litigation is being discussed then written material should be prepared with the prospect clearly in mind that it may have to be disclosed in due course;

(*b*)   the defendant should be mindful that there will be 'legal privilege' for some of the documents which it generates and receives. It is a fundamental principle that a person has a right to seek and obtain legal advice from his or her lawyer in total confidence. This is known as legal privilege. Communications attracting legal privilege are commonly divided into two types. The first is 'legal advice' privilege which protects from disclosure confidential communications between a client and his solicitor which have come into existence for the sole or dominant purpose of giving or obtaining legal advice. The second (wider) type of privilege is 'litigation' privilege which protects confidential communications between a lawyer and his client and a lawyer or his client and a non-professional agent or a third party (such as an expert witness), but only where the communications come into existence after proceedings are contemplated or pending and for the purpose of obtaining legal advice in those proceedings. In order to claim this privilege, a company would have to show that the investigation of a potential problem had taken place, and the documents had been generated, whether internally or by a firm of consultants, at the request of the lawyers for the purpose of providing legal advice to the company. Whether or not such a claim for privilege would be upheld by a court would depend on what was found to be the dominant purpose for which the document was created, regardless of the label attached to it by the company or its lawyers. In order to succeed therefore the company would have to show that the document was genuinely generated for the dominant purpose of obtaining legal advice or assisting the lawyers in preparing the case for litigation and that it was not simply an attempt to avoid disclosure in the legal proceedings.

3.27 *Insurance*

An employer is required by law to take out and maintain insurance cover against liability for personal injury or disease sustained by his employees whilst at work. [*Employers' Liability (Compulsory Insurance) Act 1969, s 1(1)*]. (See Tolley's Health and Safety at Work Handbook 1994, paragraph 16.8.) Thus, liability to employees arising from health hazards and occurrences in the workplace should in all cases be insured. Usually, industrial concerns will also take out third party or general liability ('GL') insurance. This may cover them for claims resulting from injury to members of the public or damage to property resulting from pollution or an environmental incident. Since the late 1980s, however, largely as a result of the claims experience in the United States, there has been a tendency for such policies to exclude automatically injury, loss or damage arising out of pollution of the air, ground, water or atmosphere. Sometimes the exclusion is total; in other cases the cover is restricted to 'sudden and accidental' or 'unintended' pollution. The object of this is to exclude gradual pollution of the sort which occurred in the *Cambridge Water Company* case. The scope of such exclusion and limitation clauses has not, however, been free from controversy. 'Foreseeability' may be an important issue. The effect which advances in scientific knowledge and technical development may have on the question of the foreseeability of damage, which lay at the heart of the *Cambridge Water Company* case (see above), was interestingly foreshadowed in the insurance coverage dispute in *AF & G Robinson v Evans Bros Pty Ltd (1969) VR 885*. In this case, the Australian Court had to interpret policy wording which restricted the insurer's indemnity to liability arising from 'accident'. The liability in question related to damage caused to growing crops from several years' exposure to chemical emissions from the insured's plant. The insured was aware of scientific debate as to the possible damaging effect of emissions of this sort, but it took the calculated risk that the scientific view that there was no such effect was correct. The Court held that, in principle, the taking of this sort of risk did not permit the damage which in fact resulted was caused as 'an accident'. The New Zealand Court of Appeal, in the subsequent case of *NZ Municipalities Co-operative Insurance Co Ltd v City of Mount Albert (1984) 3 ANZ Ins. Cas 60-444* puts on this earlier Australian decision the gloss that, even where risks of this sort are run, the resultant damage may still be accidental if the risk in question was not, on reasonable grounds, treated as a high or substantial risk.

To meet the demand for a degree of protection new forms of specific environmental impairment liability ('EIL') are being underwritten, often covering liability for impairment of, or interference with, legal rights and amenity, as well as normal bodily injury and damage to property. Gradual pollution, other than deliberate pollution, may also be covered. Such insurance is, however, at the moment generally restrictive in the monetary amounts covered and is subject to consultants' site surveys and audit for which the policy holder must pay. EIL coverage is still in its infancy in the United Kingdom and, at the present time, a very small number of EIL policies have been purchased. GL policies containing a general pollution exclusion but with special cover for environmental risks arising from specified operations or subject to special limits on indemnity (e.g. the so-called 'SEPTIC Pollution Endorsement') are also available, but these policies have also not been widely underwritten.

Insurance for site clean-up is of increasing importance because of the development of the powers of the regulatory authorities to impose remedial liability (see 3.2 and 3.20 above). Whether a standard GL policy covers the cost of complying with a statutory clean-up obligation, as well as the common law liability for damages to a third party whose property has been contaminated (to which GL coverage is conventionally directed), would depend in each case on the precise policy wording and the definition of the events expressed to be insured. Under most EIL policies currently available in the United Kingdom, 'off-site' clean-up is covered, but underwriters have so far resisted the temptation to follow certain US insurers in insuring 'own-site' clean-up where carried out pursuant to a regulatory requirement or on a voluntary basis to minimise or avert subsequent off-site contamination. In many instances, industrial concerns face the dilemma, upon discovering a historic source of contamination in the soil on their site, or in the aquifer beneath it, of doing nothing and allowing eventual migration of the pollution to neighbouring properties, thereby risking future legal liability (which may, if all relevant and prompt disclosures are made to insurers, prove to be covered by the insurance) or incurring immediate costs in remediating their site with a view to avoiding such liability, but probably on an uninsured and irrecoverable basis.

The relief with which the insurance community has greeted the recent House of Lords' decision in the *Cambridge Water Company* case may not be wholly justified. Where there is a source of pollution on the insured's site which results from historic activities but is still a continuing pollution source (e.g. solvents in the soil on site which are still migrating into a groundwater or the aquifer) and which at the present time, if not at the time the source of pollution was created, can reasonably be foreseen as presenting a hazard to neighbouring properties or to public health, then the possibility of nuisance or negligence claims still arises for the reasons given in 3.11 above.

In short, industry in this country is still greatly reliant on old-style GL policies. With their pollution exclusion clauses, this has created a situation where a substantial amount of the potential liability for environmental risks which manufacturing businesses face is effectively self-insured.

When faced with environmental claims the insured will first have regard to his current policy which is likely to be a GL policy and written on a 'claims made' basis with, as indicated above, pollution exclusions. However, previous older-style policies may still be relevant. In the case of gradual pollution, previous years' policies which contain no pollution exclusions and which were written on a 'losses arising' basis, may provide the insured with at least partial cover for claims relating to health effects with a lengthy latency period or delayed diagnosis, or for damage arising from land contamination which has been continuing, undetected, over a number of years.

It is essential that, in all cases, where a potential defendant becomes aware of a possible environmental claim, he should review his insurance cover with advisers and comply promptly with the terms of all relevant policies which require notification of claims or 'relevant circumstances' to insurers.

4 Atmospheric Pollution

4.1 INTRODUCTION

This chapter describes:

(a)   the controls over atmospheric emissions under the systems of Integrated Pollution Control and Local Authority Air Pollution Control. [*Environmental Protection Act 1990, Part I*]. These controls are superseding and will extend the scope of the former controls, dating from the *Alkali Acts 1863* and *1874*, contained in the *Alkali etc. Works Regulation Act 1906* and the *Health and Safety at Work etc. Act 1974*;

(b)   the provisions of the *Clean Air Acts 1956* and *1968*;

(c)   certain regulations made under the *Health and Safety at Work etc. Act 1974* which relate to safety in the context of atmospheric emissions;

(d)   the substance of, and the procedures associated with, the concept of statutory nuisance [*Environmental Protection Act 1990, Part III*];

(e)   controls over atmospheric pollution from mobile sources; and

(f)   measures relating to ozone depleting chemical emissions.

4.2 AIR POLLUTION CONTROL UNDER THE INTEGRATED POLLUTION CONTROL SYSTEM

The system of Integrated Pollution Control (IPC), being introduced under *Part I* of the *Environmental Protection Act 1990*, is considered more fully in Chapter 16. For the present, in the context of air pollution control, the following brief description will suffice.

IPC is a system of pollution control which is targeted on certain processes and substances which are considered to have the greatest potential for environmental harm. These processes and substances are defined in the *Environmental Protection (Prescribed Processes and Substances) Regulations 1991 (SI 1991 No 472, as amended)*: see further, INTEGRATED POLLUTION CONTROL (16.5).

It is a system of control administered by HMIP (and is to become a function of the proposed new Environment Agency when that Agency is established in 1995).

It is being introduced, superseding controls under the *Alkali etc. Act*, in accordance with a published timetable (see further, 16.7). It came into operation as regards all *new, or substantially modified*, prescribed processes, on 1 April 1991. In respect of *existing* processes the system of control is being introduced sector by sector on a series of dates extending as far ahead as 1996. For the list of processes controlled under the *Alkali etc. Act* see the *Health and Safety (Emissions into the Atmosphere) Regulations 1983 (SI 1983 No 943) (as amended by the Health and Safety (Emissions into the Atmosphere) (Amendment) Regulations 1989 (SI 1989 No 319))*.

In respect of processes subject to Integrated Pollution Control the enforcing agency (HMIP) is required, in determining the conditions which are to be attached to the grant of the required authorisation, to consider the impact of the process on each of the various environmental media (air, water and land). Where the process is likely to involve the release of substances into more than one environmental medium the

4.2 Atmospheric Pollution

conditions should seek to ensure that the best available techniques not entailing excessive cost (BATNEEC) will be used for minimising pollution which may be caused to the environment taken as a whole having regard to the best practicable environmental option (BPEO) available as respects the substances which may be released. [*Environmental Protection Act 1990, s 7(7)*].

For further elaboration and explanation of BATNEEC and BPEO see further, INTEGRATED POLLUTION CONTROL (16).

In addition to such general guidance as to the meaning of these terms more specific guidance is being given, in respect of each prescribed process as it is brought within IPC, as regards the content of BATNEEC and the approach to be taken as regards BPEO. This is being done by an extensive series of Chief Inspector's Guidance Notes (published by HMSO). It is in these Guidance Notes that detailed information as to the likely terms of IPC authorisations as regards atmospheric emissions is likely to be found.

In addition to the statutory obligation that IPC authorisations should require the application of BATNEEC and seek to achieve the BPEO as regards emissions to air, water and land, the *Environmental Protection Act 1990, s 7(2)* also provides that the terms of an IPC authorisation must comply with:

(*a*)   any directions by the Secretary of State given for the implementation of any obligations of the United Kingdom under EC Treaties or international law relating to the environment;

(*b*)   any limits or requirements and achievement of any quality standards or quality objectives prescribed by the Secretary of State;

(*c*)   any requirements applicable to the grant of authorisations specified by or under a plan made by the Secretary of State under *EPA 1990, 3(5)*.

In the context of atmospheric pollution this provision gives to the Secretary of State necessary powers to seek to secure compliance with such obligations as those contained in:

(*a*)   the various EC *ambient air quality Directives* (sulphur dioxide and suspended particulates: *Directive 80/779/EEC* as amended by *Directives 81/857/EEC, 89/427/EEC* and *91/692/EEC*; lead: *Directive 82/884/EEC* as amended by *Directive 91/692/EEC*; nitrogen dioxide: *Directive 85/203/EEC as amended by Directives 85/580/EEC* and *91/692/EEC*. The standards set by these *Directives* are incorporated into UK law by the *Air Quality Standards Regulations 1989 (SI 1989 No 317).

(*b*)   the *EC Directive on emissions of sulphur dioxide, nitrogen oxides and dust from large combustion plants: Directive 88/609/EEC*. In addition to requiring such emissions from new plant to be minimised to BATNEEC levels this *Directive* imposes obligations on each Member State to reduce its aggregate emissions from existing plant in accordance with percentage decreases (as against 1980 levels) set for each of the gases. The decreases which are required differ as between the various Member States and are expressed in terms of obligations to be met by 1993, 1998 and by 2003. The Secretary of State has made formal directions to HMIP as regards the conditions to be imposed on new plant (*Large Combustion Plant (New Plant) Directions 1991*); and in December 1990 issued a plan for the progressive reduction of total annual emissions of sulphur dioxide and oxides of nitrogen for existing large combustion plant. This plan indicates how it is proposed that the reduction be allocated between the electricity supply industry, oil refineries and other industry.

4.3 **LOCAL AUTHORITY AIR POLLUTION CONTROL (LAAPC) UNDER ENVIRONMENTAL PROTECTION ACT 1990, PART I**

In addition to the numerous processes which are, or which will become, subject to atmospheric emissions control (by HMIP) as an aspect of Integrated Pollution Control (IPC) there is also a larger number of processes which are prescribed as subject to the new system of Local Authority Air Pollution Control (LAAPC), also contained in *Part I* of the *EPA 1990*.

This scheme of control extends the air pollution functions of local authorities beyond their pre-existing, and continuing, functions under the *Clean Air Acts* and their powers in respect of statutory nuisances caused by atmospheric emissions.

The list of processes coming within LAAPC is contained, alongside those which are subject to IPC, in the *Prescribed Processes and Substances Regulations 1991*. The *Regulations* list categories of 'Part A' processes which are subject to IPC; and 'Part B' processes which are subject to LAAPC.

Unlike IPC which is being introduced in accordance with an introduction programme extending into 1996, LAAPC was fully introduced both for new and existing processes during 1992.

In order to advise industry as to the content and nature of the air pollution control requirements to be imposed under LAAPC, and to assist local authorities as regards their authorisation decisions, there have been issued, process by process, a large number of Secretary of State's Guidance Notes.

The various provisions of *EPA 1990* in relation to the requirement to obtain an authorisation from the enforcing authority [*section 6*] and the conditions to be attached to authorisations [*section 7*] apply equally to IPC and LAAPC, subject to the limitation that local authority control is restricted to emissions to air [*section 7(5)*]. This limitation also means that local authorities are not required to consider, in respect of Part B processes, the BPEO in respect of the various emissions from those processes [*section 7(7)*].

Most of the other general provisions of *EPA, Part I* apply equally to IPC and LAAPC. For example, the general provisions as to fees and charges [*section 8*], transfers of authorisations [*section 9*], variations of authorisations [*sections 10, 11*], revocation of authorisations [*section 12*], enforcement notices [*section 13*], prohibition notices [*section 14*], appeals [*section 15*], powers of inspectors [*sections 17, 18*], public registers of information [*sections 20–22*], offences [*section 23*], enforcement by the High Court [*section 24*], and the powers of the criminal courts to order a convicted person to remedy matters in respect of which he has been convicted [*section 26*].

For further discussion of these aspects of *EPA 1990, Part I* see INTEGRATED POLLUTION CONTROL (16).

The powers under *section 27* to remedy harm (caused by an offence of operating without or in breach of an authorisation, or in breach of a prohibition or enforcement notice) and to recover the costs involved from the convicted person are exercisable in respect both of IPC and LAAPC by the chief inspector of HMIP. The power is exercisable only with the consent of the Secretary of State.

4.4 **THE CLEAN AIR ACTS**

Dark smoke

The *Clean Air Act 1956* (the *1956 Act*) prohibits the emission of dark smoke from any chimney, industrial or domestic [*section 1*]. This prohibition is extended by the *Clean*

4.4 Atmospheric Pollution

Air Act 1968 (the *1968 Act*) to cover, also, emissions of dark smoke from any industrial or trade premises even though not from a chimney (*Clean Air Act 1968, s 1: Sheffield City Council v ADH Demolition Ltd, The Times, 18 June 1983* – offence committed by emission of dark smoke from fire on building site).

The 'chimney' offence under the *1956 Act* is committed by the occupier of the building from which the dark smoke is emitted or the person having possession of the boiler or plant served by a chimney not being a chimney of a building. In the case of the 'non-chimney' offence under the *1968 Act* the offence may be that of the occupier of the premises and also 'any other person who causes or permits the emission' (*Clean Air Act 1968, s 1(1) as amended by Control of Smoke Pollution Act 1989, s 2(1)*).

'Dark smoke' is defined as smoke which appears to be as dark as, or darker than shade 2 on the British Standard Ringelmann Chart. [*Clean Air Act 1956, s 34*]. It is not necessary for there to have been any actual comparison made between the smoke and such a chart: it is sufficient if from the evidence a court is satisfied that the smoke was 'dark' as thus defined [*section 34(2)*]. Moreover, by virtue of the *Clean Air Act 1968, s 1(1A)* (added by *Control of Smoke Pollution Act 1989, s 2*) there shall be taken to have been an emission of dark smoke from industrial or trade premises in any case where –

(a)   material is burned on those premises, and

(b)   the circumstances are such that the burning would be likely to give rise to the emission of dark smoke,

unless the occupier or any person who caused or permitted the burning shows that no dark smoke was emitted.

Certain exceptions exist to the scope of the dark smoke offences. Thus, in any proceedings it is a defence to prove:

(a)   that the contravention complained of was solely due to the lighting up of a furnace from cold and that all practicable steps were taken to prevent or minimise the emission of dark smoke; or

(b)   that the contravention was solely due to some unforeseeable and unavoidable failure of the furnace or of apparatus used in connection with the furnace; or

(c)   that the contravention was due to the use of unsuitable fuel in circumstances where suitable fuel was unobtainable, and that the least unsuitable fuel which was available was used and that all practicable steps were taken to prevent or minimise the emission of dark smoke. [*Clean Air Act 1956, s 1(3)*].

Equally no offence is committed provided the dark smoke emissions come within the terms of the *Dark Smoke (Permitted Periods) Regulations 1958* (*SI 1958 No 498*). These *Regulations* permit the emission of dark smoke for a period not exceeding a defined number of minutes during any period of eight hours, the permitted period depending on the number of furnaces served by the chimney and whether or not the emission involves the blowing of soot (in cleaning operations) from the chimney. In any event the continuous emission of dark smoke must not at any time exceed four minutes, and the continuous emission of black smoke must not at any time exceed two minutes in any period of thirty minutes ('black' smoke is defined by reference to shade 4 on the Ringelmann Chart).

Nor is an offence committed where the emission of dark smoke comes within the terms of the *Clean Air (Emission of Dark Smoke) (Exemption) Regulations 1969* (*SI 1969 No 1263*). These *Regulations* apply to dark smoke produced by the burning of certain specified materials: these include, timber and other waste matter (other than rubber or flock or feathers) resulting from the demolition of a building or the clearance of a site in connection with any building operation or work of engineering construction; explosive which has become waste and any material contaminated by such explosive; tar, pitch, asphalt and other matter burnt in connection with the preparation or laying of any surface, or which is burnt off in connection with any resurfacing; carcasses of animals and poultry which have died or been slaughtered because of any disease; and containers which are contaminated by any pesticide or by any toxic substance used for veterinary or agricultural purposes. In each case one or more of certain defined burning conditions must be satisfied. These are variously that there is no other reasonably safe and practicable method of disposing of the matter; that the burning is carried out in such a manner as to minimise the emission of dark smoke; and that the burning is carried out under the direct and continuous supervision of the occupier of the premises concerned or a person authorised to act on his behalf.

Environmental health officers are required to notify 'as soon as may be' the occupier of premises of their belief that a dark smoke offence has been committed. This notification must be confirmed in writing before the end of a period of four days commencing the day after the offence was noticed. Failure to comply with these notification obligations affords the defendant a defence to prosecution. [*Clean Air Act 1956, s 30*]. These notification provisions apply also to the offence of emitting smoke in a smoke control area under *Clean Air Act 1956, s 11* (see further, below at 4.10).

4.5 New furnaces

Local authorities must be notified of the installation in any buildings (or boiler or industrial plant attached to any building) of any new furnaces. This does not apply, however, to domestic boilers rated at less than 55,000 Btu/hr (i.e. domestic furnaces). All such new furnaces must be capable, so far as practicable, of operating continuously without emitting smoke when burning the type of fuel for which the furnace was designed. Any person who installs a furnace in contravention of these provisions, or on whose instructions a furnace is so installed, commits an offence. Any furnace installed in accordance with plans and specifications submitted to, and approved by, the local authority, is deemed to comply with the above requirements. [*Clean Air Act 1956, s 3*].

4.6 Grit and dust

The *Clean Air (Emission of Grit and Dust from Furnaces) Regulations 1971 (SI 1971 No 162)* prescribe limits on the rates of emission of grit and dust from certain categories of furnaces: boilers (not being a domestic boiler rated at less than 55,000 Btu/hr), indirect heating appliances in which the material being heated is a gas or a liquid, other indirect heating appliances, and furnaces in which combustion gases are in contact with the material being heated but that material does not in itself contribute to the grit and dust in the combustion gases.

If on any day grit or dust in excess of the prescribed limit is emitted from a chimney serving such a furnace the occupier of the building in which the furnace is situated is guilty of an offence. [*Clean Air Act 1968, s 2(2)*]. However, in any such proceedings it is a defence to prove that the best practicable means had been used for the minimisation of the alleged emission. [*Clean Air Act 1968, s 2(3)*].

In the case of furnaces other than those in respect of which grit and dust emission limits have been prescribed by the *1971 Regulations* it is an offence generally for an occupier to fail to use any practicable means for the minimisation of the emission of dust and grit from the chimney. [*Clean Air Act 1968, s 2(4)*].

All furnaces installed after 1 October 1969 must be equipped with local authority approved grit and dust arrestment equipment if the furnace is to be used:

(*a*)   to burn pulverised fuel; or

(*b*)   to burn solid fuel at a rate of 45.4 kg or more an hour, any other solid matter; or

(*c*)   to burn, at a rate equivalent to 366.4 kilowatts or more any liquid or gaseous matter. [*Clean Air Act 1956, s 6; Clean Air Act 1968, ss 3, 5*].

The occupier of the building containing the furnace is guilty of an offence where the furnace is not so equipped, or where the equipment is not properly maintained and used. [*Clean Air Act 1956, s 6(1)*].

Against local authority refusal to approve equipment a right of appeal lies to the Secretary of State. [*Clean Air Act 1956, s 6(5)*].

Certain exemptions exist to these grit and dust arrestment obligations. These are:

(*a*)   those contained in the *Clean Air (Arrestment Plant) (Exemption) Regulations 1969* (*SI 1969 No 1262*) made under the *Clean Air Act 1968, s 4*; and

(*b*)   where on application by the occupier of a building the local authority are satisfied that the emission of grit and dust from any chimney serving a furnace in that building will not be prejudicial to health or a nuisance. [*Clean Air Act 1968, s 4(4)*]. Against refusal by a local authority to grant such exemption there lies a right of appeal to the Secretary of State. [*Clean Air Act, s 4(5)*].

In either case if an exempt furnace is used for any purpose other than that in respect of which the exemption applies an offence is committed. [*Clean Air Act, s 4(7)*].

4.7   Measurement of grit, dust and fumes emitted from furnaces

Where a furnace in a building is used:

(*a*)   to burn pulverised fuel; or

(*b*)   to burn, at a rate of 45.4 kg or more an hour, any other solid matter; or

(*c*)   to burn, at a rate equivalent to 366.4 kilowatts or more any liquid or gaseous matter,

the local authority may, by notice in writing served on the occupier of the building, require the occupier to comply with requirements contained in the *Clean Air (Measurement of Grit and Dust) Regulations 1971 (SI 1971 No 161)*. [*Clean Air Act 1956, s 7*]. These requirements relate to the measurement of grit, dust and fumes. Where such a furnace is used:

(*a*)   to burn, at a rate of less than one ton an hour solid matter other than pulverised fuel; or

(*b*)   to burn at a rate of less than 28 million Btu/hr any liquid or gaseous matter,

the occupier of the building containing the furnace may, by notice in writing served on the local authority, request the local authority to make and record those measurements. [*Clean Air Act 1968, s 5(3)*]. On receipt of such a request the local authority is required from time to time to make and record such measurements. [*Clean Air Act 1968, s 5(5)*].

4.8   Fume and gaseous emissions

The *1968 Act* authorises the Secretary of State to make regulations to extend certain provisions of the *1956* and *1968 Acts* to fume emissions as well as emissions of grit and dust. The *Environmental Protection Act 1990, s 85* has added *section 7A* to the *1968 Act* empowering regulations to be made extending those provisions also to prescribed gases. In neither case have these regulation-making powers been exercised.

4.9   Chimney heights

Local authorities have powers of control over the height of chimneys. [*Clean Air Act 1956, s 10; Clean Air Act 1968, s 6*]. An application must be made to the local authority in any case where:

(*a*)   a new chimney is erected to serve a new or an existing furnace; or

(*b*)   a furnace served by an existing chimney is enlarged;

(*c*)   a furnace served by an existing chimney is removed and replaced by one with larger combustion space, where the furnace:

—   burns or is to burn pulverised fuel; or

—   burns solid matter at a rate of 45.4 kilowatts or more an hour; or

—   burns any liquid at a rate equivalent to 366.4 kilowatts or more.

The application must be accompanied by the information which the authority will require in order to do the appropriate chimney height calculations. The calculations are done in accordance with an HMSO document of 1981, the *Third Memorandum on Chimney Heights*.

The local authority must not approve a chimney unless satisfied that its height will be sufficient to prevent as far as practicable the emissions becoming prejudicial to health or a nuisance. [*Clean Air Act 1956, s 10(1); Clean Air Act 1968, s 6(4)*]. Approval may be without qualifications or may be subject to conditions as to the rate and quality of emissions from the chimney. [*Clean Air Act 1968, s 6(5)*]. Against refusal of approval or against conditions imposed a right of appeal lies to the Secretary of State. [*Clean Air Act 1968, s 6(7)*].

Chimney height approval is not necessary in respect of chimneys falling within the terms of the *Clean Air (Heights of Chimneys) (Exemption) Regulations 1969 (SI 1969 No 411)*.

In addition to these provisions as regards chimney height approval note should be taken of the more general provisions of the *Building Act 1984* and the *Building Regulations 1991 (SI 1991 No 2768)*.

4.10   Smoke control areas

A local authority may declare the whole or any part of its area a smoke control area. [*Clean Air Act 1956, s 11*]. Such an order may apply to specific buildings only; or may apply more widely but with specific buildings exempted from the order. [*Clean Air Act 1956, s 11(3)*].

The consequence of such designation is that, in any such area, an occupier of a building is guilty of an offence if smoke is emitted from a chimney of that building. It is a defence, however, for the occupier to prove that the emission resulted only from the use of an authorised fuel. [*Clean Air Act 1956, s 11(2)*]. For authorised fuels, see the *Smoke Control Areas (Authorised Fuels) Regulations 1991 (SI 1991 No 1282)*. Equally, no offence is committed if the emission has resulted only from the use of a fireplace falling within numerous *Smoke Control (Exempted Fireplaces) Orders*. These *Regulations* list classes of fireplace which can be used for burning fuels other than authorised fuels without producing any substantial quantity of smoke.

The Secretary of State has power to require a local authority to make a smoke control order. [*Clean Air Act 1968, s 8*].

It is an offence to acquire solid non-authorised fuel for use in a smoke control area

4.11 Atmospheric Pollution

(otherwise than in an exempt fireplace); and it is an offence to sell by retail such fuel, for such use, for delivery within a smoke control area. [*Clean Air Act 1968, s 9*].

The *1956 Act* contains certain provisions under which the local authority are empowered, and may be required, to pay grants to owners and occupiers of dwellings built prior to August 1964 in respect of the costs of fireplace adaptations. [*Clean Air Act 1968, ss 12, 13*].

4.11 Clean Air Acts consolidation

The Clean Air legislation, considered above, is to be consolidated (i.e. incorporated into a single Act, with only minor amendments of substance) by the Clean Air Bill (currently – May 1993 – before Parliament).

The following table indicates the location in the new consolidating measure of the principal sections which have been referred to.

Table 4.1	
1993 Act	**Derivation**
s 1	*1956 Act s 1*
s 2	*1968 Act s 1; 1989 Act s 2*
s 3	*1956 Act s 34(2)*
s 4	*1956 Act s 3*
s 5	*1968 Act s 2*
s 6	*1968 Act s 3*
s 8	*1956 Act s 6*
s 10	*1956 Act s 7*
s 14	*1968 Act s 6*
s 18	*1956 Act s 11*
s 19	*1968 Act s 8*
s 20	*1956 Act s 11*
s 25 and 2 Sch	*1968 Act s 12*
s 51	*1956 Act s 30*

4.12 HEALTH AND SAFETY AT WORK ETC. ACT 1974

Section 5 of this Act provides that it shall be the duty of the person having control of any premises (of a class prescribed under the Act) to use the best practicable means for preventing the emission into the atmosphere from the premises of noxious or offensive substances and for rendering harmless and inoffensive such substances as may be so emitted. Failure to comply with this duty is an offence. [*Health and Safety at Work etc. Act 1974, s 33*].

In addition to this general duty a number of significant sets of regulations have been made under the Act. These include:

(a)   *The Control of Industrial Major Accident Hazard Regulations 1984 (as amended in 1990): CIMAH*

These *Regulations* seek to implement *EC Directive 82/501/EEC* (*Seveso Directive*). The purpose of the *Directive* is to seek to prevent, and to minimise the health, safety and environmental consequences of, major industrial accidents. It imposes obligations to notify major hazard sites, to undertake appropriate risk assessments in respect of such sites, and to report on matters of safety and emergency planning. In respect of certain

54

industrial activities covered by the *Directive* there is also an obligation to provide the public with information as to the nature of the hazard and the action to take in the event of the occurrence of an accident (amendment to *Directive, 87/216/EEC*).

(b)   The Control of Substances Hazardous to Health Regulations 1988 (as amended in 1991): COSHH

These *Regulations* apply to all substances defined in the *Regulations* as hazardous and apply to all places of work. Hazardous substances include various gases, vapours, fumes and dusts. The *Regulations* require that employers whose activity may expose workers to any hazardous substance must make a suitable and sufficient assessment of the risk to the health of the employees and the precautions which are necessary. Appropriate measures must be taken to prevent or control the risks assessed. Monitoring of exposure to the hazardous substances must be undertaken. Employees must be properly instructed as to the risks and the precautions to be taken.

The Health and Safety Executive have issued Guidance Notes in respect of Occupational Exposure Limits (EH 40). These list 'control limits', which should not be exceeded; and 'recommended exposure limits', which represent levels to be aimed for and which are considered to be achievable by means of good practice.

(c)   The Control of Asbestos in the Air Regulations 1990

These *Regulations* seek to implement *EC Directive 87/217/EEC*. The *Regulations* impose emission limits on asbestos works which produce raw asbestos from ore, or are engaged in the manufacture or finishing of products containing asbestos.

Occupational exposure to asbestos is regulated by the *Control of Asbestos at Work Regulations 1987*. For exposure limits see Health and Safety Executive Guidance Note EH 10.

4.13   STATUTORY NUISANCE

The *Environmental Protection Act 1990, Part III (EPA 1990, Pt III) [ss 79–82]* has consolidated the substance of the law relating to statutory nuisance and has streamlined procedures. It supersedes the statutory nuisance provisions formerly contained in the *Public Health Act 1936*, the *Clean Air Act 1956*, and the *Control of Pollution Act 1974*.

For the purpose of *Part III* of the *Environmental Protection Act 1990* the following matters constitute statutory nuisances:

(a)   any premises in such a state as to be prejudicial to health or a nuisance;

(b)   smoke emitted from premises so as to be prejudicial to health or a nuisance;

(c)   fumes or gases emitted from private dwellings (see *section 79(4)*) so as to be prejudicial to health or a nuisance;

(d)   any dust, steam, smell or other effluvia arising on industrial, trade or business premises and being prejudicial to health or a nuisance;

(e)   any accumulation or deposit which is prejudicial to health or a nuisance;

(f)   any animal kept in such a place or manner as to be prejudicial to health or a nuisance;

(g)   noise emitted from premises so as to be prejudicial to health or a nuisance;

(h)   any other matter declared by any enactment to be a statutory nuisance. [*EPA 1990, s 79*].

4.14 Atmospheric Pollution

It is categories (*b*), (*c*) and (*d*) (smoke, fumes, gases, dust, smell or other effluvia) which are of particular relevance in the context of the control of atmospheric pollution.

'Smoke' is defined as including soot, ash, grit and gritty particles emitted in smoke; 'fumes' means any airborne solid matter smaller than dust; 'gas' includes vapour and moisture precipitated from vapour. [*EPA 1990, s 79(7)*].

The expressions 'prejudicial to health' and 'nuisance' are alternative defining conditions: if the matter in question is in law a 'nuisance' it does not have also to be prejudicial to health (*Betts v Penge UDC [1942] 2 KB 154*). To be a 'nuisance', however, the matter in question must fall within the common law concepts of private or public nuisance (*National Coal Board v Neath Borough Council [1976] 2 All ER 478*). It may be that the nuisance must relate to personal comfort and that statutory nuisance procedures are not applicable in respect of nuisance which involves only the despoilment of property (*Wivenhoe Port v Colchester Borough Council [1985] JPL 175*).

From the general definition of statutory nuisances the following exclusions apply [*EPA 1990, s 79(3)*]:

(*a*)   smoke emitted from the chimney of a private dwelling within a smoke control area;

(*b*)   dark smoke emitted from a chimney of a building;

(*c*)   dark smoke emitted from industrial or trade premises.

For provisions in respect of such emissions see 4.4–4.10 above.

Local authorities are under a statutory duty to inspect their areas from time to time to detect any statutory nuisances which ought to be dealt with under the procedures to be described below. They are also required to respond to any complaints made by persons residing within the area by taking such steps as are practicable to investigate such complaints.

4.14 LOCAL AUTHORITY PROCEEDINGS

Where a local authority is satisfied that a statutory nuisance exists, or is likely to occur or recur, it is required to serve an abatement notice imposing all or any of the following requirements:

(*a*)   the abatement of the nuisance, or prohibiting or restricting its occurrence or recurrence;

(*b*)   the execution of such works, and the taking of such steps, as may be necessary to comply with (*a*) above.

The notice served must specify the time or times within which the requirements of the notice are to be complied with. [*EPA 1990, s 80(1)*].

The notice must be served on the person responsible for the nuisance, except that:

(*a*)   where the nuisance arises from any defect of a structural character it is to be served on the owner of the premises; and

(*b*)   where the person responsible for the nuisance cannot be found or the nuisance has not yet occurred it should be served on the owner or occupier of the premises. [*EPA 1990, s 80(2)*].

A person so served with an abatement notice has 21 days within which to appeal against the notice to the magistrates' court. [*EPA 1990, s 80(3)*]. The grounds of appeal are set out in the *Statutory Nuisance (Appeals) Regulations 1990 (SI 1990 No 2276)*.

A person upon whom an abatement notice has been served commits an offence if, without reasonable excuse, that person contravenes or fails to comply with any requirement or prohibition contained in the notice. [*EPA 1990, s 80(4)*].

It is a defence to such a prosecution to show that the 'best practicable means' were used to prevent, or to counteract the effects of, the nuisance. [*EPA 1990, s 80(7)*]. However, this defence is not available in respect of:

(a)   nuisances falling within categories (*a*), (*d*), (*e*), (*f*) or (*g*) of the list of statutory nuisances set out above, except where the nuisance alleged arises on industrial, trade or business premises;

(b)   nuisances within category (*b*), except where the smoke is emitted from a chimney;

(c)   nuisances falling within categories (*c*) or (*h*). [*EPA 1990, s 80(8)*].

The meaning of 'best practicable means' is explained in *section 79(9)*. Thus, 'practicable' is to be judged by reference to, amongst other things, local conditions and circumstances, the current state of technical knowledge, and financial implications. It is also provided that regard should be had to any promulgated Codes of Practice.

In a case where an abatement notice has not been complied with the local authority may, instead of or in addition to taking criminal proceedings, itself take steps to abate the nuisance. Any expenses which it reasonably incurs in such action may then be recovered from the person by whose act or default the nuisance was caused. The court may apportion such expenses between persons whose acts or defaults have caused the nuisance in such manner as the court may consider fair and reasonable. [*EPA 1990, s 80(3)(4)*].

4.15   Proceedings by persons aggrieved

A person aggrieved by a statutory nuisance may make a complaint to a magistrates' court. [*EPA 1990, s 82(1)*]. The proceedings are brought against the person responsible for the nuisance. However, where the nuisance arises from a defect of a structural character the proceedings should be against the owner of the premises; and where the person responsible for the nuisance cannot be found, the proceedings should be against the owner or occupier of the premises. [*EPA 1990, s 82(4)*].

If the magistrates' court is satisfied that the alleged nuisance exists (or, although abated, is likely to recur) the court must make an order:

(a)   requiring the defendant to abate the nuisance within a time specified in the order, and to execute any works necessary for such abatement; and/or

(b)   prohibiting a recurrence of the nuisance, and requiring the execution of necessary works. [*EPA 1990, s 82(2)*].

It is an offence, without reasonable cause, to contravene any requirement or prohibition contained in such an order. [*EPA 1990, s 82(8)*]. The defence of best practicable means is available in the same circumstances as in the case of proceedings brought by the local authority. [*EPA 1990, s 82(9)(10)*].

Before a person aggrieved institutes such proceedings that person is required to have given written notice to the potential defendant of his intention to bring proceedings. The notice must specify the matter complained of as constituting a nuisance. [*EPA 1990, s 82(6)*]. The written notice must precede the application to court by a period of 21 days (or three days in the case of noise nuisances). [*EPA 1990, s 82(7)*].

Where a person is convicted following proceedings brought by a person aggrieved the court may direct the local authority to take abatement action or do the works specified in the order that has been contravened. [*EPA 1990, s 82(11)*].

Where at the proceedings for an order at the suit of a person aggrieved it is proved that the alleged nuisance existed at the date of the making of the complaint to the magistrates, the court is required to order the defendants to pay to the complainant such amount as the court considers reasonably sufficient to compensate him for any expenses properly incurred in the proceedings. This obligation to order the defendant to compensate the plaintiff applies regardless of whether the nuisance still exists (or is likely to recur) at the date of the hearing (seeking an order under *section 82(2)*).

In a case where it appears to the magistrates' court that neither the person responsible for the nuisance nor the owner or occupier of the premises can be found the court may direct the local authority to do anything which the court would have ordered such a person to have done. [*EPA 1990, s 82(13)*].

4.16 MOBILE SOURCES

Sulphur content of gas oil

EC Directive 76/716/EEC (*amended by Directive 87/219/EEC*) imposes a limit on the sulphur content of 'gas oil', a term which covers Derv fuel for diesel engined vehicles. From 1 January 1989 the sulphur content of such oil has been limited to 0.3 per cent. Member States may set a standard not lower than 0.2 per cent where this is necessary in order to meet air quality obligations in relation to sulphur dioxide. In relation to diesel fuel for motor vehicles the 0.3 per cent limit has been incorporated into UK law by the *Oil Fuel (Sulphur Content of Gas Oil) Regulations 1990* (*SI 1990 No 1096*), made under the *Control of Pollution Act 1974*.

4.17 Lead in petrol

EC Directive 78/611/EEC imposed limits on the lead content of petrol. It was superseded and its scope extended by *Directive 85/210/EEC* (amended by *87/416/EEC*).

The 1978 measure set the maximum permitted lead content in petrol at 0.40 grammes per litre. Member States may set stricter limits so long as these are not stricter than 0.15g/l.

The *1985 Directive* is aimed at promoting the availability and use within Member States of unleaded petrol. It also requires States to reduce the maximum lead limit to 0.15g/l as soon as they consider it appropriate. The *1987 Directive* permits the prohibition of the sale of 2-star petrol.

In the UK the *1978 Directive* has been implemented by the *Motor Fuel (Lead in Petrol)(Amendment) Regulations 1979* (*SI 1979 No 1*) and the *Motor Fuel (Lead Content of Petrol) Regulations 1981* (*SI 1981 No 1523*) (*as amended by the Motor Fuel (Lead Content of Petrol) (Amendment) Regulations 1985* (*SI 1985 No 1728*)). These *Regulations* have reduced the maximum permitted lead content to 0.15g/l.

Construction and Use Regulations have since late 1990 required that all new vehicles shall be capable of running on unleaded petrol.

4.18 Vehicle emissions

A large number of EC measures have been passed imposing ever stricter emission limits on motor vehicles.

The present provisions may be summarised as follows.

4.19   *New models and new vehicles*

Passenger cars:

Directive 91/441/EEC: applicable to all new model of cars as from 1 July 1992, and all new car registrations as from 1 December 1992.

CO emissions must not exceed 2.72 g/km; HC + Nox must not exceed 0.97 g/km. Other limits are prescribed for VOCs, particulates and CO at idling speed.

This *Directive* requires the EC Council to adopt stricter limits in respect of each of these matters, and also CO_2 emissions, to come into force on 1 January 1996.

Commercial vehicles:

Directive 91/542/EEC: this *Directive* is introducing, in two stages, stricter limits in relation to CO, HC and Nox emissions from diesel commercial vehicles (over 3.5 tonnes). It also introduces limits to particulate emissions. The staged introduction of the new limits is as follows:

Stage 1: applicable to new models as of 1 July 1992 and new registrations as of 1 October 1993.

Stage 2: applicable to new models as of 1 October 1995 and new registrations as of 1 October 1996.

For UK implementation of these EC requirements see the *Road Vehicles (Construction and Use) (Amendment No 2) Regulations 1990 (SI 1990 No 1131)*.

4.20   *Testing of road vehicles*

EC Directive 77/143/EEC requires, *inter alia*, the testing of goods vehicle exhaust emissions; *Directive 91/328/EEC* will introduce a common EC roadworthiness test for private cars as of 1998 (applicable to cars registered from 1994 onwards).

The current UK test requirements are set out in the *Road Vehicles (Construction and Use) (Amendment) Regulations 1991 (SI 1990 No 1526)*.

4.21   MEASURES TO PROTECT THE OZONE LAYER

At international level this matter has been addressed by the 1987 *Agreement on Substances which Deplete the Ozone Layer: The Montreal Protocol*. This agreement, subsequently revised in London in June 1990 and Copenhagen in November 1992, obliges ratifying States to achieve the following principal reductions:

(*a*)   CFCs: to reduce production levels by 75 per cent as from 1 January 1994 (based on 1986 levels) and by 100 per cent as from 1 January 1996;

(*b*)   Halons: to eliminate their use by 1 January 1994.

The revision of 1990 added two other substances to the *Protocol*, carbon tetrachloride and methyl chloroform, and set timetables for the phase out of each, which were modified at Copenhagen. The former is to be reduced by 85 per cent by 1 January 1995 and to be eliminated by 1 January 1996; the latter to be reduced by 50 per cent by 1 January 1994 and eliminated by 1 January 1996.

At Copenhagen, three new substances entered the *Protocol*: HCFCs, on which there will be a freeze in consumption in 1996 (at 1989 levels), and elimination by 2030;

4.21 Atmospheric Pollution

HCFCs, which will be eliminated by 1 January 1996; methyl bromide, which will be limited to its 1991 levels from 1995, and a 75 per cent reduction by 2000 is planned.

At EC level a somewhat shorter phase out timetable had been agreed. *Regulation 594/91* set a prohibition of CFC production after 30 June 1997; on production of carbon tetrachloride after 31 December 1997; and on production of Halons after 31 December 1999; and on production of methyl chloroform/1,1,1 – trichloroethane after 31 December 2004. Subsequently, in March 1992, the EC Council agreed a still shorter phase out period, agreeing that *Regulation 594/91* should be amended to require a complete phase out of all production of ozone depleting substances (except for essential uses) by 31 December 1995. And in December 1992 EC Environment Ministers went further still and agreed to the phase out of CFCs and carbon tetrachloride by 1995. It is expected that the European Commission will also propose earlier phase out targets in respect of HCFCs and methyl bromide.

5　Control of Dangerous Substances

5.1　INTRODUCTION

The hazard presented by a substance may vary according to the conditions in which it is transported, stored, used or handled. For example, a substance being transported may require precautions to be taken to prevent fire whilst that same substance in use in an industrial setting may be toxic. For the consumer however, because of the necessity to use only relatively small amounts of that same substance the risks may be minimal.

Dangerous substances include:

—　Substances listed as very toxic, toxic, harmful, corrosive or irritant;

—　Substances which have a maximum exposure limit;

—　Micro-organisms which pose a health hazard;

—　Substantial quantities of dust of any kind;

—　Other substances which create comparable hazards.

5.2　CONTROLS OVER ENTRY OF DANGEROUS SUBSTANCES INTO THE MARKET

Consumer Protection Act 1987

The *Consumer Protection Act 1987*, provides important safeguards for the consumer. *Part 1* of the Act implements *EC Directive 85/374/EEC* which was adopted on 30 July 1985. The Act imposes civil liability for damage caused wholly or partly by a defective product. That liability will normally extend to the producer; anyone who holds himself out as such by putting his name on the product, or by using a trade mark or other distinguishing mark in relation to the product; or anybody who has imported the product into the EC in order to supply it to another. Suppliers may be liable if they fail to identify the producer, importer, or their own specific supplier. Other legal liabilities are expressly preserved.

Specific factors to be taken into account include marketing information and instructions or warnings given. The term 'defect' is defined on the basis that the product is below a safety standard which persons generally are entitled to expect. Other provisions set out defences; define 'damage', limiting it to death or personal injury, or loss or damage to property ordinarily intended for private use provided the damages awarded would exceed £275; apply and modify relevant legislation dealing with fatal accidents, congenital disability, contributory negligence, etc.; prevent liability being excluded or limited; and allow the legislation to be amended by delegated legislation to give effect to later EC rules.

5.3　Health and Safety at Work etc. Act 1974

Health and Safety at Work etc. Act 1974, section 6 (as amended by Consumer Protection Act 1987, s 36 and Sch 3) provides that persons who manufacture, import or supply any substance, including micro-organisms, must ensure that so far as is reasonably practicable the substance will be safe and not a risk to the health of those at work when being used, handled, stored or transported by a person at work. A substance is defined

5.4 Control of Dangerous Substances

in the Act as 'any natural or artificial substance, whether in solid or liquid form or in the form of a gas or vapour'. There is an obligation on the part of those manufacturers, importers or suppliers to carry out such testing and examination as is necessary to comply with this duty and adequate information must be supplied with the product concerning inherent health and safety problems, together with stringent requirements to provide information (updated as necessary) concerning any relevant tests and conditions concerning the safe handling etc. and disposal of substances. Additional duties have been imposed on manufacturers of substances to carry out research to discover health and safety risks and to eliminate or minimise them so far as is reasonably practicable.

Notification of New Substances Regulations 1982 (SI 1982 No 1496) (as amended) obliges manufacturers to notify the supply of new substances to the Health and Safety Executive at least 45 days in advance of the supply of the new substance being one tonne or more within any period of twelve months. Further tests may be required at the instigation of the Health and Safety Executive. The Health and Safety Executive is required to send details of such tests to the Department of the Environment and the Commission of the European Communities and other Member States. Disclosure of the information provided by manufacturers to the Health and Safety Executive is restricted. Finally, the importation of unnotified substances into the United Kingdom is prohibited and the Executive is empowered to prohibit the supply or disposal of a substance.

5.4 Dangerous preparations

A person who places a preparation containing a harmful substance on the market may, instead of identifying the most important functional chemical groups, provide an alternative designation to avoid putting at risk the confidential nature of the property (see *Directive 88/379/EEC as amended*). The information which should be supplied to the appropriate national authorities in such cases is set out in an annex to *Commission Recommendation 92/214/EEC*; a further annex contains a lexicon of generic names which may be used for the purpose.

5.5 Pesticides and agrochemicals

The *Food and Environment Protection Act 1985 (as amended by the Pesticides (Fees and Enforcement) Act 1989)* regulates the use of pesticides. Two of the principal aims of *Part III* of the Act are the protection of human health and the protection of the environment. Extensive powers are available to ministers to prohibit the importation, sale, supply, storage, use and advertisement of pesticides. Importers, manufacturers and users of pesticides may be required to disclose information in order that proper controls might be put in place and the Government's international obligations be fulfilled.

Additional provisions concerning the aerial spraying of pesticides are to be found in the *Air Navigation Order 1989 (SI 1989 No 2004)*.

Fertilisers Regulations SI 1990 No 887

The *Fertilisers Regulations 1990 (SI 1990 No 887)* make it an offence to sell or have in one's possession with a view to sale any substance described as an EC fertiliser, unless that substance complies with all the requirements as to its composition and labelling.

5.6 Controls under the Environmental Protection Act 1990

The Secretary of State is empowered under *Environmental Protection Act 1990, section 140(1)* to make regulations prohibiting or restricting the importation into or the landing or unloading in the United Kingdom and the use, supply or storage of any specified substance or articles to prevent pollution of the environment or harm to human, animal or plant health. The Secretary of State may direct that the substance or article may be treated as waste or controlled waste or disposed of or treated. He may direct that such a substance should be treated in or removed from the United Kingdom. Before regulations are made the Secretary of State is obliged to seek advice from the Advisory Committee on Hazardous Substances.

The Secretary of State may short circuit procedural safeguards and make regulations swiftly where it appears to him that there is an imminent risk that serious pollution of the environment would otherwise be caused.

5.7   Packaging and labelling

The *Classification, Packaging and Labelling of Dangerous Substances Regulations 1984* (*SI 1984 No 1244*) (*as amended*) impose duties with regard to the supply of prescribed dangerous substances, identified in an approved list. No prescribed dangerous substance may be supplied to any person unless it is in a container, which includes any receptacle or wrapper or other form of packaging which is designed, made and fastened so as to stop the escape of contents when the container is handled normally and subject only to the normal stresses and strains. The container and its fastening must be made of material not likely to be adversely affected by its contents.

The container must show the following particulars:

(a)   the name of the substance being one of the names by which it is described in the approved list;

(b)   the name and address of the manufacturer, the importer, the wholesaler or the supplier of the substance;

(c)   the descriptive words or symbols indicated in *Schedule 1*;

(d)   the risk referred to in *Part IV* of the approved list. This sub-paragraph does not apply to 125 millilitres capacity or less where the substance it contains is not an explosive, toxic or corrosive substance;

(e)   the indication of safety precautions listed in *Part V* of the approved list. This sub-paragraph does not apply to 125 millilitres capacity or less.

The *Regulations* use graphic illustrations and easily understood symbols. A person injured in consequence of a contravention of these *Regulations* has grounds for a civil action for damages by virtue of *section 47(2)* of the *Health and Safety at Work etc. Act 1974*. A defence is provided in respect of criminal proceedings that a person took all reasonable precautions and exercised all due diligence to avoid the commission of the offence.

These *Regulations* which were originally framed to implement *Directive (67/548/EEC)*, a *Directive* which has been amended seven times and adapted to technical progress twelve times, are now being replaced and re-issued in a much revised form and renamed the *Chemicals (Hazard Information and Packaging) Regulations* in order to meet the extensive requirements of the latest EC Directives.

These new *Regulations* will affect those who supply or consign dangerous chemicals in Great Britain or offshore and set out the duties of those who supply chemicals as part of a transaction, including manufacturers, importers and distributors. Many of the provisions of the *Packaging and Labelling of Dangerous Substances Regulations 1984* (*as amended*) outlined above, will now be re-introduced.

5.8 Control of Dangerous Substances

The proposed *Chemicals (Hazard Information and Packaging) Regulations* will form part of an extended network of regulation with links to the *Control of Substances Hazardous to Health Regulations 1988 (SI 1988 No 1657)* and the *Control of Industrial Major Accident Hazards Regulations 1984 (SI 1984 No 1902)*. The proposed *Chemicals (Hazard Information and Packaging) Regulations* will require a supplier to decide whether the chemicals which he is putting on the market are dangerous or not. The proposed *Regulations* identify the following categories of danger.

(*a*) substances and preparations dangerous because of their physical or chemical properties:

— explosive

— oxidising

— extremely flammable

— highly flammable

— flammable;

(*b*) substances and preparations dangerous because of their health effects:

— very toxic

— toxic

— harmful

— corrosive

— irritant

— carcinogens

— teratogens.

Some 1,400 substances have been included within a more detailed approved list. If a substance is not included within the approved list the supplier must classify it in accordance with the Approved Guide on Classification and Labelling.

The proposed *Chemicals (Hazard Information and Packaging) Regulations* also include provisions for the classification of preparations using the same system as substances.

For the first time safety data sheets will need to be provided for dangerous chemicals which are supplied for work. A safety data sheet must be provided for the use of the recipient by the supplier and must indicate the precautions to be taken. (See the Approved Code of Practice on Safety Data Sheets.)

5.8 Storage, treatment and use of dangerous products

Health and Safety at Work etc. Act 1974, s 1(1) provides that the provisions of *Part 1* shall have effect with a view to

(*c*) controlling the keeping and use of explosive or highly flammable or otherwise dangerous substances, and generally preventing the unlawful acquisition, possession and use of such substances. The general duties of the Act have the effect of ensuring, so far as is reasonably practicable, the availability of adequate information about dangerous substances in the workplace.

The *Control of Substances Hazardous to Health Regulations 1988 (SI 1988 No 1657) (as amended by Control of Substances Hazardous to Health (Amendment) Regulations 1991 (SI 1991 No 2431))* were made under the *Health and Safety at Work etc. Act 1974*. These

Regulations, which are accompanied by a number of approved codes of practice (ACOPs), contain one set of rules governing virtually every chemical substance which pose a risk to the working population. Only lead, asbestos, radioactive material, explosive substances, flammable and high or low temperature substances below ground in mines and substances administered during medical treatment are excluded because they are separately regulated. A substance which is hazardous to health will include those which are very toxic, toxic, harmful, corrosive or irritant; any substances having a designated maximum exposure limit (MEL) or an occupational exposure standard (OES); micro-organisms; dust in substantial concentrations; and any substance which might constitute a health hazard. The *Regulations* provide that every employer must make a 'suitable and sufficient' assessment of the risks created by the work done. For an assessment to be 'suitable and sufficient', an employer must identify hazards and then assess the risk to his employees and others. The hazard presented by a substance is its potential to cause harm. The risk is the likelihood that it will cause harm in the circumstances of its use. The assessment must be recorded. The importance of well kept records is a thread that runs throughout all recent health and safety legislation relating to dangerous substances.

The assessment must be reviewed by an employer if there is reason to suspect that it is no longer valid or if there have been significant changes in the work. The assessment must be revised if, for example, adverse health effects become apparent, or if new control methods are available. Exposure to chemical substances must be prevented but if prevention is not reasonably practicable, the exposure of employees to these substances must be adequately controlled. If it is not reasonably practicable to control exposure by other methods, personal protective equipment should be used.

Employees have a responsibility to make full and proper use of any control measure or protective equipment made available. Once control measures are in place, they must be maintained in an efficient state, in good repair and efficient working order.

Records relating to maintenance measures must be full, easily available, easy to read and kept for a minimum of five years.

Where the failure of control would cause a serious health effect; where uncertainty exists regarding MES or OES; where carcinogens are present; or where any substance listed in *Schedule 4* to the *Regulations* is present an employer must monitor the exposure of employees to hazardous substances and keep a suitable record of that monitoring.

The records must be able to be easily understood and retrieved. If they do not identify individual workers, they must be kept for five years. If they can identify an individual, they must be kept for 30 years.

Where an employee is exposed to substances where there is an identifiable health effect associated with exposure and there is a reasonable chance of that health effect occuring, and valid techniques are available to detect the effect the employer must ensure that the employee is under suitable health surveillance (unless the exposure is not significant).

In such cases the employee must subject himself to examination at regular intervals by an employment medical adviser or a doctor appointed by the Health and Safety Executive. The examinations must be at least every twelve months. The records will invariably identify an individual and must be kept for 30 years. Such records must be made available to the employee on reasonable request.

Employers must provide information and training to enable their employees both to know the risks and the precautions that are available. The information provided by way of training must include the results of any monitoring and the collective results of any health surveillance undertaken. There is a defence to any contravention of the

5.9   Control of Dangerous Substances

Regulations if the accused can show that he took all reasonable precautions and exercised all due diligence to avoid the offence.

The HSE may exempt employees, including the armed forces from the full rigour of the *Control of Substances Hazardous to Health Regulations* in certain circumstances. In any proceedings it is likely that reliance will be placed on the approved codes of practice (ACOP) issued by the Commission and available from HMSO. Non-compliance with the ACOP is not an offence *per se* but it will be persuasive evidence in any investigation. Any employer who has not followed the ACOP has a heavy burden to discharge in showing that he did take all reasonable precautions and exercised due diligence.

For an offence triable summarily by magistrates, an offender can face imprisonment for a period up to six months and/or a fine of up to £2,000. For more serious offences, triable in the Crown Court, the fine is without limit and the maximum prison sentence increased to two years.

5.9   Notification of Installations Handling Hazardous Substances Regulations 1982 (SI 1982 No 1357)

These *Regulations* provide that, subject to certain exceptions, a person may not undertake any activity in which there is or is liable to be at any one time a notifiable quantity or more of a hazardous substance at any site, or in any pipeline within the meaning of the *Pipe-lines Act 1962*.

In order to determine whether there is a notifiable quantity of a hazardous substance at a site account shall be taken of any quantity of that substance which is

(*a*)   in that part of any pipeline under the control of the person having control of the site, which is within 500 metres of that site and connected to it;

(*b*)   at any other site under the control of the same person any part of the boundary of which is within 500 metres of the said site; and

(*c*)   in any vehicle, vessel, aircraft or hovercraft under the control of the same person which is used for storage purposes either at the site or within 500 metres of it;

but no account shall be taken of any hazardous substance which is in a vehicle, vessel, aircraft or hovercraft used for transporting it.

Waste at any site which is licensed for the disposal of such waste by a licence issued in pursuance of *section 5* of the *Control of Pollution Act 1974* is outside the ambit of the *Regulations*.

Where an activity has been notified in accordance with the *Regulations* and the person having control of that activity makes a change in it which affects the particulars specified in that notification or any subsequent notification made under the *Regulations* he must immediately notify the Executive of that change.

Where an activity at a site has been notified to the Executive in accordance with *Regulation 3(1)*, the quantity of a substance notified under *paragraph 7, Part I* of *Schedule 2* must not be increased to an amount three or more times that originally notified unless the activity has been re-notified under that *Regulation* as if it were a new activity; and accordingly *Regulation 4* shall not apply to that increase.

Subject to certain exceptions, the Executive may, by certificate in writing, exempt any person or class of persons, activity or class of activities to which these *Regulations* apply from any requirement or prohibition imposed by these *Regulations* and any such exemption may be granted subject to conditions and to a limit of time and may be revoked by a certificate in writing at any time.

A 'notifiable quantity' means:

(*a*)   in the case of a substance specified in column 1 of *Part I* of *Schedule 1*, the quantity of that substance specified in the corresponding entry in column 2 of that Part;

(*b*)   in the case of substances of a class specified in column 1 of *Part II* of that Schedule, the total quantity of all substances of that class specified in the corresponding entry in column 2 of that Part;

and in either case the quantity shall be determined in accordance with *Regulation 3(2)*.

SCHEDULE 1

List of Hazardous Substances (Named Substances)

1 Substance	2 Notifiable quantity tonnes
Liquefied petroleum gas, such as commercial propane and commercial butane, and any mixtures thereof held at a pressure greater than 1.4 bar absolute	25
Liquefied petroleum gas, such as commercial propane and commercial butane, and any mixture thereof held under refrigeration at a pressure of 1.4 bar absolute or less	50
Phosgene	2
Chlorine	10
Hydrogen fluoride	10
Sulphur trioxide	15
Acrylonitrile	20
Hydrogen cyanide	20
Carbon disulphine	20
Sulphur dioxide	20
Bromine	40
Ammonia (anhydrous or as solution containing more than 50 per cent by weight of ammonia)	100
Hydrogen	2
Ethylene oxide	5
Propylene oxide	5
tert-Butyl peroxyacetate	5
tert-Butyl peroxyisobutyrate	5
tert-Butyl peroxy isopropyl carbonate	5
Dibenzyl peroxydicarbonate	5

5.9   Control of Dangerous Substances

List of Hazardous Substances (Named Substances) – contd

1 Substance	2 Notifiable quantity tonnes
2,2-Bis(tert-butylperoxy)butane	5
1,1-Bis(tert-butylperoxy)cyclohexane	5
Di-sec-butyl peroxydicarbonate	5
2,2-Dihydroperoxypropane	5
Di-n-propyl peroxydicarbonate	5
Methyl ethyl ketone peroxide	5
Sodium chlorate	25
Cellulose nitrate other than (a) cellulose nitrate to which the *Explosives Act 1875* applies; or (b) solutions of cellulose nitrate where the nitrogen content of the cellulose nitrate does not exceed 12.3 per cent by weight and the solution contains not more than 55 parts of cellulose nitrate per 100 parts by weight of solution	50
Ammonium nitrate and mixtures of ammonium nitrate where the nitrogen content derived from the ammonium nitrate exceeds 28 per cent of the mixture by weight other than	
(a) mixtures to which the *Explosives Act 1875* applies; or	
(b) ammonium nitrate based products manufactured chemically for use as fertiliser which comply with *EC Directive 80/876/EEC*	500
Aqueous solutions containing more than 90 parts by weight of ammonium nitrate per 100 parts by weight of solution	500
Liquid oxygen	500

Classes of Substances not specifically Named in Part II

1 Substance	2 Notifiable quantity tonnes
1. Gas or any mixture of gases which is flammable in air and is held in the installation as a gas.	15
2. A substance or any mixture of substances which is flammable in air and is normally held in the installation above its boiling point (measured at 1 bar absolute) as a liquid or as a mixture of liquid and gas at a pressure of more than 1.4 bar absolute.	25 being the total quantity of substances above the boiling points whether held singly or in mixtures.

68

Classes of Substances not specifically Named in Part II – contd

1 Substance	2 Notifiable quantity tonnes
3. A liquefied gas or any mixture of liquefied gases, which is flammable in air, has a boiling point of less than 0 degrees C (measured at 1 bar absolute) and is normally held in the installation under refrigeration or cooling at a pressure of 1.4 bar absolute or less.	50 being the total quantity of substances having boiling points below 0 degrees C whether held singly or in mixtures.
4. A liquid or any mixture of liquids not included in items 1 to 3 above, which has a flash point of less than 21 degrees C.	10,000

The particulars to be included in a notification of a site are:

1. The name and address of the person making the notification.

2. The full postal address of the site where the notifiable activity will be carried on and its ordnance survey grid reference.

3. The area of the site covered by the notification and of any adjacent site which is required to be taken into account by virtue of *Regulation 3(2)*.

4. The date on which it is anticipated that the notifiable activity will commence, or if it has already commenced a statement to that effect.

5. A general description of the activities carried on or intended to be carried on there.

6. The name and address of the planning authority in whose area the notifiable activity is being or is to be carried on.

7. The name and maximum quantity liable to be on the site of each hazardous substance for which notification is being made.

The *Notification of Installations Handling Hazardous Substances Regulations 1982* are supplemented by the *Dangerous Substances (Notification and Marking of Sites) Regulations 1990 (SI 1990 No 304)*. Subject to certain exceptions the *Dangerous Substances (Notification and Marking of Sites) Regulations 1990* require the notification to the local fire authority and the enforcing authority for the *Health and Safety at Work etc. Act 1974* for any site with a total quantity of 25 tonnes or more of dangerous substances. These are those substances identified as dangerous for transport under the *Classification, Packaging and Labelling of Dangerous Substances Regulations 1984 (as amended)*. They also require the display of signs warning of the presence or possible presence of dangerous substances at the access points to any site with a total quantity of 25 tonnes or more of dangerous substances whether or not the site is excepted from notification requirements; and allow an inspector to direct the display of signs at locations of dangerous substances at such a site, if necessary.

The principal aims of the *Dangerous Substances (Notification and Marking of Sites) Regulations 1990* are to ensure that:

(*a*)   fire authorities and enforcing authorities are in possession of information which will help them in defining priorities for carrying out inspection programmes for their separate purposes;

(b)   firefighters arriving at an incident are warned of the presence of dangerous substances and of the need to make use of the information previously gathered for fighting purposes.

These *Regulations* do not apply to waste deposits in a hole in the ground, waste disposal sites operated under the provisions of the *Control of Pollution Act 1974* nor do they apply to radioactive materials. Sites which are notifiable under the *Nuclear Installations Act 1965, Notification of Installations Handling Hazardous Substances Regulations 1982* or covered by the *Control of Industrial Major Accident Hazards Regulations 1984* do not need to be re-registered under these *Regulations*.

5.10   Control of Industrial Major Accident Hazards Regulations 1984

These *Regulations* (*SI 1984 No 1902*) implement for Great Britain *EC Directive 82/501/EEC* (the 'Seveso Directive') on the major accident hazards of certain industrial activities and thus introduce new requirements with a view to preventing and limiting the effects of accidents arising from industrial activities involving dangerous substances. Safety measures and a prior notification procedure were established.

Following a number of serious accidents in the Community, including the release of dioxins at Seveso, Italy a *Directive* was adopted in 1982 on the major accident hazards of certain industrial activities, which covers approximately 2,000 industrial plants in the Community. The *Directive* was extended following the Sandoz accident in Basel in 1986. The *Regulations* cover not only in-plant storage, but storage in general of dangerous chemicals and impose special requirements where the quantities of such substances are large. Plant operators have to take whatever measures are necessary to avoid serious accidents. Thus at least three months before commencing an activity which might give rise to a major accident manufacturers have to make and forward to the competent authorities safety audits for the plant, draw up risk-avoidance and emergency plans, and notify in detail any accident with serious consequences for either man or the environment to the Health and Safety Executive who must in turn notify the Commission of the European Communities. Local authorities which prepare and keep up to date an off-site emergency plan may recover from the manufacturer the costs reasonably incurred for the purpose.

5.11   Special waste

The *Environmental Protection Act 1990, section 62* gives the Secretary of State extensive powers to make regulations in respect of waste which is difficult or dangerous to dispose of. This waste is known as 'special waste'. Such regulations may allow Waste Regulation Authorities to give directions in connection with the treatment, keeping or disposal of special waste and the setting up and maintenance of records.

5.12   Planning (Hazardous Substances) Act 1990

The *Planning (Hazardous Substances) Act 1990* came into force on 1 June 1992. Since its passage through Parliament the Act has been amended both by the *Environmental Protection Act 1990* and by the *Planning and Compensation Act 1991*. On 11 March 1992, the *Planning (Hazardous Substances) Regulations 1992* were made and came into force on 1 June 1992. The measure was originally introduced in *Part IV* of the *Housing and Planning Act 1986* which inserted into the *Town and Country Planning Act 1971* provisions introducing a new system of control over hazardous substances. Now, the presence on, over or under land of any hazardous substance in excess of the controlled quantity will require consent from the hazardous substances authority. That authority is the council of the district or London borough in which the land is situated or where the land is used for mineral working or waste deposits in shire counties the appropriate authorities will be the shire counties. Certain other bodies, for example, Urban Development Corporations and Housing Action Trusts may be hazardous substances authorities in certain circumstances.

As can be seen hazardous substances authorities have been defined in such a way that on almost every occasion the relevant authority will be the same council or other body which would act as local planning authority in dealing with an application for planning permission in respect of that land.

The hazardous substances authority may grant consent either unconditionally or subject to such conditions as it thinks fit, or it may refuse consent. In dealing with applications it is required to 'have regard to any material considerations' and in particular to a number of specified material considerations including any advice which the Health and Safety Executive have given following consultations.

There is a right of appeal to the Secretary of State against refusal or conditions imposed on a grant of consent, a call-in right in favour of the Secretary of State and a general power to revoke or modify hazardous substances consents.

The 1992 *Regulations* made under *section 5* of the Act specify what is a 'hazardous substance' for this purpose; and set out the description of the controlled quantity in each case. The *Regulations* also provide for a number of exemptions from the need for hazardous substances consent, the procedure to be followed for an application for such consent, claims for deemed consent, enforcement procedures, a consents register and fees for applications and deemed applications.

Applicants are entitled to receive consent if a hazardous substance was present on, over or under the land at any time within the period of twelve months preceding the commencement date of the legislation (provided that such consent is claimed within the period of six months following the commencement date).

A number of consequential amendments have been made to the *Town and Country Planning (Use Classes) Order 1987 (SI 1987 No 764)* and to the *Town and Country Planning General Development Order 1988 (SI 1988 No 1813)* by amending statutory instruments. These also came into force on 1 June 1992.

5.13   **SPECIAL REGIME RELATING TO THE TRANSPORT OF DANGEROUS SUBSTANCES**

As a signatory to the European Agreement concerning the International Carriage of Dangerous Goods by Road, the United Kingdom is obliged to allow road vehicles carrying certain dangerous goods on international journeys to carry such goods in the United Kingdom providing that the provisions of the agreement are complied with. The carriage of dangerous goods by rail is in certain circumstances subject to the provisions of international regulations concerning the carriage of dangerous goods by rail. British Rail has adopted 'Conditions of Acceptance of Dangerous Goods' which control rail carriage of such materials. Packaged goods carried by sea or by air must be classified, packaged and labelled in accordance with the International Maritime Dangerous Goods Code or the regulations of the International Air Transport Association.

Dangerous Substances (Conveyance in Road Tankers and Tank Containers) Regulations 1992 SI 1992 No 743 (as amended)

The *Dangerous Substances (Conveyance in Road Tankers and Tank Containers) Regulations 1992* came into force on 31 May 1992 and apply throughout the United Kingdom.

These *Regulations* provide for the safe transportation by vehicle of dangerous substances in bulk. Requirements are imposed for notices to be displayed on vehicles used for this purpose. An approved list sets out all those chemicals included within the term 'dangerous substances'. Associated with these *Regulations* is an approved code of practice on the classification of dangerous substances, which enables a substance not on the approved list or a mixture, to be identified as dangerous or otherwise, and the correct warning sign to be allocated. The *Regulations* do not apply even to these substances when they are being transported in such dilution that they pose no risk to health and safety. Conversely some substances may not be transported by road in this way and some may be transported only after precautions are taken to reduce the likelihood of fire and explosion. Vehicles used for the transport of 'dangerous substances' must be suitably constructed and examined and tested regularly. Specified fire fighting equipment must be carried on these vehicles. Drivers must be provided with sufficient information, instruction and training to enable them to be aware of the identity of these substances and the risks created by their carriage and necessary emergency action. Hazard warning panels and weather resistant labels must be displayed on the vehicle at all times when it is carrying dangerous substances.

Road Traffic (Carriage of Dangerous Substances in Packages etc.) Regulations (SI 1986 No 1951) for the most part came into force on 6 April 1987. Their introduction marked the third stage in the development of comprehensive controls over all aspects of the carriage of all dangerous substances except intentional explosives and radioactive substances. They introduce operational provisions which extend controls to all methods of carrying significant quantities of the more dangerous substances by road. Every effort has been made to harmonise these requirements with the corresponding requirements of the *European Agreement concerning the International Carriage of Dangerous Goods by Road (ADR)*.

Pressure Systems and Transportable Gas Containers Regulations (SI 1989 No 2169) for the most part came into force on 1 July 1990 and 1 January 1991; the *Regulations* will be brought fully into force on 1 July 1994. These *Regulations* impose safety requirements with respect to pressure systems and transportable gas containers which are used or intended to be used at work. They also impose safety requirements to prevent certain vessels from becoming pressurised.

5.14   EXPLOSIVES

The controls on the safety and security of explosives are mainly contained in the *Explosives Acts 1875* and *1923* and regulations discussed below.

The *Classification and Labelling of Explosives Regulations 1983 (SI 1983 No 1140)* came into force on 1 November 1983. These *Regulations* provide for the classification of explosive articles, explosive substances and combinations and unit loads thereof by the Health and Safety Executive or, in the case of military explosives, by the Secretary of State for Defence, according to the type of explosive hazard which they present and their compatibility with other hazards.

The *Road Traffic (Carriage of Explosives) Regulations (SI 1989 No 615)* for the most part came into force on 3 July 1989, *Regulation 14* which deals with the training and instruction of drivers and attendants came into force on 3 January 1990. These *Regulations*, which are accompanied by an Approved Code of Practice with Guidance Notes impose requirements with respect to the safety and security of explosives carried by road.

Some explosives may not be transported by road and some explosives may be transported only in vehicles not used for the carriage of passengers for hire and reward, certain controls are imposed on mixed loads of explosives and other dangerous substances. Vehicles used for the transport of explosives must be suitable for the safety and security of the explosives having regard to the type and quantity of explosives being carried. Drivers of these vehicles must be provided with sufficient information, instruction and training to enable them to be aware of the identity of these substances and the risks created by their carriage and necessary emergency action. Operators have a duty to ensure safe and secure carriage.

Control of Explosives Regulations (SI 1991 No 1531) came into force on 1 November 1991 and update, extend, and simplify the legislative provisions dealing with explosives generally.

The main provisions extend and simplify the present system of police controls on the acquisition and keeping of explosives; rationalise the types and quantities of explosives which may be kept for private use and not for sale; require the occupier of a licensed explosives factory to appoint a person responsible for the security of explosives; widen the existing requirements for keeping records of explosives to enable accurate accounting and identification of any losses; and require thefts of explosives to be reported to the police.

5.15 RADIATION

All nuclear waste transported by road must be appropriately and safely packaged in a manner sufficient to withstand accident. A stringent legislative code has recently been introduced in the *Radioactive Material (Road Transport) Act 1991*.

5.16 DANGEROUS SUBSTANCES IN HARBOUR AREAS

Dangerous Substances in Harbour Areas Regulations 1987 (SI 1987 No 37) came into force on 1 June 1987. These *Regulations* provide for the control of carriage, loading, unloading and storage of dangerous substances in harbours and harbour areas. See also *Merchant Shipping (Dangerous Goods) Regulations (SI 1981 No 1747)* and *Merchant Shipping (Dangerous Goods) (Amendment) Regulations (SI 1986 No 1069)*.

EC Directive 92/29/EEC

Member States are required by *EC Directive 92/29/EEC* by the end of 1994 to ensure that vessels carry on board medical supplies meeting prescribed requirements and vessels which carry dangerous substances carry the prescribed antidotes. Owners of vessels will be responsible for providing and replenishing medical supplies. Suitable information about medical supplies and antidotes will have to be carried on vessels and provision will have to be made for medical training; free medical advice will have to be available by radio. Medical provision on board vessels will be subject to annual inspection.

The *Directive* will apply to vessels flying the flag of any Member State or registered under its plenary jurisdiction, excluding inland navigation vessels, warships, pleasure boats used for non-commercial purposes and not manned by professional crews, and tugs operating in harbour areas.

6   Energy Management and Green Buildings

6.1   INTRODUCTION

There are many good environmental reasons for conserving energy but perhaps a stronger motive for most managers is simply the financial savings that sensible energy management can produce.

About 50 per cent of all energy is used in buildings and in most buildings there exists considerable scope for reducing energy consumption.

6.2   METHODS OF CONSERVING ENERGY IN BUILDINGS

There are many effective energy conservation techniques already used in the United Kingdom. Some of these are described below.

6.3   Combined heat and power

Combined heat and power means that electricity is generated on site and the waste heat is available for process heating, heating the building or even driving the air conditioning plant using absorption refrigeration equipment.

To be effective it is necessary to have a reasonably constant heating load and for this reason it is particularly suitable for hotels, hospitals, swimming pools and factories where there is a large heating load for domestic hot water or process heating.

One of the best known examples of CHP is the Greenpeace Headquarters in north London which uses a small CHP unit to provide electricity as well as heating.

Combined heat and power units can be cost-effective and quite small and quiet. The electricity is generated at a competitive price using gas and the heat generated is virtually free.

6.4   Thermal storage for air conditioning plant

Thermal storage means storing cooling energy at night for use during the day. The refrigeration plant is operated at night to cool a special insulated storage vessel.

The main advantage of running the refrigeration plant at night is that it is possible to use off-peak electricity (approximately half price). The refrigeration plant can use the stored chilled water to provide additional cooling during the day. This means that the size of the refrigeration plant can be reduced and the maximum electrical demand on the building is also reduced.

A schematic diagram of a thermal storage system is shown below (Figure 6.1.) The refrigeration plant is used to generate chilled water or ice in an insulated store. The chilled water is used as required by the air conditioning plant.

Detailed calculations are necessary to establish the optimum size of the storage vessel and the refrigeration plant to ensure the best use is made of off-peak electricity.

6.5   Heat recovery

It is possible to reclaim the heat from equipment (such as computers) and reuse this heat, to pre-heat the incoming outside air. This can be achieved by using heat recovery

6.6 Energy Management and Green Buildings

Schematic of thermal storage system for a cooling system

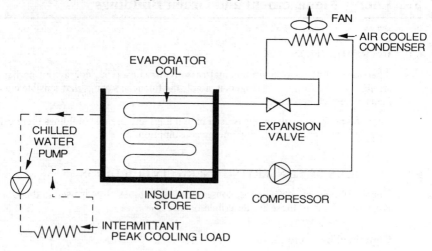

Figure 6.1

devices such as 'run-around' coils, thermal wheels, and plate heat exchangers. These devices can also be used to transfer cooling from the central exhaust system to pre-cool the incoming air.

Thermal wheels are normally the most efficient form of air to air heat recovery and 'run-around' coils are usually the least efficient.

However, each case must be carefully examined and plant selected to suit each application, as problems such as cross contamination between air streams and space required for equipment must also be considered.

6.6 Energy efficient design

Heating – boilers

Condensing boilers are boilers which manage to extract 90 per cent of the heat in the fuel by cooling down the flue gases. They are more expensive than normal boilers, but are much more efficient. Normal boilers only have efficiencies between 70 per cent and 80 per cent.

It is important to isolate boilers when not in use, to avoid wasting energy and install controls to ensure energy is used efficiently. The controls should include 'optimum start' and weather compensation to ensure that heat is supplied at the correct temperature.

Optimum start means varying the time the boilers are switched on each morning to suit the external temperature. For an office building which normally opens at 9 am, on a cold frosty morning the boilers would start at 7 am and on a mild morning they would start at 8.30 am.

It should be noted that the statutory maximum for non-residential buildings is 19°C. Unfortunately this is a very uncomfortable temperature (CIBSE recommends 21°C) but to date no one has been prosecuted for breaking this law (the answer to a parliamentary question in June 1992 stated, 'no prosecution to date').

Insulation

Thermal insulation for walls, floors and roofs can be very cost-effective. The levels in the current *Building Regulations* should be regarded as a minimum as they are well below the levels currently used in Northern Europe.

At present the *Building Regulations* specify a thermal transmittance of 0.45 W/m²K for walls and 0.25 W/m²K for roofs with 0.40 W/m²K for floors.

The Chartered Institution of Building Services Engineers (CIBSE) has been recommending for some time that 0.30 W/m²K should be used for walls, 0.20 W/m²K for roofs and 0.40 W/m²K for floors.

Extra insulation should also be applied to all pipework and ductwork to avoid wasting energy.

Glazing

At present the *Building Regulations* do not insist on double glazing in new buildings. The heat loss through single glazing is approximately twice the heat loss through double glazing.

It is cheaper to install double glazing when a building is being constructed and it also means that the size of the boiler plant can be reduced. As double glazing improves the level of comfort inside a building, (by avoiding down draughts and condensation), it makes sense to install double glazing.

The use of low emissivity coatings in addition to double glazing can reduce the thermal transmittance without significantly reducing light transmittance as shown in the following table:

Table 6.1			
A comparison of different types of glazing			
Glazing type	**U-value W/m²K**	**Total solar transmittance**	**Light transmittance**
Single glazing	5.70	0.83	0.87
Double glazing	2.80	0.72	0.76
Double + one coat low-e coating	1.90	0.69	0.73

(NB. U-value = Thermal transmittance)

Low emissivity coatings on double glazing reduce the heat loss and the solar heat gain without significantly reducing the amount of daylight inside the room.

The total amount of glazing on a building should be reduced to provide sufficient daylight and reduce solar gains and heat losses to a minimum.

Shading

Ideally glazing should be shaded to reduce solar gains in Summer and take advantage of free heating by the sun in the Winter.

This can be provided by providing horizontal shading as shown in the attached sketch below. Figure 6.2. Shading needs to be carefully designed to avoid excessive solar gains on south, east and west faces of a building.

6.7 Energy Management and Green Buildings

Effective shading can reduce energy consumption by minimising load on air conditioning plant, improving comfort conditions for the occupants and add to the interest of the building facade.

Effective window shading

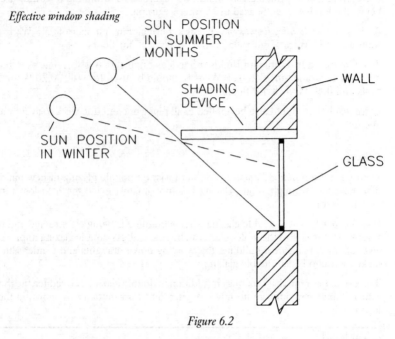

Figure 6.2

Lighting systems

The electrical load from the lighting system is usually the major energy load on the building. This load can be reduced by use of low energy fluorescent fittings instead of tungsten lights which consume much more energy.

Energy consumption can be reduced by providing 'task' lighting at the work place instead of providing a uniform lighting level throughout the building.

The new Health and Safety (Display Screen Equipment) Regulations 1992, which came into force on 1 January 1993, mean that glare must be avoided at display screens.

Considerable savings can be made by switching off all the lights at midday. It has been found that lights switched on at 9 am in the morning tend to be left on all day. If all the lights are switched off automatically and the occupants are forced to reset the lights they need, then the energy consumed by the lights will be greatly reduced.

6.7 Building Energy Management Systems (BEMS)

Building Energy Management Systems are used to control all the services inside a building. This can provide full control of energy, security and fire, etc.

With the addition of 'intelligent' controls the BEMS can learn when to switch on and switch off heating and cooling plant to suit predicted weather conditions and ensure the minimum consumption of energy.

It can also reduce the maximum electrical demand on a building by anticipating peak loads and shutting down non-essential plant.

One of the main advantages of BEMS is the control of operation and maintenance of the building services. The operation of the plant can be tailored to suit different occupancy patterns and the maintenance controlled precisely to suit the plant requirements.

Faults can be identified and rectified before the occupants realise there is a problem. Critical faults can be identified immediately and non-critical faults scheduled for maintenance at a convenient time.

Full details of all plant can be stored in the BEMS together with drawings, wiring diagrams, etc., so that all the information is stored and controlled centrally.

Intelligent outstations can operate independently and be interrogated at regular intervals. In this way several offices or factories in different areas can be controlled and monitored centrally, (using the telephone system).

There are already many cases of BEMS being used for larger buildings such as prisons, airports and hospitals in the United Kingdom, but it is essential to have an experienced energy manager to operate and control the system as well as full back-up from the BEMS manufacturer's agent.

6.8 Solar energy

Solar energy can be used to generate hot water for showers, baths and hand basins etc. Solar panels are readily available but not normally installed at the present time due to the relatively high capital cost and long payback periods. This situation is unlikely to change unless fuel prices increase dramatically.

6.9 General

Some of the most effective ways of reducing energy consumption are the cheapest.

It is possible to reduce air infiltration by draught proofing around doors and windows and fitting automatic door closures on external doors. This is normally very cost-effective and improves the comfort level inside the building by eliminating cold draughts.

The fabric heat loss can be reduced by insulating roof voids and adding insulation to flat felt roofs during refurbishment. Cavity wall insulation is also very cost-effective.

The operating efficiency of the boiler plant can be improved by regular maintenance checks and improving the insulation on boilers, pipe work and hot water storage tanks.

6.10 GREEN BUILDINGS

Introduction

There is a growing awareness of environmental issues affecting property, which is being generated through public concern and European legislation.

The overall aims for any 'environmentally friendly' building should be to consider the following:

(i)   minimising energy consumption, thus reducing carbon dioxide emissions;

(ii) selecting environmentally acceptable materials;

(iii) minimising 'sick building syndrome'.

6.11 Energy Management and Green Buildings

6.11 BREEAM

There was no real guidance on such matters, until the UK Building Research Establishment in association with a number of Developer Sponsors, published BREEAM, (The Building Research Establishment Environmental Assessment Methods) in 1990.

This now applies to new offices, houses and superstores and consideration is currently being given to an assessment method for existing buildings. The original version of BREEAM which covered new offices has been revised and a new expanded version is now available. These documents give a checklist of areas that the design should address, in order to achieve credits towards an environmentally friendly score.

The Building Research Establishment suggest there is no pass or fail figure and it is not the intention that buildings should be compared on the number of credits. It is not suggested that the assessment is considered the ideal solution, but it does make a start in addressing such problems and reflects increasing waves of European legislation.

To obtain an assessment, plans, specifications etc., are submitted to the BRE assessors, who give advice on how the design can be changed to meet the environmentally friendly criteria and upon amendment, the details are reassessed and a certificate issued.

The main ways of ensuring that a building is designed to be environmentally friendly are looking at the global effects, the neighbourhood effects (Legionnaire's Disease), and indoor environment.

6.12 Global effects

Carbon dioxide emissions

Whatever form of energy is used to heat buildings will result in carbon dioxide emissions.

Carbon dioxide emissions for different fuels

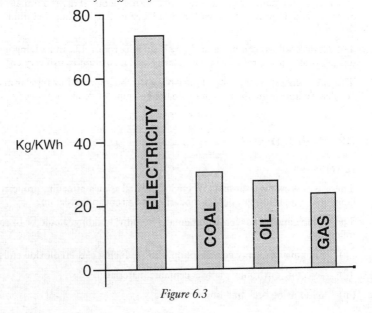

Figure 6.3

The graph above (Figure 6.3) shows the carbon dioxide emissions for different fuels. This table is based on data published in BREEAM version 2/91 (superstores and supermarkets).

Unfortunately the current UK *Building Regulations* do not specify how airtight a new building should be. As approximately 50 per cent of the heat in a building is used for dealing with air infiltration this is obviously an area which should be carefully considered.

For air conditioned buildings generous quantities of clean outside air are needed to maintain a high quality of indoor air. The quantity of outside air will depend on the number of people inside the building and the equipment likely to be used, as well as the type of furnishings and materials used. Ideally, the air extracted from the building (from toilets, etc.) should be used to pre-heat or pre-cool the incoming fresh air by using a heat recovery device, (see paragraph 6.5).

The design of the building services and their control systems should take advantage of the latest techniques to ensure that comfortable conditions are maintained at all times and energy is used efficiently.

CFCs

Although it is now normal to use HCFC-22 as a refrigerant in air conditioning plant and this has a relatively low ozone depletion potential, it is anticipated that HCFC-22 may be banned from use in the future.

As a great deal of refrigerant is used in servicing the refrigeration plant for the air conditioning system, BREEAM rightly encourages attention to the design of the refrigeration plant with regard to the ease of maintenance. It awards credits for including a comprehensive CFC leak detection system and the provision of a refrigerant receiver to store refrigerant during servicing. These are both relatively cheap improvements and should be incorporated in any well designed refrigeration plant.

Halons used in fighting computer fires have a very high ozone depletion potential and if possible alternatives should be considered.

Insulants free from CFCs should be specified. This is not a particularly onerous requirement as many satisfactory alternatives already exist (i.e. fibreglass, rockwool etc.).

Legionnaire's Disease

Legionnaire's Disease bacteria is at its most dangerous at a temperature of 37°C. Contaminated water presents a special risk when it is dispersed into the atmosphere as an aerosol. This is why cooling towers, showers, whirlpools and spas are considered the greatest risk. Even the impact of tap water hitting wash basins, sinks and baths can generate aerosols if the pressure is too high.

The new Health and Safety Executive's Approved Code of Practice means that the Building Manager is fully responsible for the safety of the occupants.

Air conditioning plant can be water-cooled or air-cooled. As a cooling tower has to be very carefully maintained to avoid the risk of Legionnaire's Disease, it is safer to use air-cooled refrigeration plant for an air conditioned building. The air-cooled plant uses more electrical energy, but does not consume any water and the maintenance costs are less.

Domestic water systems must be very carefully designed to eliminate the risk of Legionnaire's Disease. Special care must be taken to keep the cold water storage tanks

6.12   Energy Management and Green Buildings

and heating calorifiers clean and at the correct temperature (i.e. cold water below 20°C and hot water above 55°C). 'Dead legs' must be kept to a minimum so that hot water is delivered at the point of use within seconds. ('Dead legs' are branches connected to fittings where no circulation takes place and the temperature drops below 55°C.)

Indoor environment

Insufficient quantities of fresh air, (and lack of maintenance) are the most common causes of 'sick building syndrome', (this is the term applied to a building which appears to make its occupants ill).

'Sick building syndrome' is normally blamed on the air conditioning plant, but this is not always the main cause, as indoor pollutants also have a contributory effect. Although our knowledge of 'sick building syndrome' is limited we now know sufficient to analyse the problem and take remedial action.

BREEAM also identifies the flicker from lights, as a source of eye strain and recommends using solid state high frequency ballasts instead of switch start choke circuits. Fortunately these light fittings are now readily available and normally specified for all new buildings.

Humidifier fever is also a cause of 'sick building syndrome', and BREEAM recommends a steam-based humidifier and again this has been normal practice in this country for some time.

Displacement ventilation offers one of the best ways of improving the internal environment in offices. Fresh air is supplied at low level and gently drifts upward. It is then exhausted at high level and the heat is recovered to treat the incoming fresh air. The diagram (figure 6.4) below shows a typical system.

Displacement ventilation

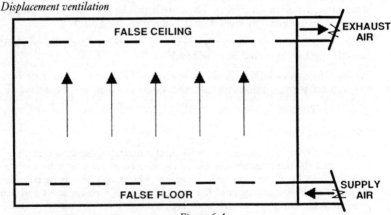

Figure 6.4

The new workplace (Health, Safety and Welfare) Regulations 1992, which came into force on 1 January 1993, states that every enclosed workplace must be 'ventilated by a sufficient quantity of fresh or purified air'.

Water economy

BREEAM also refers to water economy and recommends the use of 'low water use washdown WCs'. These use about half the water needed for a conventional WC, but unfortunately are not available in ceramics.

If the present trends continue we may have to consider using vacuum toilet systems. These use a fraction of low water use WCs and rely on a vacuum to transport the sewage. They are relatively new in Europe and although they use more electricity they have the advantage of allowing the sewage to flow uphill.

A control device attached to a urinal system can save as much as 83 per cent of the water which would flow through an unregulated cistern.

6.13 BUILDING REGULATIONS

The insulation and glazing requirements of the current *Building Regulations* are discussed at 6.6 above under the headings 'Insulation' and 'Glazing' respectively.

At present the *Building Regulations* are being revised and are due for re-issue in 1993. The DoE appears to be considering the use of energy targets or energy rating for domestic buildings and will probably eventually extend this concept to cover commercial buildings. This will depend on how rapidly the CIBSE Energy code can be extended to cover air conditioned buildings, (the energy code already applies to normally heated and ventilated buildings).

The draft *Building Regulations* issued for comment early in 1993 did include double glazing for all new buildings.

Energy targets refer to the energy consumed and at present a typical office building uses $500/600$ kWh/yr/m^2 but the Energy Efficiency Office is currently recommending that this should be reduced to about 250 kWh/yr/m^2 for air conditioned offices and 200 kWh/yr/m^2 for naturally ventilated offices.

6.14 CONCLUSIONS

Energy conservation is normally very cost-effective and most proposals for reducing energy consumption have a payback period of less than two years. There are also environmental reasons for reducing energy consumption. Global warming is mainly caused by the increased content of carbon dioxide in the atmosphere and the energy used for heating is a major contributor.

BREEAM is a very useful tool for establishing the basic parameters of a green building. However we should be looking forward to the next century and building new energy efficient buildings (or alternatively refurbishing existing buildings) which will still be considered 'green' in 20 years time.

Energy efficient 'green' buildings will be more friendly to the environment and more healthy for their occupants.

7 Environmental Assessment

7.1 INTRODUCTION

An Environmental Assessment (EA) is a methodology whereby all possible potential effects of a project are assessed before it is authorised to proceed. Although an EA is now required by statute for all significant projects, it only formalises, defines, and expands upon a procedure which has been followed in a somewhat haphazard way for many years.

Through the system of planning permission and public enquiries, major developments such as mines and quarries, motorways, estuary crossings, out-of-town shopping precincts, road widening, developments in national parks or near sites of special scientific interest (SSSIs), airport runways, waste disposal and destruction in landfills, incinerators, etc., have been subject to the scrutiny of the general public and special interest groups. Issues such as odours, dust, traffic, effects on vegetation and wildlife, landscape, visual intrusion, destruction of buildings and movement of population and more intangible concepts such as the quality of life have all been debated at great length at enquiries and in the press as part of the EA process.

This chapter explains the statutory requirements for an EA, what it should contain, and how to go about preparing one. Because of the legal requirements as well as established custom and practice, it is aimed primarily at the UK reader, although the general principles may be universally applied. An EA requires a considerable depth of expertise in a great many disciplines, and therefore it is not intended that the reader should be fully equipped to prepare his own assessment. Rather he should

- be aware of the need for an EA

- be able to judge whether one is required

- know the required contents of an acceptable Environmental Statement (ES)

- be able to bring all the necessary expertise to the project

- be able to judge whether it will meet the needs and requirements of the planning or permitting authority and all the likely consultees.

7.2 DEFINITIONS

Environmental Assessment (EA)

This term describes all aspects of the process relating to the study of the effects of a project on the environment. It includes the gathering of information from the project initiator and developer or other sources, the studying of the pertinent environmental documents, and consultation with the statutory consultees (defined in *Regulation 8* of *SI 1988 No 1199*) and other interested parties. The culmination of the EA is the production of a synthesis report which is the Environmental Statement (ES).

The ES is a document defined by statute and is primarily used in the planning and authorisation process. However, an assessment may be required not only by planning authorities but also by national governments, international agencies, grant making institutions, banks and finance houses. The planning authorities take over the assessment once the Statement has been submitted and in conjunction with the statutory consultees assess the Statement. They are required to take the ES into account when forming a judgement as to whether to award or refuse planning consent. The EA is sometimes referred to as the Environmental Impact Assessment (EIA) although this term is not now used in the UK.

7.3   Environmental Statement (ES)

The ES is the document in which the scope, activities and waste arisings are documented and their environmental effects are assessed. It is recommended that extensive consultation is carried out with the planning authority statutory consultees and other bodies which are judged to be appropriate during its preparation.

There is no fixed format but the ES must be prepared in a systematic and objective manner. There is, however, a list of required information which must be provided, and this is given in Appendix 7C.

Note: As far as planning applications are concerned the EA and the ES may be only the first stages in the authorisation process. Many manufacturing processes will need to be authorised by Her Majesty's Inspectorate of Pollution (HMIP). A permit will be required to discharge liquid effluents to a sewer or watercourse. Waste which is generated, stored, processed or disposed of will need a licence from the local licensing authority. Much of the data generated for the ES can be used for these purposes also.

7.4   Environment

The environment is generally accepted as describing all areas both within and outside the boundary of the development and refers not only to all life forms in the plant and animal kingdoms but also natural features and topography and man-made features such as archaeology, buildings and other features of artistic or historical interest.

7.5   Waste

Waste is all substances which are allowed to escape to the environment or are disposed of as being surplus to the manufacturing process.

Air

Waste emitted to atmosphere includes all gases and vapours emitted from defined release points such as vents and chimneys as well as 'fugitive' releases due to leaks or open processing. Solvent vapours, acid gases and the gaseous products of combustion all have effects on the local, national or global environment.

Water

Water-borne impurities are discharged to natural water courses such as streams and rivers (including canals) and the sea or to sewers which eventually discharge into one of the above with or without treatment. These same impurities can also leak into the ground and pollute either surface water or underground aquifers which may be used for drinking water.

Land

All solid waste which is deposited in a landfill site is regarded as a release to the environment. Even material which is incinerated could lead to discharges to land, water and air, and residues such as heavy metals could give rise to serious and expensive disposal problems.

7.6 PRESSURES LEADING TO REQUIREMENT FOR AN EA IN THE UK

Public concern over various environmental issues in the nineteen seventies and nineteen eighties was patchy, and tended to be voiced by environmental pressure groups, which were in their infancy, or special interest groups concerned with loss of wildlife or plant habitats. There was little co-ordination and the local and national authorities responsible for overseeing environmental protection were not giving a lead in requiring environmental issues to be discussed.

7.7 USA

The first developments in formal assessments took place in the USA where the *National Environmental Protection Act (NEPA)* was enacted in 1970. The Act was far-reaching in its requirements as all national agencies involved in proposals for legislation or other activities significantly affecting the environment had to prepare and make public a detailed statement on environmental impacts termed an Environmental Impact Statement (EIS), or in situations where a less comprehensive study was required, an Environmental Assessment. There had to be an open discussion of the positive and negative effects, and of the possible alternatives. American industry was soon adopting this procedure and the first systematic approach in Europe was when American multi-nationals started to require EISs for their European projects. These were prepared privately for internal consumption but helped in making manufacturing, technical and business staff aware of the consequences of their proposals.

7.8 European Community

The next major development was the formulation of Community Action Programmes on the environment by the European Community, the first of which was published in 1973. It was influenced by, and incorporated many of the provisions of *NEPA*. The need to make Environmental Assessments at an early stage in the development of a project was a logical consequence of the adopted principle of preventing the generation of pollution and nuisances at source. This is even more true today, as to incorporate pollution control equipment or mitigation measures into a project at a late stage can make the whole scheme financially non-viable, or can cause long and costly delays. Further action programmes were published in 1977 and 1983, the latter being approved not only by the EC Council but also by the representatives of Member governments. It was this 1983 programme which led to the *EC Directive* in 1985.

7.9 EC Directive

The *EC Directive* on the assessment of the effects of certain public and private projects on the environment was adopted on 27 June 1985. It was introduced so that assessments conducted within the EC would be comparable and of a uniform standard and content, and so that no country or industrial sector could gain a competitive advantage, thus frustrating the proper functioning of the common market.

The *Directive* gave Member States three years to enact the necessary national legislation which would require assessments, specify industries, processes or types of development for which assessments would be required, and define their scope and content.

7.10 UK LEGISLATION

The *1985 EC Directive* was incorporated into UK legislation by means of a series of regulations, the most important being the *Town and Country Planning (Assessment of*

7.10 Environmental Assessment

Environmental Effects) Regulations 1988 (SI 1988 No 1199) which came into effect on 15 July 1988. These _Regulations_ only apply to England and Wales. However, the general principles pertain in Scotland and Northern Ireland even though the legal and administrative arrangements are different.

Some developments not subject to control through the planning system, but subject to approval by the appropriate Secretary of State are covered by other, specific, regulations. These projects are:

- trunk roads and motorways
- power stations and overhead power lines
- oil and gas pipelines
- afforestation
- land drainage improvements
- ports and harbours
- marine salmon farming
- marine dredging for minerals.

Developments in all these areas require Environmental Statements, mostly without exception, although sometimes at the discretion of the appropriate authority.

Projects approved by private Act of Parliament are excluded from the _Regulations_ but parliament will require an ES if one would have been required under the _Regulations_. Simplified Planning Zones (SPZs) and Enterprise Zones (EZs) have less formal planning permission requirements. However, _Schedule 2_ projects (see Appendix 7B) will need to be notified to the planning authority which will consider whether an ES is required. _Schedule 1_ projects (see Appendix 8A) are excluded from SPZs, and require ESs in EZs.

Recently the government has announced its intention to end the special status of the Crown in planning law, so the Crown will be legally required to submit a statement where the _EC Directive_ applies. In practice, several ministerial departments have been preparing statements on a voluntary basis to demonstrate that they are behaving in an environmentally responsible manner.

On 25 July 1992 the _Planning and Compensation Act_ inserted a new _section 71A_ in the _Town and Country Planning Act 1990_. It gives the Secretary of State powers to require assessments not covered by the _EC Directive_. The latest amendment to the _Town and Country Planning (Assessment of Environmental Effects) Regulations 1988_ came into force in July 1992 (_SI 1992 No 1494_). The additional developments included are:

- salmon and other fish farming
- water treatment plant
- wind generators
- motorway service areas
- coast protection works
- golf courses
- privately financed toll roads.

88

7.11   THE REGULATIONS IN PRACTICE

How to determine if a statement is required

Any proposed development which covers a large area of land (over five hectares in urban areas), emits pollutants to air or water, generates solid wastes, has an adverse visual impact, could generate nuisances such as odours, dust, noise, or traffic or could affect wild animal and plant life is likely to need a statement. The developer will need to study the requirements for an ES (see Appendix 7C) and collect data before he can make a judgement. In any case data may need to be collected to demonstrate to the planning authority that no statement is formally required. It must also be remembered that local Environmental Health Officers will require engineering process data to enable nuisances to be predicted. All water discharges must be estimated in order that a permit can be obtained from the NRA or the local water plc. Additionally the developer may wish to go beyond the legal requirements to maintain good relationships with the local authorities, residents and the press.

The *1988 Regulations* divide projects into two categories

> Schedule 1 Projects – A statement is mandatory   *Annex 1*

> Schedule 2 Projects – A statement is only required if the project is likely to   *An II*
> give rise to significant environmental effects.

The problem is that the word 'significant' has not been defined. This is also true of other words and phrases in environmental legislation, and it will take some time before a body of information, experience and case law is built up.

Some guidance is given in DoE Circular 15/88 which is intended to help local planning authorities decide whether to call for a statement. Helpful guidelines on various size criteria are included. *Schedule 1* and *2* projects are given in Appendices 7A and 7B.

7.12   THE ENVIRONMENTAL STATEMENT

How to prepare it and what it should include

The spirit of the *EC Directive* is to develop the best environmental option which minimises the creation of pollution and nuisances at source rather than subsequently trying to counteract their effects after release. The way to achieve this is to consider all possible effects on the environment at the earliest possible stage in the planning and project definition process.

It is in everyone's interests that a statement is prepared, at least in outline form as early as possible. The developer will need to consult his internal or external environmental advisers in order to highlight key features of the project. It is also very important to involve the planning authority at this early stage in order to discover which issues are important to them, and what may be important to the statutory consultees. Thorough compilation of existing data, research, and consultation at the initial stages can reap substantial dividends by the time the project comes to fruition. Changes to the project after studying alternatives, incorporation of mitigation measures to counteract adverse effects, and possible enhancement of positive effects can be included at little extra cost before detailed planning has started.

7.13   Statutory requirements

Schedule 3 of the *1988 Regulations* specifies the information required in an ES and reflects the requirements of the *EC Directive*. For full details see *Schedule 3* in Appendix 7C. Broadly the ES is a comprehensive document which:

7.14 Environmental Assessment

- describes the proposed development and gives an idea of scale;
- presents quantitative data on environmental impacts;
- lists the likely significant effects on the whole environment of the region including not only natural resources but the human population and items which may be part of our cultural heritage;
- outlines measures envisaged to avoid, reduce or remedy any significant adverse effects.

Part of the ES may consist of highly technical data provided by experts. The developer is required by the *Regulations* to include a non-technical summary so that members of the public, local councillors and other interested bodies may have a full understanding of the consequences and implications of the project.

7.14 Preparation

The ES is comprehensive in the way it addresses environmental issues. Unless the developer is a major multi-national company or a conglomerate with a wide range of technical expertise at its disposal, some or all of the work in preparing the statement will need to be contracted to a consultant. In any case an in-house co-ordinator may need to be appointed. This person will be responsible for collecting all relevant data and for commissioning the necessary tasks which cannot be handled in-house.

7.15 Qualifications

What qualifications and experience are required by the co-ordinator and contributors to the statement?

Co-ordinator

The co-ordinator needs to be aware of global and local environmental issues, and have an overview of environmental legislation. For a development involving manufacturing or warehousing he needs to have a knowledge of available pollution control or treatment measures and be familiar with the permits required for air emissions, liquid discharges, water abstraction, waste storage and disposal etc. Familiarity with planning authority procedures is also necessary. Many years related experience, or a focused training course will give the necessary qualification. The reason so much emphasis is placed on knowledge and experience is that it is essential to collect data which to an uninvolved person may seem unnecessary or even irrelevant, but which may be crucial in addressing the concerns of the planning authority and the consultees.

Other contributors

Depending on the scope of the development, the following expertise may be required:

- chemical engineer
- health and safety specialist
- mechanical engineer, particularly with combustion expertise
- waste water treatment engineer
- air dispersion modeller/climatologist/meteorologist
- road traffic engineer
- geographer

90

—   ecologist

—   biologist

—   zoologist

—   marine and freshwater biologist

—   chemist

—   botanist

—   forester

—   landscape specialist

—   architect

—   noise specialist

—   geologist

—   hydrogeologist

—   hydrologist

—   socio-economist

—   archaeologist

—   agriculturalist.

Other specialists may be required in the fields of nuclear radiation, leisure and tourism etc. It should also be borne in mind that special skills are required to prepare the non-technical summary from a mass of data provided by a number of different technical experts. It is this summary which may be given the widest circulation and the most publicity. The statement will be made available to the public, and therefore environmental pressure groups, special interest groups, residents associations and the press can (and do) apply for copies.

It is also important that the ES is a self-contained document and all necessary data, maps and diagrams are included even if they have already been submitted to the regulatory authority for a different purpose.

7.16   THE ES: CONTENTS IN DETAIL

Description of the proposed development

As much detail as possible should be given on the type of activity or business to be carried out.

It should include:

—   the total area and the area occupied by buildings, storage, roads, as well as paved, tarmacadamed or concreted areas

—   plant and machinery to be installed

—   number of people employed and hours of working

—   raw materials, annual purchase in tonnes

—   main processing steps

—   main products, annual production in tonnes

7.17   Environmental Assessment

utility services – water, power, gas, sewerage, drainage.

Other specific details such as:

Industrial estates – number of units and types of business to be encouraged or discouraged

Leisure, hotels, conference centres – number of guests and visitors

Waste treatment and disposal – complete analysis of all expected materials, transfers and disposals.

7.17   Data relevant to environmental issues

This is not an exhaustive list but is a guide relating to manufacturing industry which should be used as a starting point.

— Emissions to atmosphere. Include not only the emissions from each stack or vent but also fugitive emissions of solvents. An estimate can be made from the planned annual purchases. For boilers give the type and quantity of fuel and for fuel oil and coal give the sulphur content. In all cases, include gases, vapours, acid gases and dusts.

— Discharges to sewer or watercourse. Give details of volumes and compositions for every discharge point.

— Solid waste generated. Give tonnages, compositions disposal routes or treatment methods.

— Materials storage. Detail all raw materials, intermediates and finished products, as well as all solid and liquid wastes. State volumes in storage tanks and drums.

— For warehousing state likely volumes of various types of materials and any categories of materials not to be stored.

— Methods of fire protection.

— Estimates of noise at the boundary fence and at other strategic points such as residential areas. State the potential for dust and odour releases.

— Number of vehicle movements per day, broken down by type of vehicle and loads carried. Specify the routes local to the facility.

Note: For all chemicals listed include Material Safety Data Sheets and all available toxicity data.

7.18   Significant effects (direct and indirect)

The developer is required to consider not only long term or permanent effects, but also short term or temporary effects due to construction, land development, creation of infrastructure or product or process trials. For any adverse effects the proposed mitigation measures and their effectiveness should be described.

The term 'indirect' refers to subsequent or secondary effects of a polluting substance. For example pollution of a watercourse could lead to fish being affected by disease, sterility or deformities due to accumulation of the pollutant in the main body organs. A secondary effect could result if the fish were consumed by other animals (including man), with further bioaccumulation of pollutants.

An example of diverse effects is acidic gases being emitted from combustion plant. These gases can not only affect the ozone layer in the upper atmosphere and the absorbance of the sun's rays (the greenhouse effect) but also these gases can dissolve in atmospheric water droplets and fall as acidic rain, affecting trees, aquatic life and buildings. Loss of a particular plant, animal or insect species could affect the other species which feed or otherwise depend on it.

It is prudent of a developer to consider alternatives from the earliest stages of a project. Potential objections may become apparent after an initial survey or after consultation with experts or the planning authority. It may be necessary to avoid ecologically sensitive areas, switch from our road to rail transport, provide separate access, modify the process to reduce air emissions or waste generation etc. One or two of the most acceptable alternatives should be studied in some depth to be sure that the developer has selected the plan which has the least environmental impact and is at an acceptable cost. To anticipate possible objections, or suggested alternatives from the authorities or consultees, the incremental costs of a wide range of elements of the plan should be established. To present alternatives to the authorities would only cause confusion but it would do no harm when discussing potential impacts to state that alternatives have been considered and give the reasons why they were discounted.

7.19 BASELINE DATA

For all those features which may be affected by the development proposed it is necessary to assess the current environmental situation before considering the likely significant effects of the proposed actions. A baseline should be established against which developments can be measured. The EA and ES should focus on the important issues, with a brief discussion of non-significant ones. The following data may need to be included.

7.20 Human beings

Population surveys, socio-economic data, transport and land use patterns, description of communities, utilities and facilities, local and regional development and zoning plans.

7.21 Flora and fauna

Review existing surveys giving varieties and numbers or areas of occurrence. List all endangered and protected species and others of special significance. State whether any species are thriving or declining, either by consulting local naturalists or by studying historical data.

7.22 Soil

By the use of soil maps and field visits describe the types of soil found, the vegetation or crops they support and other factors such as its stability, and vulnerability to flooding, erosion or other threats. Drainage problems should be listed.

7.23 Water

An assessment of water in its many forms and uses will be quite extensive.

It can include dynamic systems such as streams, rivers, canals, estuaries and seas, as well as static waters such as ponds, lakes and reservoirs and areas such as wetlands and marshes. Water has many uses as potable supply, recreation, sport, commercial use and power generation.

7.24 Environmental Assessment

Not only should surface water, including water courses, ditches, surface run-offs and drainage be covered but also subterranean supplies and aquifers. The hydrogeology of the region will be described.

7.24 Air

It is most important for any project where pollutants are likely to be emitted; combustion plant and other thermal processes, manufacturing, roads, radiation sources etc., that a complete analysis of the atmosphere local to the site is undertaken, under varying atmospheric conditions. What is to be looked for depends on the type of project and likely associated pollutants.

For traffic, combustion plant, or high voltage discharges one would need to monitor for oxides of sulphur, nitrogen and carbon, and ozone. Other acid gases such as chlorine and hydrogen chloride may be important. In other cases the total amount of organic compounds or certain classes or organics, and dioxins, furans and PCBs may be required. In all cases particulates must be measured, with a breakdown, if possible, into building and construction dust, soil, dust from industrial processes and the products of incomplete combustion (carbon, tars etc.). A background radiation survey may be necessary.

All these measurements should be related to local national or international standards and any prevailing or expected air quality standards for the region should be listed.

7.25 Climate

Most aspects of climate are readily available and should be given in tabular form with a short overview. Data is usually available from the Meterological Office and relates to a fixed point which may be a town, airfield or coastal location. Other data may be available from the local authority or from amateur enthusiasts but levels of pollution are not generally available. The developer needs to study the terrain and take local advice as to whether the available data (which may relate to a point 50 km or more away) is relevant to the chosen project location. Monthly, seasonal and annual averages with the two extremes (high and low) should be given for sunshine, temperature, precipitation (snow and rain) and wind speed. Additionally wind roses showing direction frequencies should be included.

Much more detailed information is available on computer disk for use in air dispersion modelling of pollutants. Any local effects of wind funnelling, thermal effects from power station complexes, downdraughts or unusual wind patterns due to natural or man-made features should be described.

7.26 Landscape

In this section should be described all features which have a visual impact, and not just idyllic rural scenery. Urban areas, skylines, industrial complexes, cultivation, crop patterns, orchards and plantations, hedgerows all have their distinctive features. People become attached to familiar views, and trying to achieve a more 'natural' vista may not be regarded as a benefit and may encounter local resistance. The scale of the landscape is also important, whether it is varied and changing frequently or whether there is little change over a large distance. This section can also act as a focus for other parts of the database. The geology, hydrogeology, land use, drainage, topography, water courses, lakes, reservoirs, tourist areas, local beauty spots and local viewpoints from hills, outcrops and footpaths as well as SSSIs, parks and nature reserves, and areas of outstanding natural beauty (AONBs) are all data which may be required when the impacts of the project are being assessed.

94

7.27   Interaction

The developer is required to discuss in the ES the interaction between some or all of the above. It may be necessary to bring together an economist, a scientist, a geographer and an ecologist in order to be able to fully describe the dynamics of the region. Employment, types of industry, traffic patterns, leisure, farming, wild life, settlements have all developed over many centuries. Before the age of mass transport many regions were self-contained economies in most respects and some regions have been remarkably resistant to change over the last few decades.

7.28   Material assets

This section will probably cover local issues, although there may be cases when a project has regional or even national impacts, such as a pipeline, refinery or a motorway. A description of local residential and industrial property values and other assets which might affect regional prosperity, for example, the tourist trade, mineral assets or commercial forest and woodland would be appropriate.

7.29   Cultural heritage

Several aspects included above, such as landscape, material assets and leisure could be brought together here if the site is in an area with many historical associations. The interest could range from prehistoric settlements or field patterns to Roman or Norman architecture, mediaeval towns, centres of the industrial revolution and nineteen thirties architecture.

7.30   DESCRIPTION OF SIGNIFICANT EFFECTS

Human beings

People need to be considered both as individuals and as a group or in the community in which they live. Issues such as the future of the community, means of gaining a livelihood, means of growing food crops, means of transport, opportunities for leisure and sport, and intangibles which contribute to the quality of life may need to be addressed. The individual may be affected by any of the statutory nuisances already mentioned and also the ability to breathe 'fresh air' and enjoy the beauty of the countryside and the landscape. People may, of course be directly affected by airborne pollution from a factory and great care must be taken in not only accurately predicting the emissions of all toxic pollutants but also the way in which they will disperse in the atmosphere and what their concentrations will be at ground level. Extensive computer modelling is an essential tool in this predictive process. The allowable upper concentration is generally 1/30 of the exposure limit allowed within the factory. There may be temporary effects such as traffic dust, noise etc. which should be detailed.

7.31   Flora

There will be a permanent reduction in vegetation as a result of most developments, although developers may wish to create other areas of garden or parkland where possible. There could also be destruction due to construction access or materials storage, but these areas could be allowed to re-establish themselves later. Dust caused by construction or construction traffic can severely affect plant life. Changes to local water courses, drainage or the soil characteristics will affect the types of vegetation which can be supported. Mitigation measures, plans for restoration and provision of alternatives such as extending new nature reserves or woodland should be described.

7.32 Fauna

The baseline survey of occurrence of various species should be studied to assess the effects on animals, birds, insects and aquatic life. Encroachment of industrial development can cause shy animals and birds to move away even if their habitat has not been destroyed. Destruction of ponds, ditches and lakes can affect migratory species such as birds, frogs, newts and toads. Wetlands generally support insect life and other fauna which feed on them. Mitigation measures could include reducing human access to certain areas and providing special routes for badgers, hedgehogs, frogs etc. A code of practice may need to be developed to control the activities of construction workers.

7.33 Soil

Significant items such as topsoil removal, excavation and attempts at landscaping by large-scale earth movement will have effects on fertility, compaction, drainage and erosion. Soil could become either waterlogged or dried-out by even minor changes to drainage. Dumping of soil and underlying rock which affects the existing strata should be described. The emission of pollutants may affect soils and therefore crops or natural vegetation. Mitigation measures such as replacement of topsoil, retaining of drainage patterns, diking and bunding or otherwise containing pollutants should be included where appropriate.

7.34 Water

Water in all its occurrences is likely to be the resource most affected by any development. Significant issues to be addressed include the following.

—   Pollution or changing the flow of aquifers, especially if used for potable water.

—   Pollution of surface waters either by direct discharge or by surface run-off from industry and farming.

—   Civil works which alter water courses and flows or dam them up, change river levels, lead to silting or bank erosion. Note that for estuaries extensive modelling may be required.

—   Abstraction which may affect other boreholes, springs, streams and river flows.

—   Discharges of inert materials such as building rubble, raw materials, or quarry waste which can clog stream beds and destroy aquatic life.

—   Discharges which affect water temperature or acidity or contain materials sometimes not regarded as pollutants such as water treatment chemicals, food-stuffs, milk, and food processing waste. Any organic matter in an effluent discharge will be broken down by aerobic bacteria. Oxygen is needed for this process and aquatic life which require this oxygen will be deprived and are likely to perish.

—   Effects of pollutants on aquatic life. Toxicity data for the major pollutants on freshwater and marine fish and crustaceans as well as aquatic vegetation should be given wherever possible.

7.35 Air

Effects can be global, national and local. All pollutants, including those from power plant and traffic should be listed with a statement as to whether they might contribute to the destruction of the ozone layer or to the 'greenhouse effect'.

Acidic gases from high stacks can affect air quality in other countries. It is claimed that northern Europe and Scandinavia are affected by emissions from UK power plants. Conversely the incident at Chernobyl in Russia affected upland areas in the UK.

Local effects include dust and vapour emissions of both organic and acidic gases. Traces of toxic components can exist due to thermal or catalytic degradation or incomplete combustion, and several of these may be identified as carcinogens or have other serious immediate or cumulative effects. Odours are very difficult to predict, as their threshold is often down to several parts per billion. Even odours regarded as pleasant such as some foodstuffs, perfumes and fragrances can be objectionable when experienced for 24 hours per day, seven days per week. Pleasant odours can also be oxidised by the air and sunlight to give unpleasant byproducts.

All proposed containment and treatment measures should be fully described with their designed effects.

7.36 Climate

Most projects in the UK are unlikely to have any significant effects on the national or local climate. Large emissions of heat or water vapour should be listed. Any changes in wind pattern due to large buildings or other constructions should be studied by computer modelling or wind tunnel testing.

7.37 Landscape

The effects on landscape can result from topographical, agricultural or industrial developments. The use of artists' impressions or photo-montages will be useful to both the developer and the planning authority and will help in planning any mitigation measures. Remember that the project must be assessed from many different viewpoints.

7.38 Interaction

All possible effects should be studied using the approach given in 7.27 above.

7.39 Material assets

This generally refers to residential property values, but other interests can be affected such as sports and recreational centres or other commercial activities. There is the general problem of dust, noise, odours or extra traffic, but a change in the pattern of residential, industrial and recreational areas can affect land and property values. Buildings which seem out of place or badly designed can meet local resistance.

As a wider issue, the effect of the project on the local economy in creating temporary or permanent jobs, or using local firms for goods and services may be a most important issue.

7.40 Cultural heritage

The effects of a project may range from destruction of prehistoric settlements to demolition of buildings of historical significance and less dramatic effects such as vibration or acid rain. Other effects could be on local dialects, customs or festivals. Codes of practice may need to be developed to allow items of archaeological significance to be identified and investigated during excavation.

7.41 Environmental Assessment

7.41 PRESENTATION OF ASSESSMENT OF EFFECTS

The developer is only required to describe the results which he considers to be significant. As this involves a degree of subjectivity there is a danger that the consultees and others involved in assessing the statement may have a different opinion. It is recommended that the developer demonstrates that all possible potential effects have been considered, with insignificant effects stated to be of little or zero significance.

The presentation can be in textual form or else can be in the form of a matrix or table where the degree of significance can be concisely shown for each effect.

Where effects are significant then an attempt at a semi-quantitative assessment can be made and shown on the matrix. The advantage of this approach is that temporary and permanent, positive and negative effects can all be shown on the same table. After planned or recommended mitigation measures are taken into account a second matrix will show the final effects of the project on which the project application will be judged.

Attempts have been made to use positive and negative scales from one to five or one to ten or to use single, double and triple negatives and positives. In the author's experience it is unrealistic to be able to award in effect a score of, say, six or seven, and to be able to distinguish between these two values. A scale of one to three should suffice for most ESs.

An example is shown here of the initial assessment of a major engineering project as defined, with an explanatory table, the mitigation proposals, and the final effects after the mitigation measures have been taken into account.

A study of the potential impacts (Table 7.2) shows that in most areas the project will have no significant impacts although it seems that more survey work is required in all areas or else the finds have not been fully identified and characterised. Zone 3 stands out as being the area where the greatest impacts are likely to be. The study team produced some proposals for the construction phase and during operations. (Table 7.3).

Provided that all the mitigation proposals are fully implemented, Table 7.4 shows that the potential impacts are predicted to reduce to zero, or in some cases be slightly positive, or in the most sensitive area would be of only minor significance.

Table 7.1			
ENVIRONMENTAL IMPACT SCALES			
Types of Impact	*Importance of Archaeological Element*		
	International	*National*	*Local*
Negative	– – (major significance)	– (minor significance)	– (minor significance)
No Known Impact	0 (insignificant)	0 (insignificant)	0 (insignificant)
Positive	+ + (major significance)	+ (minor significance)	+ (minor significance)
Negative Impacts:	(Direct) (Indirect)	Destruction of artifacts and activity sites Increased human activity and access – disturbance and damage to artifacts and sites	
Positive Impacts:		Opportunity for survey recording and identification of archaeological features/artifacts	

This matrix-based method, using evaluation hierarchies to standardise the assessment of the significance of impacts has been developed by BIOSCAN (UK) Ltd. through their experience in undertaking Environmental Assessments.

98

Possibly as Appendix (Scanner)

Table 7.2						
POTENTIAL ENVIRONMENTAL IMPACTS						
Source of Impact			*Archaeological Component*			
Element	*Activity*	*Impact*	*Prehistory*	*Garamante*	*Romano–Libyan*	*Islamic*
ZONE 1:						
Wellheads and conveyance	Construction	Direct	-/0?	-/0?	0	0
	Operation	Indirect	0	0	0	0
Haul Road	Construction	Direct	-/0?	-/0?	0	0
	Operation	Indirect	-?	-?	0	0
OS&M Camps	Construction	Direct	-/0?	-/0?	0	0
	Operation	Indirect	-/0?	-/0?	0	0
ZONE 2:						
Conveyance	Construction	Direct	0	-/0?	0	0
	Operation	Indirect	0	-/0?	0	0
Haul Road	Construction	Direct	0	-/0?	0	0
	Operation	Indirect	0?	-/0?	-?	0
ZONE 3:						
Conveyance	Construction	Direct	-?	0	- -	0
	Operation	Indirect	-?	0	- -	-?
Aggregates	Extraction	Direct	-?	0	- -(?)	0
Turnouts	Agriculture	Direct	-?	0	- -	0
Haul Roads	Construction	Direct	-?	0	- -	0
	Operation	Indirect	-?	0	- -	-?
ZONE 4:						
Conveyance	Construction	Direct	-/0?	0	-/0?	-/0?
	Operation	Indirect	-/0?	0	-/0?	0
Haul Road	Construction	Direct	-/0?	0	-/0?	-/0?
	Operation	Indirect	-/0?	0	-/0?	0
Tunnel	Construction	Direct	-/0?	0	-/0?	0
ZONE 5:						
Distribution System	Construction	Direct	-/0?	0	-	0
	Operation	Indirect	-/0?	0	-	0
Water Utilisation	Agriculture	Direct	-/0?	0	-	0

?   Uncertain impacts due to lack of survey information

Table 7.3			
MITIGATION PROPOSALS			
Source of Impact			*Mitigation Proposals*
Element	*Activity*	*Impact*	
Construction	Haul roads Conveyance route Camps Distributions systems/ turnouts Tunnel excavation	Direct	• Reconnaissance survey of Project area to identify features/artifacts of significant value. • Detailed recording and recovery of important features. • Excavation and recovery of significant features. • Controlled blasting of trench for pipeline. • Investigation of archaeological significance of Wadi Wirvirig and aggregate extraction. • Watching brief during construction of distribution systems for turn outs, tunnel excavation and trench development. • Procedures to ensure area of human activity during construction is maintained to a minimum. • Archaeological maps zoning areas and features of significance to regulate contractor activity. • 'Rescue' capacity for sites of archaeological importance.
Operation	Increased access of human activity	Indirect	• Publication of archaeological findings from survey. • Protection/conservation measures/ procedures for sites made more accessible by Project.

100

Table 7.4						
POTENTIAL IMPACTS AFTER MITIGATION						
Source of Impact			*Archaeological Component*			
Element	*Activity*	*Impact*	*Prehistory*	*Garamante*	*Romano-Libyan*	*Islamic*
ZONE 1:						
Wellheads and Conveyance	Construction	Direct	0/+?	0/+?	0	0
	Operation	Indirect	0/+?	0/+?	0	0
Haul Roads	Construction	Direct	0	0	0	0
	Operation	Indirect	-/0(?)	-/0(?)	0	0
OS&M Camps	Construction	Direct	0	0	0	0
	Operation	Indirect	0	0	0	0
ZONE 2:						
Conveyance	Construction	Direct	0/+?	0/+?	0	0
	Operation	Indirect	0	0	0	0
Haul Road	Construction	Direct	0	0	0	0
	Operation	Indirect	0	0	0	0
ZONE 3:						
Conveyance	Construction	Direct	0/+?	0	-	0
	Operation	Indirect	0/+?	0	-	0
Aggregates	Extraction	Direct	0	0	-	0
Turnouts	Agriculture	Direct	-/0?	0	-	0
Haul Roads	Construction	Direct	0	0	-	0
	Operation	Indirect	-/0?	0	-	-/0?
Tunnel	Construction	Direct	0/+?	0	0	0
ZONE 4:						
Conveyance	Construction	Direct	0	0	0	0
	Operation	Indirect	0	0	0	0
Haul Roads	Construction	Direct	0	0	0	0
	Operation	Indirect	0	0	-/0?	0
ZONE 5:						
Distribution System	Construction	Direct	0/+?	0	0/+?	0
	Operation	Indirect	0/+?	0	0/+?	0
Water Utilisation	Agriculture	Direct	0/+?	0	0/+?	0

Direct impact: Destruction of artifacts, increased human activity – disturbance and damage to sites.

Indirect impact: Increased access and human activity - disturbance and damage to sites.

•   Assumes regulated contractor activity.

Appendix 7A

TOWN AND COUNTRY PLANNING (ASSESSMENT OF ENVIRONMENTAL EFFECTS) REGULATIONS 1988 (SI 1988 No 1199)

Schedule 1

Regulation 2

Descriptions of developments

(1)   The carrying out of building or other operations, or the change of use of buildings or other land (where a material change) to provide any of the following–

1.   A crude-oil refinery (excluding an undertaking manufacturing only lubricants from crude oil) or an installation for the gasification and liquefaction of 500 tonnes or more of coal or bituminous shale per day.

2.   A thermal power station or other combustion installation with a heat output of 300 megawatts or more, other than a nuclear power station or other nuclear reactor.

3.   An installation designed solely for the permanent storage or final disposal of radioactive waste.

4.   An integrated works for the initial melting of cast-iron and steel.

5.   An installation for the extraction of asbestos or for the processing and transformation of asbestos or products containing asbestos:–

(a)   where the installation produces asbestos-cement products, with an annual production of more than 20,000 tonnes of finished products; or

(b)   where the installation produces friction material, with an annual production of more than 50 tonnes of finished products; or

(c)   in other cases, where the installation will utilise more than 200 tonnes of asbestos per year.

6.   An integrated chemical installation, that is to say, an industrial installation or group of installations where two or more linked chemical or physical processes are employed for the manufacture of olefins from petroleum products, or of sulphuric acid, nitric acid, hydrofluoric acid, chlorine, or fluorine.

7.   A special road; a line for long-distance railway traffic; or an aerodrome with a basic runway length of 2,100m or more.

8.   A trading port, an inland waterway which permits the passage of vessels of over 1,350 tonnes or a port for inland waterway traffic capable of handling such vessels.

9.   A waste-disposal installation for the incineration or chemical treatment of special waste.

(2)   The carrying out of operations whereby land is filled with special waste, or the change of use of land (where a material change) to use for the deposit of such waste.

Appendix 7B

Schedule 2

Regulation 2(1)

Descriptions of development

Development for any of the following purposes–

1. *Agriculture*

    (a)   water-management for agriculture

    (b)   poultry-rearing

    (c)   pig-rearing

    (d)   a salmon hatchery

    (e)   an installation for the rearing of salmon

    (f)   the reclamation of land from the sea

2. *Extractive industry*

    (a)   extracting

    (b)   deep drilling, including in particular–

    (i)   geothermal drilling

    (ii)   drilling for the storage of nuclear waste material

    (iii)   drilling for water supplies

    but excluding drilling to investigate the stability of the soil

    (c)   extracting minerals (other than metalliferous and energy-producing minerals) such as marble, sand, gravel, shale, salt, phosphates and potash

    (d)   extracting coal or lignite by underground or open-cast mining

    (e)   extracting petroleum

    (f)   extracting natural gas

    (g)   extracting ores

    (h)   extracting bituminous shale

    (i)   extracting minerals (other than metalliferous and energy-producing minerals) by open-cast mining

    (j)   a surface industrial installation for the extraction of coal, petroleum, natural gas or ores or bituminous shale

    (k)   a coke oven (dry distillation of coal)

    (l)   an installation for the manufacture of cement

3.   *Energy industry*

(a)   a non-nuclear thermal power station, not being an installation falling within Schedule 1, or an installation for the production of electricity, steam and hot water

(b)   an industrial installation for carrying gas, steam or hot water, or the transmission of electrical energy by overhead cables

(c)   the surface storage of natural gas

(d)   the underground storage of combustible gases

(e)   the surface storage of fossil fuels

(f)   the industrial briquetting of coal or lignite

(g)   an installation for the production or enrichment of nuclear fuels

(h)   an installation for the reprocessing of irradiated nuclear fuels

(i)   an installation for the collection or processing of radioactive waste, not being an installation falling within Schedule 1

(j)   an installation for hydroelectric energy production

4.   *Processing of metals*

(a)   an iron-works or steelworks including a foundry, forge, drawing plant or rolling mill (not being a works falling within Schedule 1)

(b)   an installation for the production (including smelting, refining, drawing and rolling) of non-ferrous metals, other than precious metals

(c)   the pressing and drawing or stamping of large castings

(d)   the surface treatment and coating of metals

(e)   boilermaking or manufacturing reservoirs, tanks and other sheet-metal containers

(f)   manufacturing or assembling motor vehicles or manufacturing motor-vehicle engines

(g)   a shipyard

(h)   an installation for the construction or repair of aircraft

(i)   the manufacture of railway equipment

(j)   swaging by explosives

(k)   an installation for the roasting or sintering of metallic ores

5.   *Glass making*

the manufacture of glass

6.   *Chemical industry*

(a)   the treatment of intermediate products and production of chemicals, other than development falling within Schedule 1

(b)   the production of pesticides or pharmaceutical products, paints or varnishes, elastomers or peroxides

(c)   the storage of petroleum or petrochemical or chemical products

7.   *Food industry*

    (a)   the manufacture of vegetable or animal oils or fats

    (b)   the packing or canning of animal or vegetable products

    (c)   the manufacture of dairy products

    (d)   brewing or malting

    (e)   confectionery or syrup manufacture

    (f)   an installation for the slaughter of animals

    (g)   an industrial starch manufacturing installation

    (h)   a fish-meal or fish-oil factory

    (i)   a sugar factory

8.   *Textile, leather, wood and paper industries*

    (a)   a wool scouring, degreasing and bleaching factory

    (b)   the manufacture of fibre board, particle board or plywood

    (c)   the manufacture of pulp, paper or board

    (d)   a fibre-dyeing factory

    (e)   a cellulose-processing and production installation

    (f)   a tannery or a leather dressing factory

9.   *Rubber industry*

the manufacture and treatment of elastomer-based products

10.   *Infrastructure projects*

    (a)   an industrial estate development project

    (b)   an urban development project

    (c)   a ski-lift or cable-car

    (d)   the construction of a road, or a harbour, including a fishing harbour, or an aerodrome, not being development falling within Schedule 1

    (e)   canalisation or flood-relief works

    (f)   a dam or other installation designed to hold water or store it on a long-term basis

    (g)   a tramway, elevated or underground railway, suspended line or similar line, exclusively or mainly for passenger transport

    (h)   an oil or gas pipeline installation

    (i)   a long-distance aqueduct

    (j)   a yacht marina

11.   *Other projects*

    (a)   a holiday village or hotel complex

    (b)   a permanent racing or test track for cars or motor cycles

(c) an installation for the disposal of controlled waste or waste from mines and quarries, not being an installation falling within Schedule 1

(d) a waste water treatment plant

(e) a site for depositing sludge

(f) the storage of scrap iron

(g) a test bench for engines, turbines or reactors

(h) the manufacture of artificial mineral fibres

(i) the manufacture, packing, loading or placing in cartridges of gunpowder or other explosives

(j) a knackers' yard

12. The modification of a development which has been carried out, where that development is within a description mentioned in Schedule 1.

13. Development within a description mentioned in Schedule 1, where it is exclusively or mainly for the development and testing of new methods or products and will not be permitted for longer than one year.

Appendix 7C

TOWN AND COUNTRY PLANNING (ASSESSMENT OF ENVIRONMENTAL EFFECTS) REGULATIONS 1988 (SI 1988 No 1199)

Schedule 3

Regulation 2(1)

1.   An environmental statement comprises a document or series of documents providing for the purpose of assessing the likely impact upon the environment of the development proposed to be carried out, the information specified in paragraph 2 (referred to in this Schedule as 'the specified information').

2.   The specified information is–

(a)   a description of the development proposed, comprising information about the site and the design and size or scale of the development;

(b)   the data necessary to identify and assess the main effects which that development is likely to have on the environment;

(c)   a description of the likely significant effects, direct and indirect, on the environment of the development, explained by reference to its possible impact on–

human beings;
flora;
fauna;
soil;
water;
air;
climate;
the landscape;
the inter-action between any of the foregoing;
material assets;
the cultural heritage;

(d)   where significant adverse effects are identified with respect to any of the foregoing, a description of the measures envisaged in order to avoid, reduce or remedy those effects; and

(e)   a summary in non-technical language of the information specified above.

3.   An environmental statement may include, by way of explanation or amplification of any specified information, further information on any of the following matters–

(a)   the physical characteristics of the proposed development, and the land-use requirements during the construction and operational phases;

(b)   the main characteristics of the production processes proposed, including the nature and quality of the material to be used;

(c)   the estimated type and quantity of expected residues and emissions (including pollutants of water, air or soil, noise, vibration, light, heat and radiation) resulting from the proposed development when in operation;

(d)   (in outline) the main alternatives (if any) studied by the applicant, appellant or authority and an indication of the main reasons for choosing the development proposed, taking into account the environmental effects;

(e)   the likely significant direct and indirect effects on the environment of the development proposed which may result from–

    (i)   the use of natural resources;

    (ii)   the emission of pollutants, the creation of nuisances, and the elimination of waste;

(f)   the forecasting methods used to assess any effects on the environment about which information is given under subparagraph (e); and

(g)   any difficulties, such as technical deficiencies or lack of know-how, encountered in compiling any specified information.

In paragraph (e), 'effects' includes secondary, cumulative, short, medium and long term, permanent, temporary, positive and negative effects.

4.   Where further information is included in an environmental statement pursuant to paragraph 3, a non-technical summary of that information shall also be provided.

Appendix 7D

Further reading

1.   Canter, L W, *Environmental Impact Assessment* (McGraw-Hill 1977).

2.   Cheremisinoff, P N, and Morresi, A C, *Environmental Assessment and Impact Statement Handbook* (Ann Arbor 1977).

3.   Fortlage, C A, *Environmental Assessment, A Practical Guide* (Gower 1990).

4.   *Overseas Development Administration, Manual of Environmental Appraisal* (ODA 1989).

5.   *Environmental Policy and Practice*. Frequent useful articles (Quarterly Journal EPP Publications).

8 Environmental Audits

8.1 WHY AUDIT?

Environmental auditing is a management tool designed to provide information on environmental performance to the right people at the right time. At the time of writing, there are no legislative requirements requiring a company to prepare an environmental audit; nor are there any Codes of Practice or even generally accepted guidance on exactly what should be included in an audit or how it should be carried out.

There is, however, a set of principles that needs to be followed to ensure that the goal of monitoring environmental performance is achieved; and a set of decisions that needs to be explicitly taken before establishing an environmental audit programme in a particular plant or company.

This chapter examines the goals, principles and decision requirements of environmental auditing; it includes a description of the steps in a 'typical' audit and offers guidance for the audit process.

8.2 What is an environmental audit?

An environmental audit is a systematic means of providing environmental management information:

(*a*)   to all levels of management;

(*b*)   for a variety of purposes.

The term 'environmental audit' is therefore used to refer to a number of different information and assessment activities. These can be categorised as follows.

(*a*)   *A technical review.* Such an audit will involve the systematic collection of information about the existing and potential impact of the organisation's activities on the environment; it will normally cover compliance with pollution control and waste management legislation. It will not cover management practices.

(*b*)   *A management review.* This will focus more on the management procedures and record keeping and will also gather information on compliance with legislation. It may also review procedures in the context of company policies, programmes and other requirements. It will not examine the existing or likely impact of the operation on the surrounding environment from a technical standpoint.

(*c*)   *Due diligence review.* This will examine the likely cost of implementing pollution control and site remediation actions and will take account of existing and future legislation (see Chapter 10). Such liability reviews are normally carried out in the context of mergers, acquisitions and long range company planning.

It is not unusual to hear any of the above referred to as 'audits' and many of the principles discussed at 8.3 below will be relevant. However, the term environmental audit is increasingly used primarily to refer to a systematic examination of an individual site carried out within an overall company-wide audit plan and designed on a regular basis to provide management with information on whether the company's policies and programmes are being achieved and the extent to which the company is in a position to comply with existing and developing environmental legislation. In other words, the output from an environmental audit is the information that allows managers to measure the organisation's environmental performance (see Figure 8.1).

8.3   Environmental Audits

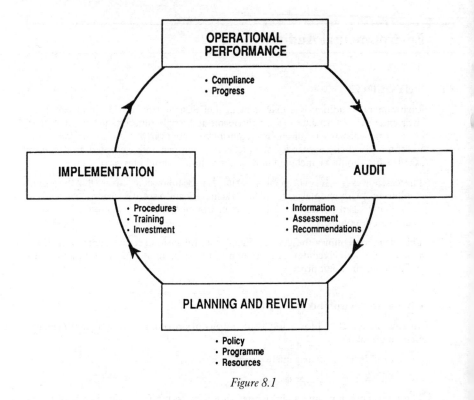

Figure 8.1

8.3   The eco-management and audit objective

The European Commission in its *Regulation for an Eco-Management and Audit Scheme* (EMAS), *formerly known as Eco-Audit*, has suggested the following definition, *based on a definition*, as developed by the International Chamber of *Commerce*:

'An environmental audit means a management tool comprising a systematic, documented, periodic and objective evaluation of the performance of the organisation, management system and processes designed to protect the environment with the aim of:

(i)   facilitating management control of practices which may have an impact on the environment;

(ii)   assessing compliance with company environmental policies'.

The Regulation specifies that an audit should include at least the following steps:

'—   Planning of the audit activities, including definition of responsibilities for the audit;

—   Review of the environmental protection policy of the company;

—   Assessment of the organisation, management and equipment;

—   Gathering of data and of all relevant information;

—   Evaluation of the overall performance;

—   Identification of areas for improvement;

—   Internal reporting to the top management;

112

and that all these steps shall be documented. A follow up policy statement by the top management shall conclude the auditing procedure'.

The EC Regulation specifies that at least the following aspects shall be considered by the audit:

'(*a*)   Relevant information and data on material and energy exchanges with the environment due to the industrial activity.

(*b*)   Compliance with community, national and local regulations and standards applicable to the industrial establishment concerned.

(*c*)   Significant incidents or operation disturbances occurred, and complaints received.

(*d*)   A review of the available policy, equipment, organisation and management systems related to the following aspects:

— pollution discharge control, monitoring and reduction;

— other nuisances;

— energy choice and reduction of energy use;

— raw materials choice and transportation; reduction of water and raw material use;

— waste transportation, elimination, recycling and reuse;

— products planning (design, packaging, transportation, use and elimination);

— prevention and mitigation of accidents;

— staff training and participation;

— external information.'

8.4   British Standard 7750

The recent British Standard specifying Environmental Management Systems places audits firmly within the organisation's management system noting that

'on their own reviews and audits cannot provide an organisation with the assurance that its performance not only meets, but will continue to meet, legislative and policy requirements. To be effective, they need to be conducted within a structured management system, integrated with overall management activity and addressing all aspects of desired environmental performance.'

Within this context, environmental management audits have the following aims:

'The organisation shall have established and maintained procedures for audits to be carried out, in order to determine: (*a*) whether or not environmental management activities conform to the environmental management programme, and are implemented effectively; (*b*) the effectiveness of the environmental management system in fulfilling the organisation's environmental policy.'

The British Standard proposes that where an organisation has no management system in place there will be a need for a preparatory environmental review that should cover the following four key areas:

'(*a*)   legislative and regulatory requirements;

(*b*)   an evaluation and registration of significant environmental effects;

(c)   an examination of all existing environmental management practice and procedures;

(d)   an assessment of feedback from the investigation of previous incidents and non-compliance'.

They note that such a review should cover both normal and 'abnormal' operations and include the implications of emergency conditions.

8.5 SETTING UP AN AUDIT PROGRAMME

Developing an audit programme requires decisions to be taken on:

—   the scope of the audit: what information is to be collected;

—   the frequency with which each site (or issue) is to be audited;

—   who is to carry out the audit;

—   what, if any, information is to be made available to the public.

It is also necessary to develop an audit protocol: that is, the detailed plan to be used by each auditor when carrying out the audit.

8.6   Scope and frequency of the audit

The scope of the audit will depend on the information that is required by management to monitor environmental performance. A full environmental audit will cover (i) compliance with environmental regulations, (ii) implementation of company's environmental policies and procedures, (iii) good environmental management practice and (iv) past activities. In so far as it provides the information to determine an organisation's environmental performance it may be expected to cover not only waste streams from plants but also wider management and operational issues.

8.7   The Eco-Management and Audit Regulation suggests that the following should be covered within the framework of the wider environmental protection system:

—   assessment, control and prevention of the impact of the activity concerned on the various sectors of the environment;

—   energy management, savings and choice;

—   raw materials, management, savings, choice and transportation; water management and savings;

—   waste avoidance, recycling, reuse, transportation and disposal;

—   selection of production processes;

—   production planning (design, packaging, transportation, use and disposal);

—   prevention and limitation of accidents;

—   staff information, training and participation in environmental issues;

—   external information, public participation and handling of public complaints.

8.8   In their guidance on environmental auditing the CBI includes a similar listing, amplified into more detailed questions (CBI, June 1990). So, for example, on wastes and transport the detailed questions include the following.

Wastes. How and where is waste of all types generated? Can it be minimised/ eliminated/recycled? Where production of waste is unavoidable, would it provide a suitable raw material for another organisation, either business or voluntary group? Are you losing recycling opportunities or increasing disposal costs by not segregating different types of waste? Who removes your waste – is it carried and disposed of responsibly?

Transport. Are you using the most efficient and environmentally sound systems for transporting your goods and materials? Would alternative systems make less demands on the environment? Do staff travelling on business use the most efficient system or merely the most 'convenient'? Would use of public transport bring about cost savings without significant increase in travelling times? Do you encourage staff to travel to work by public transport and could you increase availability of communal transport by providing additional company funded services?

8.9   The frequency with which a particular plant or activity is audited will depend on the use of the information: how frequently does management want to review the environmental performance in order to feel secure that the expected actions are taking place and that concerns noted in the previous audit are being properly addressed?

The EC Eco-Management Audit Regulation proposes that audits should be conducted at intervals of between one and three years. It notes that the frequency will need to take account of the potential overall environmental impacts of the activities at the site including:

— the importance and urgency of the problems detected;

— the potential for environmental problems;

— scale and complexity of the activities;

— volume of emissions;

— history of environmental problems.

It may be that an organisation decides to implement a self-reporting or self-auditing programme that provides key information about environmental performance in the time period between the full audits.

8.10 | **Who should carry out the environmental audit?**

To be of maximum value an environmental audit should be objective and the environmental auditor should be free from pressure from within the organisation; in other words it is important that the audit report should be objective and the auditor should feel able to make critical comments without fear of the effect of such comments on his future career within the organisation.

A number of major companies have established audit teams within their corporate environmental health and safety department. In some cases, the staffing of these teams relies on secondment from different departments within the company. In so far as individuals are then auditing different parts of the company this has a benefit that they understand the business but have no internal line responsibility to the activity being audited.

Some organisations have used external consultants to carry out some or all of the audits; in this case it is often valuable for the external auditor to work with the company's team.

Environmental auditing requires an understanding of the activity to be audited (this may be a plant, an abandoned site or a corporate headquarters); an understanding of management systems, environmental regulations and permitting procedures; and also a broad understanding of environmental impacts. A qualified auditor will in addition need to be systematic, able to deal in a constructive way with a range of management and technical staff, have an enquiring mind and be observant.

It is quite clear that such paragons are few and far between. This means that companies establishing environmental audit programmes will need to put a considerable emphasis on training: both 'in the classroom' and on site.

8.11   Qualified environmental auditor schemes

There are two schemes currently under development in the UK: the first organised by the Association of Environmental Consultancies and the second by the IEA.

The Association of Environmental Consultancies' scheme addresses the responsibility of external environmental audit companies. It lays down guidance designed to ensure that (i) the audit work is undertaken to a high standard by suitably qualified and experienced individuals and (ii) that the consulting firm itself is 'audited' by an external verification panel on a regular basis to ensure that the Code of Practice is being fully complied with. The issues covered include (i) the ethical standards to be followed by all the consultants, (ii) the way in which the audit is to be managed in order to ensure that client needs are met and the work is undertaken to a high professional standard, (iii) the selection of teams and their qualifications, (iv) issues of confidentiality. The Code of Practice stresses the need for regular training within the consultancies to ensure that all staff maintain a high level of professionalism.

The IEA scheme focuses in particular on the qualifications of individuals. This proposes to classify into one of three categories. Points will be allocated according to the individual's academic qualifications, membership of professional bodies, training and practical experience. The three levels of membership are:

(*a*)   Provisional Environmental Auditor,

(*b*)   Environmental Auditor,

(*c*)   Principal Environmental Auditor.

The Scheme will be administered by the National Environmental Auditors Registration Board, a new organisation whose composition is yet to be finalised. Currently it is proposed that the Board will be mainly made up of representatives from industry and environmental audit practitioners. In addition, representatives from academia, the government and an environmental NGO will be invited to attend.

A register of environmental auditors will be published by the IEA; this will be available to business and industry who will therefore be able to determine the suitability of individuals for audit work.

8.12   Public disclosure

Unlike financial audits, environmental audits are not carried out for the purposes of providing information to the regulatory authorities or the public at large. They are intended to assist management understand the impact their operations are having upon the environment and to provide a basis for taking action to remedy any problems. To this extent companies are likely to be unwilling to make the results of their environmental audits public; or, if the audit is carried out with this objective, it is likely that it will be a far less valuable management tool. The ICC has noted that if environmental audits are to be successfully used as part of company policy 'it is essential that the procedure should be seen as the responsibility of the company itself, should be voluntary and for company use only'.

8.13   The Eco-Audit proposal does however propose that certain information should be made available to the public on the environmental performance of the company. This would be an 'environmental statement' specific to each site audited and prepared with the same frequency as the environmental audits. Such a statement would:

— describe the company's activities at the site;

— provide a detailed assessment of all the significant environmental issues of relevance;

— summarise the figures on pollutant emissions, waste generation, raw material, energy and water consumption and other significant environmental aspects;

— include the company's environmental policy programme as well as the specific objectives for the site considered;

— include an evaluation of the environmental performance of the environmental management system and note the date for the submission of the next statement;

— publish the name of the accredited environmental verifier for the Statement: this requirement for external, independent evaluation is a crucial component of the Regulation.

Simplified statements must be drawn up for the intervening years in the audit cycle. These must draw attention to significant changes from the previous statement and include details of pollutant emissions. Where no significant changes have occurred, no further statement is required until the completion of the next audit.

It will be appreciated that for many plants and processes within the UK information on emissions, wastes and environmental effects is already on the public register (through the provisions of the *Environmental Protection Act 1990*) and increasingly the larger companies are providing a clear statement of their environmental policies and programmes in order to make it clear to the public that they are aware of their environmental responsibilities.

So while the environmental audit remains the internal document (like management accounts) companies may wish to provide a general summary in order to demonstrate to the public that they are carrying out audits and are happy to make some of the information more widely available. It should perhaps be noted that such internal systematic reviews may also become public should there be a serious pollution incident at the plant or a civil action with the result that the documents are placed before an inquiry or any other form of legal hearing.

8.14   The audit protocol

The protocol represents the plan to be used by auditors in conducting an audit. It establishes what information is to be collected; it provides a systematic basis to the audit; and it also gives a step-by-step guide to the environmental auditor on how evidence is to be collected. The protocol is an important tool in so far as it not only serves as the auditor's guide to conducting the audit but also acts as a record of the audit procedures and the notes completed by the team. In addition a completed audit protocol provides a record for the rationale for any changes in audit procedures or deviations from plan if these prove necessary during the audit.

Specifically the protocol:

(*a*)   contains a basic questionnaire covering each environmental topic;

(*b*)   provides the hard copy record to assist the auditor as the work progresses and provides a basis for referencing working papers and copies of documentation collected during the audit;

(c)   the completed protocols with the supporting documents are the record of the audit and form the basis for the formal audit report.

The protocol is therefore the key step in establishing the audit programme in so far as it informs managers and others about the scope of the audit and provides the opportunity to request that the changes are made either to collect additional information or to delete information that will not be used.

8.15   TYPICAL AUDIT PROCESS

The following typical audit process reviews the work required prior to the audit; activities at a site; and post-audit activities. It is specifically applicable to a manufacturing site rather than, for example, a corporate headquarters. The issues that are likely to be addressed in the audit are shown in Table 8.1.

Table 8.1

Items to be addressed in audits

Environment	Safety	Occupational health	Product safety
Site history	Safety policy/procedures	Employee exposure to air contaminants	Product safety programme
Processes/materials used	Accident reporting	Exposures to physical agents e.g. noise, radiation, heat etc.	Product quality control
Storage of materials above ground below ground	Accident recording Accident investigation	Measurements of employee exposure	Product packaging, storage and shipping
Air emissions	Permit to work systems	Exposure records	Product recall/ withdrawal procedures
Water discharges Solid wastes	Special procedures for: — confined space entry	Ventilation/ engineering controls	Customer information on product handling and quality
Liquid/hazardous wastes	— work on electrical equipment — breaking into pipelines, etc.	Personal protective equipment	Regulatory compliance
Asbestos, PCBs		Information and training on health hazards	Labelling
Waste disposal on site off site	Emergency response Fire fighting	Medical surveillance programme	Specifications for purchased materials/ products/packaging
Oil/chemical spill prevention	Job safety analysis Safety training	Hearing conversation	Material safety data
Permits/licences		First aid	Vendor qualification programme
Pollution control	Safety communications/ promotion	Regulatory requirements	QA testing and inspections
Contractors on site	Housekeeping		
Past incidents	Regulations compliance		Record keeping
			Product literature
			Process control

8.16   **Pre-audit activities**

(*a*)   Select and schedule facility to audit based on:

— selection criteria

— priorities assigned.

(*b*)   Select audit team members

— confirm their availability

— make travel and lodging arrangements

— assign audit responsibilities.

(*c*)   Contact facility and plan audit

— discuss audit programme

— obtain background information

— administer questionnaire (if necessary)

— define scope

— determine applicable requirements

— note priority topics

— modify or adapt protocols

— determine resource needs

— identify facility staff to be interviewed, confirm availability.

8.17   **Activities at site**

Step 1: Identify and understand management control systems

— review background information

— opening meeting

— orientation tour of facility

— review audit plan

— confirm understanding of internal controls.

Step 2: Assess management control systems

— identify strengths and weaknesses of internal controls

— adapt audit plan and resource allocation

— define testing and verification strategies.

Step 3: Gather audit evidence

— apply testing and verification strategies

— collect data

— ensure protocol steps are completed

— review all findings and observations

— ensure that all findings are factual

8.18 Environmental Audits

— conduct further testing if required

— liaise with regulatory authorities.

Step 4: Evaluate audit findings

— develop complete list of findings

— assemble working papers and documents

— integrate and summarise findings

— prepare report for closing meeting.

Step 5: Verbal report of findings to facility

— present initial findings at closing meeting

— discuss findings with plant personnel.

8.18 Post audit activities

(*a*) Issue draft report

— corrected closing report

— determine distribution list

— distribute draft report

— allow time for corrections.

(*b*) Issue final report

— corrected draft report

— distribute final report

— highlight requirement for action plan

— determine action plan preparation deadline.

(*c*) Action plan and preparation and implementation

— based on audit findings in final report.

(*d*) Follow up on action plan.

8.19 CARRYING OUT THE AUDIT

Collecting information

Environmental auditing requires the auditor to develop a full understanding of the controls, procedures and practices that are in place or are thought to be in place. These are likely to include formal procedures and practices; all forms of records (including monitoring); existing inspection and maintenance programmes; physical controls and other measures to contain spills and other incidents, etc. The auditor will need to understand how responsibilities are defined; how personnel are trained and how competent those on the site appear to be; how procedures are carried out and other standard management issues. In addition to the use of the detailed questionnaire (forming part of the protocol) the auditor will gain information through observation, interviewing individual staff, reviewing specific documentation and speaking to the appropriate regulatory authorities.

8.20   Audit interviews

Since interviewing is one of the primary techniques used in gathering audit information, good interviewing skills are essential to the successful completion of the audit. Attention to the following elements of interviewing skills during the audit process will assist in establishing a good rapport with the facility personnel as well as obtaining the information required. Take notes during the interview and record the name, title and job description of the person interviewed; be alert and responsive to the interviewee when asking questions and listening to responses; control the interview, but ensure that you appear relaxed and that your interviewee feels relaxed; go to the interviewee's workplace/office where possible; plan the interview so that you introduce yourself, explain the purpose of the interview and gather the appropriate information; know when to end the interview and thank the interviewee; end the interview on a positive note.

8.21   Documentation

It is a central principle that the audit should be fully documented; there should therefore be a clear, written, audit trail. The working papers from an audit will include completed protocols, associated questionnaires, auditor notes and copies of documents collected during the audit itself. It is important that each auditor ends the audit with a complete set of field notes and papers for each protocol step assigned to that auditor; that there is documentation (1) to ensure that an adequate audit was conducted and (2) to substantiate compliance and non-compliance issues, both with respect to regulatory requirements and company procedures; that there is a record of reference copies of documents collected during the audit; and there is the data to support the audit report, which may be helpful in subsequent follow-up.

The working papers should therefore contain all the information that the auditor believes may be necessary to support the audit findings and should contain a description of environmental management and control systems – including flow charts, diagrams, copies of documents, etc.; a description of the action taken to complete each step of the audit protocol; details of answers to questions in the protocol and other questionnaires used; details of any 'tests' conducted during the audit (e.g. checking that consignments of hazardous waste had the relevant documentation for each disposal).

8.22   Management systems

Throughout the audit, the auditor should evaluate the effectiveness and appropriateness of the management system.

Definition of roles and responsibilities. Are roles and responsibilities clearly defined, established and communicated; are personnel who need to know responsibility assignments made aware of them; are any key responsibilities overlapping, shared or conflicting?

Authority/authorisation. How is authority granted to those with assigned environmental responsibilities; who has authority to waive adherence to an established standard or requirement; how are authorities to depart from standard procedures made and recorded; what potential exists for 'conflicting interests' in accomplishing key environmental tasks?

Personnel training and experience. What formal training have key personnel had to assist in performing environmental tasks and functions; what training and awareness activities are conducted to provide an understanding of environmental obligations?

8.23   Environmental Audits

Documentation. What records are routinely developed and retained; are exception reports developed; how does the importance of the item relate to the records/ documentation kept?

8.23   Communicating and reporting

It is important that environmental auditors are not seen as 'policemen'. Clearly the very fact that there is an audit programme with regular inspections will raise environmental compliance higher on the agenda of the plant manager and all plant personnel. Nevertheless the aim is to work with the plant staff to bring about improvement rather than just identify shortcomings. To this extent involvement of the plant management personnel is important; this can be done through a series of meetings (though often availability of senior staff poses a problem) and it is very important that the draft findings are checked with the plant manager (and indeed opportunity given to rectify problems) before the findings are distributed more widely. The audit can include recommendations for action; but many companies prefer the report simply to address facts and outstanding concerns, leaving the operational managers to take the necessary remedial action.

8.24   BENEFITS OF ENVIRONMENTAL AUDITING

A properly implemented environmental audit plan provides a range of benefits for an organisation. These are as follows.

(i)   It provides a framework for measuring (and therefore managing) environmental performance.

(ii)   It reinforces accountability for the environmental dimension of the business: the audit process requires managers to be clear about their responsibilities and how these are being implemented.

(iii)   It raises awareness of the importance of professional environmental management throughout the organisation.

(iv)   To the extent that external reporting will be required, it provides a sound basis that enables companies to feel sure that what is included in the reports is an accurate record.

(v)   It provides valuable information for future planning. This includes the future design of processes and products as well as inputs into future financial plans where pollution control and other investments are to be made.

(vi)   It allows senior managers to feel secure that all the environmental aspects of their business are being professionally managed: it will not remove all possibility of environmental incidents but will at least reduce their likelihood.

9 Environment and the Balance Sheet

9.1 Those who believed that business could only reduce its environmental impact in a climate of growth have been proved wrong. Deep within the world's worst recession, industry is systematically 'greening' itself because it knows that the quality of its environmental performance is inextricably linked to profitability.

A multi-national oil company that recently cut jobs and capital spending in the face of heavy losses, maintained its environmental initiatives planned well before its forced restructuring. A global electronics player which suffered unprecedented losses in 1992 continued to drive hard for an improved environmental performance. The story is the same in the car and chemicals industries.

Businesses in these and many other sectors realise that environmental improvements are not optional extras but, like quality, have a direct impact on the profitability. There are, of course, costs that have to be borne, but these produce tangible and quantifiable business benefits too. And such benefits can be extracted from every facet of the operation.

This does not mean that the pursuit of environmental excellence is either easy or cheap. Winners in this game are those companies that possess vision, and more importantly, managerial skills that are both creative and efficient. It is these skills that are needed to solve problems that are both interdisciplinary and labyrinthine in nature.

9.2 LOOKING FOR BENEFITS

The benefits bestowed by an improved environmental performance have been likened to a fruit tree. It is relatively simple for any organisation to pick the fruit from the lower branches, but the ripest benefits are often higher up and getting there demands delicate footwork.

Benefits can be divided into two broad groups: hard and soft. Take the hard. Industry damages the environment by using it as a rubbish dump for wastes, which are emitted to land, air and water. This dump, while once almost entirely free, is getting more expensive as a result of new laws and restrictions brought about by public pressure to reduce pollution. This means that industry is faced with an ever rising bill to get rid of its waste products.

It is this increased cost, combined with the knowledge that heavy polluters get a bad press, that is driving companies to look carefully at ways of reducing wastes. Initial efforts concentrated on merely cleaning wastes to meet higher emissions standards. These so-called 'end-of-pipe solutions' proved inadequate and the emphasis is now on reducing wastes at source so that there is less to dump. Cutting wastes demands a new way of thinking about industrial processes, which often involves a redesign of the process and the use of new, cleaner technology.

9.3 UP-FRONT COSTS

There is, of course, an up-front cost, but industry is finding that the process of reducing waste not only cuts costs but helps make the business more efficient and therefore more profitable. Leading companies, such as 3M, have reaped the benefits from this philosophy for over a decade. Pressure to reduce waste to the point of

123

eradication is set to continue under the widely adopted polluter pays principle. This is beginning to force companies to include the cost of pollution – the environmental cost – into the cost of their products. Cutting this cost, by reducing pollution, is becoming essential if products are to remain competitive.

Reducing energy consumption leads to other hard benefits. Energy is an environmental issue because most of the energy used by business is derived from fossil fuels – a finite resource. Furthermore, the burning of fossil fuels creates gases, some of which can contribute to the formation of acid rain and photochemical smogs. Carbon dioxide, the major by-product of burning fuel, is a strong greenhouse gas and contributes to the suspected warming of the globe.

Emissions can be reduced dramatically simply by using energy more efficiently. More importantly, companies can save quite considerable amounts of money by becoming more energy efficient. Even in the current economic climate where energy prices are low, payback periods on a range of energy-saving schemes are relatively short and the effect on the balance sheet can be substantial – as demonstrated by Japanese industry, which is probably the most energy efficient in the world.

Direct benefits from a more efficient use of energy will increase when governments introduce carbon taxes. Although there is a concerted effort by industry throughout the world to fend off such taxes on the ground that it damages competitiveness, it seems inevitable that energy prices will have to rise if governments are to meet internationally agreed targets to reduce carbon dioxide emissions. Business itself is not against a rise in energy prices – the UK's business committee that advises the government has supported this idea – but it wants such increases to be fair so that it can compete equitably on a global scale.

9.4   ECONOMIC INSTRUMENTS

Market mechanisms, such as carbon taxes and tradeable pollution permits, are set to become one of the favoured official methods to control the environmental impact of business in all OECD countries. These mechanisms link environmental performance directly to the balance sheet because a clean company stands a better chance of being more profitable than a dirty competitor.

Further hard benefits are to be found in the many business opportunities created by environmental pressures. Tighter laws are the principal driver of the pollution control market which, according to OECD estimates, will be worth between $200 billion and $300 billion a year by the end of the decade. German, Swiss and Swedish manufacturers of pollution control equipment, such as flue-gas scrubbers, have discovered that the demand for their products is high. The story is the same for many companies producing the products, such as monitors and sensors, that contribute to the making of cleaner technologies.

9.5   MUTUALLY BENEFICIAL RELATIONSHIPS

However, many of the benefits produced by a sound environmental performance are what business considers to be soft: difficult to measure and complex to quantify, but still essential to the process of making profits. These benefits are tied into the relationships that business has with its stakeholders – shareholders, customers, employees, suppliers and the local community. If a business is to prosper it has to build sound and mutually beneficial relationships with these groups because it is these stakeholders who are generating much of the environmental pressure on business.

Shareholders realise that profitable companies are those that avoid high environmental costs and investors are beginning to choose to invest in companies with a good environmental performance. The entire financial community, insurers, banks and other investors, is beginning to adopt the same attitude.

Customers are starting to demand products that, compared with traditional products, are less damaging to the environment when they are made and used. The opportunities to pursue the green consumer are being increased with the introduction of the EC's eco-labelling scheme which will bestow a green mark of approval on certain environmentally sound products.

Employees prefer to work for companies with a good green record, as any recruitment officer will confirm. This remains an important issue even in a recession when jobs are scarce because difficult markets demand the most able employees. It is these talented and sought-after people who are the most insistent that employers have a good environmental record.

Suppliers, most companies are both buyers and suppliers, are coming under pressure to guarantee that their products are produced without causing environmental damage. This is because the buyer, who usually resells the product, cannot afford to be tainted by a supplier's environmental misdemeanours. Companies such as B&Q, the UK's biggest DIY chain, BT and IBM UK, now insist that suppliers conform with a strict environmental checklist. Such pressure percolating down the supply chain was one of the important motivators for many companies to conform to quality management standards, such as BS5750. It looks likely that the new environment management standard, BS7750, might soon become as popular with companies who need to improve their competitive positioning in the greener markets of the nineteen nineties.

9.6   BUILDING TRUST

The general public, and particularly the local community that plays host to a plant, are also influential in determining the fortunes of a company. In the words of BP, 'it is the public that provides business with its licence to operate'. And every day a company, especially those organisations involved in messy or potentially hazardous activities, have to earn the public's trust. Without such trust the company can quickly lose public support, market credibility and its ability to compete.

These soft benefits might at times seem excruciatingly soggy. But in the fast-changing markets of this decade and into the next millennium, soft issues are playing an important role in profitability. Take a company such as IBM. In the past this giant has succeeded by making high-quality products and providing its customers with the confidence that they would enjoy top-rate support. Customers bought in the knowledge that they might not get the latest technology, but they certainly would buy good quality without any risk of being let down in the long term.

But rapidly changing markets and stiff competition from manufacturers in the East have eroded IBM's ability to provide this service and remain profitable. IBM is now moving away from its manufacturing base and attempting to expand its project management abilities. The company has always prided itself on its social responsibilities and it was one of the first multi-nationals to take the environment seriously. IBM is now finding that its environment management skills developed over the past two decades are playing an important role in bolstering its image as an efficient and caring manager of projects. This is vital to its success because image helps attract and win customers. Furthermore, IBM finds that its green management skills are a potentially profitable service that it can sell to companies who need to improve their environmental performance quickly.

9.7 Environmental and the Balance Sheet

9.7 COMBINING HARD AND SOFT BENEFITS

Companies now acknowledge that the combination of hard and soft benefits from managing environmental pressures have an important effect on profitability. But more important, those organisations that have taken up the environmental challenge have discovered that the wide range of demands for information that these pressures exert has had the knock-on effect of helping them to understand better the dynamics of their business. This knowledge has given them the power to make their operations more efficient and therefore potentially more profitable. Greening the balance sheet helps keep companies in the black.

10 Environmental Due Diligence

10.1 INTRODUCTION

The increase in the number and severity of environmental protection laws, initially in the United States, but more recently in the UK and Europe, has brought with it the growing importance of 'environmental due diligence' investigations. Typically, such investigations are undertaken either as part of a corporate transaction such as a company merger or acquisition or in property acquisitions. They are however seen in a very wide range of situations including lending decisions, underwriting share issues, privatisations, etc.

10.2 The new environmental laws emanating from Westminster and Brussels all have one common thread running through them: namely that the cost of disregarding the environment is set to rise whether it be by way of increased fines for non-compliance or by the increased expenditure required to meet higher standards. It is therefore vital, when embarking on a transaction, to take steps to identify the other party's environmental obligations and legal compliance record at an early stage in order to avoid the possibility of oneself inheriting liabilities arising from the other party's failings. Buying land, for example, which turns out to be contaminated or buying a company with an environmental prosecution pending, is likely to prove a costly error.

10.3 As the practice has developed, it has become increasingly common for banks and other funding institutions also to insist on an environmental due diligence investigation before they commit funds. Sellers themselves are also beginning to carry out their own 'pre-divestiture' reviews primarily to avoid being disadvantaged by a purchaser's findings which might weaken their negotiating position.

10.4 THE INHERITANCE OF ENVIRONMENTAL LIABILITIES

There has long been considerable scope for inheriting environmental liabilities in both the criminal and civil law. An acquisition of the shares of a company will transfer to the purchaser the legal personality of the company and with it any pending environmental liabilities to which the company may be subject, including pending criminal prosecutions.

10.5 In civil law, some types of environmental liability can pass whether it is a company which is acquired or merely its assets. In the law of nuisance, for example, an occupier of property may be liable for any damage caused by the state of affairs on that property even if he did not originally create that state of affairs if he 'adopts' the nuisance by using the state of affairs for his own purposes or even if he merely 'continues' the nuisance by failing to take steps to abate it once it comes to his attention.

10.6 In public law a local authority seeking to 'clean up' contamination from former waste sites, will be entitled to recover its expenses from the person who is currently the owner of the land in question – even if he was not responsible for the contamination but merely acquired the site subsequently (*Environmental Protection Act 1990, s 61*).

10.7 Environmental problems may be inherited in other ways. If the original owner was carrying out operations without the necessary statutory licences and consents, or in breach of a condition imposed on such consent, any purchaser would also commit a criminal offence if he continued in the same way without putting the deficiency right. Again, a new owner of property may find that his plans to redevelop the land are made far more expensive by problems of contamination created by his predecessor, or that his ability to resell the land is hampered by a prospective buyer's concern over previously undiscovered contamination.

10.8 THE RISKS OF ASSUMING ENVIRONMENTAL PROBLEMS

These ways of inheriting environmental liabilities are not new. What is new are the increased risks associated with them. This is due to a number of causes.

10.9 Legal constraints

The first and most obvious source, the growing number of environmental legal controls on industry, has already been mentioned. Since 1973 the European Community has adopted some 300 Directives and Regulations relating to the environment and there is no sign of an abatement in the tide. International treaties and protocols have been adopted covering a wide range of environmental concerns from ozone layer protection to trading in endangered species. In the UK, the *Environmental Protection Act 1990* has introduced a number of radical new environmental protection regimes – integrated pollution control, local authority air pollution control, new controls over waste management and disposal and new controls over genetically modified organisms. With these new laws have come tougher penalties for infringements: fines of up to £20,000 in the magistrates' court and unlimited fines in the Crown Court. Imprisonment is also a possibility. Directors and other corporate officers and managers may personally face criminal proceedings if their actions or omissions result in their company breaching these laws.

10.10 Public awareness

The second factor, the growth of public awareness of environmental issues, is seen by many as one of the main reasons for the first, the growth in environmental laws. The publicity given to the major environmental stories of recent times such as the Exxon Valdez disaster and the coverage of issues such as global warming, ozone layer destruction and deforestation, have resulted in a much better educated and more demanding public. The profile of 'the environment' as an issue has been raised to a level where people are much more concerned about 'green' issues. The consequences can be seen in the growth of green purchasing, green investing and other consumer-led developments.

10.11 Regulatory restructuring

With the new laws has also come a radical restructuring of the way the environment is policed. Perhaps the most dramatic step in this process came with the privatisation of the water industry in 1989 and the simultaneous creation of a new pollution watchdog, the National Rivers Authority (NRA) with wide powers to control and monitor industrial discharges to water and to clean up or take legal action against polluters. For the first time the functions of policing compliance and the provision of water services (by the new water and sewerage companies) were separated.

Prior to that, in 1987, Her Majesty's Inspectorate of Pollution (HMIP) had been formed by amalgamating the existing central government inspectorates for air pollution, radiochemicals and hazardous waste. HMIP is charged with primary responsibility for overseeing and policing the introduction of IPC. During 1992, the government announced plans to amalgamate the NRA and HMIP, together with the waste regulation duties carried out by local government, into a new Environment

Agency. Plans announced in 1990 for a European Environment Agency have so far not come to fruition due to wrangling between Member States over where the Agency should be based. However, it is clear from the EC's recently adopted Fifth Environment Action Programme that the Agency is seen as having a crucial role to play in implementing the EC's environmental policies.

10.12 Access to information

A fourth factor making the inheritance of environmental problems more risky is the increased rights given to the public to have access to environmental information held by public bodies. The currently high, and increasing, level of public awareness of environmental issues has already been mentioned. It is however recognised, particularly at the European level, that the public is considerably lacking in essential information, without which its important role as an environmental 'watchdog' is hampered. The EC has set about redressing the balance by a Directive passed in 1990 requiring environmental information held by public bodies to be made available to the public. The EC also hopes that the European Environment Agency, when fully operational, will be responsible for the evaluation, improvement and dissemination of environmental information.

10.13 In the UK, publicly disclosable environmental information has traditionally been held in the form of registers, maintained under a number of different statutes and containing categories of information prescribed in the statute or regulations. 'Raw data' has generally not been disclosed and so it has not been possible, for example, for a member of the public or an environmental organisation to discover from the registers precise details of substances discharged into the air, water or land and to compare these with the levels permitted in the relevant permit or consent.

This is changing. The *Water Act 1989* (now the *Water Resources Act 1991*) required the NRA to maintain registers containing details of discharge consents and of water or effluent samples taken by the NRA and the action (if any) subsequently taken. Similarly, under the *Environmental Protection Act 1990*, HMIP and local authorities are required to keep registers containing full details of authorised processes and their emissions and discharges. The guiding principle is that such information should be freely available to the public. Information may only be capable of being withheld on grounds of commercial confidentiality or in the interests of national security if a clear and convincing case can be established. The amount of information withheld from the register in such circumstances is limited to the minimum necessary.

10.14 THE LIMITATIONS OF WARRANTIES AND INDEMNITIES

In addition to the increased risks associated with inheriting environmental liabilities, the second major reason for the emergence of environmental due diligence has been the growing awareness of the limitations inherent in the traditional method of protecting a party to a transaction against risk – the taking of warranties and indemnities.

10.15 Warranties and indemnities have, and will continue to have, a vital role to play in providing protection against environmental risks. However, sole reliance on them has the following disadvantages.

(1)   They are only as good as the creditworthiness of the person who gives them. An ability to sue for breach of warranty is of little use if the other party has gone into liquidation or has insufficient assets to cover the loss.

(2)   In the case of pollution, it is often very difficult to demonstrate when it occurred. Where, for example, the new owners of a factory carry out the same processes as

were carried out before their ownership, involving the same raw materials, process and waste discharges, the discovery some time after completion of the transaction of a pollution problem, such as sub-surface contamination, may lead to unresolved argument as to whether it occurred before or after completion and is therefore covered by a warranty which stated that the site was clean.

(3)   Warranties and indemnities, even where given, do not necessarily reflect the true environmental position of the property. They may be given by senior management located many miles from the site and with only a limited amount of knowledge of the site and its environmental practices.

(4)   Warranties often do not last a sufficiently long time for them to be effective in the enviromental field. Sub-surface contamination, for example, may only be discovered several years after completion of the sale – long after the warranties have ceased to be valid.

10.16 THE FORMS OF ENVIRONMENTAL DUE DILIGENCE

An environmental due diligence investigation is a study carried out to ascertain the extent to which a purchaser is at risk in acquiring a company or a property. The degree of sophistication to be employed in the study can vary from case to case and depends on a range of factors:

(1)   the nature of the processes carried on at the site, the raw materials used, the by-products and waste products produced etc.;

(2)   the value of the transaction;

(3)   the financial strength of the vendor and the extent to which he is prepared to provide warranties;

(4)   the nature of the proposed after-use of the site. Particularly if the site is to be redeveloped, the extent of any ground contamination that might inhibit that development needs to be ascertained;

(5)   the compliance record of the present operator;

(6)   the policy of the purchaser. In particular, a number of multi-national companies have policies whereby their global operations are carried out to the standard required by the most rigorous jurisdiction in which they operate;

(7)   previous uses of the site;

(8)   the timescale of the transaction.

10.17 The starting point for an environmental due diligence investigation is a legal investigation to ensure that the facility has the benefit of all necessary licences, consents, permissions etc.; to check that these are current; to examine whether they contain any particularly onerous or unusual conditions; to check whether the conditions are being complied with and to ascertain whether the site is the subject of any enforcement action on behalf of a regulatory agency.

The legal investigation will involve the examination of documents supplied by the operator, examination of information made publicly available in the statutory registers held by the regulatory agencies and, in the majority of cases, interviews with those officials from enforcing bodies able to comment about the environmental performance of the facility. In the UK these are principally HMIP, NRA, the water companies (who regulate discharges to sewers), local authorities, the Health and Safety Executive and fire authorities. With the making of the *Environmental Information Regulations 1992*, a considerable amount of information may be gleaned from the various regulators and other public bodies.

Another important role for the lawyer is to examine and explain to the client on whose behalf the investigation is being conducted the legal constraints currently affecting the operation and, given the speed of legal developments in the environment field, likely future constraints.

10.18 It may be that information is uncovered by the legal study which requires the employment of specialist environmental scientists to ascertain the extent of a problem. More often, however, a decision whether to make such an appointment is made at the outset, based on the factors already mentioned. In that case it is important that the legal and scientific work is well co-ordinated. In the same way that the legal investigation may reveal matters which require the employment of scientific expertise, the scientist may uncover problems which are then best pursued by the lawyer.

If scientific consultants are brought in, the level of sophistication of their work can also vary enormously, depending on the factors above and on the results of the legal investigation and their own initial findings.

At one extreme, the scientific study can be as simple as a single site visit, sometimes known as a 'walk-through' or 'phase 1' audit. If it is evident that the process is 'clean', that the site is tidy, that storage tanks are well maintained etc. it may be that nothing more sophisticated is justified. At the other extreme, the full facts may not be discovered unless the consultant takes samples of effluent and soils for laboratory analysis, digs boreholes to ascertain the presence and extent of sub-surface contamination, and generally investigates fully all likely environmental problems in a complete 'phase 2' audit.

10.19 THE USES OF ENVIRONMENTAL INFORMATION

The information produced by the environmental due diligence exercise can be used in a variety of ways in the transaction. The following are some examples.

(1)   It will enable more specific warranties to be given, tailored to the environmental situation uncovered by the exercise. Whilst, as explained above, warranties do have major limitations, their role is still important. They need to cover two major areas – criminal/public law liabilities and private law liabilities.

The first category, criminal/public law liabilities, can be covered by the vendor warranting that he has obtained all the necessary statutory permissions required for his operations, that they are current and are transferable. It is also usual to warrant that the regulatory bodies have not and are not taking enforcement action under any of the statutory provisions.

With regard to potential private law liabilities, warranties usually provide that there are no pending civil actions being brought against the vendor for environmental damage and, moreover, that there are no circumstances which would justify the bringing of such an action.

It is also possible to provide warranties relating to the state of the land or equipment even if neither a criminal/public nor a private law liability is involved. For example, it is common for vendors to warrant that there have been no spills or leaks from storage tanks or no other source of ground contamination. Often, of course, warranties extend 'only so far as the vendor is aware', which limits the degree of protection afforded.

(2)   It may be used to negotiate a reduction in purchase price, for example, to reflect the cost of a clean-up exercise.

(3)   A formula may be devised whereby the buyer assumes an increasing proportion of the contingent risks. For example, the seller may assume 80 per cent of the risk after the first year and 0 per cent after the fifth year with decreasing proportions in the intervening years.

(4)   It may enable insurance to be effected, with the insurer being able to fix a premium in the light of the information revealed by the environmental due diligence exercise.

(5)   The seller may simply be required to put the deficiency right as a pre-condition of proceeding with the transaction.

(6)   The information may be used as a bargaining chip in relation to other, unrelated, aspects of the deal.

(7)   In extreme cases, the environmental problem highlighted by the environmental due diligence exercise might be sufficiently serious for the transaction to be called off completely. In the case of acquisitions involving several sites, only some of the sites may be acquired with the most heavily polluted being withdrawn from the transaction.

(8)   If pending criminal liability is discovered, it would be possible for the purchaser to shift from an acquisition of shares to an acquisition of assets only. Acquisition of assets as opposed to the legal personality of the company would normally involve no transfer of criminal responsibility.

Even if techniques such as those described above are not employed as part of the transaction, this does not mean that the information revealed by the due diligence exercise is wasted. The study will provide a corpus of knowledge of great value for the future management of the site. The location and state of repair of underground storage tanks, the areas of the site which may be unsuitable for redevelopment for reasons of contamination, the extent to which equipment does not represent best modern standards, etc. is all useful information for the incoming management.

10.20 CONCLUSION

Environmental due diligence exercises in the context of major transaction work are becoming increasingly common in the UK. As environmental controls become more complex and as society comes to demand increasing levels of enforcement on the part of public bodies, this is an area which is likely to see considerable growth in the future. Increasingly a company involved in a take-over or merger or major land acquisition will ignore at its peril the environmental profile of the other company or property involved. Environmental due diligence investigations, of varying degrees of sophistication, are designed to ensure that any contingent environmental risks are identified and are taken into account at the stage at which their relevance and importance to the transaction in question can be used with maximum effect.

11 Environmental Health

11.1 INTRODUCTION

Although the subject areas within the discipline of environmental health are very extensive, this particular chapter is limited to topics relevant to domestic properties. These include, for example, the control of smoke from house chimneys and garden bonfires, nuisances, noise of all-night parties, pollution from obstructed drains and regulation of waste disposal routines. These complement the industrial and commercial applications found in the chapters on ATMOSPHERIC POLLUTION (4), NOISE (18), WASTE MANAGEMENT, RECYCLING AND REUSE (28) and WATER ENVIRONMENT (29) respectively. Environmental standards at dwellings themselves are generally the responsibility of local authorities (LAs), and are mostly, but not exclusively enforced by environmental health officers (EHOs). The harmonisation processes through which much UK legislation has recently passed because of the issue of directives, decisions, recommendations etc. by the European Commission (which is such an important feature in certain of the environmental subject areas) has not, as yet, had a major impact on the subject area of this chapter.

11.2 Background

The time honoured concept of the Englishman's home (however unhealthy or insanitary), being his castle and hence impregnable to enforcement agencies intent on environmental cleansing, has not been a viable proposition since the birth of the public health movement in the UK more than a century and a half ago. However, although LAs do have a wide spectrum of legislative authority to enter houses, search for problems and enforce certain standards, it goes without saying that because LAs are themselves creatures of statute, they are very much subject to the principle of *ultra vires*, and hence do not have unlimited powers to deal with every infringement of environmental codes, wherever they might find them. Indeed, even the powers of entry themselves are closely prescribed by the enabling legislation and do not offer carte blanche access.

11.3 Air pollution from domestic sources

The burning of raw coal in unsophisticated domestic fireplaces was the single most important source of the massive air pollution burden which has traditionally affected UK cities. But leaving aside a prohibition on the burning of sea coal in the capital in Elizabethan times, effective powers to control smoke from domestic chimneys had to wait until the city of Manchester introduced its own private legislation in the early nineteen fifties. As a result of the media attention directed to the notorious London smogs (4,000 extra deaths were attributed to air pollution in the capital during one nineteen fifties winter) the *Clean Air Act 1956* (*CAA 1956*) was introduced which made it an offence to emit smoke from a domestic chimney within a smoke control area. Grants jointly funded by central and local government (under *section 11*) became available to install approved appliances which burn approved (smokeless) fuels, or use means other than solid fuel to heat houses. LAs are responsible for delineating and administering such smoke control areas and enforcing the prohibition of smoke within them. [*Clean Air Act 1956, s 11*]. Many cities and large centres of population have now been incorporated in what is beginning to approach a comprehensive programme, with central government using additional central powers of direction under the *Clean Air*

11.4 Environmental Health

Act 1968, s 8 to overcome the objections of certain LAs. Some urban LAs now have 100 per cent coverage which also includes their rural hinterlands, so that even the burning of wood in domestic stoves in such areas is prohibited. Paradoxically, however, because many smaller towns and villages (particularly in traditional coal mining areas) are yet to be scheduled as smoke control areas, atmospheric sulphur dioxide levels from the burning of coal can nowadays be greater in such villages than in many city centres.

Apart from smoke control areas, the LA has strictly limited statutory powers over air pollution arising on domestic premises. For example, despite widespread concern over the contribution made to the depletion of the ozone layer by the domestic use of CFCs, the concept of enforcing emission limits on individual properties is clearly impracticable. Certain LAs do, however, interpret the powers provided in *Control of Pollution Act 1974, s 20* as empowering them to offer a recycling service which includes the collection of discarded domestic refrigerators and the return of the CFC gases they contain to the manufacturers. In addition, the *Clean Air Act 1956, s 25* empowers LAs to spend money on publicising general clean air issues.

11.4 Contaminated land

LAs were charged in the earliest public health legislation with a duty to reject plans submitted for the erection of dwellings on land filled with 'offensive' material (continued by virtue of the *Public Health Act 1936, s 54*), however the very narrow definition of this term provided no control over many forms of pollution of land and cases are still being discovered of houses which have been built on, or closely adjacent to, contaminated land. In order to provide a database to permit a quantification of this problem, LAs were to have been required to survey their areas and to publish registers of land (under the *Environmental Protection Act 1990, s 143 (EPA 1990)*) in their area which has been put to contaminative use. This section is no longer, however, to be brought into effect. Nevertheless, financial losses have already been suffered by owners of some dwellings merely because they are sited on particular estates which include a small number of houses adjacent to landfill sites emitting methane.

11.5 Dangerous substances

The last few decades have witnessed a considerable increase in the amount of toxic and corrosive chemicals used in and around the home. The powers possessed by the Secretary of State in the *Environmental Protection Act 1990, s 140(1)* to make regulations for prohibiting and regulating the use, storage and supply of any specified substance or articles in order to prevent environmental pollution or harm to the health of animals, humans or plants, are an extension of the powers in the *Control of Pollution Act 1974, s 100*, and provide harmonisation with *76/769/EEC (as amended)* and can be exercised on domestic premises if there is a proven risk. New regulations (including the *Environmental Protection (Controls on Injurious Substances) Regulations 1992*) have recently been introduced. The ambitions of some gardeners for a totally pest free environment sometimes seem to fly in the face of common sense and environmental concern, but recognition by the public that most pesticides also kill the natural enemies of the pests, is slow. In fact nature can often do a much better job of protecting appropriate plants if left to her own devices, and there are now, by virtue of the *Control of Pesticides Regulations 1986* some specific restrictions on the types of pesticides which can be used in the domestic garden. These were introduced under the *Food and Environment Protection Act 1985* in order to minimise the access of certain classes of chemicals to the food chain and of course, were primarily intended to control agricultural use of pesticides on cash crops.

Householders also come under pressure from advertisers to use significant quantities of strong disinfectants to kill 'germs' which are portrayed as lurking within household drainage systems. Powerful organic solvents are also on sale to dissolve old paintwork, alongside strongly corrosive acids (for killing off growths of algae on paving surfaces) and other hazardous chemicals. Although the labelling requirements for these products are becoming more onerous, there are no corresponding regulations for domestic premises to match those which are enforceable in the workplace to control the way in which these same materials are used and stored. Hence poisonous and corrosive substances bought by householders, regularly figure in the cases of accidental poisoning, particularly in the case of young children. Not even domestic servants, such as home helps, are provided with any statutory reinforcement of their common law rights to a safe place of work, as they constitute exempted persons under the *Health & Safety at Work etc. Act 1974, s 51*. Concerns expressed by environmentalists over the widespread and sometimes indiscriminate use of pesticides have some relevance on the domestic scene not only because of the extensive use made of pesticides (and fertilisers) by gardeners as noted above, but also due to the statutory obligations imposed on occupiers of dwellings to maintain their property free from insects and vermin. The legislation emphasising occupiers' obligations is contained in the provisions of the *Public Health Act 1936, ss 83–86* which allow action to be taken against verminous premises, articles and persons respectively. The *Prevention of Damage by Pests Act 1949 (PDBPA)* also empowers LAs to deal with infestations (including insects and mites) but only where food supplies are implicated.

Legal protection is separately provided for certain animals which householders may generally regard as pests if they are encountered in dwellings, (bats, for example are a protected species).

11.6   Drainage

The owner (or occupier) of a dwelling has the statutory right (by virtue of the *Water Industry Act 1991, s 106 (WIA)*), to discharge foul or, (with authority granted under the *Public Health Act 1936, s 34*) surface water to a public sewer, although the local planning authority could refuse planning permission for a new development on the grounds that the local sewerage works are already overburdened. The *Water Industry Act 1991, s 111* makes it clear that the rights to discharge effluents do not extend to liquids which would damage sewers or affect sewage treatment processes, thus any DIY car mechanic who empties dirty sump oil into a domestic drainage system could be guilty of an offence. *Section 112* empowers Sewerage Undertakers to order that particular premises should be connected to the local sewerage system and also to specify whether they should be drained in combination with other buildings. These powers extend to the rejection of plans of houses submitted to LAs for approval if the drainage arrangements do not meet with approval.

By virtue of the *Public Health Act 1961, s 17 (as amended)* LAs are empowered to exercise extensive powers to remedy stopped up and defective drains without recourse to summary action in magistrates' courts (except at the stage of recovery of their costs). These additional powers of LAs to speedily remedy stopped up drains at dwellings makes a significant contribution to the maintenance of a healthy and safe environment in crowded urban centres.

11.7   Housing

Despite having their role as landlords of council houses very significantly diminished as a result of recent Government policy, LAs still undertake important duties in enforcing standards regulating many of the contributions which houses make to the physical environment. They wield specific controls over both the physical construction and topographical setting of new domestic dwellings by virtue of the *Building Act 1984* and the *Town and Country Planning Acts*. Although this latter legislation has important environmental connotations in respect of the issues related to transport and the encouragement of other means of moving people than by the use of the private motor car, it is beyond the scope of this chapter. LAs are also the channel through which specific grants flow under the various *Housing Acts* to facilitate the demolition of unfit properties, to secure the improvement of substandard houses and to raise levels (in certain restricted cases) of sound and heat insulation. The extent to which LAs spend their government allocations for such improvements varies considerably and many LAs have failed to exercise their options to their full extent with complaints being voiced over the lack of take up of grants in some areas. Nevertheless the Government does have a Green House Programme and a Housing Minister has recently expressed satisfaction with the progress which is being achieved. The scheme aims to show how energy efficiency improvements in council housing could help in the fight against global warming. LAs are expected to give higher profile to energy efficiency in their Housing Investment Programmes (first introduced under the *Local Government Planning and Land Act 1980*). Overall the Government is expecting that such schemes will deliver carbon dioxide savings of 50 per cent over current levels with a 40 per cent reduction in energy consumption, and it has reminded LAs that one quarter of their annual expenditure on mainstream repair and improvement of their stock was devoted to energy related measures and if best practice were followed LAs could achieve higher output from this investment.

The controls possessed by LAs over the levels of indoor air pollution within houses are limited. In contrast to their extensive powers to regulate the indoor working environment (using prohibition and enforcement notices under the *Health & Safety at Work etc. Act 1974* and the specific provisions in the *Control of Substances Hazardous to Health Regulations 1988 (COSHH)*) in offices, shops and certain other workplaces, LAs are not empowered to take general action to control indoor air pollution levels which have arisen as a result of normal domestic activities. Their impotence in the face of the extensive health risk to non-smoking members of households from secondary tobacco smoke provides an obvious and topical example. LA Building Control Officers do pay attention to the provision of adequate means of ventilation when dwellings are first constructed or refurbished under the *Building Regulations 1991, Schedule 1, Part F* (note that underground rooms constitute a special case). EHOs can take account of ventilation rates in their assessment of the standards of fitness for habitation under the *Housing Act 1985, s 604* and the World Health Organisation Healthy Housing Guidelines also make reference to the need to provide sufficient ventilation (*Environmental Health Series EH13 WHO Copenhagen 1988*).

The emission of radon gas from both the land on which a house has been built and the materials from which it has been constructed are both relevant to the question of ventilation. The UK action level of $10mSv\,y^{-1}$ (a somewhat less onerous standard than that adopted in the USA, but four times that of Norway's level) was fixed in 1990 and includes by virtue of the *Building Regulations 1985, Part C* a requirement for radon proofing measures to be automatically included in certain high-risk locations (notably Cornwall and parts of Devon) which have been formally identified as affected areas.

11.8   Noise

A recent Building Research Establishment survey has indicated that 14 per cent of adults are bothered by noise in their neighbourhood. Complaints about noise also represent the fastest growing category in a survey of complaints made to LAs and reported by the Institution of Environmental Health Officers.

Noise from domestic premises (notably rowdy parties) is actionable by LAs using the Statutory Nuisance provisions in the *Environmental Protection Act 1990* (see NOISE (18) above). The *Control of Pollution Act 1974, s 62* also bans the use of loudspeakers (with exceptions for emergencies) in streets after 9pm and before 8am. The use of loud-speakers to advertise in public places is only allowed by vehicles selling perishable foodstuffs and then only between 12 noon and 7pm. The Secretary of State for the Environment is empowered by the *Control of Pollution Act 1974, s 71* to issue or approve codes of practice dealing with certain emissions of noise from domestic premises (such as burglar alarms), although these will not have the force of law their very existence may be persuasive.

The problem of finding a legal regime to deal with social noise will require a radical solution, and the United Kingdom Environmental Law Association has proposed a range of possible devices which could be employed. Several suggestions have been made for improvement in the current controls which are based on the cumbersome statutory nuisance procedure (see below), such as the adoption of a set of model byelaws by the residents. The Noise Review Working Party Report in 1990 suggested an equivalent to the crime prevention 'Neighbourhood Watch' schemes. This would involve local residents themselves in the resolution of disputes. There has also been the development of mediation, which can have the effect of lowering the aggravation level by involving a palpably neutral third party, with a role not of arbitration and decision taking, but just of mediation. Clearly there is much more to be done, especially with respect to improving the noise insulation afforded by buildings. It is significant that there are already *EC Directives* dealing with noise from certain appliances, (principally lawn mowers) used on domestic premises, for example, *Permissible sound power levels of lawnmowers (84/538/ EEC as amended)*, and *Airborne noise emitted by household appliances (86/594/EEC)*.

11.9   Statutory and other nuisances

The concept of nuisance is a very flexible tool for environmental control, and has played a crucial role in the development of UK environmental law (EHOs themselves evolved from the original 'Inspectors of Nuisances'). The basis of a private nuisance action at common law lies in the concept of reasonableness, witness *Saunders Clark v Grosvenor Mansion Company Limited & D'Alles-Sandry [1900] 2 Ch 373*: 'If [the defendant] is using [his property] reasonably there is nothing which at law can be considered a nuisance; but if he is not . . . then the plaintiff is entitled to relief'. Of course the notable distinction drawn in *Sturges v Bridgman (1879) 11 Ch D 852* needs to be borne in mind (Thesiger LJ holding in a much quoted judgment that 'what would be a nuisance in Belgrave Square would not necessarily be so in Bermondsey'). The separate category of public nuisance has been defined as an act or omission which materially affects the material comfort and quality of life of a class of Her Majesty's subjects, and can be distinguished from private nuisance by virtue of the fact that the latter consists of interference by an owner or occupier of property with the use or enjoyment of neighbouring property.

Many enforcement activities of LAs on domestic premises utilise the concept of 'statutory nuisance' (SN) and its associated abatement procedure, which was first introduced in the last century. SNs are a limited group of precisely defined nuisances for the prevention of which LAs are empowered to serve abatement notices (using the procedure outlined in Chapter 18).

Lord Wilberforce said in *Salford City Council v McNally [1976] AC 379* that it was important to keep close to the wording of the Act when deciding what constituted a SN.

The *Environmental Protection Act 1990, s 79* (and by extension a number of additional statutes) defines SNs which are relevant to domestic properties in the following terms:

11.10 Environmental Health

11.10 *(a)* *Premises*

'Any premises in such a state as to be prejudicial to health or a nuisance'

[*Environmental Protection Act 1990, s 79(1)(a)*].

This category centres on the physical state of the premises (defined as including land but excluding sewers), not the use to which they are put. The use of the disjunctive 'or' makes it clear that health and nuisance are alternatives (see *Salford City Council v McNally* [*1976*] *AC 379, Betts v Penge UDC* [*1942*] *2 KB 154*). The judgment in *Coventry City Council v Cartwright* [*1975*] *1 WLR 845* holds that for activities to fall within the 'prejudicial to health' category there must be some likelihood of disease, and the remote threat of physical injury is insufficient (so that an accumulation of putrescible waste which attracted vermin would be included whereas a pile of broken glass would not). An early decision regarding this same definition held that it was something which caused sick persons to become worse (*Malton Urban Sanitary Authority v Malton Farmers Manure Co* (*1879*) *4 EXD 302*). According to the Divisional Court in *National Coal Board v Thorne* [*1976*] *1 WLR 543* the appropriate test for the definition of nuisance as used in the second of the two categories, is the common law concept of nuisance, and the persons affected must constitute a class wider than just the occupants of the premises. If the latter conditions do not apply, the aggrieved person might use the facility provided by virtue of the *Environmental Protection Act 1990, s 82*, and institute individual action by laying a direct complaint about the existence of a SN to a magistrates' court.

With respect to disrepair to dwellings, it has become common practice for pressure groups to facilitate action by tenants against their landlords (often LAs) under the *Public Health Act 1936, s 99* (which is replicated by the *Environmental Protection Act 1990, s 82*), using these provisions to force them to carry out repairs or upgrade their housing stock. See the *London Borough of Southwark v Ince* (*1989*) *21 HLR 504* where the judgment was that SN procedure could be used against LA housing which was not insulated against noise. But note that in *Birmingham District Council v McMahon* (*1987*) *151 JP 709* (*Div CT*) it was held that in the case of a block of flats where the complainant did not personally suffer from the nuisance, the tenant in question was not 'a person aggrieved' hence the action must fail.

11.11 *(b)* *Smoke*

'Smoke emitted from any premises so as to be prejudicial to health or a nuisance'

[*Environmental Protection Act 1990, s 79(1)(b)*].

Smoke, defined in *section 79(7)* as including soot ash grit and gritty particles emitted in smoke, emitted from the chimney of a house is unlikely to be actionable, (but see the smoke control provisions noted above). In fact, the greatest number of complaints to LAs about smoke from domestic premises relate to the vexed question of domestic bonfires, and however much of a problem this might be to neighbours who are annoyed by perhaps copious quantities of pungent smoke, the lighting of a domestic bonfire is only an actionable offence if the results can be proved to constitute a SN within the tight constraints outlined above. In this connection it is worth remembering that the act of burning rubbish can sometimes be a weapon used in disputes between neighbours and EHOs much prefer that such cases should be settled by direct litigation between the disputing parties using the common law definitions of nuisance or the provisions of *section 82* (see 11.10 above).

11.12 *(c)* *Fumes and gases*

'. . . fumes or gases emitted from premises so as to be prejudicial to health or a nuisance'

[*Environmental Protection Act 1990, s 79(1)(c)*].

Fumes are defined as any airborne solid matter smaller than dust, and gases as including vapour and moisture precipitating from vapour [*Environmental Protection Act 1990, s 79(7)*]. By virtue of *section 79(4)*, this new category only applies to private dwellings and in addition to applying to everyday domestic emanations, such as steam from a clothes dryer, it could also be expected to cover activities such as regular paint spraying by an avid car enthusiast who was annoying neighbours or a watersports enthusiast who spent all winter building fibreglass canoes in a domestic garage, always providing that these emissions were substantial in amount yet did not constitute actual businesses where action under *section 79(1)(d)* would be more appropriate.

11.13 *(d)   Effluvia from business premises*

Environmental Protection Act 1990, s 79(1)(d) is not relevant to domestic premises.

11.14 *(e)   Accumulations*

'Any accumulation or deposit which is prejudicial to health or a nuisance'

[*Environmental Protection Act 1990, s 79(1)(e)*].

Although this (and the following) category of nuisance may be held to be largely local in its impact, certain aspects may be widespread enough to be of relevance to readers of an environmental handbook. *Bland v Yates (1914) 58 SJ 612* held that a pile of garden manure which gave off smells and attracted flies was a nuisance. An accumulation of soil which was causing dampness in a neighbour's house was similarly identified in *Hardman v North Eastern Railway (1873) 3 CPD 169*. Note that any accumulation which causes vermin to be attracted in large numbers may also be actionable under the *Prevention of Damage by Pests Act 1949, s (4)*.

11.15 *(f)   Animals*

'Any animal kept in such a place or manner as to be prejudicial to health or a nuisance'

[*Environmental Protection Act 1990, s 79(1)(f)*].

Smith v Waghorn (1863) 27 JP 744 held that horse dung accumulated to the extent that neighbours were obliged to shut their windows was actionable. *Galer v Morrisey (1955) 1 All ER 380* similarly ruled in respect of a noisy animal.

The *Public Health Act 1936, s 81(b)* also provides powers for LAs to make byelaws to control the keeping of animals, but the trifling remedies available for non-compliance with byelaws mean that most LAs would prefer to use the SN procedure, cumbersome though it is.

11.16 *(g)   Noise*

'Noise emitted from premises so as to be prejudicial to health or a nuisance'

[*Environmental Protection Act 1990, s 79(1)(g)*].

Although noise is defined as including vibration [*section 79(7)*] and sounds made by model aircraft [*section 79(6)*] this subsection is particularly widely applied to the control of noise from parties in dwellings, and continues procedures established under the *Control of Pollution Act 1974*. Significant amounts of publicity have recently followed the actions of several LAs which mount flying squads of EHOs on party patrols (notably London Boroughs such as Croydon) and who have also seized the source of the offending noise in the shape of powerful amplifiers, loudspeakers etc. However not every LA can muster the necessary police presence to guarantee that severe public disorder will not follow the seizure operation, if the occasion is a large scale party or rave. Derby's EHOs have recently expressed disquiet at the minor sentence passed on a persistent offender against the provisions of this section, who regularly ran noisy parties which lasted for three days at a time.

In connection with noisy activities in streets adjacent to houses, the effect of *Tower Hamlets London Borough Council v Manzoni* (*1983*) *148 JP 123* was to hold that, because streets are not 'premises', SN provisions, do not apply. The premises themselves can fall within the provisions of *section 79(1)(a)* if the noise is of such a character as to be injurious to health *London Borough of Southwark v Ince* (*1989*) *21 HLR 504* (see 11.10 above).

11.17 *(h)   Other statutory nuisances*

'Any other enactment declared by any enactment to be a statutory nuisance'

[*Environmental Protection Act 1990, s 79(1)(h)*].

The relevant categories which apply to domestic premises comprise:

Public Health Act 1936, s 141 (any well, tank, cistern or water-butt used for supply of water for domestic purposes which is so placed, constructed or kept as to render the water therein liable to contamination prejudicial to health);

Public Health Act 1936, s 259 (any pond, pool, ditch, gutter or watercourse which is so foul or in such a state as to be prejudicial to health or a nuisance); and

Public Health Act 1936, s 268(2) (a tent, van, shed or similar structure which is so overcrowded or is so deficient in sanitary accommodation as to be a nuisance or prejudicial to health).

Each of these sections is to some extent amended by the *Environmental Protection Act 1990, 15 Sch 4.*

Action under the *Public Health Act 1936, s 141* is not very common nowadays because of the spread of piped water supplies and the virtual demise of the custom of storing rainwater for domestic purposes in cisterns. However the current level of public interest in gypsies and persons of nomadic habits is bound to be responsible for certain LAs occasionally considering the use of the powers conferred by the *Public Health Act 1936, s 268*, cumbersome though they might be.

Note that the best practical means defence provided under the *Environmental Protection Act 1990, s 80(7)* is not available for such SNs and any local authority which anticipates a nuisance can serve a prohibition notice by virtue of the *Environmental Protection Act 1990, s 81(5)*. The use of a High Court injunction is unlikely to be considered an appropriate recourse when dealing with the categories of nuisances which usually originate on domestic premises.

The *Control of Pollution Act 1974, s 57* is reproduced in the *Environmental Protection Act 1990* by a provision which imposes a duty on a local authority to inspect its area from time to time in order to identify cases in which action should be taken to initiate proceedings for statutory nuisance. It is widely felt that there should be a positive duty on the authority to investigate such complaints.

11.18 Wastes and recycling

WASTE MANAGEMENT (28) focuses on the duty of care obligations imposed upon the occupiers of industrial premises by virtue of the *Environmental Protection Act 1990*. Because of the clear exemption for the wastes arising on domestic premises provided in *section 34(2)*, this might leave domestic householders feeling that there are no statutory extensions to their common law obligations such as have been established for example by decisions such as *Wandsworth Corporation v Baines* [*1906*] *1 KB 470* (which held that if a waste receptacle is placed for collection on a roadway in anything otherwise than an approved manner, the resulting obstruction is unlawful). In fact, waste collection authorities (which mostly means LAs) are also empowered to specify collection arrangements for household waste and particulars of the storage receptacles by virtue of the *Environmental Protection Act 1990, s 45*, and some of these requirements are quite specific. The powers of LAs extend to the right to refuse to collect certain categories of material (notably garden waste) but do not include the ability to direct householders to undertake recycling or composting their wastes.

In addition, house occupiers do have a number of additional obligations which reinforce their common law duties to act in a responsible manner. As an example, anyone engaged in domiciliary care of a patient suffering from certain diseases needs to be aware of the *Public Health (Control of Disease) Act 1984, s 26* which restricts the placing of certain infectious materials in dustbins.

The statutory nuisance provisions in *Part III* of the *Environmental Protection Act 1990* effectively, *inter alia*, limit the extent to which bonfires can be employed to incinerate solid wastes (see 11.11(b) above).

There are additional legislative restrictions under the *Water Industry Act 1991, s 111* on the composition of waterborne wastes which leave the domestic premises by drainpipes (the discharge of material which may damage sewers or interfere with sewage treatment is not permitted). In this latter case, the relatively small volumes involved would provide an obvious impediment to the effective enforcement of these requirements, although a highly visible material such as used engine oil from a car or a very specific material generated by the activities of homeworkers could be exceptions.

There can be other instances where highly toxic waste materials are generated on domestic premises by ambitious hobbyists, who may effectively be operating small scale industrial processes which of necessity enjoy much less regulation than those on industrial premises. There is no statutory obligation to have undertaken a rigorous analysis of the operation and its waste production for the purposes of *COSHH* and yet enthusiastic model makers may be using substances which are highly toxic, corrosive or flammable in scaled down versions of industrial processes. In view of the relatively small quantities of wastes involved the *de minimis non curat lex* rule might be expected to apply (although this would not provide protection in any common law action by a waste disposal worker injured as a result). Certainly the environmental impact of discarded pesticides is a proper cause for concern along with the improper disposal of unwanted medicines. Regional Health Authorities have been encouraging householders to clear out unwanted drugs from first aid cabinets but the new duty of care provisions in the *Environmental Protection Act 1990, s 34* have introduced difficulties for pharmacists who operate the DUMP (Disposal of Unwanted Medicines and Poisons) scheme now that each batch must be accompanied by a detailed consignment note. Perhaps exemptions are appropriate, otherwise not only will there be the threat of dumping by householders of unwanted medicines but in addition the target of reducing accidental domestic poisonings by a third (set in the 1992 Health of the Nation White Paper CMND 1986), is unlikely to be met.

Although the record of the UK is often cited in unfavourable comparisons with our European neighbours, most LAs are currently seeking a higher recycling profile and the Secretary of State for the Environment promised in 1989 that the record of UK local authorities on recycling would reach a target of 25 per cent of collected tonnage by the year 2000. More recently the DoE has published an 86 page guidance memorandum on recycling in the Waste Management Paper Series but councils are still being criticised by action groups for failing to provide a strong enough emphasis on sustainable development, and not relegating recycling to its proper context as a second best option.

Authoritative comparisons will eventually be possible using the data forthcoming from LAs now that they are under a statutory imperative (contained in the *Environmental Protection Act 1990, Part II*) to publish recycling plans, although one district council has refused to publish any plan on the grounds that the resources are not available which would enable the plan to be implemented. Although some imaginative recycling initiatives have emerged, and the payment of 'recycling credits' permitted in the *Environmental Protection Act 1990, s 52* has increased the extent of interest in the topic, it makes little sense to devote extensive publicity to recycling if this merely results in householders loading their own motor cars with piles of sunday supplements, empty chianti bottles or whatever, and driving long distances to recycling centres just to assuage their consciences (especially so if the paper or glass is being collected to court favourable publicity and still ends up in a landfill site).

11.19 Water supply

LAs have specific responsibilities to satisfy themselves that the water supplied in their district is wholesome by reference to the standards set in the *Water Supply (Water Quality) Regulations 1989*. These *Regulations* incorporate the standards set in the *Drinking Water Directive (80/778/EEC)*. They must keep a register of private water supplies to domestic premises and can use powers now contained in the *Environmental Protection Act 1990* to control wells, tanks etc. (see 11.17 above). There seems to be no doubt that the significant increase in the sales of bottled water to domestic outlets is at least partly driven by fears over the wisdom of drinking water direct from the public mains. Enquiries are also made to LAs by householders concerning the advisability of utilising domestic filtration and purification equipment which is widely advertised. These range from jug filters to sophisticated under-sink installations utilising reverse osmosis and salt recharging. Although complaints about colour and taste of mains water are not uncommon, Statutory Water Undertakings will issue orders requiring consumers to boil water if they are of the opinion that there is an actual health risk from the mains supply, and in practice a poorly maintained domestic filtration unit can result in significant contamination of the supply which it is supposed to be purifying.

12 Environmental Information

12.1 INTRODUCTION

The dominant force in environmental legislation is likely to remain in Brussels. Unified or harmonised action seems required for legislation to have any impact on many environmental issues because real solutions to global or regional problems must be trans-national. It is an area in which the application of the principle of subsidiarity is difficult to argue. For that reason, companies and organisations wanting to form policy which will parallel and anticipate trends must, almost certainly, look to European rather than nation state approaches.

12.2 This chapter deals with the *Environmental Protection Act 1990* and the *EC Access to Environmental Information Directive* (*90/313/EEC*). Both carry significant implications for companies in their disclosure of environmental information. Importantly, as is spelled out at 12.19 *et seq.* below, the *Directive* will allow interested parties and individuals access to the process of judicial review.

This is part of a shift away from the demand that waste regulation authorities simply maintain proper registers of information towards 'right to know' legislation which empowers anybody with any concern about the environmental impact of any undertaking to discover the relevant facts and challenge corporate practice.

12.3 INDUSTRIAL HERITAGE

In the public mind, industry and commerce bear much of the responsibility for past and continuing damage to the environment. There is no argument that such damage has been done and it is seldom excused for having been committed unknowingly or unwittingly. Contaminated land, for example, is not just a commercial problem for its owners or an inconvenience and threat to those who live on or close to it. It serves as a living reminder of a very dark industrial environmental heritage.

It is this sense of dark heritage, reinforced by major disasters such as the leak of dioxins in Seveso in Italy, which has given credence to and hastened the arrival of a new 'right to know' approach to information about what processes are being conducted in a locality, with what by-products and with what risks.

Specifically, in areas where communities are surrounded by intensive industrial and manufacturing processes, the *Directive* makes it possible for interested parties to scrutinise the entire locality. Concern is no longer restricted to the conduct of individual businesses but may consider the total cocktail of overall effects that they may be jointly or unwittingly producing.

12.4 INFORMATION: THREAT AND OPPORTUNITY

Threat

Initially, many companies may be dismayed at the prospect of placing complex information on the public record, especially when they cannot be sure how, or by whom, it might be used. For UK companies these are uncharted waters and it will take time and testing before the passage becomes clearer and more certain.

143

12.5   Environmental Information

But, however reluctant a company might be, the risks in failure to comply or in partial compliance, could be considerable – if only because of the interpretation which will be placed on such failures by those who believe they are being obstructed.

Those who believe themselves to have concerns, whether or not commercial companies consider them to be legitimate, place a premium on knowledge and will challenge reasons for withholding it, including commercial confidentiality. Quite simply, those who consider themselves to be at risk, whether such a view is justified or not, are unlikely to accept a commercial explanation as an adequate reason for being denied information which they consider relevant.

12.5   Opportunity

It is, therefore, not a moment too soon for companies to consider their reputation in their own communities. Companies which are perceived as open and enjoy a reputation as responsible members of the community are less likely to come under hostile scrutiny than companies perceived as uncaring, inaccessible or controversial. A good reputation will not succeed in hiding a less than good reality but it will set the climate.

Good companies, as stressed in PROJECTING A GREENER IMAGE (23), will not be satisfied with mere compliance. Companies wishing to retain control over the conduct of their business will seek to do so with the willing consent of their communities or, at least, without their active opposition. Good companies will need to decide not just how to comply with legal requirements, but how to make the information available through voluntary action.

12.6   VOLUNTARY DISCLOSURE

Before examining the legislation, however, the issue of the voluntary disclosure of environmental information is considered, as this is a growing trend on behalf of those companies who wish to project a 'green' image.

Voluntary public disclosure may sound like an impossible counsel of perfection. It is not. There are considerable gains to be made from it.

Voluntary public disclosure allows a company to present its own information in its own way, to audiences for whom it is relevant, in ways which are timely and in forms which make it comprehensible.

12.7   Identifying best practice

Voluntary disclosure of environmental information is probably practised at its best by larger corporations. Understandably, for reasons such as constraints on money and management time, small and medium size companies have found it difficult to address environmental issues with the same vigour.

However, there are elements of best practice which smaller enterprises can emulate and there are good reasons for developing a proper understanding of the environmental impact of any business and making that information publicly available, even where that is not a legal requirement.

Voluntary public disclosure may sound like an impossible counsel of perfection. It is not. There are considerable gains to be made from it.

12.8   **Potential financial gains**

Perhaps the strongest reason for having hard environmental data is that what is not measured cannot be managed and the active management of environmental impact contributes both to competitive positioning and cost savings. Energy savings and the minimisation of raw materials waste, for instance, produce cost savings in the long run and make a significant contribution to environmental improvement.

As part of open environmental communications it is also becoming common to see the voluntary disclosure of a wide range of data, including, for instance, information relating to lost-time injuries and for the reduction of these to be part of corporate targets. The human costs of unsafe working conditions speak for themselves. The financial costs of accidents add commercial impetus to proper concern.

ICI's four major environmental objectives reflect the combination of self-interest and environmental concern. They relate to:

—   the environmental performance of new plant

—   reduction of waste

—   saving of energy and resources

—   recycling.

12.9   **Other gains**

Openness can enhance a company's credibility in dealing with all its interest groups whether customers, shareholders, employees or environmental activists. BP, ICI, Shell and others seek to achieve environmental excellence out of self-interest rather than altruism. They understand the value of reputation and the part that credibility plays in it.

There is a further compelling reason for openness. Information from industry ensures a better informed public: a public that has an enhanced appreciation of the importance of the environment and, particularly importantly, of the contribution of industry to the whole of society.

12.10 **INFORMATION MANAGEMENT**

Voluntary public disclosure allows a company to present its own information in its own way, to audiences for whom it is relevant, in ways which are timely and in forms which make it comprehensible.

12.11 **Information which is timely**

The timing of the release of information can be critical to the way in which it is received and whether it is believed.

If information has to be sought out, the anxious researcher will be less likely to take it at face value. The very act of placing information on a register, under legal compunction rather than willingly, implies that it has been through many sifting processes; legal, technical, commercial etc. It is likely to be regarded as the least the company can 'get away with'.

Far better to be aware of growing community concerns or issues arising in public debate and to provide information which is timely in its response to that mood.

Information which is timely also allows far greater control over the communication of the issues. Timeliness is crucial to being able to set the tone of debate and to capturing the available high moral ground. Too frequently, organisations find themselves reacting and responding, denying and refuting. Wherever possible, the strategy should be aimed at a position in which the company can, and is seen to, exercise leadership and proper authority.

12.12   Information which is relevant

The concept of relevant information takes the process a step further. It means information which directly addresses the specific concerns of interested parties.

The task is not to work out a minimum statement but to identify what questions need answering. Spotting the right questions is more successful as a communications strategy, though harder, than simply deciding what to say.

For example, as someone living within 100 yards of a factory will have quite different questions from someone who lives 100 miles away. Understanding what each needs to know will ensure that each gets relevant information – and it is unlikely to be the same information.

Ensuring that information is relevant also helps to ensure that it is high quality. And in order for it to be relevant and of high quality, companies need to be in active and listening relationships with the communities from which they derive their profit and with the decision-takers and opinion-formers who have power of influence.

It is useful to remind ourselves that misconceived legislation is as much the fault of industry and business when they fail to provide the Government with manageable and intelligent information as it is of the bureaucrats whose business it is to write such legislation.

12.13   Information which is clear

Clarity is also easier to achieve under voluntary circumstances. The technical and scientific substance may not change but the tone, style and language of information communication can be tailored to the needs of those whose questions need answers.

Clarity is greatly reassuring. It tends to encourage more questions and hence a mutually helpful discourse. Obfuscation raises doubts, closes down discourse, encourages confrontation and, put bluntly, causes more trouble.

It seems unlikely that information which is required on a register by which experts will be talking with experts will be of sufficient clarity (i.e. accessibility) to assist discourse which is helpful.

Information on a register is unlikely to provide any explanation of what it means or how it should be interpreted. Voluntary disclosure which aims to provide information which is clear can achieve these things.

12.14   TESTING THE BOUNDARIES

Ultimately, however, no matter how well companies behave, community groups and others will wish to test the law; exploring for weaknesses and stretching the boundaries. And they will probe both where the law seems at its weakest and where industrial and commercial behaviour seem most vulnerable.

But, however irritating this might be for executives with a business to run, it still argues for 'compliance plus' – behaving in the spirit of the law rather than within the strictest confines of its letter.

146

For that reason, I recommend that every attempt is made to find ways in which even potentially critical commercial information can be presented in good faith but with minimum risk. Some would describe this too as seeking the high moral ground.

It is, for instance, possible to imagine coalitions of competing concerns overcoming their rivalries to pool information through a neutral professional third party, thereby producing overall figures without revealing company specific figures or competitor sensitive information. A 'compliance plus' solution that addresses public concern, may go further than required but sets out to avoid the unintended commercial damage which new laws and fresh interpretations might carry in their wake.

12.15 It is also worth remembering that the public regard which is given to environmental issues is such that commercial issues are regarded as of second order. It is for that reason that Danish legislation requiring all beers sold in that country to be sold in bottles was upheld on environmental grounds, even though many saw it as trade restraint hiding under a green skirt.

12.16 Environmental legislation is likely to be dominated by the EC on the reasonable grounds that real solutions require transnational responses.

The law is shifting from an emphasis on the provision of information to a belief in freedom of information and individuals' right to know.

Present industrial, manufacturing and commercial enterprise must recognise their legacy of environmental cost and damage, no matter whether it was unwittingly caused.

The provision of information and increasing moves towards 'right to know' legislation are easily perceived as threats. They can be turned to advantage.

A concern for real reputation and an acknowledgement of legitimate public interest are inescapable modern requirements.

12.17 Voluntary public disclosure is not an impossible counsel of perfection. Unlike information held on a register, it permits three highly desirable characteristics for successful communications; timeliness, relevance and clarity.

No matter how hard corporate UK tries in meeting both the spirit and the letter of legislation, that legislation will be tested for weaknesses so that its boundaries can be stretched.

12.18 A policy of 'compliance plus' may be the right answer and there may be ways of providing environmental information which could be commercially disadvantageous in such a way as to minimise risk and at the same time, meet the highest reasonable public expectation.

Protection of the environment is demonstrably more important to many than protection of commercial undertakings. Protecting commercial interests may therefore dictate that more, not less, information is made available.

12.19 EC ACCESS TO ENVIRONMENTAL INFORMATION DIRECTIVE

The *EC Directive* on the freedom of access to information on the environment (*90/313/EEC*) was issued on 7 June 1990 under *Article 130s* of the *EC Treaty*. Its aim is to improve environmental protection by giving access to environmental information held by public authorities. Member States must implement its provisions through domestic legislation and administrative action no later than 31 December 1992. [*Article 9*].

12.20 Environmental Information

12.20 Under *Article 2(a)* of the *Directive* 'information relating to the environment' means any available information in written, visual, aural or database form on the state of water, air, soil, fauna, flora, land and natural sites – presumably in the UK this would mean sites of special scientific interest – and on activities (including those which give rise to nuisances such as noise) or measures adversely affecting them, or likely to do so. It also encompasses such information on activities or measures designed to protect these media or features, including administrative measures and environmental management programmes.

12.21 For the purposes of the *Directive* a public authority means any public administration at national, regional or local level with responsibilities, and possessing information, relating to the environment with the exception of bodies acting in a judicial or legislative capacity. This definition would therefore cover the Secretary of State for the Environment, the National Rivers Authority and local authorities but not water or sewerage undertakers.

12.22 Water and other undertakers may however be caught by *Article 6* of the *Directive*. This requires Member States to ensure that bodies with public responsibilities for the environment and under the control of public authorities reveal environmental information held by them in the same way as public authorities. This could cover the activities of water and sewerage undertakers in at least some of their roles. For example, they have conservation duties under *sections 3 to 5* of the *Water Industry Act 1991* that are supervised by the Secretary of State for the Environment. Those duties impose, it may be said, a public responsibility for the environment. Similarly sewerage undertakers exercise a public responsibility for the environment in discharging their trade effluent and sewage disposal functions. These duties are supervised by the Secretary of State, the Director-General and other authorities. The water supply duties of an undertaker might not be considered a responsibility for the environment but the duty to supply wholesome water, supervised by the Drinking Water Inspectorate, may be.

12.23 *Article 3* requires Member States to ensure that public authorities are obliged to make available information relating to the environment to any natural or legal person at his request and without his having to prove an interest. The use of the term 'natural or legal person' might provide difficulties for unincorporated associations but they can always act through a member. States must define the practical arrangements under which such information is effectively made available. A charge may be made for supplying information under the *Directive* but that must be limited to the reasonable cost of providing it. [*Article 5*].

12.24 Normally the information requested should be provided. However it may be refused where it affects public security, matters that are under preliminary investigation or are *sub judice*, commercial and industrial confidentiality, personal information, material supplied voluntarily by a third party and material that, if disclosed, could lead to environmental harm. Information may also be refused that affects the confidentiality of the proceedings of public authorities, international relations and national defence. [*Article 3.2*]. This may cause some problems as almost any information could relate to the proceedings of the public authority to whom it is supplied. Where a request is made that concerns material that can be refused under these provisions but it is possible to separate out the confidential aspects of it, this should be done and partial information provided. In addition a request may be refused where it would involve the supply of unfinished documents or data or internal communications, or where the request is manifestly unreasonable or formulated in too general a manner. [*Article 3.4*].

12.25 Once a request for information is received the authority should reply as soon as possible and within two months at the latest. If they refuse to comply with the request they must state their reasons for so doing. Anyone who considers that his request has been unreasonably refused or ignored, or that he has been given inadequate answers, may seek a judicial review of the decision in accordance with the relevant national legal system. [*Article 4*].

12.26 In addition to the information provided by specific requests, Member States should also provide general information to the public on the state of the environment. This should be accomplished by the periodic publication of descriptive reports. [*Article 7*]. The report of the National Rivers Authority under *section 187* of the *Water Resources Act 1991* could be adapted to achieve this in respect of the water environment.

12.27 The *Directive* has been implemented in Great Britain by the *Environmental Information Regulations 1992* (*SI 1992 No 3240*) which came into force on 31 December 1992. The *Regulations* follow the *Directive* but with some amplification. They apply to information that relates to the environment. Information so relates if, and only if, it relates to the state of any water or air, any flora or fauna, any soil or the state of any natural site or other land or it relates to any activities or measures – including activities giving rise to noise or any other nuisance – which adversely affect them or are likely to do so, or any activities or administrative or other measures, including any environmental management programmes, which are designed to protect them. [*Environmental Information Regulations 1992, Reg 2(2)*].

12.28 For these purposes relevant persons are all such Ministers of the Crown, government departments, local authorities and other persons carrying out functions of public administration at a national, regional or local level as, for the purposes of or in connection with their functions, have responsibilities in relation to the environment. Further, any body with public responsibilities for the environment not encompassed by this definition but under the control of such a person will also be a relevant person under the *Regulations*. [*Reg 2(3)*]. Thus a voluntary nature conservation organisation operating as an agent of English Nature could be a 'relevant person' for the purposes of the *Regulations*.

12.29 The *Regulations* apply to all such information apart from that which is already required to be provided to the public on request or information that is contained in statutory records. [*Reg 2(1)(c), (4)*]. This means that information in registers under the *Water Resources Act 1991* or the *Environmental Protection Act 1990* could not be obtained using these *Regulations* as it is available anyway. However the fact that there is a statutory requirement of secrecy in relation to certain information – such as under *section 204* of the *Water Resources Act 1991* – cannot, in itself, prevent the application of these *Regulations* to it. [*Reg 3(7)*].

12.30 Generally a relevant person who holds any information to which the *Regulations* apply must make that information available to every person who requests it. [*Reg 3(1)*]. Indeed such a person has a duty to make arrangements to ensure the prompt handling of requests – at least to deal with it within two months of it being made – and, if the request is refused, that written reasons are given for the refusal. [*Reg 3(2)*]. A charge may be made in respect of the costs reasonably attributable to the supply of the information and the supply can be conditional on the payment of that charge. [*Reg 3(4)*].

12.31 *Regulation 4* provides exceptions to the right to information. This, together with *Regulation 3(3)*, follows *Article 3* of the *Directive*. The restriction on disclosure of information relating to legal proceedings is defined in *Regulation 4(5)* as applying to local and public inquiries, statutory hearings and appeals by way of written representations.

12.32 By *Regulation 3(6)*, without prejudice to any other available remedies, the obligation of a relevant person to make information available in pursuance of *Regulation 3(1)* will be a duty owed to the person who has requested; giving that person standing to bring an action for judicial review.

12.33 PUBLIC REGISTERS IN THE UK

Environmental information is often made available to the public through registers maintained by public authorities under the relevant statutes. In each case it is the duty of the authority to ensure the register is kept at its relevant offices and made available for free public inspection at all reasonable times. Copies of entries in the register may be obtainable on payment of a reasonable charge. A list of such registers is set out below.

12.34 Registers of abstraction and impoundment licences granted under *Part II* of the *Water Resources Act 1991* must be kept by the National Rivers Authority in accordance with *section 189* of the *Water Resources Act 1991*. Information about the flow, volume or level of water in inland waters should also be supplied to anyone asking to inspect the relevant records under *section 197* of the Act.

12.35 Ancient monuments scheduled under *section 1* of the *Ancient Monuments and Archeological Areas Act 1979* must be shown on a list published by the Secretary of State under *section 1(7)* of the Act. Lists must also be published by the Historic Buildings and Monuments Commission for England by virtue of *section 2(2)* of the Act.

12.36 Registers of potentially contaminated land are compiled and maintained under *section 143* of the *Environmental Protection Act 1990* by district or London Borough Councils or, in Scotland, planning authorities, showing land in their areas that has been or is being put to a 'contaminative use' as defined.

12.37 The dumping of waste at sea is controlled under *Part II* of the *Food and Environment Protection Act 1986*. *Section 14* of that Act, as substituted by *section 147* of the *Environmental Protection Act 1990*, requires each licensing authority to maintain registers containing details about licences they have issued.

12.38 For genetically modified organisms, under *section 122* of the *Environmental Protection Act 1990* the Secretary of State must maintain a register of notifications and consents concerning the importation, release and marketing of GMOs and other matters relating to them.

12.39 Authorities that are 'hazardous substances authorities' must keep a register showing details of applications for consents and other matters under *section 28* of the *Hazardous Substances Act 1990*. The form of the register is prescribed by *Regulation 23* of the *Planning (Hazardous Substances) Regulations 1992 (SI 1992 No 656)*.

12.40 As part of integrated pollution control, and local authority air pollution controls under *Part I* of the *1990 Act*, public registers are required to be kept by HMIP and local authorities under *section 20* of the Act. The contents of these registers are prescribed under the *Environmental Protection (Applications, Appeals and Registers) Regulations 1991 (SI 1991 No 507)*.

12.41 Listed buildings are shown on the lists compiled by the Secretary of State for the Environment. Under *section 2(5)* of the *Listed Buildings Act 1990* they must be made publicly available at local planning offices and, under *section 2(4)* at the National Monuments Record.

12.42 Litter registers are provided for under *section 95* of the *Environmental Protection Act 1990*. Each principal litter authority – other than a county council, regional council or joint board – must maintain a public register containing copies of any orders they have made designating an area as a litter control area and any street litter control notices they have issued.

12.43 Planning registers are held by local planning authorities under *section 69* of the *Town and Country Planning Act 1990*. Their contents are prescribed by *Article 7* of the *Town and Country Planning General Development Order 1988* (*SI 1988 No 1813*). They will include details of planning applications. In addition registers will also be held by the authority showing the results of determinations under *section 64* of the Act, enforcement and stop notices issued by the authority, [*T&CPA 1990, s 188*], tree preservation notices. [*T&CPA, s 214*].

12.44 Maps of land on which the public have a right of access will be maintained by local planning authorities under *section 78* of the *National Parks and Access to the Countryside Act 1949*.

12.45 Radioactive substances consents etc. issued under the *Radioactive Substances Act 1960* must be made available to the public by the chief inspector and relevant local authorities by virtue of *section 13A* of the Act.

12.46 Details of trade effluent consents or agreements for discharge into sewers must be kept on a register by every sewerage undertaker by virtue of *section 196* of the *Water Industry Act 1991*.

12.47 Waste registers are provided for by *section 64* of the *Environmental Protection Act 1990* which will require waste regulation authorities to maintain public registers of information about waste management operations in their areas. These may include information about imports and exports of waste by virtue of regulations made under *section 141(5)(f)* of the Act.

12.48 Registers of carriers of waste must be kept under *section 2* of the *Control of Pollution (Amendment) Act 1989* and *Regulation 3* of the *Controlled Waste (Registration of Carriers and Seizure of Vehicles) Regulations 1991* (*SI 1991 No 1624*).

12.49 Water quality objective notices, consents for discharges into waters and other matters relating to water pollution control must be shown on the pollution control registers of the National Rivers Authority under *section 190* of the *Water Resources Act 1991*. These registers will also contain details of authorisations by HMIP under *Part I* of the *Environmental Protection Act 1990*.

12.50 OTHER SOURCES OF INFORMATION

Some statutes or regulations provide for information to be made available to the public for various purposes.

12.51 Under *Regulation 8* of the *Control of Pesticides Regulations 1986* (*SI 1986 No 1510*) the Minister has a discretion to give information about evaluations on which the approval of the use etc. of a particular pesticide was based.

12.52 Statutory plans may be available to the public. For example, waste collection, disposal and recycling plans made under *Part II* of the *Environmental Protection Act 1990* must be open to public inspection.

12.53 Authorities may have a duty to publish reports of their activities. For example, the nature conservancy councils have a duty to make an annual report to the Secretary of State under *paragraph 20* of *Schedule 6* to the *Environmental Protection Act 1990*. The National Rivers Authority must make an annual report under *section 187* of the *Water Resources Act 1991*. These, and other, reports must be laid before Parliament and will usually be published as part of the Command Papers series.

12.54 *Part VA* of the *Local Government Act 1972* (as inserted by the *Local Government (Access to Information) Act 1985*) provides for public access to meetings and documents. It

12.55 Environmental Information

enables the public to see agendas for meetings, officers' reports and background papers. However certain information may be kept confidential. It is an offence for a council to deny access to information the public have a right to see.

12.55 Under *Regulation 5* of the *Environmental Information Regulations 1992 (SI 1992 No 3240)* where such information is not covered by those *Regulations* the relevant person who asked for it must ensure that the request is dealt with as soon as possible and in any event no later than two months after the request. If the request is refused written reasons must be given for the refusal and any charges for the information must not exceed a reasonable amount for making it available.

12.56 COMMERCIAL CONFIDENTIALITY

Section 66 of the *Environmental Protection Act 1990* enables an individual or business to apply to the waste regulation authority for information relating to their affairs to be excluded from the waste register on the grounds that it is commercially confidential. Similar provision is made in *section 22* of the Act, in relation to the registers established under *section 20*, concerning information on integrated pollution control authorisations by HMIP and on authorisations granted by local authorities under *Part I* of the Act for air pollution control purposes.

12.57 *Section 20(1)* of the *Environmental Protection Act 1990* imposes a duty on an authority to maintain a register containing matters prescribed in regulations. *Regulation 15* of the *Environmental Protection (Applications, Appeals and Registers) Regulations 1991 (SI 1991 No 507)* states that, 'subject to section . . . 22, a register maintained by an . . . authority shall contain – (a) all particulars of any application for an authorisation made to the authority'. Thus where an application is made it is the duty of the authority to enter all of its particulars on the register. In practice this will be done by putting a copy of it on the register.

12.58 At this stage the authority, subject to *section 22(4)*, has no discretion in the matter. It cannot determine itself that information is commercially confidential, nor can it exclude it from the register on any of the other grounds set out in the *Access to Environmental Information Directive*.

12.59 By *section 22(1)* no information relating to the affairs of any individual or business can be included on the register without the consent of that individual or someone carrying on the business, if and so long as the information:

'(a) is in relation to him commercially confidential . . .'.

This will not apply to information which is the subject of a direction by the Secretary of State under *section 22(7)* that requires it to be entered on the register. However information is not commercially confidential unless it is determined to be so by the authority or, on appeal, by the Secretary of State.

12.60 *Section 22(11)* of the Act states that information is, for the purposes of any determination under this section, commercially confidential, in relation to any individual or person, if its being contained on the register would prejudice to an unreasonable degree the commercial interests of that individual or person.

12.61 There is no definition of 'commercial interest' in the statute. Thus the phrase should bear its ordinary meaning. The type of information that can be confidential would include details of processes or equipment, costings, sources of materials or fuels, and future intentions of the company.

12.62 Under *section 22(2)* where someone furnishes an authority information in relation to an application for an authorisation or its variation, or for the purpose of complying with a condition in it or in response to a request under *section 19(2)*, he may apply to the authority for a determination that it should be excluded from the register on the grounds of commercial confidentiality.

12.63 *Section 22(4)* requires an authority to notify a relevant person about information it receives, for example under *section 19* of the Act, about his process so that he can object to its going on the register on the same basis.

Nothing in the *Regulations* concerns applications under *section 22(2)* or *(4)* themselves. However, where an application is made in conjunction with an application for an authorisation, the authorisation application procedure is modified by *Regulation 7* of the *Environmental Protection (Applications, Appeals and Registers) Regulations 1991*.

12.64 Guidance on determining applications is given in General Guidance Note 1 (GG1(91)) and in 'Integrated Pollution Control – a Practical Guide' (IPC). These suggest that the guiding principle is that information should be freely available to the public about matters that should be entered on the register (GG1 paragraph 54, IPC paragraph 8.78.7). Where an operator requests confidentiality it is suggested that 'it is for him to demonstrate that disclosure of the information would negate or significantly diminish the commercial advantage he has over a competitor . . . the onus is on the applicant to provide a clear justification for each item he wishes to be kept from the register' (GG1 paragraph 56, IPC paragraphs 8.9 and 8.10).

12.65 An application for exclusion from the register on grounds of commercial confidentiality must be determined. If it is not then the authority will be deemed to have accepted the application. [*EPA 1990, s 22(3)*]. This period can be altered by order. [*EPA 1990, s 22(10)*].

12.66 If the authority reject the application they must not enter the information on the register for a further 21 days. [*EPA 1990, s 22(5)(a)*]. The applicant may appeal to the Secretary of State against the rejection within that 21-day period. [*EPA 1990, s 22(5)(b); Environmental Protection (Applications, Appeals and Registers) Regulations 1991 (SI 1991 No 507), Regulation 10(1)(e)*].

12.67 Information that is granted confidentiality status will be treated as ceasing to have that status after four years from the date it was determined to be confidential by the authority. However the person who furnished it may renew his application for confidentiality in respect of it on the ground that it is still confidential. The authority must then make a new determination on the matter. [*EPA 1990, s 22(8)*]. If it rejects the renewed application the applicant has the same right of appeal as he had initially. [*EPA 1990, s 22(9)*].

12.68 In addition *section 22(1)* states that 'no information . . . shall be included on the register . . . *if and so long as* the information is . . . commercially confidential'. It would appear that information may cease to be confidential before the end of the four-year period provided in *section 22(8)* and if so it would then be placed on the register. *Section 22(8)* does not say that the information shall be treated as confidential for four years but merely that it ceases to be confidential after four years. Thus HMIP and local authorities will be able to propose registration of exempt information either during the four-year period or at its end.

13 Environmental Insurance

13.1 In recent years insurance companies have become aware of the very large potential liabilities to which they are exposed resulting from the problems of environmental pollution.

13.2 Historically the insurers had made little or no reference to pollution in their liability policies. This led to circumstances, initially in the United States, where insurers were often being asked to contribute to the clean-up of past environmental damage, often in circumstances where there had been no fortuitous loss.

13.3 An atmosphere of instability then developed in the US courts with regard to the interpretation of the insurance policy wordings; definitions of environmental damage, residual liabilities and the definition of 'sudden and accidental' loss as opposed to 'gradual loss'.

13.4 Pressure from the reinsurance industry forced insurers, initially in the USA, and now worldwide, to specifically exclude cover for environmental damage, although in certain instances some are prepared to offer some limited cover for sudden and accidental damage, as it is generally possible to be specific about the timing and the circumstances surrounding the polluting event.

13.5 Central to the problems facing insurers is this distinction between the sudden and accidental and the gradual pollution. The categories are critical because insurers treat each entirely differently as they try to identify those risks which are insurable and those which they believe are not.

13.6 As recently as 1991 the last British insurer, following the American example withdrew environmental cover, introducing a total pollution exclusion. It is advisable now to act on the assumption that there is no insurance generally available for environmental damage as a result of gradual pollution.

13.7 Insurers cannot be expected to pay for the past failures of management and society in general. The role of insurance is to protect the insured's balance sheet from fortuitous loss in the future. It is on this basis that certain insurers are now looking to design some form of environmental insurance cover that will give some protection from identifiable fortuitous losses.

13.8 The insurance solutions that are emerging will be offered only to those companies who are prepared to make a commitment to a strict risk management approach. Extensive environmental surveys will have to be carried out prior to the offer of insurance cover, insurers will insist that effective systems and techniques to manage the risks are to be in place. Only then may insurers be prepared to offer some form of cover. There are stringent requirements and many of the more 'at risk' industries will find the cover is either not available to them or does not provide a cost-effective option.

13.9 Some companies are already offering a measure of gradual pollution cover, others are offering solutions which involve an element of self-funding over a period of time. Some attempts have been made to develop pure risk financing vehicles to fund potential losses; these are unlike the traditional risk transfer methods and may offer an insured a means of smoothing losses on the balance sheet over a period of time in a financially efficient manner.

13.10 The first 'Environmental Impairment Liability' policies are now appearing in the UK. Written for specific sites on a claims made basis they provide third party liability

155

coverage for bodily injury and property damage, including clean-up costs and legal defence costs. A further specific 'Liability Insurance Programme' has been devised to address the problems of underground storage tanks. It is designed to involve a rigorous management programme, that will minimise the pollution risks to such a level that extensive insurance can be provided at a reasonable cost.

13.11   At present whilst it is difficult to judge the state of EC environmental legislation in the future, contribution by the insurance industry will be significant, but the role still remains relatively vague and unco-ordinated. Whilst insurers in the UK and Europe continue to give some commitment to environmental impairment liability insurance, they have little experience at present and until confidence grows in their own ability to provide this type of insurance, as well as confidence that industry and the legislature understand their role, it is unrealistic to expect insurers to provide significant capacity in this particular area.

13.12   Companies seeking to address their environmental liability exposures need to involve an insurance broker or risk management advisers at the earliest possible opportunity in order to identify the exposures and begin to develop solutions to provide some protection for the balance sheet. Solutions that emerge will involve a combination of risk management and risk funding, with insurance forming only a part of the equation.

14 Environmental Management

14.1 THE KEY FACTORS DRIVING ENVIRONMENTAL MANAGEMENT

External pressures

The management of environmental performance has only recently emerged as an important issue not only for businesses, small and large, but for public bodies. Its rise to prominence and its appearance on the boardroom agenda have occurred mostly because of direct pressures from external sources. It is increasingly being recognised by business that if these pressures are not addressed the profitability and viability of the business could be impaired. Failure to respond through improving environmental performance can result in missed business opportunities and significant costs being incurred.

The pressures come from various quarters but all have one interest in common, that is to minimise the adverse impacts of business activity on our environment and on our health. This is the task of environment management.

Figure 14.1 overleaf shows the range of external pressures on organisations, which are discussed in the sections that follow.

14.2 Legislation

Legislation is a key driver of better environmental performance. One of the major pieces of UK environmental legislation which aims to prevent pollution is the *Environmental Protection Act 1990*. The key elements of the Act which businesses must be alert to are: the requirements for authorisation of specified processes and substances likely to generate pollution from releases to the air, water or land; the introduction of a duty of care for waste imposed on all concerned in the chain of waste disposal; the tightening of waste licensing and the Register of potentially contaminated land, listing sites which may be contaminated due to their past or current uses. Despite a change of mind by Government on the Register, it has served to focus the minds of companies affected on clean-up. Similarly the *Water Act 1989* seeks to control direct or indirect discharges made by companies into our rivers and coastal waters.

These are just two of a host of primary legislation, rules, orders and regulations which business managers must be aware of and respond to.

Notwithstanding the UK legal pressures, there is a growing body of Directives and Regulations emerging from Brussels which companies have to anticipate and plan for (see Table 14.1 below). Such developments have become a centre piece of European Community policy aimed at making significant improvements to the quality of our environment, to our use of non-renewable natural resources and to the protection of health. It is estimated that there have been some 300 items of EC environmental legislation since the first measure was adopted in 1967.

To enforce these legal instruments in the UK there is a body of regulators, including Her Majesty's Inspectorate of Pollution, the National Rivers Authority, local Waste Regulation Authorities and the Environmental Health Departments of Local Authorities.

Given the array of legislation that exists or is planned, it is clear that one element of good environment management must be awareness in the company of what legislation

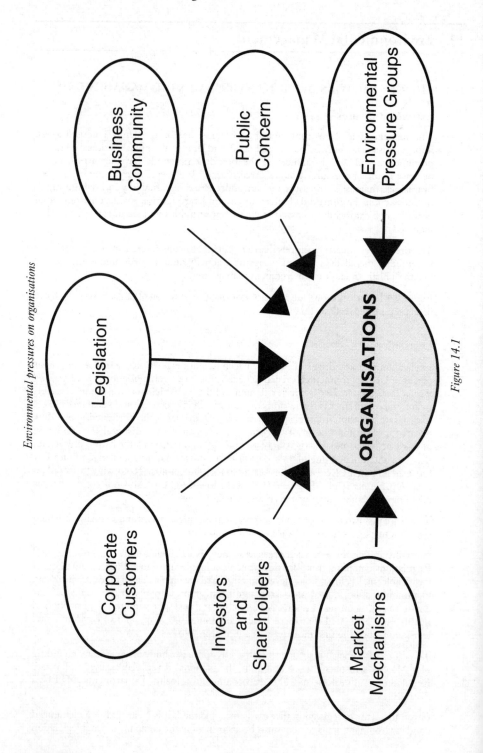

Environmental pressures on organisations

Figure 14.1

Table 14.1

Examples of topics covered in existing and proposed EC environmental legislation

Air
- Air quality
- Industrial plant emissions
- Hazardous waste incineration
- Climate change convention
- Volatile organic compounds
- Large and small combustion plants

Water
- Drinking water and groundwater
- Trade effluents
- Dangerous substances
- Surface waters
- Detergent biodegradability

Hazardous substances
- CFCs and the ozone layer
- Pesticides
- Dangerous chemicals export/import consents
- Transport of hazardous substances
- Packaging and labelling of dangerous substances

Waste
- Hazardous transshipments and waste disposals
- Landfills
- Waste shipment
- Contaminated land
- Packaging waste

Other
- Eco-labelling
- Eco-Management and Auditing
- Integrated permitting
- Liability for environmental damage
- Freedom of access to information

will directly affect it, what the implications are for the business, such as the nature and cost of replacing plant and equipment, the consequences of non-compliance, changes necessary to management procedures, the training of staff and the needs for environmental information.

14.3 Market mechanisms

While the command and control approach embodied in pollution legislation and regulations represents a significant pressure on business, policy makers have begun to examine new tools to encourage better management of environmental performance.

A range of measures are beginning to emerge designed to influence the economics of polluting activities. These so-called market based instruments impose costs on pollution causing activities and provide incentives for companies to look for ways of minimising environmental damage. Such instruments being discussed or implemented within the European Community include:

(a)   a carbon tax aimed at raising the cost of all fossil fuels, and those with a high carbon content becoming more expensive than others. This is designed to encourage energy conservation and a switch to cleaner fuels. Thus businesses will need to manage carefully their use of energy;

(b)   tradeable emissions permits which set pollution quotas. Companies that reduce their emissions below the quota can sell the unused part of their quota to other firms. Businesses thus have the incentive to improve their emissions performance;

(c)   levies and credits. Landfill levies are being considered which aim to force companies to reduce their waste streams. Recycling credits are designed to encourage collectors of waste to recycle more of the materials they collect. The management of waste streams thus becomes an important business activity for environment managers to focus on.

14.4 Investors and shareholders

Another growing pressure on companies is that from investors and shareholders. UK financial institutions control some 70 per cent of UK shares and provide large amounts of loan finance secured against the assets of the business. They have a very direct interest in the performance of their investment and are increasingly seeking information from companies on how legislation is likely to impact on the financial position of the business, and hence on the risks to their continuing involvement as investors or lenders. They will want to see that the company is not in breach of its legal requirements with the consequent threat of fines and bad publicity. They will need to be aware that the assets in the form of plant, equipment and land, against which they have lent money, are correctly valued in the light of the possibility that clean-up or better process equipment is required. New investment requirements can have an impact on gearing. Raw materials used or the finished product may have to be modified or discontinued where usage is either banned (e.g. CFCs) or where public pressure and attitudes are such that the demand for environmentally less friendly products begins to decline. Research and development costs associated with either modification of material or product may also be material. Insurance cover may no longer be adequate.

Investors will want to understand the financial implications of these issues and reassess the risk of their involvement. It is thus becoming more common for investors to ask their clients for information on these matters and to expect more detail in company reports and statements of environmental performance and planned improvements.

Investors also play an important part in facilitating acquisitions, mergers, flotations, buyouts, or divestments. Environmental matters are becoming an increasingly important factor before deals are being struck. The pressure is being put on management and the target company to demonstrate that environmental liabilities do not constitute an unacceptable risk for the investor. The issues to consider are the same as those for existing shareholders and investors. In making their decisions on whether to back the project the acquirors will want to be assured that the company is complying, is geared up for the new pollution control requirements, having made adequate provision for expenditure, is accurately stating land values and is committed to on-going improvements in the way it manages environmental performance within its operations.

14.5 Corporate customers

The management of environmental performance is not only an internal issue for companies. Most businesses are dependent on others for inputs to their products and services; they are both substantial buyers and suppliers. This interdependence means that one company can directly impact on the environmental performance of another.

As more and more companies are striving to minimise the adverse environmental effects of their own activities they are also looking to their suppliers to measure up to their own environmental standards and policies. Company environmental policy statements frequently include the intention to ensure that suppliers carry out sound environmental practices. In following through this policy the purchasing company will be seeking from its suppliers a range of information about their environmental performance covering such aspects as raw material use, manufacturing processes, packaging, disposal methods and associated management practices.

14.6   Public concern and environmental pressure groups

Most pressures on companies from the public arise from local communities which experience the direct effects of pollution. Many businesses have to deal with such complaints as noise, bad odours, dusts, smoke, unsightly waste, polluted rivers, ugly buildings and the loss of wildlife, flora and fauna. Such complaints bring adverse media coverage and a lack of confidence by the local community in the company's commitment to the environment and to health.

Environmental pressure groups, often with legal and technical expertise to match the best that management can provide, are actively seeking out poor environmental performance. They are exposing bad practice or abuses of compliance, they are carrying out their own emissions testing and are tracking the words of intent found in company statements against their actions and the improvements achieved.

14.7   Business community

Both in the UK and in the international business community, trade associations and business groups such as the Confederation of Business Industry, and the International Chamber of Commerce, are encouraging leading businesses to set the pace in adopting commitment to environmental management systems and principles.

For example, the ICC *Business Charter for Sustainable Development* is a set of 16 principles for environmental management. The ICC urges that these be adopted by any organisation concerned with its environmental performance.

These principles require adherents to make environmental management a high priority with detailed programmes and practices for its implementation integrated with existing management systems and procedures. It highlights such areas as employee and customer education, research facilities and operations, contractors and suppliers and emergency preparedness.

It requires organisations to support the transfer of technology, be open to concerns expressed by the public and employees and carry out regular environmental reviews and report progress.

Already a large number of leading organisations have signed the *Business Charter*. The pressure is on for others to follow.

Another example of environment management leadership in the UK is Business in the Environment (BIE). This is a team of leading business people drawn from a variety of sectors, which aims to raise business awareness on the environment and to devise and promote practical tools for improving performance. Following two earlier publications on environmental management, it has recently published *Guidelines for Measuring Environmental Performance* comprising a series of 14 case studies, and *Buying into the Environment*, a Supplier Code of Practice. Both guidelines are written by KPMG.

The Responsible Care Programme is an initiative from the chemical industry which commits members to demonstrate continuous improvement in all aspects of health, safety and environmental performance. In the UK, the chemical industry has agreed voluntarily to a system of annual reporting of performance.

In 1991 a new Advisory Committee on Business and the Environment was announced by the Government consisting of 25 senior executives of UK based companies, set up to report on ways of improving environmental performance through both Government and voluntary measures amongst businesses.

The CBI too has urged companies to sign up to its Green Club and commit themselves to evaluating the environmental impacts of their operations, setting targets and publicly reporting performance.

14.8   Environmental Management

Standards for environmental management

What constitutes best practice in environmental management, given these many pressures on UK businesses to minimise damage to the environment and health?

The subject is still relatively undeveloped as a management tool. Various guidelines exist but whether they work in practice and how they should fit with existing business management systems remain open questions. This latter point is particularly important. As BIE in its recent publication on performance indicators states:

'managing the environmental impact of business activities is for many businesses a relatively new idea and one which calls for both change in business culture and in day to day management systems. It is the recognition that environmental management cannot stand alone as a discipline, and that environmental thinking must be integrated with normal business practices, that forms the basis of current thinking in environmental management development'.

Effective environment management, like quality management or financial management requires *inter alia*:

(*a*)   the setting of objectives and performance measures;

(*b*)   the definition and allocation of responsibilities for monitoring, evaluating and improving performance;

(*c*)   the collection and reporting of information on performance for both internal and external uses;

(*d*)   a process for ensuring feedback on systems and procedures so that the necessary changes can be actioned.

There are two main developments which are currently helping to shape best practice in environmental management. The first is the EC Eco-Management and Audit Scheme Regulation which was published in July 1993. The second is the British Standard for Environment Management BS 7750, which is likely to form the basis of an international standard.

14.9   The Eco-Management and Audit Scheme (EMAS)

This voluntary scheme has two main aims:

(*a*)   to encourage better environmental management in industry, and

(*b*)   to improve the disclosure of information on the impacts of particular industrial sites on the environment.

The combination of these aims has led to some compromises; in particular the proposal focuses on individual industrial sites rather than companies as a whole. Nevertheless, the proposal puts environmental management clearly on the map at EC level.

Figure 14.2 illustrates the procedure envisaged in the EMAS. Following the adoption of a company level policy, an initial environmental review is made to identify the impacts of a site on the environment, and an internal environmental protection system must be established. The system must include specific objectives for environmental performance and procedures for implementing them. The system, and the results of the initial environmental review, must be described in an initial environmental statement. The statement must be validated by an accredited external organisation

Eco-Management and Audit Scheme Procedure

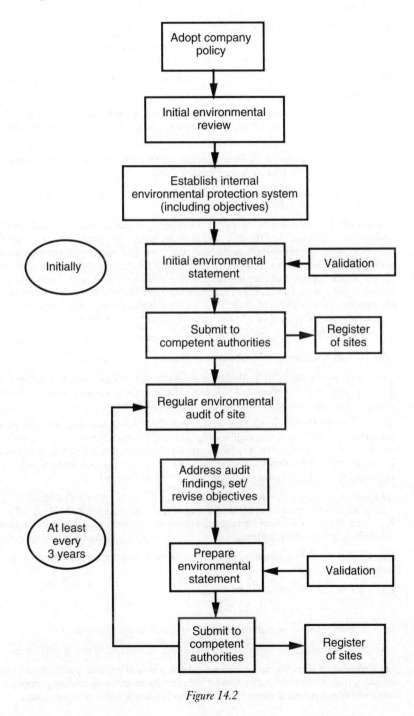

Figure 14.2

14.10 Environmental Management

before being submitted to national authorities for registration of the site under the eco-audit scheme.

There are a number of key points here:

(a) the first stage in developing environmental management is to carry out a thorough review of impacts on the environment;

(b) setting up an environmental management system is a pre requisite of registration under the scheme;

(c) it is envisaged that international standards for environmental management systems will be developed, similar in form to the British Standard described below;

(d) external validation of the environmental statement is intended to ensure consistency in environmental management systems;

(e) the description of the environmental management system within the statement will be on the public record.

Once a site has been registered under the scheme, it will require regular audits to review the effectiveness of the environmental management system as well as giving information on environmental impacts of the site. The subject of environmental auditing is discussed in ENVIRONMENTAL AUDITS (8). Here it is sufficient to note that development of procedures for internal auditing is a crucial part of an environmental management system. In addition to the audit, the preparation and external validation of an environmental statement, submitted to the competent authority for continued registration, and made public are elements of an on-going procedure.

14.10 The British Standard on Environment Management Systems (BS 7750)

In its own words BS 7750 'is designed to enable any organisation to establish an effective management system, as a foundation for both sound environmental performance and participation in "environmental auditing" schemes'.

In essence, the British Standard provides guidelines for an internal environmental protection system. In practice it will enable companies to participate who do not wish to or are unable to become accredited under the full requirements of EMAS, particularly the publication and verification of information on environmental performance. An outline of the British Standard procedure is shown in Figure 14.3.

The standard follows closely the procedures and manuals approach of BS 5750 on quality management, and it is envisaged that organisations operating to BS 5750 will readily be able to extend their management systems to incorporate the new standard. BS 5750 is not, however, a prerequisite for the environmental management standard.

Like EMAS, the British Standard procedure begins with an initial review covering four main areas:

(a) legislative and regulatory requirements;

(b) significant environmental effects;

(c) existing environmental management practices and procedures;

(d) feedback from the investigation of previous incidents and non-compliance.

On the basis of this review, an environmental policy should be developed. Critically the standard requires that the policy should include a commitment to continual improvement of environmental performance and to the publication of that commitment.

BS 7750 procedure

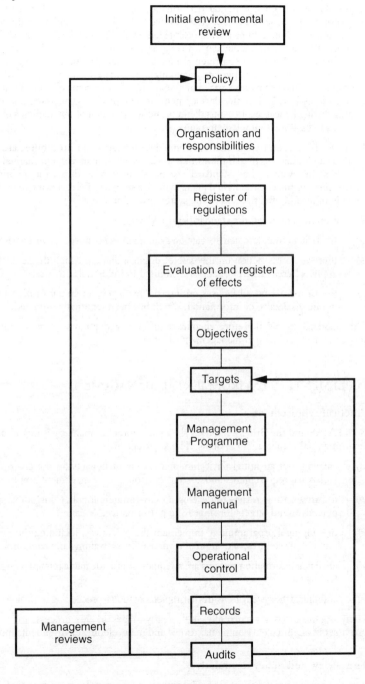

Figure 14.3

14.11 Environmental Management

Following the pattern of BS 5750, the standard places emphasis on allocating responsibilites for environmental performance management and for ensuring that sufficient resources and personnel are available for implementation of the system. Communication and training are important elements of the standard, to ensure that the message of good environmental performance is passed down through the organisation. In setting objectives and departmental targets the standard notes that such targets should form components of personal accountability and performance appraisal. At the heart of the system is an environmental management programme of actions relating to such areas as purchasing, the development of new products, planning and design, manufacturing processes, new installations and waste. Each of the actions will reflect what has to be done to implement policy.

There is also a requirement that environmental management procedures are documented, including the preparation of an environmental management manual which describes the system. The standard also sets down procedures for auditing the effectiveness of the environmental management system and for reviewing the continuing suitability and effectiveness of the system over time.

Key differences between the standard and EMAS are:

(*a*)   the British Standard can operate on a company-wide basis, not just at site level;

(*b*)   there is no restriction on the type of organisations to which the standard can apply; whereas EMAS is currently limited to industrial activities;

(*c*)   the British Standard focuses on internal management systems rather than on public disclosure of information, which has been externally validated.

The standard should therefore encourage an even wider range of organisations to adopt good environmental management practice.

14.11 IMPLEMENTING ENVIRONMENTAL MANAGEMENT

Practical requirements

Both EMAS and the British Standard set a pattern for companies wishing to develop environmental management systems. The key steps are:

(*a*)   carrying out an initial environmental review of impacts on the environment, legislative requirements and current environment management practices;

(*b*)   drawing on this review to develop an environmental policy, including specific objectives and targets for improving performance;

(*c*)   developing a programme to implement the objectives, including the development of procedures, allocation of responsibilities, training and communication;

(*d*)   ensuring information systems are adequate to provide management with regular feedback;

(*e*)   auditing of the system to ensure that implementation is proceeding according to plan.

Many organisations are currently at the early stages in this process, focusing on carrying out an initial environmental review and in developing environmental policies.

14.12 The review and policy formulation

Before a business can manage its environmental performance, it needs to understand how its activities interact with the different components of the environment (air, water, land, natural resources). A judgement on the basis of quantified and subjective assessments will be made to assess which activities have the greatest potential impact on the environment. For many companies the use of energy, process air emissions, and waste volumes will be significant impact areas. Some of these impacts will be felt globally, some within the local community and others within the factory gates.

Life-cycle analysis (LCA) is one tool which some companies are grappling with to help them make these judgements about environmental impacts.

LCA generally comprises inventory analysis and impact analysis. The inventory analysis is mainly the collection of data on sources and quantities of resouces consumed, and quantities and treatment/disposal routes of wastes and emissions generated. This information is, in theory, required at all points of the product life-cycle, from cultivation/extraction to intermediate processing, to final processing, to packaging and distribution, to use, to disposal and to transportation movements at each stage of this activity. The impact analysis involves prescribing a measure of environmental value to the impact at each point in the inventory. In an ideal world an overall environmental rating for the product produced could be determined. There are, however, many difficulties involved in applying life-cycle analysis including:

(a)   the quality and availability of data is critical to both inventory and impact analysis. There are important shortcomings in existing information systems and value models, severely hampering the ability to provide quantitative analyses and to aggregate impact analysis;

(b)   at some point, it is inevitable that the analyses require value judgements to be made, although there are some methods for applying values more scientifically/ quantitatively. This affects how useful LCA can be as a 'management tool';

(c)   the complexity of inventory analysis for many companies makes this a massive exercise, not only within company boundaries but especially in long supply chains;

(d)   there remains the question as to whether we need a full LCA to be able to achieve the objectives of identifying those activities which have the areas of greatest environmental impact, and hence are areas for potential improvement.

It is for these reasons that LCA is still in its early stages of application.

In conjunction with the initial identification of potential impacts a review is needed of what legislation the company must comply with now or in the near future. This review stage also offers the opportunity to set out a base line of actual management organisation, systems and procedures, its compliance record and the range of initiatives already in place to improve performance. For a number of companies, managing aspects of environmental performance will not be new, particularly at specific sites with regulated processes. What is likely to be new, however, is the presence of a corporate framework embracing a clear policy with objectives, coordinated programmes for improvement and company-wide procedures which are audited regularly.

14.13 Setting objectives

Setting objectives which are measurable and achievable is an area which can cause considerable difficulties in practice. KPMG's National Environment Unit has tracked the published objectives of a wide range of organisations and has found few examples of specific, measurable environmental objectives, against which progress can be reported regularly. This is understandable because to set objectives, such as a 10 per cent reduction in energy or water use per unit of output, requires hard information about current use volumes and the reasonableness and cost effectiveness of the objective to be set. A considerable amount of work, therefore, is often required to develop sensible objectives.

It is important that the objectives set at the top level in an organisation are reflected down through that organisation, so that at each level there are targets appropriate to that particular function. A key part of ensuring continuous improvement in environmental performance is to review and update them in the light of progress and changing regulations and standards. In successful organisations this is incorporated in the overall process of setting and reviewing business objectives and targets.

The process of objective setting also needs to consider the types of performance measures which will be used to ensure the objectives are achieved. For example, if the objective is to reduce waste by 20 per cent over five years, management will need to consider what kind of performance measures are appropriate and at what levels in the business.

In the recent BIE publication produced in conjunction with KPMG, entitled *Guidelines on Measuring Environmental Performance*, a number of measures are discussed including:

(*a*)   impact measures such as quantities of waste by volume going to landfill;

(*b*)   contributor measures which relate to, for example, investment in plant and equipment, or the materials and management systems that can affect the amount of waste being produced;

(*c*)   external relations measures which reflect the consequences of the impacts, such as the number of complaints or prosecutions;

(*d*)   risk measures such as the probability of groundwater contamination arising from poor waste management.

Performance measures will need to be set at different levels of the organisation and where possible tied in to the appraisal system of business units or individuals.

14.14 Definition and allocation of responsibilities

Allocation of responsibilities is vital for successful environment management. Its implementation will typically involve changes in management systems and operations, training and awareness of personnel at all levels and in marketing and public relations.

A wide range of business functions will therefore need to be involved in developing and implementing environmental management systems. The commitment of senior personnel to introduce sound environmental management throughout the organisation, and to communicate it to all staff is vital.

Companies have adopted a range of organisational approaches as part of their environment management systems. In some cases there is a single specialist function with responsibility for monitoring and auditing the system. An alternative is to have a central environmental function with an advisory role which can also undertake verification of the internal audits carried out by divisions or departments. The approach needs to be adapted to the culture and structure of the organisation, but whatever system is adopted, there are a number of crucial elements:

(*a*)   access to expertise in assessing environmental impacts and developing solutions;

(*b*)   a degree of independence in the auditing function;

(*c*)   a clear accountability for meeting environmental management objectives;

(*d*)   adequate information systems to help those responsible for evaluating performance against objectives, to identify problem areas and to ensure that action is
taken to solve them.

14.15 Training and communications

BS 7750 puts internal training and communication as a key ingredient of the environmental management system requirements. In particular, it focuses on ensuring that
employees, at all levels, are aware of company policy and objectives; of how their own
work activities impact on the environment and the benefits of improved performance;
what they need to do in their jobs to help meet the company's environmental objectives;
and the risks to the organisation of failing to carry out standard operating procedures.

This can involve a significant investment for companies, but if integrated with existing
training modules and reinforced regularly, many hours of essential training can be
achieved. An important benefit of training is that it can be a fertile ground for new ideas
to minimise adverse environmental impacts.

Communications with, for example, regulators, investors, public bodies and local
communities is an important part of good environment management and requires a
preparedness to be open, honest and informative. It also requires clear procedures for
liaising with external groups.

14.16 Operational controls

The range and effectiveness of operational controls is as important for environment
management as it is for any other form of management. The EMAS requirements, for
example, cover such controls as:

(*a*)   documentation of policy, objectives, programmes, roles and responsibilities;

(*b*)   the compilation and maintenance of a register of significant environmental
effects such as emissions, discharges, wastes and use of natural resources;

(*c*)   the establishment and documentation of operating procedures;

(*d*)   the recording, monitoring and reviewing of performance;

(*e*)   systematic and periodic audits;

(*f*)   investigation of non-compliance and corrective action.

14.17 Information management

The cohesion factor in any environment management system is the quality and
timeliness of information. The demand for environmental information is growing fast
for both internal and external users. Most new pieces of legislation at national and EC
levels require companies to provide or make information available. More and more
companies are now providing information on their environmental performance in their
annual reports or in separate environmental reports. Without good information
systems such reports are merely green gloss.

The complexity of information needs is also increasing. Although much environmental
data has common basic characteristics such as information on toxic substances, waste,
or air emissions, different regulators will set different definitions and requirements.
Furthermore data has to be gathered from many sources such as suppliers, externally
or internally across several sites and process control systems.

14.18   Environmental Management

The full range of systems applications will be needed including database management, modelling, measuring, monitoring and flexible reporting. The key issues for businesses to consider are:

(a)   how can such a wide range of information be managed to ensure effective environmental management? Management will need to cover different geographic locations, different processes and different business functions. There is likely to be a need for setting data and reporting standards and providing some company-wide application tools;

(b)   what information technology system developments are needed to meet information needs? There will at least be a need to develop some new applications, raising the question of how environmental information systems will interface with existing systems (in particular those used for managing health and safety). This is likely to require some investment and the setting of technical development parameters/standards.

To identify and manage the environmental information requirements is a significant challenge facing many companies.

14.18   BENEFITS OF ENVIRONMENTAL MANAGEMENT

Effective environmental management

Effective environmental management will involve changes across all business functions. It requires commitment from senior management and is likely to need additional human and financial resources initially. However, it can also offer significant benefits to businesses. These include:

(a)   the avoidance of liability and risk. Good environmental management allows businesses to choose when and how to invest in better environmental performance, rather than reacting at the last minute to new legislation or consumer pressures. Unforseen problems will be minimised, prosecution and litigation avoided;

(b)   the gaining of competitive advantage. A business with sound environmental management is more likely to make a good impact on its customers. The business will be better placed to identify and respond rapidly to opportunities for new products and services, to take advantage of 'green' markets and also respond to the increasing demand for information on supplier environmental performance;

(c)   the achievement of a better profile with investors, employees and the public. Increasingly investors and their advisors are avoiding companies with a poor environmental record. Environmental performance of businesses is an increasing concern for existing staff and potential recruits. Some businesses are finding that a good environmental record helps to boost their public image.

(d)   the achievement of cost savings from better management of wastes through attention to recovering, reusing and recycling; and reduced bills from more careful use of energy.

Effective environmental management can turn environmental issues from an area of threatened cost to one of profit and opportunity. As standards for environmental management are adopted and are widely applied, the question will increasingly become, as with quality management, can a company afford not to adopt environmental management? The external pressures on organisations to improve environmental performance are unlikely to abate. Environmental management systems can help companies respond to the pressures in a timely and cost-effective way.

15 Green Investment

'Every professional investor should filter investment ideas through an ecology screen.'
(Chief Strategist, Morgan Stanley, *Global Investor*, No 27, 1989)

15.1 INTRODUCTION

The origins of green investment in the UK can be found in the emergence of ethical funds in the early nineteen eighties. The demand for ethical investment came from religious groups and concerned individuals who wished to refrain from investment in companies linked to South Africa, gambling, the production of tobacco or the trade in armaments. The UK's first ethical fund, the Friends Provident Stewardship Fund, was launched in 1984 and incorporated a range of positive social investment criteria and negative 'avoidance' criteria.

Investors sought to support enterprises on positive grounds, for example, encouraging the involvement of companies in the community and those implementing equal opportunity initiatives. The natural extension of this was concern for the environment and in 1988, the Merlin Jupiter Ecology Fund was launched. Its aim was to invest in companies which made a positive contribution to social justice, protection of the environment and wise use of natural resources. Within the context of the sustainable development debate, environmental issues are now central to socially responsible investment.

Socially responsible investment (SRI) in the UK has grown in size and influence and there are now 30 funds, 13 pension schemes and eleven PEPs guided by social or environmental criteria. To 1992, total investments amounted to approximately £320 million, whereas in 1989 the figure stood at £144 million. This represents a 120 per cent increase compared to the unit trust business as a whole, which rose by 20 per cent over the same period. This rate of increase has continued. According to the *Ethical Investor* newsletter, of July 1992 and published by the Ethical Investment Research Service (EIRIS), over the period June 1991 to June 1992, the amount of money invested in ethical funds increased by more than 17 per cent, whereas the total invested in general unit trusts only rose by 3 per cent. In September 1993, according to the PIRC Intelligence Newsletter, ethical investment products have a combined value of £621 million, of which £391 million is in unit trusts.

As well as responding to the marketing opportunities, financial institutions now recognise that with the problems of contaminated land, they may be affected by environmental liability costs. This has the potential of eroding the value of investments. Two of the first sectors to have been affected have been the property and insurance sectors. The Government set up the Advisory Committee on Business and the Environment to make recommendations on future environmental policy. One of the key taskforces was the Financial Sector Working Group, which reported its findings in March 1993. One of its recommendations is that the London Stock Exchange should consider adopting standards of environmental disclosure by companies as one of its listing particulars. Another is that each company or firm in the financial sector should publish an environmental policy statement, which should include quantifiable objectives and targets for environmental performance.

This chapter attempts to disentangle various investor responses to the environmental agenda, and to summarise the UK experience of integrating environmental issues into investment decisions. Examples refer to the UK, unless otherwise stated. Issues covered include definitions of green investment, analysis of the objectives of green funds, an assessment of the methodology employed by some of the funds and finally, integration of environmental concerns into the running of institutional investment funds.

15.2   DEFINITIONS

In the specialist field of SRI, there is considerable overlap in the choice of definitions and the investor's understanding of the practice of ethical and green investing. The term 'green investing' is wide reaching in definition. It is used by both ethical funds and environmental funds. It embraces the management of funds by ethical criteria, for example, the avoidance of companies with military, tobacco or nuclear connections, as well as avoidance of companies which cause pollution and other types of environmental damage.

Green investing embraces positive values, ranging from services provided to the green consumer and to industry, through to the encouragement of companies leading in the development of internal environmental management systems. The fact that a company does not provide environmental services as their core business, would not necessarily preclude them from a green fund. Furthermore, because the nuclear, tobacco and defence industries (often treated as ethical issues) have their own environmental impacts, a number of green funds screen out companies with involvement in these businesses.

15.3   Environmental investing

The terms 'green investing' and 'environmental investing' are often used interchangeably. Environmental investing is commonly used by the City to describe the management of funds invested in companies providing environmental services. Typically, these are specialist waste management or pollution control technology services. Environmental service providers are treated by a number of fund managers as a sub-division of the stock market and companies are analysed purely on market share and financial merit, rather than assessed on their overall contribution to sustainable development.

Some environmental funds do not apply social assessment to their investments. The Eagle Star Environmental Opportunity Trust, for example, states in its Manager's Report that it is not an SRI fund:

> 'Since the provision of superior investment performance is considered by the managers to be no less important than the environmental issue, the trust should in no way be labelled as green, or ethical'.

Simply because of the environmental nature of their services or products, some environmental funds may invest in companies unacceptable to ethical investors. For example, the most popular sector amongst environmental funds has been the waste management sector, even though many companies within this sector are avoided by some ethical or green investors. The reasons for avoidance are poor environmental standards and the use of controversial technologies such as incineration. Some of the companies in environmental funds, have been the target of focused campaigns by groups such as Greenpeace.

15.4   Green investing

Because green investing has its historical roots in the ethical investment movement, this group of investors, rather than environmental investors described above, have perhaps the most important contribution to make in the debate on definitions. Green investors are equally interested in seeing a company keep to high standards of internal environmental excellence, as well as supporting a particular environmental product or service they might provide. Ethical investors who invest in environmentally responsible companies have adopted two broad approaches.

15.5   Negative screening

Many ethical funds make environmental claims, principally, they seek to avoid companies which cause environmental damage. By using specialist screening services, investors can avoid companies which, for example, produce or use CFCs, tropical hardwood or gases which contribute to global warming. These funds are only 'green' in the sense that they avoid the worst environmental offenders, rather than positively seeking to invest in companies on the cutting edge of the sustainable development debate.

Negative screening tends to treat individual environmental issues as ethical issues, (in much the same way as gambling or tobacco is treated), which a screening process will eliminate. It does, however, have the effect of treating environmental issues in isolation. It can exclude whole sector groups such as the water and chemical sectors. This form of screening benefits neutral companies and, by ignoring issues not covered by a screen, can even favour companies which cause other forms of environmental damage. Some funds which claim to be both ethical and green, consequently invest in industries such as the building materials, textiles, property, printing or dry cleaning sectors. These sectors may have greater environmental impacts (and financial liabilities in the case of property) than those companies and sectors which have been 'screened out' environmentally.

Whilst some funds treat environmental issues in isolation, a study of Environmental Investment Funds by Magne Y Orgland for Beitrage zu Okonomie und Okologie of Switzerland in 1990 found that some funds exclude whole industrial sectors. The Commercial Union Environmental Exempt Pension Fund for example, will

'neither invest in industries where environmental abuse is commonplace like building, heavy chemicals, oil or mining industries nor industries which are only passively beneficial like engineering, electricals or electronics'.

15.6   Positive screening

Positively invested green funds seek to invest in responsible companies with good environmental track records. The Merlin Jupiter Ecology Fund, for example, employs this positive approach whilst seeking to avoid environmental offenders. This approach operates alongside a negative ethical screen which excludes companies making more than 1 per cent of pre-tax profits from the tobacco, defence and nuclear industries or South Africa.

Unlike negative screening, which attempts to introduce objectivity in the appraisal of companies, positive screening often involves making subjective judgements. A priority is placed upon looking at all factors together, rather than treating environmental issues in isolation. Hence the considerable emphasis placed upon in-depth research.

Positive screening may define a green company as one operating in an environmentally beneficial sector, such as recycling and energy conservation. In addition, green funds seek to invest in companies which strive to improve their overall environmental performance, no matter what business or industrial sector they are in. This definition sees 'greenness' as an internal attitude or commitment by companies to introduce products, processes, management controls and systems which minimise environmental

15.7 Green Investment

impact. This broader vision of what constitutes a green company, is increasingly being applied by green investors who try to pick companies exemplifying best practice within industrial sectors.

15.7 ENVIRONMENTAL/GREEN FUNDS

The most common form of green investment fund is the unit trust. A number of green funds come in the form of an investment trust, an investment bond, or a Personal Equity Plan (PEP) and pension funds (retirement plans) which are outlined below. Investors may select between these funds depending upon financial objectives and security.

The UK's first green fund, the Merlin Jupiter Ecology Fund (managed by Jupiter Tyndall Merlin) was launched in 1988. 1989 saw the launch of the Eagle Star Environmental Opportunities Trust, the TSB's Environmental Investor's Fund, the Merlin International Green Investment Trust plc and Commercial Union's Environmental Exempt Pension Fund. 1990 saw the launch of the Clerical Medical Evergreen Trust, the Homeowners Friendly Society Green Chip Fund, the TR Ecotech Environmental Fund and the CIS Environ Trust. In 1992, the Commercial Union Environmental Investment Trust was launched. 1992 saw the launch of the Citibank Life Green Fund (managed by Jupiter Tyndall Merlin) and the Sun Life Ecological Fund.

15.8 Environmental/green unit trusts

Unit trust investment is one of the most popular means of investing in the UK and the majority of green funds come in this form. According to the Unit Trust Association, up to September 1992, there were over 4.4 million corporate and individual unit holder accounts, with 1,423 unit trusts in existence, accounting for £51,632 billion worth of investments. Of these funds, around 30 are green/ethical unit trusts. As SRI funds together account for approximately £320 million, this figure represents only a very small proportion of unit trust investment overall.

Unit trusts are a form of collective investment where investors pool their money in a professionally managed fund which provides investors with a simple and cost efficient access to world stock markets. The actual markets and sectors invested are determined by the stated objectives of the trust and selected by the fund manager. The trust is divided into units of equal value and the value of each unit is determined by the underlying value of the shares of the companies in which the fund is invested.

The following looks at some of the objectives of the main green unit trusts and the volume of funds under management. The figures are up to date to September 1993.

Merlin Jupiter Ecology Fund

Green: Invests worldwide in companies making a positive commitment to social well-being and the protection and wise use of the natural environment.

Ethical: The fund seeks to avoid investment in companies which make more than 1 per cent pre-tax profits from armaments, nuclear industries, tobacco or South Africa. In addition, companies are also assessed on social criteria such as policies on animal testing, attitude to women, minorities and the community.

Funds under management: £10 million

174

Eagle Star Environmental Opportunities Trust

Green: To invest in companies which take a positive approach to environmental issues and thereby share in their success.

Ethical: None

Funds under management: £10.3 million

TSB Environmental Investor Fund

Green: To invest in companies that demonstrate a positive commitment to the protection of the environment and preservation of the natural environment.

Ethical: None

Funds under management: £22.9 million

Clerical Medical Evergreen Trust

Green: To invest internationally in shares of companies whose products, processes or services contribute to the restoration and renewal of the earth's ecology or to a cleaner or healthier environment. Avoids companies engaged in the fur trade, production of tropical hardwoods and harmful pesticides and animal testing for cosmetics use. Some company categories are eliminated due to the harmful nature of their activities upon the environment.

Ethical: Will seek to avoid companies engaged in the manufacture of armaments, companies involved in South Africa or other oppressive regimes to the extent of 10 per cent of their turnover and eliminate companies engaged in tobacco, gambling and the production and distribution of pornography.

Funds under management: £11.9 million

CIS Environ Trust

Green: Investment will be limited to companies which are likely to benefit from measures taken to improve the environment, human welfare and the quality of life.

Ethical: Excludes companies with more than 10 per cent exposure to countries with oppressive political regimes; engaging in unnecessary experiments causing distress to animals; the production of armaments; and the manufacture of tobacco-related products.

Funds under management: £19.7 million

Citibank Life Green Fund

Green: To invest worldwide in companies that demonstrate a commitment to conducting their business in an environmentally responsible way as well as companies who are directly involved in environmental protection.

Ethical: The fund will not invest in companies which derive more than 1 per cent of pre-tax profits from tobacco, armaments and the nuclear industries.

Funds under management: £1.2 million (Launched July 1992)

15.9   Personal Equity Plans

Personal Equity Plans (PEPs) were introduced in 1987 and through being free of taxes on capital growth and income, were designed to encourage small investors to invest directly in equities.

15.10 Green Investment

Henderson Green PEP

Green: Invest in well managed, environmentally conscious companies that are actively involved in providing cleaner air, water treatment and pollution controls, waste disposal processes or products that contribute towards healthier living.

Ethical: According to Henderson, although the Green PEP 'is not an ethical fund as such, you can rest assured that we are unlikely to choose companies which are heavily involved in the tobacco or defence industries. Nor will we support companies that test drugs on animals or that deal with repressive regimes'.   (September 1992)

Funds under management: £7 million

15.10 Life assurance bond funds

A number of green funds, such as the Eagle Star Environmental Opportunity Trust and the Clerical Medical Evergreen Trust offer a bond facility. The bond differs from a unit trust, most significantly in taxation.

The Homeowners Green Chip Fund is available only as a bond and is a single-premium life assurance bond. In the event of the death of the investor, 101 per cent of the investment value (the number of units held at the bid price) of the units held would be payable as a lump sum.

Homeowners Green Chip Fund

Green: Invest in those companies that are making a positive contribution to the protection or enhancement of the environment, both physical and social.

Ethical: Activities regarded as 'areas of concern' are companies seen to be taking advantage of a situation arising in a country with an oppressive regime; have military contracts; are involved in the nuclear power industry (except where acting in a clean up capacity); conduct experiments on animals for the purpose of developing cosmetic products; pollute the environment; or 'have involvement' with either tropical hardwoods or pesticides.

Funds under management: £6.9 million

15.11 Pension funds

Changes in pensions legislation, for example, enabling contracting out of the State Earnings Related Pension Scheme, have made it easier for individuals to select an ethical/green option. A number of funds have a pension choice available, such as the Clerical Medical Evergreen and Citibank Life Green Funds. The following example is of a specialist pension fund, the Commercial Union Environmental Exempt Pension Fund, which is only available as an exempt unit trust pension fund with a minimum initial investment of £25,000.

Commercial Union Environmental Exempt Pension Fund

Green: Invest in companies which are directly involved in the provision of products and services which improve the environment. This includes areas such as water treatment; recycling; emission control systems; waste collection treatment and disposal; hazardous waste facilities; and energy and conservation.

Ethical: None.

Funds under management: £10.1 million

15.12 Investment trusts

An investment trust is a company quoted on the London Stock Exchange whose sole business is to invest in the shares of other companies. There are currently two funds of this type available, the Merlin International Green Investment Trust plc, which was launched in 1989, and the Commercial Union Environmental Investment Trust plc, launched in 1992.

Merlin International Green Investment Trust plc

Green: As for the Merlin Jupiter Ecology Fund.

Ethical: As above.

Funds under management: £30 million

Commercial Union Environmental Investment Trust plc

Green: As for Commercial Union Environmental Exempt Pension.

Ethical: None.

Funds under management: £16.5 million

15.13 GREEN/ENVIRONMENTAL FUND CRITERIA

Outlined below are examples of the criteria for a typical green fund, the CIS Environ Fund and a typical environmental fund, the TSB Environmental Investors Fund.

15.14 *CIS Environ Fund*

This fund combines environmental objectives with an ethical screen. The principal environmental criteria are positive ones, with selection of companies according to the following guidelines.

(*a*)   Companies whose activities are totally involved in helping to protect the environment, human health, safety and the quality of life.

(*b*)   Companies which have a significant subsidiary or division involved in the types of activities described in 15.1 above.

(*c*)   Companies which are expected to be long term beneficiaries of changing attitudes towards the protection of the environment and the enhancement of human health and safety.

CIS literature notes that companies which are known to produce significant amounts of pollution are not excluded totally, since investments might be justified in cases where the management have shown a constructive attitude towards environmental issues and are making efforts, significantly greater than those required merely to comply with advancing legislation, to clean up their processes.

CIS: ethical criteria

The literature notes that the Trust does not invest in companies where a significant proportion of turnover arises from activities with which most of its potential investors would not wish to be associated. The proportion regarded as significant for this purpose will vary according to circumstances but in no case will it be greater than 10 per cent. The activities concern:

(i)   countries with oppressive regimes;

15.15 Green Investment

(ii)   unnecessary experiments which cause distress to animals;

(iii) the production of armaments;

(iv)   the manufacture of tobacco and tobacco-related products.

15.15 *TSB Environmental Investor Fund*

The TSB Environmental Investor Fund is an environmental fund with no explicit ethical criteria. With £22.9 million of funds under management, it is one of the largest funds in this sector. Its aim is to invest in companies which demonstrate a positive commitment to conserving the natural environment.

Companies are selected by the fund manager for compliance with TSB's eleven areas of consideration and their investment potential. The Conservation Foundation sends companies an environmental questionnaire from which it prepares a report. This is presented to a committee chaired by Dr David Bellamy, to ascertain whether a company is approved for the fund. The TSB has identified eleven areas of consideration. Some companies may qualify in one only, some in several.

(*a*)   *Forestry*: companies that use acceptably and sustainably managed forest plantations to supply wood as raw materials. They would be unlikely to manage or retail tropical rainforest woods.

(*b*)   *Ozone layer*: companies that have taken steps to stop the use of chloroflourocarbons (CFCs) in aerosols or foam packing or who have controlled CFC emissions from refrigeration plants.

(*c*)   *Recycling*: companies that have taken initiatives in the following areas: recycled paper or cardboard; bottle banks or refundable glass bottles; recycling waste; biodegradable packaging; the use of reverse vending machines.

(*d*)   *Sensitive land use*: companies that demonstrate leadership in the use of derelict inner-city land; the screening of sites; or the reinstatement of the environment after extraction or development.

(*e*)   *Acid rain*: companies that make efforts to significantly reduce sulphur dioxide emissions; that actively prevent or clean up acid rain; or that look for new production methods to avoid the problem.

(*f*)   *Energy conservation*: these companies fall into two categories: those that have achieved a significant reduction in fuel bills by efficient energy conservation, and those that use energy efficiently in the production of goods, for example, those using insulation materials or solar heating.

(*g*)   *Transport*: this could range from the use of lead-free petrol in company cars; the production and/or sale of more energy efficient or environmentally friendly transportation, such as cars with fuel efficient engines and corrosion-free bodies.

(*h*)   *Pollution control*: companies involved in the control of emissions of nitrates, oil, chemicals, and so on into waterways or the atmosphere; controlling the use of bleaches for paper products; or water or sewage treatment.

(*j*)   *Animal and plant welfare*: companies that actively avoid the use of endangered species of raw material, for example, jewellery or cosmetics manufacturers, and companies that take steps to preserve the natural habitats of flora and fauna threatened by developments of that company and others.

(*k*)   *Healthy eating*: is the company involved in growing, producing or retailing organic produce to Soil Association standards? Does the company actively avoid the production or use of drugs or hormones used to promote yields through intensive farming?

(*l*)   *Community*: does the company sponsor environmental projects? Does it have evidence of comprehensive employee health and safety initiatives?

15.16 RESEARCH METHODOLOGIES

The CIS Environ Fund and the TSB Environmental Investor Fund employ different criteria. Especially in the case of ethical funds, the criteria the funds adopt can dictate the research methods used. Investors and financial advisors are keen to ensure that the criteria for green funds are clearly defined. Company managers are also interested in the assessment process.

Jupiter Tyndall Merlin (JTM) employs its own team of environmental/social scientists, the Merlin Research Unit, to assess corporate environmental performance. It has published a criteria paper entitled 'The Assessment Process for Green Investment', details of which are outlined below.

15.17 'The Assessment Process for Green Investment'

In the JTM investment process, a full profile of the company is built up involving the assessment of management, process and product. Particular regard is given to the following.

(*a*)   *Management and policy*

Enlightened and effective management is fundamental to improving corporate environmental performance. Aspects targeted are:

  (i)   *management quality*: general competence and integrity of management, proper management systems, whether the company is registered under the British Standards Institute BS 5750 scheme for Quality of Management, or is pursuing BS 7750 Environmental Management accreditation;

  (ii)   *stance*: the seriousness and sympathy with which problems raised are treated, the involvement of the board in environmental matters, the resources available for action;

  (iii)   *corporate policies towards the environment*: adequacy of the policies, for example, whether there is a formal Environmental Policy Statement, how well it is communicated, effectiveness of implementation;

  (iv)   *focus*: the level of designated responsibility for the environment, the quality of leadership and how far it is likely to sustain motivation;

  (v)   *staff*: how fully employees are informed and involved, the provision of training, environmental performance as a criterion for promotion;

  (vi)   *monitoring*: how well the company monitors its own environmental performance, how often and in what manner its policy is reviewed, whether it is submitting factory sites for the EC Eco-Management and Audit Regulation;

  (vii)   *corporate disclosure*: how open the company is to external enquiries, how fully it makes available information especially on environmental and social matters;

  (viii)   *procurement*: whether there is a purchasing policy related to environmental and social concerns; and

(ix)   *community involvement*: membership of Business in the Community, the Per Cent Club and other initiatives, level and nature of sponsorship and donations to community projects, secondment programmes.

(*b*)   *Process*

A company's processes are assessed in order to find out how far the policies and intentions stated are brought to bear in practice. Research also seeks to assess the willingness to invest in cleaner technologies, whilst recognising that something more is required than 'end-of-pipe' remedial measures. Equally, compliance with current legislation is expected to be regarded as a minimum rather than simply a target.

Aspects targeted are:

(i)   *pollution*: the nature and extent of emissions to air, water and land, and noise and other nuisances, and the approach to reducing or avoiding them, including track record in meeting or improving standards set by regulatory bodies;

(ii)   *waste*: the efforts being made to minimise the creation of waste matter, the extent to which it is reused, the methods of disposal;

(iii)   *energy*: how diligently the company is trying to conserve energy and to switch to less polluting and renewable sources;

(iv)   *materials*: the extent to which the use of non-renewable materials is minimised, the care taken to obtain materials from sustainable sources where possible;

(v)   *transport*: the steps being taken to reduce the need for and the environmental impact of the movement of raw materials and products; and

(vi)   *land use*: whether new buildings and operations are designed to protect and improve the environment and are sited to avoid places of amenity or wildlife value; whether neglected land is favoured; extent and nature of landscaping of existing sites.

(*c*)   *Products*

The assessment of products, covering goods and services, aims to be as objective and penetrating as possible. Claims of greenness are not taken at face value. Environmental data is gleaned from investigations in consumer publications, though in some areas it is recognised that information is not readily available. Implementation of the EC's eco-labelling scheme will be helpful in this assessment area.

The key aspects targeted are:

(i)   *worth*: to what extent the goods or services produced are necessary and useful;

(ii)   *R & D*: the emphasis in research and development on improving environmental performance of future products;

(iii)   *environmental impacts*: to what extent current products are energy efficient, long lasting, not damaging on disposal, capable of being reclaimed etc.;

(iv)   *packaging and labelling*: whether packaging is the least necessary and is biodegradable or reclaimable, the information given to the consumer about contents, energy rating, correct use and disposal; and

(v)   *overseas markets*: whether products banned in one country are marketed in others, whether standards are maintained in selling to other countries, whether due care is taken to label (see above) for users overseas.

At the beginning of 1993, JTM was approached by the Chartered Association of Certified Accountants (ACCA) for permission to publish the criteria paper as part of their occasional series on green accounting.

15.18 GATHERING INFORMATION ON ENVIRONMENTAL CLAIMS

Compared to SRI practitioners in the US, researchers in the UK lack the same freedom of access to information. Green investors in the UK have to make assessments on corporate environmental performance based on a combination of public registers, questionnaires, news services and from information supplied by companies. Only a few companies bring all the relevant information together in one place, in an environmental report, and of these, only a few of these are independently verified.

The Body Shop's Managing Director, John Jackson, states that

'we believe that there is an important role to be played by investment funds in *insisting* [their emphasis] that companies in green portfolios do meet public disclosure and independent verification criteria. Without this it is very hard to see how investors can be really sure of the environmental performance of companies in the portfolio'. (Personal Communication 16 December 1991).

More companies are providing detailed information to green investors on their environmental impacts in clear and precise form. However only a few have gone as far as producing environmental reports. Of these, the majority tend to be from the ex-State owned industries such as British Telecom, British Gas and some of the water companies. These reports, though sometimes lacking in the attention to detail which can be found in their American or German counterparts, nonetheless are beginning to play a key role in the environmental assessment process. British Airways, for example, held in the TSB Environmental Investors Fund published an in-depth report which later went on to win the prestigious Environmental Reporting Awards Scheme run by ACCA, the Chartered Association of Certified Accountants.

15.19 A MODEL GREEN FUND

The following model fund is a selection of companies which regularly feature in ethical/green funds, and is used to illustrate how the above definitions, criteria and research methodology lead to the creation of a green investment portfolio.

(a)   *Body Shop International*: Retail chain renowned for bringing social and animal welfare issues to the high street, with an excellent environmental record.

(b)   *British Polythene*: Leading recycler of polythene and manufacturer of polythene products with a high recycled content.

(c)   *California Energy*: An American company which has successfully specialised in the exploration and development of geothermal 'hot rocks' energy.

(d)   *Casket*: One of the UK's leading manufacturers and distributors of bicycles.

(e)   *Freeman Group*: As a supplier of insulation material to the domestic and industrial markets, energy conservation is its key business.

(f)   *Grontmij*: A Dutch company specialising in the remediation of contaminated land and cleansing polluted water.

(g)   *Halma*: Manufacturer of health and safety equipment for pollution monitoring and disinfection uses.

(h)   *IMCO Recycling*: The world's largest independent recycler of used aluminium cans.

(j)   *Manweb*: With environmental issues central to the company's policy making process, they have commissioned a six megawatt wind farm in Cornwall and are researching wind projects with 40 megawatt potential.

(k)   *New World Power*: The first listed windpower company engaged in the refurbishment of Californian windfarms.

(l)   *Neotronics Technology*: Manufactures instruments for the detection, measurement and analysis of gases. Winner of Queen's Award for Industry for its Fuel Efficiency Monitor (FEM).

(m)   *Powerscreen*: Leading manufacturer of mobile crushing equipment, for recycling building aggregate, and manufacturer of equipment for sewage waste processing and recycling.

(n)   *Wellman*: The largest recycler of plastic (PET) and fibre wastes in the USA.

(o)   *Wessex Water*: A water and waste management company which has adopted an innovative sewage processing facility. Has the best environmental record from amongst its competitors.

15.20 INSTITUTIONAL INVESTORS

'Like it or not, the days when portfolio decisions could be made in a complete moral and social vacuum are numbered.' (*Financial Times* Editorial 14 April 1990)

Growing numbers of institutional investors, faced with pressure from investors or fund trustees, are incorporating environmental concerns into investment management. Mr Philip Scott, Senior Investment Manager of Norwich Union Fund Managers stated in a speech to the Institute for International Research (IRR) in September 1989 that

'the funds of our customers are entrusted to us and as they become more environmentally aware then so must we in the management of these funds'.

The State is no longer seen as the principal mechanism for achieving social goals. In the words of a *Green Alliance* news editorial in June 1992

'it is increasingly evident that private capital is the means by which wider social and environmental values will be met in the future'.

Because of investment constraints, larger institutions are adopting a proactive approach which seeks to influence company management on environmental matters. This is part of the wider corporate governance debate in which institutions are encouraged to take a more active interest in the companies in which they invest. The type of pressure being applied by institutions varies according to the objectives of the funds.

The funds of local authorities, for example, are likely to be more proactive than the general funds managed by traditional investment houses. The most notable example of pension funds working together can be found in the signatories, representing assets of more than £10 billion, to the PIRC (Pension Investment Research Consultants) *UK Environmental Investor Code*. Signatories include the Lewisham Superannuation Fund and the South Yorkshire Authority Pension Fund. Two of the points of the *Code* call upon companies to establish procedures that will lead to incremental improvements in environmental performance, and to make available to shareholders regular progress reports on implementation of environmental policy.

15.21 *Richmond Council: example of the proactive approach*

Richmond Council, a local authority in Greater London, is well known amongst environmentalists for its activities in the fields of recycling and nature conservation. Its Investment Panel has taken a keen interest in the subject of ethical investment in the past. But being constrained by laws governing fiduciary responsibility, councillors took the path of the proactive approach, principally by scrutinising the credentials of some of the companies in which it invests.

The Investment Panel, made up of Officers and Members, exists to oversee the investment of pension contributions made by the Council and its employees. The fund has approximately £70 million invested in the shares of many well-known companies. The Panel invited Anglian Water plc, in which it is an investor, to make a presentation on its approach with particular emphasis on environmental matters. The Group Director of Finance of Anglian Water and their Director of Quality were asked to outline policies on metering, water loss, fluoridation, removal of pesticides and nitrates from drinking water, safe bathing and recreational amenities.

The Panel Chairman, Councillor Serge Lourie, commented that

'we wanted to take a more active shareholder approach and try to influence the attitudes of some of the companies in which we invest. We chose Anglian Water as a pilot and were very satisfied with the way they demonstrated their concerns for the environment. It is obviously a company which is aware of current environmental issues and which takes its responsibilities seriously'.

It plans to invite other companies in which it invests to come and make similar presentations.

15.22 *Norwich Union Fund Managers*

Norwich Union is an example of a fund management group which has set an investment policy to influence corporate environmental strategies at every level. According to Philip Scott,

'We feel that all of our funds should have a green tinge and we should use our financial muscle to bring about change where appropriate. This method of effecting change from within is likely to yield far greater results than simply setting up a green unit trust. Think of it in money terms – a green unit trust would take £20 million . . . compare this with the power of continuing to invest all £16,900 million of Norwich Union's assets in a socially responsible manner!' (IRR Speech)

Norwich Union have implemented a programme of dialogue with company management on environmental grounds. The company has released a statement of its environmental policy, which is to use its influence to encourage high standards of environmental performance in the companies in which it invests.

Norwich Union Fund Managers (NUFM) are to:

(a)   encourage companies to:

    (i)   monitor regularly the environmental impact of their business operations

    (ii)   establish procedures which will lead to improvements in environmental performance

    (iii)   comply, as a minimum, with current environmental legislation and anticipate future legislative demands and to adopt environmental good practice

    (iv)   make available to shareholders environmental reports relating to their business practices

     (v)   recognise the need for commitment to environmental issues;

(b)   operate a structured programme of communication and contact with company chairmen, senior management and investor relations managers on business strategy, including environmental policy and performance;

(c)   maintain records of a company's environmental performance which will be regularly updated;

(d)   report regularly to investment management on the environmental performance of companies within the investment portfolio;

(e)   communicate Norwich Union policies to staff, customers and companies in which Norwich Union invests to encourage Norwich Union's overall environmental policy objectives.

Philip Scott concludes that

'there is no doubt that companies will have to provide much more information on the green impact of their operations. Such information on corporate activities is essential if investors are to make investment decisions based on environmental as well as financial considerations. It's no good if a company spends millions to promote a conservation-minded image on the one hand, if it helps to destroy the Amazon with the other and does not present shareholders with the whole truth'.

15.23 CONCLUSIONS

This chapter has overseen the development of green investing, with particular focus on fund criteria. It has ended with a discussion of the role of institutional funds in taking a greater interest in the environmental consequences of companies in which they invest. SRI continues to grow in influence and because the wider public and the trustees of pension funds are always likely to care about environmental issues, the phenomenon of the socially aware investor is unlikely to go away.

For companies seeking the attention of the ethical investor, they could start with a corporate policy commitment to act as 'good citizens'. The work of the Institute of Business Ethics is particularly helpful in this respect. Future business strategy and current business activities could be re-evaluated in the light of ethical considerations. Resources are required to ensure that corporate citizenship is understood in word and deed by the wider community, shareholders and company personnel.

The challenge to pension fund trustees and to the wider investing public is to consider whether, through the direction of their shareholdings, they have an indirect impact upon the environment. One of the first tasks might be to review existing portfolios, by taking specialist advice from organisations such as EIRIS and the Merlin Research Unit. Investors might also contact an independent financial advisor who specialises in green/ethical investment (names available from the UK Social Investment Forum) and consider the investment options available.

Appendix 15A

Useful addresses

Ethical Investment Research Service (EIRIS)
4.01 Bondway Business Centre
71 Bondway
London SW8 1SQ

Tel: 071 735 1351
Fax: 071 735 5323

Merlin Research Unit
Jupiter Tyndall Merlin
Knightsbridge House
197 Knightsbridge
London SW7 1RB

Tel: 071 412 0703
Fax: 071 581 3857

Pensions Investment Research Consultants
Challoner House
19–21 Clerkenwell Close
London EC1R 0AA

Tel: 071 972 9060
Fax: 071 972 9061

UK Social Investment Forum
Vassali House
20 Central Road
Leeds LS1 6DE

Tel: 0532 429600

Institute of Business Ethics
12 Palace Street
London SW1E 5JA

Tel: 071 931 0495

15.23   Green Investment

Appendix 15B

Further reading

1. Miller, Alan, *Socially Responsible Investment, the financial impact of screened investment in the 1990s* (Financial Times Business Information, London 1991).

2. Kinder, Lydenbery and Domini (Ed), *The Social Investment Almanac, a comprehensive guide to socially responsible investing* (Henry Holt & Company, New York, 1992).

3. Simpson, Anne, *The Greening of Global Investment, how the environment, ethics and politics are reshaping strategies* (The Economist Publications 1991).

4. Gray, RH, *The Greening of Accountancy: The Profession After Pearce* (Certified Research Report 17, The Chartered Association of Certified Accountants, London: 1990).

5. Hill, Julie, *Towards Good Environmental Practice: A Book of Case Studies.* (Institute of Business Ethics, London: 1992).

6. Clutterbuck, Dearlove and Snow (Ed), *Actions Speak Louder: A Management Guide to Corporate Social Responsibility* (Kogan Page, London 1992).

7. Mackenzie, Craig, *The Shareholder Action Handbook: Using Shares to make Companies more Accountable* (New Consumer Ltd, Newcastle 1993).

8. Deloitte Touche Tohmatsu, *IISD and Sustainability. Coming Clean, Corporate Environmental Reporting: Opening Up for Sustainable Development* (Published by Deloitte Touche Tohmatsu, London 1993).

9. Campanale, Willenbacher and Wilks, *Survey of Ethical and Environmental Funds in Continental Europe* (Merlin Research Unit, 1993).

16 Integrated Pollution Control

16.1 THE CONCEPT

Integrated pollution control (IPC) was introduced into the law of England and Wales by *Part I* of the *Environmental Protection Act 1990* to regulate emissions from the most potentially polluting industries. The concept is a simple one. It is a system of regulation that recognises that the three elements that may be polluted by industrial activity – water, air and land (the three 'receiving media') – are not self-contained, but interrelate. Waste deposited on land may contaminate water. Atmospheric emissions can return to the earth, for example, in the form of 'acid rain'. 'The environment' operates not in discrete elements, but as an integrated whole.

IPC takes account of this 'cross-media' dimension and recognises that the sensible approach to pollution control is to seek to ensure that the right balance is struck – that in prescribing emission standards and techniques for industry, the best overall option is selected which minimises pollution in the round. A trade-off between the three elements may be necessary. For example, it may be necessary to accept a lower standard of water quality than might be possible if that better standard can only be achieved at the expense of worse air pollution. The point at which this balance is to be struck is called the 'best practicable environmental option'. *Section 7* of the *Environmental Protection Act 1990* places on the regulatory body, Her Majesty's Inspectorate of Pollution (HMIP), the task of minimising pollution caused by designated processes:

> 'to the environment taken as a whole . . . having regard to the best practicable environmental option available'.

16.2 THE DEVELOPMENT OF IPC

Before the *Environmental Protection Act*, legal controls over emissions took the form of a patchwork of controls operated by a patchwork of official bodies each concerned with a single medium (air, water, land) and sometimes with a single type of pollutant, such as radioactive substances or hazardous wastes. There was some recognition of the inter-dependency of the receiving media. Under the *Control of Pollution Act 1974*, for example, a local waste disposal authority could not grant a licence for a landfill waste site without consulting with the local water authority (later the National Rivers Authority) in case the waste contaminated water supplies or local streams and rivers. But this type of liaison did not amount to a fully integrated approach to environmental protection.

In the UK, the first suggestion for an integrated approach to pollution control was made in 1976 in the fifth report of the Royal Commission on Environmental Pollution – 'Air Pollution Control – An Integrated Approach'. The Report identified the need for a single integrated enforcement agency as the first step in establishing cross-media control. However, twelve years were to pass before the first steps were taken to implement the Report's recommendations by the establishment of Her Majesty's Inspectorate of Pollution. IPC was not introduced until 1 April 1991, following the enactment of *Part I* of the *Environmental Protection Act*.

16.3 HMIP was created by bringing together the various central government Pollution Inspectorates into a single body. The constituent inspectorates were:

— the Industrial Air Pollution Inspectorate (IAPI), (formerly the Alkali Inspectorate) concerned with emissions into the air from heavy industry;

16.4 Integrated Pollution Control

— the Radiochemical Inspectorate, responsible under the *Radioactive Substances Act 1960* for controlling the storage and use of radioactive materials and radioactive waste;

— the Hazardous Waste Inspectorate, whose function was to establish a consistency of approach between the various local waste disposal authorities; and

— the Water Pollution Inspectorate which was responsible for regulating discharges to water by the former (pre-privatisation) water authorities.

16.4 Establishing a new regulatory agency was an essential first step to introducing IPC. But it was not enough, and in July 1988, the Department of the Environment published a consultation paper on integrated pollution control proposing that HMIP take responsibility for a range of processes, the operators of which would be required to use the best practicable environmental option for reducing pollution. The processes proposed to be controlled under this new system fell into three categories:

(1) processes already controlled by the IAPI;

(2) processes which discharged 'red list' (i.e. toxic) substances to water and sewers 'in significant quantities'; and

(3) processes which produced large amounts of hazardous waste.

Following the consultation exercise the Environmental Protection Bill was introduced into Parliament receiving Royal Assent on 1 November 1990.

16.5 To which industries does IPC apply?

The processes which are subject to IPC are set out in the *Environmental Protection (Prescribed Processes and Substances) Regulations 1991* under six 'chapters':

Chapter 1: Fuel and power industries
Chapter 2: Metal production and processing
Chapter 3: Mineral industries
Chapter 4: The chemical industry
Chapter 5: Waste disposal and recycling
Chapter 6: Other industries (these include paper and pulp manufacture, di-isocyanate processes, processes involving uranium, coating processes and dye stuffs and printing ink manufacture).

16.6 However, none of these processes will require an authorisation under the Act unless it releases a 'prescribed substance'. The *Regulations* set out lists of prescribed substances for releases to air, land and water. The water release substances are those found on the 'red list' of toxic substances. The land release substances are 'special wastes', as defined in the *Control of Pollution (Special Waste) Regulations 1980*. However, once a process falls within the new controls because it releases, say, a 'red list' substance, then *all* its releases, whether of prescribed substances or other substances, are made subject to control under IPC.

16.7 Timetable for implementation

IPC is being brought into effect in a phased way. Since 1 April 1991, all *new* prescribed processes have required an authorisation. Similarly, if an *existing* process is substantially changed after 1 April 1991, an authorisation will be required immediately. For the great majority of *existing* processes, however, different dates are set in the *Regulations* for the new system to be operational. The first tranche of *existing* processes to come under the new regime were combustion processes (e.g. thermal power stations).

Their operators were required to apply for authorisations during April 1991. The last group (including paper and pulp manufacture, dye stuffs and printing ink manufacture and other industries) are not due to come into the new system until 1996.

16.8   **The authorisation procedure**

The heart of the new controls are the authorisation provisions contained in *sections 6–12* and *Schedule 1* of the *1990 Act.*

The Act makes it an offence to carry on a prescribed process except under an 'authorisation' granted by HMIP and in accordance with any conditions to which it is subject.

16.9   Applications for an authorisation must contain such information and be made and advertised in such manner as is prescribed in the *Environmental Protection (Applications, Appeals and Registers) Regulations 1991.* The amount of information required is considerable. It includes administrative information such as a map showing the location of the premises, releases into watercourses and internal drainage, the name and addresses of the applicant's trading partners, the applicant's company registration number etc.; process information such as a full description of the process, details of management arrangements and staff training and the extent to which the process achieves the objectives of the Act. In addition, releases of prescribed substances to the environment must be given together with an assessment of their consequences. Details of storage arrangements for raw materials, intermediates and wastes produced are to be provided and a statement on how the applicant proposes to comply with possible authorisation conditions relating to matters such as monitoring of releases and record keeping.

16.10   HMIP may serve a notice requiring specified additional information to be given.

HMIP must give notice of any application for an authorisation, together with a copy of the authorisation to consultees prescribed by the *Regulations* who have 28 days within which to make representations.

HMIP must determine an application within four months or such longer period as may be agreed with the applicant. Otherwise, it is deemed to have been refused at the end of that period, if the applicant notifies HMIP in writing that he so treats it.

16.11   The Secretary of State may call in any individual application (or class of applications) for determination by himself and he may, without calling in an application, give HMIP directions as to whether or not to grant the authorisation.

16.12   If an authorisation is granted, it must be made subject to conditions. The Act sets out, in *section 7*, types of conditions that are to be imposed. They are:

(i)   those necessary to achieve certain statutory objectives;

(ii)   those specified by directions given by the Secretary of State; and

(iii)   any other conditions which HMIP considers appropriate.

16.13   The statutory objectives are:

(i)   ensuring that, in carrying on a prescribed process, the best available techniques not entailing excessive cost (BATNEEC) will be used:

—   for preventing the release of prescribed substances or, where that is not practicable, for reducing their release to a minimum and for rendering harmless all substances which are released;

(ii)   compliance with any directions given by the Secretary of State for the implementation of international environmental obligations;

   (iii)   compliance with any limits or requirements and quality standards set by the Secretary of State;

   (iv)   compliance with any plan made by the Secretary of State under *section 3(5)* of the Act. (This section enables the Secretary of State to publish plans for limiting particular types of pollution.)

16.14 Conditions cannot address every aspect of a plant's operations and so the Act states that a condition is implied into every authorisation that best available techniques not entailing excessive cost (BATNEEC) must be used to control pollution even in the absence of a specific condition.

✳ 16.15   The concept of integrated pollution control is introduced into the system by *section 7(7)* which provides that the statutory objectives shall include the objective of ensuring that BATNEEC will be used for minimising pollution which may be caused to the environment 'taken as a whole' having regard to the 'best practicable environmental option available'.

16.16 Overlapping controls

Since the very concept of IPC is to have a single source of control, *section 28* of the Act seeks to avoid an overlap of controls. However, this does not mean that all controls over a prescribed process rests with HMIP. Conditions must not be attached to an authorisation regulating the final disposal by deposit on land of waste generated by the process. This is the province of waste regulation authorities, not HMIP. Again, in the event of conflict between an authorisation under *Part I* of the Act and a registration or authorisation under the *Radioactive Substances Act 1960*, the latter will prevail.

16.17   In the case of releases into water, they are to be covered solely by conditions attached to IPC authorisations. However, HMIP must not grant an authorisation if the National Rivers Authority certifies that the release will cause a failure to achieve any statutory water quality objective. If an authorisation is granted, it *must* contain any conditions which the NRA considers appropriate, (although HMIP may impose more onerous conditions). In other words, the NRA is able to specify minimum conditions, but HMIP may impose more restrictive ones.

16.18 Fees and charges

Provision is made in *section 8* of the Act for a scheme for fees for applications for new authorisations and variations and charges for continuing authorisations to be paid to HMIP.

The charges are set out, in theory, at a level sufficient to recover HMIP's costs. There is a flat rate charge per specified 'component' of a process for each application for a fresh authorisation or for substantial changes requiring a fresh authorisation. There is no charge for non-substantial changes that do not require a fresh authorisation – the costs of this are covered by the flat rate annual charge which also covers the costs of inspection and monitoring.

16.19 Transfers of authorisation

An authorisation can be transferred by its holder to another person who proposes to carry on the process. However, the transferee must notify HMIP within 21 days and HMIP may vary or revoke the authorisation if this is considered necessary.

16.20 **Variation of authorisations**

HMIP has power to vary an authorisation at any time if it considers that achievement of any of the statutory objectives, described above, requires a variation to be made. It is obliged to review the conditions of an authorisation in any event at least every four years. Central to the concept of BATNEEC is the need for HMIP to keep abreast of developments in techniques and their availability and a variation (usually a tightening) of an authorisation may be required as a result. It is achieved by issuing a 'variation notice' on the operator specifying the changes in the authorisation needed and the date or dates on which they are to take effect. The operator will have to respond by informing HMIP of the action he intends to take to meet the new terms, for example, what new control equipment or new process technology he will introduce to meet any new emission standards set out in the notice.

16.21 Holders of authorisations may apply to HMIP for a variation of conditions of their authorisations if a change in the process is proposed which is a 'relevant change' – i.e. one which is capable of altering the substances released from the process or of affecting the amount or any other characteristic of a substance released. The provisions are designed to cover cases such as the replacement of plant, changes in feedstock or products. Where a process includes frequent changes in inputs, outputs etc. and, therefore, needs to be able to operate with some flexibility, the authorisation will define an appropriate 'envelope' of release limits within which the operator will be able to make adjustments without the prior approval of HMIP.

16.22 **Enforcement powers**

HMIP have a variety of powers of enforcement. They may revoke an authorisation or serve an enforcement or prohibition notice.

16.23 An enforcement notice is served where HMIP believes that the operator is contravening a condition of the authorisation, or is likely to do so. It must set out the matters constituting the contravention and specify the steps that must be taken to remedy it and the period within which those steps must be taken.

16.24 A prohibition notice must be served if HMIP considers that carrying on a prescribed process under an authorisation or continuing to carry it on in a particular manner involves an imminent risk of serious pollution of the environment.

A prohibition notice, requiring the cessation of the process in whole or in part, may be served whether or not the manner of carrying on the process contravenes a condition of the authorisation.

16.25 To help HMIP in carrying out its enforcement powers, it is given the ability to:

- enter premises;

- direct that premises or anything in them be left undisturbed for the purpose of examination;

- take samples or articles for testing;

- require any person whom it is reasonable to believe is able to give relevant information to answer questions; and

- require the production of (or extracts from) any records required to be kept.

16.26 **Appeals**

Appeals lie to the Secretary of State against:

(*a*)   the refusal of a grant of an authorisation;

(*b*)   the conditions attached to an authorisation;

(*c*)   the refusal of a variation of an authorisation;

(*d*)   the revocation of an authorisation;

(*e*)   an enforcement notice; and

(*f*)   a prohibition notice.

16.27 Publicity

Public access to information is an important part of the new system of control. The Act provides that HMIP must maintain a public register containing particulars of:

(*a*)   applications for authorisations;

(*b*)   authorisations granted;

(*c*)   variation notices, enforcement notices and prohibition notices issued by HMIP;

(*d*)   revocations of authorisations;

(*e*)   appeals made to the Secretary of State;

(*f*)   convictions;

(*g*)   information obtained or given pursuant to conditions attached to authorisations; and

(*h*)   directions given to HMIP by the Secretary of State.

16.28 Provision is made in *sections 21* and *22* for the exclusion from the registers of information affecting national security and commercially confidential information.

Information is commercially confidential if its inclusion on the register would prejudice to an unreasonable degree the commercial interests of the person concerned. The Secretary of State has made it clear that the test will be a stiff one. Commercial confidentiality will normally only be accepted if disclosure would negate or significantly diminish a commercial advantage enjoyed by the operator. In the case of commercially confidential information, an application for withholding the information must be made to HMIP. If HMIP decides that the information is not confidential, the operator has 21 days to appeal to the Secretary of State. Information kept off the register by this process will cease to be confidential after four years unless the confidentiality determination is renewed.

16.29 Offences

Section 23 of the Act creates a number of criminal offences and the maximum penalties awardable by the court vary depending on the severity of the offence.

16.30 Contravention of *section 6* – operating without or in breach of an authorisation – will render the operator liable on summary conviction (i.e. in the magistrates' court) to a fine not exceeding £20,000 and on conviction on indictment (i.e. in the Crown Court) the operator will be liable to an unlimited fine or to imprisonment for a term not exceeding two years, or to both.

16.31 The operator will be similarly liable for failing to comply with an enforcement or prohibition notice.

16.32 The operator is liable to a lower maximum fine of £2,000 on summary conviction (but still on conviction on indictment to an unlimited fine or to imprisonment for a term not exceeding two years, or to both) for the offences of failing to provide information requested by HMIP, making a false or misleading statement or falsifying records.

16.33 Other offences, such as intentionally obstructing an inspector in the course of his duties, render the offender liable only on summary conviction to a maximum fine of £2,000.

16.34 The offences are 'common informer' offences which means that it is not only HMIP who may bring a prosecution. Private individuals and environmental pressure groups may also do so. If the alleged offence consists of failure to comply with the condition implied by *section 7(4)* into all authorisations that BATNEEC is used for reducing pollution, the onus will lie on the operator to prove to the court that there was no better available technique entailing excessive cost that he could have used.

16.35 BATNEEC

A key component in IPC is BATNEEC. The concept stems from the *EC Dangerous Substances Directive (76/60/EEC)* and the *EC Air Framework Directive (84/360/EEC)*. In its early draft, the *Air Framework Directive* required Member States to give prior authorisation to industrial plants likely to cause air pollution. Certain conditions were to be met before authorisations were given. One of these was to require all appropriate measures to be taken 'in accordance with the state of the art'. This was replaced in the adopted version with 'best available technology not entailing excessive costs'. In determining what technology was appropriate to bring existing plant up to the standards required of new plant, a number of factors were to be considered, including the life expectancy of the plant, its rate of utilisation, and

'the desirability of not entailing excessive costs for the plant concerned, having regard in particular to the economic situation of undertakings belonging to the category in question'.

The *Air Framework Directive* uses the term 'best available technology'. The term BATNEEC is wider in the *1990 Act* as it refers to 'techniques' rather than technology.

16.36 The meaning of BATNEEC

In general terms, it can be said that the obligation imposed under *section 6* of the Act is to use the best available techniques with due concern being paid to economic considerations where it can be proved that, in relation to the protection of the environment, the costs of applying the best available techniques would be excessive.

In more specific terms, it should be noted that:

— 'Best' is taken to mean the most effective in preventing, minimising or rendering harmless polluting emissions. There may be more than one set of techniques that achieve the same degree of effectiveness.

— 'Available' means that which is generally obtainable by any operator of the class of process in question. It does require general accessibility, but it does not imply that the technology is in general use.

— 'Techniques' includes both the process used and how that process is operated. Included are non-technical matters such as staff numbers, working methods, training and supervision as well as the manner of operating the authorised process.

— The term 'not entailing excessive costs' must be measured, in relation to *new* processes, against the resulting benefits to the environment. A marginal environmental gain may not justify a significantly higher level of cost.

—   In relation to *existing* processes matters to be taken into account include such things as the plant's remaining length of life, the technical characteristics of the plant, the nature and volume of polluting emissions it creates and the economic situation of the category of undertakings to which the plant belongs.

16.37   Specific guidance, or process notes are issued by HMIP to clarify the meaning of BATNEEC in relation to each type of process to be affected by its implementation. Those notes specify what amounts to BATNEEC for new plant and the timescale within which existing plant will normally be expected to be upgraded. Ultimately over 200 guidance notes are to be published.

16.38   New plant will be expected to meet the set standards. For existing processes, the guidance notes indicate the timescale which will generally be regarded as appropriate for upgrading.

16.39   The question of affordability is looked at from the point of view of the whole sector of the industry concerned, not just the particular operator whose process is in question. An operator who is less profitable is not allowed to continue to operate at an environmental standard below that of his more profitable competitors.

This approach has two consequences. First, it may put less profitable firms out of business, if they cannot afford to implement the required techniques. Secondly, it will allow more profitable firms who can afford state of the art abatement technology to raise the BATNEEC standard, forcing their competitors to pay out sums which they cannot easily afford. In this, the BATNEEC concept might be used as a weapon to drive out smaller or less competitive companies. BATNEEC may therefore come to be used as an opportunity to create a competitive edge.

16.40   THE DRAFT EC DIRECTIVE ON INTEGRATED POLLUTION PREVENTION AND CONTROL (IPPC)

Part I of the *Environmental Protection Act* has been taken as a model in the development of an EC Directive which will introduce IPC throughout the Community.

The draft Directive follows the UK approach in a number of key areas:

—   it will apply to both new and existing installations;

—   it will be up to the operator to justify the granting of an authorisation;

—   'best available techniques' is recognised as an evolving concept.

If adopted, it is anticipated that permits will be required under the Directive for *existing* processes by July 2000, earlier for new processes. The draft Directive uses the term 'best available techniques' (BAT) rather than BATNEEC. The definition of 'available' includes, however, not only that the technique has been proved at an industrial level but also that it must be industrially viable from a technical *and economic* point of view.

An important effect of the Directive, if and when adopted, is likely to be the harmonisation throughout the Member States of emission standards and other pollution controls.

17 Minerals

17.1 GENERAL POSITION

The extraction of minerals is an inevitable contributor to and consequence of economic development. Fuel minerals (e.g. oil, coal and natural gas) and construction and industrial minerals (e.g. limestone, metal ores and bulk aggregates such as sand and gravel) not only constitute the raw materials for physical development itself, but also make an important contribution to the national economy. Conversely, some degree of environmental harm is an inevitable result of mineral extraction: not only might land be 'removed' by surface working, but some nuisance from extractive operations and ancillary works caused by dust, noise, vibration, traffic and visual intrusion is almost inevitable. This intrusion is compounded by the incidence in the UK of a wide range of minerals (often in environmentally sensitive areas), the potential duration of mineral workings and high (if fluctuating) demand. The results are widespread environmental effects in many varied local environments.

Recognition of the need to regulate mineral extraction in the public interest is long-standing, but certainly not static. Whilst having their roots in the general planning system, controls over mineral extraction have been influenced by the individual characteristics of minerals and their exploitation. In particular, unlike other uses of land, there is little choice in the location of mineral workings: minerals can only be worked where they are found, although minerals need not be worked *everywhere* they are found.

The result is a system of control largely *within* mainstream planning, but with its own rules. Some circumstances have proved beyond the flexibility of planning, e.g. onshore hydrocarbon exploitation and marine extraction. Alternative systems have emerged for their control.

17.2 Regulatory responsibilities

The division of central government responsibility for minerals compounds the lack of cohesion in minerals law. The Department of the Environment (DoE) is central in policy making for, and the overseeing of, planning and environmental matters. It has responsibility for bulk minerals and is at the centre of a wide consultative 'web' which includes the Departments of Trade and Industry and Transport, and the Ministry of Agriculture Fisheries and Food (MAFF). The latter has a crucial role in considering the loss of agricultural land to extraction and ensuring satisfactory restoration. Responsibilities for onshore hydrocarbons, coal and non-DoE minerals rest with the Department of Trade and Industry. Controls over marine extraction in Crown ownership are exercised by the Crown Estates Commissioners, whilst a wide range of non-government bodies are also consulted regarding any proposal to exploit minerals.

Local planning control over minerals is exercised by mineral planning authorities (MPAs). [*Town and Country Planning Act 1990, s 1(4)*]. Thus, county, London borough and metropolitan district councils generally have responsibility for, *inter alia*: the winning and working of minerals in, on or under land (whether by surface or underground working) and the construction or operation of ancillary development; the use of land or construction of buildings for mineral processing where the land forms part of, or is adjacent to, an extraction site or onto which minerals are brought by means such as a conveyor or private roadway; mineral exploration; the depositing of mineral waste; the use of land in connection with the rail or water transport of bulk aggregates; the

17.3 Minerals

carrying out of operations in, on, over or under land, or a use of land, where the land is or forms part of a site used or formerly used for the winning and working of minerals and where the operation or use would conflict with or prejudice compliance with a restoration or aftercare condition (see below). These activities are collectively known as 'county matters'. [*TCPA 1990, Sch 1; Planning and Compensation Act 1991, Sch 1*].

17.3 'Minerals'

For planning purposes, 'minerals' are defined non-exhaustively to include all substances of a kind ordinarily worked by underground or surface working, except peat cut for purposes other than sale. [*TCPA 1990, s 336; PCA 1991, 12 Sch 1*]. The lack of a comprehensive definition seems to have been of little practical consequence. Further definitions for the purposes of onshore hydrocarbon exploitation are provided by the *Petroleum (Production) Act 1934, s 1*. In cases of doubt recourse might be had to the 'vernacular used in the mining world' (*Earl of Lonsdale v A-G [1982] 3 All ER 579*).

17.4 Policy framework

In addition to particular statutory variations, the adaptation of non-subject-specific planning controls to minerals is enabled by dedicated minerals policy guidance notes (MPGs). There are currently ten: *General Considerations and the Development Plan System* (January 1988), *Applications, Permissions and Conditions* (1988), *Opencast Coal Mining* (May 1988), *The Review of Mineral Working Sites* (September 1988), *Minerals Planning and the General Development Order* (December 1988), *Guidelines for Aggregates Provision in England and Wales* (1989), *The Reclamation of Mineral Working* (1989), *Planning and Compensation Act 1991: Interim Development Order Permissions (IDOs) – Statutory Provisions and Procedures* (September 1991), *IDOs – Conditions* (March 1992) and *Provision of Raw Material to the Cement Industry (1991).*

Maintenance of a steady supply to meet industrial demand is central to existing minerals policy (see e.g. MPG 6, paragraph 8). That is not to say that environmental factors are of little importance – 'due regard' must be given to protection of the environment – but considerable emphasis is given to reducing to 'acceptable levels' environmental damage or loss of amenity caused by mineral workings and ancillary operations (MPG 1, paragraph 5). Simply put therefore, the law regulates a three-stage process: quantification of the demand, or 'need', for minerals; identification of appropriate sites (which will include an initial consideration of environmental factors); and minimisation of environmental harm at sites themselves. Throughout this process, policy is ubiquitous; and the law becomes increasingly complex.

A fundamental policy shift may be indicated by the draft revised MPG 6 and accompanying *Policy Issues Paper* (DoE, January 1993) which suggest enhanced reliance on supply by more use of waste, other recyclable secondary materials and non-standard sources of primary aggregates (e.g., superquarries and marine sources). The DoE has recognised 'clear indications that the areas which can be worked in an environmentally acceptable manner are likely to decrease'. An incremental shift towards supply-led, rather than demand-led, policy may therefore be in prospect (although the draft MPG itself is not imperatively phrased).

17.5 POSITIVE PLANNING

Strategic plans

Structure plans and Part I of Unitary Development Plans ('strategic plans') must contain 'general policies' for mineral extraction and with mandatory local plans [*TCPA*

1990, s 36(1)], these comprise the 'development plan'. Where, in making any determination under the Planning Acts, regard is to be had to the development plan, that
determination shall be made in accordance with the plan unless material considerations indicate otherwise. [*TCPA 1990, s 54A*]. Although it has been said that this
provision makes the planning system 'plan-led', central policy provides local
government with considerable latitude in the formulation and interpretation of plans
and an examination of their content illustrates considerable potential for conflict in
their application. Given this built-in flexibility, local influences upon local decision-
making are of crucial importance.

Broad guidelines exist as to the content of strategic plans. Mineral development is a
'key topic' (PPG12) and aspects which must be considered include the following.

(*a*)   Scope of provision, consistent with national and regional policy. Central guid-
        ance requires provision for a sufficient stock of *permitted* reserves with planning
        consent (a 'landbank') to secure continuous supply during the plan period
        considering fluctuations in demand, the long lead-in times of mineral sites and
        necessarily high levels of capital investment. Quantitative forecasts for *aggregates*
        are compiled by Regional Aggregates Working Parties (RAWPs): advisory
        bodies comprising representatives from industry, MPAs and government
        departments (MPG 1, paragraph 57; MPGs 6 and 10). Estimates of demand
        and supply are notoriously difficult to compile – a factor which, when combined
        with quickly changing environmental perceptions, makes the weight which a
        plan is likely to be accorded vitally dependent upon its age.

(*b*)   General location for development – although site-specific policies must be
        confined to MLPs (PPG12, paragraph 5.13).

(*c*)   Broad areas of restraint – this conversely entails the prevention of unnecessary
        sterilisation of mineral resources by *other* forms of development (MPG 1,
        paragraph 5).

(*d*)   Policies to ensure that land taken for mineral extraction is reclaimed at the
        earliest opportunity and is capable of an acceptable afteruse after working has
        come to an end.

(*e*)   Policy variations or peculiarities for individual minerals or groups of minerals.

Environmental factors must receive 'comprehensive and consistent consideration': a
structure plan must include policies in respect of the conservation of the natural beauty
and amenity of land, the improvement of the physical environment and the management of traffic. [*TCPA 1990, s 31(2)*]. Plans should include proposals to secure the
extraction of minerals whilst minimising harm to the environment (MPG 1, paragraph
21).

17.6   Minerals local plans

The role of the MLP is to relate the general policies of the strategic plan to identifiable
areas of land. It must be in general conformity with the relevant strategic plan [*TCPA
1990, s 36(4)*] and contain an authority's policies relating to the winning and working of
minerals or involving the depositing of mineral waste. Where no separate waste local plan
is prepared, a MLP may additionally contain detailed policies in respect of development
which involves the depositing of refuse or waste materials. [*TCPA 1990, s 38*].

In formulating its MLP, an authority shall have regard to central policy guidance, the advice
of RAWPs and other affected authorities (e.g. non-metropolitan district and adjoining
county councils), statutory consultees (e.g. the National Rivers Authority), public representations received and any other matters prescribed by the Secretary of State.

17.7 Minerals

In addition to the factors listed above, MLPs should consider in appropriate detail those areas within which there would normally be a presumption for or against mineral working. The relative weight of such policies might vary, e.g., from broad areas of search to preferred areas, depending upon the MPA's knowledge of mineral resources, the precision of demand forecasts and competing land use pressures. Much emphasis is thus placed upon proactive mineral site designation. (MPG 1, paragraphs 21–31). Further, and in addition to statutorily designated sites of environmental importance, MPAs may designate areas of special landscape or nature conservation value, which must then be considered in relation to mineral extraction. (MPG 1, paragraph 33).

17.7 REGULATORY PLANNING

Mineral development

'Mining operations in, on, over or under land' constitute an act of development requiring planning permission. [*TCPA 1990, s 55*]. This includes: the removal of material of any description from a mineral working deposit, a furnace ash or clinker deposit, or a deposit of metallic slag; and the extraction of minerals from a disused railway embankment. A 'mineral-working deposit' is further defined as being any deposit of material remaining after minerals have been extracted from land or otherwise deriving from the carrying out of operations for the winning and working of minerals in, on or under land. [*TCPA 1990, s 336*]. 'The winning and working of minerals', whilst not otherwise explained, includes extraction from a mineral working deposit – a rather circuitous definition which seems to result in 'the winning and working of minerals' being treated as generally synonymous with 'mining operations', although this is not explicitly stated (but see the *Town and Country Planning General Development Order 1988 (SI 1988 No 1813, article 1(2))*).

'Depositing mineral waste', also a 'county matter', is any process whereby a mineral-working deposit is created or enlarged and 'depositing of refuse or waste materials' includes the depositing of mineral waste. [*TCPA 1990, s 336; PCA 1991, 12 Sch 1*].

Elaboration has been provided by the Court of Appeal describing 'every shovelful' as being a separate mining operation: *Thomas David (Porthcawl) Ltd v Penybont RDC [1972] 3 All ER 1092*. Exploratory drilling of deep boreholes is development, although transitory sample boring may not be – the distinction is one of fact and degree (*Bedfordshire County Council v CEGB [1985] JPL 43*).

17.8 Environmental Assessment (EA)

Where an MPA considers that the environmental effects of a proposal to extract minerals are likely to be significant by virtue of factors such as its size, nature or location, it may require that an EA be undertaken (*Town and Country Planning (Assessment of Environmental Effects) Regulations 1988 (SI 1988 No 1199)*). EAs are not undertaken as often as might be expected for such major development, largely, it seems, as a result of a common perception that the detailed process of pre-application consultation and discussion encouraged for mineral development, coupled with the need to submit detailed working and restoration schemes, makes them superfluous.

17.9 Permitted development

Planning consent for activities otherwise constituting development may be granted by a development order. [*TCPA 1990, s 59*]. The *General Development Order 1988 (as amended)* permits the following specifically mineral-related development.

(a)   Development ancillary to mining operations (although prior notice may be required. [Sch 2, Part 19].

(b)   Waste tipping at a mine. [Sch 2, Part 21].

(c)   Mineral exploration for defined periods (although not the drilling of boreholes for petroleum exploration). [Sch 2, Part 22].

(d)   Removal of material from a mineral working deposit or stockpile. [Sch 2, Part 23].

(e)   The winning and working of minerals on land held or occupied for agriculture of minerals reasonably required for agricultural purposes. [Sch 2, Part 6, Class B].

(f)   British Coal mining development. [Sch 2, Part 20].

Permitted development rights (PDRs) may be removed by a local authority (subject to the approval of the Secretary of State). Additionally, and where it considers it expedient, a planning authority may require a formal planning application for certain classes (Part 22, Class B – exploratory drilling for a period of up to four months; and Part 23, Class C – removal of minerals from a deposit other than a stockpile) where the development, or any part of it: is in a National Park, an area of outstanding natural beauty, a site of special scientific interest, or a site of archaeological interest; would adversely affect the setting of a Grade 1 listed building or cause serious detriment to the amenity of the proposed location; or would cause a nuisance to residential occupiers, a hospital or a school. There is thus provision to remove permitted development rights where their implementation would interfere with sites of recognised environmental value.

It seems to be accepted that PDRs may also be removed by a planning condition (e.g. Dunoon Developments v Secretary of State for the Environment and Poole BC [1992] JPL 937), although policy restricts this to 'exceptional circumstances' and where there is a 'real and specific threat to an interest of acknowledged performance' (Planning and Noise, Draft PPG, paragraph 43).

17.10 Notification and consultation

The particularly controversial nature of mineral development demands wide consultation on individual applications. Local liaison committees, where they exist, can have an important role in defraying contention (MPG 2, paragraphs 5–6). Applications to develop minerals must be publicised by newspaper advertisements and either the erection of site notices or notification of adjoining landowners/occupiers [TCPA 1990, ss 65–68; DoE Circular 15/92]. Proposals for underground mining necessitate separate notification [General Development Order 1988, article 12(2)], whilst owners of mineral rights in land to which a proposal relates must also receive separate notification. [TCPA 1990, s 67]. Where the Crown Estates Commissioners, British Coal or the Secretary of State for the Environment have notified an MPA that land in their area contains gold, silver, coal or oil, the MPA must notify the designator of any proposals for mineral development in those areas. Similarly, and to prevent sterilisation of mineral resources, MPAs may designate 'minerals consultation areas' wherein any development proposals must be notified to the MPA, whether a county matter or not. [Local Government, Planning and Land Act 1980, s 86(2)].

The General Development Order 1988 specifies a broad range of mandatory consultees to a mineral development proposal, which includes the National Rivers Authority, MAFF, English Heritage, the relevant Nature Conservancy Council (NCC) and Parish Councils: article 18. This protracted consultation invariably affects the time taken to make a determination – which is often far longer than the prescribed eight weeks.

17.11 Minerals

17.11 Planning conditions

Central to continuing environmental control over mineral extraction is the imposition of conditions on planning consents. [*TCPA 1990, s 70*]. Conditions may regulate the development or use of any land under the control of the applicant, whether or not it is included within the application, where it appears expedient to the MPA for the purposes of or in connection with the development authorised by the permission. [*TCPA 1990, s 72(1)*]. Although planning control was not designed with the particular demands of mineral control in mind, being rather based upon the notion of 'once-and-for-all' consent, planning conditions have evolved into the principal means of ensuring that long term mineral sites meet acceptable environmental standards throughout their lifetimes. Comprehensive on-going control by numerous, and increasingly detailed, conditions is now standard practice (although subject to local variation).

Such control is also consistent with government policy that the cost of meeting acceptable environmental standards should fall on industry: an application of the 'polluter pays' principle. (MPG 1, paragraph 10). Once a consent is granted, an authority has only limited powers of compulsory alteration or revocation – powers reluctantly used by reason of resulting liability on MPAs to pay compensation (see below). Whilst more modern consents might make provision for the periodic review of their conditions, 'modernisation' of existing environmentally inadequate consents is still heavily reliant upon negotiation between planning authorities and mineral operators. Considerable weight is placed upon an effective partnership between the industry and the mineral planning authorities. That partnership should precede the date of an application: extensive pre-application consultation is recommended. (MPG 2, paragraph 5).

Planning authorities currently have no power to charge for participating in pre-application consultations (*R v Richmond-upon-Thames LBC, ex parte McCarthy & Stone (Developments)* [*1992*] *JPL 467*), although the Secretary of State has an enabling power. [*Local Government and Housing Act 1989, s 150*].

The power to impose planning conditions, although broadly stated, is not unrestricted. Conditions must: be necessary [DoE Circular 1/85, paragraphs 12–14]; be imposed for a planning purpose (*Newbury District Council v Secretary of State* [*1981*] *AC 578*); fairly and reasonably relate to the development permitted (*Pyx Granite Co. Ltd v Minister of Housing and Local Government* [*1958*] *1 QB 554*); not be unreasonable in the *Wednesbury* sense (i.e. *Associated Provincial Picture House v Wednesbury Corporation* [*1948*] *1 KB 223*; *Newbury District Council v Secretary of State* [*1981*] *AC 578*). Policy further dictates that conditions should be precise and enforceable. Enforceability will be dependent upon the ease with which a breach could be detected and the practicability of subsequent enforcement action. (MPG 2, paragraphs 55, 63). An applicant may appeal against the imposition of a planning condition. [*TCPA 1990, s 78*].

Conditions commonly relate to such matters as: construction or alteration of site access; protection of highways, e.g. provision of on-site wheel-cleaning facilities (although conditions *cannot* specify off-site routes to be taken by works traffic); hours of working; progressive working and restoration; soil movement, storage (including 'screening'), treatment and replacement (see MPG 7); and the provision of screens of vegetation. Such conditions are clearly intended to help minimise environmental harm. Wider use of conditions to secure environmental protection is also common by, e.g., nuisance abatement and controls over the use of sites for waste disposal. The interface between planning controls and other dedicated statutory regimes may therefore become more vague, whilst the principle that planning should not duplicate specific statutory controls remains (*Fawcett Properties Ltd v Buckinghamshire County Council* [*1961*] AC 636). Conditions may sometimes, therefore, be imposed to minimise dust, noise, light and vibration nuisance. The provision of impervious bunds to prevent groundwater pollution from, e.g., fuel storage tanks is also common. It should be borne in mind, however, that

'planning control is primarily concerned with the type and location of new development and changes of use. Once broad land uses have been sanctioned by the planning process, it is the job of pollution control to limit adverse effects that an operation may have on the environment'. [Cm 1200, September 1990, paragraph 6.39].

The border between planning controls and other statutory systems is ambiguous. (See *Planning and Pollution*, Draft PPG).

Conditions are statutorily implied as to duration and commencement of mineral development. All development consisting of the winning and working of minerals must commence within ten years of the grant (*Town and Country Planning (Minerals) Regulations 1971, Regulation 6*) or before the expiration of a specified period after the completion of other development consisting of the winning and working of minerals or the depositing of mineral waste which is already being carried out by the same applicant [*TCPA 1990, s 91(4)*], and must cease after the expiry of 60 years [*TCPA 1990, 1 Sch 5*]. These periods may be varied by the MPA.

Common law liability in nuisance *may* still arise (*Medway (Chatham) Dock Co. Ltd v Gillingham BC (1992) 4 LMELR 119*).

17.12 Restoration and aftercare

Where a permission for development involving the winning and working of minerals or involving the depositing of refuse or waste materials is granted subject to a restoration condition (a condition involving reclamation with subsoil, topsoil or soil-making material) it may also be made subject to an 'aftercare condition'. [*TCPA 1990, 2–6 Sch 5 (as amended)*]. Such a condition may require that land be brought up to a specified standard for agriculture, forestry or amenity purposes, and include provision for planting, cultivation, draining or otherwise treating land. Steps required under an aftercare condition may only extend during the aftercare period: currently five years. An MPA may alternatively require the submission of an 'aftercare scheme' for its approval after the grant of consent. Neither an aftercare condition nor a scheme can make provision for such matters as the erection, construction and maintenance of fencing, gates and paths, although provision for leachate control from site-fill materials is permissible. Before imposing an aftercare condition, an MPA must consult MAFF (for agricultural afteruses) and/or the Forestry Commission. [*TCPA 1990, 4 Sch 5*]. Progressive reclamation is the subject of detailed technical policy advice which includes soil handling, filling, landform creation and aftercare: see MPG 7.

The power to impose aftercare conditions, created after the landmark Report of the Stevens Committee, 'Planning Control over Mineral Working' (1976), is arguably the most significant advance in planning control over minerals since 1947. It also clearly demonstrates the need for planning to provide for long term monitoring and control over mineral sites.

17.13 Reserved matters

Although planning permission may not be granted subject to a condition requiring further consent from another person or body, it may be appropriate to leave some matters for an MPA's detailed consideration after consent proper. In addition to schemes of progressive working and reclamation, these might relate to, e.g., soil

17.14   Minerals

handling, tree planting, drainage provision or (very frequently) general landscaping. Such matters are not necessarily 'reserved matters' within the meaning of the *General Development Order 1988, article 2(1)* as they often derive from full, rather than outline, planning permission. They result in 'hybrid' consents, where powers to approve detailed later submissions are often delegated to officers. [*Local Government Act 1971, s 101*].

The LPA must respond to applications for approval of such matters within eight weeks [*General Development Order 1988, article 24*], although a recent decision suggests that in certain, limited, circumstances development may commence before approval is given and before the initiation of enforcement action in order to prevent a permission from lapsing. [*F G Whitley & Sons Co Ltd v Secretary of State for Wales [1992] JPL 856*].

17.14 Planning obligations

Obligations provide a useful supplement to conditions as a means of minimising environmental harm. Any person interested in land in the area of an MPA may, by agreement or otherwise, enter into a planning obligation restricting the development or use of the land, requiring specified operations or activities to be carried out in, on, under or over the land, or requiring the land to be used in any specified way. [*TCPA 1990, s 106*]. Obligations may involve the payment of money to an MPA, whilst conditions may not, and whilst planning conditions must 'fairly and reasonably relate to the development permitted', obligations need not (*R v Gillingham BC, ex parte Parham Ltd [1988] JPL 336*).

Obligations are widely used to regulate, e.g., vehicle routing and off-site screening, and less frequently, to make provision for local on-going consultation by the establishment of 'liaison committees'. Recent policy advice also recommends their use to offset the loss of or impact on any amenity or resources present on a site prior to development (DoE Circular 16/92). More controversial are obligations entered into as part of negotiations over a 'new' site which restrict a mineral operator's rights over an older site which itself was granted subject to what have come to be regarded as 'inadequate' environmental protection conditions. The MPA gains from not having to *require* alteration of the old consent, and the operator from the advantages of cooperation with the regulator – a 'win-win' situation.

Policy suggests that where a developer is dissatisfied with unduly protracted negotiations, or considers that an MPA is attempting to place unreasonable demands upon it, it might consider a unilateral obligation (DoE Circular 16/91). The use of unilateral obligations may also reduce the delay often associated with mutual agreement. ('The Use of Planning Agreements', DoE Research Report, 1992).

17.15 Review and monitoring

Review of planning permissions takes two forms: that which is statutorily required, and that which is not. First, MPAs are under a duty to undertake periodic reviews of the winning and working or minerals and the depositing of mineral waste in their areas with a view to deciding whether to use their regulatory or alteration/revocation powers. [*TCPA 1990, s 105*]. This statutory review embraces every 'mining site' in an MPA's area and is presently to be conducted at such intervals as an MPA thinks fit, although the Secretary of State may prescribe its periodicity and coverage. A similar duty has existed since 1981, but has been of little effect in 'modernising' old permissions, largely because of compensation liability on compulsory alteration (MPG 4). The extended power vested in the Secretary of State to specify the incidence and scope of the review is intended to resolve this problem.

Second, planning consents themselves may provide for periodic review or revision. This might be either by explicit provision (e.g. a condition allowing for a five-yearly review of the effects of traffic from a development) or the use of phraseology allowing for adaptation to changing demands (e.g. a requirement that 'all reasonable steps' be taken to minimise environmental nuisance). The advantage is flexibility, as potentially expensive periodic review and compulsory alteration becomes unnecessary; the disadvantages are uncertainty and a further blurring of the borderline between planning controls and specialist statutory regimes.

17.16 Modification and revocation of minerals consents

The effective implementation of the review of mineral working sites is not solely dependent upon voluntary modifications to development practices by minerals operators. Both the local authority and the Secretary of State have powers to modify or revoke planning permissions consisting of the winning and working of minerals or involving the depositing of refuse or waste materials if, having had regard to the development plan and other material considerations, they consider it expedient. [*TCPA 1990, ss 97 and 100*]. Orders so made may only relate to operations yet to be completed or changes of use remaining to be made, and are subject to notification of owners and occupiers of affected land and other persons who, in the opinion of the LPA, will be affected by the order. Confirmation by the Secretary of State of an order under *section 97* is required unless it is unopposed [*TCPA 1990, s 99*], whilst a notified objector may require an inquiry to be held.

A modification or revocation order may include an aftercare condition if the permission to which it relates is already subject to a restoration condition or if a restoration condition has previously been imposed upon it. [*TCPA 1990, 7 Sch 5*]. If a minerals consent is *revoked*, full compensation is payable to any person interested in the affected land or minerals for any expenditure incurred carrying out work which is rendered abortive by its revocation or other loss or damage sustained which is directly attributable to the revocation. Where a minerals consent is merely *modified*, reduced compensation may be payable. [*TCPA 1990, s 116*]. It is therefore possible to improve the environmental standards to which a minerals consent is subject, whilst reduced compensation recognises that the financial burden of that improvement should not be borne entirely by a mineral operator. The Government has recently published proposals which suggest that present compensation entitlements may be reduced or removed to facilitate more effective modernisation. ('Review of the Provisions of the Town and Country Planning (Minerals) Act 1981: Old Mining Permissions', Department of the Environment Consultation Paper, March 1992; *(1992) 4 LMELR 81*). This might entail the forced submission by developers of proposals to modify existing minerals consents, at their own cost, similar to those which have been introduced to regulate 'Interim Development Order Permissions'. [*Planning and Compensation Act 1991, 2 Sch*]. See *(1992) 4 LMELR 81*.

17.17 Discontinuance and suspension of minerals consents

It is not normally possible to abandon by disuse a planning permission for operational development (*Pioneer Aggregates (UK) Ltd v Secretary of State for the Environment* [*1985*] *AC 132*). However, MPAs have other powers to 'modify' minerals consents after they have been granted. They may require that any *use* of land for development consisting of the winning and working of minerals or the depositing of refuse or waste materials should be discontinued or be made subject to further conditions regulating its continuance. [*TCPA 1990, s 102, 1 Sch 9*]. *Section 102* therefore extends beyond *section 97* to include permitted development under the *General Development Order 1988*. Conditions which may be imposed include restoration and aftercare conditions. An MPA may further require the alteration or removal of any buildings, works, plant or machinery on such land or used for the purposes of mineral extraction of waste depositing. A discontinuance order is therefore a wider power than simple revocation under *section 97*.

Section 102 also differs as to the matters for which compensation is payable. Where an order is made under *section 102*, compensation is payable to any person who has suffered damage in consequence of the order by depreciation of the value of an interest in land or minerals or by being disturbed in the enjoyment of such minerals. [*TCPA 1990, s 115*]. Works carried out in compliance with an order under *section 102* are also compensatable.

Where it appears to an MPA that mineral development has permanently ceased, it may prohibit the resumption of working *and*: require the removal of plant or machinery; require that specified steps be taken to remove or alleviate any injury to amenity which has been caused by that development; require compliance with a previously imposed restoration condition; or impose restoration or aftercare conditions. [*TCPA 1990, 3 Sch 9*]. An MPA can assume permanent cessation only when no development has been carried out to any substantial extent for at least two years and, on the available evidence, resumption seems unlikely. The Secretary of State's approval is needed.

Where permitted mineral development has not been carried out to any substantial extent for at least twelve months, but it appears that resumption is likely, an MPA may issue a suspension order requiring the specified steps be taken 'for the protection of the environment'. The approval of the Secretary of State is also required for such orders, which may include steps for the purpose of preserving the amenities of the area in which the land is situated, protecting that area from damage or preventing any deterioration in the condition of that land during the period of suspension. The order must specify the period in which the required steps must be taken. [*TCPA 1990, 5 Sch 9*]. Suspension orders are registerable as local land charges, and may be modified after issue by a supplementary suspension order. This latter power is intended to provide a means of 'up-dating' environmental requirements on suspended sites, and also provides a means of effecting the results of the review of suspension orders which MPAs are also under a duty to conduct. [*TCPA 1990, 9 Sch 9*].

Suspension orders do not prevent the recommencement of mineral development, but impose an obligation upon a developer to inform the MPA of intention to resume. An MPA (or the Secretary of State on appeal) must revoke a suspension order if development recommences 'to a substantial extent'. [*TCPA 1990, 10 Sch 9*]. Breach of an order under *section 102* or *Schedule 9* is an offence. [*TCPA 1990, s 189*]. Where an order under *section 102* or *Schedule 9* has been issued but not complied with, the MPA may enter upon land and execute required steps, costs for which are recoverable from the defaulter. [*TCPA 1990, s 190*].

17.18 Modified compensation

The *TCPA 1990* provides for the reduction of compensation payments in some cases of modification of minerals consents: *section 116*. The *Town and Country Planning (Compensation for Restrictions on Mineral Working) Regulations 1985 (as amended by SI 1989 No 992 and SI 1990 No 803)* apply as if made under *section 116* [*Town and Country Planning (Compensation Restrictions on Mineral Working) Regulations 1985, paragraph 16(2)*]. Essentially, compensation is reduced only if fundamental planning issues relating to the site (e.g. its basic acceptability) are not reopened by the review and modification process. (See generally, *Town and Country Planning (Compensation for Restrictions on Mineral Working) Regulations 1985*.)

17.19 COAL

Generally coal is embraced by the foregoing provisions. In practice, the concentrated expertise and co-ordinated management provided by BCC results in unusually formalised and rigorous consultation and formulation of proposals. There are some other differences. Modifications have been made of compensation payable upon revocation and modification of planning consent and as a result of adverse decisions by the Secretary of State in relation to underground coal workings. These modifications are limited to the BCC's 'specified land', i.e.: unworked coal; unworked minerals other than coal only capable of economic exploitation in conjunction with coal extraction; and surface land acquired before 15 July 1974 which is in the immediate vicinity of mine shafts or elsewhere where coal industry activities are carried on. (*Town and Country Planning (British Coal Corporation) Regulations 1974 (as amended) SI 1974 No 1006*).

Also, opencast coal mining (now subject to planning control: *Housing and Planning Act 1986*), by virtue of its extreme environmental effects and relative economic advantages over deep-mined coal, has a separate policy regime. Central to this policy (and uniquely) is that the overall level of opencast production should be determined by market forces. It is not incumbent upon the developer, as with all other surface minerals, to establish the need for the extraction in question. (See generally MPG 3).

17.20 ONSHORE OIL AND GAS

Onshore oil and gas exploitation is regulated by the *Petroleum (Production) Act 1934 (as amended)*. There are two stages: exploration and development licensing and planning regulation. Since 1984 the licensing system on shore has comprised: first, advertisement of a new round of licensing awards; second, issuance of 'exploration licences' by the Secretary of State for the Environment valid for six years covering 10×10 km blocks conferring rights to carry out seismic tests and drill exploratory boreholes (*subject to planning permission*); third, award of 'appraisal licences' for renewable five-year periods to enable site specific development programmes to be drawn up leading to application for planning permission; and fourth, issuance of 'development licences' with 20-year renewable lives for specific areas of discovery, *after* planning permission has been obtained and satisfactory development programmes submitted to the Secretary of State. [*Petroleum Production (Landward Areas) Regulations 1991* (SI 1991 No 981)]. Adherence to good oilfield practices, and provision of a pollution contingency plan, to provide safeguards against pollution and spillage, drawn up in consultation with authorities responsible for pollution control and mineral planning authorities, are conditions of development licences.

As regards planning control, MPAs should include policies in structure and local plans to provide a policy background against which proposals can be assessed. (See generally DoE Circular 2/85.) Exploitation must be consistent with the protection of the environment and proposals in statutorily designated areas will be subject to 'the most rigorous examination', with the burden upon a developer to show that environmental objections are outweighed (MPG 1). Specialist advice is provided by the Petroleum Engineering Division of the Department of Energy.

17.21 MARINE EXTRACTION

To help minimise the environmental disruption associated with onshore sites, policy states that the dredging of construction aggregates 'should be encouraged wherever possible without unacceptable damage to sea fisheries and coastal erosion' (MPG 6).

Yet whilst offering some environmental advantages, marine extraction presents its own environmental problems, including fisheries and habitat destruction, coastal erosion, effects on water quality, dangers to marine navigation and problems associated with the siting of wharfage and processing facilities.

Marine extraction of aggregates does not fall within terrestrial planning control. Consent must instead be sought from the owners of the mineral resource: generally the Crown [*Crown Estate Act 1961; Continental Shelf Act 1964*]. The Crown Estate Commissioners (CEC) issue prospecting and production licences on the Crown's behalf. Prospecting licences have a normal duration of four years with a ceiling tonnage on the material which may be extracted and are not subject to any formal consultation. Production licences are subject to a complex process of consultation. *Outline* proposals must be submitted to the CEC, who consult, e.g., local coastal protection authorities, the NRA, local fisheries interests, local offshore operators, the Department of Transport, the Ministry of Defence, the relevant Nature Conservancy Council, Trinity House and the relevant MPA. Consultants are also commissioned to assess whether a proposal presents an unavoidable risk of coastal erosion, in which case it will be automatically rejected. An environmental assessment may be required. An application for a production licence may only be made after this pre-application consultation.

The application should include a response to the pre-application consultation, including any measures proposed to remove or alleviate objections. The application is then subjected to the 'government view procedure' where the 'coordinating department', generally the Department of the Environment, initiates wide ranging inter-departmental discussion. If agreement that a proposal is in the public interest can be reached, then a favourable (often conditional) 'government view' is given. If any department has an overriding objection, an unfavourable view would result. On average, 50 per cent of applications receive a favourable response, 25 per cent do so when initial objections have been overcome, whilst 25 per cent are rejected outright.

An extractor might also need consent from the Department of Transport or the local coast protection authority [*Coast Protection Act 1949, ss 34 and 18*], MAFF [*Food and Environmental Protection Act 1985, Pt II*] or an adjoining MPA (where the extraction would extend below low water in an estuary).

18 Noise

18.1 INTRODUCTION

Noise is sound which is undesired by the recipient: one man's music can be another man's nuisance. Ordinances to control noise can be dated back to the Roman era, but in the UK the seminal study of modern times is that undertaken by the Wilson Committee on the Problem of Noise (the Wilson Report), published in 1963 [Cmnd 2056].

Almost the whole of current UK practice can be traced back to the Wilson Report, but in 1990 a Noise Review Working Party was set up under the chairmanship of W J S Batho, which reported in August of that year. The Working Party recommended a number of wide ranging revisions to current practice which have yet to take effect. The reader of this chapter should be aware that the UK approach is likely to change rapidly over the next few years and that it is more important than ever to ascertain that this guidance is still valid. Where a change is known to be in the pipeline, this is indicated in the text. Reference has been made only to material of principal importance in environmental noise, as an exhaustive treatment would defeat the objectives of this chapter.

18.2 THE PERCEPTION OF SOUND

Sound is a rapid fluctuation in air pressure. The human ear can hear a sensation of sound when the fluctuations occur between 20 times a second and 20,000 times a second. This is called the frequency of the sound and is measured in Hertz (Hz). The loudness of the sound depends on the amount of fluctuation in the air pressure. Typically, the quietest sound that can be heard (the threshold of hearing) is 0 dB and the sound becomes painful at 120 dB. Surprisingly perhaps, zero decibels is not zero sound. The sensitivity and frequency range of the ear varies somewhat from person to person and deteriorates with age and exposure to loud sounds.

However, the human ear is not equally sensitive to sounds of different frequencies (i.e. pitch): it tends to be more sensitive in the frequency range of the human voice than at higher or lower frequencies. When measuring sound, compensation for these effects can be made by applying a frequency weighting, usually the so-called 'A' weighting, although other weightings are sometimes used for special purposes.

The ear has an approximately logarithmic response to sound: for example, every doubling or halving in sound pressure gives an apparently equal step increase or decrease in loudness. In measuring environmental noise, sound pressure levels are therefore usually quoted in terms of a logarithmic unit known as a decibel (dB). To signify that the 'A' weighting has been applied, the symbol of dB(A) is often used. However, current practice tends to prefer the weighting letter to be included in the name of the measurement index, see below, e.g. dB(A) L_{eq} and dB L_{Aeq} – both refer to the 'A' weighted equivalent sound level in decibels.

Depending upon the method of presentation of two sounds, the human ear may detect differences as small as 0.5 dB(A). However, for general environmental noise the detectable difference is usually taken to be about 3 dB(A). A 10 dB(A) change in level corresponds, subjectively, to an approximate doubling or halving in loudness. Similarly, a subjective quadrupling of loudness corresponds to a 20 dB(A) increase in sound pressure level (SPL). When two sounds of the same SPL are added together, the resultant SPL is approximately 3 dB(A) higher than each of the individual sounds. It would require approximately *nine* equal sources to be added to an original source before the subjective loudness is doubled.

The sound pressure level of environmental sound fluctuates continuously. A number of measurement indices have been proposed to describe the human response to these varying sounds. It is possible to measure the physical characteristics of sound with considerable accuracy and to predict the physical human response to characteristics such as loudness, pitch and audibility. However, it is not possible to predict *subjective* characteristics such as annoyance with certainty. This should not be surprising: one would not expect the light meter on a camera to be able to indicate whether one was taking a good or a bad photograph, although one would expect it to get the physical exposure correct. Strictly speaking, therefore, a meter can only measure sound and not noise: nevertheless, in practice, the terms are usually interchangeable.

18.3 NOISE INDICES

Statistical levels – L_{A10} and L_{A90}

The Wilson Committee used 'statistical sound levels' to describe varying noise levels, principally L_{A10} and L_{A90}, since these were relatively easy to measure with the instruments available at that time.

18.4 *'Typical maximum noise level'* – L_{A10}

L_{A10} is the level of sound exceeded for 10 per cent of the measurement period. In modern usage, the letter 'A' denotes the frequency weighting. It can be regarded as being representative of the typical maximum levels of the fluctuating noise. This index is now principally used in the measurement of road traffic noise. Research has shown that this parameter, when expressed as the average of the 18 one-hourly L_{A10} noise levels between 0600 and 2400 hours, is correlated with annoyance from road traffic noise. The symbol for this index is L_{A10} (18-hour).

18.5 *Background noise level* – L_{A90}

L_{A90} is the level of sound exceeded for 90 per cent of the measurement period. It is therefore a measure of the background noise level, in other words, the sound drops below this level only infrequently. (The term 'background' should not be confused with 'ambient', which refers to *all* the sound present in a given situation at a given time.) The range of noise levels between L_{A90} and L_{A10} is sometimes called the 'noise climate' of an area.

18.6 Equivalent continuous 'A' weighted sound pressure level – L_{Aeq}

This is a modern unit which also takes into account fluctuations in sound pressure levels. This unit takes into account both steady and impulsive noises and is defined as the steady, continuous sound pressure level which contains the same energy as the actual, fluctuating sound pressure level. It is necessary to state the time period over which the sound is measured, e.g. $L_{Aeq, (18-hour)}$.

This unit is now being put forward as a universal noise index, because it can be used to measure all types of noise, although it has yet to supplant older units in a number of areas where calculation techniques and regulatory criteria have not been updated.

Levels measured in L_{Aeq} can be added using the rules mentioned earlier. There is also a time trade-off: if a sound is made for half the measurement period, followed by silence, the L_{Aeq} over the whole measurement period will be 3 dB less than during the noisy half of the period. If the sound is present for one-tenth of the measurement period, the L_{Aeq} over the whole measurement period will be 10 dB less than during the noisy tenth of the measurement period. This is a cause of some criticism of L_{Aeq}: for discontinuous noise, such as may arise during construction work, it does not limit the maximum noise level, so it may be necessary to specify this as well.

18.7   Maximum 'A' weighted sound pressure level – L_{Amax}

This is the maximum root-mean-square (rms) sound pressure level during the measurement period. Sound level meters indicate the rms sound pressure level averaged over a finite period of time. Two averaging periods are defined S (slow) and F (fast) having averaging times of one second and one-eighth of a second. It is necessary to state the averaging period. Maximum SPL should not be confused with Peak SPL which is a measure of the instantaneous peak pressure. This can only be measured with specialist instruments and is used in the assessment of explosive sounds, e.g. in blasting and hearing damage assessments.

18.8   ENVIRONMENTAL PROTECTION ACT 1990

Statutory noise and vibration nuisance

Environmental Protection Act 1990, s 79 defines noise (*inter alia*) as a statutory nuisance when emitted from premises so as to be prejudicial to health or a nuisance, and therefore subject to the provisions of the Act. 'Noise' includes 'vibration' throughout *EPA 1990* and the *Control of Pollution Act 1974*.

EPA 1990, ss 79–82 supersede similar provisions for noise in the *Control of Pollution Act 1974 (COPA)*, ss 57–59. *Section 79* applies to any premises, including land and any vessel except one powered by steam reciprocating machinery. However, defence establishments are exempt from action against noise nuisance, as are aircraft, except model aircraft.

18.9   Noise abatement notices

Where the local authority is satisfied that a noise nuisance may occur or recur, it shall serve a 'noise abatement notice' which may require the abatement of the nuisance, or prohibit or restrict its recurrence, and it may require the execution of remedial works or other steps for those purposes. The time for compliance must be stated. The notice is to be served on the person responsible for the nuisance, or on the owner of the premises if the nuisance is caused by a structural defect; or if the person responsible cannot be found, or if the nuisance has not yet occurred, on the owner or occupier of the premises. Failure to comply with the notice will result in an offence, with penalties continuing until the offence ceases. There is a right of appeal to the Magistrates' Court within 21 days of the service of the notice.

18.10   Defences

It is a defence to show:

(*a*)   that the 'best practicable means' were used to prevent or counteract the nuisance, where it arises on industrial, trade or business premises;

(*b*)   that the alleged offence was covered by a notice under *COPA 1974*, s 60 or a prior consent under s 61, relating to construction sites.

Where the premises are in a noise abatement zone, three further defences exist:

(c)   the noise level did not exceed that stipulated in a consent under *section 65*, relating to registered levels in a noise abatement zone;

(d)   that the noise level did not exceed that stipulated in a noise reduction notice under *COPA 1974, s 66*;

(e)   that the noise level did not exceed that stipulated in an order under *COPA 1974, s 67* relating to noise emissions from a new building.

A local authority may take action against a source of nuisance arising outside its area. Where a notice is not complied with, a local authority may undertake works to abate a nuisance and to recover its reasonable expenses from the persons responsible.

If the local authority feels that action in the Magistrates' Court will be inadequate, it may take action in the High Court: however, if the offence relates to a construction site, it will be a defence to show that the noise was authorised by a notice or consent under *COPA 1974, s 60* or *61*.

18.11 Complaint by an individual

Under *EPA 1990, s 82*, any individual may make a complaint to a Magistrates' Court that he is aggrieved by a noise nuisance. If the court is satisfied that a nuisance exists or, although abated is likely to recur on the same premises, the court shall make an order requiring the defendant to abate the nuisance within a specified time and to execute any works necessary; the same applies to prevention of a recurrence. A fine may also be imposed. Before instituting proceedings for a noise nuisance against anyone, the aggrieved person must give him at least three days' written notice. Where the nuisance arises on industrial, trade or business premises, it is a defence to show that the 'best practicable means' of control have been applied: however, the defence that the works were covered by local authority notices or consents is not available. The court may require the local authority to undertake works to abate a nuisance if the person responsible for the nuisance fails to comply with an abatement order, or if he cannot be found. Successful complainants shall be awarded costs.

18.12 Assessment of nuisance

There are no proven health risks associated with the levels of noise and vibration typically encountered in the environment, although there is a risk of hearing damage from long term exposure to high levels of noise: occupational exposure is dealt with under the *Noise at Work Regulations* which are outside the scope of this chapter. Occupational exposure to high levels of vibration can also have adverse effects on health.

Consequently, noise and vibration nuisance are largely subjective effects which depend on the level of amenity expected by individuals and by the public at large. This leads to considerable debate and dispute about objective criteria for assessment of acceptability. A local authority or complainant need not provide objective measurements of noise or vibration to prove his case, although it is quite common for the noise to be rated in accordance with BS 4142:1990 or to be compared with guidance in various Government Circulars, or Guidance Notes or other British Standards.

18.13 CONTROL OF POLLUTION ACT 1974

Construction sites

Where it appears that construction works are being, or will be, carried out, the local authority may serve a notice under *COPA 1974, s 60* imposing requirements on the way the works are to be undertaken, including the plant or machinery which is, or is not, to be used; the hours of working; and the level of noise at specified times which may be emitted from the premises, or at any specified point on the premises.

In doing so, the local authority must have regard to the need to protect persons in the locality from the effects of noise; any relevant code of practice for noise control issued pursuant to *section 71*; and to the need for ensuring that the best practicable means of noise control are employed. Before specifying particular methods, plant or machinery, the authority must consider whether the operator may prefer an equally effective alternative. Appeals against a notice may be made to the magistrates' court.

Section 60 applies to all types of engineering construction, alteration, repair and demolition, including works on roads, buildings, structures and dredging work.

18.14 Prior consent

Where a person intends to carry out work of the type referred to in *section 60*, he may apply for prior consent under *section 61*, on or after building regulation approval has been sought (where applicable). The application must give particulars of the works, the method by which they will be carried out and the noise control measures which will be used.

The local authority shall give consent if it considers that the proposals are adequate, or it may attach conditions to the consent, limit its duration and limit or qualify the consent to allow for a change of circumstances.

The local authority must respond within 28 days. If it does not, or if it refuses, or if it gives qualified consent, the applicant can appeal within 21 days.

It is an offence to break the terms of the consent. Whilst the consent gives protection against proceedings for nuisance by the local authority, it does not protect against proceedings by a private individual.

18.15 Commentary

Contractors have been generally unwilling to risk an application for prior consent, but with improved methods of noise prediction and control, and the need for more detailed environmental assessments, major construction contracts increasingly require prior consent to be sought. In some cases, this is a condition of the planning consent. Even motorway and trunk road construction projects are becoming subject to such applications, following the loss of Crown immunity. [*EPA 1990, s 159*].

18.16 NOISE ABATEMENT ZONES

Noise abatement orders

A local authority may designate any part or all of its area a noise abatement zone by means of a 'noise abatement order' which must specify the classes of premises to which it applies. Before an order is made, all owners, lessees and occupiers in the area are to be notified and given at least six weeks to lodge an objection with the local authority itself. [*COPA 1974, s 63*].

18.17 Noise level registers

The local authority must measure the level of noise emanating from relevant classes of premises within a noise abatement zone and record the results in a 'noise level register'

18.18 Noise

(the Register) which is available for public inspection. Owners and occupiers are to be supplied with a copy of their entry. They may appeal against it to the Secretary of State within 28 days of notification, who may direct the authority as he thinks fit, regarding the entry. Once an entry has been registered, its validity or accuracy may not be questioned in any following proceedings. [*COPA 1974, s 64*]. The *Control of Noise (Measurements and Registers) Regulations 1976* set out exhaustive requirements for the measurement procedure which it is not appropriate to detail here.

18.18 Consent to exceed the registered noise level

It is an offence to exceed the registered noise level without the authority's consent, which may be subject to conditions regarding the amount and duration of the excess. The consent must be recorded in the Register. The local authority is deemed to have refused consent to exceed the registered level if it does not reach a decision within two months: the applicant may appeal to the Secretary of State within three months of the decision or deemed refusal. [*COPA 1974, s 65*].

18.19 Noise reduction notices

The local authority may issue a 'noise reduction notice' for any premises to which a noise abatement order applies, requiring the level of noise emanating from the premises to be reduced to stated levels, which may be given for different times of the day and different days of the week. The notice may specify what steps are to be taken to reduce noise and it must specify a time for compliance of not less than six months. The noise reduction should be practicable at reasonable cost and afford a public benefit. An appeal against a noise reduction notice must be made to the magistrates' court within three months. [*COPA 1974, s 66*].

In any proceedings against failure to comply with a noise reduction notice, it is a defence to show that 'best practicable means' have been used, provided the noise arises in the course of a trade or business.

18.20 New buildings in a noise abatement zone

The owner or occupier of a new or altered building in a noise abatement zone may apply to the local authority for determination of the acceptable level of noise for his building, or the local authority may do this of its own initiative, and the level will be added to the Register. The applicant may appeal to the Secretary of State within three months, either against the determined level, or against the failure of the local authority to determine a level within two months. [*COPA 1974, s 67*].

If no level of noise has been determined for a new or altered building within a noise abatement zone, the local authority may issue a noise reduction notice if it appears that an unacceptable level of noise is emanating: in such a case, there is no requirement that the reduction of noise should be at reasonable cost and of public benefit; no more than three months need be allowed for compliance, and the 'best practicable means' defence is not available in proceedings for non-compliance. [*COPA 1974, s 67(5)*].

18.21 Commentary

The legislation on noise abatement zones has not been a great success. Noise registers are difficult to set up, because the measurements require considerable manpower, technical expertise and expensive equipment. It is often difficult to determine the precise contribution from individual premises, especially where there is extraneous noise, such as from a road. Noise reduction notices could be difficult to sustain, requiring justification as to practicability and need. Where noise problems arise, it is quicker, simpler and more certain to take action for noise nuisance, whilst proper planning will alleviate problems in the longer term. Consequently, very few noise abatement zones have ever been set up: the concept is in need of some overhaul if its original intentions are to be achieved. However, in many districts, transportation noise is probably the more serious problem, which noise abatement zones cannot alleviate.

18.22 Codes of practice

The Secretary of State may prepare, issue and approve codes of practice giving guidance on minimising noise, including the use of specified types of plant and machinery. He may also approve codes of practice issued by other bodies for the same purpose. [*COPA 1974, s 71*]. A number of codes of practice have been approved, although some prepared by vested interests have not received approval.

The following codes of practice have been approved by statutory instrument (the statutory instrument itself does not contain the code of practice):

(*a*)   BS 5228: Noise control on construction and open sites:

Part 1: 1984 Code of practice for basic information and procedures for noise control [*SI 1984 No 1992*];

Part 3: 1984 Code of practice for noise control applicable to surface coal extraction by opencast methods [*SI 1984 No 1992*];

Part 4: 1992 Code of practice for noise control applicable to piling operations (not yet approved; Part 4: 1986 was approved by *SI 1987 No 1730*);

(*b*)   Ice cream van chimes [*SI 1981 No 1828*];

(*c*)   Burglar alarms [*SI 1981 No 1829*];

(*d*)   Model aircraft [*SI 1981 No 1830*].

18.23 Regulations governing noise from machinery

The Secretary of State may make regulations requiring the use of noise reduction devices on plant or machinery, or for limiting the level of noise produced by construction machinery. [*COPA 1974, s 68*].

No such regulations have been made and it appears to be unlikely that these provisions will ever be used as the current approach is now different. The *Construction Plant and Equipment (Harmonisation of Noise Emission Standards) Regulations 1985* (*SI 1985 No 1968*) (supplemented by *SI 1988 No 361* and *SI 1992 No 488*) require certain such plant to carry a label indicating the sound power level it produces. These *Regulations* were introduced as part of the EC approach to the single European market, but should help to bring market forces to bear in producing quieter plant as contractors face more stringent controls on the noise they can create.

18.24 BRITISH STANDARDS

BS 4142:1990 Method for Rating Industrial Noise affecting Mixed Residential and Industrial Areas

This is a procedure for assessing the likelihood of complaints arising as a result of noise from factories, other fixed installations and sources of industrial noise in commercial premises. The original concept arises from work reported by the Wilson Committee,

18.25 Noise

but it was very substantially modified in the 1990 revision. The procedure is often used as an objective method of assessing nuisance, although the foreword to the procedure emphasises that quantitative assessment of general community annoyance and the assessment of nuisance is beyond the standard.

The procedure is rigorously defined: considerable skill and care is needed in using it. In summary, it requires the 'rating' level of the noise under investigation to be compared with the background L_{A90}. If the intruding noise exceeds the background by 10 dB or more, this indicates that complaints are likely. An excess of 5 dB is of marginal significance, and at 5 dB below background, there is less likelihood of complaints. At 10 dB below background, there is a positive indication that complaints are unlikely. The main requirements of the procedure are as follows.

The noise should be measured preferably with a Type 1 (precision) sound level meter, preferably giving a direct measurement of L_{Aeq}, and having a calibration certificate. The intruding noise is measured over a one-hour period in the daytime and over a five-minute period at night. (This allows noisy events to be averaged over a longer period in the daytime, which may result in a lower average level.) If the intruding noise has a distinguishable discrete note (e.g. whine, hiss, screech, hum), distinct impulses (bangs, clicks, clatters, thumps) or it is sufficiently irregular to attract attention, a penalty of 5 dB is added to the measured level to give the 'rating' level. (Only a single 5 dB penalty is added.) The background noise level may be measured over any time period which gives a representative value – usually at least five minutes. All measurements are made outside buildings at a location free from reflecting surfaces other than the facade in question, and the influence of wind, rain and electrical noise must be minimised.

18.25 BS 5228:Part 1:1984 Noise Control on Construction and Open Sites

Part 1 of this standard is a code of practice for basic information and procedures for noise control. It contains a comprehensive set of tables describing the noise levels produced by a wide variety of construction and demolition operations, along with a procedure for calculating the L_{Aeq} emanating from a construction site. The procedure has been validated for small sites: for large sites (e.g. trunk road construction and surface mineral workings), it may be necessary to use enhanced calculation procedures (Control of Noise at Surface Mineral Workings, HMSO 1990 and MPG II).

18.26 CIRCULAR 10/73 'PLANNING AND NOISE'

This circular is the extant Government advice, although a replacement (PPG 20) is currently in the draft consultation phase. The circular recommends various criteria in now out-moded units (Noise and Number Index, Corrected Noise Level) and is therefore becoming difficult to use. However, some of the policy statements are still useful in planning work.

The general approach is that noise-sensitive developments and noise sources should be kept apart by adoption of suitable planning policies. Where other constraints make this impracticable, then planning conditions must be used to ensure that the siting and design will minimise the effect of noise. Sometimes this will require a comprehensive approach to the planning of developments. The circular stresses the need to avoid increases in ambient noise levels affecting noise-sensitive areas. It also advises that applicants for industrial developments should provide predictions of noise levels and, if a BS 4142 assessment shows that they are 'likely to give rise to complaints', *even if reasonable sound insulation is provided*, 'it will hardly ever be right to give permission'. This now appears to be a confusing statement, because BS 4142 relies on external noise levels, which noise insulation cannot affect. It arises through the many changes to BS 4142 since 1973. The intention, however, is indicated in the following standards, which the circular suggests should apply to sites proposed for noise-sensitive development.

Table 18.1

Standard	Traffic Noise	Industrial Noise	
	L_{A10} (18-hour) dB(A)	Corrected Noise Level dB(A) (Approximately equal to 'rating noise level' see BS 4142:1990)	
		Day	Night
Site Standard	68*	75	65
Maximum noise level within dwellings with windows closed	50	55	45
'Good standard' of noise within dwellings with windows closed	40	45	35

* *Revised figure*

The site standard is the recommended maximum noise exposure of a site proposed for noise-sensitive development. Noise insulation would be required to obtain the 'good standard' of internal noise on a site exposed to the site standard level.

The circular gives criteria for aircraft noise in terms of NNI which have now been effectively superseded by a recent Government decision to change to the L_{Aeq} index.

18.27 Revision of Circular 10/73 'Planning and Noise' : draft PPG 20

The Noise Review Working Party recommended that Circular 10/73 should be revised: a Planning Policy Guidance Note (PPG 20) to replace the circular is currently in draft for consultation. This draft takes into account powers and procedures under the *Town and Country Planning (Applications) Regulations 1988* and the *Town and Country Planning (Assessment of Environmental Effects) Regulations 1988* to require information from planning applicants. The basic tenet of the guidance remains that noise-sensitive developments should be kept apart from sources of noise, and vice versa. The earlier recommendation for a 'comprehensive approach to the planning of developments' is reinforced through recommendations that local plans or Part II of Unitary Development Plans should contain noise control policies. PPG 20 is intended to assist planning authorities in formulating these policies, but leaves it open to them to propose variations to deal with local circumstances.

An important innovation is the definition of 'action levels' for noise, as suggested by the Noise Review Working Party, in four categories:

(a)   Noise exposure category A

Noise need not be considered a determining factor in granting planning permission, but noise at the high end of the category should not be regarded as a desirable level.

(b)   Noise exposure category B

Noise should increasingly be taken into account and require noise control measures.

18.28 Noise

(c)   Noise exposure category C

There should be a strong presumption against development, but where it is considered that permission should be granted, conditions must ensure adequate insulation against noise.

(d)   Noise exposure category D

Permission should normally be refused. There are different limits for dwellings and schools, and for road, air, rail and mixed sources of noise, in terms of L_{Aeq} (0700–2300 hours). There is a single set of limits for night-time (2300–0700 hours). They are not quoted here as they may change following the consultation period: furthermore, each authority would be entitled to devise alternatives.

It should be noted that industrial, construction and surface minerals sites are omitted from the noise exposure categories. There is much controversy over limits for industrial developments and further research is being conducted into this. The draft discusses the use of BS 4142:1990 for assessing the likelihood of complaints and some of the difficulties in using it. However, it shrinks from imposing this approach, discussing the alternative possibilities of noise abatement zones.

Similarly, powers under *COPA 1974, ss 60, 61* are cited as a means of dealing with construction noise. MPG 11 gives guidance on noise at surface mineral workings, discussed below.

18.28 Control of noise at surface mineral workings, MPG 11

These guidelines provide advice on how the planning system can be used to keep noise within environmentally acceptable limits without imposing an unreasonable burden on minerals operators. They will replace the general advice on noise control in MPG 2, MPG 9 and PPG 20 (the replacement of Circular 10/73). The guidelines recommend:

(a)   a modified form of the BS 5228 Part 1: 1984 noise calculation method;

(b)   a method of setting noise limits for incorporation into planning conditions which take into account the particular features of each site and which should be straightforward to monitor;

(c)   monitoring procedures;

(d)   noise control practices which can be made the subject of planning conditions and/or can be incorporated into good practice by the operator.

It is suggested that much of the guidance would also apply to waste sites. The suggested noise limits for noise-sensitive properties are 55 dB L_{Aeq} (one-hour) free field in the daytime (0700–1900 hours), and 42 dB L_{Aeq} (one-hour) free field at night (1900–0700 hours). It may be appropriate for dawn and evening periods to have intermediate limits. For open-cast coal, it may be necessary to accept a higher daytime limit up to 60 dB L_{Aeq} (one-hour) free field in exceptional cases. Also, it may be necessary to permit higher limits during temporary works, such as site preparation and restoration and during the construction of baffle mounds. A daytime limit of 65 dB(A) L_{Aeq} (one-hour) is suggested for certain areas of open space heavily used by the public for quiet relaxation, but the effect on the feasibility of the proposed operation is a material consideration. SSSI's may be noise-sensitive in exceptional circumstances.

18.29 ROAD TRAFFIC NOISE

The construction and maintenance of roads is the responsibility of the Highway Authority, generally the Department of Transport for motorways and trunk roads and

216

the county council, London borough or metropolitan borough in the case of all other roads. There are no noise standards set down for the construction and use of new roads. However, the *Highways (Assessment of Environmental Effects) Regulations 1988 (SI 1988 No 1241)* require an environmental statement (see ENVIRONMENTAL AUDITS (8)) to be prepared for all trunk roads over 10km in length, other trunk roads over 1km in length which pass within 100m of a National Park, an SSSI, a conservation area or a designated nature reserve, or through an area where more than 1,500 dwellings lie within 100m of the centre line of the road. New motorways, trunk roads and improvements to them which may have a significant effect on the environment also require an environmental statement. The *Town and Country Planning (Assessment of Environmental Effects) Regulations 1988 (SI 1988 No 1199)* stipulate that 'special roads' (generally motorways) are *Schedule 1* schemes requiring an environmental statement. Other roads are regarded as *Schedule 2* schemes, requiring an environmental statement where the scheme is likely to have a significant effect on the environment. The *Regulations* do not stipulate how such an assessment is to be made.

The Department of Transport's *Design Manual for Roads and Bridges, Volume 11 'Environmental Assessment'* (June 1993) provides guidance on the assessment of trunk road schemes, including motorways. It applies to the whole of the UK, including Northern Ireland, and supersedes a number of earlier standards. It envisages three key stages in the development of a road scheme, the detail of the assessment increasing at each stage.

At Stage 1 (pre-programme entry assessment) the assessment is related to broadly-defined route corridors. The main steps are to identify existing roads and new routes or corridors where traffic flows may change by 25% (corresponding to 1 dB(A) in noise level) in the year of opening; to consult with the local authority for information on existing nuisance from roads or industry, and for noise constraints from Local Plans; to identify sensitive areas for noise and vibration (including certain non-residential buildings and recreational areas); and to estimate the number of houses at various distances bands within 300m of the road.

Stage 2 (pre-public consultation assessment) is intended to assist in developing and refining route options. It includes the requirements of Stage 1, but with the additional requirement to determine changes in noise level at sensitive properties, taking agreed mitigation into account. The changes should be annotated on a map, which should show the distances at which changes will not be discernible. (There is an implication that this should be within 300m, but this may not hold for busy motorways.) An estimate of vibration nuisance can be made from a chart, where appropriate.

Stage 3 is the assessment required for the Environmental Statement. It requires all the information in Stage 2 to be worked up in more detail for the 'Preferred Route' and the 'Do Minimum' Option. The changes of noise level are to be classified in bands of 1 to 3, 3 to 5, 5 to 10, 10 to 15, and over 15 dB(A), and also according to the prevailing ambient noise level in bands of below 50, 50 to 60, 60 to 70, and above 70 dB(A). A complex new requirement is to estimate the change in noise nuisance and potential risks of sleep disturbance resulting from the scheme. A series of charts are provided for the purpose, but it is not appropriate to detail the procedure here.

18.30 Land Compensation Act 1973

Compensation under Part 1 of the Land Compensation Act

Owners of property which depreciates in value as a result of direct physical factors (such as noise) arising from the use of a new or substantially altered road are entitled to claim compensation for any resultant loss in value of the property, which is assessed at a

18.31   Noise

point one year after the opening of the road. This is additional to, but takes into account, any noise insulation which may have been offered. Claims for compensation must be made within a limited period which comes into operation one year after the road is opened.

18.31 *The Noise Insulation Regulations 1975 (as amended 1988)*

These *Regulations* impose a duty on highway authorities to offer a package of noise insulation and associated measures for living rooms and bedrooms in dwellings and other residential buildings against noise from new roads including roads to which an extra carriageway has been added. This duty applies to eligible buildings within 300 metres of the new road where the future noise level within a period of 15 years is expected to be 68 dB(A) L_{10} (18-hour) or greater, provided that this level is at least 1.0 dB(A) greater than the pre-construction noise level and that traffic on the new highway contributes at least 1.0 dB(A) to the total noise level. [*Reg 3*].

The *Regulations* also give the highway authority discretionary powers to insulate dwellings against noise from substantially altered highways and, in limited circumstances, to extend insulation from qualifying properties to adjacent properties which do not otherwise meet the noise exposure criteria for insulation. [*Reg 4*].

The highway authority also has discretionary powers to provide insulation against construction noise where this could seriously affect the enjoyment of a dwelling for a substantial period of time. [*Reg 5*].

18.32 *The noise insulation package*

The noise insulation package applies only to living rooms and bedrooms in dwellings and other buildings used for residential purposes. [*Reg 7*]. Thus staff quarters in a hotel would be eligible, but guest rooms would not. A nurses' home would qualify, but a hospital ward would not. The kitchen of a dwelling would not qualify unless it is also used as a dining room. Noise insulation consists of weather-stripping (draught-proofing) the existing primary window and providing an openable secondary window inside the primary window. The air space between the two windows ranges between 100 and 200mm depending on the thickness of the secondary pane of glass; this is necessary to provide adequate attenuation of low-frequency sound. The window reveal is lined with sound absorbent material. [*Schedule 1*].

A venetian blind must also be fitted between the two windows if they face towards the sun, unless there is some other means of controlling exposure to heat from the sun.

Each insulated room must be fitted with a silenced mechanical ventilator (an electric fan contained in an acoustically-lined box). A fixed vent must also be provided. These are usually enclosed in the same box which must normally be mounted on an outside wall of the building. A room containing a combustion appliance which draws air from the room may require additional permanent vents. The *Regulations* specify the use of fan-failure valves on the supply to gas cookers, but these have been found to be unsatisfactory in practice and therefore rooms with gas cookers or any other flueless combustion appliance cannot be insulated unless there are adequate openable windows on a non-insulated facade. [*Reg 9(2)*].

The *Regulations* spell out the terms in which an offer must be made [*Reg 8*], with an appeals procedure. [*Reg 13*]. The Highway Authority must make an offer of insulation to the occupier of the premises, who must notify his landlord, if any. The authority must offer the choice of doing the work or of paying a grant for the occupier to do the work. Although there are cost yardsticks for the grant, these are out of date and therefore the amount of the grant is limited to what it would cost the Highway

218

Authority to do the work, or the actual cost to the claimant, whichever is the less. [*Reg 11*].

Many occupiers wish to take the grant as a contribution towards 'sealed unit' replacement-type dual glazing, which is usually more expensive. However, it does not conform to the specification for noise insulation and the *Regulations* prohibit the payment of grant except on installations completed to specification. [*Reg 10*]. Where a building is subject to a tenancy agreement, either the landlord or tenant can accept insulation, even if the other party does not consent. [*Reg 12*].

18.33 Calculation of Road Traffic Noise

Range of applications and procedure

This is the statutory calculation procedure for assessment of entitlement under the *Noise Insulation Regulations*, but it is also applicable to ENVIRONMENTAL ASSESSMENT (7) of road schemes, highway design and land use planning. Two methods of calculation are provided: prediction and measurement. Prediction is the preferred method, but measurements are permitted where traffic conditions fall outside the range of validity of the prediction method, where traffic or site conditions are unusually complex, or measurement is a more economical method of determining the noise level. Measurements can only be made when the wind direction is generally towards the reception point, its speed not more than 10 m/s and the road surface is dry. Whilst members of the public often expect measurements to be made as a check on calculations, it is often difficult to obtain the right weather conditions, it may not be possible to ascertain the contribution from different parts of the road network, and it may still be necessary to apply a calculated factor to allow for future changes in traffic flows.

The prediction method is complex and, whilst manual calculations are feasible, the use of a computer program is a great advantage. The method has been refined over a number of years and is very reliable when properly applied.

18.34 RAILWAY NOISE

Railway noise is measured in terms of the L_{Aeq} index. Following the Report of the Mitchell Committee, the Government has decided that separate assessment of daytime (0600–2400 hours) and night-time (2400–0600 hours) periods is desirable and has stated that noise insulation would be appropriate, for equity with the standard for road traffic noise, when the daytime exposure reaches 68 L_{Aeq} (18-hour) or the night-time exposure reaches 63 L_{Aeq} (6-hour). In October 1993, *The Noise Insulation (Railways and Other Guided Transport Systems) Regulations 1993* were issued in draft for public comment. These are analogous to the *Noise Insulation Regulations* for road traffic, but with trigger levels for insulation as set out above. At the same time, the Department of Transport issued a draft calculation method for railway noise.

18.35 AIRCRAFT NOISE

Civil Aviation Act 1982

Protection from action

Noise from aircraft is protected from action against trespass or nuisance by the *Civil Aviation Act 1982, ss 76, 77*, provided that the *Rules of the Air, Air Traffic Control Regulations* and normal aviation practice are observed. *CA 1982* also makes the

18.36 Noise

Secretary of State for Transport responsible for noise abatement measures for aircraft taking off or landing at airports designated for the purposes of *section 78*, and for noise insulation schemes for airports designated for the purposes of *section 79*. Presently, three airports are designated: Heathrow and Gatwick for both sections and Stansted under *section 78* only. However, a number of regional airports have noise insulation and abatement schemes as a condition of their planning consent.

18.36 *Consultation facilities*

Under *section 35*, the Secretary of State may require an airport to establish suitable consultation facilities with users, local authorities and local representative organisations. All national and regional airports and some general aviation airfields have been designated. The general policy is to designate airports with a turnover in excess of £1m, and smaller airfields in response to requests where designation is likely to help in alleviating local problems. Some airfields also have voluntary consultation facilities.

18.37 *Environmental considerations when licensing*

Under *section 5*, the Secretary of State may require the Civil Aviation Authority (CAA) to consider environmental matters when licensing or re-licensing an aerodrome, but this power has not been used. Under *section 6*, the Secretary of State may direct the CAA, where it has power, to take action to deal with noise, vibration, etc., attributable to civil aviation.

18.38 Aircraft noise indices

Following the work of the Wilson Committee, aircraft noise in the UK was assessed by the Noise and Number Index (NNI). There were concerns about its validity, especially for smaller airfields [DR Report 8402], and it has now been superseded by the L_{Aeq} (0700–2300 hours) index for daytime aircraft noise exposure, which is thought to have more general applicability although it is more complex to calculate. There is no policy decision on an index for aircraft noise exposure at night.

18.39 Aircraft noise and sleep disturbance

Research by the CAA [DR Report 8402] suggests that aircraft movements outside daytime hours should be included in an index, but not weighted to penalise such movements. The Report concluded that L_{Aeq} (24-hour) gives good correlation with noise disturbance. 55 L_{Aeq} (24-hour) represents the point of onset of community disturbance and 70 L_{Aeq} (24-hour) is a point of high disturbance.

Other research into sleep disturbance at Heathrow and Gatwick [DORA Report 8008] suggests that a satisfactory measure of aircraft noise exposure, i.e. one which correlates well with sleep disturbance is L_{Aeq} (2300–0700 hours). The research seems to indicate that aircraft noise causes additional awakening at levels of 65 L_{Aeq} (2300–0700 hours). However, the research does not claim that this index is superior to a 24-hour index, nor that separate day and night indices are needed. The Report also supports the approach of some noise insulation policies which are based on the noise footprint produced by individual aircraft, with the 95 PN dB (approximately 82 dB(A)) footprint being taken as the criterion for sleep disturbance. Research on this matter is continuing.

18.40 Calculation of aircraft noise

There is no standardised UK calculation procedure but the CAA and a number of consultancies have developed their own techniques, which require sophisticated computer programs to operate from a comprehensive database of aircraft noise and performance data.

18.41 OTHER TRANSPORTATION PROJECTS

Proposals for new railways, tramways, other guided transport systems and certain works relating to canals or interfering with rights of navigation will require an environmental statement unless waived by the Secretary of State [*Transport and Works (Applications and Objections Procedure) Rules 1992* (in draft)].

18.42 CONTROL OF NOISE AND VIBRATION

Introduction

The control of noise and vibration forms an integral part of good design and should not be regarded as something which can be simply added on as an afterthought. Whilst environmental statements raise the question of noise and vibration, the matter is treated too often as a simple reporting exercise rather than as a procedure which should have a beneficial effect on the design process. Good design starts from a proper understanding of the performance requirements of the project: for noise and vibration, this will mean assessing the likely emissions from noisy areas and the targets to be achieved in sensitive areas.

18.43 Site layout

The whole issue can be made less critical if noisy areas are kept away from sensitive areas, preferably with an intermediate buffer zone. Consequently, the importance of a good site layout cannot be over-emphasised. On open sites, it may be possible to locate service buildings to screen noisy activities; in the case of surface mineral sites, overburden mounds may be able to serve this purpose, and even the direction of working may be arranged so that the working face screens the noisy activities. On industrial sites, sources such as ventilation units are often highly directional, so it may be possible to locate these so that they face away from sensitive areas.

With ingenuity, measures such as these need cost little or nothing, but because questions of site layout tend to be settled early in the design process, it may not be possible to take advantage of them unless noise is considered from the outset.

18.44 Dealing with noise problems

Whenever a noise problem is encountered, it is essential that a proper study is undertaken to identify the causes, or potential causes, and then to verify these by means of proper acoustical calculations and possibly other studies relating to the operation of the process itself. There have been many cases where silencers, speed controllers and the like have been installed, only to make matters worse. The calculations need to demonstrate that the cause has been correctly identified and that the proposed remedial work is adequate for the purpose. Whilst the calculations require skill and practical experience of the type of plant and process involved, the solution of noise problems need not be, and should not be, a haphazard procedure of trial and error.

18.45 Design of noise control schemes

The first priority, when designing a noise control scheme, is to identify and cure the major sources of noise, no matter how difficult and expensive this may be. For example,

18.46 Noise

if two sources are contributing 63 and 53 dB(A) respectively at a receiver, the total noise will still add up to about 63 dB(A). This is because the louder source is producing ten times the sound intensity of the quieter source. It is therefore obvious that to reach a target of, say, 60 dB(A) at the receiver, no amount of work to reduce or even eliminate the quieter source will achieve that target. However, if the louder source is reduced by 4 dB(A) to 59 dB(A), the target level of 60 dB(A) will be achieved.

For this reason, the usual procedure in designing a noise control scheme is to rank the noise sources in order of significance and to reduce them, starting from the loudest, until the desired target is achieved.

18.46 Methods of reducing noise

Noise and vibration can be controlled at its source, along its propagation (transmission) path, or at the receiver. If at all feasible, it is preferable to control noise at source, since this avoids the need to identify and treat possibly a multitude of propagation paths and receivers. However, this may require a complete change to the process in question and is often impracticable in an existing installation. It is only practicable to control noise at the receiver when there are a limited number of identifiable reception points: for environmental noise, this option may not be feasible because there are too many potential reception points and they are not accessible to the originator of the noise. Consequently, much noise and vibration control takes place along the propagation path.

18.47 Control of noise at source

The control of noise at its source is usually dependent on finding a way of undertaking the process in a smooth and gradual manner, avoiding sudden impacts and changes. Examples include the use of rotary rather than reciprocating machinery, using belts instead of gears, breaking things by bending or slicing rather than hammering or chiselling and reducing pressure in several gradual steps, rather than in one sudden step. It is quite often found that such changes make the process more energy efficient and, indeed, developments designed to improve energy efficiency frequently produce lower noise levels as a side-effect.

Where existing plant is causing a noise problem, it may be tempting to scrap it and replace it with new equipment, but it would be unwise to assume that new plant will be automatically quieter. Plant should be ordered against a carefully thought-out specification, preferably requiring the supplier to guarantee to achieve the required noise targets. Where components are bought from a number of sources, the performance of the total system should be specified and the main contractor, engineer or noise consultant should have a duty to see that this is met, otherwise there can be serious disputes over who is at fault should a problem arise.

18.48 Fans

Fans are often required for the cooling of motors, pumps, compressors, engines and many types of electrically-powered equipment; they can be the prime source of noise in these devices. They are also used for cooling buildings, which not only creates noise in itself, but can also form a weak link through which noise can escape to the exterior. Whilst some designs of fan are much quieter than others for a given duty, those commonly fitted to equipment are selected primarily for small size and price rather than efficiency. Some designs of fan are particularly susceptible to the creation of a strong hum or whine which adds disproportionately to the annoyance. The selection of the best fan for the job requires thought as to the duty (i.e. the volume and pressure of the air that needs to be moved) and to the noise targets. There is an enormous variety of silencers available for fans, but their selection is a specialist subject in itself, as certain types of fan will not work efficiently against any resistance to air flow. It is futile to fit a silencer in such cases as the fan will continue to make a noise, but will fail to shift any air. Thermostatic controls on cooling fans may add to the cost, but prevent noise and wasted energy when cooling is not needed.

18.49 Reduction of radiated noise

Noise is often radiated from the outer surfaces of objects which are set into vibration by the motion of masses within them. The principal ways of reducing this effect are to strengthen casings to avoid resonances, to fix damping materials (such as rubber or bitumastic sheets) onto the casing to 'kill' the vibration, or to contain the vibration by lagging the casing. Lagging usually requires an inner flexible layer (such as mineral fibre) faced with an outer heavy and airtight skin. The inner flexible layer prevents vibration from reaching the outer skin.

18.50 The propagation path

There are many ways of reducing noise as it travels along its propagation path; perhaps the most obvious is to fit an enclosure around the machine. Enclosures are capable of giving very significant reductions in noise: the main drawbacks are that they impede access to the machine, which can be a problem when materials must be fed into the machine and products must be taken from it; enclosures may cause a heat build-up, requiring cooling fans to be fitted; they take up space around the machine and may become a dirt trap, especially problematic in the food and pharmaceutical industries.

18.51 Design of enclosures

An enclosure is only as good as its weakest link: even small air gaps can cause a serious loss of performance. Devising and maintaining an adequate seal, particularly on doors which have to withstand frequent use, is a special difficulty. Even the minute interstices in the mortar of a brick wall have a measurable reduction in its noise performance, so where maximum performance is needed, it is usual to require these to be plastered.

A further problem is to eliminate 'flanking' transmission, whereby noise skirts around the wall or enclosure that is intended to stop it. Very often, this occurs when vibration from the machine gets into the supporting structure, travels through it and is re-radiated by walls or floors on the other side of the partition. It is, therefore, important that the machine is supported on flexible 'antivibration' mounts and that pipework and electrical conduits contain flexible connections to provide a vibration break.

18.52 Reduction of reverberation

Some buildings are highly reverberant and in such cases it may be possible to reduce noise levels by putting acoustically absorbent materials, such as acoustic tiles, on the walls or ceiling, or by hanging sound absorbers above the working area. The noise reduction is generally fairly small, around 5 dB(A), so this tends to be a relatively inefficient solution, particularly as absorbers do little to reduce noise levels close to the source where occupational noise exposure is important.

18.53 Noise barriers

Noise barriers are not very effective within a building because of the effect of reverberation, but they can be helpful in the open. The effectiveness of a barrier depends on the degree to which it cuts off the direct line of sight between the source and the receiver and on the frequency of the sound. Barriers are more effective at reducing high-frequency sound than low-frequency sound and, for preference, should be positioned either close to the source or close to the receiver.

18.54 Noise control at the receiver

As mentioned previously, control of environmental noise at the receiver can be problematic because the receiver is usually in a different ownership from the source of the noise. Noise insulation, discussed under the heading 'Road traffic noise' at 18.29 above, is the most obvious form of control at the receiver, along with rearranging the space so that noise-sensitive usages are moved to a quieter area. A further possibility is to use a bland 'masking noise' which disguises the intruding noise. Masking noises are usually broad-band 'pink' noise, giving a gentle 'rushing' sound so as to be reasonably effective without being excessively intrusive. Noise control within a building is particularly difficult because noise will travel through the structure and services such as pipework, with very little attenuation. It is crucial to provide air-tight partitions and vibration breaks, which requires particular attention to detail and a high quality of workmanship. Proper advice should be obtained whenever very low noise levels are needed at the receiver as this may require special designs, maybe even mounting a whole building on springs to avoid ground-borne noise, especially new railways.

18.55 Active noise control

This is the cancellation of an offending noise by the use of an anti-phase or negative copy of the original signal. Significant advances have been made in recent years, but currently the principle tends to be applied to low-frequency tonal noises, generally propagating along a duct or in a confined space. ANC systems require sophisticated electronics with high capital and maintenance costs. Consequently, they are found where performance is the criterion, typically aerospace and military applications.

18.56 Obtaining advice

Many acoustic hardware manufacturers provide a free advisory service, usually relating to their own products, whilst a full, independent professional service is provided by acoustics consultants such as those who belong to the Association of Noise Consultants, which requires its members to be qualified and to give an independent service. The Institute of Acoustics is the governing body of the profession. Noise consultants will provide a free quotation for their services and are increasingly willing to do fixed-price work. Where competitive quotations are sought, this should be against a properly drawn-up specification, otherwise there can be big differences in the depth and scope of the various proposals put forward, making fair comparisons impossible.

19 Northern Ireland

19.1 INTRODUCTION

The legal system in Northern Ireland is broadly similar to that of England and Wales. The main way in which law differs in Northern Ireland relates to the mechanism for enacting legislation. Since the abolition of the legislature at Stormont in 1972 and the institution of direct rule from Westminster, most of Northern Ireland's legislation is carried into effect by *Orders in Council*. Under the *Northern Ireland Act 1974, Orders in Council* are used to make laws for Northern Ireland on subjects which are 'transferred matters' under the *Northern Ireland Constitution Act 1973*. Only 'excepted' matters, e.g. terrorism, need to be legislated for by an Act of Parliament at Westminster. Unlike primary legislation these *Orders in Council* can be challenged by the courts. However this procedure does not provide Parliament with any mechanism for amending the Government's legislative proposals – an *Order* must be accepted or rejected as a whole, though it can be withdrawn and re-laid later in a revised form. In consequence, there is a clear political vacuum/democratic deficit in terms of accountability. A further consequence, at least so far as progressive legislation is concerned, is that Northern Irish law often lags behind that of the rest of the UK.

Certainly this is the case with environmental policy and legislation. Northern Irish environmental law is characterised by a backlog of legislation waiting to be implemented, a failure to implement *EC Directives* and international covenants and an unsatisfactory position in relation to protective statutory designations. Therefore, despite the Government's commitment in its White Paper on the Environment (*This Common Inheritance: Britain's Environmental Strategy* (Cm 1200, 1990)) to the imposition and maintenance of identical environmental standards for the whole of the United Kingdom, Northern Ireland lags far behind the rest of the United Kingdom in terms of environmental protection. Indeed, concern over the process of legislating for Northern Ireland prompted the Rossi Committee (Environment Committee First Report, *Environmental Issues in Northern Ireland* HC 39 (1990–91)) to recommend that:

'the Government pay more attention in the future to ensuring that disparities between the substance of environmental legislation in Northern Ireland and the rest of the United Kingdom is minimal'. (paragraph 33)

Rather than enacting a comprehensive legislative programme as with the *Environmental Protection Act 1990*, the Government's plan is to introduce a number of separate *Orders in Council* for Northern Ireland dealing with disparate pieces of United Kingdom legislation. Moreover, the comparatively trivial aspects of the British legislation are to be the first to be implemented here. So far the only part of the *1990 Act* to have been implemented in this jurisdiction is the section on Genetically Modified Organisms which was implemented in the *Genetically Modified Organisms (Northern Ireland) Order 1991 (SI 1991 No 1714)*. The next proposed *Order* is to be a *Litter (Northern Ireland) Order* (now in draft), before the more substantial issues like statutory nuisances and the duty of care in relation to waste are tackled. Already the legislative timetable is behind schedule. Moreover, it is noteworthy that, whereas in other areas vast sums of money are pumped into the Northern Ireland economy, considerably fewer resources have been devoted to the cause of environmental protection. The Department of the Environment for Northern Ireland, which has a broad remit in relation to environmental issues, is severely under-resourced. Although the Rossi Report acknowledged the existence of the pressing economic and security issues which have dominated the activities of politicians and civil servants (paragraph 107) they were of the view that the resulting situation, whereby mechanisms and bodies to protect the environment are lacking, or under-resourced, needed to be tackled.

19.2 European and international obligations

Because the passage of an *Order in Council* takes a minimum of 64 weeks, and the process of legislating for Northern Ireland usually begins after the *EC Directive/ Regulation* in question has been implemented in the rest of the UK, the resulting delay often means that the UK is in breach of EC legislation in respect of Northern Ireland. For example, when the UK was recently found by the European Court of Justice to be in breach of the *Drinking Water Directive*, one of the grounds of complaint by the European Commission was the fact that the *Directive* had not been implemented in Northern Ireland or Scotland. (See N Schoon and A Marshall, 'Britain guilty of breaching EC water laws' *The Guardian*, 26 November 1992.)

19.3 The players

The lack of accountability which affects the process of legislating for Northern Ireland extends to the body responsible for implementing and policing most of the legislation.

The most significant player in relation to the environment in Northern Ireland is the Department of the Environment for Northern Ireland (DoE(NI)) which is charged with a wide range of responsibilities for issues including planning, roads, water, housing, transport, collection of rates (the poll tax has never applied here), land registration, mapping, nature reserves and environmental protection. This centralisation of power within the DoE(NI) has arisen largely as a consequence of the economic and political situation in Northern Ireland, and has certainly been detrimental to the cause of environmental protection within Northern Ireland. For instance, many of these wide-ranging functions would appear to have mutually conflicting goals – e.g. in relation to water pollution, the DoE(NI), which both operates sewage works, and is responsible for policing pollution, is perceived as both poacher and gamekeeper. Another consequence is that important environmental issues within or between departments are rarely debated in the public domain, e.g. the cross-border drainage scheme at the Blackwater River, or salmon fishing in Strangford Lough, or the designation of Marine Nature Reserves. Moreover, the problems faced by the DoE(NI) appear to have been intensified by its narrow focus upon the negative or restrictive aspects of conservation. None of the more positive measures adopted in Britain, such as the national parks and management plans, have been attempted in Northern Ireland. Nor has the DoE(NI) been able to achieve the high profile and popular initiatives of British agencies like English Heritage and the Countryside Commission. The Rossi Committee concluded that it was imperative that a more positive approach was taken (paragraph 124). The DoE(NI) is also hampered by the fact that environmental issues are positively underfunded in comparison with other areas of government activity.

The centralisation of environmental functions in Northern Ireland may be contrasted with the pattern of environmental administration in Great Britain, which has been for independent bodies to take responsibility for different aspects of the environment. Within a statutory remit and subject to statutory limitations they are able to set their own agenda and engage freely in debate.

However, recent years have witnessed a fragmentation of functions within the DoE(NI), with different functions being allocated to separate units. This has largely occurred in response to the report of the Balfour Committee (J Balfour, *A New Look at the Northern Irish Countryside* (1984)) which decided that there was no need for an environmental protection agency separate from the DoE, although commitment to environmental protection needed to be strengthened within the department.

Thus, in 1984 a new Environmental Protection Division was established within the DoE(NI) through the amalgamation of the Countryside and Wildlife Branch with the Historic Monuments and Buildings Branch, and the Conservation Service was expanded. However, the status and resourcing of these services within the DoE remains inadequate. Both the EPD and CS are headed by a Director (Grade 5) rather than an Under- Secretary (Grade 3). This subordinates the status of these services and the importance of environmental issues and countryside conservation within the DoE(NI) in comparison to other services like planning, water and sewage and roads which are headed by Directors (Grade 4); and in comparison to functions exercised by the Departments of Agriculture and Economic Development.

In 1989 a new advisory body – the Council for Nature Conservation and the Country-side (the CNCC), chaired by Professor Newbound, was created by the *Nature Conservation and Amenity Lands (Amendment) (Northern Ireland) Order 1989 (SI 1989 No 492)* to advise the DoE(NI) on nature conservation and the countryside. This body consists of 20 members, 18 of whom are voluntary, plus a Chairperson and Deputy Chairperson appointed by the Secretary of State. Its aims are:

(1)   to advise, assist and encourage the Countryside and Wildlife Branch of the DoE(NI) in designating Areas of Outstanding Natural Beauty (AONB) and Areas of Special Scientific Interest (ASSI); to manage National Nature Reserves and Country Parks; to award grant aid, to take part in research and surveys and in interpretation and publication;

(2)   to develop policy guidelines in themes such as tourism, waste disposal and water pollution; and

(3)   to perform the role of honest broker between the Government and the voluntary sector.

In 1990 a new Director of Environmental Services within DoE(NI) was appointed at management level; in addition the decision was taken to separate the Department's environmental protection functions from its day-to-day responsibility for water and sewage through the establishment of a new government-owned body responsible for such functions.

It is, however, debatable how much impact these changes have made. Certainly one subsequent survey has concluded that Dr Balfour's intentions for the conservation branch have not become a reality, thus making it necessary to re-examine the issue of creating a separate environmental protection agency. (See K Milton, *Our Countryside, our concern* (1990) (Report for the Northern Ireland Environment Link).)

The then Environment Minister, Peter Bottomley dismissed such calls on the grounds that:

(a)   the small size of Northern Ireland negated the need for a proliferation of agencies;

(b)   the CNCC was more influential operating within the DoE than outside it;

(c)   it would be difficult for a small agency to wield real power;

(d)   there was a need to give the CNCC time to establish itself. (Rossi Report, paragraph 126)

Nonetheless, Rossi concluded that:

'We do not think that the DoE(NI) can be an effective protector of the environment, given its present structure'. (paragraph 123)

In view of the fact that there was a need for more weight to be given to environmental protection, and that the DoE(NI) was too constrained to act as an effective guardian and watchdog for the environment, it recommended the creation of an independent body to ensure that this happened (paragraph 110). It envisaged that such a body would carry out functions equivalent to English Heritage, the National Rivers Authority, Her Majesty's Inspectorate of Pollution, the Countryside Commission and the Nature Conservancy Council:

> '. . . we consider that a Northern Ireland environmental agency could develop its own character, could be a focus for local pride in the environmental heritage and could play a full part in relationships with other national agencies and contribute to UK conservation'. (paragraph 129)

Ironically, if such a recommendation were implemented, Northern Ireland would lead the rest of the UK in terms of a meaningful system of integrated pollution control (see INTEGRATED POLLUTION CONTROL (16)). However, there are no signs that such a body will be established in the near future.

In addition to the DoE(NI) there are also 26 district councils which have some environmental responsibilities, e.g. in relation to waste disposal, environmental health, nuisances and litter prevention. They are extremely varied in size – ranging in population from 15,000 to 302,000 with a consequent variation in resources. Education and Library Boards and the Northern Ireland Housing Executive also have a minor role to play.

There is also an Historic Buildings Council. Under *article 105, Planning (Northern Ireland) Order 1991 (SI 1991 No 1220)* the Historic Buildings Council is continued and charged with the duties of:

> '. . . reviewing, and periodically reporting to the DoE on the general state of preservation of listed buildings and advising the DoE on such matters relating to the preservation of buildings of special architectural and historic interest as the DoE may refer to it, and any other functions as are conferred on it by any statutory provision'.

Under *article 106* the DoE(NI) may make grants or loans for the preservation or maintenance of listed buildings to the National Trust, or (under *article 107*) may purchase any listed building or land adjacent to it which it considers should be administered by the National Trust, Government department, district council or other suitable body.

Article 109 provides for compulsory purchase of listed buildings where this is necessary for the building's preservation.

Voluntary bodies

Most of the national evironmental and conservation organisations have branches in Northern Ireland which contribute a great deal to the cause of environmental protection in terms of gathering information and applying pressure on Government agencies.

19.4 Published information

The quantity and quality of published environmental information is generally poor. For example, the statistics on waste disposal are incomplete. The general impression of the Rossi Committee was that environmental data for Northern Ireland was less comprehensive than for England and Wales. A recurrent complaint from environmental organisations in their submissions to the Rossi Committee was the lack of statistics or annual reports on various aspects of the environment. This problem has been compounded by the restructuring of environmental bodies in the UK. For example, the establishment of HMIP means that Northern Ireland is no longer included in the annual reports by the controlled waste inspectorate.

The Rossi Committee recommended that the Government publish annual environmental statistics for the whole of the UK, and that, as soon as they acquire the necessary resources the DoE(NI) should produce an annual report on the environment in Northern Ireland (paragraph 134).

19.5 Countryside/wildlife/nature conservation

It is in the field of conservation that the slow development of environmental protection in Northern Ireland is most marked. Unlike the rest of the UK, in this jurisdiction there is no independent statutory body charged with the role of nature conservation. Although Northern Irish interests are represented on the Nature Conservation Committee established by the *Environmental Protection Act 1990*, the two Northern Irish members, appointed by the DoE(NI) have no vote.

The pattern of nature conservation in Northern Ireland broadly mirrors the practice in the rest of the UK but is of more recent origin. The 1984 Balfour Report noted its concern at the lack of status accorded to conservation within the DoE(NI); and the lack of attention paid to conservation in other aspects of DoE activity. They found a lack of co-ordination regarding investment in the countryside. Also staffing levels were insufficient to cope with the workload on conservation. The Report identified the need for the strengthening of policy on nature conservation and the countryside.

The current legislation is largely a response to such criticisms, and is designed mainly to bring Northern Ireland into line with the rest of the UK. It is based on three *Orders in Council* enacted 1985–1989, which are roughly equivalent to the *National Parks and Access to Countryside Act 1949* and the *Wildlife and Countryside Act 1981* in Great Britain.

19.6 The *Wildlife (Northern Ireland) Order 1985 (SI 1985 No 171)* makes provision with respect to wildlife in Northern Ireland. It affords protection to certain wild birds, animals and flora. *Article 4* makes it an offence to intentionally kill, injure or take any wild bird, to take, damage or destroy the nest of a wild bird, or to take or destroy the eggs of any wild bird; or [*article 7*] to offer such birds for sale or purchase them. *Schedule 1* lists birds which are protected by these provisions, either at all times or in the close season; whilst *Schedule 2* lists those birds which may be killed or taken outside the close season, or by authorised persons at all times. *Article 10* makes it an offence to intentionally kill, injure or take certain wild animals listed in *Schedule 5*; or [*article 13*] to offer them for sale or purchase them. Under *article 14* it is an offence to intentionally pick, remove, uproot or destroy any plant listed in *Part 1* of *Schedule 8*, or to offer such plants for sale or purchase them.

Article 15 makes it an offence to release, or allow to escape into the wild, any animal which is of a kind not ordinarily resident in, or not a regular visitor to, Northern Ireland. *Article 18* provides that the above provisions do not apply where the DoE(NI) has granted a licence for scientific or educational purposes, or for photography, or in order to prevent the spread of disease or to preserve public health, or public or air safety. *Article 19* affords special protection to deer, making it an offence to intentionally kill, injure or take any deer of a species or description listed in *Schedule 10* during the close season prescribed in *Schedule 10*, unless under licence. [*Article 20, 21*].

This law conforms with *Directive 79/409 EEC* (conservation of wild birds) and *Directive 82/461 EEC* (conservation of migratory species of wild animals).

229

19.7   The *Nature Conservation and Amenity Lands (Northern Ireland) Order 1985 (SI 1985 No 170)* restates, with amendments, the *Amenity Lands Act (Northern Ireland) 1965*. It makes provision with respect to nature conservation, enjoyment and conservation of the countryside, and amenity lands. It imposes on the DoE(NI) the duty of formulating and implementing policies for nature conservation and for the conservation and enhancement of the natural beauty and amenity of the countryside. [*Article 3*]. The *Order* established a Committee for Nature Conservation to advise the DoE(NI) on matters in relation to conservation [*article 5*]; and an Ulster Countryside Commission to advise the Department and to inquire into and report upon matters affecting the natural beauty and amenity of any area of Northern Ireland. [*Article 11*]. Subsequently however, both bodies were abolished by the *Nature Conservation and Amenity Lands (Amendment) (Northern Ireland) Order 1989* which established the Council for Nature Conservation to which the functions of the pre-existing bodies were transferred (*articles 3, 4 of 1989 Order* – see 19.3 above). The *1985 Order* also deals with the acquisition of land, either for conservation purposes or in order to establish nature reserves; and with the disposal and use of amenity lands. [*Articles 6–8*]. It empowers the department to enter into management agreements with the owners and occupiers of land to conserve its natural beauty or promote its enjoyment by the public. [*Article 9*]. The *Order* empowers the Secretary of State to declare national nature reserves [*article 18*] and marine nature reserves. [*Article 20*]. Under the *Order* district councils are able to provide or secure the provision of nature reserves on any land in their district. The *Order* also provides for the establishment and conservation of areas of special scientific interest (ASSIs) by the DoE(NI) after consultation with the Council for Nature Conservation and the Countryside. [*Article 24*].

The *1989 Order* empowers the DoE(NI) to declare as a nature reserve, to carry out works and provide facilities on, and to make byelaws in respect of, land acquired as an ASSI. It makes it mandatory for the DoE(NI) to declare an ASSI, where it is satisfied that an area is of special scientific interest. The *Order* also enables the Department to consent to certain operations or activities proposed to be carried out in such an area without previous written notice.

In the years following the enactment of these provisions, most of the criticisms levelled by conservationists have concerned the slow pace of designation of protected sites.

Although *article 12* of the *1985 Order* introduced a system for the designation of national parks in Northern Ireland, no national park has yet been declared. In the absence of such a scheme, nine areas have been designated Areas of Outstanding Natural Beauty, but this designation offers inadequate protection to these fragile environments which remain vulnerable because of inadequate planning regulations (see below). In the view of the National Trust a more positive approach was needed, which would create a policy-making and executive body which would carry out active management as well as an advisory role. (Rossi Report, p 3). Nor have any areas been designated Nature Marine Reserves. Lough Neagh designated in 1976 remains the only Ramsar site in Northern Ireland (i.e. protected under the Ramsar Convention). Forty ASSIs have been designated since the first one in 1986; and 45 Nature Reserves are now specifically managed for conservation.

19.8   In their evidence to the Rossi Committee the National Trust and the Royal Society for the Protection of Birds (RSPB) were both highly critical of the slow pace of designation of protected areas. This can be partly accounted for by the fact that the process of designation was started from scratch in Northern Ireland in 1985, unlike in the rest of the UK, where there was a pre-existing nature conservation framework. However, the pace of designation does seem excessively slow.

In response Mr Phillips, the Director of Conservation in the DoE(NI) did declare his intention to complete the process of ASSI designation within ten years, although no such targets had been set in the White Paper on the Environment. The DoE(NI) is also currently reviewing Northern Ireland's areas of outstanding natural beauty (AONBs).

19.9   In relation to international obligations to protect endangered species the *Control of Trade in Endangered Species (Designation of Ports of Entry) Regulations 1985 (SI 1985 No 1154)* prohibit the import of live animals specified in the *Schedule* except at one of the ports or airports designated in the *Schedule* in relation to animals of that kind. The *Control of Trade in Endangered Species (Enforcement) Regulations 1985 (SI 1985 No 1155)* provide for offences in respect of the contravention of certain provisions of European Community legislation relating to the implementation in the EC of the *Convention on International Trade in Endangered Species of Wild Flora and Fauna 1984.*

19.10 A particular problem has concerned peat bogs. The Rossi Committee recommended that the DoE(NI) should give priority to the designation of representative peat bogs as ASSIs and to other means of ensuring their survival (paragraph 47).

19.11 *Tree preservation*

Under *Article 64* of the *Planning (Northern Ireland) Order 1991* a duty is placed upon the DoE(NI) to ensure, where appropriate, that in granting planning permission adequate provision is made, by the imposition of conditions, for the preservation or planting of trees. Under *article 65* the department is empowered, where it appears to it expedient, to make 'tree preservation orders' with respect to trees, groups of trees, or woodlands, in order to prevent the cutting down, topping, lopping or wilful destruction of trees except with the consent of the department, or to secure replanting of any part of a woodland which is felled. *Article 82* empowers the DoE(NI) to issue enforcement notices where trees are not replaced.

19.12 *Historic buildings*

These are protected by the *Historic Monuments (Northern Ireland) Act 1971.*

In Northern Ireland there are many fewer historic buildings than in the rest of the UK – few buildings in rural or urban areas tend to be more than 200 years old. Under *article 42* of the *Planning (Northern Ireland) Order 1991* the DoE(NI) is charged with the duty of compiling and periodically revising lists of buildings of special architectural or historic interest, after consultation with the Historic Buildings Council and the appropriate district council. Written consent must be obtained from the department for the execution of any works for the demolition, alteration or extension of such buildings. Anyone who executes, or causes to be executed, any works for the demo-lition of a listed building, or for its alteration or extension in any manner which would affect its character is guilty of an offence. *[Article 44].*

Additionally, buildings within conservation areas may not be demolished without the consent of the DoE(NI). *[Planning (Northern Ireland) Order 1991, article 51].* However, *article 52* empowers the department to make grants or loans for the purpose of defraying in whole or part any expenditure incurred in connection with the promotion, preservation or enhancement of the character or appearance of the area.

Where works carried out on listed buildings contravene *article 44* the department may issue a 'listed building enforcement notice' specifying the alleged contravention and requiring specified steps to be taken to restore the building to its former state, or alleviate the effects of the work. *[Article 77].* Such an order may be appealed to the Planning Appeals Commission. *[Planning (Northern Ireland) Order 1991, article 78].*

19.13 Northern Ireland

19.13 Planning

Planning practice and policy in Northern Ireland differ significantly from the rest of the UK. Unlike most of the UK, Northern Ireland's present pattern of rural and urban settlement is largely the creation of the last 400 years, following the plantation by English and Scottish colonists in the early seventeenth century. In 1972 planning became a central Government (DoE(NI)) responsibility, and the framework for development was established by *The Regional Physical Development Strategy* (1975–1995). This identified towns and villages as growth points and set out a policy of limited development in the countryside, unless the applicant could demonstrate a particular need related to employment or personal circumstances. The result has been that 2,500–3,000 houses are built annually in the Northern Irish countryside – more than permitted annually in the rest of the UK. This has given rise to the phenomenon of 'bungalow blight' – the indiscriminate construction of inappropriate hacienda-style bungalows, particularly in areas close to the larger towns and cities. The policy has been defended by the DoE(NI) on the basis of both traditional patterns of dispersed housing in Northern Ireland, and the current economic situation in which house-building generates employment. Significant pressure groups like the Ulster Farmers' Union have stressed the need for an adequate supply of housing for farmers' families.

The other main problem in relation to planning control in Northern Ireland has been the reluctance of the DoE planning services to attach environmental conditions to planning permissions. They appear to hold the view that pollution should be controlled by environmental pollution legislation after the development has proceeded – a policy which has been criticised by the Institute of Environmental Health Officers, who take the view that planning control can be used in a more positive way to enhance the environment (Rossi Report, paragraph 103).

According to the CNCC, the planning situation in Northern Ireland has:

'. . . got right out of hand. Throughout most of Northern Ireland there seems to be a presumption in favour of permission to build . . . There is a tradition here of dispersed settlement. Northern Ireland is cited by the Planning Departments in Scotland and Wales as the worst-case example, on no account to be followed' (Rossi Report, paragraph 100).

This situation has largely resulted from the recommendations of the Cockcroft Report (WH Cockcroft, *Review of Rural Planning Policy* HMSO (1978)) which in its review of planning policy favoured a relaxation of the existing rural planning policy and recommended that more houses be allowed in the countryside by widening the categories of people permitted to live there, and looking favourably on applications to build well-designed factories and workshops in the countryside, even in AONBs. The report contended that the adoption of a policy which allowed for the provision of more jobs in the countryside would lessen the drift away from the land and ensure that traditional patterns of rural settlement in Northern Ireland were preserved.

In Practice Notes subsequently issued by the DoE(NI) in 1979 on *Policy for the Control of Development in Rural Areas*, it was declared that, apart from 'areas of special control' where a number of single houses despoiling the countryside would be unacceptable, or where it was necessary to prevent 'urban sprawl' or 'ribbon development', it would no longer be necessary to demonstrate any special 'need' in order to obtain planning permission to build in the countryside.

The Rossi Report concluded:

'We are concerned about what we have learned about the planning system in NI, of which indiscriminate development in the countryside and the lack of environmental conditions in planning consents are two aspects. We shall consider whether to carry

232

out an inquiry into the operation of the planning system, unless we receive assurances in the Government's reply that appropriate changes are being made.'

It recommended that the DoE(NI) carry out a revision of the effect of policy on residential development in the countryside and reconsider the changes introduced following the Cockcroft Report (paragraph 101).

19.14 The main legislation is now the *Planning (Northern Ireland) Order 1991 (SI 1991 No 1220)*. However, this *Order* has effected little substantive change. It repeals and consolidates most of the *Planning (Northern Ireland) Order 1972 (SI 1972 No 1634)* and the provisions amending it. *Article 3* imposes a duty on the DoE(NI) to formulate and co-ordinate policy for securing the orderly and consistent development of land and the planning of development. *Article 4* allows the department to propose the making, alteration, repeal or replacement of a development plan for an area. The department must consult with the appropriate district council [*article 5*], publicise and invite representations as to the plan [*article 6*] and may cause a public inquiry to be held by the planning appeals commission (PAC). [*Article 7*]. The PAC consists of a Chief Commissioner and a number of other Commissioners appointed by the Secretary of State. [*Article 110*]. After considering objections and the report of the inquiry (if held) the department may adopt the plan.

Any development of land – i.e. the carrying out of building, engineering, mining or other operations in, on, over or under land, or the making of any material change in the use of any buildings or other land [*article 11*] – requires planning permission to be granted by or under a development order of the DoE(NI). [*Articles 12, 13*]. *Articles 14–18* deal with 'simplified planning zones' which, when adopted, have the effect of granting planning permission for specified classes of development. *Article 19* provides for planning permission to be automatically granted for specified developments under the *Enterprise Zones (Northern Ireland) Order 1981 (SI 1981 No 607)*.

19.15 An application for planning permission must be made in such manner as may be specified in a development order. [*Planning Order 1991, article 20*]. The DoE(NI) must then publish notice of the application in at least one local newspaper. [*Article 21*]. The application must be accompanied by a certificate relating to the legal and equitable interests in the land. [*Article 22*]. If a development has been carried out without requisite permission the DoE(NI) may, within four years, by notice require an application for planning permission [*article 23*], although there is a right of appeal to the PAC. [*Article 24*].

When the department receives an application for planning permission it must have regard to the development plan for the area insofar as it is material to the application, and to any other material considerations, and may then grant planning permission, with or without conditions, or refuse it. [*Article 25*]. The department may grant planning permission 'for a limited period', which requires works to be done, or works or buildings to be removed, or certain uses of land to be discontinued within a specified time. [*Article 27*]. Where an application involves a major development or access to a trunk road the DoE(NI) may require a public local inquiry to be held by the PAC. [*Article 31*].

If planning permission is refused, or if any consent or approval required by the DoE(NI) is refused, the applicant may appeal to the PAC by notice served within six months; each party has a right to appear and be heard. [*Article 32*]. The applicant can appeal to the PAC where the department fails to give its decision within the due time. [*Article 33*].

19.16 Unless otherwise stated, planning permission is conditional upon the development being begun within five years. [*Article 34*]. Outline planning permission – i.e. permission under a development order subject to approval of details – is conditional upon approval of the details within three years. *[Article 35]*. If a development has been begun, but not completed within the period, the DoE(NI) may serve a notice of intention on the applicant to make a 'completion order' whereby the planning permission will cease to have effect at the expiration of a further period specified in the *order. [Article 37]*.

Planning permission may be revoked or modified if it appears to the DoE(NI), having regard to the development plan and any other material consideration, that it is expedient to do so. The department must notify the owner/occupier of the land and any person affected. They then have a right of appeal to the PAC. *[Article 38]*. If expedient or in the interests of proper planning and amenity, the department may require use to be discontinued or a building to be removed, upon the service of notice. *[Article 39]*. Any person who uses land, or causes or permits land to be used after the expiry of the period allowed for compliance with an order under *article 39* shall be guilty of an offence. *[Article 83]*.

19.17   The DoE(NI) may enter into agreements under seal as to the use of land, enforceable against the owner and any successor in title. *[Article 40]*. A person who wishes to work on land or change its use, may apply to the DoE(NI) for a determination that planning permission is not required; and the department may make such determination on an application for planning permission. *[Article 41]*.

19.18   If it appears that there has been a breach of planning control after 25 August 1974 the DoE(NI) may, within four years, issue and serve an enforcement notice to take effect at least 28 days after service. *[Article 68]*. This will specify the matters alleged to constitute a breach of planning control and the steps required to remedy the breach. At any time before it takes effect, any person with an estate in the land may appeal in writing to the PAC stating which of a number of specified grounds they are relying upon, and the DoE(NI) must publish notice of the appeal. *[Article 69]*. On appeal, the PAC may uphold, quash or vary the enforcement notice *[article 70]*; and may grant planning permission. *[Article 71]*. Non-compliance with the enforcement notice is a summary offence, and if the defendant has ceased to be the owner of the land, he/she may join a subsequent owner. *[Article 72]*. Upon service of an enforcement notice the DoE(NI) may serve a 'stop notice' to prevent further development. *[Article 73]*. Where an enforcement notice is not complied with, an authorised official is empowered to enter the land and take remedial steps, the expenses of which are recoverable summarily as a debt. *[Article 74]*. Unless planning permission is subsequently granted *[article 75]* the enforcement notice is of continuing effect. *[Article 76]*.

19.19   Where the refusal or revocation of planning permission has rendered the land useless, the owner may serve a notice requiring the DoE(NI) to purchase it. *[Article 94]*. The department may serve a counter-notice objecting to purchase *[article 95]*, in which case the owner may refer the matter to the Lands Tribunal. *[Article 98]*. If the purchase notice is not objected to or is upheld by the Lands Tribunal, the department is deemed to have agreed to purchase the land for a sum equivalent to compulsory purchase compensation. *[Article 98]*.

19.20   *Article 121* allows authorised officials to enter land for a number of specified purposes. *Article 124* requires a planning register to be kept containing information about applications made and notices issued under this legislation. *Article 125* empowers the DoE(NI) to seek information as to estates in land.

19.21   Particular criticism has been directed at the lack of protection afforded to Northern Ireland's extensive coastline. Despite the variety and richness of the Ulster coastline and the importance of tourism to the local economy, there is no policy for planning or coastal protection, although the need for such a policy was identified as long ago as 1947. (See *The Ulster Countryside* – A report by the Planning Advisory Board on

Amenities in Northern Ireland, Belfast HMSO 1947.) According to the National Trust, there is a need for a coastal protection strategy to deal with both the day-to-day problems of continuing exploitation of coastal resources as well as the projected problems associated with the anticipated rise in sea levels. At present there is only very limited protection contained in the *Water (Northern Ireland) Act 1972* and the *Food and Environmental Protection Act 1985*. These are wholly inadequate to address important issues such as visual amenity and wildlife disturbance. As recent commercial developments like cage fish farms and marinas have demonstrated, there is a need for more comprehensive legislative protection.

The National Trust recommended to the Rossi Committee that the Government should develop a comprehensive coastal planning and protection strategy for Northern Ireland's coastline, and that consideration should be given to the drafting of legislation which would ensure that comprehensive assessment and control applied to the marine environment in coastal waters (Rossi Report, p 3).

19.22 Waste disposal

Waste disposal is one of the most significant functions still exercised by district councils in Northern Ireland. Local authorities are responsible for the collection and disposal of controlled wastes, for the preparation of waste disposal plans and for licensing waste disposal sites. There are 73 landfill sites – 28 are operated by district councils and 45 by private operators. These range considerably in size. The present arrangements are unsatisfactory. The unregulated choice of landfill sites often disrupts wildlife and destroys valuable habitats. There are also frequently leachate problems which affect watercourses. It is clear that many of the sites should never have been given planning permission, others are badly run, and producing polluting leachates (Rossi Report, paragraph 59).

19.23 The legislation governing waste disposal is the *Pollution Control and Local Government (Northern Ireland) Order 1978 (SI 1978 No 1049)*. The situation obtaining here is broadly comparable to that in England and Wales prior to the passage of the *Environmental Protection Act 1990*. District councils are under a duty to ensure that adequate arrangements are made for the disposal of all controlled waste within their districts. [*Article 3*]. After consultation with the DoE(NI), any other relevant district councils, and representatives of trade and business, the district council must prepare, and periodically revise, a waste disposal plan, relating to the kinds and quantities of controlled waste in the district and methods for disposing of it. [*Article 4*]. *Article 5(1)* prohibits anyone from depositing, or causing, or knowingly permitting controlled waste to be deposited on land; or allowing plant or equipment to be used for those purposes, unless the land is occupied by the holder of a licence to dispose of waste. Contravention of this provision is an offence triable summarily or on indictment, in which case there is a maximum prison sentence of two years.

19.24 A person charged under *Article 5(1)* may avail of one of four defences [*article 5(4)*]:

(a)   that he

(i)   took care to inform himself, from persons who were in a position to provide the information, as to whether the deposit or use to which the charge relates would be in contravention of *Article 5(1)*; or

(ii)   acted under instructions from his employer and neither knew nor had reason to suppose that the information given to him was false or misleading or that the deposit or use might be in contravention of *article 5(1)*.

(b)   in the case of an offence of making, causing or permitting a deposit or use otherwise than in accordance with conditions specified in a disposal licence, that he took all such steps as were reasonably open to him to ensure that the conditions were complied with; or

(c)   that the acts specified in the charge were done in an emergency in order to avoid danger to the public and that, as soon as reasonably practicable after they were done, particulars of them were furnished to the district council in whose district the acts were done.

19.25 An application for a waste disposal licence can only be rejected if the district council is satisfied that such rejection is necessary for the purpose of preventing danger to public health. Conditions may be attached relating to matters such as the duration of the licence, supervision by the licence holder of activities to which the licence relates, precautions to be taken etc. Each district council must keep a register of all disposal licences issued which is available to the public. [*Article 8*]. A district council may on its own initiative, or upon application by the licence holder, serve notice modifying the conditions specified in the licence; or may revoke the licence where the activities to which it relates would cause danger to public health, or be seriously detrimental to the amenities of the locality affected, provided such danger or detriment cannot be avoided by modifying the conditions specified in the licence [*Article 9*]. The licence may be transferred or relinquished upon notice to the district council. [*Article 10*]. Appeals can be made to the DoE(NI) where an application for a licence or modification of a licence is rejected; or against conditions imposed or modified in a licence, or where a licence is revoked. [*Article 12*]. The district council is under a duty to provide for the collection and removal of all household waste in its area. [*Article 14*].

19.26 In 1990 the DoE(NI) employed Aspinall & Co (Consultants) to review waste disposal in Northern Ireland. Their report concluded that the present arrangements did not adequately address the requirements of waste management. It identified the lack of existing landfill sites, and lack of joint ventures between districts which, combined with the inadequacies of current waste management arrangements, resulted in varying standards and the duplication of resources. Aspinall recommended that, whilst responsibility for collection and disposal should be retained by district councils, reorganisation should take place at regional level by districts on the same basis as that which obtains for environmental health. (See Aspinall & Co, *A Review of Waste Disposal in Northern Ireland*, Report to the DoE(NI) 1990.)

19.27 In their submission to the Rossi Committee the National Trust proposed that the DoE(NI) should develop a waste disposal policy for Northern Ireland which would increase the opportunity for regulation and waste minimisation, and require the adoption of a more rational approach to landfills which would require the co-operation of adjacent district councils. In time they envisaged such an approach leading to a reduction in the number of landfill sites and attendant problems, due to more careful site selection as well as landfill and engineering practices. The Rossi Report recommended that the DoE(NI) should seek to establish a system of regional waste licensing for Northern Ireland based on groups of district councils (paragraph 61).

19.28 Particular problems are presented by hazardous special wastes. There is no co-ordinated or forward planning approach to hazardous waste disposal in Northern Ireland, and there are few facilities for the disposal of such wastes, although *Regulation 17* of the *1978 Order* empowered the DoE(NI) to make special provision in regulations for the disposal of 'special waste' which is dangerous or intractable. Two co-disposal landfill sites are licensed to take special wastes in Belfast and Derry, whilst some waste is transported to England for incineration and treatment.

The Aspinall Report revealed that many local authorities were unaware of the arisings of special wastes and that 'not all hazardous wastes were being disposed of in a correct and legal manner'. Statistics about the generation and disposal of special wastes are incomplete and confused. Disposal costs tend to be low in comparison with other regions of the United Kingdom. Aspinall concluded that realistic pricing of special waste disposal, reinforced by increased regulation and enforcement was needed to stimulate a change in attitude to waste disposal. Rossi identified a lack of facilities for toxic waste disposal (paragraph 64). This apparently contradicts the Government's commitment to regional self-sufficiency in waste disposal in its White Paper on the Environment (see 19.1). Having noted public disquiet about toxic waste in regions which are net importers, and the likelihood of it becoming increasingly difficult to export waste for treatment, plus the fact that, in order to attract investment and industry in future to Northern Ireland it is essential that satisfactory waste disposal facilities exist, the Rossi Report therefore recommended that:

> 'the Government [should] encourage better regulation of special waste disposal and more realistic pricing, and then, as more information about arisings becomes available, start to plan for the provision of suitable facilities for disposal and treatment within Northern Ireland'. (paragraph 64)

19.29   In response, the *Planning (Northern Ireland) Order 1991* provides in *article 53* that the presence of a hazardous substance in, over or under land requires the consent of the DoE(NI) unless the aggregate quantity of the substance is less than the controlled quantity. It requires regulations to be made regarding applications for 'hazardous substances consent'.

19.30   The DoE(NI) may either refuse hazardous substances consent, or grant it unconditionally, or subject to such conditions as it thinks fit. [*Article 55*]. In determining the outcome of the application the department must have regard to any material conditions, including:

(*a*)   any current or contemplated use of the land;

(*b*)   the way in which land in the vicinity is used, or is likely to be used;

(*c*)   any planning permission that has been granted for the development of land in the vicinity; and

(*d*)   the provisions of the development plan for the area.

19.31   A special procedure applies to major applications, where the DoE(NI) considers that the presence of a hazardous substance would involve a substantial departure from the development plan for that area; or be of significance to the whole, or a substantial part of Northern Ireland, or affect the whole of a neighbourhood. In such cases the department may cause a public local inquiry to be held by the PAC. Where they decide that this is necessary the applicant has a right to be heard by the PAC. [*Article 56*]. If the consent is refused, or granted subject to conditions, the applicant may appeal in writing to the PAC within six months of notification of the decision. [*Article 57*].

19.32   Under *Article 59* the DoE(NI) may revoke or modify hazardous substances consent, if it appears that there has been a material change of use of the land to which the consent relates, or if planning permission has been granted which would involve a material change, or if the hazardous substance to which the licence relates has not been present on or over or under the land to which the licence relates in amounts which exceed the controlled quantity, or if it appears expedient to revoke or modify the hazardous substances consent having regard to any material consideration. A hazardous substances consent shall also cease to have effect if there is a change of the person in control of part of the land to which the consent relates, unless an application for the continuation of the consent has previously been made to the DoE(NI). [*Article 60*].

19.33   Any contravention of hazardous substances control amounts to an offence. The defendant has a defence if he/she took all reasonable precautions and exercised all due diligence, or had no knowledge of the presence of the substance in amounts exceeding the controlled quantity. [*Article 61*]. In emergencies, where the community would otherwise be deprived of an essential service or commodity the DoE(NI) may direct that the presence of a hazardous substance does not breach the order.

19.34 Contaminated land

Contaminated land presents an environmental problem throughout the UK. (See HC 170 (1989–90) Cm 1161 1990 for criticisms of the English position.) A similar situation obtains in Northern Ireland, where there is a lack of legislative or financial provision to deal with such sites, allied to a lack of means and expertise. Once again the relevant legislation is the *Pollution Control and Local Government (Northern Ireland) Order 1978* which is inadequate to deal with the problem. Under this legislation it is uncertain who bears responsibility for contaminated land in Northern Ireland. It is up to the district council, the Industrial Science Division (of the DoE(NI)) and the new owner to decide how land is to be dealt with.

A number of old industrial and landfill sites have been abandoned by their original operators with toxic or potentially polluting substances present. This has aroused little Government attention, and it has generally been left to the landowner to decide whether to take remedial action. The Rossi Committee deplored the position whereby industry has been allowed to contaminate land and then divest itself of responsibility for that contamination (paragraph 67). This is particularly problematic in Northern Ireland, where considerable financial inducements to industry to locate there exist; but there is nothing to prevent them from withdrawing after the minimum period leaving behind a contaminated site for the Government to sort out.

The Rossi Committee recommended that the Government should take steps to prevent the contamination of land by industries in NI by:

(i)   enacting provisions equivalent to those of the *Environmental Protection Act 1990* relating to the after-care of landfills and integrated pollution control;

(ii)   prepare a Code of Practice ensuring that contamination is addressed when the land is sold; and

(iii)   ensure that long-term environmental considerations are fully taken into account when financial inducements are given to incoming investors (paragraph 68).

There has been no attempt to landscape sites, which allows spillage to continue for years. The Rossi Committee recommended that a register of contaminated land should be created, and that a clearly defined system of grant aid should be introduced specifically directed at the clean up of contaminated sites. They also recommended that the specific duties of the DoE(NI), local authorities and other interested bodies with regard to contaminated land should be clearly defined and delineated (paragraph 71).

19.35 Statutory nuisances

The situation in relation to statutory nuisances in Northern Ireland is similar to England and Wales, although there the *Environmental Protection Act 1990* has simplified matters by consolidating the list of statutory nuisances, streamlining procedures for dealing with them, increasing the powers of local authorities to deal with them, and significantly increasing penalties. In Northern Ireland responsibility for dealing with statutory nuisances rests with the district councils. The definition of statutory nuisances still dates from the *Public Health Act 1878* (*PHA 1878*).

Section 107, as amended, defines nuisances as follows:

— premises being in such a state as to be a nuisance or prejudicial to health;

— any pool, ditch, gutter, watercourse, privy, urinal, cesspool, drain or ashpit so foul or in such a state as to be a nuisance or prejudicial to health;

— animals kept so as to be a nuisance or prejudicial to health;

— accumulations or deposits which are a nuisance or prejudicial to health (although in this case it is a defence that such accumulations or deposits are necessary for the effectual carrying on of any business or manufacturing process; that they have not been kept for longer than is necessary; and that the best available means have been used to prevent injury to public health);

— any house or part of a house so overcrowded as to be dangerous or prejudicial to the health of the inmates;

— any factory, workshop, or workplace not kept sufficiently clean or sufficiently ventilated to render harmless, as far as practicable, any gases, vapours, dust or other impurities generated in the course of work carried on therein that are a nuisance or prejudicial to health; or which are so overcrowded while work is carried on that they are dangerous or prejudicial to the health of those working therein (although in this case it is a defence that 'best practicable means', as defined in the *Clean Air (Northern Ireland) Order 1981*, have been used to abate the nuisance, or to prevent or counteract the effects of the grit, dust or effluvia);

— any trade, business, manufacture or process which is a nuisance; or which causes any grit, dust or effluvia which is a nuisance to, or injurious to the health of, any of the inhabitants of the neighbourhood.

All of the above are nuisances liable to be dealt with summarily.

Under *section 108* a duty is imposed upon district councils to inspect their district for the detection of nuisances. *Section 109* enables any person aggrieved by a nuisance, or two householders in the district, or a police constable or officer to give information about nuisances to the district council. If the district council is satisfied of the existence of the nuisance it is under a duty to serve a notice on the person responsible, or the owner/occupier, requiring them to abate the nuisance within a specified period. The district council is under a duty to abate the nuisance if such persons cannot be traced. [*PHA 1878, s 110*]. If a person defaults in respect of such a notice, the district council can complain to a court of summary jurisdiction which can make a court order imposing a penalty [*PHA 1878, ss 111, 112*]; and further penalties will be imposed if it is not complied with. [*PHA 1878, s 114*]. *Sections 128, 129* impose restrictions on the carrying on of certain offensive trades.

19.36 *Noise*

Noise is beginning to feature more prominently as a matter of concern in Northern Ireland. The relevant legislation is the *Pollution Control and Local Government (Northern Ireland) Order 1978*. *Article 38* of this *Order* empowers a district council, where it is satisfied that noise amounting to a nuisance exists, or is likely to occur or recur within its district, to serve a notice requiring the abatement of the nuisance or prohibiting or restricting its occurrence or recurrence; and requiring the execution of works, or the taking of any other steps as may be specified in the notice. *Article 37* provides for periodical inspections by district councils for the purposes of detecting anything which ought to be dealt with under *article 38*; and deciding how to exercise its powers concerning noise abatement zones. A district council may by order designate all or any part of its district a noise abatement zone. [*Article 43*]. It is then under a duty to

239

measure noise levels emanating from premises within the zone which are of any class to which the noise abatement order relates. [*Article 44*]. The level of noise recorded must not exceed that contained in the noise level register, unless consent has been obtained from the district council. [*Article 45*]. If it appears to the council that the level of noise emanating from any premises to which a noise abatement order applies is not acceptable having regard to the purposes for which the order was made, and that a reduction in that level is practicable at reasonable cost, the council may serve a 'noise reduction notice' requiring the person responsible to reduce the level of noise, to that level specified in the order, to prevent any subsequent increase in the level of noise, and to take such steps as may be specified in the order to achieve those purposes within a specified time. [*Article 46*].

Where it appears to the district council that a building is going to be constructed and that a noise abatement order will apply to it when it is erected, or that any premises will, as the result of any works, become premises to which a noise abatement order applies, the council may, on the application of the owner or occupier of the premises or a person who satisfies the authority that he is negotiating to acquire an interest in the premises, or on its own iniative, determine the level of noise which will be acceptable as emanating from the premises. [*Article 47*].

Article 48 imposes restrictions upon noise emanating from plant and machinery.

In addition, any occupier of premises is permitted to take summary proceedings on the ground that he is aggravated by noise amounting to a nuisance. [*Article 39*]. *Article 40* deals with control of noise on construction sites and enables the district council to serve a notice imposing requirements as to the way in which the works are to be carried out. A person who intends to carry out works to which *article 40* applies may apply to the district council for a consent under *article 41*.

Although highway authorities have been under a duty to insulate since 1973 in England and Wales, there are no noise insulation regulations in Northern Ireland for buildings adjacent to new roads. A further problem here is the reluctance of the planning service to impose conditions related to noise. Another issue peculiar to Northern Ireland is nuisance caused by helicopters in the vicinity of army landing bases.

The Rossi Committee recommended that the provisions of the *Environmental Protection Act 1990* in relation to noise should be speedily enacted in Northern Ireland. [*Article 106*].

19.37 **AIR POLLUTION IN NORTHERN IRELAND**

The control of air pollution in Northern Ireland is governed by the *Clean Air (Northern Ireland) Order 1981* (*SI 1991 No 158*) and the *Alkali, etc. Works Regulation Act 1906, as amended*. The collection of information concerning atmospheric pollution is governed by the *Control of Pollution and Local Government (Northern Ireland) Order 1978*. The *Alkali, etc. Works Regulation Act 1906* is enforced by the Alkali and Radiochemical Inspectorate which mirrors the English positions before HMIP was established in 1987. The *Clean Air (Northern Ireland) Order 1981* is enforced primarily by the district councils.

One of the most important points which emerged from the Rossi Report concerning air pollution was Northern Ireland's dependence on coal and oil as a source of energy. Seventy per cent of households rely on coal as their main source of energy as compared to 12 per cent in the rest of the UK (Rossi Report, paragraph 85). The *EC Directive* on smoke and sulphur dioxide (*80/779/EEC*) obliges the UK to achieve the air standards set out in the *Directive*, however the UK had a derogation until April 1993. The Rossi

Report states that smoke limit values have been exceeded during winter at Belfast, Londonderry and Newry where air monitoring has been conducted. Local authorities in NI have introduced legislation to bring Northern Ireland into compliance with the *Directive*. This is covered in more detail at the end of this section. Northern Ireland also suffers from rising levels of sulphur dioxide, in contrast with a pattern of steady decline on the mainland. In their report to the Rossi Committee, the Coal Advisory Serivce stated that there was no one reason for this trend; the IEHO has suggested that the absence of natural gas supplies in NI and the resultant widespread use of coal is possibly to blame. The DoE(NI) reported that although recent sulphur dioxide levels in NI had breached the *Directive*, recent figures showed a decrease in the quantity of sulphur dioxide in the atmosphere (Rossi Report, Figure 1, paragraph 86). The Rossi Report recommends that the Government introduce legislation in NI making it an offence 'to sell unauthorised fuels in a smoke-control area and to sell fuel with an excessively high sulphur content' (paragraph 88). Derry City Council raised the question of the possible hardship which this could cause.

19.38 The DoE(NI) has exercised only some of its powers under the *Clean Air (Northern Ireland) Order* and the *Alkali, etc. Works Regulation Act 1906* to make regulations concerning clean air. This has led to a number of weaknesses in the legislative control of air pollution in NI. Most noteably, the DoE(NI) has failed to introduce regulations controlling emissions of grit and dust from furnaces, arrestment plant exemptions, heights of chimneys exemptions and the measurement of grit and dust emissions, all of which have existed in the rest of the UK for some time. The DoE(NI) stated that these delays were caused either by the fact that changes were being made to draft *Directives*, or, that other DoE(NI) projects were given greater priority until they had extra staff.

19.39 The DoE(NI) provided the Rossi Committee with the following as a list of their legislative commitments concerning air pollution. These range from regulations to fill in details to comprehensive reviews of policies. DoE(NI) target dates are also included; however, many of these have not been met; where the measure has been made the date is indicated in brackets:

Alkali and Works (Northern Ireland) Order 1991
Alkali Works (Regulation) (Northern Ireland) Regulations 1991
Oil Fuel (Sulphur Content of Gas Oil) (Northern Ireland) Regulations 1991
Control of Asbestos in the Air (Northern Ireland) Regulations 1991
Clean Air (Emissions of Grit and Dust from Furnaces) (Northern Ireland) Regulations 1991
Clean Air (Measurement of Grit and Dust from Furnaces) (Northern Ireland) Regulations 1991
Clean Air (Northern Ireland) Order (no target date has been set)
Smoke Control (Exempted Fireplaces) (Northern Ireland) Regulations 1991
Smoke Control (Authorised Fuels) (Northern Ireland) Regulations 1991
Clean Air (Arrestment Plant for New Furnaces) (Northern Ireland) Regulations 1991.

19.40 Clean Air (Northern Ireland) Order 1981

The *Clean Air (Northern Ireland) Order 1981* consolidates the *Clean Air Act (Northern Ireland) 1964*. Like the *Clean Air Act 1956* which operates in England and Wales, the *Clean Air (Northern Ireland) Order 1981* essentially controls and monitors the emission of dark smoke, smoke, dust, grit and fumes from certain categories of chimneys and furnaces, including those which service buildings, industrial plants, vessels, and railway engines. Its terms also regulate the building of chimneys, the height of chimneys and the creation of smoke control zones. The *1981 Order* creates a variety of statutory offences and *article 38* sets out the penalties incurred by the person on whom liability falls. District councils are given the task of enforcing the provisions of this

Order [article 39]; however, *article 39(1)* states that nothing in this *Order* shall be construed as extending to the enforcement of any provisions of the *Alkali, etc. Works Regulation Act 1906* (the *1906 Act*) or any of the building byelaws. There is however a significant inter-relation between certain provisions of the *1981 Order* and the *1906 Act*; this is explained in the section which specifically concerns the provisions of the *Alkali, etc. Works Regulation Act 1906*. *Article 40* of the *Clean Air (Northern Ireland) Order 1981* sets out the application of the *Public Health Acts (Northern Ireland) 1878–1962* to the function of the district councils conferred by the *1981 Order*. The *Clean Air (Northern Ireland) Order 1981* has been amended by the *Local Government (Miscellaneous Provisions) (Northern Ireland) Order 1985 (SI 1985 No 1208)*, and where relevant these amendments will be addressed below.

19.41 *Dark smoke*

Article 3 of the *1981 Order* is phrased in almost identical terms to the *Clean Air Act 1956* (the *1956 Act*). Under both pieces of legislation it is an offence to emit dark smoke from the chimney of any building [*Clean Air Order 1981, article 3(1); Clean Air Act 1956, s 1*], and the occupier will be held liable in the event that this provision is contravened. The penalties incurred for violation of *article 3* are laid down in *article 38(1)*. As under the *1956 Act*, 'dark smoke' is defined as being smoke which is as dark or darker than shade 2 on the Ringelmann Chart. [*Article 2(3)*]. *Article 2(3)(a)* and *(b)* explains the manner in which the nature of the smoke emitted can be established in proceedings brought under this *Order*. For the purposes of this *Order* a 'chimney' includes

> 'structures or openings of any kind from or through which smoke, grit, dust or fumes may be emitted, and in particular, includes flues, and references to the chimney of a building include references to a chimney which serves the whole or part of a building but is structurally separate from it'. [*Article 2(2)*].

The prohibition in *article 3* is not limited to chimneys of buildings. *Article 3(4)* identifies other categories of chimneys to which this article will apply. *Article 3* will apply to a chimney 'which serves the furnace of any boiler or industrial plant, where the boiler or plant is attached to a building or is fixed or attached to any land'. Where a prohibited emission is made from the chimney of a boiler or plant, *Article 3(5)* states that any reference to the 'occupier' of the building shall be construed to mean the person 'having possession' of the boiler or plant. *Article 3(3)* of the *NI Order* and *section 1(3)* of the *1956 Act* afford the defendant the same statutory defences to the offence in *article 3(1)*. These defences are set out in full in ATMOSPHERIC POLLUTION (4). In terms of the enforcement of *article 3*, *article 39(2)* states that a district council 'may institute proceedings for an offence under *article 3* where any smoke affects any part of its district notwithstanding that the smoke is emitted from a chimney outside its district'. As under the *Clean Air Act 1956*, district councils are obliged to notify 'as soon as may be' the person deemed liable under the *Order* of the council's belief that an offence has been committed under *article 3*. Failure to do so will provide a defence for the defendant. *Article 37(1)* and *(2)* contains the specific rules governing the form of the notice and the time limits within which the notice must be given. These broadly approximate to the terms of *section 30* of the *Clean Air Act 1956*. *Article 3(2)* states that certain emissions of smoke can be exempted from the operation of *article 3(1)*. These include emissions which have been permitted for certain periods of time and under certain conditions and are contained in the following regulations: *Dark Smoke (Permitted Periods) Regulations (Northern Ireland) 1965 (SI 1965 No 73); Dark Smoke (Permitted Periods) (Vessels) Regulations (Northern Ireland) 1965 (SI 1965 No 74)*; and *Clean Air (Emissions of Dark Smoke) (Exemption) Regulations (Northern Ireland) 1981 (SI 1981 No 86)*.

19.42 *Emissions of dark smoke from industrial and trade premises*

Like the *Clean Air Act 1968, article 4(1)* of the *Northern Ireland Order 1981* extends the prohibition in *article 3* to emissions of dark smoke from industrial and trade premises. This prohibition operates even if the emission is not from a chimney. [*Article 4(2)*]. Once again liability for any violation of *article 4(1)* will fall on the occupier of the trade or industrial premises in question. Penalties incurred for an offence under *article 4* are set out in *article 38(6)*. *Article 4(5)* defines an 'industrial or trade premises' as meaning a 'premises used for any industrial or trade purposes or premises not so used on which matter is burnt in connection with any industrial or trade process'. Where one is prosecuted under *article 4(1)*, it is a defence to prove that the violation in question was 'inadvertent' and that 'all practicable steps had been taken to prevent or minimise the emission of dark smoke'. *Article 4(3)* empowers the DoE(NI) to make regulations exempting certain emissions of dark smoke from trade or industrial premises from the prohibition in *article 4(1)*, these exemptions are contained in the *Clean Air (Emission of Dark Smoke) Regulations 1981* (*SI 1981 No 340*). As is the case under *article 3*, the district council are obliged to notify the person held liable as soon as may be, of the council's belief that a violation of *article 4* has occured. Failure to give such notice within the time limit set down in *article 37(1)* and *(2)* will once again provide the defendant with a defence.

19.43 *New furnaces*

Both *section 3* of the *Clean Air Act 1956* and *article 5* of the *1981 NI Order* prohibit the installation of a furnace in any building, boiler or industrial plant (even where they already contain a furnace) unless the district council is notified. *Article 5* also applies to reconstruction work on a furnace which is prescribed in relation to the installation of any furnace. *Article 5* divides new furnaces into two categories. *Article 5(4)* requires that notice be given to the district council of the proposed installation of a new furnace, while *article 5(5)* states that after such date as may be prescribed, a new furnace cannot be installed unless the plans and specifications of the furnace have been submitted to the district council for approval. The power to prescribe this date has not been exercised to date. *Article 5(6)* goes on to provide that where plans and specifications have been submitted to the district council (whether or not they are required to be submitted under *article 5(5)*), the furnace cannot be installed except in accordance with approved plans, which shall be deemed to comply with *article 5(1)* of the *1981 Order*. *Article 5(7)* and *Schedule 1* govern the procedure to be followed when making an application for such approval, while *article 5(8)* controls the power of the district council to grant the approval. Essentially they cannot approve plans for a furnace which is not, 'in so far as is practicable, capable of being operated on a continuous basis without emitting smoke when it is burning fuel for which it was designed'. A person who installs a furnace, or on whose instruction a furnace is installed in violation of *article 5* is guilty of an offence under *article 5(9)* or *5(10)* depending on whether the furnace is one to which *article 5(6)* applies. Penalties incurred for an offence under *article 5* are set out in *article 38(2)*. *Article 5* will not apply to furnaces designed solely or mainly for domestic purposes, that is the furnace of a boiler which has a maximum heating capacity of less than 55,000 or more British thermal units per hour. Nor will *article 5* apply where the installation of a furnace has begun, or an agreement for the installation of a furnace has been reached before 1 July 1965.

19.44 *Grit and dust from furnaces*

Article 7(1) empowers the DoE(NI) to make regulations controlling the rate at which grit and dust is emitted from the chimneys of furnaces to which this article applies. This power has not been exercised to date. If grit or dust is emitted at a rate which exceeds prescribed rates, the occupier of the building in which the furnace is situated will be guilty of an offence, penalties for which are set out in *article 38(6)*. It is a defence to prove that the 'best practicable means were used' to minimise the alleged emission. *Section 2* of the *Clean Air Act 1968* which applies in England and Wales and *article 7* of the *Clean Air (Northern Ireland) Order 1981* provide that even where there is no prescribed rate for a particular chimney servicing a furnace, the occupier of the building will be guilty of an offence if he did not use 'any practicable means' in order to minimise the emission of dust or grit. *Article 7* does not apply to furnaces designed 'mainly or solely' for domestic purposes, however, it will apply to any other type of furnace in which 'solid, liquid or gaseous matter' is burnt.

Article 16 allows the DoE(NI) to make regulations which apply all or some of the provisions of *articles 7, 9, 10, 26(3), 27(4)* and *29(1)* to fumes in the same way as they apply to grit and dust. This power has not been exercised yet. Similarly the DoE(NI) is allowed to make regulations which apply the terms of *article 5* (requiring new furnaces to be smokeless) to fumes in the same way that it aplies to smoke. The DoE(NI) may also make whatever modifications are necessary when these provisions are being applied to fumes.

19.45 *Equipment to arrest emissions of grit and dust from furnaces*

Article 8 of the *1981 Order* concerns the provision of equipment to arrest the emission of grit and dust from furnaces and broadly approximates to *section 6* of the *Clean Air Act 1956* and *sections 3, 5* of the *Clean Air Act 1968*.

Article 8 applies to any furnace which is used to 'burn fuel or solid waste'. *Article 8(2)* goes on to make provisions for furnaces which are situated 'in buildings', however these provisions also apply (with certain changes) to 'outdoor furnaces', that is the furnace of a boiler or industrial plant which is attached to a building, or fixed to land. [*Article 13(1)*]. The provisions of *article 13* are dealt with in more detail below.

Article 8 states that a furnace (in a building) may not be used to burn fuel or solid waste unless that furnace is provided with equipment to arrest emissions of grit and dust. *Article 8* also requires that the plans and specifications for such equipment must be submitted to, and approved by, the district council. The equipment must also be properly installed, used and maintained. Violation of the above obligation is an offence for which the occupier of the building will be liable [*article 8(3)*], penalties for violation of *article 8* are set out in *article 38(6)*. *Schedule 1* of this *Order* governs the application for approval. The district council cannot give its approval if the furnace, to which the application relates, does not satisfy prescribed minimum standards concerning the concentration and/or rate of dust and grit emissons from furnaces. The power to set down such prescribed rates has not been exercised to date. *Articles 8(7)* and *(8)* of the *Clean Air (Northern Ireland) Order 1981* have been repealed by *Schedule 3* of the *Local Government (Miscellaneous Provisions) (Northern Ireland) Order 1985.*

Article 9(1) essentially restates the obligation imposed in *article 8(2)*. It provides that it is an offence to violate this obligation; the occupier of the building will be liable; penalties incurred are set out in *article 38(6)*. *Article 8* does not apply to furnaces installed, or where their installation began, or where an agreement was entered into to install or purchase a furnace before 1 July 1965 [*article 8(4)*], or before *article 62* of the *Pollution Control and Local Government (Northern Ireland) Order 1978 (SI 1978 No 1049)* came into force. [*Article 9(2)*]. *Article 9(3)* has been amended by *Schedule 3* of the *Local Government (Miscellaneous Provisions) (Northern Ireland) Order 1985* and should read as follows:

> '*Article 8(2)* shall not apply to a furnace to which paragraph (1) applies and *Article 8(5)* and *(6)* shall apply in relation to an approval under paragraph (1) as they apply in relation to an approval under *Article 8*'.

Article 10(1) allows the DoE(NI) to pass regulations exempting certain furnaces from the effects of *article 9(1)*; this power has not been exercised yet. *Article 10(2)* gives the district council the power to exempt furnaces used in violation of *article 9(1)* from the provisions of *article 9(1)* if the district council is satisfied that the emission of grit and dust from the chimney serving the furnace would not be 'prejudicial to health or a nuisance'. The occupier of a building must apply to the district council for an exemption. *Article 10(4)–(6)* governs the procedure to be followed when such an application is being made; the response of the district council; the position in the event that the district council fails to respond; the right of appeal to the DoE(NI); and the DoE(NI)'s possible response to such an appeal. *Article 10(7)* provides that it is an offence to use the furnace for a purpose other than that for which it is exempted under *article 10(4)–(6)*. The occupier of the building will be held liable. *Article 10(3)* has been repealed by *Schedule 3* of the *Local Government (Miscellaneous Provisions) (Northern Ireland) Order 1985*.

19.46 *Measurement of grit and dust from furnaces*

Much like *section 7* of the *1956 Act*, *article 11(1)* of the *Clean Air (Northern Ireland) Order 1981* concerns the measurement of grit and dust emitted from furnaces. *Article 11* gives the district council the power to serve a notice on the occupier of a building in which a furnace (to which *article 8* applies) is situated concerning the measurement of grit and dust emitted from the furnace. *Article 11(2)* states that where this provision is applied to a furnace, the occupier of the building must comply with 'such requirements as may be prescribed' concerning the recording of emissions of dust and grit; altering the chimney for the purposes of making such measurements; providing and maintaining apparatus for making such recordings; and making available to the district council the results of such recordings. The power to establish such requirements has not been exercised yet. *Article 11(3)–(9)* governs the issuing of notices under *article 11*. District councils may revoke any notice concerning any of the sub-paragraphs of *article 11(2)* but this does not prejudice their power to issue another notice under *article 11(2)*. [*Article 11(3)*]. Failure to comply with a notice under *article 11(2)* is an offence [*article 11(4)*], penalties incurred are set out in *article 38(6)*. The occupier of a building containing a furnace to which *article 8* applies may also request that the district council measures the emission of dust, fumes and grit. [*Article 11(5)*]. This request, which must be made in writing, can be withdrawn by the occupier or any subsequent occupier. In the event that an occupier requests that the district council take measurements of dust, fumes and grit emissions, the district council is then empowered to take and record the requested measurements for as long as the request remains in force. However, the occupier cannot be obliged to comply with any of the requirements set out in *article 11(2)* except the requirement set out in *article 11(2)(b)*, namely, that the occupier should make adaptations to the chimney of the furnace for the purposes of making and recording the said emissions. [*Article 11(7)*]. If the district council serves a notice under *article 11(1)* and *(2)*, the notice must state the effects of *article 11(5)* and *(7)*, detailed above. In the event that the occupier is obliged to measure the emissions, the occupier must permit the district council to be present during the making and recording of the measurements. [*Article 11(9)*].

19.47 *Information about furnaces and fuel consumed*

Article 12 empowers the district council to request information from the occupier of a building concerning furnaces in the building and the fuel or waste burnt in those furnaces. It is an offence to fail to comply with the request for information or knowingly to supply information which is false in a material particular; penalties incurred are set out in *article 38*.

19.48 *Grit and dust emissions from outdoor furnaces*

Article 13 states that *articles 7–12* of this *Order* apply to outdoor furnaces in the same way as they apply to furnaces in a building. The effect of this is that the furnace of a boiler or industrial plant, which is either attached to a building, or, which is fixed to or installed on any land, will be governed by *articles 7–12* in the same way as furnaces in buildings. All references to 'the occupier of a building' contained in *articles 7–12* must be construed to mean 'the person having possession of the boiler or plant' when these articles are being applied to a furnace which is not in a building. *Articles 11(3)* also provides that when *articles 7–12* are being applied to a furnace which is 'already contained in a boiler or industrial plant', the references in *articles 8* and *9(3)* to the 'installation of a furnace' must be construed as references to 'attaching the boiler or plant to the building or fixing it to or installing it on any land'. Furthermore, any reference in *articles 8* and *9(3)* to the 'purchase of a furnace' must be construed as a reference to 'the purchasing of the boiler or plant'.

19.49 *Height of chimneys*

Where it is proposed to erect a chimney, the plans for the chimney must be submitted to the district council for its approval. *Article 14(1)* applies to all chimneys, including those within the meaning of *article 15* (that is chimneys serving furnaces, see 19.50 below), but does not apply to the chimney of a building 'used or wholly used as a residence or residences, a shop or shops or an office or offices'. *Schedule 1* of this *1981 Order* governs the procedure for making an application for such approval. *Article 14(3)* has been repealed by *Schedule 3* of the *Local Government (Miscellaneous Provisions) (Northern Ireland) Order 1985. Article 14(4)* (which approximates to *section 10* of the *Clean Air Act 1956*) states that the district council cannot give its approval unless it is satisfied that the height of the chimney will be sufficient to prevent, 'in so far as is practicable, the smoke, grit, dust or gases from becoming a nuisance or prejudicial to health'. The district council must have regard to certain factors, listed in *article 14(4)* when making this determination. Where a chimney is erected in violation of approved plans, the district council is empowered to have that part of the chimney which is built not in accordance with the plans to be either 'altered, pulled down or removed'. The district council is also empowered to recover summarily expenses which they incur in the process of doing any work in this context from the person who caused the chimney to be built. [*Article 14(4)*].

19.50 *Height of chimneys serving a furnace*

Article 15 deals in more detail with applications to build chimneys which are designed to serve furnaces to which *article 8* applies (a furnace in which fuel or solid waste is burnt). *Article 15* overlaps with the provisions of *article 14* to a considerable degree; it essentially provides that a furnace cannot be used to burn fuel or solid waste unless the height of the chimney serving that furnace has been approved by the district council. However *article 15* goes on to state that it is an offence to allow a furnace to be used to burn fuel or solid waste without obtaining the required approval or to violate any conditions attached to the approval. In the case of a furnace in a building, the occupier of the building will be held liable, and in the case of a boiler or industrial plant attached to a building or fixed to or installed on to land, the person in possession of the boiler or plant will be held liable for any offence under this article. Penalties incurred are set out in *article 38. Article 15(2)* exempts certain categories of boiler or plants from the operation of *article 15. Article 15(11)* defines them as being boilers or plants used 'wholly for any prescribed purposes'. The power to make regulations concerning the height of chimneys under *article 15* has not been exercised to date.

Article 15(3)–(9) also contains detailed provisions governing the procedure to be followed when approval is sought for a chimney; the possible responses of the district council; the right of appeal to the DoE(NI); and the possible responses which the DoE(NI) can make. Finally *article 15(10)* lists certain categories of furnaces which are governed by *article 15* and others which are outside the operation of this article.

19.51 *New buildings over-reaching adjacent chimneys*

Article 24 provides that where a person 'erects or raises a building' (referred to as 'the taller building') to a height greater than the height of an adjoining building and the chimneys or flues of the adjoining building 'are in a party wall between the two buildings, or are six feet or less from the nearest part of the taller building', the district council may, by notice in writing, require that person to build up the chimneys and flues of the adjoining building so that 'the top of them is at the same height as the top of the chimneys of the taller building, or the top of the taller building, whichever is the higher'. The council may also (by notice in writing) require the owner or occupier of the adjoining building to allow the person served with the notice to enter and execute whatever work is necessary in order to comply with the notice.

Article 24 only applies to buildings that are erected or raised after *article 62* of the *Pollution Control and Local Government (Northern Ireland) Order 1978* has come into effect. [*Article 23(1)*]. Furthermore, the district council can only require the chimneys or flues of an adjoining building to be raised in so far as is practicable. The notice requesting the alterations, may specify a time within which the work is to be completed.

Article 24 also allows the owner or occupier of the adjoining building to serve a 'counter-notice' on the first-mentioned person and on the district council to the effect that he himself will carry out the necessary alterations to the adjoining building. A counter-notice must be served within 14 days of notice being served on the owner or occupier and such persons are then obliged to do the work, but can recover expenses incurred from the first-mentioned person.

It is an offence to fail to comply with any notice served by a district council under this article and similarly it is an offence to fail to fulfil the terms of a counter-notice. If the first-mentioned person has been refused entry by the owner or occupier of the adjoining building, or has been refused permission to carry out the necessary work, or a counter-notice has been served on them, they will not be deemed to have violated this article. Penalties incurred for violation of *article 24* are dealt with under *article 38(3)*. The district council is empowered to carry out the necessary work and recover its expenses in the event that a notice is violated.

19.52 *Smoke control areas*

Like *section 11* of the *Clean Air Act 1956*, *article 17* of the *Clean Air (Northern Ireland) Order 1981* gives the district council the power to control the emission of smoke in particular areas, and to this end the council may declare a particular area to be a smoke control area. Once an area is declared to be a control area, it is an offence to emit smoke from the chimney of any building; the occupier of the building will be held liable; penalties incurred for violation of *article 17* are dealt with under *article 38(2)*. Smoke control orders may also apply to chimneys serving the furnaces of any boilers or industrial plants which are either attached to buildings or are fixed to or attached to land (substituted terms of reference are dealt with in *article 17(11)*). It is a defence to prove that the emission of smoke was 'not caused by the use of any fuel other than an authorised fuel'. An authorised fuel is defined in *article 2(2)* of the *1981 Order* as being a fuel which has been prescribed by the DoE(NI) as 'authorised' for the purposes of this *Order*. Three regulations have been introduced so far specifying categories of authorised fuels. They are: the *Smoke Control Areas (Authorised Fuels) Regulations (Northern Ireland) 1982 (SI 1982 No 216)*; *1986 (SI 1986 No 313)*; *1992 (SI 1992 No 70)*.

Article 17(4)–(9) and *(12)–(14)* governs the district councils' power to make or revoke smoke control orders under this article; the councils' power to create exemptions from the provisions of this article; the suspension or relaxation of those provisions; and the bringing into effect of such orders. As under *articles 3* and *4*, a district council is obliged to notify the person deemed liable under the *Order* of their belief that a violation of *article 17* has occurred. If this notification is not given within the time limits set down in *article 37(1)* and *(2)* this will provide the defendant with a defence. *Article 41* gives district councils the power to act jointly for the purpose of declaring an area to be a smoke control area. In the event that district councils do act jointly in this context *article 41(1)* contains a number of modifications of the terms of *articles 17* and *18* and *Schedule 2* and a number of substituted references. *Article 41(2)–(4)* sets out the district councils' powers in this context.

19.53 *Adaptations of fireplaces in private dwellings*

Numerous regulations have been introduced between 1970 and 1985 exempting certain types of fireplaces from the operation of *article 17* of the *1981 Order*. These are contained in nine sets of regulations passed between 1970 and 1985 entitled *Smoke Control Areas (Exempted Fireplaces) Regulations (Northern Ireland) (SI 1970 No 222, SI 1971 Nos 74* and *330, SI 1972 No 180, SI 1974 Nos 40* and *275, SI 1977 No 347, SI 1983 No 405* and *SI 1985 No 53*). In the event that the district council declares an area to be smoke controlled, and this leads to 'the owner or occupier of, or any person with an estate or interest in, a private dwelling' incurring expenses on 'adaptations in or in connection with the dwelling' in an effort to avoid violating *article 17*, the district council is required, under *article 18*, to repay the owner or occupier or other person for expenses incurred. This provision does not apply to a 'new dwelling'. *Article 18(2)* sets out the amounts which the council is required to repay, the conditions which govern these repayments and the situations in which the council will not be required to repay. Under *article 18(3)* the district council may require the owner or occupier of a private dwelling to carry out adaptations to the property in order to avoid violation of *article 17*. These adaptations must be carried out within 21 days of service of the notice to do the work, but this period may be extended by the council. *Article 18(5)–(10)* sets out the procedure which the district council must follow when it seeks to request an owner or occupier to carry out adaptations under *article 18*. Also laid down in these provisions are the grounds on which a notice to carry out adaptations may be appealed; the procedure to be followed when making an appeal; and the appeal court's jurisdiction in this regard. *Article 18(11)* and *(12)* deals with the situation where the person served with the notice fails to make the adaptations or fails to obey a notice which has been confirmed on appeal, in such an event the district council is empowered to carry out the work itself. The provisions of *Article 18(11)* and *(12)* also govern the council's power to recover its expenses in this situation.

Article 20 contains definitions of a variety of terms and phrases used in the provisions of *articles 18* and *19* of this *Order*. In particular it elaborates on the meaning of the phrase 'adaptations in or in connection with a dwelling to avoid contraventions of article 17'. [*Article 20(1)–(3)*]. *Article 20(4)–(6)* and *(8)* explain references to 'expenditure' or 'expenses incurred' in the carrying out of works under *article 18* or *19*, and finally, *Article 20(7)* and *(8)* concern the extent to which a district council can dictate the type of appliance which is installed when a dwelling is being adapted to avoid violation of *article 17*.

The Head of the DoE(NI) may, with the approval of the Head of the Department of Finance, vary the provisions of *articles 18, 19* and *20* in certain specific areas listed in *article 21* of this *Order*.

Article 22 empowers district councils to make grants towards the adaptation of certain categories of premises, listed in *Article 22(1)*. The *Clean Air Act (Grant Extension)*

Order (Northern Ireland) 1969 (SI 1969 No 57) has been introduced under *article 22*. The Armagh District Council submitted complaints to the Rossi Committee that cost limits for grants for the conversion of fireplaces were not reviewed often enough.

19.54 *Smoke nuisances*

Where smoke is a nuisance to any of of the inhabitants of a neighbourhood it will be regarded as a nuisance under *article 23* within the meaning of *section 107* of the *Public Health (Ireland) Act 1878* (the *1878 Act*). The provisions of the *1878 Act* (except *section 288*), will apply to such nuisances, subject to the provisions of this *Order*. Where legal proceedings are brought under this article in relation to smoke emitted from a chimney, it is a defence to prove that the 'best practicable means had been employed to prevent the nuisance'. Under *article 37(1)* and *(2)* a district council is obliged to notify 'as soon as may be' the person deemed liable under this section of their belief that a violation of *article 23* has occurred. Failure to comply with this obligation will provide a defence for the defendant, penalties incurred are dealt with under *article 38(7)*. *Article 23* does not apply to the following categories of smoke:

'(a)   smoke emitted from a chimney of a private dwelling; or

(b)   dark smoke emitted from a chimney –

(i)   of a building; or

(ii)   serving the furnace of a boiler or industrial plant attached to a building or for the time being fixed to or installed on any land; or

(c)   dark smoke emitted otherwise than as mentioned in sub-paragraph (b) from industrial or trade premises within the meaning of article 4'.

19.55 *Emissions from railway engines*

In the case of railway engines *article 26* states that *article 3* of this *Order* (which prohibits dark smoke from chimneys) will apply to railway locomotive engines in the same way as it applies in relation to buildings. References to the occupier of the building must be substituted for references to the owner of the engine. The owner of a railway engine must 'use all practicable means there may be' in order to minimise the emission of smoke from the engine's chimney. Failure to do so is an offence. Unless provided for in this article, the provisions of this *Order* do not apply to smoke, dust or grit emitted from railway engines.

19.56 *Emissions from vessels*

Article 27 provides that *article 3* of this *Order* shall also apply in relation to vessels in waters governed by this article in the same way that it applies to buildings. References to the occupier of the building must be substituted for references to 'the owner of, and the master or other officer or person in charge of, the vessel'. References to a furnace include references to the vessel's engine. *Article 27(2)* and *(3)* detail the waters to which this article applies. Nothing in this *Order* shall apply to smoke, grit or dust emitted from a vessel unless this article provides for it.

19.57 *Emissions from Crown premises*

A district council is also obliged to report any emissions of smoke, dark smoke, grit or dust from Government premises listed in *Article 27(1)*; it is also obliged to report any emissions of dark smoke from a vessel of Her Majesty's navy or 'any Government ship in the service of the Admiralty while employed for the purposes of Her Majesty's navy' which appears to the council 'to constitute a nuisance to any of the inhabitants of the neighbourhood'.

Article 27(2) obliges the Government department responsible to make an inquiry into the complaint and if it is revealed that there is cause for complaint, the department responsible must 'employ all practicable means for preventing or minimising the emission of smoke, dust or grit, or abating the nuisance and preventing a recurrence of it'. *Article 27(3)* and *(4)* details the types of premises or vessels which are not governed by this article, while *Article 27(5)* includes another category of premises (namely a premises occupied 'for the service of a visiting force') within the categories of premises governed by this article. *Article 27(6)* defines the terms used in this article. Any penalties incurred for violation of any of the above articles is laid out in *article 38.*

19.58 *Exemptions from the provisions of the Clean Air (Northern Ireland) Order 1981 in the interests of research into atmospheric pollution*

Article 28 gives district councils the power to exempt:

'(*a*)   chimneys from the operation of *articles 3, 7, 17, 23,* and *26*;

(*b*)   any furnace, boiler or industrial plant from the operation of *article 5(1)*;

(*c*)   any premises from the operation of *article 4*;

(*d*)   any furnace from the operation of *articles 8, 9* and *11'*.

where the council deems it 'expedient' to do so in the interests of carrying out research and investigations into the problem of air pollution.

19.59 *Heating and cooking arrangements*

Article 30 states that regulations may be introduced to govern heating or cooking arrangements in buildings to prevent the emission of smoke in so far as is practicable. Regulations introduced under this article must be made in accordance with the *Building Regulations (Northern Ireland) Order 1979 (SI 1979 No 1709)*. *Schedule 4, Part II* of the *Clean Air (Northern Ireland) Order 1981* amends *Schedule 2* of the *1979 Regulations*. The *New Buildings (Prevention of Emissions of Smoke) Regulations (Northern Ireland) 1969 (SI 1969 No 6)* were enacted pursuant to the *Clean Air Act (Northern Ireland) 1964* which was consolidated by the *Clean Air (Northern Ireland) Order 1981*. The *1969 Regulations* are now deemed to be passed pursuant to *article 30* of the *1981 Order.*

Article 35 gives the DoE(NI) the power to make regulations extending the provisions of the *Clean Air (Northern Ireland) Order 1981* to certain emissions from chimneys; this power has not been exercised to date.

19.60 *Disclosures of trade secrets*

Under *article 36* it is an offence to make an unjustified disclosure of any information concerning a trade secret which has been obtained by a person under this *Order* or in connection with the execution of this *Order*. *Article 36* also contains a list of three possible justifications for the disclosure of such information. Penalties incurred under *article 36* are set out in *article 38(4).*

19.61 *Premises in two or more districts*

Article 42 states that any premises which extends into the 'districts of two or more district councils' will be treated as being wholly within which ever district is agreed by the two councils for the purposes of this *Order*. *Schedule 3* of the *Local Government (Miscellaneous Provisions) (Northern Ireland) Order 1985* repeals the phrase 'or in default of agreement, as may be determined by the DoE(NI)'.

19.62 **ALKALI, ETC. WORKS REGULATION ACT 1906**

The *Alkali, etc. Works Regulation Act 1906* consolidates and amends the *Alkali Acts 1881* and *1892*, and is equivalent to the English position prior to the passage of the *Water Act 1989*. The *1906 Act* has been amended by the *Alkali, etc. Work Order (Northern Ireland) 1977 (SI 1977 No 152)*; however, the latter was revoked by the *Alkali, etc. Works Order (Northern Ireland) 1987 (SI 1987 No 123)* which in turn was revoked by the *Alkali, etc. Works Order (Northern Ireland) 1991 (SI 1991 No 49)*. The *1991 Order* was enacted pursuant to the DoE's powers under *article 25(9)* of the *Clean Air (Northern Ireland) Order 1981 (SI 1981 No 158)*. *Schedule 4, paragraph 2* of the *Clean Air (Northern Ireland) Order 1981* substitutes a number of new provisions in place of *sections 1(2), 2(2), 6(3), 7(2)* and *9(8)* of the *1906 Act*. *Schedule 4, paragraph 3* inserts a *section 16A* into the *1906 Act*. *Section 16A* sets out the fines and liabilities incurred by a person who is found guilty of an offence under the *1906 Act* for which no express penalty is provided. *Article 25* of the *Clean Air (Northern Ireland) Order 1981* inter-relates to a considerable extent with the terms of the *1906 Act*. The *Pollution Control and Local Government (Northern Ireland) Order 1978 (SI 1978 No 1049)* makes a number of changes to the *1906 Alkali Act*. *Schedule 7* of the *1978 Order* repeals certain words from *sections 9(1), 11(b), 18(1), 20*, and *22(1)* of the *1906 Act*, the exact words will be highlighted below. *Schedule 7* also repeals the following sections of the *1906 Act* in their entirety: *sections 3, 4, 5, 8, 12(1)(d), 14, 15, 17, 18(1) (4)* and *19*. The *Alkali, etc. Works (Metrication) Regulations (Northern Ireland) 1985 (SI 1985 No 35)* were introduced pursuant to the DoE's powers under *article 82(1)* of the *1978 Order*. The *1985 Regulations* substitute amounts expressed in metric units for amounts not so expressed.

19.63 *Gases*

Section 1 of the *1906 Act* states that every 'alkali work' must be carried out in such a way that:

(1) the 'muriatic acid gas' which evolves from the work condenses to the extent required by the terms of *section 1(1)* of the Act [*section 1(1)*]; and

(2) the best practicable means are used to prevent the escape of 'noxious or offensive gases' by the exit flue of the apparatus used in the process; and

(3) the best practicable means are used to prevent the direct or indirect discharge of such gases into the atmosphere; and

(4) the best practicable means are used to render harmless and inoffensive any gases which are discharged. [*Section 2(1)*].

The definition of 'noxious or offensive gases', contained in *section 27* of the *1906 Act*, has been amended by *Schedule 1* of the *Alkali, etc. Works Order (Northern Ireland) 1991 (SI 1991 No 49)*. All of the above are subject to the overall proviso that *section 1* or *2* of the *1906 Act* will not have been violated if the amount of gas discharged into the atmosphere does not exceed the amount set out in *section 1(1)*, namely, that there is no more than one-fifth part of a grain of muriatic acid in each cubic foot of air, smoke or chimney gases, escaping from the works into the atmosphere. The procedure for calculating the proportion of acid per cubic foot or air, smoke or gas is set out in *section 16* of the *1906 Act*.

The list of 'works' provided in *Schedule 1* of the *1906 Act*, has been amended by the *Alkali, etc. Works Order (Northern Ireland) 1991*; the current list of works is contained in *Schedule 2* of the *Order*. Violation of either *section 1(1)* or *2(1)* of the *1906 Act* is an offence under *sections 1(2)* and *2(2)* respectively; the owner of the works in question will be held liable in both instances; penalties incurred are set out in *sections 1(2)* and *2(2)*.

19.64 Sulphuric acid works

Section 6(1) of the 1906 Act states that every sulphuric acid work (as defined in Schedule 2 of the Alkali, etc. Works Order (Northern Ireland) 1991) must be carried out in such a way that the acid gases which are produced are condensed to the extent laid out in section 6(1). Once again the procedure for determining the proportion of acid to a cubic foot of air, smoke or gas is laid down in section 16. Violation of section 6 is an offence under section 6(3); the owner will be held liable.

19.65 Muriatic acid works (hydrochloric acid works)

There is a similar obligation imposed on the manufacture of muriatic acid. The extent of the condensation required is laid out in section 6(2) of the 1906 Act and the procedure for determining the proportion of acid to a cubic foot of air, smoke or gas is laid down in section 16. Once again it is an offence to violate this obligation and the owner is deemed to be liable.

19.66 Scheduled works

Section 7(1) imposes an obligation on the owner of any work specified in Schedule 2 of the Alkali, etc. Works Order (Northern Ireland) 1991 (SI 1991 No 49) (known as a 'scheduled work') to use the best practicable means to prevent the escape of 'noxious or offensive gases' by the exit flue of the apparatus used in the process, or the direct or indirect discharge of such gases into the atmosphere. The phrase 'noxious or offensive gases', defined in section 27(1) of the 1906 Act, has been amended by Schedule 1 of the Alkali, etc. Works Order (Northern Ireland) 1991 (SI 1991 No 49). Similarly the owner is also obliged to use the best practicable means to render 'harmless and inoffensive' any gases which are discharged. Section 7(1) is subject to the qualification that an inspector does not object to the amount of muriatic or other acid gas 'per cubic foot of air' which has been released from a scheduled work into the air. The quantities of gas concerned are set out in section 7(1)(a) and (b) and the procedure for determining the proportion of acid per cubic foot of air, smoke or gas is set out in section 16. It is an offence to knowingly fail to use the best practicable means as required under section 7; liability falls on the owner of the work in question; penalties incurred are set out in section 7(2). Section 15 concerning the making of special rules for employees of an alkali work (outlined above) also applies in relation to the employees of a scheduled work.

Section 26 provides that for the first three years after the commencement of this Act, section 26(b) will apply to the 'over-heat pan' process for concentrating sulphuric acid as though 'two grains of sulphuric anhydride were substituted for one grain and a half of sulphuric anhydride'.

19.67 Burning cable

Article 56 of the Pollution Control and Local Government (Northern Ireland) Order 1978 prohibits the burning of insulation from a cable for the purposes of recovering the metal from the cable unless this is done at a location which is registered as a 'work' under section 9 of the Alkali, etc. Works Regulation Act 1906. Section 16A of the 1906 Act will apply to an offence under article 56 of the 1978 Order. Section 16A was originally inserted into the 1906 Act by Schedule 3, paragraph 2 of the Clean Air Act (Northern Ireland) 1964, consolidated by the Clean Air (Northern Ireland) Order 1981. Section 16A is now deemed to be inserted by Schedule 4, paragraph 3 of the 1981 Order. Section 16A concerns the penalties which will be incurred for violation of provisions of the Alkali, etc. Works Regulation Act 1906.

19.68 *Registration of works*

Section 9(1) of the *1906 Act* prohibits the carrying on of an alkali or scheduled work unless it is certified as registered. Stamp duty will be charged on the issuing of every certificate of registration. Failure to comply with this obligation is an offence, for which the owner of the work will be liable to a fine. Where a work is being registered for the first time, the application for registration may be made at any time; thereafter, the application must be made in January or February. In the event that a certificate of registration is already in force for the work, the new certificate will continue in force for a year after the expiration of the previous certificate; where there is no existing certificate, the new certificate will continue in force until 'the following first day of April'.

Where an alkali or scheduled work is either being registered for the first time or the work has been closed for the preceeding year, the inspector or, on appeal, the DoE(NI), may require that the work be fitted with whatever equipment they deem necessary to ensure that the work complies with the provisions of this Act. Where it applies, this requirement is a condition of registration, and the work cannot be issued with a certificate of registration unless it is complied with. The DoE(NI) may dispense with this condition '. . . in the case of work erected before the commencement of this Act which were not before the commencement of this Act required to be registered'. The owner of the work is obliged to send written notice of any change in ownership of the work, or any change in the particulars stated in the register. No expense will be incurred for making such changes and no new certificate will be issued. Failure to do so will mean that the work is no longer registered. Notice must be sent within one month of the change in question.

19.69 *Relationship between the Clean Air (Northern Ireland) Order 1981 and the Alkali, etc. Works Regulation Act 1906*

Article 25 of the *1981 Order* will apply to '. . . so much of any work registered under *section 9* of the *Alkali, etc. Works Regulation Act 1906* . . . as is directly concerned in the processes which necessitate its registration under that section'. [*Article 25(1)(a)*]. *Article 25* will also apply to so much of any work being altered or erected, which when complete, will be directly involved in processes which will necessitate its registration under *section 9* of the *1906 Act*. [*Article 25(1)(b)*]. The DoE(NI) will conclusively determine 'how much of any work' would be directly involved in these processes. The DoE(NI) must be given notice of any proposal to alter a work, to which *article 25* applies, in such a way that it alters the processes which necessitate its registration. The DoE(NI) must also be notified of any alterations or erections of a work as described in *article 25(1)*. Violation of this obligation is an offence under *article 25(7)*. The person who carries out the alteration or erection, or on whose instruction it is carried out will be guilty of the offence.

Articles 3–24 of the *Clean Air (Northern Ireland) Order 1981* will not apply to works caught by *article 25*. [*Article 25(3)*]. *Article 25(3)* will not affect the application of *articles 3, 7* or *23* of the *1981 Order* to works to which *article 25* applies. However a district council can only institute proceedings under *articles 3, 7* and *23* of the *1981 Order* or *section 107(4)* or *(7)* of the *Public Health (Ireland) Act 1878* without the DoE(NI)'s consent.

The *Alkali, etc. Works Regulation Act 1906* will apply in relation to smoke, dust and grit from any works to which *article 25* of the *1981 Order* applies. In this regard the *1906 Act* will operate in the same way as it does in relation to noxious or offensive gases.

Where it considers it expedient to do so, the DoE(NI) can order *article 25(8)* to apply to the whole or part of any works to which *article 25* applies. In this event, *article 25(3)–(7)*

'. . . shall not apply to the works or, as the case may be, to the specified part of the works'. [*Article 25(8)(a)*]. However, *article 25(8)(b)* provides that it will be a defence to '. . . any proceedings under *article 3* in respect of dark smoke from the works or, as the case may be, from the specified part of the works, to prove that the best practicable means' were used '. . . to minimise or prevent the emission of dark smoke from the works' in question, and if proceedings are brought under *article 23* in relation to smoke nuisances from the whole or part of the works in question, the defence contained in *article 23(2)* will be available irrespective of whether the smoke was emitted from a chimney or not.

Article 25(13) empowers the DoE(NI) to order an inspector to enter and inspect any work (even one which is not caught by the *Alkali, etc. Works Regulation Act 1906*) where the DoE(NI) regards the work in question as likely to cause the evolution of any noxious or offensive gas. The provisions of the *1906 Act* concerning the powers of inspectors will apply to a work referred to in *article 25(13)* of the *1981 Order. Article 25(15)* qualifies this power to the extent that an inspector acting under *article 25(13)* is not authorised to enter and inspect a work in connection with an emission of grit, smoke or dust.

19.70 *Inspection*

Inspectors, appointed under *sections 10* and *11* of the *1906 Act*, are given extensive powers of entry and inspection under *section 12* for the purposes of executing their functions under this Act. Failure to furnish an inspector with information which he is entitled to demand, or obstruction of the inspector in the execution of his duties is an offence under *section 12(4)*. The owner of the work in which the inspector was obstructed and the person obstructing the inspector will be held liable under the Act.

19.71 *Legal proceedings under the Alkali, etc. Works Regulation Act 1906*

Section 18 contains the rules concerning legal proceedings for offences under all provisions of the *1906 Act* and the defendant's liability to cumulative fines under this Act. The *Pollution Control and Local Government (Northern Ireland) Order* has extensively amended the provisions of the *1906 Act* concerning the fines which can be imposed for violation of the latter's provisions. Essentially it is sufficient for the plaintiff to allege that the work in question is a 'works' to which the Act applies and to state the name of the registered or ostensible owner of the work, or the name by which the business is usually known.

Where an action is being taken against the owner of a work on the grounds of a failure to secure the condensation of any gas to the satisfaction of the chief inspector, or a failure to use the best practicable means as required by the Act, the inspector must give the owner of the work at least 21 days' notice in writing, stating either the facts on which the inspector has based his opinion, or the means which the owner has failed to use, and the means which the inspector will accept as sufficient. A copy of this notice must be produced before the court hearing the case. *Section 21* governs the service of any notice, summons or document which is required to be served on the owner under this Act.

Section 20 states that the owner of a work will not be liable for any violation of the *1906 Act* if the owner can prove that 'he used due diligence to comply with and enforce the execution of this Act, and that the offence in question was committed, without his knowledge, consent or connivance, by some agent, servant or workman, whom he shall charge by name as the actual offender'. Proceedings may be taken against the actual offender.

Section 22 provides that where a complaint is to the central authority by any sanitary authority, on the basis of information given to them by any of their officers or by any ten inhabitants of their district, to the effect that a nuisance is being created by a work which is being carried on in violation of this Act, the central authority is empowered to carry out an inquiry into the matter and may direct inspectors to take legal proceedings if necessary. If the nuisance in question is being wholly or partially caused by the acts or defaults of several works, a person injured by the nuisance may take an action for damages against any one or more of the owners of such works. The owners of the works in question will be obliged to pay that proportion of the damages which reflect the owners' contribution to the nuisance, even where the act or default of the owners would not alone have caused the nuisance. Where the owners of the work can produce a certificate from the chief inspector to the effect that the work in question was carried on in accordance with the requirements of this Act and those requirements were being complied with at the time of the complaint, the owner of such work is not liable to pay damages under *section 23*.

19.72 European directives concerning air pollution

Once again the pattern of very slow implementation of *EC Directives* into Northern Irish law has been repeated in this context. The following *Directives* have been implemented to date:

The *Air Quality Standards Regulations (Northern Ireland) 1990 (SI 1990 No 145)* has been introduced to implement *Directive 80/779/EEC (Suspended Particles Directive)*; *Directive 82/884/EEC (Lead in Air)*; *Directive 85/203/EEC (Nitrogen Dioxide Directive)* as amended by *Directive 85/580/EEC*. These *Regulations* also implement *article 17* of the *Clean Air (Northern Ireland) Order 1981* concerning smoke control areas.

Directive 80/779/EEC has been amended by *Directives 81/857/EEC, 89/427/EEC* and *91/692/EEC; Directive 82/884/EEC* has been amended by *Directive 91/692/ EEC*; and *Directive 85/203/EEC* has also been amended by *Directive 91/692/EEC*; however, none of these amendments have been incorporated into Northern Irish law yet.

The *Alkali, etc. Works Order (Northern Ireland) 1991* implements *Directive 84/360/EEC* on the combating of air pollution from industrial plants and also *Directive 87/217/EEC* on the prevention and reduction of environmental pollution by asbestos. Plants belonging to the categories outlined in Annex I to *Directive 84/360/EEC* are made subject to the provisions of the *Alkali, etc. Works Regulation Act 1906*.

The *Oil Fuel (Sulphur Content of Gas Oil) Regulations (Northern Ireland) 1991 (SI 1991 No 235)* implement *Article 2.3* of *Directive 87/219/EEC* which allows for exemptions from the prohibition on the use of gas oil containing an excess of sulphur.

19.73 Pollution Control and Local Government (Northern Ireland) Order 1978 (the 1978 Order) (SI 1978 No 1049)

This *Order* is equivalent to *Parts I, II* and *IV* of the Control of Pollution Act 1974. Aside from the extensive amendments made to the *Alkali, etc. Works Regulation Act 1906*, only *Part IV* of the *1978 Order* relates to air pollution, in particular, information concerning air pollution.

19.74 *Sulphur content of oil fuel*

Article 55(1) of the *1978 Order* gives the DoE(NI) the power to make regulations imposing limitations on the sulphur content of oil fuel used in furnaces or engines; regulations concerning this issue are contained in *Oil Fuel (Sulphur Content of Gas Oil) Regulations (Northern Ireland) 1991* (the *1991 Regulations*) *(SI 1991 No 235)*. The *1991*

Regulations also implement *Article 2.3* of *EC Directive 87/219/EEC* which gives exemptions from the prohibition on the use of gas oil containing an excess of sulphur.

19.75 *Information concerning air pollution*

Articles 57–61 of the *1978 Order* deal with various aspects of the collection of information concerning atmospheric pollution. *Article 57* is entitled 'research and publicity' and gives the district council a range of powers concerning the financing and organisation of research into air pollution and the publication of information on that problem. *Article 57* also empowers the district council to obtain information concerning the emission of pollutants and other substances into the air. References in *Part IV* of the *1978 Order* to 'the emission of substances into the atmosphere' shall be construed as applying 'to substances in a gaseous or liquid or solid state or in any combination of those states'. [*Article 63(2)*]. To this end *article 63(2)(a)–(c)* establishes the procedure whereby the council can obtain this information. Essentially the council may obtain this information by issuing a notice (under *article 58*) requiring the occupier of any premises in its district to provide, 'whether by periodical returns or by other means' the information that is specified in the notice concerning the emission of pollutants and other substances into the air. Alternatively the council may obtain the information by entering any premises (either by agreement or under *section 98* of the *Local Government Act (Northern Ireland) 1972*) for the purpose of measuring or recording the emissions. A final option is that the council may enter into an agreement with the occupier of premises whereby the occupier carries out the measurements and recording on behalf of the council. None of these options apply to private dwellings.

Where the district council decides to obtain such information by entering any premises the council is obliged under *article 57(3)* to give the occupier of the premises 21 days' notice of its intention to enter for these purposes. *Article 57(3)(a)* dictates the contents of the notice which must be served. If the occupier requests that the council serves him with a notice under *article 58* (during the 21-day period) then the council cannot enter the premises. Where the emission is from a 'work' which is subject to the *1906 Act*, a district council is not permitted to gather information concerning the emission unless it does so pursuant to a notice served under *article 57* or *58*, and does not enter the premises in question. The details of the procedure under *article 58* will be dealt with in more detail below.

In the event that the council exercises its powers to serve a notice and enter under *article 57*, the council is obliged to publish any information gathered in such a way that trade secrets are not disclosed. This is the case unless the council is given written consent by an authorised person or the DoE(NI)'s consent. [*Article 57(5)*]. Violation of this obligation is an offence and it will be a defence in criminal or civil proceedings to prove that the information was disclosed in accordance with this article. This will apply in particular to proceedings brought under *article 36* of the *Clean Air (Northern Ireland) Order 1981 (SI 1981 No 158)* which also makes it an offence to unjustifiably disclose trade secrets. District councils are obliged under *article 57(8)* to consult at least twice in each financial year with persons

> 'carrying on any trade or business in the council's district, or such organisations appearing to the council to be representative of those persons, and such persons appearing to the council to be conversant with the problems of air pollution or to have an interest in local amenity as appear to the council to be appropriate'

about the manner in which the council uses its powers under *articles 57* and *58* and about the 'extent to which and manner in which, any information collected under those powers should be made available to the public'.

19.76 *Notices served under article 58*

Where a notice is served under *article 58* the person on whom the notice is served must comply with the notice within six weeks of the date of the service, or a longer period which the district council has (by notice) allowed. A person served with a notice under *article 58* cannot be required to supply information at intervals of less than three months, and notices under *article 58* cannot require information 'covering a period of more than twelve months'. *Article 58* will also apply to premises 'used for, and to persons in' the 'public service of the Crown' in the same way as it applies to other premises and persons. However, where *article 58* is applied to premises or persons in the Crown service, a district council may not exercise any of its powers under *article 72* of the *1978 Order*, or *section 98* of the *Local Government Act (Northern Ireland) 1972*. Where a person is served with a notice under *article 58* it is an offence under *article 58(7)* to fail, 'without a reasonable excuse' to comply with the requirements of the notice, or in providing the required information, knowingly or recklessly to make a statement which is false in a material particular. The person will be liable to a maximum fine of £400 on summary conviction. Where a person is convicted under *article 58(7)*, nothing in *article 57(3)* will prevent the district council from exercising its power to enter under *article 57(3)* in respect of the premises in question.

Article 58(3) states that where a notice is served under *article 58* in relation to a 'work' subject to the *Alkali, etc. Works Regulation Act 1906*, the person on whom the notice is served is not obliged to supply any information which is not supplied to an inspector appointed under the Act for the purposes of the Act.

19.77 *Appealing a notice served under article 58*

Article 59 of the *1978 Order* allows any person served with a notice or any person with an 'interest' in the premises to which the notice relates, to appeal the notice to the DoE(NI). *Article 59(1)(a)* and *(b)* lays down two main grounds upon which the appeal can be based. *Article 59(1)(a)* states that an appeal may be based on the ground that giving all or part of the information required to the district council or making all or part of it available to the public would:

' (i)   prejudice to an unreasonable degree some private interest by disclosing information about a trade secret, or

(ii)   be contrary to the public interest'.

Article 59(1)(b) states that an appeal may be brought on the basis that the 'information required by the notice is not immediately available and cannot readily be collected or obtained by the recipient of the notice without incurring undue expenditure for the purpose'. *Article 59(2)* gives the DoE(NI) the power to direct the district council to 'withdraw or modify' the notice if the appeal is allowed. Alternatively, the DoE(NI) may direct the council to take certain specified steps to ensure that 'prejudicial information is not disclosed to the public'. The district council is obliged to comply with the DoE(NI)'s direction. *Article 59(3)* gives the DoE(NI) the power to make regulations concerning the logistics of bringing an appeal under *article 59*; this paragraph also contains a list of representatives who must be consulted by the DoE(NI) before any such regulations are made.

19.78 *Regulations concerning the district council's powers under articles 57 and 58*

Article 60(1) gives the DoE(NI) the power to make regulations concerning the methods by which and the manner in which district councils can exercise their powers under *articles 57* and *58*. *Article 60(2)–(5)* sets out the persons who must be consulted by the DoE(NI) before such regulations are made, and the possible contents of the regulations.

19.79   Northern Ireland

19.79 *Provision of information for the DoE(NI)*

The DoE(NI) may, for the purposes of obtaining information about air pollution, require district councils to make the necessary arrangements for 'the provision, installation, operation and maintenance of apparatus for measuring and recording air pollution; and for transmitting the information so obtained to the DoE(NI)'. [*Article 61(1)*]. *Article 61(2)* and *(3)* concern the defraying of expenditure incurred by the council in providing the required apparatus, the DoE(NI)'s obligation to consult the district council before giving such a direction and the council's obligation to comply with the direction.

19.80 WATER POLLUTION IN NORTHERN IRELAND

The principle measures governing water pollution in Northern Ireland are the *Water Act (Northern Ireland) 1972* (the *1972 Act*); the *Water and Sewerage Services (Northern Ireland) Order 1973* (the *1973 Order*) (*SI 1973 No 70*); the *Pollution Control and Local Government (Northern Ireland) Order 1978* (*SI 1978 No 1049*); and the *Water and Sewerage Services (Amendment) (Northern Ireland) Order 1985* (*SI 1985 No 756*). In addition to these measures there is also the *Laganside Development (Northern Ireland) Order 1989* (*SI 1989 No 490*), and numerous regulations concerning fishing in the Foyle Area. The *Water Act (Northern Ireland) 1972* and the *Water and Sewerage Services (Northern Ireland) Order 1973* are central to the control of water pollution in NI, and together they broadly approximate to the position in England and Wales prior to the passage of the *Water Act 1989*.

19.81 Unlike the situation in England, no special body like the National Rivers Authority exists to oversee water pollution. The DoE(NI) is the principal player in both the *Water Act (Northern Ireland) 1972* and the *Water and Sewerage Services (Northern Ireland) Order 1973*. Under the *1972 Act* the DoE(NI) is made responsible for the conservation and 'cleanliness of inland and coastal waters' in Northern Ireland. While under the *1973 Order* the DoE(NI) is made responsible for the supply and distribution of water, the provision and maintenance of sewers for draining domestic sewage, trade effluent and surface water, and finally to deal effectively with the contents of its sewers. The most frequent complaint made to the Rossi Committee concerning water services in NI resulted from the lack of a special body to oversee water pollution, namely, that the DoE(NI) is perceived as both 'poacher and game-keeper' in relation to water pollution laws. It both operates sewage works and polices pollution. Although the Rossi Committee were satisfied that it took its role seriously, it remarked that 'while a situation exists in which the Water Service cannot be publicly held to account for water pollution incidents', it is inevitable that their role will be viewed with suspicion (Rossi Report, paragraph 78).

19.82 The Environmental Protection Division of the DoE(NI) is made up of a small team of scientists; the DoE(NI) also employs a number of agents, for example, the Department of Economic Development, the Fisheries Conservancy Board for NI, the Foyle Fisheries Commission, and environmental health officers who are responsible for pollution from domestic septic tanks and also investigate urban pollution incidents. There is also the Water Appeals Commission (set up under the *1973 Order*), and the Northern Ireland Water Council, established under *section 4* of the *1972 Act*. The Department of Agriculture is also given some power concerning the prevention of water pollution. One of the DoE(NI)'s most significant achievements in the context of water, related to beaches in NI. Sixteen beaches have been designated under the *EC Bathing Water Directive* and in 1989 all 16 complied. 'Designation' simply means that the beaches in question must meet with the standards set by the EC. The Rossi Report noted that the DoE(NI) had an 'impressive record on prosecution for water pollution offences, particularly when compared with the situation in Great Britain'. There were 227 prosecutions in NI in 1987 and 1988, compared with 292 in England, although this was prior to the establishment of the NRA. In Northern Ireland 18 per cent of pollution incidents led to prosecution, compared to less than 2 per cent in Scotland. However the levels of fines imposed as a consequence of successful prosecutions remained low. The Rossi Committee recommended that Resident Magistrates should give consideration to the level of fines imposed for breaches of water pollution laws. They also recommended that the DoE(NI) should 'publicise data on the full environmental costs of a number of selected pollution incidents, so as to engender a broader understanding of the costs of water pollution' (paras 76–77).

A number of local authorities reported coastal discharges of raw sewage in areas where the *EC Bathing Water Directive* does not apply. In response, the Rossi Report recommended that 'a more extensive system of sampling beaches for water quality should be instituted and that the DoE(NI) should endeavour to raise the quality of coastal waters generally'. In addition the Committee recommended that wherever possible all sewage should receive 'at least primary and secondary treatment, with disinfectant, subject to further research' and, where appropriate, the removal of nutrients from the liquid effluents which result. The Rossi Report also points out that 'half of all NI water pollution incidents are caused by agriculture'. The Report also pointed out that many other EC states have more rigourous control over slurry disposal and that the imposition of EC legislation in this area is likely to result. The Committee's recommendation in this context was 'that the government should give high priority to reducing pollution by farm slurry, including supporting slurry recycling services through its own purchasing policy as well as through other powers' (paragraph 78).

19.83 The following is a list of known DoE(NI) legislative commitments in the context of water pollution; where the legislation is actually in place, the date passed will be included in brackets:

Water and Sewage Services (Amendment) (Northern Ireland) Order 1991
Pollution of Groundwater by Dangerous Substances (Northern Ireland) Order 1991/1992
Environmental Assessment (Discharges to Water) (Northern Ireland) Regulations 1990
Bathing Waters (Northern Ireland) Regulations – no date specified
Freshwater Fish (Northern Ireland) Regulations 1991
Shellfish Waters (Northern Ireland) Regulations – no date specified
Water (Miscellaneous Provisions) (Northern Ireland) Order 1992
Disposals at Sea (Exemptions) (Northern Ireland) Order 1991
Pollution Control (Ships' Tanks Workings) (Northern Ireland) Regulations 1991
Pollution Control (Landed Ships' Waste) (Northern Ireland) Regulations 1991.

19.84 Water Act (Northern Ireland) 1972

The *1972 Act* contains 33 sections and is divided into three parts, there are also four schedules attached to the Act. *Part I* of the Act sets out the powers of the DoE(NI) in the context of water. *Part II* contains the provisions concerning the prevention of water pollution, while *Part III* contains a wide variety of miscellaneous and general provisions concerning the management of water resources and the control of water pollution. The *Water Act (Northern Ireland) 1972* has been amended on two occasions to date, by *Schedule 3* of the *Pollution Control and Local Government (Northern Ireland) Order 1978* and by *Schedule 3* of the *Water and Sewerage Services (Northern Ireland) Order 1973*. *Section 31* of the *Water Act (Northern Ireland) 1972* amends *Part 3* of *Schedule 1* of the *Radioactive Substances Act 1960*. *Section 31* also repeals the *Rivers Pollution Prevention Acts 1876* (except *section 7*) and *1893* and *section 78* of the *Public Health (Ireland) Act 1878*. *Section 7* of the *1876 Act* was later repealed by the *Water and Sewerage Services*

(Northern Ireland) Order 1973. The *Water Act (Northern Ireland) 1972* does not apply to the use of sanitary appliances on vessels in tidal waters, from which polluting matter passes or can pass into such waters, but which are used for ordinary sanitation purposes. This is the case unless regulations are enacted under *section 12(1)(b)* which apply to tidal waters; this power has not been exercised to date. *Section 32(3)* states that *section 5* of the *1972 Act* shall not affect the operation of *section 448(2)* of the *Merchant Shipping Act 1894.*

19.85   Part I: The Powers of the DoE(NI)

Part I of the *1972 Act* confers principal responsibility on the DoE(NI) for the management of water resources and the prevention of water pollution in Northern Ireland. *Part I* also refers to the Department of Agriculture(NI) (DA(NI)) as having functions in this context; however, the DA's specific functions are set out in the *Drainage Acts (Northern Ireland) 1925–1964.* The DA(NI) and DoE(NI) are given the power to prepare 'water management programmes', the possible contents of which are outlined in *section 3(2)* of the 1972 Act. *Section 26* of the *1972 Act* states that legal proceedings under this Act must be instituted by the DoE(NI) or the Attorney-General or with the consent of the Attorney-General. This includes legal proceedings in respect of all offences except for an offence under *section 16(3)*. Legal proceedings under *section 16(3)* must be instituted by the Department of Agriculture or by the Attorney-General, or with the Attorney-General's consent. Water management programmes must be reviewed by the two departments at maximum intervals of seven years [*section 3(3)*] and *Schedule 1* of the Act governs the procedure to be followed when such programmes are being drawn up. *Section 4* of the Act establishes the NI Water Council whose function is to advise the DoE(NI) and the DA in the exercise of their functions under the *Water Act (Northern Ireland) 1972.*

19.86   Part II: The Prevention of water pollution

Part II contains the provisions concerning the pollution of water, and therefore its terms will be examined in detail. *Section 5* prohibits the discharge or deposit of polluting matter in such a way that it enters water. Defences to, exemptions from, liability incurred and directions to repair damage are all dealt with in *section 5. Section 6* allows the DoE(NI) to take preventative action in the event that a violation of *article 5* seems likely to occur or has occurred. *Sections 7* and *8* prohibit the direct discharge of effluent or polluting matter into water. However, these and subsequent sections also contain a system of statutory consents (similar to that operating in England and Wales under *section 88* of the *Water Resources Act 1991*) which allow such discharges. Finally *section 13* gives the DoE(NI) the power to prohibit or restrain any person from depositing or discharging any matter on to any land or into water notwithstanding that it has already given consent under *section 7* or *8.*

19.87   *Section 5: depositing or discharging polluting matter in such a way that it enters water*

Essentially *section 5* prohibits the depositing or discharging of 'poisonous, noxious or polluting matter' in such a way that it enters water. Defences, exemptions, liability incurred and directions to repair damage are all dealt with in the provisions of *section 5* (see below).

Section 5(1) provides that it is an offence to

'knowingly or otherwise –

(*a*)   discharge or deposit of any poisonous, noxious or polluting matter so that it enters a waterway or water contained in any underground strata; or

(b)   discharge or deposit of any matter so that it enters a waterway or water contained in any underground strata and tends either directly or in combination with similar acts (whether his own or another's) to impede the proper flow of the water of the waterway or strata in a manner leading or likely to lead to pollution or a substantial aggravation of pollution due to other causes or of its consequences.'

Any reference in *section 5(1)* to 'matter entering a waterway or water contained in any underground strata', includes a matter which enters the waterway or water by being carried into it. [*Water Act (Northern Ireland) 1972 s 5(6)*].

However, where a person discharges matter into a sewer or sewage disposal works, owned by a local authority, and it enters a waterway or water contained in underground strata, an offence will not have been committed if:

'the authority are bound to receive the matter, or they have consented to do so unconditionally, or they have consented to do so subject to conditions and the person observes the conditions'. [*Water Act (Northern Ireland) 1972, s 5(2)*].

In proceedings under *section 5* it is a defence to prove that all reasonable care was exercised to prevent the discharge or deposit of the matter in question. [*Water Act (Northern Ireland) 1972, s 5(3)*].

On conviction of an offence under *section 5*, the Court making the conviction, may direct the person in question to take such measures as the Court deems necessary to 'remedy or nullify' any violation of this section [*section 5(4)*]. However, the Court may only make such an order if the DoE(NI) makes an application to the Court for such a direction, and the person charged has been given at least ten days' notice of the application.

Failure to comply with a direction under *section 5(4)* is an offence under *section 5(5)*. This offence is regarded as an offence which is 'substantially a repetition or continuation of an offence' under *section 5*. Liability for such an offence is dealt with under *section 5(7)*, see below.

Section 5(7) provides that a person found guilty of an offence under *section 5* shall be liable:

'(a)   on conviction on indictment, to a fine;

(b)   on summary conviction, to a fine not exceeding £400;

but if it is shown to the satisfaction of the court by or before which the person is convicted that the offence was substantially a repetition or continuation of an earlier offence by him after he had been convicted of the earlier offence (whether under this Act or otherwise), he shall be liable –

(i)   on conviction on indictment, to imprisonment for a term not exceeding two years or to a fine, or to both;

(ii)   on summary conviction, to the greater of a fine not exceeding £400 or a fine not exceeding £40 for each day on which the offence was so repeated or continued'.

19.88   *Section 6: prevention of violations of section 5*

The *1972 Act* also allows the DoE(NI) to take preventative action in the event that a violation of *section 5* seems likely to occur. To this end *section 6* contains a system of notices which the DoE(NI) may serve on an actual or potential polluter of water, (i.e., a user or proposed user of any land, water, vessel or vehicle), restraining or prohibiting their activities. It is an offence to violate a notice served under *section 6* but it is also possible to appeal such notices.

Section 6(1) provides that if it appears that a violation of *section 5* ('whether it be a new or repeating/continuing violation') is likely to occur by reason of

'any use or proposed use of:

(*a*)   a waterway or land for the disposal of any matter;

(*b*)   land for the storage of any matter;

(*c*)   a vessel or vehicle from which poisonous, noxious or polluting matter may enter a waterway or water contained in any underground strata;'.

The DoE(NI) may serve a notice either:

'(i)   prohibiting the use complained of, or

(ii)   permitting the use only subject to conditions which remove the grounds of complaint, or

(iii)   requiring it to be stopped within a period of time which is specified in the notice'.

This notice may be served on either:

(i)   the owner of the land, or

(ii)   the user or proposed user of the waterway, land, vessel or vehicle.

Where an individual is served with a notice under *section 6(1)*, any violation of *section 5* which is shown to have been wholly or partly due to a contravention of a valid notice, will be treated, for the purposes of *section 5(7)*, as a repetition or continuation of an offence for which he has been convicted under *section 5*. [*Water Act (Northern Ireland) 1972, s 6(2)*].

A notice under *section 6(1)* may require the removal, from the waterway, land, vessel or vehicle, of any matter which has been used in a manner complained of in the notice. [*Water Act (Northern Ireland) 1972, s 6(3)*]. In the event that the notice does require the removal of matter referred to in *section 6(3)*, but it is not removed as required, the DoE(NI) may remove the matter in question and dispose of it in whatever way it considers appropriate [*section 6(4)*]. The DoE(NI)'s power to defray expenses incurred in this context are dealt with in *section 6(6)*. It is possible for any interested party to obtain from the DoE(NI), on request but at their own expense, details of any notice served under *section 6(1)* concerning the use or proposed use of any land. [*Water Act (Northern Ireland) 1972, s 6(5)*].

19.89   *Appeal notices served under section 6(1)*

It is possible to appeal the service of a notice served under *section 6(1)*. *Section 6(7)* as amended by *Schedule 3* of the *Water and Sewerage Services (Northern Ireland) Order 1973* provides that the appeal must be commenced within four weeks of the date when the notice was served and must be taken to the Water Appeals Commission for Northern Ireland. The Appeals Commission may quash the notice if it is satisfied that *section 5(1)* is not likely to be violated by the use or proposed use complained of in the notice.

19.90   *Sections 7 and 8: the discharge of effluent or polluting matter into waterways or underground stratum*

Sections 7 and *8* address the situation where effluent or polluting matter is discharged directly into waterways or underground stratum. Although each section will be dealt with in more detail below, the following is a brief outline of their terms. *Section 7* concerns waterways, while *section 8* concerns underground stratum. Although the direct discharge of such matter is prohibited in the first paragraph of both sections, the remainder of *sections 7* and *8* go on to provide a system of statutory consents, which may be granted by the DoE(NI), rendering the discharge in question lawful. *Section 9*, as amended by the *Water and Sewerage Services (Northern Ireland) Order 1973*, lays out the procedure to be followed by the applicant and the DoE(NI) when an application for consent is made; the effect of a consent; liability incurred for violation of a consent; and the extent to which the DoE(NI)'s decision can be appealed. *Section 10* provides for the review of consents under *section 7* or *8*, while *section 13* allows the DoE(NI) to restrain or prohibit the depositing or discharge of any matter notwithstanding the fact that the DoE(NI) has already given its consent to such activity.

Sections 7(1) and *8(1)* prohibit the discharge into a waterway or underground stratum of:

(*a*)   any trade or sewage effluent;

(*b*)   poisonous, noxious or polluting matter not falling within paragraph (*a*).

However, the discharge of such matter is possible if the DoE's consent is obtained. The DoE(NI) may grant its consent subject to such conditions as it considers 'proper to impose'. The operation of a consent obtained under either section is dealt with in *section 7(2)* or *8(2)*. Conditions imposed under *section 7(2)*, concerning discharge into waterways, will bind any person discharging effluent or matter 'from land or premises to which the consent relates'. Conditions imposed under *section 8(2)*, concerning discharges into underground stratum, shall bind any person 'using any land or premises to which the consent relates'.

19.91   Where effluent or matter referred to in *sections 7* and *8* are discharged without the DoE(NI)'s prior consent, the DoE(NI) may serve that person with a notice imposing such conditions on the discharge as it would have imposed had an application been made for its consent. [*Water Act (Northern Ireland) 1972, s 9(2)*]. Schedule 3 of the *Pollution Control and Local Government (Northern Ireland) Order 1978* has inserted the following provision for appeal into *section 9(2)* of the *1972 Act*. Essentially it provides that a person served with a notice under *section 9(2)* may appeal the notice to the Water Appeals Commission within 28 days of the notice being served. Any reference to a condition in *section 9* includes a condition 'varied, imposed or substituted' under *section 10*. [*Water Act (Northern Ireland) 1972, s 9(12)*].

The remainder of *section 9* deals with applications for consent under *section 7* or *8*. *Section 9(1)* provides that an application for consent must contain particulars 'with respect to such matters as the DoE(NI) may determine in relation to any application or class of application'. The applicant may be required by the DoE(NI) to publish notices of the application in newspapers specified by the DoE(NI). [*Water Act (Northern Ireland) 1972, s 9(3)*].

Section 9(4), as amended by *Schedule 3* of the *Water and Sewerage (Northern Ireland) Order 1973*, provides that when the DoE(NI) is making its decision on an application for consent under *section 7* or *8* of the *1972 Act*, the DoE(NI) is obliged to give notice of its decision on that application to the person making the application and either to the Foyle Fisheries Commission, where the discharge will occur, or is occurring, in the Londonderry Area, or to the Fisheries Conservancy Board for Northern Ireland, where the discharge will occur, or is occurring, outside that area. *Section 9(4)*, as amended, allows the above parties to appeal the DoE(NI)'s decision to the Water Appeals Commission for NI. This appeal must be brought within 28 days of the date on which they received notice of the DoE(NI)'s decision.

Where an application for consent under *section 7* or *8* is made, but the DoE(NI) fails to respond, giving notice of its decision, within three months of the date on which it received the application (or within an extended period agreed in writing between the DoE(NI) and the applicant), the DoE(NI) will be taken to have granted its consent without any conditions attaching to the discharge. [*Water Act (Northern Ireland) 1972, s 9(5)*]. The word 'intended' in *section 9(5)* is repealed by the *1973 Order.*

Where an application for consent to discharge is made under *section 7* or *8*, but there is an existing discharge of matter, which, in the DoE(NI)'s opinion is similar to the discharge for which the consent is sought, the DoE(NI) must have regard to the following factors when deciding whether or not to give its consent:

'(*a*)   the length of time during which the effluent or matter has been discharged;

(*b*)   whether all reasonably practicable steps are being taken to prevent the effluent or matter causing the pollution;

(*c*)   whether it is reasonably practicable to dispose of the effluent or matter in any other manner;

(*d*)   whether the discharge constitutes a significant threat to public health, fisheries or any persons using water.' [*Water Act (Northern Ireland) 1972, s 9(6)*].

Discharge will be deemed to be 'similar' within the meaning of *section 9(6)* if, in the DoE(NI)'s opinion the discharge is:

'similar in nature, composition and temperature to, and is of a similar volume and made at a similar rate to, a discharge of effluent or matter during any corresponding period within the period of 12 months immediately before the appointed day under *section 7* or *8*, as the case may require'. [*Water Act (Northern Ireland) 1972, s 9(7)*].

Consent granted under *section 7* or *8* will cease to have effect at the end of a three-year period from 'the date on which it was granted if no discharge is made, or, from the date of the last discharge in any other case'. [*Water Act (Northern Ireland) 1972, s 9(8)*]. A register of consents and conditions still in force must be kept by the DoE(NI). This register shall be open for inspection, to any persons, at all reasonable hours. The register will also act as conclusive evidence of the terms of such consent or conditions that have effect where this would favour the case of a person charged with an offence. [*Water Act (Northern Ireland) 1972, s 9(9)*].

Violation of *section 7* or *8*, or any conditions imposed under those sections, is an offence under *section 9(10)*. A person found guilty of such an offence is liable in terms identical to those set down in *section 5(7)* of this Act, see above. However, until the DoE(NI) has either refused or granted its consent (unconditionally or subject to conditions) under *section 7* or *8*, a person will not have committed an offence by breaching *section 7* or *8*, or any condition imposed under those sections, by discharging effluent or matter if he has applied for the DoE(NI)'s consent before the appointed day under *section 7* or *8* and the discharge corresponds to the description of the discharge specified in the application.

19.92   *Section 10: review of consents granted under section 7 or 8*

Section 10(1) of the *1972 Act* allows the DoE(NI) to review any consent given under *section 7* or *8*. However these reviews must take place at minimum intervals of three years from the date when the consent was given or, from the date of the last review of the consent. In the event that the person making the discharge applies for a review, the review can take place at any time. During a review the DoE(NI) is empowered to vary its consent or any conditions to which the consent is subject. [*Water Act (Northern Ireland) 1972, s 10(2)*]. Under *section 10* any reference to 'varying a condition' is deemed to include a reference to the imposition of new conditions and to the substitution of conditions. [*Water Act (Northern Ireland) 1972, s 10(4)*]. Where the

DoE(NI) varies its consent or conditions, it is obliged to give notice of that variation to the parties listed under *section 9(4)*. As under *section 9(4)*, the parties concerned with the variation may appeal the decision to the Water Appeals Commission for NI if the appeal is brought within 28 days of the date on which they received notice of the variation.

Section 11(1) of the *Water Act (Northern Ireland) 1972* states that where effluent or matter is discharged in accordance with consent, which has been varied or substituted under *section 10*, this shall not be regarded as an offence under, or violation of any legislation listed that *section 11(1)*. *Section 11(2)* states that 'consent' in this context does not include consent granted under *section 9(5)* of this Act.

Section 12 allows the DoE(NI) to make further regulations governing the use of waterways; the focus of these regulations is outlined in *section 12(1)*. These powers have not been exercised to date.

19.93 *Notices served notwithstanding DoE(NI) consent under section 7 or 8*

Even where the DoE(NI) has granted its consent under *section 7* or *8*, or has imposed a condition under *section 9* or *10*, it is still possible for the DoE(NI) to serve any person with a notice prohibiting them from 'depositing or discharging any matter' on to any land or into any waterway or underground stratum if the Ministry considers it 'necessary in the public interest' to do so. [*Water Act (Northern Ireland) 1972, s 13(1), (2)*]. A notice served under *section 13(1)* will continue in force until it is either revoked by the DoE(NI), or the DoE(NI) gives its consent to the discharge in response to an application, made under *section 7* or *8*, by the person served with the notice under *section 3*, or it is quashed or varied by the Water Appeal Commission under *section 13(3)*, see below.

19.94 *Section 13: appealing a notice served under section 13*

Section 13(3), as amended by the *Water and Sewerage Services (Northern Ireland) Order 1973*, states that the person served with the notice under *section 13(1)* may appeal the notice to the Water Appeals Commission for NI. The appeal must be brought within four weeks of the date when the notice was served. *Section 13(3)*, as amended, allows the Appeals Commission to vary or quash the notice if it considers any provision of the notice to be unreasonable. *Section 13(4)* (also amended by the *1973 Order*), provides that where a notice is served and complied with, but is subsequently quashed or varied on appeal, the DoE(NI) is obliged to pay, to that person, an amount equal to the loss suffered, or expenditure incurred by the person complying with the notice. *Section 13(4A)* (inserted by *Schedule 3* of the *Water and Sewerage Services (Northern Ireland) Order 1973*), states that any dispute under *section 13(4)* concerning the loss suffered or expenditure incurred, shall be resolved by the Lands Tribunal.

19.95 *Section 13: violation of a notice served under section 13*

Any person who violates *section 7* or *8* in the context of notices served under *section 13* is guilty of an offence under *section 9(10)*. The liability for this offence is the same as detailed under *section 9(10)*, see above. [*Water Act (Northern Ireland) 1972, s 13(5)*].

In the context of any consent under this Act, it is important to note that *section 21(2)* states that it is an offence to 'knowingly or recklessly' make a statement which is false in a 'material particular' for the purpose of obtaining a consent. The liability for such an offence is detailed in *section 22*.

19.96 *Section 13: remedial action by the DoE(NI)*

Section 13(6), as amended by *Schedule 3* of the *Pollution Control and Local Government (Northern Ireland) Order 1978*, states that where any poisonous, noxious or polluting matter or any solid waste matter, other than matter discharged in accordance with a consent under *section 7* or *8* is likely to enter, or is or was present in, any waterway or water contained in underground strata, the DoE(NI) may take whatever action it deems appropriate to either prevent its entry into such waters, or to remove and dispose of it where it has already entered such waters. The DoE(NI) is also given the power to take whatever action it deems necessary in this situation to remedy or mitigate any pollution caused or to restore the state of the waters (including the flora and fauna in them), in so far as is reasonably practicable to do so, to their condition immediately before the polluting matter entered the water. *Section 13(7)*, concerning DoE(NI) constructions of a temporary nature, has been repealed by the *Pollution Control and Local Government (Northern Ireland) Order 1978.*

Expenses reasonably incurred by the Ministry, as a result of operations carried out under *section 13(6)*, shall be recoverable in terms identical to those set out in *section 6(6)* of this Act.

19.97   Part III: miscellaneous and general

Part III of the *1972 Act* deals with a variety of miscellaneous and general matters concerning the powers of the DoE(NI) in relation to water. Among the powers conferred on the DoE(NI) in this context are the following: the power to make regulations concerning abstractions of water; the power to impose charges on persons abstracting water or making discharges into water (these powers have not been exercised to date); the power to carry out 'minor works' for the purpose of promoting the recreational use of water; the power to acquire land for any purpose under this Act; the power to execute any engineering or building operations which are necessary for the purposes of its functions under this Act; and finally the power to collect data and information for the purposes of fulfilling its functions under this Act.

19.98   *Power to obtain information*

Under section 21(1) the DoE(NI) may obtain information concerning the abstraction of water from, or the discharge of effluent into, waterways or underground stratum from persons carrying out the abstraction or discharge. The DoE(NI) may direct the times and form in which the information is to be supplied by such persons at the time and in the form that is specified in the direction. *Section 21(2)*, as amended by the *Water and Sewerage Services (Northern Ireland) Order 1973*, states that any person given a direction to supply information under *section 21(1)* may appeal the direction to the Water Appeals Commission within four weeks of the day on which the direction is given to him. The Appeal Commission is empowered to quash or vary the direction where it deems that it would be 'unreasonable or unduly onerous' for the person in question to comply with the direction. Failure to comply with a direction to supply information is an offence under *section 21(3)*, the liability for which is a maximum fine of £20 upon summary conviction. It is an offence to knowingly or recklessly give information under *section 21(1)* which is false in a material way, or to 'knowingly or recklessly' make a statement which is false in a material way in an effort to obtain any consent under this Act. *Section 22* sets out the liability for such an offence as follows:

' (i)   on conviction on indictment, to imprisonment for a term not exceeding two years, or to a fine, or to both;

 (ii)   on summary conviction, to imprisonment for a term not exceeding three months, or to a fine not exceeding £100, or to both'.

19.99   *DoE(NI)'s right to enter and inspect any land, vessel or vehicle*

Section 23(1) gives the DoE(NI) quite extensive powers to enter and inspect any land, vessel or vehicle, at a reasonable time, for the purposes of performing any function conferred on the DoE(NI) under this Act. *Section 23(1)* outlines in more detail the extent of the DoE(NI)'s powers in this context. Under *section 23(2)* a justice of the peace may warrant, that persons referred to in *section 23(1)* gain entry by force, if it is shown to the satisfaction of the JP (on sworn information in writing), that any of the situations laid down in *section 23(2)* exist, and that there are reasonable grounds for entry for the purpose for which entry is required. *Section 23(3)* governs the binding nature of the warrant. The remaining subsections of *section 13* set out a variety of supplementary provisions concerning the DoE(NI)'s right to enter and inspect land, vessels or vehicles.

19.100 *Right to take samples*

Section 25(1) of this Act empowers persons authorised by the DoE(NI) to 'obtain and take away' samples of water from a waterway or underground strata or samples of water or of any effluent or matter which is passing, or is likely to pass, from any land, vessel or vehicle into a waterway or underground stratum. Any sample of effluent taken at 'an inspection chamber, manhole or other place provided in compliance with a condition imposed under this Act', shall be presumed in legal proceedings, to be a sample of 'what was passing from the land or premises to the waterway or underground strata' in relation to which the sample was taken. [*Water Act (Northern Ireland) 1972, s 25(2)*]. This presumption will continue until the contrary is shown. *Section 25* also allows the DoE(NI) to fix the points at which samples are taken and to maintain a register of such points. *Section 25(3)* governs the procedure to be followed by the DoE(NI) where it wishes to fix sampling points and the use of samples taken at such points in legal proceedings under this Act. *Section 25(5)* governs the use of the results of sampling in legal proceedings, while *section 25(7)* states that it is an offence to 'wilfully obstruct' the taking of samples.

19.101 **The Water and Sewerage Services (Northern Ireland) Order 1973 (the 1973 Order) (SI 1973 No 70)**

Under the *1973 Order* the DoE(NI) is given the specific functions of supplying and distributing water and providing for the draining and treatment of domestic sewage, trade effluent and surface water in Northern Ireland. Once again the DoE(NI) is the primary player, however, *Part I* of the *1973 Order* also establishes the Water Appeals Commission which is conferred with jurisdiction to hear appeals from decisions of the DoE(NI) under this *Order* and the *Water Act (Northern Ireland) 1972*. The *1973 Order* contains 61 articles and is divided into eight parts and has four schedules attached. There have been two amendments to the *Water and Sewerage Services (Northern Ireland) Order 1973*. *Schedule 3* of the *Pollution Control and Local Government (Northern Ireland) Order 1978* amended several articles of the *1973 Order*, the most relevant of which are dealt with below, and in 1985 the *Water and Sewerage Services (Amendment) (Northern Ireland) Order 1985 (SI 1985 No 756)* extended the civil liability of the DoE for loss and damage caused by escaped water (this is also dealt with in more detail below). *Schedule 4* of the *1973 Order* repealed *section 7* of the *Rivers Pollution Prevention Act 1876* and amended and repealed several sections of the *Public Health (Ireland) Act 1878*. *Schedule 3* of the *1973 Order* amended *Schedules 1, 2* and *4* of the *Water Act (Northern Ireland) 1972*.

19.102 *Part I* contains the definitions of terms used in the *Order*, while *Part II* confers on the DoE(NI) a number of specific functions (outlined above) concerning water and sewerage services in NI and also establishes the Water Appeals Commission. *Part III* is entitled 'Works and Land' and essentially gives the DoE(NI) the power to acquire land, compulsorily or otherwise, for the purpose of carrying out its functions under the *Order*. It also enables the DoE(NI) to acquire rights to water contained in any waterway or underground strata, but where it exercises this right, the DoE(NI) is obliged to either pay compensation for any loss or damage caused or to provide compensation water. Any dispute concerning compensation will be determined by the Lands Tribunal. Persons aggrieved by the DoE(NI)'s actions in this context are given a right to appeal to the Water Commission. *Part II* also entitles the DoE(NI) to take over private water supplies or sewage treatment works; similarly the DoE is entitled to execute any works it considers necessary to carry out its functions under this Order.

19.103   For present purposes *Parts IV–VIII* are the most important and therefore their terms will be dealt with in some detail. *Part IV* concerns the rights and duties of owners and occupiers in relation to the provision of water and sewerage services in NI. *Part V* deals with trade effluents. *Parts VI* and *VII* contain a variety of miscellaneous provisions concerning water and sewerage respectively. *Part VIII* sets out general provisions concerning the DoE(NI)'s functions in the context of this *Order*, in particular it extends the DoE(NI)'s civil liabilty for damage or loss caused by escaped water.

19.104   *The rights and duties of owners and occupiers in relation to the provision of water and sewerage services in Northern Ireland*

Article 17 concerns the making of new connections or the altering of existing water mains and sewerage pipes. It is an offence to connect into the DoE(NI)'s water mains or sewerage pipes without the DoE's consent. Similarly it is an offence to do so in violation of any condition attached by the DoE(NI) to consent given under *article 17*. *Article 17* does not apply to the discharge of trade effluent, this is dealt with in *Part V* of the *Order*. *Article 18* addresses the rights of owners and occupiers following lawful connections under *article 17*. *Article 18(1)* states that a person who has been lawfully connected under *article 17* may 'take a sufficient supply of water for his domestic purposes from that main or may drain domestic sewage and surface water from his premises into the sewer or works'. *Article 18(2)* goes on to provide that *article 18* does not allow such persons to:

'(*a*)   discharge domestic sewage into a sewer reserved for the conveyance of surface water; or

(*b*)   discharge, without the approval of the DoE, surface water into a sewer reserved for the conveyance of domestic sewage'.

Article 19 addresses the situation where new buildings are being built. Under *article 19* the DoE(NI) may enter into an agreement with the builder concerning the provision of water, mains, pipes, sewers and sewage treatment works to serve the new buildings. Under such an agreement the DoE(NI) may specify the terms and conditions on which the building can be carried out; however if an agreement cannot be arrived at, *article 19(2)* allows the builder to appeal to the Appeals Commissioner.

19.105   *Trade effluents*

this part of the *Order* essentially deals with the extent to which occupiers of trade premises can discharge trade effluent from those premises into sewers or sewage treatment works which belong to the DoE(NI). *Article 33* states that *Part V* may also apply to other effluents as it applies to trade effluents. Several orders have been made in this regard; due to their local nature, they are contained in the classified lists of local orders.

Article 20(1) authorises the occupiers of trade premises to discharge trade effluent into sewers or sewage treatment works which belong to the DoE(NI). However, such persons may be required under *Part V* of this *Order* to obtain the DoE(NI)'s consent in order to do so. *Article 20(2)* states that where such person discharges trade effluent without the DoE(NI)'s consent or in violation of directions imposed under this *Order*, they shall be guilty of an offence and shall be liable, on conviction on indictment, to a fine, or on summary conviction, to a maximum fine of £400.

However, where it is shown to the satisfaction of the Court convicting such persons, that the offence was

'substantially a repetition or continuation of an earlier offence by him after he had been convicted of the earlier offence (whether under this Order or not), he shall be liable:

(i)   on conviction on indictment, to imprisonment for a term not exceeding 2 years or to a fine, or to both;

(ii)   on summary conviction, to the greater of a fine not exceeding £400 or a fine not exceeding £40 for each day on which the offence was so repeated or continued'.

In terms of allowing the discharge of trade effluents, *Part V* distinguishes between what are termed 'new discharges' of trade effluent and 'existing discharges'. The control of 'existing discharges' is relatively straightforward, while the situation in relation to 'new discharges' is much more complex, requiring application for the DoE(NI)'s consent under *article 22*. Alternatively, the *1973 Order* makes provision for agreements 'in lieu' of consent under *article 32*. Each system of control will now be described in more detail.

19.106 *Existing discharges*

An existing discharge is defined in *article 28(1)* as being a lawful discharge of trade effluent which has been made from trade premises into the sewers or sewage treatment works of a local authority during the two years immediately prior to 1 October 1973. In the case of an existing discharge *article 29* provides that, except where an alternative agreement has been arrived at between the DoE(NI) and the person making the discharge, an existing discharge shall be allowed to continue. This is subject to the other provisions contained in *Part V* of this *Order*. Any disputes between the DoE(NI) and the person making the trade discharge as to whether the discharge is an 'existing discharge' or not must be determined by the county court. [*Article 28(3)*]. The decision of the Court is final except on points of law. *Article 28(2)* also states that where a local authority and the person making the trade discharge came to an agreement before 1 October 1973 stating that the nature or composition of the discharge may be altered, or that the temperature, volume or rate of discharge may be increased, *article 28(2)* will also regard any discharge made in accordance of such an agreement as being an 'existing discharge'. *Article 23(2)* empowers the DoE(NI) to request information from the owner or occupier of a premises making an existing discharge concerning the discharge. The request for information must be in writing and may also require information concerning the period for which the discharge has continued.

Article 31 states that the DoE(NI) may review an existing discharge; however the DoE(NI) is obliged to carry out the review if it is requested to do so by the person making the discharge. The DoE(NI) may direct that any continuance of the discharge be unconditional or subject to such conditions as the DoE(NI) considers appropriate. *Article 31(2)–(6)* sets out the procedure to be followed by the DoE(NI) when making reviews of existing discharges under this *Order*. These paragraphs also allow representations to be made to the DoE(NI) in this regard and allows for the review to be appealed to the Appeal Commission. The provisions of *article 31(2)–(6)* are identical to those detailed in respect of 'new discharges' under *articles 24–27* of this *Order* (see below).

A new discharge is defined in *article 21* as being a discharge of trade effluent into the sewers of sewage treatment works of the DoE(NI) where the discharge:

'(*a*)   has not previously been lawfully made into such sewers or works or the sewers or works of a local authority;

(*b*)   not being an existing discharge by virtue of *Article 28* and whether commenced before or after 1st October 1973, has become substantially altered in nature or composition or whose temperature, volume or rate of discharge has been substantially increased since 1st October 1973; or

(*c*)   has been discontinued for a period of two years or more, the whole or part of which period occurs after 1st October 1973, and is thereafter resumed'.

As already mentioned, the control of 'new discharges' of trade effluent is more complex. Essentially an occupier or prospective occupier of a trade premises who wishes to discharge trade effluent, must obtain the DoE(NI)'s consent under *article 22*. The requirement to obtain consent is subject to *article 32* under which an agreement can be made with the DoE(NI) in lieu of an application for consent. *Article 23* contains the procedure governing an application for consent under *article 22*. In applying for consent the person seeking to make the new discharge must serve a 'trade effluent notice' on the DoE(NI). *Article 23(2)* states that this notice must state

'so far as is reasonably practicable:

(*a*)   the nature, composition and temperature of the effluent;

(*b*)   the maximum quantity of the effluent which it is proposed to discharge on any one day;

(*c*)   the maximum hourly rate at which it is proposed to discharge the effluent'.

If the person seeking to make the new discharge is not the owner of the trade premises, then that person must also send a copy of the trade effluent notice to the owner of the premises and inform the owner that he has 28 days from the date when he received a copy of the notice to make representations to the DoE(NI) in respect of the application for consent. [*Article 23(3)*]. The DoE(NI), for its part, is obliged to take into account any representations made under *article 23(3)* when it is making its decision on the application. [*Article 23(4)*].

Article 24 lays down the time limit (three months) within which the DoE(NI) must make its decision on the application under *article 22*, the possible responses which the DoE(NI) can make and the effect of its decision. The DoE(NI)'s decision will continue to have effect even where there has been a change of ownership or occupancy of the trade premises in respect of which the decision was made. [*Article 24(3)*]. *Article 25* obliges the DoE(NI) to inform the owner, occupier or prospective occupier of the premises of its decision and the reasons for its decision. Notice of the DoE(NI)'s decision must draw attention to the effect of *article 24(3)* and must refer to the fact that the applicant has a right to appeal the decision under *article 26*, and the possibility of obtaining a review of the decision under *article 27*.

Article 26 allows an applicant under *article 22* to appeal the DoE(NI)'s decision within 28 days of the date on which he received notice of the DoE(NI)'s decision. The appeal must be brought before the Appeals Commission. *Article 27* provides for a system of review of the DoE(NI)'s decision. *Article 27* provides that the DoE(NI) may review its decision made under *article 24* at intervals of not less than two years. The two-year period shall run from the date of the decision under *article 24* or from the date of the last review under *article 27*. The DoE(NI) may review its decision at any time if the person making the new discharge requests the review. Once again the DoE(NI) must inform the owner and occupier of the trade premises of its intention to review its decision concerning the new discharge. The DoE(NI) must also inform the owner and occupier of its reasons for having the review and that they have a right to make representations to the DoE(NI) in respect of the proposed review within 28 days of receiving notice of the review. *Article 27(3)* obliges the DoE(NI) to take any representations into account when it is reviewing its decision. The occupier of the trade premises may appeal the DoE(NI)'s review to the Appeal Commission within 28 days of the date of the review. A review under *article 27* can take effect from a date specified in the review, but must not take effect earlier than three months after the date of the review.

19.108 *Agreements 'in lieu' of consent*

Part V of the *1973 Order [article 32(1)]* also allows the DoE(NI) to come to an agreement with the owner or occupier of a trade premises for the 'reception, treatment or disposal by the DoE(NI) of any trade effluent produced on those premises'. This system operates 'in lieu' of the system of consents which operates under *article 22*. *Article 32(2)* also enables the DoE(NI) to enter into such agreements in relation to the 'varying or renewing' of an existing agreement. This is permissible whether the existing agreement was entered into before or after 1 October 1973. Where the person entering into the agreement is the occupier, but not the owner of the trade premises, the DoE(NI) must notify the owner of the proposed agreement. The owner may make representations to the DoE(NI) in this regard within 28 days of the date on which he recieved notification. [*Article 32(3)*]. The DoE(NI) is obliged under *article 32(4)* to take into account any representations made under *article 32(3)* before it enters into any agreement with the occupier. *Article 32(5)* states that a discharge made in accordance with an agreement reached under *article 32* does not require the DoE(NI)'s consent (so *articles 22–26* cannot apply in this situation), nor can it be reviewed by the DoE(NI) under *article 27* or *31*. However, if the parties to the agreement fail to renew the agreement on or before the date on which it expires, the DoE(NI) may review the making of the discharge by direction; the DoE(NI) is obliged to do so where the person requests a review. [*Article 32(6)*]. A review in this situation will be governed by the terms of *article 27(2)–(5)*. In the event that the DoE(NI) fails to issue a direction under *article 32(6)* reviewing the agreement, the discharge may continue in accordance with the agreement. [*Article 32(7)*]. *Article 32(8)* states that all references to an occupier shall include prospective occupiers.

19.109 *Pollution of water which belongs to the DoE(NI)*

Article 34(1) states that it is an offence to do anything which causes water which belongs to the DoE(NI) to be polluted, the liability for which is set out in *article 34(3)*. *Article 34(2)* states that it is a defence to prove that all reasonable care was taken to prevent the act which caused the pollution.

19.110 *Water shortages*

Article 36 concerns the management of water resources in the event of water shortages and has been amended by *Schedule 3* of the *Pollution Control and Local Government (Northern Ireland) Order 1978*. Essentially any person who suffers loss or damage due to the actions of the DoE(NI) in the event of water shortages is entitled to compensation from the DoE(NI); disputes in this context will be determined by the Lands Tribunal.

19.111 *Discharge of matter into sewers*

Article 39(1) prohibits any person from passing, or permitting the passage of any matter or substance into sewers or sewage treatment works which belong to the DoE(NI), or into a drain connecting with these two which, either alone, or in combination with any substance it is likely to contact while passing through the DoE(NI)'s sewers or works, is likely to 'injure the sewer or works, or to interfere with the free flow of their contents, or to effect prejudicially the treatment or disposal of their contents or to be prejudicial to health'. *Article 39(2)* states that violation of *article 39(1)* is an offence and *article 39(3)* provides that a person convicted of an offence under *article 39* shall be liable, on conviction on indictment, to a fine; and on summary conviction to a maximum fine of £400 and a further fine of not more than £40 for every day that the offence is continued after conviction for the offence. *Article 39(2)* provides for a defence in the following terms. Essentially it is a defence to prove that at the time the matter or substance was passed or permitted to pass into the DoE(NI)'s sewers or works, 'the accused did not know, and could not reasonably have been expected to know', that the passage of the matter or substance in question would have been likely to lead to the effects specified in *article 39(1)*. The prohibition contained in *article 39* operates without prejudice to the provisons of *Part V* of this *Order*.

19.112 *Maintenance of water and sewerage services in NI*

Part VIII of the *1973 Order* contains a variety of general provisions concerning the DoE(NI)'s functions in the context of water and sewerage services in Northern Ireland. The DoE(NI) has made a number of regulations pursuant to *articles 40* and *51–53* concerning the proper provision and maintenance of water and sewerage services in NI. They are the *Water and Sewerage Services Regulations (Northern Ireland) 1973 (SI 1973 No 344)*; the *Water Regulations (Northern Ireland) 1974 (SI 1974 No 143)*; and the *Water Regulations (Northern Ireland) 1991 (SI 1991 No 50)*. The DoE(NI) has not exercised its powers under *articles 42(2), 43* and *57* to make regulations concerning the recreational use of water and the construction, inspection, maintenance and repair of reservoirs and dams.

19.113 *Interferences with works and fittings which belong to the DoE(NI)*

Articles 41 and *44* concern interferences with works or water fittings which belong to the DoE(NI), which are offences under these provisions. Similarly it is an offence under *article 5* to 'wilfully obstruct' an officer authorised by the DoE(NI) in the execution of any functions under this *Order*. An offender is liable to a fine not in excess of £100 on summary conviction for such an offence.

19.114 *The DoE(NI)'s power to gather information concerning water and sewerage services*

Articles 46–52, as amended by the *Pollution Control and Local Government (Northern Ireland) Order 1978*, gives the DoE(NI) the power to collect information concerning water and sewage services. *Article 46* enables the DoE(NI) to request, from an owner or occupier of any premises, a statement in writing of the nature of their ownership of the premises. It is an offence to fail to provide the information requested or to knowingly misstate any detail of the information, for which one is liable on summary conviction to a maximum fine of £25. Similarly, an owner or occupier of land can be required by the DoE(NI) to produce plans and information in their possession (or which they can reasonably be expected to obtain) concerning drains or pipes under the land they occupy or possess and any sewage discharged from such pipes or drains. Failure to comply with such a request is an offence under *article 47(2)* for which one is liable to a fine not exceeding £25. The DoE(NI), for its part, must make available for inspection and/or copying, maps showing and distinguishing all mains and sewers which belong to the DoE. [*Article 48(1)* and *(2)*].

19.115 *Disclosures of information obtained in the course of work carried out under this Order*

This *Order* also prohibits the disclosure of information concerning 'manufacturing processes or trade secrets' obtained by any person in the course of work carried out under this *Order*. The prohibition is framed in terms identical to *section 24(8)* of the *Water Act (Northern Ireland) 1972*.

19.116 *The DoE(NI)'s power to enter*

Article 50 of the *1973 Order* gives the DoE(NI) certain powers to enter land at reasonable hours for the purposes of various functions listed in *article 50(1)* of the section. *Schedule 3* of the *Pollution Control and Local Government (Northern Ireland) Order 1978* adds

'(h)   taking away for analysis samples of water'

to this list. In determining whether the time of entry is reasonable, regard shall be had to whether there is an emergency. [*Article 50(10)*]. *Article 50(2)–(9)* gives the DoE(NI) rights to enter without notice in emergency situations; with heavy equipment; by force; and accompanied with any other persons that are necessary to the carrying out of the works. The rights conferred on the DoE(NI) in this regard are all drafted in terms identical in all material respects to the terms of *sections 23* and *24* of the *Water Act (Northern Ireland) 1972*. The DoE(NI) is also obliged to leave premises as effectively secured against trespass as they were when first entered by the DoE(NI). [*Article 50(6)(b)*]. *Article 50(8)* states that it is an offence to wilfully obstruct any person who is legally entitled to enter under this *Order*; such a person shall be liable to a maximum fine of £100 on summary conviction. The DoE(NI) is also obliged to reinstate lands upon which it has carried out works, this must be completed as soon as possible. [*Article 50(9)*].

19.117 *Admissibility of samples in legal proceedings*

Article 51, as amended by *Schedule 3* of the *Pollution Control and Local Government (Northern Ireland) Order 1978*, sets out the position concerning samples taken under *article 50* (other than a sample taken under *article 50(1)(h)*), which may be admitted as evidence in legal proceedings concerning 'sewage, matter or substance discharged from any premises or of any water in, on or under land'. The provisions of *article 51* governing the admissibility of such samples are identical to those contained in *section 25(5)* and *(8)* of the *Water Act (Northern Ireland) 1972*.

19.118 *Financial provisions*

Articles 53–56 of the *Water and Sewerage Services (Northern Ireland) Order 1973 (SI 1973 No 158)* set out the extent to which the DoE(NI) can impose charges for services rendered under this *Order*, recover expenses incurred while carrying out work under this *Order* and the provision of compensation by the DoE(NI).

19.119 *Violation of regulations made by the DoE(NI) concerning water and sewerage*

Article 57 states that the violation of regulations made by the DoE under this *Order* is an offence, for which one is liable to a maximum fine of £400 on summary conviction.

19.120 *Civil liability of the DoE(NI) for escapes of water*

Article 57A has been inserted into the *Water and Sewerage Services (Northern Ireland) Order 1973* by the *Water and Sewerage Services (Amendment) (Northern Ireland) Order 1985 (SI 1985 No 1209)* and essentially extends the civil liability of the DoE(NI) to loss or damage caused by escapes of water. More specifically, *article 57A(1)* imposes a civil liability on the DoE(NI) for loss or damage caused to 'agricultural land or forestry land' by water which has escaped from a main or service pipe. This liability is subject to the provisions contained in the remaining paragraphs of this article.

Article 57A(7) defines 'agricultural land' as meaning land:

'used for agriculture for the purposes of a trade or business, and "agriculture" includes horticulture, fruit growing, seed growing, dairy farming and livestock breeding and keeping, the use of land as grazing land, meadow land, market gardens and nursery grounds, and the use of land for woodlands where that use is ancillary to the farming of land for other agricultural purposes'.

'Forestry land' is also defined in *article 57A(7)* as meaning:

'land used for forestry for the purposes of a trade or business, and "forestry" means the growing of woods and forests for the production of timber and other forest products and the growing of trees for planting in such woods and forests'.

Article 57A(7) states that the term 'land' does not include any house or other building, and 'service pipe' means pipes that are vested in the Department. 'Damage' includes 'the death of, or injury to, any person (including any disease and any impairment of physical or mental condition)'.

Article 57A(2) provides that the DoE(NI) shall not be liable for any loss or damage caused by escaped water if the escape was 'due wholly to the fault of the person who suffered the loss or damage or of any servant, agent or contractor of his'. *Article 57A(7)* defines 'fault' as having the same meaning as it does in the *Law Reform (Miscellaneous Provisions) Act (Northern Ireland) 1948*.

Article 57A(3) goes on to state that the DoE(NI) will not be liable for loss or damage caused to any of the following categories or bodies or persons:

'(*a*) any person authorised by any statutory provision to carry on any railway or road transport undertaking or any undertaking for the supply of electricity or gas; or

(*b*) any person to whom the telecommunications code applies falling within section 10(1)(a) of the Telecommunications Act 1984 (persons authorised by licence to run a telecommunication system); or

(*c*) the post office'.

This exemption operates if the DoE(NI) would not be liable for that loss or damage apart from *article 57A(1)*.

The following shall apply in relation to any loss or damage for which the DoE(NI) is liable under this article as if the damage were the DoE(NI)'s fault, but which is not due to the fault of the DoE(NI) (*article 57A(4)*):

Law Reform (Miscellaneous Provisions) Act (Northern Ireland) 1948;
Limitation Acts (Northern Ireland) 1958–1982;
Fatal Accidents (Northern Ireland) Order 1977 (SI 1977 No 1251).

The provisions of *article 57A(1)* shall not effect any entitlement which the DoE(NI) may have to recover contributions under the *Civil Liability (Contribution) Act 1978*. Any loss for which the DoE(NI) is liable under *article 57A(1)* shall be treated as if it were damage for the purposes of the *1978 Act*. [*Article 57A(5)*]. The DoE(NI) shall not incur any liability for any loss or damage under *article 57A(1)* if the DoE(NI) is also liable for that loss or damage under an agreement or statutory provision made before the commencement of the *Water and Sewerage Services (Amendment) (Northern Ireland) Order 1985*.

19.121 **European Directives concerning Water Pollution**

The implementation of *EC Directives* concerning water pollution has been very slow. So far only the following *Directives* have been implemented into Northern Irish law.

19.122 *Dangerous substances*

The *Pollution of Waters by Dangerous Substances Regulations (Northern Ireland) 1990 (SI 1990 No 38)*, implement the provisions of *Directive 76/464/EEC (Aquatic Environment Directive)* and the following *Directives* which concern specific types of dangerous substances: *Directive 82/176/EEC; Directive 84/156/EEC; Directive 83/513/EEC; Directive 84/491/EEC; Directive 86/280/EEC*; and *Directive 88/347/EEC*. The *Pollution of Waters by Dangerous Substances (Amendment) Regulations (Northern Ireland) 1992 (SI 1992 No 401)* amend the *1990 Regulations* to take account of the requirements of *Directive 90/415/EEC*.

19.123 *Environmental impact of drainage activities*

The *Drainage (Environmental Assessment) Regulations (Northern Ireland) 1991 (SI 1991 No 376)* was introduced to implement *Directive 85/337/EEC* concerning the assessment of the environmental impact of certain public and private drainage projects. 'Public drainage works' are specified in the *Drainage (Northern Ireland) Order 1973* as being works by the Department of Agriculture 'for the purpose of draining land or preventing or mitigating flooding or erosion to which land is subject'. This definition goes on to specify numerous categories of such activities which affect watercourses.

19.124 **ENERGY IN NORTHERN IRELAND**

Because of its complete dependence on fossil fuels, mainly oil, the supply of electricity in Northern Ireland has been a matter of concern for the past two decades. The supply of electricity has been examined recently on two occasions, in 1988 by the Energy Committee (House of Commons 679 (1987–88), and in 1990 by the Rossi Committee (paragraphs 90–96). The Rossi Report in particular, highlighted the lack of diversity in the Northern Irish energy supply as being a major problem, and one which will intensify as EC restrictions on the use of fossel fuels increase. The UK is presently working towards implementing the *EC Large Combustion Plants Directive*. This will result in greater pressure to reduce SO_2 and NO_2 emissions. NIE officials reported to the Rossi Committee that it will be much more expensive to achieve this result in Northern Ireland than on the mainland and they urged that 'the apportionment of SO_2 reductions should be determined on the basis of equal cost rather than *pro rata*' (paragraph 94). The Rossi Report also pointed out that NI may encounter considerable difficulties in achieving a mixture of energy supplies which does less damage to the environment than the present system.

19.125 The Northern Ireland Electricity Service was established as the statutory body responsible for the supply of electricity in NI by the *Electricity Supply (Northern Ireland) Order 1972*; it was renamed *Northern Ireland Electricity* (NIE) by the *Electricity Supply (Amendment) (Northern Ireland) Order 1987*. The *1972 Order* as amended by the *1987 Order* governs the supply of electricity in NI; certain fines and penalties in this context are dealt with in the *Fines and Penalties (Northern Ireland) Order 1984*. The *1987 Order* essentially removed the ban on private generation in NI, thereby paving the way for private generators to supply the NI grid. However private generators are also obliged to give the NIE notice of construction of any private generating station. The *1987 Order* also extended the functions and borrowing powers of the NIE; it made some new provisions concerning the NIE's powers of entry; it obliges the NIE to adopt and support schemes for the use of heat produced from the generation of electricity; it empowers the NIE to require a person to remedy any electric line rendered unsafe by his actions; and finally, it increases the time within which prosecutions for certain offences can be brought. Parts of *articles 2(2)*, *8(3)* and *36(1)* of the 1972 Order are repealed by the *1987 Order*, and all of *articles 30* and *54(1)* are repealed.

20 Packaging

20.1 A WIDE RANGE OF ENVIRONMENTAL CONCERNS

Each stage of the packaging product life cycle has given rise to environmental concerns. Attention has focused on the raw materials and energy used in production, the existence of environmentally harmful substances in packaging materials, the uses to which packaging is put, and the problems associated with recycling and disposal. All of these issues have received attention from the public, the media, and policy-makers in recent years.

20.2 The problems in perspective

It can be argued that the level of concern about packaging is out of proportion to its environmental significance. The risks which packaging poses to the human and natural environment are far less than those caused by many other industrial products. In its contribution to promoting health and improving the quality of life, the benefits of packaging are clear. Advances in packaging have assisted in the efficient mass production and distribution of goods, and have enabled foods to be contained and preserved longer and transported without damage and waste.

Many of these benefits have been taken for granted. Similarly, many of the problems caused by packaging have not been recognised either. Now, the efforts of consumers, environmental groups, and legislators have ensured that packaging is under the spotlight. Although not high risk, packaging is a high profile environmental issue.

20.3 A visible problem

Packaging waste is one of the smaller elements of the total waste stream, but it is highly visible. The attention it receives is shown in the consistently high level of complaints made to local authorities about litter, for example.

20.4 Amounts of packaging waste

The composition of waste

Agricultural 58%

China Clay 6%

Industrial 12%

Sand/Gravel/Rock 3%

Coal 12%

Household 4%

Other 4%

Hazardous 1%

Figure 20.1

20.5 Packaging

The visibility of packaging waste has focused attention on the amounts of waste produced. The actual amounts, in fact, are relatively small. According to the UK Industry Council on Packaging and the Environment (INCPEN), used packaging accounts for only one-quarter of household waste by weight. Figure 20.1 shows the composition of typical household waste:

In terms of volume, packaging waste represents a small proportion of total wastes arising. It has been estimated that domestic packaging waste accounts for less than 3 per cent of the total waste generated by modern industrial economies.

Nevertheless, as an obvious component of daily waste, concerns about packaging have been linked to worries about the total amounts of waste produced by developed economies. It is clear from Table 20.1 below that the amounts of total municipal waste (including household waste and comparable waste from small commercial and industrial enterprises, collected and treated by municipalities) have grown significantly in the last two decades.

Table 20.1

Increases in amounts of municipal waste in selected OECD countries 1975–1989

	% increase in quantity			% increase per capita		
	1975–1980	1980–1985	1985–1989	1975–1980	1980–1985	1985–1989
Canada	–	27.0	2.5	–	21.2	−1.7
USA	14.3	11.3	17.3	8.4	5.9	16.2
Japan	9.0	–	16.3	4.1	−3.2	14.5
Austria	18.9	3.2	–	19.4	3.1	–
Belgium	6.3	–	–	5.7	–	–
Denmark	–	17.3	–	–	17.5	–
Finland	–	–	13.6	–	–	12.2
France	16.7	7.1	13.3	14.1	4.6	11.3
Germany	4.9	−9.5	0.5	3.9	−8.6	0.2
Greece	–	20.9	4.1	–	17.4	3.1
Ireland	15.3	71.9	–	7.7	65.1	–
Italy	−0.4	6.8	15.3	−2.0	4.1	14.5
Luxembourg	7.6	2.3	29.8	6.4	1.8	30.6
Netherlands	–	−10.8	11.7	–	−12.9	9.0
Norway	–	15.9	1.5	−1.9	14.0	−0.3
Portugal	–	18.4	–	–	8.4	–
Spain	25.8	5.0	18.4	19.5	1.9	16.9
Sweden	4.6	5.6	–	3.1	5.1	–
Switzerland	17.9	11.6	14.0	18.2	9.1	10.8
UK	−3.1	9.7	5.9	−3.4	9.0	4.9

OECD Environmental Data Compendium 1991

20.5 Waste avoidance or minimisation

The increase in the amounts of waste generated, of whatever type, has emphasised the need for improved waste minimisation.

Preventive action has long been advocated as the best way to manage waste. OECD guidelines on waste strategy recommended waste minimisation as early as 1976. This emphasis has been repeated more recently. The European Commission's Strategy for

Waste management (SEC (89) 934 final. 18 September 1989) and the Council's 1990 *Resolution on Waste Policy* (*OJC 122/02*; 18 May 1990) both stress the importance of waste minimisation.

Translating the principle of waste minimisation into action has proved difficult as levels of consumption have increased. However, there are now encouraging signs that industry in developed economies (in the packaging sector and more widely) is recognising the benefits of minimising waste. Producers and retailers, keen to promote themselves as environmentally responsible organisations, are increasingly including packaging waste reduction targets in their environmental policies. Consumers too have shown that they are willing to cut packaging consumption, although how far this happens significantly remains to be seen. It is also unknown whether developing economies will be able to reconcile increased production and consumption with waste minimisation.

20.6 Excessive packaging?

For many, packaging waste has become a manifestation of the wastefulness of the 'throw away society'. Judgements about whether packaging is excessive need to be made in a proper social and economic context. Changes in lifestyle have resulted in the production of more packaging. For example, the increased demand for fresh food has often resulted in more packaging to ensure adequate protection and shelf-life.

The view that packaging is excessive also needs to be judged in the context of technical standards and regulatory requirements. Over two-thirds of total packaging is used for food and beverages. A wealth of regulations exist which deal with materials and articles in contact with foodstuffs. The UK *Food Safety Act 1990*, for example, has provisions which deal with all the operations involved in the sale, possession for sale, delivery, preparation, labelling, storage, and import and export of food. Similar food contact legislation exists in other countries. At international level, measures have been developed by the Council of Europe, later embodied in a series of *EC Directives* from *1976–1989*. Packagers, acting as middle-men between food producers and retailers, must fulfil their obligations in ensuring that food meets required safety standards. Some of the packaging which consumers see as excessive, in multi-layered containers for example, is fulfilling different functions not generally recognised by the user.

The amount of packaging for food and consumer goods is also influenced by economic and logistical factors. Packages must meet rigorous technical standards, and must be capable of safe passage by air, road, and sea. Requirements for adequate labelling and information also influence the type and amount of packaging used.

Consumer choice, convenience and image also affect the amount of packaging used; luxury goods may have extra packaging to enhance their image. Changes in consumer attitudes can clearly play a part in bringing about reductions in packaging use. The packaging industry has been under pressure from consumers, governments and environmental groups to reduce the total amount of packaging. The UK Government's White Paper on the Environment makes clear that industry needs to achieve more in reducing the unnecessary packaging of consumer goods (*This Common Inheritance*, paragraph 14.17). The UK has not introduced mandatory measures to meet these objectives but other countries, notably Germany, have.

20.7 A consumer issue

The rise in importance of environmental issues to the consumer has also led to a sharp focus of attention on packaging waste. Consumers have shown interest in the packaging of products just as much as in the products themselves. Recent research into consumer attitudes to packaging has found that 79 per cent of people believe there should be legislation governing the environmental impact of packaging. A survey carried out by 'Which' magazine in May 1990 found that 59 per cent of consumers would buy a particular product if they thought it less likely to damage the environment.

The power of the individual purchaser, supported by consumer and environmental groups, to make product choices based on environmental criteria has been demonstrated clearly. In two well-known instances in the late 1980s, well-orchestrated campaigns targeting the use of CFCs as a propellant in aerosols and as a foam-blowing agent in the production of fast food containers resulted in retailers and manufacturers rapidly phasing out these products and using CFC-free alternatives.

Manufacturers and retailers have now recognised that a product's packaging is an integral part of its environmental acceptability. Innovations such as light-weight packages, refillable containers, designing for recyclability, and using more recycled material are increasingly common.

20.8   THE ENVIRONMENTAL IMPACT OF PACKAGING TYPES AND MATERIALS

It is difficult, however, for consumers to assess the environmental impact of different types of packaging. The following section sets out the main materials used in the packaging market, and the key environmental concerns which have arisen in connection with each.

20.9   The packaging market

The approximate market share of the principal materials used in packaging is shown below in Table 20.2.

Table 20.2	
Material	*Approximate market % by value*
Paper and board	33
Plastics	30
Metals	20
Glass	5
Wood	5
Other	7

20.10 Paper and board

Paper is an adaptable packaging material, which can be made into many grades and forms. It is suitable for transport and maintains its shape across wide temperature variations. Paper and board packages include corrugated fibre, fibreboard, rigid boxes, cartons, cardboard, paper bags and sacks, and various other types of paper products.

Much of the concern over paper and board packaging has focused on the alleged depletion of natural resources. Many of these fears are groundless; paper packaging is usually made from renewable resources or from recycled materials. Many leading paper producers have set up tree replanting programmes so that the resources are drawn from replenished and managed forests.

The manufacture of paper and board often involves the use of chemical bleaches, including chlorine. This has resulted in fears about the levels of residual dioxins (physically stable organo-chlorine compounds, most of which are highly toxic and which are allegedly carcinogenic) in paper and board products, such as milk cartons. Studies in Canada and New Zealand have found low levels of dioxin migration from cartonboard into milk, but recent Swedish studies have found virtually no evidence of this. Advances in process technology have virtually eliminated the use of chlorine as a bleaching agent, and manufacturers now claim that the levels of dioxins in pulp are inconsequential. Nevertheless, it remains an emotive topic.

Paper-based waste is the single largest component of domestic waste, representing about 30–40 per cent in most countries. Much of it is landfilled. This waste does not readily degrade and paper materials like newspapers are often used to date landfill sites. Approximately 60 per cent of used paper and board is currently recycled. Collection rates for recycling are improving both at point of sale and at municipal waste sites. Manufacturers of packaging are increasingly designing for recyclability by ensuring that their products are made of a single material. Some of the more advanced paper packages, which contain composite materials, require separation before recycling.

Practical difficulties can arise in recycling some paper-based packaging. Manufacturers have stressed the complications in recycling cartons and have emphasised the benefits of energy recovery as an alternative. With a high calorific value, carton incineration is a relatively straightforward and energy efficient means of disposal.

The problems of collection and sorting can be overcome for most paper-based products. However, the difficulty remains of finding a market for recycled paper goods. In the past, the volume of recycled waste paper goods has outstripped demand for them. This has resulted in gluts on the market and collapses in price, rendering further recycling uneconomic. The markets for recycled paper products (and other recycled goods) are notoriously fragile. Changes in international raw material costs can be devastating to developing national markets. It has been alleged that the recent German packaging legislation (discussed below at 20.20 *et seq.*) has resulted in a surplus of recycled paper packages entering the UK market, undercutting prices and making UK recycling initiatives uneconomic.

20.11 Plastics

Plastics have won a steadily growing share of the packaging market. They are light and versatile, cheap and good quality, and provide good heat insulation. They are resistant to fungi and bacteria, and are available in a wide range of types. The principal plastics used in packaging are PET (Polypropylene terephthalate) and PVC (Polyvinyl chloride), commonly used for food and drink containers such as large soft-drink bottles, and polyethylene, used for films, plastic bags, and shrink wrapping. According to INCPEN, plastics represent about 7 per cent by weight of household waste.

Plastics have a number of advantages over other packaging materials. They have often replaced other materials like glass or board because they are lighter and cheaper to transport.

However, they are at the forefront of consumer concern about packaging waste, and several countries have introduced tough measures which focus on plastics. For example, both Switzerland and Austria have banned the use of PVC, a move derived partly from a desire to stop the use of all chlorine compounds in manufacturing, and partly from frustration with the amount and visibility of PVC (and other plastic) waste.

20.12 Disposing of plastics

The principal environmental problem with plastics is the difficulty of disposing of them. This is discussed below. Other issues, however, have contributed to their

20.13   Packaging

relatively poor environmental image. Their manufacture from oil has led to concerns that they contribute to the depletion of valuable finite resources, even though they are responsible for only 2 per cent of the world's oil consumption. The use of ozone-depleting CFCs in the manufacture of polystyrene has not helped their image. The association with the chemical industry, which is still a high risk sector despite having some of industry's most advanced environmental management systems, has also tarnished their reputation.

More particularly, concern has focused on the difficulty of disposing and recycling of plastics. This is tied to the fact that they do not, in general, biodegrade. Their chemical stability makes photodegradation too slow to have a significant impact on the problem of litter, and their slow biodegradation can be an advantage in the composition of landfill waste, where some inert matter is required. Some biodegradable plastics which can be broken down organically into water and carbon dioxide are beginning to emerge, but there is a long way to go before these gain a significant market share.

Plastic waste is incinerated. Its average calorific value is higher than coal, and about twice that of paper. But although the chemical industry would prefer incineration to be accepted as a viable disposal option, it remains deeply unpopular with the public in many countries. Fears about the release of dioxins if incineration takes place at insufficiently high temperatures have undercut efforts to increase incineration capacity. The introduction of tougher emission standards for incinerators (required by *EC Directives 89/369/EEC* and *89/429/EEC*) may reduce this problem but only over the medium-long term.

20.13 Recycling plastics

Plastics are also difficult to recycle. They are often composed of several different resins bonded together so that successful recycling requires clear identification of the types of plastic contained within composite materials. At present, the market for recycled plastics is small, the technology for recycling them is relatively undeveloped, and the quality of the recycled material is often poor. There are very few collection points for post-consumer plastic waste. The expense too of recycling plastic is disproportionate to the benefit achieved.

Work is under way to tackle these problems. In the USA and Sweden efforts are being made to develop marking schemes which identify the common polymers and keep them separate. Considerable efforts are being made among American and European plastics manufacturers to develop recycling technologies and raise awareness of the potential markets for recycled plastic goods and materials. Recycling targets have been set by national and international plastics industry bodies and investments in recycling plant are being made. The greatest spur to the development of technology for plastics recycling, however, is likely to be the German packaging ordinance which requires that 64 per cent of plastic packaging output is recycled by 1995. In this case, as in others, tough regulatory standards are likely to provide the greatest impetus to the development of improved environmental technologies.

20.14 Metals

Metal packaging consists of tins, cans and aluminium-based products, mainly for household use in connection with food and drink. Industrial metal packaging includes the production of tubes, steel drums and barrels.

Environmental concerns in this area have focused on the extraction of raw materials and production processes. Metal and mineral extraction costs are high in economic and environmental terms. Aluminium production, for example, is energy intensive, requiring large amounts of electricity to break down the aluminium oxide to pure aluminium.

The costs involved in extraction and production have been one factor in the strong incentive to recycle. It has been estimated that recycling aluminium consumes only 5 per cent of the energy used to extract it initially. Another factor in promoting recycling is the relative ease of separation. Aluminium cans, for example, are easy to separate from other waste by magnetic extraction.

However, aluminium represents only a tiny proportion of total domestic waste. In the US, which is the biggest market for aluminium products, it amounts to about 1 per cent by weight. Steel/tinplate cans (which have the larger market share) require material separation prior to recycling, which has increased the costs. New lightweight all steel cans are now coming onto the market.

20.15 Glass

Most glass container sales are for food, alcohol, soft drinks, and dairy products (especially milk). However, the market share of glass as a packaging material has been eroded by plastics, which have largely replaced it in mass markets, except for milk and beer bottles. Glass has become the preferred material for high-quality, luxury goods like perfumes and alcohol.

Although the resources used in glass production (silica sand, soda ash and lime) are plentiful, extraction and production have high environmental and energy costs. However, glass is easy to recycle, and public involvement in glass recycling schemes is high. The benefits of recycling too are clear. For each tonne of cullet used, it has been estimated that an equivalent saving is made of 30 gallons of oil and 1.2 tonnes of primary raw materials. Another advantage of glass packaging is that its durability ensures it can be used several times.

The debate over the advantages and disadvantages of refillable bottles has been long-running. Switzerland and several American states have introduced laws requiring mandatory deposits on bottles to encourage their return and re-use. Most environmental groups support the use of refillable beverage containers, and have criticised packagers and retailers for their refusal to adopt a more positive approach in this area. Life cycle analyses which demonstrate the environmental benefit of refillables (provided they are used a sufficient number of times) have been used to support the argument. Packagers argue that 'one-trip' containers (i.e. those used once only) can in some cases consume fewer resources and produce less waste.

Aside from the environmental arguments, economic and logistical factors have been important in preventing refillable systems developing. There are significant economic costs in cleaning and sterilising used bottles, and in setting up the distribution and collection systems needed for an effective refillable system. In the UK, the centralisation of the distribution and collection systems of large supermarkets has prevented these schemes from taking off. Greater standardisation of bottle shapes and sizes would also assist refillables. In Denmark, specially designed bottle banks exist for the public to return them. If return and re-use schemes grow, glass will be a major beneficiary.

The refillable debate also affects the future of plastics packaging. PET soft drink containers are now being refilled in some European countries such as Holland, Austria, Denmark, and Switzerland. This increases the pressure on manufacturers and handlers to ensure that PET bottles are sufficiently strong to survive frequent use and handling.

20.16   Packaging

20.16 Evaluating packaging types: Life cycle analysis

The refillable versus the one-trip argument, in which conflicting claims are frequently made by those involved, illustrates the need for an agreed methodology of life cycle analysis. At present, there is no agreed methodology for judging the environmental credentials of the variety of packaging containers and materials. Claim and counter-claim (often made by competing packaging manufacturers) about the merits and dangers of packaging materials and systems prevail.

Despite the lack of standard procedures, more extensive use of life cycle analysis is now being made. The analysis covers four principal stages in the product cycle. These are raw material consumption, design and production; distribution; use; and disposal. But until guidelines for carrying them out are agreed, genuine comparisons will be hard to make. It will be even longer before the findings of life cycle analyses are communicated to the consumer in a user-friendly way.

20.17 A TRADE ISSUE

Packaging regulations can have repercussions on international trade. In this sense, packaging is, like many other environmental matters, a transnational issue. Packaging laws provide a good illustration of the conflict which can arise between establishing high standards of environmental protection on the one hand, and promoting free trade on the other. This is clear from experience in Europe and North America.

In North America, a variety of legal provisions exist in different states. Some states have introduced requirements governing the recycled content of glass packaging. California now requires that 15 per cent of the content is recycled, moving progress-ively to 65 per cent by 2001. Oregon requires a 35 per cent recycled content by 1995. These provisions will make it difficult for Canadian glass container manufacturers, who use a closed-loop recycling system in Canada, to meet the recycling content requirements. They may even need to import cullet from the USA to do so. On the other hand, it has been argued that Canada's refilling systems have restricted the access imported beverages can make into Canadian markets.

Environmental/international trade issues like this are likely to become increasingly common as more emphasis is given to the difference in environmental standards between trading partners. Resolving them is unlikely to be easy. If trade disputes arise between Canada and the USA over differing standards and practices, there are likely to be more serious problems now that Mexico is a signatory to the North American Free Trade Agreement, where there are virtually no environmental packaging guidelines or standards.

The problems of reconciling the conflicting interests of trade and environmental protection have also been felt in the European Community, shown in the problems faced in implementing the *Council Directive on containers of liquids for human consump-tion*, commonly known as the *Beverage Containers Directive* (*EC Directive 85/339/EEC*) (27 June 1985). It took eleven years and 15 drafts to agree this *Directive*. It was then widely held to have failed in its objectives.

20.18 The Beverage Containers Directive

The *Beverage Containers Directive* set out to reduce the environmental impact of used beverage containers, a highly visible environmental problem. It required Member States to draw up a framework of measures within two years of its entry into force which would reduce the tonnage and/or volume of beverage containers that ended up as household waste. A related objective was that these measures should save energy and raw materials. A variety of means were permitted to achieve this, such as light-weighting, refilling and re-use, and energy recovery.

In implementing the *Directive*, the different approaches adopted by Member States resulted in the creation of obstacles to trade. In Denmark, all beer and soft drink containers had to be returnable, and had to be marketed in approved re-usable containers. The effect of this was to force foreign drinks manufacturers to use special containers for the Danish market, which was not sufficiently large to justify the effort and expense. A 1988 ruling by the European Court upheld the validity of the Danish scheme. The Court's judgment gave precedence to environmental criteria over the interests of free trade.

On the back of this decision, other Member States introduced regulations on refillable bottles, which had a similarly damaging effect on trade. Germany introduced quotas for different re-fillable bottles, deposits on larger plastic bottles, and placed an obligation on industry to accept bottles when consumers returned them. It later introduced a mandatory deposit on plastic bottles, damaging the import of lightweight plastic bottles of mineral water (which was required to be bottled at source) from neighbouring countries.

The detrimental impact on trade of national measures of this type is clear. The problems created by the *Directive*, particularly in the context of the efforts devoted to establishing the single market, led the Commission to re-visit the problem of packaging waste. It has now been proposed that the *Beverage Containers Directive* is replaced by a new *Packaging Waste Directive*. This is discussed in detail at 20.27 *et seq.* below.

Outside the Community, provisions focusing on beverage containers are common. In Switzerland, legislation requires that drinks can only be marketed in refillable or recyclable containers. In Austria, targets have been set for the refilling and recycling of beverage containers, such as 90 per cent for beer and mineral waters, 80 per cent for non-alcoholic beverages and 40 per cent for fruit juice and fruit drinks. In Scandinavia, one of the four key objectives of the Nordic Council's 1990 Action Programme for Packaging is to increase the rate of recyclable material in beverage containers to 75 per cent by the end of the century.

20.19 A patchwork of European measures

The variety of approaches and targets to deal with the problem of beverage containers is a product of the patchwork of national schemes to tackle packaging waste throughout Europe.

While some countries have introduced legislation to meet their objectives, others have adopted a voluntary approach. In the UK, the Government is seeking to encourage industry to reduce the unnecessary packaging of consumer goods, set targets for packaging reduction, and introduce measures to reduce packaging. Wider ranging measures are under consideration. In Belgium, a voluntary agreement signed between packaging industry associations and the Flemish Government (26 June 1990) has set out a plan for industry to develop a collection, recycling and waste reduction programme, and to phase out the use of toxic heavy metals in packaging material. The programme covers consumer, commercial, and industrial waste. The Dutch 'Packaging Covenant' (6 June 1991) is a voluntary over-arching agreement between the Government and the Foundation on Packaging and The Environment, but its provisions are binding on individual signatories. Monitoring and compliance will be overseen by a newly-established commission comprised of industry and government representatives.

Across Europe a range of targets have been set which vary from country to country. These include targets to improve levels of recycling, to increase the recycling of

20.20 Packaging

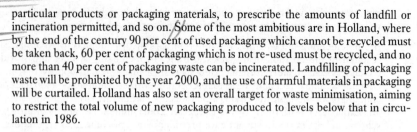

particular products or packaging materials, to prescribe the amounts of landfill or incineration permitted, and so on. Some of the most ambitious are in Holland, where by the end of the century 90 per cent of used packaging which cannot be recycled must be taken back, 60 per cent of packaging which is not re-used must be recycled, and no more than 40 per cent of packaging waste can be incinerated. Landfilling of packaging waste will be prohibited by the year 2000, and the use of harmful materials in packaging will be curtailed. Holland has also set an overall target for waste minimisation, aiming to restrict the total volume of new packaging produced to levels below that in circulation in 1986.

While the broad objectives of these various national targets are common, the differences will clearly have an impact on the market. The acceptability of different packaging materials from one market to the next, for example, will vary. Trading will be more difficult.

20.20 THE GERMAN PACKAGING REGULATION

The most contentious of the national schemes, because it is the most far-reaching and arguably has an adverse effect on foreign traders in particular, is the German national packaging waste scheme. The framework for it is set out in the '*Topfer Decree* (12 June 1991) (see 22.4 below)'. A key feature of the regulation is that it shifts responsibility for packaging waste disposal away from public municipalities towards the producers of waste.

20.21 Types of packaging; take back, re-use or recycle

The regulation defines three types of packaging and introduces obligations on the producers of waste relating to each. 'Transport' packaging is material used to ensure the safe passage of goods from manufacturer to distributor or retailer. From 1 December 1991 the producers of this waste (objects like wooden crates, pallets, paper, or cardboard wrapping and so on) have been obliged to take back and re-use or recycle the waste, outside the municipal waste disposal system.

'Sales' packaging is material such as bags, blister packs, bottles, tins, cans and so on which are used to convey the goods until they are used by the consumer. Since 1 January 1993, this has had to be taken back by the retailer at the point of sale and passed on for re-use or recycling, again outside the public waste disposal system.

'Secondary' packaging is material in addition to sales packaging such as that used to group products together for greater convenience or for improved stacking or promotion. Since April 1992, it has been required that this type of packaging is either removed by the retailer or that the consumer is able to return it at or near the point of sale. The costs of setting up systems for this to happen and subsequent costs in handling for re-use or recycling are also the responsibility of the retailer. Third parties can be involved, however, to assist manufacturers, distributors, and retailers in meeting their obligations under the law.

The ordinance covers all types of products save for those which might pose a health risk by virtue of residual contamination. There has been some initial uncertainty about the distinctions between the different classifications of packaging described above, such as the lines drawn between transport and sales packaging.

20.22 Other objectives

In addition to these provisions, the regulation has introduced a mandatory deposit on certain types of non-returnable packages, including beverage containers. It also contains tough recycling and collection targets for different types of packaging material. It aims for a collection rate of 80 per cent by 1995, with 80–90 per cent of this having to be sorted into a quality suitable for recycling or re-use.

The regulation allows for alternative means of complying with the packaging obligations. Manufacturers and retailers can devise their own systems to collect, re-use and recycle waste so long as the overall requirements of the regulation are fulfilled. If they choose to do this they must set collection and sorting quotas, guarantee certain standards of re-use and recycling, and ensure coordination with the existing municipal waste disposal system. Licence to operate such schemes has to be granted by the regional competent authority.

20.23 DSD and the green dot

In the light of this, the manufacturing, packaging, and distribution sectors set up in 1991 an independent company (called DSD – 'Duales System Deutschland') to administer and finance the collections required to fulfil the requirements of the regulation. In effect, a private system for waste collection and recycling has been created which operates in parallel (or as a 'dual system' overall) with existing municipal initiatives. However, many local authorities have reached agreement with DSD to avoid duplication of effort.

DSD's income is derived from licensing its members to mark their product with a green dot, which guarantees that the producer will take the product back to re-use or recycle. In order to gain the green dot, the DSD must be satisfied that the manufacturer or distributor will actually carry out the recycling or re-use. For some materials, a general acceptance and recycling guarantee (provided by industry federations, for example) is acceptable. For other materials, specific guarantees need to be obtained, and the DSD may need to check whether recycling will be possible when considering the licence application.

20.24 The impact on importers and foreign manufacturers

The regulation does affect imported goods. Its obligations extend to those who are responsible for bringing packaging waste into circulation. Importers are clearly subject to its provisions, and it appears as though foreign manufacturers are also subject to it. Clearly, the likelihood that this national law will impose obligations on companies lying outside its normal jurisdiction is highly controversial. The regulation has already been attacked by external parties as a barrier to trade, and is under examination by the European Commission.

20.25 What will be the impact of the German scheme?

Within Germany, the DSD system appears to be working well. A series of pilot projects in selected cities has proved successful, with high collection rates, and encouraging compliance with the requirement to separate different types of waste material. Over 7,000 firms have applied for the green dot, and an increasing proportion of packaging on German shelves now sports the green dot.

As a result of the regulation, it is likely that German retailers will increase the pressure on distributors and manufacturers to reduce amounts of unnecessary packaging material. It appears as though the measures are forcing companies to reconsider how much secondary packaging is actually needed. It is also likely to spur companies to design for recyclability. Retailers will prefer and thus may give preference to products packaged in a single material for ease of recycling.

It appears as though the regulation is also affecting the markets for recycled goods, both positively and negatively. Early indications are that levels of recycling are increasing in Germany. It seems to have prompted initiatives to develop recycling in hitherto unpromising areas, notably plastics. One estimate is that over 35 per cent of the 30,000 tonnes of polystyrene foam used in packaging in Germany is now being re-used. However, as discussed previously, the regulation to recycle paper is alleged to have hit fledgling foreign markets for recycled goods.

On the back of the regulation, other sectors of German industry are seeking to develop innovative solutions to minimise packaging waste. Others are ensuring that they will be able to meet the requirements to take back their products when their use is over. Car manufacturers are a good example, where German companies are acknowledged to be among the leaders in increasing the proportion of cars which can be recycled and re-used.

The German scheme, although controversial, may point the way ahead. Its impact on trade, however, will be closely scrutinised, and it may erect some of the obstacles to trade which the Community has been trying hard to knock down. That is why it remains a goal of the European Commission and other Member States to establish a harmonised regulatory framework for packaging across the Community as a whole. The German scheme, and others being developed, may make that objective more difficult.

20.26 EC PACKAGING PROPOSALS

It is now widely held that the Community's earlier attempts to control the packaging waste problem were too narrowly focused. The EC's draft *Packaging Waste Directive* (*COM 92/278*; *OJC 263*; 12 October 1992) is therefore wider in scope, contains a more diverse range of targets, is more flexible, and can be implemented through a range of policy instruments, including fiscal and economic incentives.

20.27 THE EC PACKAGING DIRECTIVE

The *Draft Packaging Waste Directive*, which has been in preparation since the end of 1990, was agreed on 15 July 1992, and published in the Official Journal in October (*OJC 263, Volume 35*).

The *Directive* has been proposed under *Article 100a* of the *Treaty*; that is, it is a harmonisation measure, framed within the context of the completion of the internal market. Its objective is to create a harmonised framework which will both promote free trade and protect the environment. The measure covers all packaging.

20.28 Waste management targets

The draft *Directive* contains waste management targets. Within ten years of the *Directive* entering into force, 90 per cent by weight of packaging waste must be recovered. Within the same period, a separate target of 60 per cent by weight of each packaging waste material must be removed from the waste stream for the purpose of recycling.

On waste minimisation and disposal, not more than 10 per cent by weight of packaging waste output (i.e. the residues of collection and sorting material) can be disposed of. Landfill is to be used as a last resort.

Interim targets are also set. Member States can specify intermediate recycling, recovery and re-use targets within their waste management plans. They must indicate when they will achieve a reduction of 60 per cent by weight of packaging waste for recovery, and a 40 per cent by weight removal rate by material, for the purposes of recycling.

20.29 Minimum essential requirements

The draft sets out minimum 'essential requirements' for packaging. These include general requirements relating to packaging design and production, as well as specific requirements on the concentration of heavy metals such as lead, cadmium, mercury, and hexavalent chromium. Essential requirements are also related to re-usable and recoverable packaging. For example, these set minimum calorific values which must be achieved for packaging processed for the purposes of energy recovery.

Where packaging conforms to relevant Community standards, it is presumed to comply with these essential requirements. National standards are also acceptable unless challenged, whereupon the issue will be resolved by the Commission.

20.30 Return and management systems

The proposal requires Member States to set up 'return and management systems' so that waste is effectively returned, re-used or recycled. The proposal does not prescribe the type of system which Member States adopt. The use of economic instruments to minimise waste and help finance collection, re-use and recovery systems is encouraged. Any such schemes will be examined by the Commission to ensure they comply with the aims of the *Directive*, and do not contravene rules governing indirect taxation, state aids, or competition.

20.31 Marking

Once packaging meets the essential requirements, and is subject to established return and management systems, it can display a mark which will guarantee it free circulation around the Community. These provisions will take effect not later than five years after the *Directive* comes into force.

This would effectively mean that the Danish ban on imported beverage containers mentioned previously would no longer be valid.

20.32 More information about packaging

The draft contains a number of measures relating to the provision of information about packaging. Member States must develop national databases on packaging and packaging waste and the measures they are using or proposing to tackle the issue. This data must be updated every three years, and reported to the Commission.

Packaging waste management plans will form part of the wider waste management plans required under the *Waste Framework Directive*. (*Council Directive 75/442/EEC, as amended by 91/156/EEC.*)

20.33 The timetable for implementation

Even though progress has been made with the proposal now formally adopted, it is unlikely to be negotiated and approved until the mid-1990s. Implementation will be gradual over ten years. The inevitable delay in implementing the *Directive* will have important consequences. It will ensure that the national initiatives already taken, particularly the German scheme which has introduced a tougher regime than that proposed for the Community as a whole, will shape the way the sector develops in the short term.

20.34 A continuing focus of attention

The existence of the *Directive* will ensure a constant spotlight of public attention on the packaging sector in the coming decade. There will be increasing pressure on the packaging industry to innovate to produce lighter packages, which consume less energy in production, use less potentially harmful substances, are of homogenous material, are designed for recyclability, and so on. Nevertheless, the final text is more favourable towards the packaging industry than some earlier drafts.

The most controversial element of earlier versions of the proposal has been dropped; the so-called 'Standstill proposal'. This sought to limit the total amount of packaging waste produced in each Member State within ten years to the 1990 Community average, estimated at 150kg per capita. This target, to the relief of the industry and the dismay of environmental groups, has not been included.

20.35 Tough targets for recycling and recovery

Given current levels of performance, the recycling and recovery targets are ambitious. Waste recycling activities and recovery rates are such that the Member States still have a long way to go to meet the requirements of the *Directive*. Not only do they each need to improve their total recycling and recovery performance, but they need to do so at a much faster rate than hitherto.

Environmental groups have argued that the recycling targets are not tough enough, and have fought against the inclusion of incineration as a disposal option. They have also noted that the *Directive* states that 60 per cent of materials must be removed from the waste stream for the 'purpose of recycling' rather than saying that they must be recycled. The provision that the targets can be changed in the light of scientific advance is feared to be an escape clause to permit greater recovery or re-use if recycling targets cannot be met. Packagers are keen to incorporate recovery within the overall targets, and are opposed to the idea of recycling at any cost.

20.36 THE FUTURE

Debate about recycling rates and all the other environmental issues discussed above will persist. Consumers are likely to become better informed about the environmental impact of packaging, as they are about the environmental impact of other aspects of social and commercial behaviour. The packaging sector will be under increasing pressure to improve its performance, with the threat of regulation if its progress is too slow.

The impact of tighter environmental regulations on the packaging industry is difficult to quantify. Like many other sectors, it is currently being affected far more seriously by wider economic conditions (lower consumer spending, deteriorating trade) than by tougher environmental regulations. While tighter environmental provisions may increase costs for packagers, they may also provide the seeds for future growth. Packaging companies which invest successfully in research and development into new materials, techniques, and products will be best-placed to respond to an upturn in green consumerism and waste minimisation initiatives.

20.37 A problem for developing economies

The problems of packaging and packaging waste have been of particular importance in the developed world, for obvious reasons. But it will not be long before the developing world faces similar problems. In common with many environmental matters, the issue of packaging poses questions about how best to manage the goals of development and environmental protection. While most developed economies in the west are attempting to reduce the amount of packaging waste produced, the under-developed economies of the east and south are seeking to develop the distribution systems for foods and goods which will improve health and standards of living but which will probably increase levels of packaging waste. It has been forecast, for example, that the demand for packaging in the countries of the former Soviet Union will double between now and 1995. Perhaps the greatest challenge facing the packaging sector in the decade to come is expanding in these markets, as well as their traditional ones, in a manner which is industrially and environmentally sustainable.

21 Planning and the Environment

21.1 INTRODUCTION

The mass of new environmental legislation that has been enacted in the past few years may lead practitioners and others to underestimate the environmental protection role played by the well-established system of town and country planning in Britain since 1948. The planning system in this country has been much more powerful than in any of the other nations of Western Europe or North America, where town and country planning has traditionally been regarded as a largely mechanical function to achieve pre-determined physical objectives in the urban environment, such as minimum standards for buildings and roads, maximum densities, the separation of non-conforming uses, and set-back and layout requirements.

21.2 In Britain, planning has been the principal tool of environmental protection. Through the use of planning controls and incentives, local authorities and central government have brought about the relocation of polluting industry and its physical separation from residential areas; the decongestion of the old industrial cities and the establishment of new towns; the protection of landscape and countryside areas from unrestricted urban expansion; the preservation of natural habitats and the protection of floodplains; the provision of physical infrastructure concurrently with the needs of new development, coupled with an ability to prevent development from proceeding in advance of the necessary sewerage and sewage treatment capacity and controls over the location of landfill.

21.3 Its strength derives to a large extent from the fact that it is not underpinned by any guarantee of property rights. In the US, for example, planners operate always under the threat that their regulation of the use and development of land may go so far as to constitute a 'taking' of property, requiring the payment of compensation, and this imposes a very real constraint over the planning process. Property owners in Britain, by comparison, are protected primarily by procedural safeguards – such as the right to object to draft plans, and the right to appeal to the Secretary of State against the refusal or conditional approval of planning application. Only in an extreme case, where land is left without any reasonably beneficial use and no planning permission is forthcoming from the local planning authority to allow it to be put to use, does the law allow for compensation: a landowner may serve a *purchase notice* requiring the local planning authority to buy the land itself (so sometimes called inverse compulsory acquisition) but at a price which may be above its going market value.

21.4 The British system of planning also imposes a wide ranging system of control over land-based activity and places comparatively little emphasis on 'as of right' development. Although there is a statutory instrument, the *Town and Country Planning General Development Order 1988 (SI 1988 No 1813)* (the *General Development Order*), which applies nation-wide to granting planning permission for specified types of development, such as householder and agricultural development, there is no system corresponding to US zoning, under which each municipality establishes the limits to be imposed upon development within different zones in their area. An attempt to emulate that system, through 'Simplified Planning Zone' schemes (now under the *Town and Country Planning Act 1990, ss 82–89* and *Schedule 7*), has proved largely ineffective, in part because of the reluctance of local planning authorities to relinquish planning controls, and partly because of the cumbersome nature of the procedures. Their revision by the *Planning and Compensation Act 1991* may help to revive the popularity of these measures.

21.5 Planning control is not only wide ranging, it is also highly discretionary in its application. In deciding whether or not to grant planning permission, the local planning authority must 'have regard to' the development plan and to any other material considerations. But subject to that duty, they may grant or refuse planning permission and impose any conditions they think fit. Hence the development plan is not prescriptive, even under a somewhat ambiguous 1991 amendment which requires the authority always to determine applications in accordance with the plan unless material considerations indicate otherwise [*Town and Country Planning Act 1990, s 54A (inserted by Planning and Compensation Act 1991, s 26)*]; and since the courts have generally refrained from placing any *a priori* constraints upon what may or may not comprise material considerations, the concept has proved remarkably malleable and flexible over the years. Considerations in 1993 may be 'material' to planning which in 1947, when the formula was first introduced, might not have been considered relevant at all. So it has been that environmental protection has emerged as a legitimate aim of the land-use planning system, without any need for confirmatory primary legislation.

21.6   Limits to planning control

Land-use planning focuses on changes in land-use, and it is therefore at its strongest in protecting the environment from potentially harmful development. It is largely impotent when it comes to imposing further restrictions on established industry. Local authorities are able to provide relocational incentives, and even to require the discontinuance of a use or to impose conditions on it. [*Town and Country Planning Act 1990, ss 97–100* (revocation or modification of planning permission); *102–104* (discontinuance orders)]. But these coercive powers are exercisable only with the Secretary of State's consent, and only upon payment of compensation. Planning control therefore does not provide a cost-free basis for raising environmental standards for established industry. Changing the substances used in a manufacturing process, for example, may have significant environmental consequences but does not attract planning intervention (and for this reason it has been necessary to introduce a separate but parallel system of controls over the storage or use of hazardous substances, now under the *Planning (Hazardous Substances) Act 1990*, which was brought into force in mid-1992). Likewise, most agricultural operations are outside the planning system altogether.

21.7   Yet despite all this technical compatibility between land-use planning and environmental protection, local planning authorities generally remain confused as to what their role truly is. All would claim to have been practising environmental protection for years, under the planning system. But their purpose in doing so has been, and continues to be, the pursuit of rational land-use and the preservation of amenity. The system excels at protecting agricultural land from development, and at a low cost. In countries which prevent the taking of land without just compensation, a ban on development like this would be vulnerable to legal challenge as constituting a 'taking', calling for full compensation. Hence the British system provides a powerful basis for nature conservation, for resource management and for national parks. But only indirectly has the planning system had any role in limiting polluting emissions into the environment, largely through refusing or conditioning planning permission for environmentally harmful industry, and then primarily on the basis of consultation with other agencies. Determining the most appropriate cross-over point between planning and pollution controls is one of the most difficult problems for the future. It is the subject of a consultation paper issued by the Department of the Environment in June 1992, to which this chapter will return (see 21.19 below).

21.8   The function of planning policy

Planning *law* acts as the link between planning *policy* and planning *control*. Planning policy provides the substance for decision-making; planning law provides the procedures. The processes of making planning policy are complex, because there are many conflicting interests to be resolved. They are not always reconciled in policy advice, and the maze of policy is therefore often conflicting and difficult to comprehend. Policies that are relevant to planning are adopted and pursued at different levels of government, with different degrees of formality, and with different levels of commitment. Different policies may conflict or compete when applied to particular development proposals, and therefore have to be reconciled on a case-by-case basis. A policy is in any event never a binding rule. It often takes the form of a presumption: thus, there is a presumption against 'inappropriate' development in the green belt (PPG2, *Green Belts* (1988), paragraph 12), and against non-agricultural development in the open country-side (PPG7, *The Countryside and the Rural Economy* (1992), paragraph 1.10); and there has, until recently, been also a general presumption in favour of granting planning permission. (Now superseded by new *section 54A*, and by the policy advice in PPG1, *General Policy and Principles* (1992).) Policy is not law, and these policy statements are not legally binding on local planning authorities. But their effect is similar: a local planning authority that chooses to depart from government policy must show good planning reasons for doing so if its decision is challenged on appeal. If it cannot, not only may its decision be overturned by the Secretary of State or an inspector, but the authority may be required to pay the appellants' costs of bringing the appeal.

21.9   The national policy framework

Planning policy is made nationally by the Department of the Environment (in Wales and Scotland, by the Welsh Office and Scottish Office respectively, though in close liaison with the Department of the Environment). Policy statements have traditionally been issued in the form of circulars addressed to local authorities, although they may also appear in other government documents, including white papers, written answers to Parliamentary questions, press releases and so on.

However, the format of a circular has long since become inappropriate for statements whose true audience is not just local authorities but the public at large, and it has therefore yielded in the past few years to a new series of national guidance notes published by the Department of the Environment (through Her Majesty's Stationery Office). These Notes, which are listed in Appendix 20A to this chapter, are being issued progressively and are gradually superseding many of the old circulars. Circulars have been retained as the medium for promulgation of material that is specifically addressed to local authorities, such as advice on handling planning applications. Each Note or circular sets out general policies on land-use or planning procedure. Some of the circulars that remain in effect and which have particular relevance to environ-mental protection are set out in Appendix 21B.

21.10   The practical effect of national policy

National policy statements affect environmental planning decisions at two principal levels. The first is in the preparation of development plans. In this process, sometimes known as 'forward planning', local authorities assess the development requirements and pressures in their areas, and devise appropriate policies and allocations of land for anticipated development. They undertake this in the context of government policy, which sets national priorities for development, and also provides regional guidance. National policy also guides local planning authorities in their so-called 'development control' function, which involves such tasks as determining planning applications and taking enforcement action against unlawful development. We now turn to examine these areas in more detail.

21.11 Planning and the Environment

21.11 The development plan

Outside London and the metropolitan areas (Greater Manchester, West Midlands, South Yorkshire, West Yorkshire, Tyne and Wear and Merseyside) plan preparation is a two-stage process. First, there are structure plans which are prepared by the county planning authority (i.e., the county council in its planning capacity). These are strategic plans, intended to co-ordinate national and regional policies and to accommodate anticipated demographic and employment trends. In growth regions they will identify areas suitable for major new urban settlements and establish a strategy for communications networks and the provision and funding of physical and social infrastructure. They record strategic political choices and set a balance between such issues as growth and constraint, employment and conservation, green field development and inner city regeneration. The authorities must have regard also to the availability of resources to carry out any proposals for public development contained in the plan. It is a high level exercise conducted in a sub-regional context, and is deliberately not site-specific. There are no geographical maps, only a diagrammatic representation of strategic linkages. The purpose is to avoid site-related objections to issues of general strategy, and to lessen the possibility of planning blight from major new proposals.

21.12 Second, there are local plans, prepared by the district planning authority (i.e. the district council in its planning capacity), which are intended to refine the structure plan policies and tie them down to specific locations. They have, by law, to be in 'general conformity' with the structure plan, and this requirement can cause difficulties. The county planning authority may have an overall conservation policy which attempts to concentrate all major development on one or two locations. Some of the district planning authorities within the county, which may be under different political control from the county, may try to use their local plans as a means of attracting some of that growth to their own areas.

Local plans usually allocate land to residential, commercial or industrial development and specify the circumstances under which, and the terms on which, they will be prepared to grant planning permission. The allocations are sometimes phased, so as to ensure that there will be a reasonably constant supply of land over the life of the plan – around ten years. Planning permission is still required before development may commence, and permission may be granted for development on sites not allocated, and refused on sites that are. The plan does not in itself permit or prohibit development. The local plan will also normally contain details of the authority's requirements for off-street car parking, site layout, plot ratios, infrastructure and similar physical requirements of the development, but the authority has discretion as to the amount of detail to include, and will sometimes deal with these matters instead either in a non-statutory policy document (which has no legal basis) or on a case-by-case basis. In early 1992, the districts came under a duty to prepare comprehensive district-wide local plans [*Town and Country Planning Act 1990, s 36(1), (substituted by Planning and Compensation Act 1991, 4 Sch)*], which will in due course replace the individual local plans adopted for different areas within some districts. At the same time, the counties came under a duty to produce statutory plans for minerals and waste policies. [*T & CPA 1990, ss 37, 38*]. Waste in Wales is a district council responsibility, and waste policies may be included in their district-wide plan, replacing the so-called 'subject local plans' which some (but by no means all) of them had produced under the previous arrangements.

21.13 Development plans therefore have important environmental implications, and their potential for environmental protection is coming now to be recognised. In the Environment White Paper (*This Common Inheritance*, (Cm 1200, 1990)) the Government urged local planning authorities to have particular regard to the conservation of energy as an issue in development plans, and it promised further guidance to authorities on the location of new development in relation to traffic generation as part of the need to tackle global warming:

'One aim would be to guide new development to locations which reduce the need for car journeys and the distances driven, or which permit the choice of more energy efficient public transport – without encouraging more or longer journeys – as an alternative to the private car. By the same token, the planning of transport routes should take account of the potential impact on settlement and development patterns. However, not enough is known about the relationship between choice of housing and employment location and transport mode to allow the Government to offer authoritative advice at this stage' (*This Common Inheritance*, (Cm 1200, 1990, paragraph 6.34)).

21.14 The issues to be covered in structure and local plans, and the procedures to be followed in preparing them, are now prescribed nationally by the *Town and Country Planning (Development Plan) Regulations 1991* (*SI 1991 No 2794*), and environmental issues now figure prominently in the list, and also in the Government's most recent guidance on plan preparation. These form part of an extensive reform of the development plan system, in which the Government took the opportunity to reinforce the role of development plans as instruments of environmental protection. Local planning authorities are now required by law to have regard to environmental considerations. [*Town and Country Planning (Development Plan) Regulations 1991* (*SI 1991 No 2794*)]. There are two elements to this: a requirement that authorities have regard to a broader range of environmental concerns than those traditionally falling within the ambit of land-use planning; and a requirement that they appraise the environmental impact of their proposals as a whole. This is not seen as imposing an obligation to conduct a full environmental assessment (PPG12, *Development Plans and Regional Planning Guidance*, paragraph 5.52; PPG12 (Wales), *Development Plans in Wales* (1992), paragraph 5.52); although such a requirement may yet be imposed under proposals currently under consideration by the European Community. PPG12 suggests, however, that the obligation is one to appraise the environmental implications:

'Such an environmental appraisal is the process of identifying, quantifying weighing up and reporting on the environmental and other costs and benefits of the measures which are proposed. All the implications of the options should be analysed, including financial, social and environmental effects. A systematic appraisal ensures that the objectives of a policy are clearly laid out, and the trade-offs between options identified and assessed'. (PPG12, paragraph 5.52)

21.15 Authorities are also urged (PPG12, paragraph 6.25) to make use of the Department of the Environment's publication *Policy Appraisal and the Environment* (HMSO, 1991) to assist in introducing a commonly accepted and systematic approach to the treatment of environmental issues in developing their planning policies.

As to the environmental content of plans, Chapter 6 of PPG12 emphasises the need to go beyond the traditional environmental issues of planning, such as the green belt and nature conservation, and to ensure that they also address newer environmental concerns such as global warming and the consumption of non-renewable resources. The Department acknowledges that it is not yet in a position to give advice on how different patterns of development might influence the need to travel and the choice of mode, and hence CO_2 emissions, but urges (paragraph 6.14) local planning authorities nonetheless to pursue policies encouraging the use of public transport in their settlement policies, such as:

(i)   development that makes full and effective use of land within existing urban areas without amounting to 'town cramming' (further guidance is in PPG3, *Housing*);

(ii)   growth that is closely related to public transport networks – for example near existing railway stations with spare capacity;

(iii)   location of new development types that *attract* trips (for example, office employment, shopping, higher education and leisure) at points such as town centres which are capable of acting as nodes for public transport networks to avoid encouraging substantial increase in car use; and where there may be advantages in enabling one journey to serve several purposes;

(iv)   housing (which by contrast to (iii) *generates* trips) that is located in such a way as to minimise car use for journeys to work, school and to other local facilities;

(v)   limitations (by capacity or price) on town centre parking, whether public or as part of other developments, provided that does not encourage development in more energy-inefficient locations elsewhere;

(vi)   appropriate interchange opportunities between major public transport networks; and

(vii)   positive encouragement of facilities to assist walking and cycling.

The advice acknowledges that the planning system cannot compel people to live near their work, or to use public transport when it is available, or to walk or cycle; but stresses that the system can encourage development patterns that provide that choice.

The advice also identifies other areas of environmental concern to be addressed by development plans, such the clean-up and reuse of contaminated and derelict land, protection of groundwater resources, the environmental impact of providing new water services, the siting of hazardous installations, mineral extraction operations, and securing the conservation of natural beauty and amenity of land.

21.16   Public participation

Public participation is required in the making of all development plans, although the requirements have been relaxed by the 1992 development planning reforms. The authority must undertake an extensive array of consultations on its draft proposals before placing them formally on deposit for public inspection and objections. It no longer is obliged to embark upon a full public participation exercise, but the Government is anxious that this should not be seen as a weakening of public involvement in the planning process, particularly now that structure plans and local plans no longer need to be submitted to the Secretary of State for approval.

The conservation policies of development plans tend to carry a long-term commitment, and thus to reinforce designations made by other agencies, including SSSIs declared by the Nature Conservancy Council. (Known as 'English Nature' since the break-up of the former agency by the *Environmental Protection Act 1990*. In Wales the new agency is the Countryside Council for Wales.) Hence the very process of preparation of development plans, with its extensive consultation requirements, draws together and co-ordinates the environmental protection policies of other statutory agencies.

21.17   Planning in the metropolitan areas: unitary plans

In Greater London and the metropolitan areas the arrangements outlined above existed until April 1986, when the upper-tier planning authorities were abolished. Thus it was no longer possible to maintain a two-tier system for plan making, and the planning authorities in those areas became the London boroughs and the metropolitan district councils. They have inherited all the old structure plans and the local plans, but over the coming years will be replacing them with 'unitary' plans, which will do the job of both the former plans. These are in two parts, strategic and detailed. They do not require approval by the Secretary of State, though, like structure plans, they need to accord with strategic guidance given by him to the planning authorities concerned, and he retains power to call in a unitary plan for his own approval.

21.18 Development control

Planning permission is required before any 'development' is carried out, even if it is in accordance with the development plan. Through this mechanism, a wide ranging control is achieved over all changes in land use: 'development' includes not only building operations, but also mining, engineering works and changes in use. [*Town and Country Planning Act 1990, s 55*]. But there are exceptions. Agriculture, for example, enjoys wide immunity from planning control. No planning permission is required to put land to agricultural use, to change its use between categories of agriculture, forestry or horticulture, or to cease agricultural activity altogether. Moreover, there is a national grant of planning permission for building and engineering development on agricultural land where it is required for agricultural purposes, under the *Town and Country Planning General Development Order 1988, 2 Sch, Pt 6*. Although this specifies physical limits to what may be done (in terms, for example, of the height, area and location of new farm buildings) it nonetheless allows major engineering operations, such as the draining of marshes, the filling of gullies and the removal of hedgerows, to be undertaken completely outside planning control. This permission can be withdrawn by the local planning authority in relation to specific areas or types of development (using a so-called 'Article 4 direction') but because this may require the payment of compensation, it is rarely used. Even if planning control did extend to agricultural operations such as the drainage of marshes, it would not on its own provide satisfactory protection. Since it is not a crime to breach planning control, and the local planning authority's remedies are limited to serving an enforcement notice requiring the breach to be remedied, the system creates little deterrent to undertaking works whose effects may be irreversible. Herein lies the necessity for the system of SSSI designations under the *Wildlife and Countryside Act 1981*, where, however, there is a compensation liability which makes the controls expensive to implement.

21.19 Determining planning applications

Planning control was initially conceived of as being concerned primarily with the principle, design and location of new development. In theory, regulation of pollution from that development is a matter for the separate systems of control examined in other components of this book. But in practice, the two systems overlap considerably: considerations of environmental protection and public safety must inevitably be taken into account in planning applications, and the planning system has the ability to improve environmental performance in such matters as urban densities and recycling of contaminated land. It can run parallel to, but not emulate, specific pollution controls. A draft PPG (*Planning and Pollution Control*, reproduced in the June 1992 *Monthly Bulletin of the Encyclopedia of Planning Law and Practice*) issued in 1992 by the Department of the Environment attempted to reconcile the conflict:

'1.23 The possibility that new development could cause pollution or generate waste is one aspect of the overall environmental effect of that development or the use of land. It may therefore be a material consideration to be taken into account in deciding whether to grant planning permission for it. Similar considerations may arise in deciding whether to take enforcement action against existing unauthorised development. Planning conditions can complement the pollution control regime, and thus help to secure the proper operation and rehabilitation of potentially polluting development'.

But the draft went on to stress that planning controls are not an appropriate means of regulating the detailed characteristics of industrial processes, and that planning authorities should not substitute their own judgement on pollution control issues for that of the bodies with the relevant expertise and the responsibility for statutory control over those matters. As a general rule, the dividing line should be drawn between matters affecting the protection of health and the environment, which are for specific pollution controls on the one hand, and the impact of development on the use of land and the appropriate use of land on the other; with facilities for consultation in cases of unavoidable overlap:

'1.26 . . . Where the potential for harm to man and the environment affects the use of land (e.g. by precluding the use of neighbouring land for a particular purpose or by making the use of that land inappropriate because of, say, the risk to an underlying aquifer), then planning and pollution controls may overlap. It is important to provide safeguards against loss of amenity which may be caused by pollution. The dividing line between planning and pollution control consideration is therefore not always clear-cut. In such cases close consultation between planning and pollution control authorities will be important at all stages, in particular because it would not be sensible to grant planning permission for a development for which a necessary pollution control authorisation is unlikely to be forthcoming'.

21.20 Environmental impact assessment

The extensive consultation system that is built in to development planning and development control provides an opportunity for reconciliation of the two primary control systems. The local planning authority are required to consult the National Rivers Authority and Her Majesty's Inspectorate of Pollution before determining specified categories of planning application, and in practice consult more widely than the minimum statutory requirements. Should they propose to disregard the advice they receive, the consultee may seek to persuade the Secretary of State to call in the application for his own determination; and if the authority refuse permission (or impose conditions) on the basis of advice received from the other agency, that agency must be prepared to support that advice if an appeal is made, if necessary by supplying a witness to give evidence at a public local inquiry.

These consultation regimes are formalised in cases requiring ENVIRONMENTAL ASSESSMENT (7), and this process looks likely to provide an important bridge for the future between planning and pollution control. Environmental assessment procedures were introduced in England and Wales in July 1988 to implement the *EC Council Directive 85/337/EEC* on the assessment of the effects of certain public and private projects on the environment. The process was not entirely new to Britain. Some developers, particularly in the energy sector, had already adopted a practice of preparing and submitting environmental impact statements as part of their application for planning permission for major new projects, finding that this helped to focus the environmental issues and arguments. But the *EC Directive* required a wider use of environmental assessment, and to a standard format. It was implemented through the normal town and country planning procedures, by a series of statutory instruments made under the *European Communities Act 1972*. This means that the initial implementation process has been closely tied to the *Directive's* requirements, because power under the *1972 Act* is strictly limited to what is required to give effect to an EC obligation. The main instrument has been the *Town and Country Planning (Assessment of Environmental Effects) Regulations 1988 No 1199* (hereafter '*the Regulations*'). Advice on *the Regulations*, and on the applicable criteria and thresholds, is contained in DoE Circular 15/88. The courts have held that the procedures do not extend to projects that were 'in the pipeline' when *the Regulations* were introduced, even if they had not been approved by then (*Lewin and Rowley v Secretary of State for the Environment and the Secretary of State for Transport* (*Court of Appeal, 11 January 1989*); *Twyford Parish Council v Secretary of State for the Environment and Secretary of State for Transport* (*High Court, 26 October 1990*)). That view was contested by the European Commission which in 1991 complained formally to the UK Government and proposed to institute proceedings in the European Court of Justice relating in particular to the M3 link at Twyford Down near Winchester. The complaint was later dropped following negotiations between the Commission and the UK Government.

21.21   The *Planning and Compensation Act 1991* introduced environmental assessment into the *Town and Country Planning Act 1990* so as to allow the Government to make regulations broadening the application of the regime. A consultation paper issued in July 1992 proposes the exercise of the power to extend assessment to a range of additional developments, including salmon farming; water treatment plants; wind generators; motorway and other service areas; coast protection works; golf courses and privately financed toll roads. Separate regulations were also made to deal with the special cases for which assessment is required by the *Directive*, but which in England and Wales are outside planning control, dealing with forestry, highways, land drainage, harbours, salmon farming and oil and gas lines. Many of the types of activity concerned fall within *Annex II* of the *Directive*, so that assessment is mandatory only where the characteristics of the particular proposal so require. But certain highway and harbour projects are within *Annex I*, where assessment is mandatory in all cases.

The principal regulations are those for planning, because most of the development for which environmental assessment is required by the *Directive* also requires planning permission. The type of development to which the assessment procedures apply is prescribed by *Schedules 1* and *2* to *the Regulations*, drawn in turn from *Annexes 1* and *2* to the *Directive*. In all cases falling within *Schedule 1*, except exempt development, the assessment procedure is mandatory; but in cases falling within *Schedule 2* it need be complied with only where the development would be likely to have significant effects on the environment by virtue of factors such as its nature, size or location. Indicative criteria and thresholds for identifying projects requiring environmental assessment are set out in Appendix A to DoE Circular 15/88, although the circular warns (paragraphs 18–21; 30–33) that no simple test is possible and that the criteria and thresholds are not definitive.

21.22   **The scope of the Regulations**

There is considerable discretion in determining which *Schedule 2* projects need to be subjected to environmental assessment, and a special procedure is established by *the Regulations* to allow a prospective developer to obtain a swift preliminary ruling (for which three weeks is allowed) from the local planning authority, with a right of appeal to the Secretary of State. (An environmental statement may be submitted by an applicant on a voluntary basis. If it is stated to be submitted for the purpose of *the Regulations*, the requirements of environmental assessment will apply to the application. [*Reg 4(4)(i)*]. But if it is not so stated, the requirements will have effect only if it is a *Schedule 1* application, or a *Schedule 2* application likely to have significant effects on the environment by virtue of factors such as its nature, size or location.) The appeal has been used in several instances to date, but early research has shown that the issue is in most cases resolved by negotiation between the parties, albeit with a wide range of interpretation between different planning authorities (Department of the Environment, *Monitoring Environmental Assessment and Planning* (HMSO, 1991)).

21.23   In *R v Swale Borough Council, ex parte the Royal Society for the Protection of Birds (Simon Brown J)* [*1991*] *1 PLR 6* the court concluded that the decision whether any particular proposal was or was not within the scheduled descriptions had to be decided on the application, rather than on the permission granted by the authority (which might be narrower in its terms, or made subject to conditions for the prevention of environmental damage); but the decision itself was a matter exclusively for the planning authority, subject only to challenge on the usual *Wednesbury* grounds for judicial review. The court also took the view that the question had to be considered strictly in relation to the development applied for, and not any development contemplated beyond that. However, the next question, whether it would be likely to have significant effects on the environment, should not be considered on the basis of the application in isolation if in reality it was properly to be regarded as part of an inevitably more substantial development.

21.24   In cases where assessment is required, no planning permission may be granted by a local planning authority, the Secretary of State or an inspector, unless they have first taken 'environmental information' into consideration. [*Reg 4(2)*]. First, the application for planning permission must be supported by the submission of an environmental statement; secondly, the statement must be published and subjected to consultation. Their responses and representations are also part of the environmental information. But, because the process is located in the planning system, the decision at the end is a planning decision, and is taken on broader considerations than purely environmental concerns.

21.25   The environmental statement

The requirements of assessment contained in the *EC Directive* relate to a process rather than a document. Thus the information submitted by the applicant is not itself the environmental impact assessment, but is a step in an evaluative procedure. An environmental statement comprises a document, or series of documents, which provides certain 'specified information' for the purpose of assessing the likely impact upon the environment of the development proposed to be carried out. The specified information is prescribed by *Schedule 3* to *the Regulations*, and includes a description of the development proposed, the data necessary to identify and assess its main environmental effects, a description of the likely significant effects and, where significant adverse effects are identified, a description of the measures envisaged to avoid, reduce or remedy them. There must also be a non-technical summary of the information, and the statement may contain other specified matters by way of explanation or amplification.

21.26   But *the Regulations* do not specify any standard form or format for environmental statements, and there is still widespread variation in practice. Although the strength of the process lies in raising environmental standards and encouraging developers to look at environmental impacts and alternatives from the earliest stages of project design, some statements seem to have been prepared only at a very late stage in the design of the project, when major commitments have already been made, and they contain minimal information or analysis. Others consist of nothing more than a series of apparently unrelated chapters dealing with different topics and prepared by different firms of consultants. A research study of the statements submitted in the first 18 months following the *1988 Regulations* showed that the majority were technically inadequate (Department of the Environment, *Monitoring Environmental Assessment and Planning* (HMSO, 1991)). Local planning authorities generally lack sufficient in-house expertise to evaluate submitted statements, and may be reluctant to commit funds to retain consultants to provide an independent assessment.

21.27   Availability of information

The Regulations impose a duty on the local planning authority and certain other public bodies in relation to certain types of development (including the Countryside

Commission, the Nature Conservancy Council for England (in Wales, the Country-side Council for Wales) and Her Majesty's Inspectorate of Pollution) to enter into consultation with a prospective applicant at his request to determine whether they have any information which may be relevant to the preparation of an environmental statement, and to make it available to him. [*Reg 22*].

21.28   Who decides?

All planning applications are made to the district council (or the borough, city, or London borough council) where the land is situated. They determine the great majority of applications themselves, but in the non-metropolitan areas, applications concerning minerals extraction or waste disposal are dispatched to the county council for decision. All applications are now required to be given some form of publicity by the local planning authority.

The local planning authority are required to take public objections into account when determining the application, though this is only one of the many factors they are required to consider. Decisions are usually made by elected councillors, sitting in a special development control sub-committee; although it is common to delegate decision-making on some relatively uncontroversial types of development to professional planning officers. Where it is for the councillors to decide, they will generally have a written report from the planning officers leading to a recommendation to grant or refuse; but the councillors are not obliged to take the recommended course.

21.29   The criteria

The legislation confers broad power. The authority must 'have regard to' the development plan (which for these purposes includes any statutory plan in force, including an old-style plan if it has not yet been superseded by a structure plan plus local plan, or by a unitary plan). They are also required to have regard to any other material considerations. And, under new *section 54A*, introduced in 1991, they are required to decide in accordance with the plan except where material considerations indicate otherwise. This measure, which is a reaction against the more laissez-faire days of the nineteen eighties when Ministers urged local authorities to abandon their out-of-date plans in favour of promoting economic growth, looks likely to underpin environmental protection objectives in planning decision-making.

21.30   (i) The role of the development plan

Two things flow from this formula. First, the development plan is only indicative, and not binding. The local planning authority may depart from it. There are some substantive and procedural preconditions, however. The substantive precondition depends upon what interpretation the courts will place on new *section 54A*. In the light of advice from the Secretary of State (PPG1, *General Policy and Principles* (1992)), which itself becomes a material consideration in determining applications, the correct approach appears to be that the old presumption in favour of development is to be regarded as overridden by the new section, leaving a presumption in favour of development that accords with the development plan, and a presumption against that which does not. Before a local planning authority can sanction a departure from the plan, they must now first advertise the application and, in certain cases, must also notify the Secretary of State (*Town and Country Planning (Development Plans) (England) Direction 1992*), with a view to his exercising his power to call in the application for his own decision. [*Town and Country Planning Act 1990, s 77*]. The courts have generally held that there is no error of law if the authority fail to comply with this requirement, and have pointed to the breadth of discretion exercisable by the authority in determining what is, and is not, a 'departure application'. But in one decision the court did set aside an authority's grant of planning permission to itself to build a superstore on land allocated in the development plan for a heliport: the planning officers could not reasonably have concluded that this was not a material departure from the plan (*R v Doncaster Metropolitan District Council, ex parte British Railways Board [1987] JPL 444*).

21.31 (ii) Other material considerations

Notwithstanding their legal and practical importance as formal policy commitments, development plans are nothing more than snapshots of an authority's land-use policies at the time they are prepared. It is impractical to expect them to provide a comprehensive answer to all development questions over the whole life of the plan, and discretion has therefore to be employed in applying the plan to each planning application. The scope of that discretion is reflected in the expression 'any other material considerations'. The legislation does not prescribe in any greater detail the considerations that may and may not be relied upon, and the courts have declined to provide any hard and fast definitions (although there has been a huge volume of case law on the point). They have however insisted that, to be material, a consideration must be material *in planning terms*. Although that allows us to discard considerations that can have no possible applicability to planning – such, for example, as whether the development will help or hinder the electoral chances of the authority's opposition party – it is too general a proposition to be of greater help and simply begs the question of what is the purpose of planning. It is clear that the planning process is not limited to the visual appearance of the built environment – so other material considerations cannot be restricted to considerations such as density, mass, layout and design. But beyond that, the linkages become difficult to define. It might not generally be a material consideration that the developer proposed to spend the profits from the development in a particular way, or was willing to promise to pay large cash sums to the local planning authority if permission were granted. Yet if the purpose of the transaction is to further some related planning aim, then it may well constitute a material consideration in determining the application. Thus in the *Covent Garden Opera House* case (*R v Westminster City Council, ex parte Monahan [1989] JPL 107; [1989] 1 PLR 36*) the Court of Appeal upheld the grant of planning permission by Westminster City Council for a proposal by the Opera House which included not only major improvements to the Opera House buildings, but also a major commercial development which was contrary to the local plan's policies for the area. The Opera House Trustees' objective in including the commercial development was to raise funds to apply to the Opera House improvements. The Court of Appeal held that this trade-off between the deleterious effects of allowing more commercial development in the area contrary to the plan, and the desire to retain and enhance the Opera House in the area, was a material consideration in determining the application.

An important source of material considerations is national policy. Policy advice is not, of course, law; and it is still relevant only where it is indeed 'material' to the development being considered. But where it is material, a local planning authority must have regard to it in determining applications. Thus Government advice on the relationship between planning and environmental protection is important, not only in setting the policy framework for local decision-making, but also for decisions made on appeal by the Secretary of State and his inspectors.

It is noteworthy therefore that the Department of the Environment's 1992 consultation paper on *Planning and Pollution Control* suggests that authorities should have regard to all the environmental consequences of a proposed development, including impacts on air, land and water, although they should balance these against potential benefits of the development. The advice also proposes a set of specific environmental considerations:

- the availability of land and sufficient quantities of water for potentially polluting development, as well as its proximity to other development;

- the character of the area, including any designations, or other nature conservation or archaeological interests;

- the design of the site, including for example access routes, and the visual impact of the development;

- the hours of operation required by the development;

- the potential for land contamination and measures of protection, restoration and aftercare;

- the impact of any discharge of effluent or leachates, which may pose a threat to surface or underground water supplies or to adjacent areas;

- the risk of toxic spillage, whether on site or on access roads;

- the possibility that nuisance might be caused, for example, by the release of smoke, fumes, gases, dust, steam, smell or noise, where not controlled under *Part I* of the *Environmental Protection Act 1990*;

- the waste generated by the development and proposed arrangements for storage, treatment and disposal;

- transport requirements arising from the need to transport polluting substances or waste;

- the potential for energy and materials recovery, including the recovery of gas from landfill sites.

If that list appears in formal advice given to local planning authorities, its effect will be to reinforce the powerful role of land-use planning in environmental protection.

21.32 Appeals and called in applications

Any planning application may be called in by the Secretary of State, at any time before it is determined by the local planning authority, for determination by him. This power to supplant the local authority's jurisdiction is sparingly used (in only around 200 cases per year, out of over 500,000 planning applications), and its primary function is to allow a full review of a major development proposal rather than merely to allow the local planning authority to grant planning permission in the normal way (against which third parties would have no right of appeal). If the local planning authority refuse planning permission, on the other hand, the applicant does have a right of appeal. There is also a right to appeal against any conditions imposed by the local planning authority. [*Town and Country Planning Act 1990, s 78*]. The Secretary of State and his inspectors operate on appeal within the same policy framework as the local planning authority.

21.33 Open space preservation

The planning controls outlined above are generally sufficient to preserve open spaces from development, and are the principal mechanism even in the national parks. Green belts are designated within the statutory plans (with the detailed control policies spelt out in local plans) around many of the major metropolitan areas, and especially restrictive criteria are applied in assessing planning applications within them. Planning permission will not be given, except in very special circumstances, for the construction of any new buildings or for the change of use of existing buildings for purposes other than agriculture, sport, cemeteries, institutions standing in their own grounds or other uses appropriate to a rural area. Nor will existing towns and settlements be allowed to expand, apart from a limited amount of infill development or rounding off within boundaries defined in the development plans. Local authorities are enjoined to make every effort to prevent any further industrial or commercial development in green belts, even within existing settlements, because of the additional demands that would be created for labour and hence for the allocation of further land for housing.

21.34 Agricultural land preservation

Preservation of agricultural land is a factor taken into account in the preparation of development plans and there is provision for special intervention by the Ministry of Agriculture, Fisheries and Food if their objection to the loss of agricultural land is not accepted by the local authority concerned.

The extent to which planning controls ought to be used to protect agricultural land is currently extremely controversial, because of the extent of agricultural over-production. Throughout the post-war years, and particularly since Britain's entry to the European Community in 1973, agriculture has been a favoured and heavily subsidised industry. It has been clear and constant government policy that high class agricultural land should not be lost to urban development where land of a lower quality is available, and that the amount of land taken should be no greater than is reasonably required for carrying out the development in accordance with proper planning standards. The Ministry of Agriculture has had to be consulted on planning applications for development of agricultural land involving the loss of ten or more acres, or where the direct loss would be less than that, but where further loss might follow the development.

But in 1987, the Government announced a switch in this policy. Because of the substantial surpluses of agricultural produce in western countries, there was a need to review agricultural production and to diversify rural economies. The new policy on development involving agricultural land therefore relegates agricultural land quality considerations by making them no longer pre-eminent, but matters simply to be considered alongside environmental and economic considerations. Fresh government advice to local planning authorities in their evaluation of planning applications involving non-agricultural development on agricultural land insists that:

'The agricultural quality of the land and the need to control the rate at which land is taken for development are among the factors to be included in that assessment, together with the need to facilitate development and economic activity that provides jobs, and the continuing need to protect the countryside for its own sake rather than primarily for the productive value of the land'. (DoE Circular 16/87 now superseded by PPG 7.)

The consultation requirements were also reduced, allowing less direct influence by the Ministry of Agriculture over planning decisions relating to agricultural land, and enhancing the environmental quality of land as a material consideration.

21.35 Planning agreements and planning obligations

For many years local planning authorities have made use of planning agreements to supplement their development control powers. These agreements are given statutory effect by *section 106* of the *Town and Country Planning Act 1990* (formerly *section 52* of the *Town and Country Planning Act 1971*), so as to become enforceable not only against the developer who signs them but also against all subsequent owners of the land. It has therefore been possible for the local planning authority to obtain an enforceable promise by a developer to do things which could not be secured solely by planning conditions, such as to cede land to the authority for particular purposes (for building highways, schools or community facilities; or to preserve an area as open space or as a local nature reserve) and/or to provide funding for those purposes. Because agreements reflect a negotiated style of control, they have provided a basis for so-called 'planning gains'. This is generally a trade-off arrangement, under which the local planning authority are willing to grant planning permission for a project which is not ideal in planning terms (perhaps as a departure from established policy for the area) because the planning agreement secures some counter-balancing planning gain. Such gains may take the form of facilities provided by the developer to serve the needs of people attracted to the area by the development, or even (although this is frowned upon by Government advice) to meet existing shortfalls in public facilities. Some authorities are also looking to developers to provide environmental gains, not only by improving the quality of their development proposals so as to minimise emissions and environmental losses, but also to provide collateral facilities.

Under the *Planning and Compensation Act 1991*, planning agreements were superseded by 'planning obligations' which may be entered into by developers not only in the form of agreements with the local planning authority, but also unilaterally. The Government's objective was to overcome the impasse that sometimes occurs when a planning inspector is minded to grant planning permission on appeal, but cannot do so unless the local planning authority is willing to execute an agreement to overcome some legitimate planning objection to development proceeding. Under the new provisions, a developer will be able to offer an enforceable unilateral undertaking, thus by-passing an obstructive local planning authority. However, the reforms go wider than this, because they involve a redrafting of the powers, making it clear that an obligation may contain provisions:

'(a) restricting the development or use of the land in any specified way;

(b) requiring specified operations or activities to be carried out in, on under or over the land;

(c) requiring the land to be used in any specified way; or

(d) requiring a sum or sums to be paid to the authority on a specified date or dates or periodically'.

This reformulation resolves doubts about the true scope of the existing provisions, and may encourage authorities and developers to make greater use of the powers. From a developer's point of view, the new provisions have the advantage of providing a 'review window'. Although the Secretary of State is not a party to an obligation, and has in the past had no role in relation to their execution or variation (which has, of course, made them particularly attractive to local planning authorities as an instrument of planning control), there is now to be a right for a developer to apply to the local planning authority for an obligation to be modified or discharged and, if aggrieved by their decision, to appeal to the Secretary of State.

There is a role for local planning authorities to secure environmental gains through negotiated agreements made under these powers, particularly for habitat protection and the provision of open space. A wider role in this respect is suggested by the 1990 Environment White Paper, which promises that the new legislation on planning obligations, reinforced by explicit policy guidance from the Secretary of State, will 'make it easier for local authorities and developers to provide for the interests of nature conservation and of the environment more generally when preparing development proposals' (*This Common Inheritance*, paragraph 6.42). This approach is reinforced by policy advice issued on the new system, in which the Department of the Environment 'welcomes the initiatives taken by some developers in creating nature reserves, planting trees, establishing wildlife ponds and providing other nature conservation benefits' [DoE Circular 16/91, *Planning Obligations*, paragraph B8]. Similarly, local authorities and developers are encouraged to consider the use of agreements covering the excavation of archaeological sites, and the recording and publication of the results. The advantage of agreements in these cases is that 'they are likely to provide more flexibility and be of greater mutual benefit to all the parties than could be provided for by alternative statutory means' (PPG16, *Archaeology and Planning* (1990), paragraph 26).

21.36 Contaminated land

The preventative strength of the planning system is well illustrated above, but it is in practice only as strong as its information base. In the case of contaminated land, this has regularly proved inadequate. Ideally, planning control should have regard to the fact of contamination, and should prevent development occurring upon land whose condition is potentially a danger to health or human safety. But, as the House of Commons Environment Committee's Report on *Contaminated Land* showed, there have been numerous cases where local planning authorities have granted permission, sometimes for residential development, on closed landfills and other contaminated land of whose condition they had no knowledge (indeed, it seems that in some cases planning permission has been granted even where the authority did have knowledge of contamination).

The Secretary of State has advised local planning authorities that:

'Contamination, or the potential for it, is a material planning consideration which needs to be taken into account at various stages of the planning process including the preparation of development plans and the determination of planning applications. The best way of minimising any associated risks is to ensure that areas of potentially contaminated sites are identified at the earliest stage of planning'. [DoE Circular 21/87, *Contaminated Land*, paragraph 5]

The same advice goes on to suggest that when planning permission is applied for in respect of a site which is known or strongly suspected to be contaminated to an extent which would adversely effect the proposed development, an investigation by the developer to identify any remedial measures necessary to deal with hazards would normally be required before the local planning authority can determine the application [DoE Circular 21/87 *Contaminated Land*, Annex, paragraph 13]. Where there is only a suspicion of contamination, or it seems that the degree of contamination is only slight, authorities are advised to attach conditions to any grant of planning permission, to make it clear that development should not start until a site investigation and assessment has been carried out and that the development will need to incorporate all the measures shown by it to be necessary [DoE Circular 21/87 *Contaminated Land*, Annex, paragraph 13].

The system of registers of contaminated land originally to be established under the *Environmental Protection Act 1990, s 143*, and local authorities' duties of inspection of closed landfills and other potentially polluting sites under *section 61* of that Act, have been consigned by the government to a wide-ranging review of contamination and the powers of public bodies in respect to it.

But the planning system also has a central part in securing the clean-up of contaminated land. In the absence of adequate public funds for clean-up, or effective and enforceable private liability rules, the only method of financing it is by providing the financial incentive of a sufficiently profitable after-use. Enterprise zones and (more effectively) urban development corporations have provided an indication of how selective public sector support can underwrite the economic regeneration of an area sufficient to warrant private investors undertaking clean-up costs to render land suitable for redevelopment.

21.37 Tree preservation orders

The protection of trees has been a major environmental achievement of the planning system and deserves a brief mention in this chapter. It works by, first, imposing a special duty on local planning authorities under the *Town and Country Planning Act 1990, s 197*, to ensure that when granting planning permission they make adequate provision for preserving and protecting trees by imposing conditions; and, secondly, by a special power to make tree preservation orders under which additional protection is conferred on specifically identified trees or woodlands. A tree preservation order may be made and confirmed by a local planning authority, in accordance with a Model Order prescribed by regulations. [*The Town and Country Planning (Tree Preservation) Regulations 1969 (SI 1969, No 17)*]. Once it is in force it becomes an offence to breach its prohibition of topping, lopping or felling the specified trees without consent. In conservation areas there is a form of modified tree preservation control, based on a prior notification system. There is a general prohibition [*Town and Country Planning Act 1990, s 211*] against lopping, topping or felling of any tree in a conservation area (though some exceptions are prescribed by regulations [*Town and Country Planning (Tree Preservation Orders) (Amendment); (Trees in Conservation Areas) (Excepted Cases) Regulations 1975 (SI 1975, No 148)*]); but it is a defence to show that prior notice was given to the local planning authority. [*Town and Country Planning Act 1990, s 211(3)*].

The additional control imposed by tree preservation requirements is normally exercised without liability to pay compensation, but compensation may be prescribed by the *Order* itself [*section 203*], and may also be claimed, in certain limited cases, in respect of replanting requirements [*section 204*].

The controls over trees were comprehensively reviewed in a report published by the Department of the Environment in 1990, which recommended the introduction of further controls over hedgerows (though coupled to a compensation entitlement to secure proper management), the transfer of woodlands responsibility to the Forestry Commission in place of the existing overlapping system and the clarification of various legal points.

21.38 Conclusions

The British planning system has particular strengths as an instrument of environmental protection which do not exist in the more straightforward zoning systems of planning that are common elsewhere. It follows that its role must grow in the coming years if the Government's current objectives for environmental protection are to be realised; and that the role of local government in preparing environmentally oriented development plans, and in appraising proposals for development, must also grow. Questions must remain, however, about the financial and technical resources available to local authorities to carry out these tasks, about the demarcation between planning and other complex environmental control systems.

Appendix 21A

POLICY GUIDANCE NOTES

Planning policy guidance notes

PPG1	General Policy and Principles (1992)
PPG2	Green Belts (1988)
PPG3	Housing (1992)
PPG3	(Wales) Land for Housing in Wales (1992)
PPG4	Industrial and Commercial Development and Small Firms (1992)
PPG5	Simplified Planning Zones (1992)
PPG6	Major Retail Development (1988)
PPG7	The Countryside and the Rural Economy (1992)
PPG8	Telecommunications (1988)
PPG9	Regional Guidance for the South East (1989)
PPG10	Strategic Guidance for the West Midlands (1988)
PPG11	Strategic Guidance for Merseyside (1988)
PPG12	Development Plans and Regional Planning Guidance (1992)
PPG12	(Wales) Development Plans in Wales (1992)
PPG13	Highways Considerations in Development Control (1989)
PPG14	Development on Unstable Land (1990)
PPG15	[Cancelled]
PPG16	Archaeology and Planning (1990)
PPG17	Sport and Recreation (1991)
PPG18	Enforcing Planning Control (1992)
PPG19	Outdoor Advertisement Control (1992)
PPG20	Coastal Planning (1992)
PPG21	Tourism (1992)
PPG22	Renewable Energy

Mineral policy guidance notes

MPG1	General Considerations and the Development Plan System (1988)
MPG2	Applications, Permissions and Conditions (1988)
MPG3	Opencast Coal Mining (1988)
MPG4	The Review of Mineral Working Sites (1988)
MPG5	Minerals Planning and the General Development Order (1988)
MPG6	Guidelines for Aggregates Provision in England and Wales (1989)
MPG7	The Reclamation of Mineral Workings (1989)
MPG8	Planning and Compensation Act 1991: Interim Development Order Permissions (IDOs) – Statutory Provisions and Procedures (1992)
MPG9	Planning and Compensation Act 1991: Interim Development Order Permissions (IDOs) – Conditions (1992)
MPG10	Provision of Raw Material for the Cement Industry (1992)

Regional policy guidance notes

RPG1	Strategic Guidance for Tyne and Wear (1989)
RPG2	Strategic Guidance for West Yorkshire (1989)
RPG3	Strategic Guidance for London (1989)
RPG4	Strategic Guidance for Greater Manchester (1989)
RPG5	Strategic Guidance for South Yorkshire (1989)

The Government is presently proposing also to issue PPGs on heritage, wildlife and planning and on planning, pollution control and waste management.

Appendix 21B

CURRENT DEPARTMENTAL CIRCULARS RELEVANT TO ENVIRONMENTAL PROTECTION THROUGH PLANNING

DoE Circular 36/78	Trees and Forestry
DoE Circular 32/81	Wildlife and Countryside Act 1981
DoE Circular 2/85	Planning Control over Oil and Gas Operations
DoE Circular 8/87	Historic Buildings and Conservation Areas: Policy and Procedures
DoE Circular 21/87	Development of Contaminated Land
DoE Circular 27/87	Nature Conservation
DoE Circular 15/88	Town and Country Planning (Assessment of Environmental Effects) Regulations
DoE Circular 24/88	Assessment of Environmental Effects in Simplified Planning Zones and Enterprise Zones
DoE Circular 17/89	Landfill Sites. Development Control
DoE Circular 20/89	Water Act 1989
DoE Circular 14/90	Electricity Generating Stations and Overhead Lines
DoE Circular 16/91	Planning Obligations
DoE Circular 17/91	Water Industry Investment: Planning Considerations
DoE Circular 1/92	Planning Controls over SSSIs
DoE Circular 11/92	Planning Controls for Hazardous Substances

Appendix 21C

THE POLICY HIERARCHY IN PLANNING

National planning

Secretary of State:
> departmental circulars
> planning policy guidance notes
> mineral policy guidance notes
> parliamentary answers, speeches, announcements, appeal decisions, consultation papers

Regional planning

Secretary of State
> strategic policy guidance
> regional policy guidance notes

Structure plans/unitary development plans

Outside metropolitan areas:

> County planning authority prepares and (since 1992) approves structure plan amendments

Within London and metropolitan areas:

> London borough/metropolitan district prepares unitary development plan (effectively both a structure plan and a local plan)

Local plans

Outside metropolitan areas:

> Local planning authority (usually district council) prepares and adopts local plan (unless called-in by the Secretary of State). In London and metropolitan areas, Part 2 of the unitary development plan fulfils the same function. County planning authority prepares minerals plan and (except in Wales) waste plan.

Non-statutory plans

Category includes:

- development plans in course of preparation/adoption
- plans which are not intended to be processed through the statutory procedures
- policies on issues of detail, development briefs for particular sites etc.

Appendix 21 D

Further reading

This Common Inheritance. Britain's Environmental Strategy Cm 1200 (1990): the Government's White Paper, which contains a chapter on land-use.

Cullingworth, JB, *Town and Country Planning in Britain*, 10th ed, (George Allen and Unwin 1988): provides an overview of the operation of the planning system as a whole, but contains no legal analysis.

Grant, Malcolm (Ed), *Encyclopedia of Planning Law and Practice* (6 vols looseleaf; Sweet & Maxwell): a comprehensive guide to the subject, containing all the primary and secondary legislation (with detailed commentary) plus Government circulars.

Grant, Malcolm, *Urban Planning Law* (1982, with 1990 updating supplement): detailed text.

Heap, Sir Desmond, *An Outline of Planning Law* (Sweet & Maxwell, 1991): provides a valuable overview of the subject.

Wood, Christopher, *Planning Pollution Prevention* (Heinemann, 1989): valuable study of the relationship between planning control and controls over pollution in the UK and US.

22 Power

22.1 INTRODUCTION

The need for energy, the form it takes and the methods by which it is produced raise key environmental issues, and the way they are resolved will have a dramatic effect on the power industry. Should we be using less energy? Should we be building gas-fired, not coal-fired, power stations? Should coal-fired power stations be cleaner? Should non-fossil power stations be developed, and if so where? Should nuclear power be developed or reduced?

One of the most significant factors for the last decade or so has been the appreciation of the damaging effects of using fossil fuels, notably the emission of 'greenhouse' gases and those associated with 'acid rain'. This has encouraged the development of cleaner, more efficient production and generation processes, as well as the development of non-fossil fuel resources. Even so, about 85 per cent of the country's total energy needs are met by fossil fuels.

Another major change over the last decade is the increasing amount of EC environmental legislation. Much of this has had a direct impact on the power industry. This is set to continue under the Fifth Action Programme, 'Towards Sustainability', which was adopted on 3 December 1992 in *Resolution 92/C 331/03* on industrial competitiveness and environmental protection. It focuses on establishing sustainable energy resources and greater energy efficiency over the next seven years.

These changes to the industry brought about by environmental protection are in themselves far-reaching; they have however been further complicated by the privatisation of the electricity industry in 1990. At a policy level the philosophies behind environmental protection and privatisation often appear contradictory, one essentially interventionist and the other part of a strategy for the development of a free market. It is, for example, far from clear how to combine a desire to increase profits by maximising sales with the need to conserve energy, or why a private company should concern itself with the national long-term energy needs.

Nevertheless privatisation of the power industry has in some respects allowed control to be exercised in new ways, for instance the licensing procedure for companies is an area where environmental issues can be considered, and at certain points, e.g. energy efficiency in terms of maximum returns from resources, both the philosophies are served.

Quite how the combination of these two philosophies works in practice will emerge over the next few years. In as politically sensitive an industry as this the nature of the legislation will also depend on the aims of the party in power. What is likely is that the environmental legislation for the power industry that has been enacted over the past few years will be developed and refined, and the role of the regulatory bodies will become more clearly defined in response to the demands of the industry, a better understanding of the environment and the aims of both Westminster and Brussels.

This chapter provides a comprehensive overview of the electricity industry, rather than attempting to cover all the environmental aspects of energy law. Other environmental aspects of the coal, oil and gas industry, such as mining, onshore and offshore oil and gas production and supply have not been covered. The chapter is therefore divided into six main sections: an overview of the regulatory framework for the electricity industry under the *Electricity Act 1989*, i.e. the post-privatisation structure; the regulations for the construction of power stations; the regulations for their operation; the regulation of supply and transmission; the particular issues associated with renewable resources; efficiency and conservation.

22.2 ELECTRICITY: THE PRIVATISED INDUSTRY

The electricity industry is regulated by the *Electricity Act 1989*, as amended by subsequent legislation. This Act lays down the regulatory framework for the electricity market after the privatisation of the industry in 1990.

The *Electricity Act 1989* imposes duties on, and gives powers to, the Secretary of State (following the abolition of the Department of Energy, those powers are exercisable by the President of the Board of Trade) who, in this respect, has three general functions under *section 3*:

(i) to secure that demand is met,

(ii) to secure that the supplies are properly financed, and

(iii) to promote competition.

He may appoint a Director General of Electricity Supply in order to carry out these functions.

[*Electricity Act 1989, s 1*].

Under *section 4*, a licence is required by a person who:

(i) generates electricity for the purpose of giving a supply to any premises or enabling a supply to be so given;

(ii) transmits electricity for that purpose; or

(iii) supplies electricity to any premises.

It is an offence to carry out these activities without a licence. National Power, PowerGen and Nuclear Electric, the former constituents of the Central Electricity Generating Board, are the largest generators; the National Grid Company, also formerly part of the CEGB, is the largest transmitter; the twelve regional electricity companies are the principal suppliers. There are, however, certain exemptions from the licensing requirements set out in the *Electricity (Class Exemptions from the Requirement for a Licence) Order 1990 (SI 1990 No 193)*, covering on-site generating stations, those with a capacity of less than 10MW for public supply and suppliers to the electricity pool.

A public electricity supplier is under a duty to develop and maintain an efficient, co-ordinated and economical system of electricity supply. [*Electricity Act 1989, s 9(1)*].

The holder of a licence to transmit electricity is under a duty to develop and maintain an efficient, co-ordinated and economical system of electricity transmission, and to facilitate competition in the supply and generation of electricity. [*Electricity Act 1989, s 9(2)*].

22.3 CONSTRUCTION OF POWER STATIONS

Section 36 consent

Section 36 of the *Electricity Act 1989* provides that, with some exceptions, no generating station can be constructed, extended or operated except in accordance with a consent granted by the Secretary of State.

The *section 36* consent is, however, not the same as planning permission, although planning permission may be, and usually is, deemed to be granted under *section 90*, the *Town and Country Planning Act 1990*, when a *section 36* consent is issued.

Section 36 consent is not needed for (*a*) a generating station whose capacity does not exceed 50MW, or (*b*) a generating station to be constructed or extended, whose capacity will not exceed 50MW [*section 36(2)*]; the Secretary of State has the right to vary the permitted capacity, and set a higher or lower figure. Consents may be subject to such conditions as he thinks appropriate, and continue in force for such period as may be specified in or determined by or under the consent [*section 36(5)*]. Under *section 36(4)* he can order that *section 36(1)* will not apply to generating stations of a particular class or description, either generally or for such purposes as may be specified in the order.

Environmental issues are taken into consideration in this process by the Secretary of State in deciding whether to grant consent, and if so on what terms, under the provisions of *Schedule 9*. These provide that in making an application for consent to construct or extend a generating station of not less than 10MW (or to modify its operation), or for consent under *section 37* for power lines, or for any other prescribed works, the licence holder must:

(*a*)   have regard to the desirability of preserving the natural beauty of the country-side, of conserving flora, fauna and geological or physiographical features of special interest and of protecting sites, buildings and objects of architectural, historic or archeological interest; and

(*b*)   do what he can to mitigate the effect that his proposals would have on the natural beauty of the countryside, and the flora, fauna, features, sites, buildings or objects.

Within twelve months of being granted a licence, the licence holder must prepare a statement setting out how he proposes to fulfil his obligations in this respect, and before preparing this statement he must consult with the Countryside Commission, the Nature Conservancy Council, and, if appropriate, the Historic Buildings and Monuments Commission for England or the Historic Buildings Council for Wales.

Schedule 8 to the *Electricity Act* sets out the consent procedure, both for *section 36* consent and consents under *section 37* for installing power lines. An application must be in writing, describe the land concerned by reference to a map and be accompanied by a fee, the amount of which depends on the type of power station, but ranges from £5,000 to £40,000 under the *Electricity (Applications for Consent) Regulations 1990 (SI 1990 No 455)*. The Secretary of State can direct that further information be provided. The applicant must also serve notice of the application on the relevant planning authority. If the planning authority objects, the Secretary of State can grant the consent subject to such conditions as take the objections into account. If this is impossible, then a public inquiry must be held. The Secretary of State may also prescribe any other form of notice to be made, so that other persons may object. If they do object, the Secretary of State will consider their objections; he is not under an obligation to hold a public inquiry.

22.4   Environmental assessment

For large power stations, environmental concerns must be dealt with more formally.

If the power station will have an output of 300MWth or more, or is a nuclear power station, then *section 36* consent cannot be given unless the application is supported by an environmental statement, as set out in the *Electricity and Pipe-Line Works (Assessment*

22.5 Power

of Environmental Effects) Regulations 1990 (SI 1990 No 442), which implements *Council Directive 85/337/EEC*. For any other power station, the Secretary of State will determine whether an environmental statement is necessary. These *Regulations* also apply to power lines of over 275KV and the construction or diversion of cross-country pipe-lines which may be associated with the proposed power station. The environmental impact assessment must cover:

(*a*) a description of the site and proposed development;

(*b*) the data necessary to assess its likely environmental effects;

(*c*) a description of likely effects on human beings, flora, fauna, soil, water, air, climate, the landscape, the interaction between any of the above, material assets, the cultural heritage;

(*d*) a description of measures to avoid, reduce or remedy any effects;

(*e*) and finally, a non-technical summary of the statement.

The *Regulations* go on to state the sort of issues which could be included by way of explanation or amplification of the information in the statement. These are:

(i) the physical characteristics of the proposed development, and the land-use requirements during the construction and operational phases;

(ii) the main characteristics of the production process used;

(iii) the type and amount of any residues and emissions (including water, air and soil pollutants, and noise, vibrations, light, heat and radiation);

(iv) any alternative proposals;

(v) the likely significant direct and indirect effects on the environment of the development that may result from either the use of natural resources or the emission of pollutants, creation of nuisances or elimination of waste, with a description of the forecasting techniques;

(vi) any difficulties, especially technical deficiencies and lack of know-how.

Again, a non-technical summary must be provided.

22.5 Other consents

The power station will also require consent under the *Town and Country Planning Act 1990* (see PLANNING AND THE ENVIRONMENT (21)) if planning permission is not deemed to have been given when *section 36* consent is granted. As with other planning applications affecting historical, architectural or natural features, consent may also be required under the *Planning (Listed Buildings and Conservation Areas) Act 1990*, the *Ancient Monuments and Archeological Areas Act 1979* and the *Wildlife and Countryside Act 1981*.

In addition to the application to construct and the licence to supply, if the power station is fuelled by crude liquid petroleum, any petroleum product or natural gas, or is to be converted for such use, then a proposal must be made to the Secretary of State, who can refuse, or put conditions on, the proposal, under the *Energy Act 1976, s 14*.

Any storage of hazardous substances will require Hazardous Substances consent under the *Planning (Hazardous Substances) Act 1990*, but this may be deemed to be granted when *section 36* consent is issued.

Consent will be needed for any cross-country pipelines under the *Pipe-lines Act 1962, s 1*, and an environmental statement must be prepared, as described above, for that aspect of the scheme. Cross-country pipelines are those that exceed ten miles. For any other pipeline, notice must be given to the Secretary of State. He must consult with the Health and Safety Executive if the pipeline is for hazardous substances, e.g. oil or gas, to ensure that the *Control of Industrial Major Accident Regulations 1984 (SI 1984 No 1902)*, and *Notification of Installations Handling Hazardous Substances Regulations 1982 (SI 1982 No 1357)*, are complied with.

In any proposal for consent under the *Pipe-lines Act 1962, ss 1, 2*, the person applying, and the Secretary of State in considering the proposals, must have regard, under *section 43*, to a similar set of criteria as those under *Schedule 9* to the *Electricity Act* (see 22.3 above), i.e. the desirability of preserving the natural beauty of the countryside, of conserving flora, fauna etc. Under *section 44* the Secretary of State must have constant regard to the need for preventing water pollution in relation to the exercise of his powers. Finally, under *section 45*, a person executing pipeline works in agricultural land is obliged to ensure that the land is restored to the same fitness for use as it had before the works were begun.

22.6   Nuclear power

For nuclear power, see RADIOACTIVE SUBSTANCES (25). A nuclear site licence will be required under the *Nuclear Installations Act 1965, s 1* for the installation or operation of a nuclear reactor or any other installation for the production of nuclear energy, or for preparatory processes, or for the storage of nuclear fuel. These are issued by the Health and Safety Executive, acting through the Nuclear Installations Inspectorate. This licence can only be granted to a body corporate and is not transferable. [*Nuclear Installations Act 1965, s 3*]. It can be subject to conditions, and may be revoked or surrendered at any time.

On an application, the Health and Safety Executive has the power to direct that the applicant should serve notice of the application on the local authority and the National Rivers Authority; this however will not be necessary if a *section 36* consent is required since they will have to be informed in any event.

22.7   Water

The construction of a power station will inevitably involve disruption to and alteration of the water supply and drainage system in the area. This will require authorisation.

The most important authorisations are firstly the licence to obstruct or abstract water and to discharge effluent into controlled waters, granted by the NRA, and set out in *sections 24* and *85* of the *Water Resources Act 1991*.

Secondly, consent is required from the sewage undertaker to discharge trade effluent into a public sewer, under the *Water Industry Act 1991, s 118*.

Thirdly, consent from the NRA or, if appropriate, the internal drainage board, is required for any obstruction to a watercourse, under the *Land Drainage Act 1991, s 23*.

22.8   Offshore and coastal power stations

Various licences and consents are required for offshore or coastal power stations.

Power stations in an offshore installation, e.g. an oil rig, that simply provide power to the installation are exempt from *section 36* of the *Electricity Act*, under the *Offshore Generating Stations (Exemption) Order 1990 (SI 1990 No 443)*.

Under the *Coast Protection Act 1949, s 34* consent is required from the Secretary of State for the Environment to construct, alter or improve works, or to deposit materials,

22.9 Power

on the seashore below the high water mark so as to cause a danger to navigation. Under *section 18*, the excavation or removal of materials from the seashore is prohibited.

Under the *Harbours Act 1964, s 16* an empowerment order from the Secretary of State for Transport is required to carry out works improving a harbour.

Under the *Food and Environmental Protection Act 1985, s 5* a licence is required to deposit substances or articles within UK waters, either in the sea or on the sea bed from any vehicle, vessel, aircraft etc., from a container floating at sea, or from a structure on land constructed or adapted for the purpose of depositing solids at sea. It is also required for such deposits *anywhere* at sea by British vessels, aircraft, containers etc. It is granted by the Secretary of State for Agriculture, Fisheries and Food.

Under the *Petroleum and Submarine Pipe-lines Act 1975, s 20* authorisation for pipe-lines in territorial waters must be obtained from the Secretary of State.

22.9 OPERATION OF POWER STATIONS

The principal control on the environmental impacts of operating a power station, apart from the continuing effect of any conditions that may have been imposed under *section 36* when consent for its construction was granted, are those contained in *Part I* of the *Environmental Protection Act 1990*. For power stations with a net rated output of 50MWth or more an authorisation under the system of INTEGRATED POLLUTION CONTROL (16), is required. The general requirements under this are summarised in the *Industry Guidance Note IPR1*, for the Fuel and Power Industry, issued by HMIP. For smaller stations with a capacity between 20 and 50MWth, authorisation from the local authority is needed. The major exception to this is for power stations fuelled by waste materials (see 22.12 below).

22.10 'Acid rain'

The most important substances implicated in the problem of 'acid rain' are sulphur dioxide and oxides of nitrogen, emitted when fossil fuels are burned. In 1988 the EC adopted *Directive 88/609/EEC*, which specifically concerns the limitation of emissions of certain pollutants into the air from large combustion plants, i.e. those over 50MWth, and is specifically aimed at combatting acid rain. The *Directive* is generally known as the *Large Combustion Plants Directive*. It requires that sulphur dioxide emissions from each Member State's existing large commission plants in aggregate be reduced from their 1980 levels in three stages: by 25 per cent by 1993, by 43 per cent by 1998 and by 60 per cent by 2003. Emissions of oxides of nitrogen are to be reduced in two stages: by 20 per cent by 1993 and by 36 per cent by 1998. Existing plants are those whose original construction licence was granted before 1 July 1987. The requirements for *new* power stations (i.e. those whose construction licence was granted on or after 1 July 1987) are dealt with on an individual plant basis. They must be designed such that their emissions do not exceed the limits set out in the *Directive*.

With respect to 'existing' plants, the *Large Combustion Plants Directive* has been introduced into the UK by means of a 'National Plan'. This National Plan sets emission limits of sulphur dioxide and oxides of nitrogen for the fossil fuel generating companies until 2003.

In order to retain operational flexibility, each power station of the two main generating companies is allocated its own emission limit (the sum of all the emission limits for the power stations being the limit set in the National Plan for that company). There is a degree of freedom granted to enable generation to be switched between a company's plants, provided that the overall company emission 'bubble' is not exceeded.

If a power station reaches 95 per cent of its limit, the company is required to inform HMIP; if it reaches the limit HMIP must be informed again. The power station can only continue generating if the company has applied for an extra quota, which will be balanced by a corresponding reduction in the quotas for the company's other power stations.

In the future and as the the techniques for monitoring emissions develop, the limit for each power station may be set with reference to the 'critical load' for the area in which it is located, i.e. the level of pollutant that the area is deemed to be able to tolerate. The limit will therefore depend on what the critical load is for the relevant area, and how much of the pollutant is already produced by other polluters.

22.11 'Global warming'

Fossil fuel power stations are likely to give off two greenhouse gases, carbon dioxide and nitrous oxide. Indeed, the Government White Paper, *This Common Inheritance*, Cm 1200, published in 1990, identifies power stations as the single largest source of carbon dioxide (p 68). Oxides of nitrogen are discussed above. Carbon dioxide emissions are not directly controlled; although oxides of carbon are listed as prescribed substances for IPC, only carbon monoxide emissions are limited. *This Common Inheritance* states that the *Electricity Act 1989* is likely to encourage the reduction in carbon dioxide from power stations because of the incentives for greater energy efficiency and the encouragement of non-fossil fuels. Another major greenhouse gas, methane, is discussed at 22.12 in relation to waste gas.

For the future, it is possible that a combined energy and carbon tax will be introduced. A draft proposal is currently being considered by the European Commission but the UK Government has recently signalled its opposition to the measure.

22.12 TRANSMISSION AND SUPPLY OF ELECTRICITY

Power lines cannot be installed or kept installed above ground unless consent has been granted by the Secretary of State, under the *Electricity Act 1989, s 37*. This however does not apply to an electrical line with a nominal voltage not over 20KV and to be used by a single consumer, nor in relation to a line which is or will be within premises in the occupation or control of the person responsible for its installation, or in other cases which may be prescribed. Consent under this section can be subject to conditions, and can be varied or revoked at any time. Contravention is an offence. Certain minor exemptions, e.g. temporary diversions, are set out in the *Overhead Lines (Exemption) Regulations 1990 (SI 1990 No 2035)*.

The procedure for obtaining consent is set out in *Schedule 8* to the *Electricity Act 1989*, and is broadly similar to that for *section 36* (see 22.8 above).

Just as major power stations require environmental assessments, so high voltage power lines require them too. Requirements for environmental assessments are set out in the *Electricity and Pipe-Line Works (Assessment of Environmental Effects) Regulations 1990 (SI 1990 No 442)*, and are described at 22.4 above, in relation to *section 36* consents. The National Grid Company plc has undertaken to produce an environmental statement for overhead power lines along new routes with a nominal voltage of at least 275KV. (Transmission is usually at either 400KV or 275KV.) The Secretary of State is unlikely to require an environmental statement if the nominal voltage is less than 132KV, or if the power line is less than 1 km long, although each case will be assessed individually, bearing in mind the nature of the land over which the power lines will pass.

22.13   RENEWABLE RESOURCES

At a European level the increased use of 'renewable' sources of energy is being advocated strongly, especially in the recent Fifth Action Programme, 'Towards Sustainability', which focuses on the sustainable management of national resources and a reduction in the consumption of non-renewable energy, and the 'Alterner' proposal advocating alternative resources, both introduced in 1992.

Renewable resources include solar power, wind power, tidal energy, geothermal energy and hydroelectricity. Waste incineration as a source of power is also sometimes classed as 'renewable'.

The development of renewable energy has been encouraged in various orders under the *Electricity Act 1989, ss 32, 33*. The Secretary of State may require each public electricity supplier to use a certain amount of electricity from non-fossil fuel generating stations, the 'Non-Fossil Fuel Obligation'. [*Electricity Act 1989, s 32*].

The first order was for nuclear power, the *Electricity (Non-Fossil Fuel Sources) (England and Wales) Order 1990 (SI 1990 No 263)*, as amended by an amendment order, *SI 1990 No 494*; this sets the requirements for the industry until 31 March 1998, and they decrease yearly. For the current period, 1 October 1992 to 31 March 1995, the total amount required is just over 8,200MW.

The second order sets out general requirements for renewable resources, the *Electricity (Non-Fossil Fuel) (England and Wales) (No 2) Order 1990 (SI 1990 No 1859)*, from 10 October 1990 until 31 December 1998.

The third order, the *Electricity (Non-Fossil Fuel) (England and Wales) Order 1991 (SI 1991 No 2490)*, has precise yearly requirements for different types of renewable resources for each of the twelve suppliers from 1 January 1992 until 31 December 1998; this replaces the second order for these years. The requirements either increase or remain constant each year till 1996, and for the last two years all the requirements remain constant. For example, the total requirement for wind power for the period 1 April 1993 to 31 March 1994 is about 22MW. For the period 1 April 1994 to 31 March 1995 it is 82MW. The highest individual requirement for the 1994–1995 period, on Eastern Electricity plc, is about 11MW; the lowest, on South Wales Electricity plc, is just under 3MW. The other types of renewable resources specified are hydroelectricity, landfill gas, municipal and general industrial waste, sewage gas, and other. In context, total electricity consumption is about 60,000MW.

The Secretary of State can also impose a levy on any power produced by fossil fuels, the 'Fossil Fuel Levy'. [*Electricity Act 1989, s 33*]. Fossil fuel for these purposes means coal, coal products, lignites, natural gas, crude liquid petroleum or petroleum products. The levy varies from year to year, but is about 11 per cent of the total amount charged by licensed suppliers for electricity supplied which is generated from fossil fuels.

In assessing whether a licence for the generating company under the *Electricity Act 1989, s 4* is required, the notional capacity of a renewable resource generating station is reduced by multiplying the actual wattage by a multiplier of less than 1, which varies according to the type of renewable resource. The values of the multiplier are: 0.33 for tidal or wave power; 0.43 for wind power; 0.17 for solar power. Thus while the company operating a coal-fired generating station must be licenced if its output for public supply is over 10MW, the company operating a tidal powered generating station will effectively only need a licence if its output exceeds 30MW. A multiplier of 1 has been given to forms of water power other than tides or waves, i.e. hydroelectricity, thus making no difference to the capacity. This is set out fully in the *Electricity (Class Exemptions from the Requirement for a Licence) Order 1990 (SI 1990 No 193)*.

In terms of constructing such a power station, of particular importance is the planning policy guidance note on renewable energy (PPG 22), which was published on 3 February 1993. This outlines the general policy considerations, e.g. the reduction of greenhouse gas emissions, and the appropriate environmental protection legislation. The planning authorities will have to consider the need for energy both nationally and locally, the effect on the economy, the availability of alternative sites and any drawbacks.

Two problems with most renewable resources are, first, that they cannot be transported elsewhere, but must be exploited in situ, and further, many are often best exploited in national parks, areas of outstanding natural beauty or other sensitive locations, which require special consideration. Hydroelectric stations and 'wind farms' are obvious examples.

The Annex to PPG 22 considers the problems associated with wind power. Other detailed annexes on other forms of renewable energy are planned. The most appropriate locations for wind turbines will usually be on exposed high ground where their visual impact may be considerable. Proximity to airports, roads and railways may need to be avoided. A further problem is the continuous background noise, especially in rural areas. Most current designs for wind farms do not exceed an output of 50MW and so do not require *section 36* consent. Planning permission is, however, still required, and the local planning authority can still request an environmental assessment.

Hydroelectricity is probably the best established renewable resource, indeed one of the oldest working power stations in England, at Chagford in Devon, commissioned in 1916, is an HEP station. Although HEP stations are likely to have an output of less than 300MWth, environmental assessments may well be required for *section 36* consent because of the consequences to watercourses and drainage areas. As noted above, hydroelectric power stations are given a multiplier of 1 for the purposes of a *section 4* licence, thus being treated the same as non-renewable resource fuelled power stations. The requirements for HEP under the non-fossil fuel obligation are fairly low, about 10MW for the final three periods, because HEP stations with a capacity of over 20MW are excluded from the provisions of the order; this excludes the two largest HEP stations, at Dolgarrog and Rheidol, both in Wales, with outputs of 27MW and 53MW respectively.

The use of solar energy through photovoltaic systems is unlikely to become a major energy source on a large scale in the UK because of the climate and the amount of land required. A 1MW plant could use up to 25 acres. The other problem with some photovoltaic systems is their use of toxic materials, notably cadmium, which may cause problems of the disposal of waste cells.

For tidal and wave power, the various consents for offshore and coastal power stations listed at 22.8 above are relevant.

22.14 Energy from waste

The generation of electricity from waste has environmental advantages and disadvantages. On the one hand it avoids the further use of non-renewable resources by making use of the energy potential of otherwise useless material. On the other hand the process of incineration may itself be environmentally harmful, for example, by the emission of greenhouse gases, heavy metals or dioxins.

Under *Part I* of the *Environmental Protection Act 1990*, IPC (Integrated Pollution Control) is required for a power station of 3MWth or more that is fuelled by waste oil, recovered oil, or any fuel manufactured from, or comprising, any other waste.

Authorisation from the local authority will be required for a power station of less than 3MWth that is fuelled in this way; the only exception is a power station fuelled by waste other than either waste oil or recovered oil or solid fuel manufactured from waste by a heat process, in which case an output of below 0.4MWth will not require authorisation.

The IPC limits for the combustion of various forms of waste under BATNEEC are set out in the Process Guidance Notes, IPR1/4 to 1/8, published February 1992. These supplement the general Industry Guidance Note IPR1, and cover: waste and recovered oil (IPR 1/4); municipal waste (IPR1/5); fuel from tyres and tyre rubber (IPR 1/6); poultry litter (IPR 1/7); wood waste or straw (IPR 1/8). For a detailed analysis of the treatment of waste, see WASTE MANAGEMENT (28).

Although the incineration of waste is more carefully controlled under the *Environmental Protection Act 1990* than the combustion of fossil fuels, it nevertheless benefits from being considered as a renewable resource under other pieces of legislation. Under the non-fossil fuel obligation there are increasing yearly requirements on public electricity suppliers to use municipal and general industrial waste. The total requirement by 1998 is about 260MW. The heaviest requirements in this respect are on Eastern Electricity plc, since they increase from zero in the first three periods (1 January 1992 to 31 March 1994) to about 36MW in the last two periods (1 April 1996 to 31 December 1998).

Waste gases, such as landfill gas or sewage gas, are also required to be used under the third order. The total requirement for landfill gas for the last three periods is 48MW, and for sewage gas about 27MW. Waste gas processing is subject to *Part II* of the *Environmental Protection Act 1990*, which requires anyone occupying a site on which waste is treated to obtain a waste management licence setting out the appropriate conditions. The combustion of waste gas is particularly environmentally beneficial, since waste gas contains methane, which is 21 times more potent a greenhouse gas than carbon dioxide.

22.15 ENERGY EFFICIENCY AND CONSERVATION

There is very little specific legislation on energy efficiency. This however may well change over the next few years, since energy efficiency is currently being widely discussed, most notably at a European level. The fifth action programme specifically highlights energy efficiency as a key issue. This follows on from two earlier Decisions: *89/364/EEC* on the efficiency of electricity use; *91/565/EEC* on the promotion of energy efficiency. ENERGY MANAGEMENT AND GREEN BUILDINGS (6) deals with some of the current energy efficiency legislation.

23 Projecting a Greener Image

23.1 Increasingly, commercial companies and others see marketing advantages in claiming 'environmental friendliness'. Green advertising is big business and 'green' products are an increasingly important part of the consumer scene. Projecting a greener image is, however, more than merely getting the advertisements right. It involves a fundamental commitment to environmental excellence.

23.2 COMPLIANCE PLUS

To project a green or greener image relies on the development of a system of beliefs and values rather than on meeting enforceable standards. Compliance with the law is assumed but this is unlikely to be a sufficient basis on which to project a green image. All best practice assumes compliance, it never tries to make a virtue out of it.

The framework for environmental compliance in a formal sense is set by a growing number of institutions: nation state governments, the European Community, non-governmental organisations, regulators and, increasingly, industry groupings committed to self-regulation. In an informal sense, it is set by a general climate of public opinion driven by pressure groups and charismatic individuals. (See THE PLAYERS (2).)

The issue of compliance also encompasses the kind of compliance which purchasers demand of suppliers. It is, for instance, increasingly the case that a declaration of environmental policy is required as part of the rubric for tender for Government contracts – even for service industries where the law has minimal impact on corporate environmental behaviour. (See PURCHASING DECISIONS (24).)

What this means in practice for individual companies will naturally depend on a number of factors; whether you are product or service deliverers, the essentially hazardous or non-hazardous nature of production and distribution, the opportunities for improvement, the needs and preferences of purchasers and direct customers, the number of employees, the ability to affect suppliers etc.

But there is no business activity which cannot improve its own environmental performance and there is no business activity truly exempt from an increasing and proper public expectation of environmental responsibility. Willful abuse of the environment is as unacceptable in companies as it is in individuals. The list of immediate priorities includes the minimisation of waste, car fleet management (smaller cars, unleaded petrol), the appropriate use of recycled products, energy conservation and energy efficiency measures and purchasing/supplier policies.

To fail to attend to such every day matters – matters where the company can properly be expected to behave as a moderate but 'green' individual would behave – is not only environmentally irresponsible, it is unwise organisational behaviour. At some point it will work to the disadvantage of financial performance (loss of business, damaged reputation, advantage to a competitor) or even to a legislative response which could be costly and untimely.

However, many companies wish to project a deliberately green image because there is very legitimate commercial or, in the case of local authorities, electoral and institutional advantage in doing so. There are other reasons too for wanting a greener reputation: recruitment, ability to expand, employee motivation and the positioning of products. Fortunately, there is a good deal of best practice from which to draw, though the nature

23.3   Projecting a Greener Image

of the business or undertaking will determine what best practice model is most appropriate for it.

23.3   BEST PRACTICE: PROACTIVE

The fundamental requirement is that the external image should be matched by the internal reality. Claims which prove to be false, damage those making them and undermine their credibility amongst key audiences; customers, consumers, employees, shareholders, governments, electorate, communities. Such damage is difficult to repair.

The first step is always to bring the reality as close to the image to be projected as can be achieved; ideally, the reality might even be better and the case almost understated. The environmental 'con' attracts a great deal of opprobrium, including nomination for such very public events as the Friends of the Earth 'Green Con of the Year Award'. But, communication is vital and one cannot assume that good deeds speak loudly enough for themselves.

23.4   Corporate environmental responsibility

Corporate environmental responsibility – and the greener image which it will enable companies to project – has to be endemic within the culture. It cannot be grafted on. To achieve a responsible and sustainable position, the internal culture must change. Just as 'customer focus' programmes which produce only plastic smiles are easily detectable and counter-productive, so are environmental programmes which produce only plastic daffodils.

And because internal culture must change, then so must the systems of employee incentive and reward. Which means, in the first place, that the commitment to environmental excellence must come from the top and, more importantly, be sustained by and driven from the top. Programmes which are invented at the top but where responsibility and accountability for successful implementation are delegated to the middle do not have a good track record. Therefore, there is also a need for clear, definable goals.

Furthermore, environmental issues are frequently complex, requiring sophisticated judgements. It is now believed by many, for example, that the promotion of the catalytic converter has been actually harmful; grabbing at this quick fix 'solution' has retarded by many years the more desirable innovation, the lean burn engine and provided those of us in colder climates, where for much of the time the converter is ineffective, with false comfort.

Because the issues are complicated and judgements have to be made about delicate balances, it can only be at the most senior levels and on the basis of the best possible information that sound policy can be developed and maintained and improved through constant revisiting and review.

It is also only at this level that decisions can be taken which appear to fly in the face of environmental fashion. The pressure for recycling, for instance, must be resisted when there are good grounds for saying that either there is not a market for the recycled products or where there is an economically and environmentally superior disposal route. The German *Topfer Decree*, for instance, which is driving much of European legislation on packaging (see PACKAGING (20)) and with which German industry is co-operating, is much criticised as having the potential for creating greater environmental harm than good. Yet we must also bear in mind that the best way to kill a green

326

image is to explain why the fashionable thing cannot or should not be done. Communications must always address solutions.

The first step, therefore, is to develop the commitment to environmental excellence. If the commitment is real, the outcomes will be of genuine and long lasting organisational and environmental benefit. Indeed, though inadvisable to have nothing to say, it is perhaps better to say nothing than to pretend to have zeal and to claim more than the reality or to invent quick promotional fixes which do more harm than good.

Projecting a greener image is therefore about constant movement forward as well as compliance plus.

23.5   The reality checks

Any green claims need to be credible to both an organisation's internal and external worlds and the only way of discovering whether that credibility can be maintained is to take independent soundings about both the factual content of what you are about to say and the language which you are going to use to say it.

Two issues arise here; is your assessment of environmental impact honest and credible and will you be believed? It is all too easy to believe your own evidence. The real question is whether it is sufficiently robust to stand up to external scrutiny. It is also all too easy to believe that you will be believed. Convincing and credible third parties who will back you up are also required.

Green activists are quick to spot assessments that are partial. A paper tissue manufacturer claimed that its virgin fibre paper was environmentally sound because it was made from harvested trees (a renewable resource) and because growing trees replenish the earth with oxygen. Not a sustainable argument, because it omitted to consider the impact of emissions in the transport distribution network and the emission of ozone damaging gases during burning and decomposing as the paper enters the waste stream. Fully developed methods of life cycle analysis will eventually decide whose case is the stronger but to lose the debate because the argument was badly framed made sense neither for the company nor, perhaps, for the environment.

Exaggerated or dishonest claims are also easily detected by employees who, depending on the circumstances, may be a company's worst enemies or its best ambassadors. What they say in the pub or to friends at the sports club or even to the local newspaper will travel far and if they see their company's green image as 'just PR' it will travel further still.

Starting down the path of environmental excellence, a number of reality checks can be taken through consultation.

23.6   *What do they think of you now?*

And who are they? They are all amongst that group of people who as individuals or groups have the capacity to alter the way in which you are able to do your business; shareholders, employees, communities, customers, consumers, voters, politicians, peer group companies, other organisations, pressure groups, etc. And you probably won't find out by asking them yourself. Best practice here suggests that an external agency should undertake a confidential audit of representatives of the people who matter to you, to find out what they perceive your environmental performance to be and discover the issues which matter to them.

It is also good practice to make sure that you have identified all the issues which your industry or sector has faced in recent years and the ones which are likely to be raised by pressure groups and others in the coming years and the events (such as a public inquiry) which may throw your industry or sector into high profile.

Many organisations wishing to project a green image will have a strong regional or local presence. For them, the opinion of the community is particularly relevant whether during the process of getting planning consent for new premises, expanding existing plant, maintaining high class recruitment and so on.

Your greener image must be set in the context of how you are seen by the outside world – whether or not it accords with your own view.

23.7   *What do you want them to think?*

You want them to think that you are, on environmental issues, what you say you are. And what you say you are will be contained in your published and public environmental policy, your marketing and promotional literature, annual report, public information leaflets and elsewhere. Fundamentally, your environmental vision will be a statement of how you will behave and act in order to share the sincere environmental values and concerns of your customers and others of importance to your business. And in order for your environmental vision to be credible, it will mean setting and communicating goals for improvement.

You will not claim perfection because no reasonable person expects it or will even believe it – but you will state your commitment to constant improvement. Perhaps that part of your environmental policy will be like that of National Westminster Bank plc,

> 'Our aim is to determine what is best environmental practice in all we do and then implement it. No cosmetic quick fixes. And because the National Westminster Bank is a very large organisation indeed, we hope our stone in the pond will produce much more than a ripple or two.
>
> The purpose of this message is to set out what we are already doing and going to do. We undertake to report to you how we are getting along.'

23.8   Turning the new position to advantage

Having checked what is it that 'they' really think and having decided what you want 'them' to think, you must now get your environmental house in order and then communicate your achievements to advantage.

23.9   *The internal issues*

It must now be assumed that you have decided to have an environmental position which will be at least 'compliance plus' and, if at all possible, will adopt and set best practice standards in your sector.

There are three elements; policy, procedures, programmes.

Policy will be encapsulated in your Environmental Statement. It will be concrete not abstract, it will identify measurable goals rather than produce words of good intent, it will be in plain English and, very importantly, it will relate the contribution of good environmental practice to meeting core business or organisational goals – including profitability and/or cost containment. Enlightened self-interest is always very plausible.

The policy then has to be turned into action. Your reality checks with the outside world and, perhaps, through your environmental auditors (see Chapters 8 and 9, 'Environmental Assessment' and 'Environmental Audits') will have told you much about what needs to be done in order both to comply and to meet the anxieties or expectations of those who are important to your business success. Your immediate action list will be there. But actively to seek to project a greener image which reflects the internal reality, programmes and procedures will also need to be put in place.

Fundamentally, you will require your employees, at every level, to assist and that means that they must receive rewards and incentives. There has to be a culture in which there is positive encouragement for employee participation both in identifying what needs to be done and in designing responses and action plans. Your overall Environmental Statement must make sense to them and they must be able to see what their contribution can be. The rewards and incentives are those you would normally deploy; notice board acknowledgements, celebration in the in-house magazine, prizes and awards, promotion, performance related bonuses, and so on.

There are, though, areas which many would still consider to be discretionary but which you should have considered if they are appropriate. This especially applies if you are positioning your product as green and selling it on that basis, where you are actually selling into the still niche market of the actively green consumer. The Body Shop is probably a good example. If your selling point is to be green, then there are other things to be taken into consideration.

Amongst them, is green or ethical investing (see GREEN INVESTMENT (15)). Consumers are becoming increasingly aware of the 'hidden' aspects of company policy which will affect their purchasing decisions. The publication, *New Consumer*, for instance, assesses companies not just on their environmental record but also on their investment policies, especially on some of the wider environmental issues such as whether the company invests in others with nuclear connections, forestry operations and tobacco as well as more controversial issues such as animal testing.

After honest assessment you have now delivered genuine commitment and you are fully equipped to talk about what you have done and what you will be doing and why it makes sense for you – as well as for the environment.

At this stage you are really ready to project a greener image.

23.10 *Communicating to external audiences*

The process which you began needs to be continuous; projecting a greener image depends as much on active listening as it does on active communication. It also means constant measuring which tells you whether your immediate and long-term goals are being met within the framework of enhancing your core business. A greener image is not a once-off creation, it is a continuous process.

However, the opportunities for projecting and developing a greener image are many and they generally take two major forms; description and demonstration. Description is where many organisations stop but demonstration can add much value, particularly if there are marketing advantages to projecting a greener image.

23.11 *Communicating by description*

The reception areas of many companies and local government offices are used as a point at which policy and practice are presented in leaflets and brochures which describe what is being done on environmental issues. Best practice will also ensure that such material is not simply 'environmentally correct' but that it contains information which is relevant to those who will pick it up and is written in a way which makes it accessible, including, where appropriate, translation into first languages other than English.

Such materials are also useful communications for customers, suppliers and important contacts as well as those who actually visit premises. But best practice will also encourage you to describe the practical commitment to environmental excellence in other ways, particularly in annual reports or other forms of reporting periods of activity. They are particularly important because they are moments at which the effectiveness of company policy is related to performance. They are also an opportunity to describe cost savings through, for instance, energy efficiency and to demonstrate the pay back of environmental initiatives.

Additionally, information about your 'greening' can be newsworthy, though normally only at a local level. Stories in the local paper about what you have done and about employees' contributions help communicate your image to the very important constituency of local residents and the local community.

There are also opportunities at both national and local level for using your environmental interest as a means of meeting and creating allies out of significant opinion formers.

23.12 *Communicating by demonstration*

When British Gas wanted to demonstrate its commitment to the environment, it commissioned 14 publications on 14 separate environmental topics from independent academics. It then ran its 'Energy Not Apathy' campaign in the national newspapers and received an overwhelming demand for copies of the brochures, each of which was published in summary on 14 consecutive days. It also commissioned and had published a seminal work on Environmental Corporate Responsibility. It demonstrated its green image by doing much more than attending to its internal issues.

British Gas is a big company with the resources to make it happen but smaller organisations can also demonstrate commitment, from the supermarket providing bottle and can banks in car parks to the local authority providing walking guides which describe local flora and fauna.

Many companies also see the commercial and social benefit of directing their corporate responsibility (charitable) funds towards environmental projects and recognise the importance of then communicating what they have helped others to achieve. Constructed around regional and local programmes, the active support of communities who wish to improve their environment or restore it to former glory are also effective in creating community links on which so many organisations depend.

For larger companies, cause-related marketing has proved commercially satisfying, linking the purchase of a product with a company commitment to support a named cause though there is no reason why the concept could not be adopted by other kinds of organisations. In France, for instance, a significant increase in glass bottle recovery was achieved by linking the volume collected with donations to a cancer charity. Particularly where we want people to change their behaviour, such incentives can really work.

Demonstration can also take the form of open access. Especially where hazardous or potentially hazardous processes are concerned, open days on which the public can visit the plant have proved highly successful. Openness demonstrates both commitment and the all-important balance between active communication and active listening.

And any sizeable manufacturing plant might also wish to demonstrate its green credentials by establishing a committee with representatives from the local community to discuss issues of mutual interest. The committee might contain a local head teacher, doctor, health visitor, police sergeant, fire chief, church leader or others.

23.13 BEST PRACTICE: REACTIVE

So far we have only described how organisations can deliberately set out to project a green image. It is, perhaps, worth a few thoughts on how that can best be protected when trouble strikes.

Material and financial loss can be insured against (see ENVIRONMENTAL INSURANCE (13)) but damage to reputation and credibility cannot. When the worst happens, and at some time it probably will, the only insurance against unnecessary damage to reputation and credibility lies in having prepared for it.

Just as it is prudent to consider the external threats and to have a position worked out in relation to them (e.g. the public enquiry into one company which potentially affects its whole sector) it is prudent to have considered the worst scenario from internal threats; a chemical spill, an accidental poisonous gas emission, a malicious information leak etc. The damage which environmental mishap can do to the greener image which you have projected can be minimised by having prepared a strategy for dealing with such an event.

Who will be the spokesperson? How will they control the information flow? What information will they need? What media training should they have been given? What actions will they need to take? When to attack? When to concede? What physical communications links will be needed to other offices or locations? Many questions which can be answered in advance, leaving the organisation better prepared to handle the issue with sensitivity to both organisational and public needs in a time of crisis. These aspects of dealing with the media and the public in the event of a crisis should be built into all emergency response plans. Human perception as well as legal and technical solutions to crises is a vital component of damage limitation.

23.14 *Summary*

The environment is not an issue which will go away. It is on the public and political agenda in a serious way. More and more, we will all be asked to make more out of less – less energy, less raw material, less fossil fuel – to manage waste by reducing it at source and recovering the materials and energy locked up in it and by ensuring that our business and industrial activities are clean and sustainable.

Where we fail to take action of our own accord, international, regional, national and local legislators will take the matter into their own hands.

It is, therefore, enlightened self-interest both to have a greener image and to project it. But green is complex, and sophisticated judgements need to be made; 'knee jerk' responses have the potential for more harm than good.

Overall, good, clear and honest communications matched by good, clear and honest endeavours will mark out those destined for success. The financial and other costs of pursuing a business which is dirty are now too great for that business to be sustained.

Projecting a greener image requires that the reality matches the claims. All best practice assumes compliance, it never tries to make a virtue out of it and there are also ways of ensuring that your environmental successes are turned to business advantage.

Key, however, is the requirement for a green commitment to affect and help drive corporate culture.

If these things are in place, then other goals can be supported and met; profitability, cost containment, increased customer loyalty, public reputation, better recruitment and retention of the right kind of people, employee loyalty and so on.

23.14   Projecting a Greener Image

Nothing is safely done without consultation with the external world and a process of active listening to support the use of active communications.

Communications can both describe and demonstrate your green image at work.

Finally, your green image is as important as anything else in this book because what people think of you in environmental terms is central to their willingness to trust you.

But remember, environmental communications are based on the need to communicate shared environmental values; at root it is affective not logical, emotional not statistical while, simultaneously, it comes from setting improvement goals. Concrete targets give your internal and external audiences the sense that you want to improve and intend to do so. It gives them the subtle sense of victory because you've admitted that you must do better (which they already knew) and for internal audiences it gives them something to work towards.

24   Purchasing Decisions

24.1   With world attention being paid to the environmental impact of manufacturing processes, product packaging and the products themselves, a purchasing department has considerable power within any company wishing to establish an environmentally friendly image. However, buyers need to monitor the findings of environmental research and review policy as new facts emerge, even if this means a change of direction; for example, phosphates in detergents are thought to have harmed aquatic life, but researchers now suggest that in some circumstances they could be better than alternative ingredients. Purchasing policy needs to be flexible enough to incorporate the latest scientific findings quickly.

24.2   CORPORATE STRATEGY AND ENVIRONMENTAL PURCHASING

An environmental policy needs to be developed as part of the corporate strategy if it is to be successful. The purchasing department will play a significant role in its implementation as the control point at which goods are allowed into a company.

The purchasing policy will reflect what a company wants to be and what its end product will be. The initial step in developing a policy could be an environmental risk assessment of products and services bought in order to prioritise issues to be addressed. Issues arising might include minimising use and wastage of energy, water and paper; buying the most efficient and least polluting of fleet transport; considering alternatives to hardwood furniture.

Implementing developed policies will always require balance and careful decision-making in the light of available information. For example, a manufacturing company with strong environmental ideals might specify minimal packaging for its products using recycled material but another, while wishing to acknowledge environmental issues, might be satisfied with the purchase of packaging from sustainable sources.

A buyer should seek to adopt a 'cradle-to-grave' approach when looking at all stages of the supply chain so that for any item purchased there is awareness of what raw materials have been used, what processes there are, what use will be made of the product and how it will be finally disposed of. Those having the least impact during their 'life cycle' should be sought and those with identified environmental hazards discriminated against. It nevertheless should be acknowledged that much of the information necessary for a life cycle analysis may be difficult to obtain or measure and that some of the judgments will inevitably be subjective.

24.3   THE RIGHT QUALITY

In purchasing terms the right quality is that which satisfies the need. Any purchase should be the most suitable in the market place at that time, that is, comply with the specification and provide value for money. This approach fits in neatly with internal management schemes that emphasise the need to get things right first time and seek to eliminate waste, as for example total quality management.

A specification detailing required quality should include any environmental considerations, whether this be to meet the company's own environmental policy or other standards, such as those being developed by the EC. The EC's eco-labelling system (see ENVIRONMENTAL ASSESSMENT (7)) adopts a 'cradle-to-grave' approach to the assessment of a product with the first products displaying the eco-label due to be on the market during 1993. This will not cover food and drink products and pharmaceuticals.

A buyer should seek to ensure specifications do not stipulate hazardous materials, particularly where an environmentally friendlier alternative is available. Tenderers should be made aware of the importance of the environment to the purchaser by the incorporation of a questionnaire, which could, for example, ask about the nature of packaging materials and processes.

Purchasers need to be aware that there is no legal definition for terms such as 'environmentally friendly' and need to guard against being influenced by unofficial standards devised by suppliers or misleading advertising.

24.4   THE RIGHT QUANTITY

Balancing the cost of holding stock with the cost of running out of an item has lead to the widespread adoption of JIT (just in time) policies, whereby deliveries are made on a 'little and often' basis. However the cost of more frequent journeys (using more energy and increasing vehicle pollution) needs to be brought into the equation, with decisions being based on the true cost of purchase rather than just the price.

An environmental policy will emphasise the need to use less resources by only purchasing what is needed and minimising waste, a direction which will underline any company's drive for efficiency and effective use of resources. Even encouraging office practices such as 'recycling' office memos for scrap pads could be incorporated.

Cost cutting and the achievement of savings are an important aim for purchasing staff, but these objectives may run counter to environmental policy if it proves that recycled and 'green' products are more expensive, though in the future increased demand for these may lead to lower prices. Price comparisons between alternative products should always take account of the total 'life' costs of each, that is, the cost to the environment of each product.

For those companies whose prime concern is to convey an image of being concerned about the environment a balance has to be found between the 'added value' of selling environmentally sound products, perhaps at a higher price which reflects that position, and the price the customer is prepared to pay for the goods.

24.5   THE RIGHT SUPPLIER

Where companies maintain an approved list of suppliers, environmental considerations can be made a condition for qualification; for example, the existence of a supplier's environmental policy might be one such condition but it is important that their policy follows the same direction as the purchaser's. Supplier visits and investigations can help ensure that the stated policy is translated into action. For example, check if there is site evidence of green policies within the organisation such as paper recycling bins or skips for recyclable materials such as glass; or if there is compliance with stated policy on the source and nature of packaging.

If suppliers do sell items that are hazardous, ensure they are set up for the proper disposal of these items as they have a duty throughout the life of their product.

24.6   COMPILING A LIST OF POTENTIAL TENDERERS

Sources of information for potential suppliers will include buyer's knowledge, trade organisations, Chambers of Commerce, trade journals and directories, exhibitions, salespersons visits, supplier catalogues and departmental records.

Buyers should endeavour to eliminate those companies known to have a poor environmental record. Preference should be given to those suppliers with a positive environmental attitude.

24.7   SUPPLIER APPRAISAL

Supplier appraisal is carried out before the order has been placed and is essentially a method of assessing potential performance. The appraisal would generally be divided between desk research and a supplier visit. However a balancing of the cost of time taken on assessment and the value of the business to the company must always be undertaken.

The desk research element of the appraisal system will generally include using published data such as company reports, balance sheets, references, strike record etc. To this could be added responses to a supplier questionnaire which would make a general enquiry into the company's policy on environmental matters and seek to establish whether the company complies with environmental legislation. The supplier could also be asked to provide information on the impact of his products on the environment, stage by stage throughout their life cycle.

Judge suppliers by assessing the use made of hazardous materials or processes, energy levels required in production, distribution and use and waste disposal facilities against current environmental issues and legislative requirements. A conscientious supplier will have already made 'cradle-to-grave' assessments.

Serious supplier evaluation should involve visits and inspection of the supplier's premises. While all buyers should examine working practices, staff morale, stocks etc., opportunity should also be taken to perform an informal environmental audit of the site. For example, to observe whether recycled material is being saved; whether dangerous waste is being disposed correctly; whether the company buys and holds very high levels of stock unnecessarily, pushing up production elsewhere; or whether the components have a low or high environmental cost.

Supplier appraisal could be made easier with the development of the EC's eco-audit scheme (see ENVIRONMENTAL AUDITS (8)). Though still in its pilot stage, this will provide a voluntary scheme for companies to commit themselves to a corporate policy of ENVIRONMENTAL MANAGEMENT (14). The participating company must show evidence of an environmental policy, the establishment of an accredited environmental system, such as BS 7750 1992 (Specification for Environmental Management Systems), and report annually on progress against performance. Completion of the scheme will be acknowledged with the awarding of a logo.

24.8   TENDER DOCUMENTS

Tender documents should include questions which ascertain the environmental impact of goods to be supplied. For example, tenderers could be asked to state whether CFCs are used in products or packaging which it is proposed to supply against the contract and if they are, details must be supplied. In more general terms, tenderers could be asked what measures they are taking to ensure their products or services are environmentally friendly.

Evaluation of tender returns should be with regard to the usual criteria of price, quality, delivery etc. plus the details of environmental information given. Rejection of an offer because the environmental impact would be too damaging will emphasise to suppliers the importance of the environment in today's markets.

24.9   VENDOR RATING

Vendor rating systems can be used to stress the importance of environmental considerations to suppliers. These systems are generally devised using a number of attributes that the buyer wishes to measure after orders have been placed with a supplier. These can be anything from the speed a query is dealt with to punctuality on delivery. This scheme can easily incorporate a company's performance on environmental policies which it promised to achieve at the tendering stage.

Promotion of suppliers' interest in striving to achieve better results on environmental goals could be achieved by publishing vendor rating results. Public recognition of a good performance can motivate suppliers as a way to get more business.

24.10 SUPPLIER DEVELOPMENT

The aim of supplier development is to develop the quality and number of suppliers a business needs who seek to follow an environmental policy similar to their own. Responsibility for the environment can be passed down the supply chain through buyers positively influencing suppliers. Success lies with the purchasing department creating a relationship of trust in which environmentally friendly policies can be discussed; it is essential that staff understand the issues and support them. Longer term relationships with suppliers may aid development of environmental measures.

25 Radioactive Substances and Nuclear Installations

25.1 INTRODUCTION

This chapter examines, from an environmental and public health perspective, the United Kingdom and European Community controls on the nuclear industry and on the wider use of radioactive material in industry generally. It provides an overview of the organisations responsible for establishing the radiological protection standards upon which these controls are based.

Under United Kingdom legislation, broadly separate regulatory regimes have been established for operations which handle or use radioactive substances as part of their wider activities and those which are known as nuclear installations and which are primarily involved in the nuclear energy sector and defence work.

25.2 Ionising radiation and its health effects

The nuclear industry in the United Kingdom (which includes nuclear weapons production, the nuclear power utilities and companies engaged in 'the nuclear fuel cycle' i.e. fuel preparation and production and nuclear waste reprocessing) has grown up under the strict control of legislation which recognises the associated risks of such undertakings.

The principal hazard of ionising radiation is harm to human health. Such harm is mediated through damage done to individual cells in the body by the energy deposited within them by the radiation to which they are exposed. The effects of such exposure may be seen at an early stage and have an obvious clinical presentation (such as a radiation burn). A biological effect of this sort would usually be caused by exposure to very large amounts of radiation over a short period of time and is described as a 'non-stochastic' effect. Lower doses of radiation may cause longer term effects of a type which cannot be so readily attributed to the radiation exposure since they are of a sort (e.g. cancers and inherited abnormalities) which occur naturally in the population. These effects are termed 'stochastic' and are conventionally evaluated and controlled by reference to the increased statistical probability of a person (or his offspring) suffering such an effect as a result of exposure to a given quantity of radiation.

The principal sources of ionising radiation, to which everyone is exposed throughout his or her life, occur in Nature. They include cosmic rays from outside the earth's atmosphere and radioactive gases resulting from the decay of naturally occurring minerals. There are also man-made, or artificial, sources, principally radioactive substances employed in medical diagnostic and therapeutic procedures, nuclear weapons testing fallout and radioactivity which is released into the environment as a result of industrial processes.

There are different types of ionising radiation. All are released during the disintegration of atoms as radioactive substances go through a natural decay process. They include electromagnetic waves such as gamma and x-rays which have relatively low energy but a relatively high penetrating effect on the human body and sub-atomic particles (principally alpha and beta particles) which penetrate less far but carry more energy.

The *radioactivity* of a radioactive substance is conventionally measured in becquerels (Bq).

25.3 Radioactive Substances and Nuclear Installations

The current standard unit of radiation dose is the sievert (Sv). In the context of environmental exposures and radiological protection (in contrast to laboratory experiments, where the doses studied are often very much higher) one is usually concerned with doses measured in thousandths of a sievert, the millisievert (mSv), or millionths of a sievert, the microsievert (μSv). For example, the total annual dose to the average person living in the United Kingdom from all radiation sources is estimated to be 2.5 mSv or 2500 μSv, with doses arising from man-made sources contributing some 13 per cent (about 325 μSv) to that total. These man-made sources include 300 μSv arising from medical and dental exposures and less than 1 μSv from radioactivity discharged into the environment by industry.

The health effects on the public of a radioactive substance which occurs in, or is discharged into, the environment are dependent on the 'pathways' by which people may become exposed to it. For example, alpha and beta particles have little radiological significance unless they are taken into the body by inhalation or ingestion (e.g. in milk or food stuffs) or through abrasions in the skin. These exposures give rise to 'internal radiation' doses. On the other hand, gamma and x-rays will deliver an 'external radiation' dose (often to the whole body) as a result of the physical proximity of the person to the radioactive substance from which they are emitted. Thus, the behaviour of radioactivity in the environment and human habits are key issues in radiological dosimetry and control. (For comprehensive but non-technical explanations of radiation and health see *Nuclear Radiation: Risks and Benefits*, E Pochin, Oxford Science Publications (1983) and *Living with Radiation* 4th ed. re-print (1990), NRPB, HMSO.)

The effects on the body of ionising radiation are, as a result of statistical and biological study, well understood. Of all the many harmful agents produced by industrial activity the depth of understanding of radiation's effects is probably unique. Unique, too, is the high degree of internationalism in the field of legal and regulatory controls, as is described more fully in the following paragraphs of this chapter. The control regime in the United Kingdom is based on internationally-set standards which themselves are founded on the key concept of the minimisation of doses to workers and the public so as to avoid harmful effects, in particular stochastic effects.

25.3 INTERNATIONAL ORGANISATIONS RELEVANT TO RADIOLOGICAL CONTROL

International nuclear co-operation has created a broadly harmonised system of national legislation on nuclear safety issues. It provides the basis for controls within the United Kingdom, as indicated above.

25.4 The International Commission on Radiological Protection

The principal standard-setting organisation is the International Commission on Radiological Protection (ICRP). It is a scientific body of distinguished experts who are independent of national governments and all other institutions, including the United Nations. They are elected by the International Congress of Radiology (an international association of professional radiologists many of whom work with, and are themselves exposed to, radiation, often in the medical field). The ICRP from time to time publishes recommendations on radiation protection standards and, in particular, recommendations as to permissible dose levels for the public and for workers exposed to radiation, for example in hospitals, factories and nuclear installations. In doing so, ICRP draws on current scientific and medical knowledge and on the work of the United Nations Scientific Committee on the Effects of Atomic Radiation (UNSCEAR) (see below) and of other influential bodies such as the BEIR committees of the National Research Council which operates under the aegis of the US National Academy of Sciences. The ICRP's recommendations are treated as highly authoritative and are acted on by most national and regional bodies responsible for radiological protection and nuclear safety. So far as the United Kingdom is concerned, the Government receives advice on ICRP recommendations directly from the National Radiological Protection Board (NRPB) (see 25.20 below). ICRP standards also find their way into the United Kingdom control regime through European Community Directives promulgated under the *European Atomic Energy Community* (*Euratom*) *Treaty*, as is discussed at 25.9 and 25.12.

25.5   The United Nations Scientific Committee on the Effects of Atomic Radiation

UNSCEAR was set up as a United Nations Committee in 1955 to compile and analyse the result of on-going scientific research into the effects of radiation on man. One of its principle roles has become the derivation from the scientific material of 'risk factors' which attribute a statistical probability for the occurrence of radiation-induced effects, including stochastic effects, to a given quantity and type of radiation. These serve as one of the basic building blocks for the radiological protection standards recommended by ICRP, as has been explained.

There are a number of other international agencies and bodies which have advisory and assistance functions and which themselves build on the work of the ICRP and its recommendations in promoting detailed safeguards and standards. Foremost amongst these are the International Atomic Energy Agency (IAEA) and the Nuclear Energy Agency (NEA) of the Organisation for Economic Co-operation and Development (OECD) (see 25.6 and 25.7 below).

25.6   The International Atomic Energy Agency

The IAEA is a United Nations Agency. It was set up in 1957 and has a permanent Secretariat and staff based in Vienna. Its mandate is to establish health and safety standards in order to protect health and minimise danger to life and property. To achieve this aim the IAEA consults with other relevant international organisations, such as ICRP. The IAEA's Basic Safety Standards for Radiation Protection are based on the recommendations of the ICRP. IAEA standards, regulations, codes of practice, guides and other related instruments cover such subjects as radiation protection, transport and the handling of radioactive materials and radioactive waste disposal.

The IAEA has established Radiation Protection Advisory Teams (RAPATS) which assess, on request from Member States, the quality of radiation protection in those States, determine immediate and future radiation needs, and a long-term strategy for technical assistance.

The IAEA's own recommendations are advisory only, although countries which receive materials or services from the IAEA (mainly developing nations) are required to treat such recommendations as binding on them. The IAEA's most publicised activities in recent years have been its monitoring of the effects of the Chernobyl accident and its inspection work in Iraq following the Gulf War.

25.7   The Nuclear Energy Agency of the Organisation for Economic Co-operation and Development

The OECD's NEA represents the industrialised market economies with the most advanced nuclear programmes, including most Western European states, the USA, Canada, Japan and Australia.

25.8 Radioactive Substances and Nuclear Installations

The NEA is required to contribute to the safety of workers and the public against ionising radiations and to the promotion of a system for third party liability and insurance with respect to nuclear damage. It provides a forum in which experts from national bodies can meet and exchange experiences and knowledge. The recommendations and advice of the NEA (again based on ICRP recommendations) are not binding on member governments but the NEA promotes them with the express view to seeing them incorporated in national legislation.

The NEA has an active Secretariat based in Paris and it runs a number of committees concentrating on specialist issues. Particularly influential is the Committee on Radiation Protection and Public Health which has set up an Incident Reporting System between national regulatory authorities. It systematically collects and disseminates information on nuclear reactor operating experiences.

25.8 Other United Nations bodies

The work of two other United Nations bodies, The World Health Organisation (WHO) and the Food Agriculture Organisation (FAO) embraces radiological protection issues. Both organisations undertake research and publish advice in this field, usually in relation to specific situations.

25.9 The European Atomic Energy Community (Euratom)

So far as the development of the control regime in the United Kingdom is concerned, the most important international body is the European Atomic Energy Community which was established by the *Euratom Treaty* of 1957, to which the United Kingdom acceded when it joined Europe in 1973. The European Community not only promotes the nuclear industries within Member States, but through the Community institutions, lays down uniform legislative standards for the industry and, in particular, standards for radiological protection to be implemented by Member States. The *Ionising Radiation Regulations 1985* (discussed further at 25.27 below) is a significant example of the implementation in United Kingdom law of such Community legislation.

Article 2 of the *Euratom Treaty* specifically requires the Community to promote research and to ensure the dissemination of technical information; to establish uniform safety standards to protect the health of workers and of the general public and ensure they are applied; to facilitate investment and ensure by encouragement the establishment of the basic installations necessary for the development of nuclear energy in the Community; to ensure that all users in the Community receive a regular and equitable supply of ores and nuclear fuels, and to make certain, by appropriate supervision, that nuclear materials are not diverted to purposes other than those for which they are intended.

Measures taken by the European Community to protect human health have extended beyond the operation of nuclear installations and the use of radioactive substances within Member States and have included the imposition of 'intervention' limits on levels of radioactive contamination in foodstuffs imported into the European Community and restrictions on the importation of foodstuffs from Eastern Europe in the aftermath of the Chernobyl accident.

In common with the approach adopted by most of the other international bodies described in this section, the maximum permissible doses and levels of exposure and contamination provided for in Community legislation are based on the recommendations of the ICRP.

The *Euratom Treaty* and the role of the European Community in developing the nuclear safety and radiological control regimes in individual Member States through Community legislation is discussed more fully at 25.12 below.

25.10 Summary

The international control arrangements described in this section (and more fully at 25.11 *et seq.* below) provide a complex framework which encourages the nuclear industry worldwide (and specifically within the European Community) to adopt, and operate to, broadly comparable standards of radiological protection and safety. The United Kingdom, with its long history of nuclear research and activity, follows these standards closely and, through the work of the NRPB, has often been in the forefront with its control regime.

An overview of the international control arrangements are illustrated in Figure 1.

25.11 CONVENTIONS AND INTERNATIONAL PROVISIONS

Overlaying the international control arrangements described above, there is a network of obligations arising from international conventions and agreements to which the United Kingdom is a party and which have an effect on the operations of the nuclear industry and the use of radioactive materials in this country.

At the European Community level, there is the *Euratom Treaty*, an outline of which was given at 25.9 above and the provisions of which are discussed in further detail at 25.12 below.

Numerous other relevant international treaties include:

(1)   The *Paris Convention on Third Party Liability in the Field of Nuclear Energy* (1960);

(2)   The *Convention concerning the Protection of Workers against Ionising Radiations* (1960);

(3)   The *International Convention for the Future Safety of Life at Sea* (1960);

(4)   The *Brussels Convention on the Liability of Operators of Nuclear Ships* (1962) (to which the United Kingdom is not a contracting party);

(5)   The *Vienna Convention on Civil Liability for Nuclear Damage* (1963) (to which the United Kingdom is a signatory but which it has not ratified);

(6)   The *Brussels Convention on Third Party Liability in the Field of Nuclear Energy* (1963);

(7)   The *Treaty on the Non-proliferation of Nuclear Weapons* (1968).

(8)   The *Brussels Convention relating to Civil Liability in the Field of Maritime Carriage of Nuclear Material* (1971);

(9)   The *Convention on the Physical Protection of Nuclear Material* (1980);

(10)   The *Convention on Assistance in the case of a Nuclear Accident or Radiological Emergency* (1986);

(11)   The *Convention on Early Notification of a Nuclear Accident* (1986); and

(12)   The '*Ospar Convention*' for the Protection of the Marine Environment of the North East Atlantic (1992) (awaiting ratification by the United Kingdom).

Whilst these *Conventions* are most directly applicable to radioactive substances handled and produced by nuclear installations, certain aspects of them are relevant to the use of

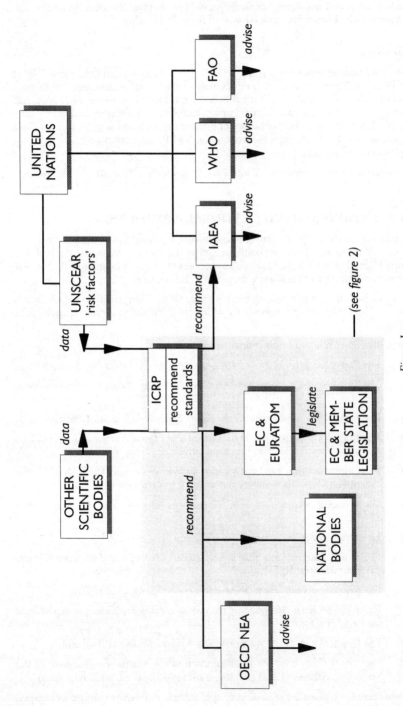

Figure 1
International advisory and control arrangements

radioactive substances in industries employing such substances as subsidiary elements in their main undertaking.

Amongst these multilateral treaties one of the most significant for the United Kingdom nuclear industry is the *Paris Convention on Third Party liability in the Field of Nuclear Energy* (1960). This *Convention* sought to harmonise for the first time the basic laws applying to the liability incurred for damage caused by nuclear incidents involving nuclear fuel and radioactive products or waste arising from land-based nuclear installations.

The main principles of the *Paris Convention* are the absolute and exclusive liability, without proof of fault, of the operator of the nuclear installation concerned; long legal limitation periods and the obligation to cover liability by insurance or other financial security arrangements.

The *Vienna Convention on Civil Liability for Nuclear Damage*, signed in 1963, is based on the same principles as the *Paris Convention* but unlike the *Paris Convention* the *Vienna Convention* has a worldwide application. The principles of the *Vienna Convention* includes provisions as to absolute and exclusive liability of the operator of a nuclear installation similar to those contained in the *Paris Convention*, although this liability is limited in time and in money – and the obligation to cover the liability with an appropriate financial guarantee.

There is a Joint Protocol to the Paris and Vienna Conventions which provides for a mutual extension of the operator's liability under the Paris and Vienna systems.

The *Brussels Supplementary Convention* to the *Paris Convention* of 1963 created a mechanism whereby the amount of compensation for victims of nuclear accidents could be increased through public funds.

The *Paris* and *Brussels Supplementary Conventions*, which were revised in 1982 through the adoption of two protocols, increased the compensation payable as provided for by the *Brussels Supplementary Convention*.

Following the Chernobyl accident, doubts have been expressed as to the adequacy of the compensation regime established by the *Paris*, *Vienna* and *Brussels Conventions*. Discussions, involving governments (including the United Kingdom Government) and interested non-governmental organisations are currently taking place in Vienna with a view to the reform of the Vienna Convention and to building on the current mutual recognition arrangements between the Paris and Vienna regimes.

The Chernobyl accident also provided a catalyst for other international agreements, including the *Convention on Early Notification of a Nuclear Accident* and the *Convention on Assistance in the Case of a Nuclear Accident or Radiological Emergency*, both of 1986. Their objective is to ensure that there is in place an efficient system for the immediate notification of a radiological incident in one country to the relevant authorities in other countries which may be affected. The latter *Convention* includes provision for the giving and receiving of assistance by signatory states. It also establishes certain immunities from civil and criminal action and from taxation to be granted to personnel from the state who provides assistance in accordance with the *Convention*. Any call for assistance under the *Convention* by the United Kingdom Government will be made public. The *Atomic Energy Act 1989* made changes to domestic legislation to implement the *Convention*.

Concerns about the discharge of radioactive effluent into seas and rivers and the dumping at sea of solid radioactive waste has prompted other treaties, for example the *Oslo Convention on Waste Dumping at Sea* (1972) and the *Paris Convention on the Prevention of Marine Pollution from Land-Based Sources* (1974). This second treaty, in particular, requires signatories to take account of the available technology in order to minimise radioactive discharges from nuclear reprocessing plants. The 1972 *Oslo Convention* and the 1974 *Paris Convention* are now being effectively replaced by the *Ospar Convention* on the Protection of the North Sea and North-East Atlantic which was signed by 13 countries in Paris in September 1992. At the time the *Ospar Convention* was concluded a 15-year moratorium on sea-dumping of radioactive waste was agreed, including by France and the United Kingdom who still retain the option to pursue this practice. If these countries maintain their position on sea dumping the Treaty Commission will have to take a formal decision before 1 January 2008 on a further extension of the moratorium.

There is at present a *Euratom/US Government Agreement* on co-operation in the nuclear field, which is due to expire at the end of 1995. The *Agreement* covers research and development, industrial and trade co-operation, safety measures, political trading, conditions and safeguards. Negotiation over the terms of a new *Agreement* have been underway since 1992 and are expected to be concluded in 1994.

The Chernobyl accident has also prompted negotiations with a view to a new international convention on nuclear safety standards. These negotiations, involving a number of governments, are at an advanced stage.

Despite the substantial number of treaties which have been signed during the past 30 years, international regulation of the safety of nuclear power is still criticised for failing to provide sufficiently tight and comprehensive control over what is undoubtedly a major ultra-hazardous transboundary environmental risk. A particular difficulty is the lack of an effective international policing organisation and the provision for only limited international inspection. The large measure of discretion as to the implementation of standards and obligations left to national governments recurs as a constant theme. For example, although the 1968 *Non-Proliferation Treaty* makes it obligatory in practice for parties to accept non-proliferation of nuclear weapons safeguards through bilateral agreements with the IAEA and to allow periodic compulsory Agency inspection for the purpose of verification, no comparable attempt has been made to enforce common adherence to the IAEA's health and safety standards. After the Chernobyl accident a UN review group recommended that the IAEA should promote better exchanges of information among states on safety and accident experience, the development of additional safety guidelines and the enhancement of the IAEA's capacity to perform safety evaluations and inspections on request. Whether Chernobyl, and the perceived risk of similar incidents, will produce more effective international control (beyond the notification and assistance arrangements outlined above) is still uncertain.

25.12   EC LEGISLATION

As explained at 25.3–25.10 above, the European Community plays an important role in developing the control regimes in Member States. Here the *Euratom Treaty* is the most important Community instrument.

25.13   The Euratom Treaty

European Community Regulations have been made under the *Euratom Treaty* providing for inspections of national facilities and for the application of Euratom safeguards. These safeguards apply to all Member States. They may be compared with the separate IAEA safeguards system for non-nuclear weapon Member States. 'Verification Agreements', which ensure the compatibility of both systems, came into force in 1977/1978 and provide for the wider application of the *Non-Proliferation Treaty Safeguards* and for co-operation between the European Community and the IAEA.

Articles 30 and *31* of the *Euratom Treaty* provide for the European Commission to lay down certain basic standards for the protection of the health of workers and the general public from the dangers of ionising radiation. These standards cover maximum permissible doses, maximum permissible exposures and contamination and principles governing health surveillance (see the *Basic Safety Standards Directive*, at 25.14 below).

In the area of environmental and public health protection the *Single European Act* of 1986 [*Article 25*] also increased generally the powers of the Community to act to safeguard the environment on the basis of the principles that a preventative approach (embodying the so-called 'precautionary principle') should be taken, that environmental damage should, as a priority, be rectified at source and that 'the polluter should pay'. A particular objective of the radiological protection standards developed by the Community is that radiation doses to workers and the public should be kept 'as low as is reasonably achievable' (the 'ALARA principle') (see *4th Environmental Action Programme* (1986)).

Another important provision of the *Euratom Treaty* is *Article 34* which concerns 'dangerous experiments' in the nuclear field. Such experiments can only take place after the Member State in question has taken 'additional health and safety measures on which it shall first obtain the opinion of the Commission' and the consent of the Commission is required where the effects of such experiments are liable to affect the territories of other Member States. The Commission is also entitled under *Article 35* to a right of access to these facilities to determine their operative efficiency.

Article 37 provides for Member States to produce data which relates to any plan for the disposal of radioactive waste. This makes it possible to determine whether the implementation of such a plan is liable to result in radioactive contamination of the water, soil or airspace of another Member State. The Commission is then required to give an opinion. Whilst this opinion may be non-binding, the European Court of Justice in *Saarland and Others v Minister for Industry, Posts and Telecommunications and Tourism and Others (1988)* (*C-187/87*), having held that the opinion must be sought prior to final authorisation of such an activity, also ruled that the Member State must accord the opinion the most searching examination and consideration.

A Commission opinion issued under *Article 37* follows a standard format. The main issues it must address include: the distance between the nuclear facility and the nearest territory of another Member State; discharge limits for liquid effluents in the case of (*a*) normal operations and (*b*) accident situations; the water body receiving the effluents, and where appropriate, the desirability of these neighbouring states concluding bilateral or multilateral agreements concerning, for example, joint regulation of the conditions governing routine discharges of radioactive waste into an international river. A number of bilateral agreements in fact already exist in respect of the siting of nuclear facilities close to international borders.

In 1982, the European Commission issued a recommendation on the application of *Article 37* to Member States and since 1987 the opinions of the Commission under *Article 37* have been published in the Official Journal of the European Communities. *Article 38* also empowers the Commission in cases of emergency to issue a *Directive* requiring a Member State to take all necessary measures to prevent infringement of basic standards relating to levels of radioactivity.

The Community, in seeking to safeguard health, has the power to lay down other safety criteria for nuclear operations, such as the transportation and management of radioactive waste (see the recent *Regulation on Shipments of Radioactive Substances between Member States (1493/93/Euratom)* which came into force on 9 July 1993). However, because of the strong sense of national interest which a number of Member States still entertain in relation to both their civil and military nuclear programmes, the Community has not yet been able to develop a comprehensive or strong role in regulating the European nuclear industry. In particular, the Commission has no enforcement powers and only minimal consultative powers in respect of the siting of nuclear installations, the storage of nuclear waste, the evaluation of different types of reactor and the setting of permissible discharge levels for radioactive effluents. In these wider areas national policy remains the determining factor.

25.14 Other European Community provisions

The Basic Safety Standards Directive

The authorisation and the subsequent operation of a nuclear installation and similar plant are governed by European Community law, namely by the *Directive on Basic Safety Standards* of 15 July 1990 (*80/836/Euratom*), as amended by a further *Directive* of 3 September 1984 (*84/467/Euratom*) ('*Basic Safety Standards Directive*'). These safety standards provide the basis for a Community policy on radiation protection which applies to any activity which may involve a risk to the population, to workers and to the environment caused by radiation or radioactive contamination. For example, *paragraph 45(4)* of the *Basic Safety Standards Directive* provides that in the event of accidents each Member State shall stipulate,

(*a*)   intervention levels, measures to be taken by the competent authorities and surveillance procedures with respect to the population groups that are liable to receive a dose in excess of the dose limits laid down in the *Directive*, and

(*b*)   the necessary resources both in personnel and in equipment to enable action to be taken to safeguard and maintain the health of the population. These measures may, if necessary, be taken by one Member State jointly with other Member States.

Quantative dose limits for various categories of workers and for members of the public are laid down (see further 25.47 below) and *Article 6* specifies a set of wide principles, including ALARA, on which approaches to dose limitation should be based.

There is currently a proposed Community Directive on standards on ionising radiation exposure limits for workers and the general public, which would amend the *Basic Safety Standards Directive*. The proposed changes are based on the publication in 1991 of the ICRP's latest recommended dose limits. However, a number of Member States are reluctant to accept the ICRP's new lower maximum exposure doses as compliance with the revised figures will be expensive.

A recent case in the European Court of Justice relating to safety standards for the health protection of the general public and workers against the dangers of ionising radiation was brought against Belgium by the European Commission. The Commission considered that Belgium was infringing Articles of the *Basic Safety Standards Directive* relating to occupational exposure to ionising radiation. The case concerned the imposition by Belgium of *stricter* standards in respect of the exposure to radiation of apprentices aged between 16 and 18. The court held, firstly, that whilst European Community dose limits were based on the ICRP guidelines these guidelines did not constitute absolute norms but are simply guidelines and the principle which governs dose limits is the principle of optimisation of protection, i.e. keeping all exposures within the ALARA principle. Having regard to the objective of the *Directive*, the court considered that, had the Community legislation intended to prohibit a higher level of protection in individual Member States, it would have expressly indicated this in its provisions (*Case C-376/90*).

The Health and Safety Commission in the United Kingdom has decided not to set lower dose standards in this country before currently anticipated revisions to the *Basic Safety Standards Directive* are adopted (HSC Policy Statement, 24 August 1993).

25.15 Environmental impact assessments

A further important Community initiative, discussed elsewhere in this Handbook, is the *Directive on the Assessment of Effects of Certain Public and Private Projects on the Environment* (*85/337/EEC*) which applies to nuclear power stations, other nuclear reactors and installations solely designed for the permanent storage or final disposal of radioactive waste. It also applies to installations for the production or enrichment of nuclear fuels, for the reprocessing of irradiated nuclear fuels and for the collection and reprocessing of radioactive waste if the relevant Member State considers that characteristics of these installations so require. The *Directive* requires the carrying out of an environmental impact assessment by relevant national regulatory bodies before consents to proceed with projects of this sort are granted. However, projects serving national defence purposes are exempt, as are those which are approved by a specific act of national legislation. In addition, Member States can exempt projects in whole or in part from the provisions of the *Directive* (see 25.46(b) below).

25.16 Intra-Community movement of radioactive materials and waste

The completion of the Single Market in Europe and the abolition of border controls present complications in monitoring the shipment of radioactive waste and radioactive substances in general. Consequently, the European Commission has been mandated by the Council of Ministers to produce standard legal documents for a system of prior authorisation and notification for shipments of such materials. A new *Regulation on Shipments of Radioactive Substances* within the European Community came into force in July 1993 (see above). It was essentially an interim measure, pending the implementation by Member States of the *Directive on the Supervision and Control of Shipments of Radioactive Waste between Member States and into and out of the Community* (*92/3/Euratom*). (The United Kingdom has now implemented this Directive through the *Transfrontier Shipment of Radioactive Waste Regulations 1993* (*SI 1993 No 3031*) which came into force on 1 January 1994 (see 25.51 below).)

The *Regulation* applies to shipments of radioactive substances between Member States whenever the quantities and concentrations of radioactive material exceed the levels laid down in the *Basic Safety Standards Directive*. The *Regulation* and the *Directive* also apply to shipments of radioactive waste. They provide that checks carried out under Community or national law on relevant shipments should not take the form of controls at frontiers but should be conducted solely within the context of routine checks performed in a non-discriminatory manner throughout the territory of a Member State.

25.17 Emergency measures and provisions

Also following the Chernobyl accident, the European Community adopted *Regulation 1707/86/EEC* which stipulated maximum permitted contamination levels of foodstuffs (being 370 Bq/kg for milk and food preparations for infants, and 600 Bq/kg for all other products specified in the Regulation) for a period of time after the Chernobyl incident. A *Regulation* laying down maximum permitted radioactivity levels for foodstuffs, feeding stuffs and drinking water in the case of abnormal levels of radioactivity or of a nuclear accident was also adopted in 1987.

The Council Decision on Community arrangements for the early exchange of information in the event of a radiological emergency was issued in 1987 (*87/606/Euratom*). This established a rapid information exchange, ECURIE, which is based on a system set up by IAEA.

A *Resolution* was also adopted in 1987 on the introduction of Community Cooperation on Civil Protection (*87/C 76/01*). It provides, in particular, a guide to civil protection in the European Community including a list of liaison officials from the Member States and the Commission who are required to hold meetings to organise 'regular authorised simulation exercises' and to work towards better use of the data banks which exist in the civil protection field.

In addition, the *Directive on Informing the Public about Health Protection Measures in the Event of a Radiological Emergency (89/618/Euratom)* defines the content of the information to be provided to the population under normal circumstances and in the case of an emergency. A system entitled the International Nuclear Event Scale classifies nuclear events at seven levels. The Chernobyl incident registered at level 7 whilst the Tomsk incident (see below) was found to be a level 3 incident.

The European Commission intends to continue its work in this field particularly in respect of upgrading safety standards, the verification of monitoring of installations, the enhancement of public information and education and the establishment of adequate training in radiation protection. The Tomsk incident in Siberia, in which a tank with nuclear waste exploded contaminating an area of 120 sq km, has produced a call by the last Danish Presidency of the European Community to set up an Atlantic environmental alliance to deal with potential catastrophes resulting from the operation of nuclear power stations in Eastern Europe.

The Community also contributes substantial sums to a multilateral nuclear safety fund operated by the European Bank for Reconstruction and Development.

25.18 Summary

As we have seen, the Euratom system and the work of the European Community generally are important elements in the present regulatory regime operated in the United Kingdom and in the international regime of co-operation and assistance established between Member States. The degree of control exercisable at the European level is, however, only partial and the Euratom regime has been criticised in the following specific areas:

(1)   a lacuna exists whereby neither the Community nor the IAEA has a right to inspect the records of military or mixed civil-military plants;

(2)   there is no agreed definition of radioactive waste within the European Community or categorisation into low, medium or high level radioactive wastes in Community law. This leads to inconsistencies between Member States as to the manner in which such wastes are handled, both domestically and in intra-Community dealings.

Even in the area of radiological protection, where the Community has been most active and effective, there is still a high degree of national autonomy. In the United Kingdom the Government looks to the Medical Research Council (MRC) to advise on the biological aspects of new standards determined by international bodies and their acceptability in the United Kingdom. There is also the NRPB which is intended to be a national point of authoritative reference on radiological protection. The NRPB, as well as conducting applied radiological research, formulates its own standards and codes of practice and advises the Government and the nuclear operators on their radiological responsibilities. Thus, there is a system within the United Kingdom which effectively 'shadows' wider international developments, including the promulgation of specific Community legislation, such as the *Basic Safety Standards Directive*. This domestic system not only provides advice on the implementation of Community *Regulations* and *Directives* but, on occasions, issues its own guidance which anticipates such legislation. This is discussed further in the following section.

25.19 UNITED KINGDOM BODIES

As we have seen, radiological protection standards, which are the cornerstone of nuclear safety, are, in the United Kingdom, based primarily on the recommendations of international organisations, the United Kingdom's obligations under international *Conventions* and European Community legislation.

Again as we have seen, advice to the United Kingdom Government on the levels of human exposure to radiation, which are acceptable from the health point of view, is given by the MRC and the NRPB. The NRPB provides advice on the recommendations of the ICRP and on relevant legislation of the European Community. It also has a prior consultative relationship with the European Commission at the stage when relevant Community legislation is being proposed.

25.20 The National Radiological Protection Board

The NRPB was established by the *Radiological Protection Act 1970*. The Board's functions are:

'(i)   by means of research and otherwise, to advance the acquisition of knowledge about the protection of workers and the general public from radiation hazards; and

(ii)   to provide information and advice to persons (including government departments) with responsibilities in the United Kingdom in relation to the protection from radiation hazards either of the community as a whole or of particular sections of the community'.

The Board is an independent and small body appointed by the Health Ministers, after consultation with the United Kingdom Atomic Energy Authority (UKAEA), and the MRC. The Board also has an advisory committee of 15 to 25 persons appointed by the Health Ministers. This committee has a duty to bring to the notice of the Board any matters on which, in its opinion, any person requires the advice or services of the NRPB.

The Board itself is comprised of persons eminent in the fields of nuclear energy and medicine, while the advisory committee is partly expert and partly representative, where the scientists work with representatives from both sides of industry.

The activities of the Board are regionalised, based on district headquarters. The Board employs a substantial team of technical and scientific staff and its extensive activities fall into two categories. First, advisory services, which consist of advice, measurement and investigation tasks on aspects of radiological protection, such as the design of laboratories and the prevention of accidents. Secondly, the Board provides technical services, for example the design and testing of film badges for monitoring the safety of personnel, monitoring of premises, design features of installations such as warning devices, testing of instruments and materials, testing for leakages and advice on incident and accident strategies and training functions.

The NRPB also produces numerous publications, both of a general explanatory nature and on specific studies it has undertaken (examples are studies of radioactivity in house dust in West Cumbria, studies of radon gas in homes in Cornwall and analyses of current work on electric and magnetic field exposure) or containing particular recommendations or guidelines.

25.21 The Medical Research Council

As discussed above, the Government also receives advice from the MRC on radiation issues, especially on the biological implications of proposed new standards and legislation. The MRC operates under the aegis of The Development of Health.

25.22 Radioactive Substances and Nuclear Installations

25.22 The Radioactive Waste Management Advisory Committee

Advice to Government on the development and implementation of policy on radioactive waste management is provided by a third body, The Radioactive Waste Management Advisory Committee (RWMAC). This Committee has an independent chairman and a majority of independent members with relevant backgrounds. RWMAC's terms of reference are to 'advise the Secretaries of State for the Environment, Scotland and Wales on the technical and environmental implementation of an overall policy for all aspects of the management of civil radioactive waste, including research and development; and to advise on any such matters referred to it by the Secretaries of State'. One of RWMAC's current tasks is to evaluate the proposals for long-term storage facility for intermediate level radioactive waste (see below).

25.23 UK Nirex Limited

A further body, UK Nirex Limited, (formerly the Nuclear Industry Radioactive Waste Executive) was set up to implement the national waste strategy, covering wastes from defence as well as civil sources. It is Nirex's responsibility to provide and manage any new facility for the disposal of low and intermediate level radioactive waste. Nirex, established by the Government in 1982, has now been incorporated as a company and its ownership is divided between British Nuclear Fuels plc, Nuclear Electric plc, the UKAEA and Scottish Nuclear plc, with the Secretary of State having a special share. The company is at the present time investigating the possibility of developing a long-term intermediate level waste disposal facility in West Cumbria.

25.24 The Committee on Medical Aspects of Radiation in the Environment

Last amongst the principal advisory bodies is the Committee on Medical Aspects of Radiation in the Environment (COMARE) which was established in 1985 in response to the report of the Independent Advisory Group chaired by Sir Douglas Black. This Group had considered suggestions of high cancer rates, in particular childhood leukaemia, in West Cumbria. COMARE's First Report, on West Cumbria, was published in 1986. It has since produced further reports, including in relation to the leukaemia incidence in the vicinity of the Dounreay nuclear installation in North East Scotland. The Committee has its own secretriat but reports to, and is funded by, the Department of Health.

25.25 The authorising bodies

The responsibility for administering the various legal and regulatory controls over the activities of the nuclear industry and the use and disposal of radioactive substances lies with a number of Government departments and agencies. These are, principally,

(i)   the Health and Safety Executive (HSE) through its Nuclear Installations Inspectorate (NII) and its Field Operations Division which includes Factory and Agriculture Inspectors;

(ii)   the Ministry of Agriculture Fisheries and Food (MAFF) which has joint responsibility for granting radioactive accumulation and disposal authorisations to nuclear installations which are licensed sites situated in England. The Secretary of State for Wales and the Department of Agriculture (Northern Ireland) have similar responsibility for nuclear installations in Wales and Northern Ireland (see below), and

(iii)   Her Majesty's Inspectorate of Pollution (HMIP) in England and Wales, Her Majesty's Industrial Pollution Inspectorate (HMIPI) and the Alkali and

Radiochemical Inspectorate perform these functions in Scotland and Northern Ireland respectively. They grant authorisations both to nuclear installations and to other concerns using radioactive substances or disposing of radioactive waste, as well as being responsible for the registration of undertakings which use radioactive material or mobile radioactive apparatus (see also below).

United Kingdom radiological control regime

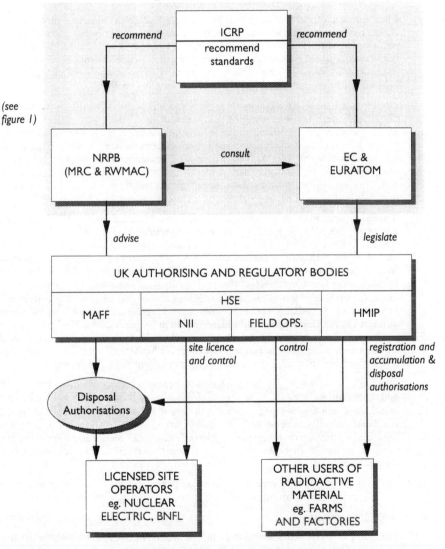

Figure 2

Note: For the bodies in Scotland and Northern Ireland corresponding to HMIP and for the departments in Wales and Northern Ireland corresponding to MAFF see 25.25 above.

A detailed discussion of the statutory framework within which each of these bodies operates and of their separate regulatory functions is given at 25.27 below. An overview of this statutory framework and the interrelationship between these various bodies is illustrated in Figure 2.

25.26 GENERAL RADIOLOGICAL PRINCIPLES AND PROTECTION STANDARDS

Most radiological protection principles are based on the recommendations of the ICRP. Its current principal recommendations are contained in ICRP Publication 60, published in April 1991. Present United Kingdom standards on radiation exposure are based on the *Ionising Radiation Regulations* (*SI 1985 No 1333*) which implement the *Basic Safety Standards Directive*. These are, in turn, founded on the ICRP's previous recommendations, published in 1977 in ICRP Publication 26.

Underpinning the ICRP recommended quantitative dose limits there is the fundamental principle that all exposures should be kept within the ALARA principle described in 25.12 above. A corresponding principle of dose limitation is found throughout the United Kingdom control regime. It requires risks from radiation to be kept 'as low as reasonably practicable' (the 'ALARP' principle). The conceptual and practical differences between ALARA and ALARP are much debated, but each operates as a basic restraint on activities involving radioactive substances and as a motivation towards continual monitoring and upgrading of plant equipment and working procedures.

The basic principles of radiological protection established by the ICRP are also adopted by the NII in their Safety Assessment Principles (SAPs). SAPs are framed as a set of objectives which are used as a reference for judgements which must be made by the NII in the evaluation of nuclear installations which require site licences under the *Nuclear Installations Act 1965*. In 1983 the NII published the 'Safety Assessment Principles for Nuclear Chemical Plant'. They include radiological principles, principles for the evaluation of radiation exposures under normal operating conditions, principles for the evaluation of fault conditions and protection systems. The document also sets out relevant engineering and management principles. The 1983 SAPs cover nuclear installations other than reactors and nuclear assemblies. They were published subsequent to the 'Safety Assessment Principles for Nuclear Power Reactors' issued in 1979 which specified similar specific principles relevant to nuclear reactors.

The policy upon which all SAPs are based is that the recommendations of the ICRP and the requirements of the *Basic Safety Standards Directive* must be followed in respect of radiation and exposures to persons both on and off nuclear sites. SAPs require a demonstration that all reasonably practicable steps have been taken to prevent plant failure, plant damage or maloperation, thus reducing the chance of accidents occurring and limiting the likelihood and consequences of such accidents. There are also specific requirements that:

(i)   as the result of normal operations, no person receives doses of radiation in excess of the appropriate limits;

(ii)   the exposure of individuals to radiation are kept as low as reasonably practicable;

(iii) the collective doses to operators and the general public as a result of operation of the facility are kept as low as reasonably practicable;

(iv)   all reasonably practicable steps are taken to prevent accidents; and

(v)   all reasonably practical steps are taken to minimise the radiological consequences of any accident.

A designer of a facility will also be required to show that the radiation risk is within the ALARP principle.

In response to recommendations made by the Inspector at the Sizewell B Public Inquiry, the HSE have published a public document entitled *Tolerability of Risk from Nuclear Power Stations* (1988). It discusses specifically the risks arising from nuclear power stations in both normal operating, and in accident, conditions and canvasses certain levels of 'tolerability' (i.e. the limits of acceptable risk) for various individual and societal risks resulting from nuclear power stations. For example, for infrequent unplanned events, targets have been set of 1 in 100,000 per year for fatal risks for workers and 5 in 10,000,000 per year for a member of the public. These risks are suggested as 'tolerable'. These and other similar statistics are reflected in the SAPS.

Risk assessments for the design for conventional hazards, as well as nuclear and radiological hazards, are usually undertaken by the NII to ensure that, where it is not reasonably practical for such hazards to be avoided, appropriate precautions are then incorporated in the construction methods and operating procedures of nuclear installations, as is required by the *Control of Substances Hazardous to Health Regulations 1988*.

25.27 UNITED KINGDOM LEGISLATION

The nuclear industry and the use of radioactive material in factories, laboratories and hospitals are regulated generally by a series of Acts of Parliament and subsidiary legislation, chief amongst which are the following.

1.   The *Radioactive Substances Acts 1948* and *1960* (as amended by the *Environmental Protection Act 1990*) – now consolidated in the *Radioactive Substances Act 1993*, the principal provisions of which came into force on 27 August 1993.

2.   The *Nuclear Installations Act 1965* (as amended by the *Energy Act 1983, Part II*), and

3.   the *Ionising Radiation Regulations Act 1985*.

The main control regime can be conveniently divided into two parts:

(*a*)   the regulation of nuclear installations and

(*b*)   the regulation of the use of radioactive substances in other situations.

In each of these areas control of the environmental effects of the use of radiation is exercised through (i) the licensing or registration of sites, premises and equipment and (ii) the granting of authorisations for the accumulation and disposal of radioactive substances and waste.

25.28 General duties

There are a number of general legislative prohibitions and restrictions on activities relating to the use of atomic energy and radioactive substances, in particular the following.

25.29 *Under the Atomic Energy Act 1946*

The UKAEA and the President of the Board of Trade have special powers in relation to atomic energy. These include powers to enter premises and to inspect documents which are, or are believed to be, related to atomic energy or other prescribed substances. There is also the power to acquire the rights as to the energy released from atomic power as a result of any process, incuding an artificial fission process, and the liabilities of persons who are parties to a contract relating to the production or use of atomic energy [*sections 5 and 9*].

Section 11 provides for the control of the dissemination of sensitive information relating to plants which are, or may be, used to produce or use atomic energy. Dissemination constitutes an offence where carried out by an unauthorised person or to an unauthorised person without the requisite Government authority. An officer of an offending company (or anyone acting in that capacity at the time of the commission of the offence) is personally guilty of that offence as well unless he proves that the offence was committed without his consent or connivance and that he exercised due diligence to prevent the commission of the offence having regard to the nature of his functions in that capacity and to all the circumstances. Penalties for this offence include, on summary conviction, imprisonment for up to three months and/or a fine not exceeding £2,000, or, on conviction on indictment, up to five years or an unlimited fine.

25.30 *Under the Radioactive Substances Act 1993*

Without the necessary registration, authorisation or exemptions (see 25.31–25.40 below) no-one may:

(*a*)   on premises which are used for the purposes of an undertaking by him, keep or use radioactive material knowing or having reasonable grounds for believing it to be such material [*section 6*];

['Radioactive material' is subject to a complex definition in the 1993 Act (see *section 1*). It does not include radioactive waste (see (*c*) below), but it may be one or both of:

(i)   a substance containing an element specified in *Schedule 1* of the *Act* (i.e. actinium, lead, polonium, protoactinium, radium, radon, thorium or uranium) whether in solid, liquid or gaseous form where the radioactivity of that element per gramme of the substance in which it is contained is greater than the relevant values also specified in *Schedule 1*, or

(ii)   a substance possessing radioactivity which is wholly or partly attributable to an artificial process of nuclear fission, or similar process, or as a result of contamination.

There is also a minimum level of radioactivity prescribed. Below this level the substance is not treated as 'radioactive material' e.g. the small quantities of radium contained in the luminescent dials of some time pieces and process control equipment may fall outside the definition. Subject to this prescribed minimum, 'radioactive material' includes both certain specified natural radionuclides as well as all radionuclides arising from man-made fission processes and any other substances which are radioactive because they carry on them or in them such radionuclides. It covers most possible sources of radioactivity, other than those occurring naturally, and anything made from or containing such a source.]

(*b*)   keep, use, lend or let on hire mobile radioactive apparatus for testing measuring or otherwise investigating the characteristics of substances or articles or releasing qualities of radioactive material into the environment or into organisms [*section 9*];

['Mobile radioactive apparatus' is also widely defined by *section 3*. It includes any apparatus, 'equipment, appliance or other thing which is radioactive material' and which is constructed or made to be transportable. It will include portable x-ray machines used throughout industry, in particular in engineering construction and metallurgy, and medical equipment used in radiological investigation and therapy.]

(c)   dispose of radioactive waste from premises which he uses as an undertaking [*section 13(1)*];

or

accumulate radioactive waste on such premises with a view to its disposal [*section 14*];

or

dispose of radioactive waste from mobile radioactive apparatus]*section 13(2)*];

or

in the course of carrying on an undertaking, dispose of radioactive waste which he has received for the purpose of disposal [*section 13(3)*].

[Under *section 2* 'radioactive waste' means 'radioactive material' which would otherwise be waste (see at (*a*) above) or material which is contaminated with radioactivity. There are special provisions for disposals and accumulations of radioactive waste arising from clocks or watches [*sections 15(1); 8(4)(5)*]. Radioactive waste may come in many forms, ranging from contaminated protective clothing used by radiation workers in nuclear power stations and contaminated soil samples analysed by laboratories for their radioactive content to the millions of gallons of dilute radioactive liquid effluent which are discharged each year into the Irish Sea from British Nuclear Fuels plc's reprocessing plant at Sellafield].

Each of these different duties described at (*a*)–(*c*) above carries with it the separate duty of not 'causing or permitting' any of the basic prohibited activities.

The contravention of all these duties is punishable, on summary conviction, by a fine of up to £20,000 or (for a private individual) by six months imprisonment, or both, or on conviction on indictment, by an unlimited fine or up to five years imprisonment, or, again, both [*section 32*].

25.31 Nuclear installations

Major nuclear facilities, such as nuclear power stations, nuclear fuel preparation and production plants and radioactive waste reprocessing plants, are subject to a special site licensing and inspection regime under the *Nuclear Installations Act 1965*. They are also governed by special arrangements with regard to the use of radioactive material and the accumulation and disposal of radioactive waste in relation to which the basic duties under the *Radioactive Substances Act 1993* were discussed at 25.30 above.

25.32 *Site licensing – the Nuclear Installations Act 1965 (the 1965 Act)*

The *1965 Act* controls certain nuclear installations and operations by means of a licensing system operated by the Health and Safety Executive (HSE) through its Nuclear Installations Inspectorate (NII) [*section 1*]. The *1965 Act* also provides for a permitting system for certain specialist operations relating to the extraction of the radionuclides plutonium and uranium from irradiated matter and the enrichment of uranium [*section 2*].

'Nuclear site licences' granted under *section 1* of the *1965 Act* are required for:

(a)   all nuclear reactors, including experimental reactors (but excluding those used in ships and aircraft);

(b)   other nuclear power plants;

(c)   plants engaged in the nuclear fuel cycle (e.g. uranium enrichment, fuel preparation and fuel assembly and storage plants);

(*d*)   sites and plants for storing and reprocessing radioactive waste; and

(*e*)   radioactive waste depositories.

Licences can only be granted to corporate bodies and are not transferable [*section 3*].

The construction, commissioning, operation and decommissioning of any nuclear installation which is granted a nuclear site licence is carried out by the licensee under the strict supervision and control of the NII. Before the licence is issued, prospective licensees are required to provide the NII with a preliminary safety report (PSR) to demonstrate to the NII's satisfaction that in principle the licensee is capable of constructing and operating the proposed facility to an acceptable standard of safety. A pre-construction safety report (PCSR) is then prepared which is based on the detailed design. It gives a design description and a comprehensive statement of the safety case which enables the safety features of the facility to be identified and its safety significance assessed. As the development proceeds the NII identify points at which they require further information on particular nuclear safety aspects of the project before issuing a consent to proceed. Consent to commence construction of the facility depends upon a satisfactory outcome of the NII's review and assessment of the PCSR.

The NII has safety assessment principles for nuclear installations which have been developed primarily for its own staff but also to assist designers and operators. The principles, which are divided into three categories, comprise (*a*) fundamental principles on radiological protection, (*b*) basic principles to limit radiological consequences in both normal and accident conditions and (*c*) engineering principles which provide a basis for good practice. In carrying out an assessment, the assessor is also required to judge the extent to which the safety submission shows conformity with the relevant SAPs (see 25.26 above).

When applying for a nuclear site licence the applicant may be required to serve notice of the application containing specified particulars on relevant bodies, such as local authorities and the National Rivers Authority (NRA). In such cases a three-month period is provided prior to any grant of a licence, during which time these bodies may make representations about the application to the NII [*section 3(3)*].

25.33 *Site licence conditions*

The NII may impose a wide range of conditions on a site licence [*section 4(1)*] and the NII has an on-going obligation to review these conditions in the light of any relevant representations which may be made by organisations such as trade unions representing workers on the site [*section 4(4)*]. The nuclear site licence may also be varied at any time to exclude parts of the site which no longer need to be licensed [*section 3(6)*] or may be totally revoked [*section 5(1)*].

During construction, conditions may be imposed requiring the licensee to provide the NII with design information which it considers necessary and to submit for approval whatever quality control system is in operation. Other matters covered by conditions during construction may be the inspection and testing of components and the setting up of a plant commissioning committee. Conditions will later be added concerning authorised personnel, the preservation of records, radiological protection control, the storage of nuclear fuel, accumulation of wastes and the preparation of emergency reports. The NII supervises the construction and commissioning of new plant and equipment on a 'step by step' basis. The site licensee can only move on to the next relevant stage of development after the NII has been satisfied on technical grounds that this is appropriate and has issued a formal licence instrument permitting it to be done. As a matter of practice, the NII liaises with HMIP, or its relevant counterparts, on plant development questions relating to radioactive waste discharges and waste management systems generally.

Once the plant becomes operational, the conditions invariably require the setting up of a permanent safety committee. They also make provision for the plant to be shut down regularly to permit detailed examination and testing of components and a search for common faults. After the examination, consent to operate the reactor again must be obtained from the Inspectorate.

Site licence conditions may also require the maintenance of an efficient system for monitoring ionising radiations from anything on the site, or from anything discharged on or from the site. This monitoring, in the case of stations operated by the nuclear generating industry, is extended in some cases to points up to 20 miles from the station. The programme may start up to a year before the station begins operation, to provide a point of reference. The results are reported to the Department of the Environment (DoE) and MAFF (which also carry out their own monitoring exercises). The NII is also now entitled to recover the costs of nuclear safety research which it sponsors from nuclear site licencees and applicants.

On decommissioning, conditions may be imposed relating to the process of decommissioning, the demolition methods employed and the disposal of the materials on the site. Further, prior to decommissioning, as installations approach the end of their design life, NII will conduct a long-term safety review of the plant.

The licensee has a duty to keep copies of the conditions which are contained in a schedule to the licence posted on the site [*section 4(5)*].

25.34 *Site licence conditions and emergency plans*

Licence conditions invariably also include an obligation to provide for an emergency plan and, at least in installations operated by the nuclear generating industry, these plans are exercised annually. The plan typically outlines the duties of fire control bodies, first aid, rescue and the monitoring of radiation within and in the vicinity of the station. These plans must also be capable of extension to deal with events resulting in large releases of radionuclides, even though the basic design philosophy is intended to make such accidents improbable. Emergency plans also depend on cooperative action between the site operator's staff, the local authorities and the emergency services, coordinated as in any civil emergency by the police who are specifically responsible for any evacuation of the local population that may be called for.

In the early stages of a major accident at a United Kingdom site, responsibility for advising the police on off-site countermeasures lies with the site operator. Within a few hours, the operator should have established an Off-Site Centre, some way from the site, at which a wider range of regional and national organisations would be represented to provide advice and assistance as required. Central Government would appoint a Government Technical Adviser (GTA) to coordinate the advice from these bodies, which would include the DoE and MAFF (or equivalents in Scotland and Northern Ireland), plus the NII and the NRPB. Each of these bodies would be supported by its own headquarters emergency organisation.

The radiological protection aspects of emergency plans require an early assessment of the magnitude and nature of the release, its dispersion in the environment, and the doses that might arise. The countermeasures that might be taken to avoid exposure of the public would depend on the projected levels of dose that would otherwise be received. The NRPB has issued advice on the levels of dose at which specific countermeasures would produce some positive overall benefit.

The site operator would carry out measurements of dose rates and activity concentrations in air and other media in the vicinity of the site. MAFF would undertake comprehensive monitoring of foodstuffs in the affected area and would extend its routine monitoring programme to provide information on a wider basis. The NRPB would make an independent assessment of the radiological impact, and would provide suitable advice to the GTA and to Central Government. The NRPB would also coordinate monitoring of the environment on a national scale, to provide reassurance to people living in unaffected areas and to enable the full impact of the accident to be assessed.

Although accidents occurring overseas by their nature are likely to have a lower radiological impact on the United Kingdom than equivalent accidents occurring within the country, a coordinated national response plan is provided by the DoE, which is currently setting up a network of automatic gamma-ray dose rate monitoring stations to provide warning of an overseas accident, should the international notification arrangements fail. In the event of an overseas accident being either notified or detected, the system would provide information on dose rates throughout the United Kingdom and the DoE would also coordinate other forms of radiological monitoring.

In relation to these type of emergencies, the United Kingdom *Regulations*, the *Public Information for Radiation Emergencies Regulations 1992* (*SI 1992 No 2997*), which came into force on 1 January 1993, implement the main requirements of the *EC Directive on Public Information in the Event of an Emergency* (see 25.26 above). The *Regulations* have two main requirements. Members of the public within any area adjacent to a working area from which the possibility of a radiation emergency is reasonably foreseeable should receive certain prescribed information. The operator is required to prepare this information and ensure its dissemination. Further, county and regional councils must prepare and keep up to date arrangements which ensure that members of the public affected by a radiation emergency receive prompt and appropriate information. This information needs to cover the facts of the emergency and advice on intended health protection measures.

An air crash on a nuclear installation is a particular hazard which is provided for in the *Air Navigation (Restriction of Flying) (Nuclear Installations) Regulations 1988* (*SI 1988 No 1138*). These *Regulations* restrict flying in the vicinity of certain specified nuclear installations where the Secretary of State considers it necessary in the public interest.

The Government Advisory Committee on the Safety of Nuclear Installations, which keeps under general review safety measures at licenced sites, monitors, in particular emergency exercise procedures.

25.35 *Reporting of 'occurrences', site supervision and enforcement*

The site licensee has a strict duty not to cause injury to people or damage to property as a result of 'occurrences' involving nuclear matter which is present on the site, or in the course of transportation to or from the site or which originally emanated from the site [*section 7(1)(a) and (2)*]. (People other than licensees have a similar general duty in respect of the transportation of nuclear matter within the United Kingdom [*section 11*].) 'Nuclear matter' is technically defined and includes some, but not all, potential sources of ionising radiations.

There is also a strict duty on licensees not to cause third party injury or damage resulting from on-site irradiation by radioactive sources other than nuclear matter or irradiation arising from radioactive waste stored at or discharged from the site [*section 7(1)(b)*].

Against this background, licensees have to report promptly certain dangerous occurrences which take place on a licensed site or in the course of transportation of nuclear matter. The NII are empowered to carry out investigations into such occurrences and to publish their reports, as well as to keep a register of occurrences [*sections 22, 23*]. The

Nuclear Installations (Dangerous Occurrences) Regulations 1965 (SI 1965 No 1824) specify the type of occurrence which must be reported to the NII and the manner in which the report must be made. Under the *1965 Act* the licensee is obliged to make the report by the quickest means available to him and this obligation is reflected in the *Regulations*.

General supervision of licensed sites is maintained by the NII, whose inspectors visit sites regularly to ensure compliance with the regulations and standards.

Operating a nuclear installation without a site licence is a criminal offence. [*Section 1(3)*]. Operating in breach of the licence conditions is also a criminal offence, and it may cause the NII to revoke the licence. [*Section 4(6)*]. In practice, there is close cooperation between the operators and the NII, and it is rare for enforcement action of this type to be required. There are infrequent prosecutions, usually relating to technical breaches of conditions – there was only one such prosecution in 1990–1991.

Proceedings relating to an offence under the *1965 Act* may be brought only by the Secretary of State, or with the consent of the Director of Public Prosecutions [*section 25*].

The power to enforce the general duties (not relating specifically to radioactivity) of operators of nuclear installations under the *Health and Safety at Work Act 1974* also lie with the HSE, through the NII.

25.36 *Information on licensed nuclear sites*

The rights of the general public to information about nuclear installations are limited primarily to information about the location and extent of licensed sites.

The Secretary of State for the Environment has a duty to maintain and make available for public inspection a list of licensed sites and maps showing the position and limits of the sites [*section 6*]. Details of each site is to be kept until the expiry of thirty years after the termination of the relevant licensee's 'period of responsibility' for the site.

Persons 'having duties' on a nuclear site, such as trade union representatives, have a right to information about the conditions attached to the site licence [*section 4(4)*].

Any person who has obtained information in the exercise of his powers under the *1965 Act* commits an offence if he discloses that information without the consent of the Secretary of State [*section 24(5)*]. Members of NII as office holders under the Crown owe separate duties under the *Official Secrets Act 1911*.

In practice, most civil nuclear installations form Local Liaison Committees in order to communicate with the local population. The Committees meet at least once a year, and include among their members elected representatives of the community and local trade union officials, as well as plant personnel and representatives of NII and Government departments. The meetings of these liaison committees are used to inform local people about the operation of the installation and, in particular, its radioactive discharge record.

25.37 *Nuclear installations operated by the UKAEA and the Crown*

Nuclear installations under the direct control of the UKAEA and the Crown do not require nuclear site licences [*sections 1, 9*]. The UKAEA is responsible for the nuclear reactor and reprocessing facility at Dounreay in Scotland as well as research operations at Harwell and certain parts of the Sellafield site. The Crown's principal nuclear activities are concerned with weapons production and Defence under the auspices of the Ministry of Defence. Major MOD nuclear installations include the Atomic Weapons Research Establishment at Aldermaston and the naval dockyards at Devonport and Rosyth.

The UKAEA and Crown installations are not, however, unregulated. Express provision is made in the *1965 Act* for the UKAEA [*section 8*] and the Crown [*section 9*] to owe the same strict duties as a licensee owes under *section 7* (see above). The NII operate informal arrangements under which they monitor and inspect safety systems UKAEA and MOD sites as if they were formally licensed.

25.38 *Disposal authorisations for licensed nuclear sites under the Radioactive Substances Act 1993*

As explained at 25.28 above, it is a criminal offence to use radioactive material or mobile radioactive apparatus or to accumulate or to dispose of radioactive waste [*Radioactive Substances Act 1993, ss 6, 9, 13, 14*] without a relevant registration, authorisation or exemption.

The regime of registration and authorisation under the *1993 Act* is discussed in detail at 25.40 below. This regime covers the use of radioactivity throughout industry. So far as nuclear installations are concerned, this regime stands alongside, and supplements, the nuclear site licence system discussed earlier. There are, however, special provisions made for the application of the *Radioactive Substances Act 1993* to licensed nuclear sites. They include:

(*a*)   licensed nuclear sites are exempt from the requirement under *section 6* to be registered as premises where radioactive matter is kept or used [*section 8*];

(*b*)   such sites are nevertheless still required to register with the inspectorates appointed under the *1993 Act* (see 25.41 below) any mobile radioactive apparatus which is used on site [*sections 9, 10*];

(*c*)   licensed nuclear sites are exempt from the requirement to secure an authorisation from the inspectorates for the accumulation of radioactive waste under *section 14* [*section 14(3)*]; and

(*d*)   The operators of licensed nuclear sites require an authorisation under *section 13* to dispose of radioactive waste. But again special rules apply to nuclear sites:

(i)   apart from nuclear sites in Scotland, the disposal authorisation is issued not, as in other cases (see 25.42 below), by the relevant chief inspector appointed under *section 4* of the *1993 Act* acting alone, but by the chief inspector acting jointly with

(*a*)   in England, the Minister of Agriculture, Fisheries and Food,

(*b*)   in Wales, the Secretary of State for Wales, and

(*c*)   in Northern Ireland, the Department of Agriculture (Northern Ireland).

[*section 16(3)*];

(ii)   the chief inspector and the relevant Minister must consult in all cases with certain consultees (including local authorities and water bodies) before a disposal authorisation is granted [*section 16(5)*];

(iii)   there is no 'deemed refusal' procedure where an application by the nuclear site operator is not determined within the prescribed period of four months (see 25.42 (*d*) below); and

(iv)   the nuclear site licensee has no right of appeal against a decision to refuse, vary or revoke an authorisation or against conditions which may be attached to it [*section 26(3)(a)*].

25.39 *Nuclear installations – the inter-relationship between the nuclear site licence (NII) and the system of disposal authorisation (HMIP and MAFF)*

As is apparent from the foregoing discussion, the dual system of control exercised over licensed nuclear sites by NII, on the one hand, and the chief inspectors and the relevant Ministers, on the other, is complex. Each regulatory body has its own area of principal responsibility, but there is a degree of overlap with aspects of off-site and on-site safety being of interest to both. For example, a plant failure may lead to a discharge of radioactivity from the site as well as creating a radiological hazard for workers on the site. The one incident may lead to breach of site licence conditions and of conditions (typically quantative limits on the discharge of certain radionuclides or of types of radioactivity) in the disposal authorisation. A specific illustration of this is the so-called 'beach incident' which occurred off British Nuclear Fuels plc's Sellafield site in November 1983 when radioactive solids were discharged through the company's marine discharge pipe. This led to a prosecution under the *Nuclear Installations Act 1965* for breach of site licence conditions (including the failure to keep adequate on-site records) and under the *Radioactive Substances Act 1960* for breach of a condition in the disposal authorisations which required all discharges to be within the ALARA principle.

In such cases the NII and the chief inspector and the relevant Minister will often conduct joint reports into the incident and, if necessary, carry out a joint audit of the facilities on the site. Under *section 5* of the *1993 Act* the Minister of Agriculture, Fisheries and Food and the Department of Agriculture (Northern Ireland) may appoint their own inspectorate in relation to nuclear sites situated in England and Northern Ireland. On 17 October 1990 the HSE and HMIP (who have been appointed as the inspectorate in England under *section 4* of the *1993 Act* (see 25.40 below) entered into a special operational demarcation arrangement with regard to environmental policing generally. This arrangement applies to the nuclear sector (see Health and Safety Commission Annual Report 1990/91).

Nuclear installations will often need to dispose of non-radioactive substances, such as heavy metals and solvents, as part of their routine operations. The discharge of non-radioactive species do not fall within the scope of the authorisation system laid down by the *Radioactive Substances Act 1993*. Where appropriate, separate consents will be required e.g. from the NRA in relation to releases into controlled waters, from the Waste Regulatory Authority for controlled waste and from the local authority for atmospheric emissions.

25.40 Radioactive Substances Act 1993 – the general regime

There are many undertakings which use radioactive materials and generate or handle radioactive waste as well as nuclear installations requiring nuclear site licences under the *Nuclear Installations Act 1965*. These undertakings include commercial laboratories, hospitals, research facilities, engineering concerns and chemical plants. They, like nuclear installations, are regulated by the system provided for in the *Radioactive Substances Act 1993*.

As with the *Radioactive Substances Act 1960* which preceded it, the *1993 Act* provides for a system of regulation and enforcement administered by inspectorates for England and Wales, for Scotland and for Northern Ireland, appointed under *section 4* of the Act. Each inspectorate is headed by a chief inspector. In England and Wales Her Majesty's Inspectorate of Pollution has been appointed as the relevant inspectorate under the *1993 Act*. The inspectorate in Scotland is Her Majesty's Industrial Pollution Inspectorate and in Northern Ireland the Alkali and Radiochemical Inspectorate.

25.41 *Permits to use radioactive material and apparatus*

The use of radioactive material or of mobile radioactive apparatus is, as explained at 25.28–25.31 above, a criminal offence unless the premises where the radioactive material is to be used is registered with the chief inspector appointed under the *Radioactive Substances Act 1993* [*sections 6, 7*] or the mobile radioactive apparatus is itself so registered [*sections 9, 10*]. In each case:

(*a*)   the application for registration requires the submission of a statutory form giving particulars, not only of the premises or the apparatus, but also of their future use by the applicant [*sections 7(2), 10(1)*];

(*b*)   the chief inspector must (subject to the need to safeguard national security) send to relevant local authorities copies of the application [*sections 7(3), 10(3)*];

(*c*)   the application for registration may be granted or refused by the chief inspector or granted subject to limitations and conditions [*sections 7(4), (5), 10(2)*];

(*d*)   if an application is not determined within a prescribed period of four months from the date on which it was made it may be treated as having been refused; and

(*e*)   the chief inspector may at any time cancel a registration under *section 7* or *10* or vary it by adding or varying limitations or conditions to which it is made subject. This must then be communicated to the person to whom the registration relates and the relevant local authority (see (*b*) above).

25.42 *Authorisations to dispose and accumulate radioactive waste*

Again, as explained at 25.28–25.31 above, it is an offence to accumulate or dispose of radioactive waste on premises used as an undertaking unless the person concerned is exempted by the *Radioactive Substances Act 1993* (or exempted by a special exclusion made by order of the Secretary of State for the Environment or the Department of the Environment for Northern Ireland under *section 15(2)*) or he has been granted statutory authorisation for such disposal [*section 13*] or accumulation [*section 14*] by the chief inspector.

No accumulation authorisation under *section 14* is needed if the waste is accumulated in accordance with an authorisation for disposal under *section 13*.

The authorisation procedure, in each case, includes:

(*a*)   subject to restrictions to safeguard national security, a requirement that a copy of the application is sent by the chief inspector to each local authority in whose area the radioactive waste is to be disposed of or accumulated [*section 16(6)*];

(*b*)   provision for the authorisation granted to be in respect of radioactive waste generally or of a particular type of waste [*section 16(8)(a)*];

(*c*)   power for the chief inspector to impose such limitations and conditions on the authorisation as it thinks fit;

(*d*)   the right of the applicant to treat the application as refused if it is not granted within the prescribed period of four months [*section 16(7)*];

(*e*)   in relation to *disposal* authorisations only [*section 13*], a requirement for the chief inspector to consult with relevant public bodies, including local authorities and the NRA, where the disposal is likely to involve the need for special precautions to be taken by such bodies [*section 18(1)*]. The cost to the local authority of taking such precautions may be charged to the applicant by the authority [*section 18(2)*]; and

(f)   provision that the authorisation should not, in normal circumstances, take effect until at least 28 days after a copy of the certificate of authorisation has been sent to the local authorities who have been notified of the application (see (a) above) [section 16(10)].

As in the case of registration of premises where radioactive materials are used and of mobile radioactive equipment (see above), the chief inspector has power to revoke or vary at any time authorisations granted for the disposal and accumulation of radioactive waste [section 17]. The scope of HMIP's power to vary such authorisations was recently examined in the case of R v HMIP and MAFF, ex parte Greenpeace, 29 September 1993. In this case, which concerned a challenge to the grant of a variation to an authorisation to dispose of radioactive waste from a nuclear installation, it was held that HMIP and MAFF had the power to grant such a variation (rather than being required to consider the grant of a fresh authorisation) where the variation did not extend the description of radioactive waste contained in the original authorisation nor purport to authorise disposals of new descriptions of such waste. The fact that the relevant disposals would arise from new plant or new discharge points which had been constructed on the licensed site was held to be immaterial.

The accumulation and disposal authorisations will usually be detailed documents specifying not only quantitative limits and the types of radioactivity to be handled, but also conditions which relate to the systems of storage and disposal which will be employed. These are frequently specified in an 'implementation document' forming part of the authorisation. A general overriding condition to employ 'best practicable means' to limit the quantity of radioactivity discharged is frequently included in the authorisation.

An industrial undertaking disposing of radioactive waste will often also need to dispose of non-radioactive substances and will require separate authorisations for this from other relevant regulators. Where the business is carrying on a 'prescribed process' within the meaning of Part I of the Environmental Protection Act 1990 and is subject to the authorisation regime laid down in that Act express provision is made (in section 28(2) of the Environmental Protection Act) for the harmonisation of any relevant conditions which may be imposed by HMIP (and its counterparts in Scotland and Northern Ireland) under the Radioactive Substances Act 1993 and by the responsible regulatory body under the Environmental Protection Act 1990. The conditions imposed under the Radioactive Substances Act effectively take priority.

On the other hand, the Environmental Protection (Prescribed Processes and Substances) Regulations 1991 provide that certain processes involving uranium (which is, of course, a radioactive material) will come under Part A, the integrated pollution control regime, of the Environmental Protection Act 1990 and not the authorisation system under the Radioactive Substances Act 1993. The relevant processes which are subject to integrated pollution control (unless carried on at a nuclear installation with a nuclear site licence) are:

(a)   the treatment of any ore, concentrate or material containing uranium, its compounds or alloys in order to produce uranium, its compounds or alloys, or

(b)   the manufacture of, and any process involving the use of uranium hexafluoride or of any other volatile compound of uranium, or

(c)   the mechanical processing or casting of uranium, its compounds or alloys.

In granting an authorisation for these processes under the Environmental Protection Act, the chief inspector will, of course, seek to ensure that 'the best available techniques not entailing excessive cost' are employed to prevent or minimise the release of any of these substances prescribed into any environmental medium, thereby controlling their radiological effect on the environment.

25.43 *Registrations and authorisations under the Radioactive Substances Act 1993 – general provisions*

There are the following further provisions of the *Radioactive Substances Act 1993* which are common to the registration of premises using radioactive materials [*section 7*] and of mobile radioactive apparatus [*section 10*] and to the authorisation for disposals [*section 13*] and accumulations [*section 14*] of radioactive waste:

(*a*)   the fees payable upon an application for registration or authorisation (and for their variation) are determined according to a charging scheme made by the Secretary of State for the Environment under the *Environmental Protection Act 1990* (see now *Radioactive Substances Act 1993, s 43*). The present scheme came into operation on 1 April 1991. A periodic 'subsistence' charge is also made during the life of the registration or authorisation. The charges are intended to enable the inspector (and the relevant minister where the authorisation relates to licensed nuclear sites) to recover their administrative costs, including the costs of on-going inspection and monitoring. Charges are made in four bands. The first two bands relate to certain major nuclear installations and are based on a 'time charge' system. The other two bands are flat fees. In these lower two bands, major laboratories and industrial users are currently charged £800 for applications and variations and an annual fee of £400. Smaller users in the lowest band are correspondingly charged £300 and £75, although in some cases, where the quantities of radiation are small, no annual fee is payable.

(*b*)   the chief inspector has wide powers to require regulated persons to keep relevant records and to provide copies to them [*section 20*]; to issue enforcement notices requiring steps to be taken to comply with the limitations and conditions imposed by the registration or authorisation [*section 21*] and to issue prohibition notices which require specified action to be taken which may suspend the operation of the whole or part of the registration or authorisation where the carrying on of an activity involves an imminent risk of pollution or harm to human health [*section 22*].

(*c*)   The Secretary of State for the Environment (and the Department of the Environment for Northern Ireland) has the power to give the chief inspector directions to grant, or to refuse the grant of, a registration or authorisation; to impose particular conditions and to vary or cancel or revoke a registration or authorisation [*section 23*]. The Secretary of State also has the power to 'call in' for his own determination an application and, if he thinks fit, hold a local inquiry into it [*section 24*].

(*d*)   Decisions of the chief inspector relating to the refusal of registration or authorisation, the imposition of limitations and conditions and variations, cancellations and revocations are all subject to a statutory appeals procedure. Enforcement and prohibition notices may also be appealed against [*sections 26, 27*]. Appeals lie to the Secretary of State for the Environment (or the Department in Northern Ireland). They may be brought only by the person who has, or is applying for, the relevant registration or authorisation. The appeal may take the form of a hearing. Detailed procedures are set out in the *Radioactive Substances (Appeals) Regulations 1990 (SI 1990 No 2504)*. There is no express provision for members of the public or other interested parties to be represented at such hearings but the person hearing the appeal probably has a discretion to allow such representations as part of his general discretion to determine his own procedure.

(*e*)   Specific exemptions may be granted from registration and authorisation by the Secretary of State for the Environment (and the Department of the Environment for Northern Ireland) by reference to classes of premises, undertakings and descriptions of radioactive materials or mobile apparatus [*sections 8(2), 15(2)*]. He may grant them subject to limitations or conditions. For example:

(i)   The *Radioactive Substances (Testing Instruments) Exemption Order 1985* (*SI 1985 No 1049*) provides exemptions and exclusions under the radioactive substances legislation in respect of testing instruments and radioactive sources used in conjunction with such instruments.

(ii) The *Radioactive Substances (Gaseous Tritium Light Devices) Exemption Order 1985* (*SI 1985 No 1047*) provides a general exemption from registration under *section 7* of the *Act* in respect of the keeping and use on certain premises of instruments, luminous and similar devices containing tritium gas in robust sealed containers.

(iii) The *Radioactive Substances (Luminous Articles) Exemption Order 1985* (*SI 1985 No 1048*) again provides a general exemption from registration under *section 7* of the *Act* in respect of the keeping and use of similar luminous articles, subject to conditions.

(*f*) Breaches of any limitations or conditions imposed on a registration or authorisation or to which an exemption is subject or a failure to comply with any requirements of a prohibition or enforcement notice are criminal offences. Each is punishable, on summary conviction, by a fine of up to £20,000 and/or six months imprisonment or, conviction or indictment, by an unlimited fine and/or five years imprisonment.

A special hearing procedure exists in relation solely to disposal authorisations sought or granted under *section 13*. Before refusal, variation or revocation of such an authorisation, and before any limitations or conditions are attached to it, the Secretary of State for the Environment, or the Department in Northern Ireland (and the relevant Minister in the case of a licensed nuclear site) must offer the applicant or holder of the authorisation concerned and all local authorities and 'other persons' the Secretary of State considers appropriate an opportunity to appear before a person appointed by the Secretary of State (and the Minister where appropriate) to make representations [*section 28(1), (2)*].

25.44 *Policing powers under the Radioactive Substances Act 1993*

In addition to their specific powers in relation to registration and authorisation outlined above, the Secretary of State for the Environment (and the Department of the Environment for Northern Ireland) and the inspectorates have been given certain general policing powers. These include the following.

(*a*) The Secretary of State may dispose of radioactive waste which is stored on premises where he considers it ought to be disposed of or where it is unlikely to be disposed of lawfully. He is entitled to recover his reasonable expenses of disposal from the occupier of the premises or, if unoccupied, the owner [*section 30*] and has a right of entry onto the premises for this purpose in certain circumstances [*section 31(5), (6)*].

(*b*) The inspectorates have substantial powers to enter premises which have been registered under *section 7* or in respect of which an authorisation under *sections 13* and *14* has been granted or to enter a licensed nuclear site, to carry out inspections and tests, to take samples and documents and to formally question the occupier or anyone responsible for the premises [*section 31(1), (2)*]. Similar powers exist where registration or authorisation has not been obtained and the inspectorate has reasonable grounds for belief that there is an unlawful keeping or use of radioactive materials or an unlawful disposal or accumulation of radioactive waste there [*section 31(4)*] – although such powers are limited in this case to situations where the occupier of the premises co-operates; a magistrate's warrant has been obtained or there is an emergency. [*Radioactive Substances Act, s 31(6), Sch 2*].

(*c*) In keeping with current policies of regulatory openness and public access to environmental information, both the inspectorate and all local authorities who hold relevant information under the *Radioactive Substances Act 1993* must, subject to special safeguards to protect trade secrets and national security, make copies of certain categories of documents available for public inspection. These documents include:

  (i)   applications for registration and authorisation under the *1993 Act*;

  (ii) certificates of registration and authorisation;

  (iii) prohibition and enforcement notices; and

  (iv) records of convictions under *section 13* [*section 39*].

It is envisaged that HMIP data on the monitoring of individual sites will also be made available for public inspection in due course (see DoE Circular 21/90, Welsh Office Circular 56/90, HMSO 1990).

25.45 *The special position of government bodies*

Until the coming into force of *Part V* of the *Environmental Protection Act 1990* in January 1990, the Crown was exempt from the control of the radioactive substances legislation. The *Radioactive Substances Act 1993* now expressly provides for its provisions to bind the Crown [*section 42(1)*], except in relation to Defence activities. No criminal liability attaches to contraventions of the Act by the Crown, but the regulatory bodies may seek High Court (in Scotland, Court of Session) declarations as to the unlawfulness, or otherwise, of acts or omissions on its part.

Probably the most significant area in which the removal of the Crown exemption would have operated is the use of radioactive materials and equipment and the disposal of radioactive waste by NHS hospitals. Such hospitals are now, in principle, required to seek relevant registrations and authorisations under the *Radioactive Substances Act 1993*. However, the *Radioactive Substances (Hospitals) Exemptions Order 1990* (*SI 1990 No 2512*) has, to a large extent, lessened the impact of this change. Under the *Order*, both NHS and private hospitals are exempt from registration and authorisation where the levels of radioactivity involved in their activities are less than prescribed limits. Most hospitals will be operating generally below these limits. Nevertheless they are still required to meet certain conditions as to storage and use of radioactive material and to keep records. Conditions as to disposal systems are also imposed.

25.46 **The interrelation between the Radioactive Substances Act 1993 and Planning Controls**

Projects to construct, enlarge, modify or change the use of premises concerned with the handling of radioactive material or the accumulation or disposal of radioactive waste will invariably require development consents e.g. under the Town and Country Planning legislation. This will be in addition to satisfying the specific authorisation requirements of the *Radioactive Substances Act 1993* and, in the case of nuclear installations, the various other licensing and consent arrangements described in paragraphs 25.31 to 25.45 above. A large development of this kind is likely to become the subject of a public or other statutory enquiries, as in the cases of *Windscale* (1978) and *Sizewell B* (1988).

HMIP and MAFF, in the case of nuclear installations and their counterparts, are charged with the specific responsibility of considering and authorising the use, accumulation and disposal of radioactive material or waste. They have a general duty in doing so to consider the public health and safety aspects of this proposed activity (*R v HMIP and MAFF ex parte Greenpeace* – see above). However, the radiological and wider environmental effects of the development may also be matters requiring consideration in the planning process – which, in most cases, will precede these other authorisation and consent processes. Of particular importance are:

(*a*)   Article 6 of the *Basic Safety Standards Directive*, which provides that:

'The limitation of individual and collective doses resulting from controllable exposures shall be based on the following general principles:

(*a*)   The various types of activity resulting in an exposure to ionising radiation shall have been justified in advance by the advantages which they produce,

(*b*)   . . .'

The scope and nature of the issues to be considered under this 'prior justification' requirement of European Community law are at present unclear. It is, however, unquestionable that one of the circumstances in which, in at least some cases, the requirement will fall to be addressed is at the initial planning stage. (Otton J goes further than this in *R v HMIP and MAFF ex parte Greenpeace* (see above) and suggests that where a benefit and disbenefit analysis has been conducted at the planning stage of a plant from which radioactive discharges will be made, the relevant activity may be regarded as being 'justified in advance' and that a re-evaluation is not required, either by *Article 6* of the *Basic Safety Standards Directive* or by the *Radioactive Substances Act 1993*, before the discharge authorisations themselves are granted.)

(*b*)   The *Directive on the Assessment of the Effects of Certain Public and Private Projects on the Environment (85/337/EEC)* and the various regulations by which this *Directive* has been implemented in the United Kingdom. (See 25.15 above.) Of particular relevance to the nuclear industry are the *Town and Country Planning (Assessment of Environmental Effects) Regulations (SI 1988 No 1221)* and the *Electricity and Pipe-line Works (Assessment of Environmental Effects) Regulations (SI 1989 No 167)*. Pursuant to the *Directive* and these *Regulations*, environmental information has to be supplied to, and taken into account by, relevant planning authorities in forming the judgment as to whether certain developments should go ahead. The *Regulations* make the following specific provisions for 'nuclear' developments:

(i)   Applications to local planning authorities for development relating to the permanent storage or final disposal of radioactive waste are 'Schedule 1' applications i.e.; applications for which, if not in respect of 'exempt development', environmental information and assessment is required *without more* (paragraphs 2(1) and 4(1) and *Schedule 1* of the *Town and Country Planning (Assessment of Environmental Effects) Regulations 1988*).

(ii)   'Schedule 2' applications for which environmental information and assessment is required if the development in question is not an exempt development *and* is one which would be likely to have significant effects on the environment. These include applications to local planning authorities for developments relating to nuclear fuel production, enrichment and reprocessing plants and installations for the collection or processing of radioactive waste, other than installations which otherwise fall under *Schedule 1* (see above) (*paragraphs 2(1)* and *4(1)* and *Schedule 2* of the *Town and Country Planning (Assessment of Environmental Effects) Regulations 1988*).

(iii)   Environmental information must be submitted to the Secretary of State for Trade and Industry in connection with applications for the construction or extension of nuclear power stations, regardless of the level of likely effects, if any, of such developments on the environment (*paragraphs 1–3* and the *Schedule to the Electricity and Pipe-line Works (Assessment of Environmental Effects) Regulations 1989*).

(c)   An emerging principle of planning law, supported by the adoption of the above-mentioned *Directive* and its implementation by the *Town and Country Planning (Assessment of Environmental Effects) Regulations 1988*, that the environmental effects in general, and the levels of emissions and pollution in particular, arising from a proposed industrial development may be relevant considerations for planning authorities to consider in relation to applications for such development. (See the Draft DoE Planning Policy Guidance on Planning and Pollution Controls (June 1992) and the case of *Gateshead Metropolitan Borough Council v Secretary of State for the Environment and Northumbrian Water Group Plc, 29 September 1993*.)

The general law and practice relating to the provision of statutory environmental information and the conducting of environmental impact assessments are discussed further in Chapters 7 and 12.

25.47 *Safety regulations in respect of exposure to ionising radiation*

In addition to the control regimes established by the *Nuclear Installations Act 1965* and the *Radioactive Substances Act 1993*, all operations involving radioactive materials and waste, including operations at licensed nuclear sites, are also subject to the *Ionising Radiations Regulations (SI 1985 No 1333) (IRR)*. As discussed above, these *Regulations* are based on European Community legislation, namely the *Basic Safety Standards Directive.*

The *IRR* are principally directed to safeguarding the health of workers and form part of the corpus of health and safety at work legislation. Breaches of the *IRR* are criminal offences and carry the same penalties as are provided for in the *Health and Safety at Work Act 1974.*

Responsibility for enforcing the *IRR* lies with the HSE. [*Health and Safety at Work Act 1974, s 19(1); Health and Safety (Enforcing Authority) Regulations 1989 (SI 1989 No 1903)*]. The NII's functions in relation to licensed nuclear sites includes enforcement of the *IRR*. Other Divisions and Inspectorates of the HSE, in particular the Field Operations Division which is responsible for factories and agriculture, carry out the enforcement function in relation to other situations in which the *IRR* are applicable.

Under the *IRR* an employer has a wide range of duties and obligations, including:

(a)   to notify the HSE of his intended work with ionising radiation and to furnish specified particulars [*Regulation 5*];

(b)   generally to ensure that all necessary steps are taken to restrict so far as reasonably practicable the extent to which his employees and other persons are exposed to ionising radiations, including by means of design and engineering controls [*Regulation 6*];

(c)   to provide necessary personal protective equipment [*Regulation 6(3)*];

(d)   to designate controlled or supervised areas with restricted entry [*Regulation 8*];

(e)   to operate a classification system so that employers likely to receive specific levels of dose (often termed 'radiation workers') are identified as such and made subject to personal monitoring and record keeping regimes. [*Regulation 9*].

The operation of the *IRR* are backed up by various other regulations, HSE guidance notes and Approved Codes of Practice (see in particular, the *Management of Health and Safety at Work Regulations 1992* (*SI 1992 No 2051*) and the HSE's guidance notes on the restriction of occupational exposure to ionising radiation 1985 and 1990 and the HSC Approved Code of Practice to the *Ionising Radiation Regulations 1985, Part IV* of 1991).

(These and other occupational health aspects of the *IRR* are discussed in Tolley's Health and Safety at Work Handbook 1994, Chapter 9.)

The scope of the *IRR* is not, however, restricted to occupational health and safety. One of its key provisions requires employers to ensure that their employees 'and other persons' are not exposed to ionising radiation emitted in the course of handling radioactive materials and waste beyond specified dose limits. These dose limits are based on the *Basic Safety Standards Directive* and, ultimately, ICRP recommended limits. The quantative limits, as indicated above, include specific limits not only for categories of employees but persons other than employees. Such persons include not only contractors and visitors at sites where radioactivity is present but, what is more significant from the point of view of the environment, all persons anywhere who may receive a dose from such activities including doses to the general public from radioactive discharges from such sites. The current dose limits for 'other persons' specified in the *IRR* [*Schedule 1*] are:

1.   Whole body dose – 5 mSv.[1]

2.   Individual organ and tissues dose (other than the lens of the eye) – 50 mSv.[1]

3.   Lens of the eye dose – 15 mSv.[2]

Notes

(1)   The dose in any calendar year, comprising the total of the effective dose equivalent (EDE) (i.e. dose actually received) from external radiation and the committed effective dose (CED) i.e. all internal doses received both in that year and to be received in future years from that year's intake of radionuclides into the body.

(2)   The average of the EDE from external and internal radiation in any calendar year.

The current dose limits in the *IRR* are derived from the recommended limits published in 1977 by the ICRP in its publication 26. The latest ICRP recommendations are those published in 1991 in publication ICRP 60 which places a limit on the annual whole body dose (as defined in Note (1) above) to members of the public from the use of radioactivity of 1 mSv, with larger annual doses being permissible so long as the annual average of any five-year period is not greater than 1 mSv. As discussed in at 25.14 above, these ICRP recommendations have not yet been incorporated into the *Basic Safety Standards Directive* regime, nor, accordingly into United Kingdom law. Nevertheless, the nuclear industry in this country, including the NII and, most importantly, HMIP and MAFF in granting disposal authorisations, have been working for some years to more rigorous standards than those presently specified in the *IRR*. Various other dose limits have been recommended from time to time in Government White Papers (in 1982 and 1986) and by RWMAC in 1984. Industry and the authorising agencies have been following generally the NRPB guidelines contained in its publication GS9 of 1987. These guidelines were amended in June 1993 and the new limits are likely to provide the bench-mark for dose limitation at least until the *Basic Safety Standards Directive* and the *IRR* are up-dated. The present timing for the revision of the *Basic Safety Standards Directive* is late 1994 at the earliest. The HSC has concluded that, whilst any revisions to the *Directive* would be implemented in the United Kingdom, there is no need to anticipate them (HSC Policy Statement, 24 August 1993).

The quantative limits for annual whole body doses to the general public contained in the two sets of NRPB guidelines referred to above are as follows:

— NRPB 1987
    (GS9)   0.5 mSv (i.e. 500 μSv) from a single radioactivity source arising from the current year's discharges of radioactivity from that source.

— NRPB 1993   (*a*)   1 mSv (total EDE) from both the current year's and previous years' discharges from *all* sources with

            (*b*)   a further constraint of

                (i)   0.3 mSv (i.e. 300 μSv) (CED) from the current year's discharges from a *single* source or

                (ii)   ALARP if the limit of 0.3 mSv cannot be achieved.

The 'package' of 0.3 mSv or ALARP from a single source (i.e. a single site or plant) described above will be particularly influential on HMIP and MAFF when granting disposal authorisations under *Radioactive Substances Act 1993, s 13* and drafting conditions for such authorisations.

25.48 The regulation of special situations and activities

The United Kingdom's radiological control regime covers not only the use and disposal of radioactive materials in nuclear installations and other work places as discussed above. It extends to other areas, including the following.

25.49 *Naturally occurring radiation*

A significant source of public exposure to radiation in the United Kingdom is to radon daughters – the radioactive decay products of radon which is a gas, itself resulting from the decay of naturally occurring uranium 238 which is found in granite rock. The principal pathway of exposure is inhalation. Radon may present a hazard where it seeps up through the ground and accumulates in buildings. Devon and Cornwall have naturally high radon levels. Other areas of relatively high radon include Somerset, Derbyshire, Northamptonshire and the Highlands of Scotland.

Building Regulations and guidelines seek to ensure that all new homes in areas of naturally high radon levels are built to standards (in particular ventilation standards) which limit those levels in the home. These *Regulations* have recently been extended to apply to certain areas in Derbyshire, Northamptonshire and Somerset. The extent of the areas in Devon and Cornwall which are already covered by *Building Regulations* have also been revised. Government financial assistance is available at certain levels of exposure for building works which will reduce these levels.

The NRPB currently estimate that a radon concentration of 20 becquerels per cubic metre of air (20 Bqm^3) gives an EDE of 1 mSv per year.

The NRPB has set its own 'Action Level' for existing houses of 200 Bqm^3 a year (i.e. giving an EDE of 10 mSv to its occupants) and an 'Upper Band' for future houses of 100 Bqm^3 per year.

25.50 Medical uses of radioactive substances

The *Ionising Radiation (Protection of Persons Undergoing Medical Examination or Treatment) Regulations 1988 (SI 1988 No 778)* implements the provisions of *Euratom Directive 84/466* which lays down basic measures for the radiation protection of persons undergoing medical examination or treatment.

The *Regulations* require:

(*a*)   every exposure of a person to ionising radiation for a diagnostic or therapeutic purpose to be carried out under the responsibility of a person who is clinically directing such exposure;

(*b*)   the exposure to be carried out in accordance with accepted diagnostic or therapeutic practice and administered only by those persons who have received adequate training; and

(*c*)   employers to ensure compliance with these training requirements, to keep a record of the particulars of training of persons they employ and a record of radiation treatment and to provide an expert to advise their staff as necessary.

Those aspects of the *Regulations* which relate to nuclear medicine are enforceable by the Secretary of State for Health. The remaining provisions are enforced by the HSE.

25.51 Transportation of radioactive materials and waste by road

The *Transfrontier Shipment of Radioactive Waste Regulations 1993 (SI 1993 No 3031)* establish a general framework of authorisations and approvals, without which the shipment of radioactive waste (including recyclable waste) from, to or through the United Kingdom is prohibited. [*Regulations 6 and 10*]. The *Regulations* are administered and enforced by the chief inspectors appointed under the *Radioactive Substances Act 1993*. They involve the prior notification of applications for shipments to the competent authorities in each other country to which the shipment relates. The approval for the shipment from these other authorities is also required. [*Regulation 7(3), (5)–(7)*]. *Regulation 5(1)* imposes the duty of making an application for shipment on the person within the United Kingdom responsible for the proposed shipment. Failure to comply with the authorisation requirements and the making of false or misleading statements in connection with applications are criminal offences punishable by a fine and imprisonment. [*Regulation 18*].

Specific provision for carriage of radioactive materials by road is made by the *Radioactive Substances (Carriage by Road) (Great Britain) Regulations 1974 (SI 1974 No 1735)* as amended by the *1985 Regulations* of the same name. The *Regulations* and codes of practice supplementing them are based on the IAEA's *Regulations for the Safe Transport of Radioactive Materials 1973* as amended in 1985. The *Regulations* apply to any radioactive substance whose specific activity exceeds 0.002 microcuries per gramme and include the following requirements:

(*a*)   radioactive substances may not be carried in a public service vehicle;

(*b*)   such substances may not lawfully be opened or wilfully damaged;

(*c*)   no label may be lawfully removed from a package in which they are kept or any hazard placard removed from any vehicle in which such substances are being carried;

(*d*)   no one other than the carrier may ride in a vehicle carrying radioactive material, unless they do so in a separate compartment and with the permission of the carrier;

(*e*)   the carrier is under a general duty to take reasonable care to ensure that no injury is caused by the carriage to the health of any person; and

(*f*)   the carrier has a specific duty to ensure that the material is safe to carry and is contained in secure packaging.

The *Radioactive Material (Road Transport) Act 1991* empowers the Secretary of State to make regulations designed to prevent any injury to health, or any damage to property or to the environment arising out of the transport of radioactive material. This gives effect to the *International Regulations for the Safe Transport of Radioactive Material* published by the IAEA. Other provisions enable the Secretary of State to appoint inspectors or examiners who may prohibit the driving of vehicles where the vehicle fails to comply with the *1991 Regulations* or has been involved in an accident or where any radioactive package which was being carried has been lost or stolen.

Enforcement notices may also be issued by inspectors requiring specific steps to be taken. Failure to comply results in the commission of a criminal offence. In order to fulfil their duties, inspectors are given powers of entry to vehicles.

25.52 *By rail*

Other than the *Transfrontier Shipment of Radioactive Waste Regulations 1993* (see above) there are no statutory controls over the carriage of radioactive materials by rail, the subject being governed by British Railways Board Regulations. The Regulations are designed to ensure the safety of personnel and livestock and to prevent damage to sensitised photographic material during normal transit. Again, material is radioactive for the purpose of the Regulations if its specific activity is greater than 0.002 microcuries per gramme. Notice must be given before any radioactive material is consigned by rail.

For the purposes of transport, radionuclides are divided into eight groups according to radiotoxicity and radiation hazard. The detailed application of the regulations may differ according to the group, but explosive radioactive material is accepted only by special arrangement with the Board and with the approval of the Department of the Environment. The Regulations also lay down packaging standards for different classes of radioactive material to assure radiological safety. They specify the handling, storage and administrative controls required and quality assurance programmes to ensure that all the requirements specified for packages and consignment are properly met. The Regulations require reviews and inspections to ensure compliance.

25.53 *By sea*

The *Merchant Shipping (Dangerous Goods and Marine Pollutants) Regulations 1990* (*SI 1990 No 2605*) regulate the carriage of radioactive substances by sea as do the *Transfrontier Shipment of Radioactive Waste Regulations 1993*. The *Regulations* essentially prohibit the transport of dangerous goods on any ship unless a written declaration is provided to the effect that the shipment is properly marked and labelled in accordance with the *Regulations* and is packaged so as to withstand the ordinary risks of handling and transport by sea. The classification and packaging of goods must be in accordance with the International Maritime Dangerous Goods Code, 1990 edition.

25.54 INDIVIDUAL RIGHTS AND COMPENSATION CLAIMS

As has been explained, the nuclear industry and the use of radioactive material generally in the United Kingdom is so regulated as to minimise the risk of people being harmed or property being damaged by radiation. The relative effectiveness of such regulation is indicated by the fact that the claims records of the nuclear industry is good and that, because of the infrequency of claims relating to radiation, there is little direct legal authority in this area.

The potential for the artificial uses of radiation to do harm for which those who may suffer from it would seek compensation is, nonetheless, real. At major nuclear installations, especially reactor facilities, there is the possibility of both nuclear and conventional explosions which could cause death and injury as well as direct physical damage to property, over a large area. There is then the special sort of damage and injury which is specific to radiation itself, namely:

(a)   the radioactive contamination of land or goods. This contamination may have no effect on the physical properties of the land or goods themselves, as would the destructive effects of, for example, an explosion. It may, however, cause an impairment in their utility, a diminution of their value or, at the least, a loss of enjoyment in them because of the ultimate risk to human health that the contamination creates. For example, farm produce may be unfit for human consumption as a result of contamination or a house that has been contaminated may be inhabitable without decontamination procedures being undertaken, and

(b)   the sort of radiation-induced health conditions, both stochastic and non-stochastic, that were discussed at 25.1 *et seq.* above.

A person who has been injured by exposure to ionising radiation or whose land and goods have been damaged as a result of such exposure or by contamination may claim compensation under one or other of the common law torts or under the several statutory provisions which expressly create compensation rights in such circumstances.

The general principles on which a person may sue for compensation for the harmful effects of environmental pollution are considered elsewhere in this Handbook in CIVIL LIABILITY AND COMPENSATION FOR ENVIRONMENTAL HARM (3). The particular position with regard to harm caused by ionising radiation is summarised below. As is the case with the regulatory controls described at 25.27 *et seq.*, there is a difference in the legal treatment of the activities of nuclear installations which are licensed under the *Nuclear Installations Act 1965* as compared with other users or producers of radioactive material and waste.

25.55 Health effects arising from occupational exposure to radiation

An employee who suffers injury or death (which may be a non-stochastic effect such as a radiation burn or a stochastic effect such as a cancer) as a result of exposure to radiation may be able to take action against his employer under the common law tort of negligence if it can be shown that the injury or death has resulted from, or has been materially contributed to by, a failure on the employer's part to discharge his duty of care to seek to avoid injury to the employee's health.

A claim of this sort may also be brought for breach of statutory duty. *Health and Safety at Work Act 1974, s 47(2)* provides that a civil action will lie for breach of *Regulations* made under *section 15* of that *Act*. Such *Regulations* include the *IRR*. Accordingly, any breach of the duties imposed on an employer by the *IRR* (e.g. the duty to take all necessary steps to restrict so far as reasonably practicable the extent to which a relevant person is exposed to radiation – *Regulation 6(1)*) which has led to the relevant injury or death will provide the ground for a compensation claim.

These will be principal grounds on which an employee, injured by radiation, (or his family in the case of fatality) would sue the responsible employer in a case where the employee was not working at a licensed nuclear site. The position of employees at licensed sites is different, and is dealt with further below.

As explained at 25.31 above, the licensee of a nuclear installation which is licensed under the *Nuclear Installations Act 1965* has a strict duty to ensure that no 'occurrences' involving nuclear matter, including nuclear matter on the site, cause injury to persons or damage to property [*section 7(1)(a)*]. Under *section 7(1)(b)* the licensee has a further strict duty to secure that no ionising radiation emitted from a source on site which is not nuclear matter causes such injury or damage. The UKAEA and the Crown have corresponding duties under *sections 8* and *9* respectively.

Where injury or damage is caused in breach of the duties under *section 7* the licensee is obliged to pay compensation under *section 12* of the *Act* in accordance with *sections 15* and *16*. There are five key features to the special compensation arrangements established by the *1965 Act*:

(*a*)   the duty under *section 7* is one of strict liability i.e. the claimant does not have to show any negligence on the part of the licensee, only that the relevant 'occurrence' or exposure to ionising radiation has caused the injury or damage;

(*b*)   the claimant has 30 years after the occurrence, or the least in a series of occurrences, which gave rise to the injury or damage (rather than the usual three-year limitation period for personal injury claims) within which to bring his or her claim. This provision recognises the special nature of radiation effects where stochastic effects may not be manifest for many years – see further below [*section 15(1)*].

(*c*)   there is a general 'channelling' procedure under which a site licensee who has caused injury or damage in contravention of *section 7* has no other legal liability (e.g. in negligence or under the IRR – see above) in respect of that injury or damage. Nor has any other person in respect of that same injury or damage. Thus, another effect of this provision seems to be that a supplier of defective equipment causing radiation injury at a licensed site has no liability to the injured employee. The 'channelling' is strict – the liability accrues only under the *1965 Act* and only against the site licensee;

(*d*)   the site licensee's liability for each occurrence which constituted a breach of duty under *section 7* is subject to a statutory cap, currently £5 million per site [*section 16(1)*]. The licensee has a obligation to make financial provision, subject to Government approval, of up to £20 million for total claims which may be made in respect of periods during which the licensee may be liable for such sums [*section 19*]; and

(*e*)   any claim which is made more than 10 years after the occurrence, or last in a series of occurrences, which gave rise to the claim is subject to a special claims procedure. Such a claim is not brought, at least initially, in the Courts but is made to the President of the Board of Trade (or the relevant Minister for Northern Ireland) who determines the claim and the amount of compensation. The Minister may refer questions, both as to liability and the amount of compensation, to the Courts. The claimant himself has a right of appeal to the Courts if dissatisfied with the Minister's decision [*section 16*].

Whether a claim for radiation-induced injury of a stochastic nature is brought under the common law or the *IRR* or under the strict liability regime of the *Nuclear Installations Act 1965*, the most problematic issue for the claimant will be that of establishing causation. As was explained at 25.1 *et seq.*, most of the cancers and hereditary effects capable of being caused by radiation may also be caused by other agents and occur naturally in the population. There is the further question as to whether the damage to individual cells in the body (which is caused by all exposure to radiation) without the presentation of a clinical condition such as cancer amounts to personal injury, both at common law and under the *1965 Act*. At the moment there is little case law directly on these important issues, but the following observations may be made:

(a)   scientific bodies, such as UNSCEAR, have developed various 'risk factors' using the observed incidence of certain health effects in populations exposed to radiation (particularly the victims of the A-bomb explosions at Hiroshima and Nagasaki) by which the statistical probability of an exposure to a given dose of radiation having caused a specific cancer or other effect may be calculated;

(b)   the likelihood of a stochastic effect actually being caused, or materially contributed to, by previous exposure to radiation may in certain cases be established by a calculation of statistical probability, but the mere increase in the statistical risk of suffering that effect as a result of radiation exposure is insufficient (*Wilsher v Essex Area Health Authority [1988] 2 WLR 557* and *Reay* and *Hope v British Nuclear Fuels plc, 8 October 1993*);

(c)   for there to be personal injury for which compensation may be claimed there has to be some real damage beyond what can be regarded as negligible (*Cartledge v Jopling [1963] AC 758*). Thus, cell damage caused by radiation which has not developed into cancer may, in principle, be a compensatable injury (*Sykes v MOD (1984) 134 NLJ 783*) but it must be identifiable physiological damage which is more than minimal;

(d)   the complexity of establishing causation for radiation injuries is recognised by the nuclear industry. Special employee compensation schemes have been established by some of the nuclear operators and representative trade unions where compensation is assessed not on strict compensation grounds but under which, subject to certain thresholds, amounts of compensation are awarded by reference to degrees of enhancement of statistical risk;

(e)   as indicated earlier, radiation may cause certain hereditary health effects. These typically occur as a result of the irradiation of the parents' gonads causing genetic damage to their germ cells which is then transmitted to the offspring at the time of conception. Previous legal uncertainties as to whether a person who had suffered health effects as a result of inheritance (the relevant bodily insult having occurred even before the person was conceived) have been resolved by the *Congenital Disabilities (Civil Liability) Act 1976*. *Section 3* of this *Act* makes express provision for children born disabled as a result of parental irradiation. Anything which affects a man's or woman's ability to have a normal healthy child is treated as an 'injury' to that person. If a child is born disabled as a result of such an injury to either of its parents caused by a breach of the duties in *section 7* (or *sections 8, 9*) of the *Nuclear Installations Act 1965*, the child's disabilities are compensatable under the *1965 Act* on the basis that the relevant injury to the child is treated as being caused at the same time as the injury to the parent. In the two recent cases in which inherited injuries resulting from parental irradiation was alleged the plaintiffs were unsuccessful, having failed to demonstrate that certain statistical associations on which they relied represented a causal relationship or that a plausible biological mechanism existed for the causation of the injuries (*Reay v British Nuclear Fuels plc and Hope v British Nuclear Fuels plc, 8 October 1993*). Similar provisions apply to pre-conception events, other than a breach of the *1965 Act*, which lead to disabilities in offspring [*section 1*]. This *section* would enable a child who was born with a disability as a result of parental irradiation otherwise than as a result of operations at a licensed nuclear site to sue the person responsible for the primary injury to the parent.

25.56 Claims for public health effects and property damage

Health effects

The main health risks to the public from the use of radioactive substances are (*a*) the possibility of a major incident at a nuclear installation causing an explosion leading to direct and immediate injury and death to those in the area and (*b*) longer term effects arising from abnormal releases of radioactive material or waste into the environment. It should be borne in mind that the systems of nuclear site licensing and disposal authorisations and the work of the NII, HMIP and MAFF are directed almost entirely to preventing, or at least substantially minimising, the risk of these eventualities.

In relation to claims by the public against the operators of licensed nuclear sites, the *Nuclear Installations Act 1965* provides the principal ground for legal action by members of the public, as it does for employees (see 25.54 above).

The *1965 Act* was passed to ratify the United Kingdom's obligations under the *Paris Convention* of 1960, the *Vienna Convention* of 1963 and the *Brussels Supplementary Convention* also of 1963 whose principal object is to safeguard the welfare of third parties in relation to the operations of the nuclear industry and to provide a special framework for compensation based on extended limitation periods and strict liability. Specifically, the *1965 Act* provides:

(*a*)   Under *section 7(1)(b)(ii)*, the duty (in addition to the other duties under *section 7* discussed at 25.54 above) to ensure that no ionising radiation from waste discharged on or from the licensed site causes such injury or damage. (The Act thus specifically contemplates compensation for injury arising from the discharge into the environment of radioactive waste.)

(*b*)   The duty under *section 7(1)(a)* to secure that occurrences involving nuclear matter present on-site or originally emanating from the site, or which is in transit, do not give rise to injury. The Act speaks of injury from the radioactive properties of that matter including those properties in combination with 'any toxic, explosive or other hazardous properties' of the nuclear matter. (Accordingly, an explosion or fire resulting from the nuclear operations being carried out at the licensed site e.g. a reactor failure or fire such as that which occurred at Windscale in 1958 will permit recovery of compensation under the *1965 Act* even if the injury resulted from the explosion itself rather than any radioactivity which may also have been released.)

Where a claim for injury to a member of the public relates to the handling of radioactive material or waste other than at a licensed nuclear site, it may be brought:

(*a*)   in negligence or as negligent trespass to the person (both amount to the same cause of action – *Letang v Cooper* [*1965*] *IQ 8 232*);

(*b*)   in public nuisance

(*c*)   under *Regulation 6* of the *IRR* (see 25.55 above);

    or

(*d*)   possibly under the common law rule in *Rylands v Fletcher* which imposes a liability for damage resulting from an 'escape' or release of dangerous substances which are kept or handled in circumstances where such keeping constitutes a 'non-natural' use of the land without the need to prove negligence. There is no direct authority for the proposition that the keeping of radioactive material or the accumulation of radioactive waste falls within this rule but in view of cases which have applied the rule to explosive manufacturers and to electricity undertakings, there is good reason to anticipate that it would apply. It is, however, an open question as to whether damages for personal injuries can be recovered under the rule in *Rylands v Fletcher* following the speech of Lord Macmillan in *Read v Lyons* [1947] *AC 156* at 170–175. One of the results of the House of Lords' recent decision in *Cambridge Water Company v Eastern Counties Leather plc, 9 December 1993*, in which the rule in *Rylands v Fletcher* was apparently assimilated into the law of private nuisance, may prove to be the resolution of this question against the prospective claimant.

The various points made above in relation to the problems for employees of establishing relevant injury and the causative link between that injury and radiation exposure equally apply to claims brought by members of the public, both under the *Nuclear Installations Act 1965* and at common law.

25.57 *Damage to property*

As indicated above, the duties of a licensee of a nuclear site under *section 7* of the *Nuclear Installations Act 1965* (and the corresponding duties of the UKAEA and the Crown) include duties not to cause damage to property, as well as to avoid personal injury, as a result of occurrences involving nuclear matter (whether on-site or off-site) or ionising radiation emitted from nuclear waste. Where damage has been caused in breach of such duties the *1965 Act* is, once again, the exclusive means of seeking compensation from the licensee. Apart from damage by fire or explosion, the most obvious manner in which the operations of a nuclear plant would affect a third party's property is by way of contamination of his land or goods with radioactive material discharged from the site, either as a result of an unplanned release or by routine discharges of radioactive waste.

The extent to which contamination may constitute 'damage to property' within the meaning of the *1965 Act* has been the source of some debate. There may seem to be little doubt that farm produce, or livestock, which are rendered unfit for human consumption because of contamination will be treated as falling within the *Act*, but there has been much greater uncertainty where the utility of the thing which has been contaminated is not so obviously affected by the contamination (e.g. the effect on woodland) or where the alleged damage is essentially economic, such as a diminution in value of the land or goods. These issues were considered in the case of *Merlin v British Nuclear Fuels plc [1990] 3 All ER 711* which concerned a claim under the *1965 Act* for the fall in value of a house which contained low level radioactive contamination from waste discharged from the defendants' Sellafield plant. In this case it was held:

(a)   'property' within the meaning of the *1965 Act* is to be construed narrowly and means tangible property – it does not include wider concepts of amenity or 'living space';

(b)   contamination of a dwelling house does not on its own amount to damage to property. Some further 'damage' must be caused by the contamination. Tangible damage to the property itself is required. The mere increased risk to human health from the contamination that may be present is not sufficient; and

(c)   the *1965 Act* does not, in any event, compensate pure economic loss.

The question remains open as to whether claims for property damage relating to contamination would be so limited if they were brought under the common law, specifically under the rule in *Rylands v Fletcher* or in public or private nuisance. Private nuisance in particular, may take the form of an interference with the use and enjoyment of land without proof of financial loss or physical damage to the property affected (*St Helen's Smelting Co v Tipping (1865) 1 HLC 642*). In public nuisance pure economic loss does appear to be recoverable (*Harper v Haden [1933] 1 Ch D 298*). A common law claim of this sort is arguably available even against the licensee of a nuclear site since the activity and its result complained of would, whilst actionable at common law, not be a breach of duty under the *1965 Act* because the loss itself would not be damage to property within the meaning of the Act (following the *Merlin* case). It would, therefore, be unaffected by the 'channelling' provision of the Act (see 25.55 above).

Claims can be brought under the *Nuclear Installations Act 1965* only against the licensees of nuclear sites licensed under that Act and only in respect of compensation for actual damage. Claims for property damage against other users of radioactive material and actions against all site operators for injunctions to restrain activities causing continuing or anticipated contamination would have to be pursued under the common law.

25.58   *Claims against foreign operators and against carriers*

Certain foreign operators who have nuclear matter which is being transported to or from relevant nuclear sites have a duty to ensure that occurrences (taking place within the territorial limits of the UK or occurrences outside these limits which involve nuclear matter), in respect of which a duty is imposed on any person by *section 7, 8* or *9* of the *1965 Act*, should not cause injury to any person or damage to any property of any other person which arises out of the radioactive properties or a combination of those and any toxic, explosive or other hazardous properties of that nuclear matter [*section 10*].

Section 11 imposes a duty on carriers of nuclear matter within the territorial limits of the UK to the same extent. *Section 12* imposes a right to compensation in respect of a breach of duty imposed by *section 7, 8, 9* or *10* of the Act, with certain exceptions and restrictions which are set out in *section 13* relating to such matters as incidents on ships and aircraft and incidents which are attributable to hostile action in the course of any armed conflict.

25.59 Appendix 25A

Glossary

ALARA	–	As low as reasonably achievable
ALARP	–	As low as reasonably practicable
Bq	–	Becquerel
CED	–	Committed effective dose
DoE	–	Department of the Environment
Euratom	–	European Atomic Energy Community
EDE	–	Effective dose equivalent
FAO	–	Food Agriculture Organisation
HMIP	–	Her Majesty's Inspectorate of Pollution
HMIPI	–	Her Majesty's Industrial Pollution Inspectorate
HSC	–	Health and Safety Commission
HSE	–	Health and Safety Executive
IAEA	–	International Atomic Energy Agency
ICRP	–	International Commission on Radiological Protection
IRR	–	Ionising Radiation Regulations
MAFF	–	Ministry of Agriculture Forestry and Fisheries
MOD	–	Ministry of Defence
mSv	–	millisievert
NII	–	Nuclear Installations Inspectorate
NIREX	–	Nuclear Industry Radioactive Waste Executive
NRPB	–	National Radiological Protection Board
OECDNEA	–	Organisation for Economic Co-operation and Development Nuclear Energy Agency
RWMAC	–	Radioactive Waste Management Advisory Committee
SAPS	–	Safety Assessment Principles
Sv	–	Sievert
UKAEA	–	United Kingdom Atomic Energy Authority
UNSCEAR	–	United Nations Scientific Committee on the Effects of Atomic Radiation
WHO	–	World Health Organisation
μSv	–	microsievert

26 Environmental Law in Scotland

26.1 INTRODUCTION

The purpose of this chapter is to draw attention to areas of environmental law and the administrative arrangements for the regulation of the environment in which Scotland differs from England. Within the space available it is not possible adequately to summarise the environmental law of Scotland but rather only to warn 'here there be dragons' and without necessarily identifying all their lairs. Certain general points must first be made as to the law and administrative structures before going on to particular areas of concern.

26.2 LAW, COURTS AND ADMINISTRATION

Law

The Scottish legal system is separate and distinct from that of England.

The Lord Advocate is the supreme law minister for Scotland and is assisted by a Solicitor General. The holders of these offices usually sit in either the House of Commons or the House of Lords.

Although over the centuries of the Union much legislation applicable to both jurisdictions has been enacted, there remain many differences traceable to conceptual divergencies, history and legal tradition. In some instances there is separate legislation specifically for Scotland; sometimes adaptations for the Scottish application of a statute are contained within an Act itself.

The common law in each jurisdiction is fully separate, English decisions being sometimes persuasive but never binding authorities in Scottish cases, and vice versa. Where in the rest of this book English cases are cited, there is usually a Scottish equivalent, but to cite such *seriatim* would be impracticable.

The separate law and court structure manifests itself in different procedures and remedies, even sometimes in divergent results. In environmental law the differences are mainly in procedures and machineries.

26.3 European Community

As part of the United Kingdom, Scotland is affected by *EC Directives* and other legislation in other environmental matters. The precise implementation of *Directives* into Scots law mirrors the different legislation for Scotland in particular areas of environmental law. Environmental statutes now routinely give power by statutory instrument to implement new EC environmental requirements.

26.4 Court structure

The Scottish court structure does not parallel that of England. In both the civil and criminal realm, as is the case for England, certain matters can be taken from Scotland to the Court of Justice of the European Communities or into the machinery of the European Convention on Human Rights.

In civil law the relevant courts begin with the Sheriff Court. Scotland is territorially divided into six sheriffdoms. Local sheriff courts are situated in most centres of population. An appeal lies from the Sheriff to a Sheriff Principal for each Sheriffdom. Above the Sheriff Court, the Court of Session sitting in Edinburgh can also have original jurisdiction. Single judges sit in the Outer House of the Court of Session. An appeal lies from the Outer House, or from the Sheriff Court level, to the Inner House of the Court of Session which sits in two divisions. Exceptionally the Divisions of the Inner House may be replaced by a Whole Court. The Inner House also acts as an appellate body for a variety of administrative tribunals and courts of special jurisdiction. A final appeal in civil matters lies from the Court of Session to the House of Lords.

The structure of Scottish criminal courts has as its base the District Court which deals with very minor offences. The Sheriff Court has criminal jurisdiction in addition to its civil powers within its territory, and deals with the bulk of criminal offences. The single judge High Court of Justiciary sitting in Edinburgh or on circuit deals with the more serious crimes.

An appeal lies from the District Court, from the Sheriff Court or from the High Court of Justiciary to the Justiciary Appeal Court sitting in Edinburgh. There is no further appeal.

Almost invariably in Scotland criminal prosecutions are conducted by a state prosecutor. The work of these prosecutors is overseen by the Lord Advocate's Department and the Crown Office in Edinburgh. Prosecutions before the Sheriff Court are normally conducted by a Procurator Fiscal; a prosecution before the High Court of Justiciary is usually conducted by a barrister, normally one of the Advocates Depute who serve under the Lord Advocate.

26.5   Remedies

The legal structures north of the Border are accompanied by a set of procedures and remedies which do not always parallel their English counterparts. In Scotland for example, the opportunities to challenge administrative action by way of an expedited judicial review are more generous than those of England. Damages, interdict (injunction) and declarator (declaration) are the commonest remedies sought. Interim interdict is issued '*ex parte*' (to use the English phrase) to preserve an existing situation until more thorough examination is made of the matter. Scottish procedures should be treated with caution by those unfamiliar with them.

Particular mention must be made of 'nuisance'. The common law concept of nuisance is not as restricted as that of England. It is not a closed category – whatever is noxious or obstructive or unsafe, or makes life uncomfortable can be caught within its ambit (*Watt v Jamieson, 1954 SC 56*). Any affected individual may act, and a member of the public can act in the interest of the generality (*Ogston v Aberdeen District Tramways Co., (1896) 24 Rettie (HL) 8*). The distinction between a private and a public nuisance is not made in Scotland. Interdict, with or without damages, is the remedy given. In addition, generally under the *Public Health (Scotland) Act 1897 (as amended)* and other statutes such as the *Control of Pollution Act 1974 (COPA 1974)* in particular matters, local authorities and other agencies have a duty to seek out and deal with so-called 'statutory nuisances' (see NOISE (18)). Alternatively a member of the public can complain to the appropriate agency, requiring it to use its powers.

It is important to note that, as Lord Fraser of Tullybelton put it in *RHM Bakeries (Scotland) v Strathclyde Regional Council 1985 SC (HL) 17*, the principle of *Rylands v Fletcher (1868) LR 3 HL 330* 'has no place in Scots Law'. *Culpa* (fault) must be both alleged and proved.

26.6 **Administration**

Environmental law in Scotland is administered through the Scottish Office, local government and through a number of statutory and other agencies.

26.7 *The Scottish Office*

The Scottish Office, functioning under the Secretary of State for Scotland, has responsibility for a variety of matters which in England are entrusted to fully separate departments or ministries. Since 1991 the Scottish Office departments have been named respectively the Scottish Office Agricultural and Fisheries Department, the Scottish Office Environment Department (formerly the Scottish Development Department), the Scottish Office Education Department, the Scottish Office Home and Health Department and the Scottish Office Industry Department. The re-naming was intended more accurately to reflect the function of the departments within the Scottish Office itself. The mere recitation of the names indicates the range of environmental responsibilities held by the Scottish Office.

26.8 *Local government in Scotland*

Under the *Local Government (Scotland) Act 1973*, mainland Scotland was divided into regions, further subdivided into districts. In addition three islands councils (for the Western Isles (the Hebrides), for Orkney and for Shetland) operated as single authorities for their areas. Environmental functions were largely allocated to regional councils.

Legislation proposed in 1993–4 will remodel local government in Scotland. The new system is one of twenty-eight single tier authorities, with three public authorities to run water supply and sewerage. The Bill may be amended during its preliminary course. It is not clear when the new system will replace the old.

26.9 **Other agencies**

The Scottish Environment Protection Agency

In January 1992 the Scottish Office issued a Consultation Paper *Improving Scotland's Environment: The Way Ahead*. This suggested the creation of a single Scottish Environment Protection Agency (SEPA) bringing together centrally in Edinburgh the environmental responsibilities of local authorities, river purification authorities and the Industrial Pollution Inspectorate. SEPA will operate independently of the Scottish Office and take an integrated approach to environmental matters. Obviously modelled on similar proposals for England, the new agency will operate from 1996.

26.10 *Scottish Natural Heritage*

Nature conservation, landscape amenity and the recreational use of the countryside are matters largely been brought together in a single agency, Scottish Natural Heritage, under the *Natural Heritage (Scotland) Act 1991*. The new body merges the Nature Conservancy Council for Scotland and the Countryside Commission for Scotland and takes over most of their powers.

26.11 *Ancient Monuments Board for Scotland*

This Board set up under *section 22* of the *Ancient Monuments and Archaeological Areas Act 1979* advises the Secretary of State in the exercise of relevant areas of his responsibilities.

26.12 *Historic Scotland*

The responsibility for historic buildings, their preservation and conservation now rests with 'Historic Scotland', the Historic Buildings Council for Scotland. The basic statute is the *Historic Buildings and Monuments Act 1953 (as amended)*. Historic Scotland has an important role under the planning legislation in advising the Secretary of State in the exercise of various of his functions.

26.13 *The National Trust for Scotland*

A separate National Trust for Scotland mirrors the activities of the National Trust in England.

26.14 *Land registration and conditions in titles*

Although not an individual agency as such, it is proper here to consider the impact of conditions in titles to land as affecting environmental control.

Scotland has operated a system of public registration of title to land for centuries, the entry of a title on the Register of Sasines being necessary for a title valid against third parties (cf. the *Registration Act 1617* and the *Land Registration (Scotland) Act 1979*). For most of the country, the system of land holding remains feudal in the technical sense and conditions in a title (which can have environmental consequences) are enforceable by the feudal superior. Depending upon how a condition is expressed it may also be enforceable by other persons. Such conditions in title are publicly available through the Sasine Register or the Land Register of Scotland.

Environmental agreements between a landholder and an environmental agency such as Scottish Natural Heritage (or more often the Secretary of State acting on the advice of such an agency) whether arrived at by negotiation or by imposition, are often registrable in the appropriate Sasine Register, and are then enforceable against successors in title.

The Scottish Law Commission has proposed the abolition of feudal tenure. If this happens it is not clear what would be the effect on environmental conditions in a title deed.

26.15   Integrated Pollution Control

The introduction of Integrated Pollution Control in the UK has been the major development of recent years (see Chapter 16). The *Environmental Protection Act 1990* (*EPA 1990*) was passed to comply with current EC law and to permit the implementation of future EC developments. Until the (possible) creation of a Scottish Environment Protection Agency with responsibility for pollution control the enforcing authorities for the *Environmental Protection Act 1990* vary.

Emissions arising from industrial processes in Scotland are dealt with under the *Environmental Protection Act 1990* and its system of Integrated Pollution Control. Her Majesty's Industrial Pollution Inspectorate in Scotland (HMIPI) is a major enforcement agency and is separate from Her Majesty's Inspectorate of Pollution (HMIP) which functions in the rest of the UK. The Secretary of State for Scotland appoints the Chief Inspector and inspectors to deal with processes prescribed under *EPA 1990*. Where *EPA 1990* applies, responsibilities are divided between Her Majesty's Industrial Pollution Inspectorate and the river purification authorities described below (see 26.19 *et seq.* below). In terms of regulations made under *EPA 1990, s 5*, water and land matters are dealt with by the river purification authorities (see 26.19 *et seq.* below). Other emissions are dealt with by the Inspectorate. However, much non-factory air pollution remains the responsibility of the local authorities (see 26.17 *et seq.* below).

26.16 PARTICULAR ENVIRONMENTS

Agriculture

Controls on agriculture having an environmental aspect are similar to those in England, but in Scotland many are operated mainly through the Agriculture and Fisheries Department of the Scottish Office or through the river purification boards (see 26.19 *et seq.* below).

Land drainage is an area where Scotland and England differ. In Scotland the position at common law is that landowners may resist alteration of drainage naturally occurring through, into or from their land. Measures unreasonably altering natural drainage, whether by increasing, concentrating or diminishing it, can be objected to by affected neighbours (*Logan v Wang (UK) Ltd 1991 SLT 580*). Landowners need not consent to drainage works affecting their land, even if they are benefited thereby. A landowner may agree to a drainage scheme, and such agreement may contain conditions as to cost, maintenance and renewal of the scheme. Appropriately expressed, such agreement can become a condition of tenure of the property, to be relied on by and enforced against successors in title.

However, such a position allows an intransigent landowner, or occupier, to impede the rational development of drainage schemes. Statutory regimes were therefore introduced, and still exist, whereby a drainage scheme can be imposed after court action. Each Act in this area has preserved the vitality of schemes set up under expired predecessors.

The main statutes now are the *Land Drainage (Scotland) Acts 1930–1958 (as amended)* and the *Agriculture (Scotland) Act 1948 (as amended)*. Within their definitions of the land to which they apply there is provision for a court to order a report from a skilled person as to the feasibility of a proposed scheme, for the imposition of a scheme found desirable, and for the appropriate allocation of its costs of construction, maintenance and renewal.

Mention should also be made here of the responsibilities of local authorities for flood control (where the main statute is the *Flood Control (Scotland) Act 1961*, with the Land Drainage statutes (above) also playing a role), and of the powers of water supply authorities to seek for and secure their supplies under the *Water (Scotland) Act 1980*. Hydroelectric undertakings also have statutory powers. In all cases drainage works may be required, and where necessary, imposed.

Other matters relevant to agriculture, including irrigation are dealt with below (see 26.24 *et seq.*).

26.17 Atmosphere

Atmospheric pollution control in Scotland mirrors that in England and readers are therefore referred to ATMOSPHERIC POLLUTION (4).

Emissions arising from industrial processes in Scotland are dealt with under the *Environmental Protection Act 1990* and its system of Integrated Pollution Control. Her Majesty's Industrial Pollution Inspectorate in Scotland is a major enforcement agency for air pollution under the *Environmental Protection (Determination of Enforcing Authority)(Scotland) Regulations 1992 (SI 1992 No 530)*. In addition local authorities have powers under the Act for certain other industrial emissions.

Local authorities also retain their responsibilities under the *Clean Air Acts 1956–1968 (as amended)*. As in England, furnaces are supervised, chimney heights are controlled, dark smoke is dealt with, smoke control areas may be designated and smoke control orders made.

Mobile sources of pollution, such as motor vehicles, are controlled through UK legislation.

26.18 Noise

The common law is still a potential mechanism of noise control (*Watt v Jamieson 1954 SC 56; Webster v Lord Advocate 1985 SLT 361*).

Statute has given powers and duties to local authorities. Noise can be dealt with under the general duty imposed on local authorities under *sections 16* and *17* of the *Public Health (Scotland) Act 1897* to suppress nuisances, although noise is not specifically mentioned. Now such matters are usually more conveniently dealt with under *COPA 1974, Part III*.

The operation of *COPA, Part III*, mirrors that in England. Noise abatement and reduction notices may be issued, noise abatement zones created, noise level registers established and their requirements enforced, noise reduction notices issued, noise from construction sites regulated, and works necessary to reduce noise may be required.

The noise provisions of health and safety at work legislation also significantly affect and control noise in Scotland.

Mobile sources of noise, vehicles and aircraft, are all subject to noise reduction requirements in terms of general UK legislation. Type approval, silencing systems, noise maxima and required certifications all have a role to play.

Specific areas where noise is unavoidable are subject to special regimes designed to minimise the impact of noise outwith the area. Aerodromes may have screening systems and embankments installed under statutory powers. The *Roads (Scotland) Act 1984* and similar legislation provides for measures directed towards the reduction of noise from major road arteries, motorways and the like.

26.19 Water

Introduction

Water is an area in which the law of Scotland differs considerably from that in England, both in common law and in statutory provision. There is no National Rivers Authority. Water supply will not be privatised, but under the local government reorganisation three public water authorities will take over sewerage and water supply functions.

A large body of common law deals with everything from rivers and streams as boundaries through to questions of the alteration of volume and flow, and matters of drainage (see, e.g., *Young (John) and Co. v The Bankier Distillery Co. (1983) 20 Rettie 76*, and *Logan v Wang (UK) Ltd 1991 SLT 580*). Common law rules exist also as to the use of water whether for power, irrigation, washing or drinking (*Buccleugh, Duke of v Alexander Cowan and Sons*, Charge to the Jury by Lord Justice-Clerk Inglis, *(1866) 5 Macpherson 214 at 215–220*). Further bodies of common law relate to navigation and to fishing, whether for salmon or otherwise. In a good many instances the substratum of common law remains a possible source of remedy available despite the introduction of a variety of statutory regimes, statute specifically preserving the common law (e.g. *Rivers (Prevention of Pollution) (Scotland) Act 1951, s 35(6); COPA 1974, s 105(2)*).

Statutory regimes exist in all the major areas of water law indicated above. They deal with water pollution, sewerage and with water supply regimes. Land drainage is indicated at 26.16 above. Fishing regimes lie outwith the compass of this work.

26.20 **Water pollution**

General

Section 1 of the *Rivers (Prevention of Pollution) (Scotland) Act 1951* lays a duty on the Secretary of State for Scotland to promote the cleanliness of the rivers and other inland waters and the tidal waters of Scotland. *Section 1* of the *Water (Scotland) Act 1980* added water quality and conservation duties. The Secretary's duties are discharged through a variety of agencies. The position broadly is now that any agency taking decisions which could affect water quality or quantity (e.g. planning or waste disposal) must take that into account. In addition there is the *Environmental Protection Act 1990* and its system of Integrated Pollution Control for processes prescribed under the *EPA 1990*. However, the enforcing mechanism for water and for water and land remains that of the system of river purification authorities described at 26.21 below. [*Environmental Protection (Determination of Enforcing Authority) (Scotland) Regulations 1992 (SI 1992 No 530)*].

Separate regimes cope with water pollution at large, the specific question of sewerage, and water supply.

26.21 *River purification*

A new Scottish Environmental Protection Agency will centralise river purification functions from 1996. Since the coming into force of the *Rivers (Prevention of Pollution) Act 1951*, mainland Scotland has been divided into seven river purification areas each with a river purification board. The three islands councils (Western Isles (Hebrides), Orkney and Shetland) act as river purification authorities for their areas. The area of jurisdiction of each River Purification Authority is so drawn that it has a source to sea competence irrespective of the local authority boundaries in that area. Each area extends into the territorial sea and may even go beyond the territorial sea by order of the Secretary of State.

A river purification board is established by order of the Secretary of State for Scotland acting under *sections 135* and *135A* of the *Local Government (Scotland) Act 1973*. As presently constituted each Board may have a membership of up to three times the number of local authority districts wholly or partly within its area. One third of each Board is appointed by the Regional Councils and one third by districts within its area. The remaining third is appointed by the Secretary of State for Scotland to represent agricultural, fishery, industrial and any other relevant interests in the area. Power has been taken but not yet exercised under *section 135A* of the *Local Government (Scotland) Act 1973* (added by *section 27* and *Schedule 10, para 6* of the *Natural Heritage (Scotland) Act 1991*) to vary the size of any Board and in particular to change the proportions of its composition to one quarter each for regional and district councils and one half for Secretary of State appointees. It is expected that this power will be used to reduce the size of Boards. When the new SEPA takes over the functions of the Boards will be subsumed within the central body, truncated local arrangements continuing for enforcement purposes.

River purification authorities administer statutory powers. The main water pollution provisions are contained in *COPA 1974, Part II* (*as amended*) and then considerably substituted by *Schedule 23* of the *Water Act 1989*.

The Secretary of State has power to classify waters in Scotland as to their purpose and as to their chemical composition. [*COPA 1974, s 30B*]. Present regulations are used to facilitate the work of water supply authorities (see 26.23 below) but require action by river purification authorities. By *section 30(3)* the Secretary of State can set water quality targets for a river purification authority and the authority is thereafter under a duty to ensure the objective is met. [*COPA 1974, s 30D*]. Each authority maintains a register of water quality objectives for its area and this is open to the public.

By *section 54* of *COPA 1974*, the Secretary of State may give general or specific directions to each river purification authority as to the carrying out of its functions, and in particular in the implementation of its international and EC obligations. Similar powers are given by *section 156* of the *Environmental Protection Act 1990*.

The major mechanism for water pollution control open to a river purification authority is that of licensing. There is a general prohibition on causing or knowingly permitting the entry of matter or pollutants into water systems except with the consent of the appropriate river purification authority. [*COPA 1974, ss 31, 32*]. Breach of the prohibition is a criminal offence, and 'causing' is construed in a commonsense way (*Lockhart v National Coal Board 1981 SLT 161*; cf. *Alphacell v Woodward [1972] AC 824*). The consent of the river purification authority may be made subject to conditions.

The consent system is used to control physical changes to a river structure (e.g. by piling for a bridge, pipe-line), and the entry of solid matter, as well as for continuing discharges into a watercourse. Continuing liquid discharges into a water system require the consent of the river purification authority as detailed below. Special provision is made for the control of the discharge of trade or sewage effluent.

An entry of matter, or a discharge of liquid material is lawful if made in compliance with the terms of a consent issued by the appropriate river purification authority. A discharge may otherwise be lawful if it is made in terms of a licence granted under *Part II* of the *Food and Environmental Protection Act 1985*, or if authorised by the mechanisms of the *Environmental Protection Act 1990*, or if covered by local orders. In each instance compliance with the terms of the licence or consent is essential. [*COPA 1974, s 31*].

Where an application for consent to a discharge is made to a river purification authority a considerable amount of information has to be supplied by the would be discharger and usually any eventual consent will reflect that information. [*COPA 1974, s 34*]. The place of discharge, construction and maintenance of the outlet, the composition and temperature of the discharge, its chemical composition, volume and rate are all matters that may be taken under review. Other conditions can be made, including as to the provision and operation of measuring and monitoring apparatus, record keeping and the forwarding of information to the authority. [*COPA 1974, s 34(4)(a)–(g)*]. Conditions can be varied as to time and different conditions set for different time periods. [*COPA 1974, s 34(4)*].

A consent may not be unreasonably refused and appeal lies to the Secretary of State for Scotland whose decision is final. [*COPA 1974, s 39(1)*].

26.22 *Sewerage*

In Scotland sewerage is governed by the *Sewerage (Scotland) Act 1968* (*as amended*). The provision of the sewerage is the responsibility of each regional or islands council acting as sewerage authority for its area. [*Sewerage (Scotland) Act 1968, s 1(1)*, as amended by *Local Government (Scotland) Act 1973, s 143*].

The sewerage authority is vested with the existing sewerage system, and has power to maintain and to add to it. [*Sewerage (Scotland) Act 1968, s 16*]. When local government is reorganised sewerage functions will be taken over by three public water authorities which will also deal with water supply.

The duty of the sewerage authority is to provide and maintain a system of public sewers necessary to deal with domestic sewage, surface water, trade effluent and to provide the necessary sewage treatment works. [*Sewerage (Scotland) Act 1968, s 1(1)*]. It is required to lead a public sewer to a point where owners of premises may at reasonable cost connect their drains or private sewers to the public system. The duty of the authority is however limited to acting at its own reasonable cost, and the decision of the Secretary of State is final as to that reasonability. [*Sewerage (Scotland) Act 1968, ss 1(2), (3)*]. The duty lies on the authority, and it is not competent for others to construct a sewer and ask for recompense thereafter (cf. *Docherty Ltd v Monifeith Town Council 1970 SC 200; Varney (Scotland) Ltd v Lanark Burgh 1974 SC 245*).

The sewerage system does not include septic tanks, and there is no duty imposed on a sewerage authority in respect of such. [*Sewerage (Scotland) Act 1968, s 10(1)*]. However, an authority may elect to assume a duty to empty all or any septic tanks, in all or part of its area. If it does so, its duty extends only to domestic sewage tanks. [*Sewerage (Scotland) Act 1968, s 10(1)*]. Where an authority does not so elect, it may agree to empty domestic sewage septic tanks on terms and conditions at its discretion. [*Sewerage (Scotland) Act 1968, s 10(4)*].

Owners connecting their buildings or sewerage systems to the public system must give notice and receive permission so to do. [*Sewerage (Scotland) Act 1968, s 12(3)–(6)*]. The right to construct a sewer through intervening property must be otherwise constituted (e.g. by agreement). Sewerage is of course a major consideration in the grant of planning permission for any new development (cf. *North East Fife District Council v Secretary of State for Scotland, 1992 SLT 373*).

The discharge of material into the public sewerage system is regulated on much the same lines as is discharge of effluent into the water system. Particular provision is made for trade effluent, where any discharge requires the consent of the sewerage authority which consent may be subject to conditions (see the *Sewerage (Scotland) Act 1968, ss 24–38*).

26.23 Water supply

Water supply in Scotland will be altered, but not privatised, as part of local government reorganisation. Three public water authorities will take over the functions of the existing authorities from a date as yet undetermined.

At present (1993) in Scotland water supply authorities are the regional and islands councils for their areas, except in central Scotland where a Central Scotland Water Development Board copes with the requirements of that major conurbation. In some other parts of Scotland regional councils co-operate in the light of economic and topographic good sense. Victorian and later agreements allow authorities to operate collection reservoirs (including some major lochs) and to lead water considerable distances to centres of population.

The *Water (Scotland) Act 1980* largely codifies water supply law in Scotland. Since 1980 *sections 76A–76L* have been added by *Schedule 22* of the *Water Act 1989* to implement European *Directives* on water quality and the *Food Safety Act 1990* and regulations thereunder deal with the special case of water required in the production of food.

Water supply authorities have extensive powers to construct reservoirs and pipe-lines as well as to seek and secure supplies of wholesome water. These powers include the prevention of contamination or pollution of water sources and a power to require the occupier of land to take steps to implement what is required. Water authorities have extensive powers to enter into agreements as to land drainage, or in the last resort to impose agreements so that the purity of supplies are preserved. They may also apply to the Secretary of State for a order permitting the taking of water from sources other than their normal sources in time of drought, and may, when needed, issue prohibitions on hose-pipe and other use of their supplies. Breach of such prohibitions and orders are offences punishable through the ordinary criminal processes.

26.24 Miscellaneous

Powers have been granted to the Secretary of State for Scotland to make regulations in a variety of matters dealing with water and to allow river purification boards, water supply and other authorities to intervene in any activity that may affect the quality or volume of watercourses (e.g. *COPA 1974, s 31A*). A growing number of regulations deal with the agricultural use of land, including the storage of silage, slurry and oil. [*Control of Pollution (Silage, Slurry and Agricultural Fuel)(Scotland) Regulations 1991 (SI 1991 No 346)*]. The use of nitrate fertilisers is also causing concern. In particular, as in England, by *COPA 1974, s 31B* an area may be designated a nitrate sensitive area and controls operated on the use of land thereafter.

The drawing of water from river or stream for irrigation purposes can be controlled through the requirement of consent of the River Purification Authority. (The provisions and mechanisms of the *Spray Irrigation (Scotland) Act 1964 (as amended)* are to be replaced by those in *Part II [sections 15–19]* and *Schedule 5* of the *Natural Heritage (Scotland) Act 1991*). In extreme cases a drought order may be imposed. Drought orders and orders permitting the taking of water not ordinarily available for water supply may be issued by water supply authorities, or by the Secretary of State.

26.25 Waste

As in England, waste is to be regulated under *Part II* of the *Environmental Protection Act 1990*. Definitions of waste and the general requirements as to how waste is treated are common to both jurisdictions. However, there are significant differences as to administrative structures.

In mainland Scotland at present (1993) district councils act as waste regulation authorities, waste collection authorities and waste disposal authorities. [*Environmental Protection Act 1990, s 30*]. Districts are not required to establish local authority waste disposal companies. [*Environmental Protection Act 1990, s 32(12)*]. It is, however, required that administrative arrangements within a district or regional council are made so as to secure that the functions of regulation and disposal are kept entirely separate. As noted, local government will be reorganised on the basis of single tier authorities from a date as yet uncertain.

Such administrative matters apart, and subject to differences as to the procedures in the case of infringements, the systems north and south of the Border are broadly equivalent.

26.26 Planning and the environment

The principal Act for Scotland is the *Town and Country Planning (Scotland) Act 1972* as considerably amended through two decades. In broad terms the Scottish system mirrors town and country planning in England. The ultimate authority is the Secretary of State for Scotland acting through the Environment Department of the Scottish Office. The detailed operation of planning for an area rests with the district or the region concerned. In the Borders, Dumfries and Galloway, Highland Region and in the three islands council Regions the regional authority is the all-purpose general planning authority for its area. [As noted, local government will be reorganised on the basis of single tier authorities. Exactly how this will affect Town and Country Planning is not yet clear.]

Over the years the Secretary of State has issued a number of policy guidance statements on planning matters. These come in the form of national planning guidelines, circulars and planning advice notes. Copies are available from the Scottish Office Environment Department.

Regional and general planning authorities are required to prepare structure plans for their areas. [*Town and Country Planning (Scotland) Act 1972, s 5*]. More detailed local plans are prepared by the district authorities or the general planning authority for all parts of their areas. [*Local Government (Scotland) Act 1973, s 176(1)*].

Planning permission is required for the development of land. In very broad terms the procedures, exemptions and remedies mirror those in England. Specific advice should be sought.

As in England, Conservation Areas may be established within the planning mechanisms. In addition under *section 6* of the *Natural Heritage (Scotland) Act 1991* an area may be designated as a Natural Heritage Area by the Secretary of State for Scotland on the recommendation of Scottish Natural Heritage.

26.27 Recreation

Access to land

Although it is technically true that the mere fact of trespass will not form the basis of an action in Scots law landowners may order persons found on their land to leave. A persistent offender may be interdicted from entry to a particularly designated piece of land.

26.28 National parks

There are no national parks in Scotland at present.

26.29 Country and regional parks, access agreements and orders

Under *section 48* of the *Countryside (Scotland) Act 1967* (*as amended*), it is competent for a local planning authority within or outwith its area to provide, maintain and manage a country park. Such a park is for recreational purposes, and is to be near a large concentration of population.

Similarly a regional park may be designated by a regional council, or by regional councils acting jointly. [*Countryside (Scotland) Act 1967, s 48A*].

Alternatively under *section 13* of the *Countryside (Scotland) Act 1967* (*as amended*), an access agreement may be entered into in respect of a particular area with a landowner or other person having the appropriate interest in land. In appropriate cases, and after confirmation by the Secretary of State it is competent for an access order to be imposed to secure such an arrangement for public access. An access agreement or order may of course be subject to financial conditions and compensation.

The Forestry Commission, the British Waterways Board, water supply authorities, the two Scottish electricity generating companies and other agencies also allow access to appropriate parts of their lands, sometimes under statutory requirement.

26.30 Access through land

At common law a right of access through a piece of land may be constituted or implied as a private servitude in favour of one piece of land over another, (e.g. for access to a house or farm). There may also be a public right of way constituted through immemorial use. The Scottish Rights of Way Society has done sterling work in identifying, occasionally marking, and defending many routes which are otherwise in danger of being extinguished or obliterated.

Apart from such products of 'time immemorial' a general or district planning authority may agree with a landowner as to the creation of a public path, and a public path creation order can in the last analysis be imposed, if approved by the Secretary of State. Such agreements or orders are registered in the appropriate Sasine Register and become conditions running with the title. [*Countryside (Scotland) Act 1967, ss 30, 31 (as amended)*]. Compensation may be agreed.

Under *sections 39–40* of the *Countryside (Scotland) Act 1967 (as amended)* long distance routes may be agreed between the appropriate local authority, Scottish Natural Heritage and the landowner, and in the last analysis the landowner may be required to permit such access. Where a new route is so constituted its existence is registered in the General Register of Sasine and becomes a burden running with the land. Whether voluntarily arrived at or imposed, an agreement for the creation and maintenance of a new country route may contain conditions and financial compensations.

26.31 *Access to water*

A navigable river (a matter of fact and practice, though rebuttably presumed in the case of a tidal part of a river), or a loch on which there is a right of public navigation, can be used for recreational purposes as well as for passage (*Wills' Trustees v Cairngorm Canoeing and Sailing School Ltd, 1976 SC (HL) 30*). At common law a right to go onshore from the river or to have access over private land to the river is not automatically included in the public right of navigation and would require to be otherwise available. Anchoring is possible only for purposes incidental to navigation (*Campbell's Trustees v Sweeney, 1911 SC 1319*). However, variants of many of the statutory mechanisms indicated above for the creation of a public access to land may now be used to provide public access to water for recreational purposes, or rivers, streams and other areas of water may be included within an access agreement. River purification authorities can regulate matters falling within their sphere of interest such as sanitation controls on vessels (*COPA 1974, ss 33, 47* and (not in force) *COPA 1974, s 48*). Fishing rights are quite separate from questions of access to water.

26.32 **Nature conservation**

Species

The *Wildlife and Countryside Act 1981* applies in Scotland. In addition, a number of species are dealt with by particular statutes (e.g. the *Deer (Scotland) Act 1959*). Laws relating to shooting and fishing, which impose close seasons or limit the methods by which these activities can be carried out, also affect the conservation of nature (e.g. the *Ground Game Act 1880* and the *Salmon Act 1986*). A range of legislation deals with game.

26.33 *Habitat protection*

The protection of particular habitats through their designation and subsequent control is a relatively recent development in Scots law. The categories mirror those available in England. Under various statutes areas may be designated as nature reserves, marine nature reserves, sites of special scientific interest, natural heritage areas or national scenic areas, and limestone pavement orders may be made. For particular areas requiring special protection nature conservation orders may be made or an area may be designated an area of special protection or a site may be designated as a world heritage site. In most instances the designating authority for such measures is either the Secretary of State or Scottish Natural Heritage. The initiative for designation may be taken variously by either the Secretary or Scottish Natural Heritage, or by the appropriate local authority.

27 Soil and Contaminated Land

27.1 INTRODUCTION

This chapter reviews the subject of contaminated land, contaminated sites and the related problem of contaminated groundwater. In particular, the chapter looks at the reasons why contaminated land is an area of growing concern, reviews the legal and liability issues and the precautions one can take to avoid running into problems. The practical steps that can be taken if one already has contaminated land problems are also addressed. The chapter therefore discusses the background to contaminated land and developing policy in the UK, addresses European Community influences and reviews the practical issues (e.g. site investigation and remediation methods) which need to be taken into account in dealing with contaminated land and groundwater.

27.2 What is contaminated land?

There is no formal UK definition of contaminated land. The UK Government's current view is that a precise or quantitative definition of contamination is not possible and that it should remain a general concept with the focus of attention on risks to human health or to the environment from the presence of contaminants in soil and water. Contaminated land has been defined by the NATO Committee on Challenges to Modern Society (CCMS) as 'Land that contains substances which, when present in sufficient quantities or concentrations, are likely to cause harm, directly or indirectly, to man, to the environment, or on occasion to other targets' (NATO/CCMS. Demonstration of Remedial Action Technologies for Contaminated Land Groundwater, Final Report, Vol. 1 1992). These substances could be deposited, kept or disposed of in such a way that they do not pollute the environment. The NATO/CCMS definition appears to be consistent with the idea that contamination is not necessarily synonymous with pollution, a distinction drawn by the Royal Commission on Environmental Pollution in its Report (Royal Commission on Environmental Pollution. *Best Practicable Environmental Option* 12th Report, Cmnd 310 (HMSO), London, 1988).

Contaminated land is not defined in the *Environmental Protection Act 1990 (EPA 1990)*, but is referred to in an indirect way. *EPA 1990, s 143* which is now not to be brought into force, would have placed an obligation on local authorities to draw up registers of land which is being, or has been put to a 'contaminative use'.

In this context, land subject to contamination is defined as land which is being, or has been, put to a contaminative use. Contaminative use means any use of land which may cause it to be contaminated with noxious substances. Substance means any natural or artificial substance, whether in solid or liquid form or in the form of a gas or vapour (e.g. methane).

In the UK the issue of contaminated land and its environmental implications was recognised as early as 1976 when the Interdepartmental Committee on the Redevelopment of Contaminated Land (ICRCL) was established as an advisory body to local authorities and others on the practical aspects of contaminated land. ICRCL has provided guidance notes on the problems of, and solutions to, the redevelopment of contaminated land and acts as a channel for advice from other government departments (e.g. Health). The guidance from ICRCL is advisory only and has no statutory force.

27.3   Soil and Contaminated Land

27.3   SCALE OF THE PROBLEM

In order to appreciate fully the ENVIRONMENTAL MANAGEMENT (14) issues associated with contaminated land, it is necessary to understand both the scale and nature of the problem of contaminated land in the UK.

Unlike some other countries in Europe, there has been no systematic national survey of contaminated land in the UK, although there have been limited, and largely desk-based, surveys of potentially contaminated land carried out on a regional basis, e.g. in Wales, Cheshire, parts of the West Midlands and Scotland (ECOTEC Research and Consulting Ltd: *Contaminated Land in Scotland* – A Report for Scottish Enterprise, 1991).

It has been suggested that the scale of the contaminated land problem in the UK is at a minimum 50,000 sites and most likely between 75,000 to 100,000 sites, or of the order of 100,000 hectares. These are potentially contaminated sites requiring investigation and possibly treatment. Experience elsewhere in Europe has shown that estimates of the scale of the problem tend to increase once formal registration systems are in place. For example, when the *Interim Soil Clean-up Act* was introduced in the Netherlands in 1983, as a means of authorising and financing investigation and remedial works, the 'contaminated land problem' was thought to comprise a few hundred sites. Subsequent survey work has indicated that the scale of potentially contaminated land in the Netherlands may actually amount to some 100,000 sites. Similarly, the number of sites where chemical wastes had been deposited in Denmark was originally (1980-1982) estimated at 500. By May 1988, this figure had been revised to 1,599 sites and it is still growing.

The UK is not alone in Europe in being the only country with contaminated land. As indicated above, a number of European countries have also been addressing the subject. It is now generally accepted, that the scale of contaminated land in Europe is of the order of 380,000 sites. The costs of clean-up by 1995 are conservatively estimated at $3.3 billion with Germany accounting for 40 per cent of this expenditure ($1.3 billion).

Thus, contaminated land in the UK is potentially a large problem and one which will impact on owners and occupiers of land, developers, those that use land and even the general public.

27.4   Sources of contaminated land

While the most significant sources of contaminated land are well known (see Table 27.1) the actual contribution of each to the overall stock of contaminated land is not known with certainty due to a lack of accurate survey data.

Table 27.1
Industries and activities commonly associated with contaminated land

Gas and electricity supply industries	Pharmaceutical industries
Scrap processing	Iron and steel works
Transport industries	Tanning and associated trades
Sewage works and farms	Wood preserving
Mining and extraction	Dockyards
Waste disposal	Chemicals
Metal smelting and refining	Oil refining, storage and
Metal treatment and finishing	distribution
Paints and graphics	Explosives manufacture
	Asbestos manufacture and use

Summary data on sources of contaminated land which are available from regional survey data and at a national level, together with the nature of enquiries made to ICRCL since its establishment in 1976, indicate that contributions to the overall contaminated land stock are likely to be heavily influenced by differences in regional industrial history (e.g. 'metal-bashing' in the West Midlands, chemicals in Cheshire, mining in Wales). In general terms, however, at a national level the most important sources of industrially contaminated land in the UK are considered to be:

(a)   waste disposal sites;

(b)   miscellaneous works and trades (e.g. tanning, timber treatment etc.);

(c)   metal processing industries;

(d)   gas works; and

(e)   chemical works.

27.5 Types of contamination

A wide range of different types of contamination can be expected to be found on contaminated sites including heavy metals, organic and inorganic pollutants and other substances (e.g. toxic gases). In practice, the full range of contaminants actually present on contaminated sites can only be established by a detailed chemical site investigation for the following reasons.

(a)   Many sites, particularly those in city or urban locations, have a long and complicated industrial history.

(b)   Process changes, local practice and the use of proprietary equipment and materials, may have introduced unusual substances onto sites.

(c)   A lack of detailed local records on the operations carried out on particular sites makes it difficult to anticipate all the materials which may be encountered in the field.

However, certain basic groups of contaminants and hazards can be identified as illustrated in Table 27.2 below.

27.6 *Problems associated with contaminated land*

(a)   There may be risks to the health and safety of those working or living on the site or living near it (e.g. from direct contact with contaminants or consumption of contaminated garden produce).

(b)   There may be concerns about the safety of a proposed or an existing development (e.g. from the effect of aggressive chemicals on building materials and services, fire and explosion or settlement).

(c)   There may be other detrimental environmental effects as a result of the disturbance of contaminants (e.g. air and water pollution, difficulty in establishing plant growth).

(d)   There may be delays while contamination problems are being remedied; in extreme cases, emergency action may have to be taken or redevelopment schemes may have to be abandoned. Such action may be very expensive.

(e)   The value of the land may be affected; both buyers and sellers of land may form unrealistic views of the costs of development. Lenders may be reluctant to advance money if the security is land which may be contaminated.

27.7 Soil and Contaminated Land

Table 27.2
Types of contamination
• *Toxic, flammable and explosive gases*, e.g. acetylene, hydrogen cyanide, hydrogen sulphide
• *Flammable liquids and solids*, e.g. fuel oils, solvents
• *Combustible materials and those liable to self-ignition*, e.g. timber, ash, coal residues
• *Corrosive substances*, e.g. acids and alkalis
• *Toxic substances*, e.g. metals, hydrocarbons, inorganic salts
• *Asbestos*
• *Pesticides*
• *Substituted aromatic compounds*, e.g. PCBs, dioxins, furans
• *Biological agents*, e.g. anthrax, polio, tetanus
• *Radioactive materials*, e.g. hospital laboratory wastes, some slag materials
• *Physically hazardous materials*, e.g. glass, unstable structures, unstable ground

Once it has been established that land is contaminated, the value of the land itself may diminish and the potential liability created by the cost of remediation can also affect the overall financial worth of the owner of such land.

Potentially, the most far-reaching effect is on the lenders, rather than the owners or occupiers of contaminated land. The provision of capital will be secured by some form of fixed security over the land or the assets of the company. Lenders may see the asset against which their money is secured reduced or, in extreme cases, effectively wiped out.

The choice of action to take once contamination is suspected or confirmed, depends on whether the site is occupied and is in active use, is being considered for redevelopment or potentially poses a serious threat to the environment (e.g. proximity to water resources). The action to be taken ranges from a 'do nothing' approach to a need to investigate and clean-up. The latter course of action depends on whether the site or land presents a health hazard, is a threat to groundwater or is being considered for redevelopment. The legal liability covering the requirement to clean-up is discussed at 27.7 *et seq.* below.

27.7 LEGISLATION

The law relating to contaminated land is complex and still under development. In this section a brief overview is provided.

Once a site is suspected of being contaminated, or has been investigated and found to be contaminated, there are various ways in which responsible parties may be held liable for the contamination and any remediation required.

27.8 LEGAL LIABILITIES

Legal liabilities may arise in relation to contaminated land under the following heads:

— liability for remedial action or 'clean-up'

— civil liability.

27.9   Liability for remedial action

In the UK there are a number of statutes under which remedial action may be required to be taken. As long ago as 1875, for example the *Public Health Act* of that year, powers were available to local authorities to take action in respect of statutory nuisances. These provisions are now contained in *Part III* of the *Environmental Protection Act 1990*. Two more recent provisions, under which public bodies may require remedial action or may carry it out and recover their costs, are discussed here.

27.10   The first is contained in *section 61* of the *Environmental Protection Act 1990*. This is designed to deal with the problems which can arise from closed waste landfill sites. *Section 61* provides that each waste regulation authority must inspect its area to see whether there are any former waste sites which, because of the presence in or discharge from the sites of any noxious gases or liquids, the site may cause pollution of the environment or harm to human health. If it believes that such risks are likely to arise, the local authority is under a duty to carry out works to avoid the risk occurring. The cost of the works are to be recovered from the person who is for the time being the owner of the land.

A number of observations might be made about this section, which is not yet in force:

— whilst the marginal note to the section reads 'duty of waste regulation authorities as respects closed landfills', it does apply to any land on which there are 'concentrations or accumulations of noxious gases or noxious liquids' arising from waste deposits. The site may not therefore have been used as a 'landfill' but could, for example, have been used for the temporary surface deposit of waste pending disposal elsewhere;

— the remedial action taken by the local authority may not simply be on the land where the waste is found. *Section 61(7)* specifically empowers the local authority to take any action 'whether on the land affected or on adjacent land' that is necessary to avoid such pollution or harm;

— crucially, the person who is liable to reimburse the local authority for the costs of carrying out the remedial work is 'the person who is for the time being the owner of the land'. That person may be wholly innocent. He may not be the person who deposited the waste. He may not even have known the land has been put to a waste disposal purpose. He may only have acquired the land in the recent past. Nevertheless, he is given no right of recourse or right to obtain a contribution towards remedial costs from anyone else (not the person who sold him the land, nor the person who deposited the waste, etc.).

At the time of writing, no date can be given for this section coming into force – the Government is reviewing generally the powers that regulators, including local authorities should have in relation to contamination.

27.11   The second provision under which clean-up may be required is found in *section 161* of the *Water Resources Act 1991*, formerly *section 115* of the *Water Act 1989*. That section provides that if the National Rivers Authority decides that any polluting matter or solid waste is likely to enter or has entered any controlled waters (i.e. rivers and streams, lakes and ponds, ground water and coastal waters) it may carry out works to prevent it entering or to remedy the problem. Again cost recovery is possible – from the person who caused or permitted the discharge.

27.12   Given these new powers, it will be increasingly important for those acquiring land not only to find out about previous uses of the land and to seek representations about those uses but also to write into acquisition documentation a private law right of recourse should a clean-up be required – a right necessitated by the absence of a general right in the legislation. This is discussed in greater detail in ENVIRONMENTAL DUE DILIGENCE (10).

27.13   Soil and Contaminated Land

27.13 *Civil liability for contamination*

Civil liability – under which a person may be required to pay damages to an injured party and/or be made subject to an injunction to stop the damage occurring – is only possible if damage has been caused or is threatened to the plaintiff. It is not possible for anyone – either a neighbour or an environmental group – to seek to prevent someone from polluting their own land in a way that does not cause injury to others.

27.14   Civil liability may arise either under statute or at common law. An example of statutory liability is found in *section 73(6)* of the *Environmental Protection Act 1990* which provides that where damage is caused by waste illegally dumped, the person who deposited it or who caused or permitted the deposit, is liable for the damage it causes as well as being liable for a penalty in criminal law. A similar provision is found in *section 88* of the *Control of Pollution Act 1974.*

27.15   Other common law remedies open to someone who alleges that he has been damaged in some way by pollution are private nuisance, the rule in *Rylands v Fletcher (1866) LR 1 Ex 265; (1868) LR 3 HL 330*, negligence and trespass.

27.16 Nuisance

Private nuisance consists of an unlawful interference with the plaintiff's use and enjoyment of his land or of some right enjoyed by him over land or connected with it. Nuisance can only be claimed if the interference is unreasonable in all the circumstances. This means that the nature of the area where the nuisance is alleged to arise is an important consideration in deciding whether the nature of the interference is such as ought reasonably to be borne, given the locality.

27.17   A recent case where these issues were considered is *Gillingham BC v Medway (Chatham) Dock Co Ltd [1992] 3 All ER 923.* In this case a former naval dockyard at Chatham was given planning permission to operate as a commercial port. Access to the port was limited to two residential roads and heavy traffic was experienced for 24 hours a day. It was known when planning permission was granted that this would be a consequence but it was considered that the economic benefit of having a commercial port outweighed the environmental disadvantages. Nevertheless, the local authority later commenced action under *section 222* of the *Local Government Act 1972* alleging that the use of the residential roads by HGVs was a public nuisance for which the company operating the port was responsible and they sought an injunction to prevent it. In defence, the company pleaded that no public nuisance could arise from a lawful act and that the grant of planning permission had made their activity lawful.

The case came before Buckley J and he considered that the grant of planning permission was analogous to statutory authority. Statutory authority can be a defence to a nuisance action and he found that here the grant of planning permission acted in the same way. The planning system acts as a delegation of Parliament's authority to planning authorities to strike a balance between community and individual interests and has elaborate provisions for objections to be heard and appeals to be made. A grant of planning permission is not a licence to commit nuisances, but an authorisation to change the character of the neighbourhood could lead to an activity previously considered tortious, losing that quality. Whether or not the use of the highway constituted a nuisance had to be judged by the character of the locality as the nuisance was based on allegations of impairment to the use and enjoyment of property. The character of the locality had changed with the grant of planning permission and the annoyance complained of resulted from the consented works which benefited from the same sort of immunity from suit as those authorised by statute. A nuisance has to be considered in the light of its existing environment, not one existing in the past.

The case echoes the language used in *Sturges v Bridgman* (*1879*) *11 Ch D 852* ('what would be a nuisance in Belgrave Square would not necessarily be so in Bermondsey') but develops the law by making it clear that the grant of planning permission in itself, or perhaps the implementation of it, may change the nature of the locality for nuisance purposes. The decision appears to leave those afflicted by nuisance arising from activities having planning permission with few remedies, especially as it appears that a planning authority is not liable in negligence to a third party in respect of a grant of planning permission (*Ryeford Homes Limited v Sevenoaks DC [1989] 2 EGLR 281*).

It has, however, been suggested that the *Gillingham* case turned essentially on its own facts and that it may not be followed in future cases.

27.18 In relation to nuisance, it is important to appreciate that the nuisance action may be brought against not only the person who created the nuisance originally, but also against those who continue to occupy land from which the nuisance emanates. This can arise whether he 'continues' the nuisance by failing to take reasonable steps to bring it to an end, or if he 'adopts' the nuisance by continuing to carry out the activity which gives rise to it. (See *Sedleigh-Denfield v O'Callaghan [1940] AC 880*.)

27.19 The rule in Rylands v Fletcher (1868)

This case established a principle of strict liability for damage caused by material escaping from land. The words of Mr Justice Blackburn were as follows:

> 'The person who for his own purpose brings on his land and collects and keeps there anything likely to do mischief if it escapes, must keep it at his peril and, if he does not do so, is *prima facie* answerable for all the damage which is the natural consequence of its escape.'

Liability can only arise following an escape, so there will be no liability under this rule for contamination of a site *per se* unless there is evidence of pollution leaching into watercourses or adjoining land or in some other way 'escaping' from the land.

The potential use of *Rylands v Fletcher* to impose strict liability for pollution incidents has been thought to be considerably weakened by a requirement which was added when the case reached the House of Lords, i.e. that the use of the land must be 'non-natural'. Here again, a recent case considered the point in some detail. This was the case of *Cambridge Water Co v Eastern Counties Leather Plc, The Times, 23 October 1991*. In this case a common solvent (tetrachlorethene) was discovered in tap water within the area of the Cambridge Water Company and it was subsequently traced to a particular borehole. Investigation of the source of the pollution indicated two leather companies as defendants and actions were commenced against them. Eastern Counties Leather were prepared to accept that at least some of the pollution probably came from its site and the Judge (Kennedy J) at first instance concluded that neat solvent had been spilled at the site, originating in the transport practice which operated until 1976 of lifting 40 gallon drums by means of fork lift trucks. The Water Company brought its action relying on the rule in *Rylands v Fletcher* and also alleging nuisance and negligence. With regard to *Rylands v Fletcher*, there had been an accumulation on the land of something which was likely to do mischief if it escaped and there had been an escape and consequential damage. The question was whether the accumulation had been a 'non-natural' use of the land. When *Rylands v Fletcher* was originally decided it was generally considered that any use of land other than for farming, mining or residential purposes was artificial and therefore a hurdle to surmount following cases such as that of *Rickards v Lothian [1913] AC 263* where the House of Lords considered non-natural meant 'a special use, bringing with it increased dangers to others'. This approach was followed by Kennedy J in the *Cambridge* case. Was the use of the land one which created special risks and was it a generally beneficial activity? To the latter question he answered 'yes' – the leather company provided employment in what could properly be called an industrial village. To the first question he answered 'no', considering that storage of chemicals takes place the length and breadth of the country, and while that represents a hazard in an industrial society it is 'part of the life of every citizen'.

The Water Company appealed to the Court of Appeal which doubted whether a 'non-natural' use of land was a requirement for liability under the *Rylands v Fletcher* rule. The Court of Appeal reversed the decision of the Court at first instance, basing its decision on *Ballard v Tomlinson (1885) 29 [1881–5] All ER Rep 688 115 Ch D*. That case is the leading authority on the protection of 'natural' rights – i.e. rights which the Courts have identified as an 'incident of the ownership of land'. The right to abstract water in its natural, unpolluted state, is such a right. The leather company was required to pay compensation.

The leather company was given leave to take the case to a higher authority and it is now before the House of Lords.

27.20 *Negligence*

To establish a case under the tort of negligence the plaintiff must be able to demonstrate that:

— a duty of care is owed to him by the defendant;

— the defendant is or has been in breach of that duty and;

— the damage of which he complains is a foreseeable consequence of that breach of duty.

27.21 In recent years there have been some examples of successful negligence actions in the environmental field such as *Thompson v Smiths Ship Repairers (North Shields) Limited [1984] QB 405; [1984] 1 All ER 881* which was concerned with unnecessary exposure of industrial workers to noise; *Tutton v AD Walter Limited [1985] 3 All ER 757 QBD* concerned with the poisoning of neighbour's bees by insecticide sprayed on agricultural land; *Scott-Whitehead v National Coal Board 53 P & CR 263; [1987] 2 EGLR 227* where a public authority responsible for the control of river pollution was found liable in negligence for failing to warn those downstream of pollution which was damaging to crops.

The principal advantage of the tort of negligence in the environmental area is that it does not require the plaintiff to have an interest in land.

In the *Cambridge* case discussed above, the questions of both negligence and nuisance were also raised. Ever since the decision in *Miller (RW) & Co v Overseas Tankship (UK), The Wagon Mound (Number 2) [1966] 2 All ER 709* it has been necessary to prove not only a causal link but also that the defendant should have reasonably foreseen the broad general type of harm that flowed from his activities. The question which therefore arises is what is the broad general type of harm that must be foreseen? In the *Cambridge* case at first instance Kennedy J refused to accept that 'pollution' was such a broad type of harm. Instead, he asked himself what a reasonable supervisor would have foreseen knowing that there had been repeated spillages for a number of years. He would not, Kennedy J concluded, have foreseen an environmental hazard. He would not have foreseen a material effect on the quality of drinking water caused by chemicals percolating through the ground and into the aquifer. Further, the Water Company had suffered loss because it could not use the affected borehole; but it could not use the borehole because of recent water quality standards. It could not have been known in 1976 that new, strict, water quality standards would apply in 1991. Kennedy J added:

'there must be many areas . . . where activities long ceased still have their impact on the environment and where the perception of such impact depends on knowledge and standards which have been gained or imposed in recent times. If . . . those who were responsible for those activities . . . should now be under a duty to undo that impact . . . that must be a matter for Parliament. The common law would not undertake such retrospective enquiries.'

This aspect of the decision was not affected by the reversal in the Court of Appeal. Reasonable foreseeability remains a vital ingredient of the tort of negligence.

27.22 *Trespass*

Trespass to land requires that the defendant's unlawful act has caused direct physical interference with the land. The leading case in the environmental field is that of *Jones v Llanrwst Urban District Council (1911) [1908–10] All ER Rep 922* which concerned the discharge of sewage into a river in such a manner that it settled on the land of the plaintiff. The question of whether the interference is sufficiently direct to constitute trespass has been discussed in a number of cases. In one case (*Esso Petroleum Co Ltd v Southport Corporation [1955] 3 All ER 864; 54 LGR 91*) there was some discussion in the House of Lords as to whether the jettisoning of oil from a stranded tanker in a river estuary which was then carried by the action of wind and tide onto the foreshore was sufficiently direct to amount to a trespass. In an American case (*Martin v Reynolds Metals Co (1959)*) the Supreme Court of Oregon held that the transmission into the air of flouride particles from the defendant's aluminium reduction plant which settled on the plaintiff's land rendering it unfit for raising livestock could amount to a trespass.

The advantage of bringing an action in trespass is that trespass, unlike nuisance, is actionable whether or not any damage was suffered as a result of the wrongful activity. However, the measure of damages which may be awarded (as opposed to an injunction) will clearly reflect the level of damage which is suffered.

27.23 *Conclusion*

The holding of contaminated land can give rise to a significant number of potential liabilties. Because of this, it is increasingly important when acquiring land, acquiring shares in a company which owns land, or lending on the security of land etc. to ensure that such potential risks are identified and catered for in the acquisition or other documentation. In English law many types of liability pass with the land. Because of the *caveat emptor* rule, a disposal of land normally involves the disposal of at least some of the risk at the same time. The two golden rules of acquisitions must be (i) to find out as many facts about potential contamination as one can and (ii) to reflect those facts and the attendant risks in the acquisition documentation, price to be paid, etc. When selling land which may be contaminated disclosure of the true state of the land is likely to be necessary and, increasingly, decontamination is likely to become regarded as an essential prerequisite of a sale.

27.24 DEVELOPMENT OF CONTAMINATED LAND

Planning legislation and building regulations provide mechanisms to encourage or require clean-up, particularly in relation to the return of contaminated land to beneficial use. Since 1985, building regulations have required measures to be incorporated into buildings to protect users from contaminants present on site.

Many of the issues involved in remediating contaminated land are dealt with under the provisions of the *Town and Country Planning Act 1990* (*TCPA 1990*). This Act

27.24 Soil and Contaminated Land

contains the framework for the development control system on which land use planning is based.

Any building, mining or engineering operation to be undertaken on land or any material change in the use of that land requires a grant of planning permission. Planning permission can be made subject to conditions and it is these conditions which are used to deal with environmental problems relating to land contamination.

The DoE issues circulars which provide current policy guidance on planning matters. Where a proposed use of a contaminated site is more sensitive to the hazards from contamination than the existing use, then such contamination will form 'a material consideration' for determining whether planning permission will be granted for a proposed development. DoE Circular 21/87, Development of Contaminated Land, makes it clear that the responsibility for assessing whether or not land is suitable for a particular purpose, including whether it is contaminated, rests primarily with the developer. The circular further states that it is in the developer's interests to make such an assessment since the presence and extent of any contamination will affect the value of the land and the costs of developing the site. In a later section of the circular on determining planning applications there is a suggestion that the developer may wish to consider whether or not to proceed depending on the contamination and the local authority requirements. Thus, it appears that refusal of planning permission on the basis of the effect of contamination on the future use can be justified in some circumstances.

A local authority may impose planning conditions on any planning permission it grants. [*TCPA 1990, s 70*]. DoE Circular 1/85 on The Use of Conditions in Planning Permissions advises that conditions related to contaminated land may be imposed in order to ensure that the development proposed for the land will not expose future users or occupiers of the site or any buildings or services to hazards associated with the contaminant present. It goes on to state that contaminated land being considered for redevelopment into sensitive areas such as housing, gardens, allotments or agriculture may be undesirable unless suitable remedial action is taken.

It should be noted that at present it may still happen that such clean-up operations may be required as a condition attached to the permission for the subsequent development (particularly if the dangers of contamination were not realised when the present development commenced). Such conditions may represent a major limitation on the commercial attractiveness of the site to subsequent purchasers.

Planning conditions are subject to strict rules as to their content, in that they must be imposed for a recognised planning purpose, they must relate to the development in question, and they must be reasonable in all the circumstances.

Many planning authorities now include on their application form a question which asks whether or not the applicant has any reason to believe that the land is contaminated. In this context it should be noted that the planning authority are entitled to be furnished with such information [*Town and Country Planning (Applications) Regulations 1988*] as they reasonably need to determine the application and this may include details of any contamination which the applicant may suspect is present on the land (see Circular 21/87).

Local authorities have used *section 106* agreements in relation to decontamination works, partly of their own volition and partly on the prompting of the National Rivers Authority in its capacity as consultee on planning matters. The practical effect is that a copy of the site investigation report and a methodology statement for clean-up, including standards, will be incorporated into the *section 106* agreement. As the agreement is registrable as a local land charge, it is a permanent record of the contamination associated with a site.

It is important when considering *section 106* agreements to deal with the question of what controls are required for the execution of the works. For example, some decontamination techniques (on-site disposal or re-disposal of controlled waste) may require a Waste Disposal Licence under the Control of Pollution Act 1974 [note that the waste management provisions of COPA 1974 will gradually be replaced by those of the EPA 1990] depending to a certain extent on what exclusion or exemption regulations are made under *EPA 1990, s 33*. Similarly where the proposed remedial strategy requires disposal in a way requiring consent of the NRA or a water company, then the need for such consent needs to be borne in mind when a developer enters into a *section 106* agreement.

27.25 Planning policy guidance on planning and pollution controls

In June 1992 the DoE published its consultation paper 'Guidance on Planning Policy & Pollution Controls' (PPG) (Department of the Environment. Consultation Paper: Planning Policy Guidance on Planning and Pollution Control. Draft Consultation, 9 June 1992). The purpose of the consultation paper is to give advice on the relationship between controls over development under planning law and under pollution control legislation. The consultation paper is an important document with a section in the draft on the development of contaminated land. The following specific paragraphs in the draft PPG are worth noting.

(*a*)   Paragraph 3.24 sets out the reasons for contamination of the land but then points out that contamination is a material planning consideration which needs to be taken into account at various stages of the planning process, including the preparation of development plans and determination of planning applications.

(*b*)   Paragraph 3.25 discusses the *section 143* registers and the rationale behind the register, i.e. to create a level playing field so that contaminated sites are identified early in the stages of planning thus permitting the owner or developer to devise a strategy which will minimise the risk of developing such land. As explained above these registers are no longer proposed.

(*c*)   Paragraph 3.27 discusses the risks of contamination, including water pollution and emission of landfill gas, and states that a balance has to be struck between these risks and liabilities and the need to bring the land into beneficial use.

(*d*)   Paragraph 3.28 and the first part of paragraph 3.29 go on to discuss requirements for a detailed investigation of a site to ascertain its history and the nature of the contamination whereupon the developer can select the most appropriate use for the land and the preventive measures to be taken.

What is extremely important to note in the draft PPG is the conclusion to paragraph 3.29, which states 'when determining a planning application for land which it has reason to believe might be contaminated, the local planning authority will need to consider whether the proposal takes proper account of contamination'.

It appears, therefore, that if the planning authority consider the proposals to treat or contain the contamination are insufficient then they can refuse consent for development.

27.26 SITE INVESTIGATION

Site investigation data provides the basis of the risk assessment, establishing both the hazards involved and the risk that specified targets (e.g. site workers, neighbouring users, environmental quality) may suffer damage as a result of the presence of contamination. Site investigation data also informs the selection of appropriate remedial methods.

Site investigation is a crucial element in the land remediation process. A comprehensive and thorough examination of ground conditions is the only reliable way of determining the actual condition of a site, in terms of the nature and extent of any contamination present. Investigations comprise at least two elements – desk-based studies and field investigation with associated chemical testing. Desk-based studies of the site history have a key role to play in establishing the framework for any such investigation. The purpose of this is to collect and collate all available existing data of relevance to the investigation. With this information, the subsequent field investigations can be safely and effectively planned and executed. The objectives of the desk study are to:

(*a*)   identify the major hazard sources;

(*b*)   identify the principal targets at risk if appropriate; and

(*c*)   provide information on health and safety precautions for the field investigations.

Guidance on procedures for desk studies and field investigation is given in published standards and Codes of Practice such as BS 5930 (1981) [note: this is currently being updated]; Code of Practice for Site Investigations; BS Draft for Development DD 75 (1988) Code of Practice for the Identification of Potentially Contaminated Land and its Investigation [note: a decision to update this is currently under review]; Construction Industry Research and Information Association (CIRIA) Special Publication 78, Building on Derelict Land (1991). Typical information sources used include site records, maps and most importantly consultation with site owners and regulatory agencies.

CIRIA is also in the process of preparing a comprehensive guidance manual on the remediation of contaminated land (CIRIA. Handbook on the Remediation of Contaminated Land (RP 443), in preparation.)

The CIRIA study covers the entire process of remediation from investigation, decommissioning and demolition, through remediation and post-treatment monitoring and will be presented in the form of a comprehensive Handbook. The Handbook is intended primarily for use by the construction industry, in particular by project and development managers, consultants and contractors acting on behalf of public and private development agencies, and other clients of the construction industry. However, it will be relevant also to central and local government bodies, other regulatory authorities, and many other organisations with a professional interest in the development funding and land transaction sectors, including those associated with operational industrial and commercial facilities.

27.27   The primary purpose of a site investigation is to answer the question: 'does contamination exist and if so does it matter?' in terms of actual or potential impacts on the environment, public health or other 'targets' such as building materials and natural resources. In order to answer this question, additional information about the site is normally required. For example, about the geology and hydrogeology of the site, surface drainage, propensity for flooding etc., and the current or future proximity of potential targets. If the site is to be developed (or redeveloped) then additional information relating to the engineering properties of the ground will be required.

In practice, the scope of the site investigation is inevitably constrained by cost. Thus the value of the information obtained from the site investigation, in terms of informing the risk assessment and subsequent remedial needs, must always be balanced against the cost of undertaking the essential elements of the investigation, in terms of:

(a)   numbers and types of exploratory excavations;

(b)   numbers and types of samples collected;

(c)   extent and duration of monitoring activities; and

(d)   range and complexity of the analytical testing programme.

In many cases, the balance between the cost and scope of the investigation is a matter for professional judgement taking into account other factors pertinent to the site, including:

(a)   its past history and likely contamination profile;

(b)   the size of the site;

(c)   the requirements of the intended use;

(d)   locational factors (e.g. proximity to housing, water abstraction points or other sensitive targets);

(e)   the extent to which the investigation for contamination purposes can be integrated with other activities, for example, investigations carried out for geotechnical purposes.

The principal aim of the field investigation is to provide the information on which the definitive assessment of the site conditions and the development of the remedial strategy will be based.

Thus the typical objectives of the site investigation work are to obtain information on:

(a)   the types, quantities, concentrations and physical presentation of the principal contaminants present on the site;

(b)   the location of the contaminants, in terms of their vertical and lateral distribution and their association with specific environmental media including, for example, water, soil and waste materials;

(c)   the geology of the site;

(d)   the geotechnical properties of the site in terms of both man-made and natural features;

(e)   other physical features, such as ground temperature due to combustion or microbial activity;

(f)   the hydrological profile of the site.

A detailed plan of the proposed investigation, sampling and analytical strategy should be prepared covering the areas to be investigated; the procedures to be used for investigation purposes; the methods, types and numbers of samples to be collected and their protection and handling prior to testing; and the analytical procedures to be used. Health and safety procedures, emergency containment measures, environmental protection measures and requirements in respect of liaison with the relevant regulatory bodies should also be specified. Sampling procedures are of particular importance since the value of the data obtained is directly related to how representative the samples are, and the nature of some materials or substances can change significantly as a result of disturbance through the process of taking and handling the samples.

With regard to sampling procedures, there are various approaches which may be adopted, including random, systematic and stratified approaches. Both random and stratified approaches are generally considered inappropriate for contaminated sites, and most sampling strategies will be on some form of systematic arrangement, usually modified to some extent by judgement, based on the findings from the desk study and in the light of site conditions.

In order to obtain the information and data required to make the necessary judgement as to how contaminated the site is and 'whether it matters' requires reliable data. Many site investigations can be let down by poor specification, lack of understanding of analytical requirements and in some cases poor quality analytical data. For example, while 'toluene extract' data may be a useful first step in testing for the presence of organic contaminants more sophisticated analysis, such as gas chromatography (GC) or GC/mass spectroscopy (MS), is required to identify and quantify specific organic contaminants such as individual phenol compounds, polyaromatic hydrocarbons or chlorinated solvents.

27.28   ASSESSMENT OF CONTAMINATION

Having carried out a properly planned and executed site investigation, the question to be asked is 'at what level of contamination should a site be considered to be contaminated and to what standard should a site be cleaned?'.

The UK Government, through the ICRCL has in the past issued guidance on the assessment and redevelopment of contaminated land (Interdepartmental Committee on the Redevelopment of Contaminated Land, ICRCL Guidance Note ICRCL 59/83 (second edition), 'Guidance on the Assessment and Redevelopment of Contaminated Land' Department of the Environment (London)). In particular, guidance is available on the redevelopment of landfill sites, gasworks sites, sewage works and farms, scrap yards and the handling of asbestos contaminated sites.

In terms of quality criteria and standards for contamination in soil, at present the UK uses a system of 'trigger values' for a limited range of contaminants and end uses, together with other environmental criteria, to assist in the determination of the significance of the presence of contamination and the need for remedial action.

Tables 27.3 and 27.4 set out the current trigger values. It will be seen that they are not comprehensive and cover only certain priority substances and environments and come with a 'health warning' to use professional judgements in their interpretation.

In contrast, in the USA there is a bewilderingly complex network of potentially applicable standards for identifying contaminants of concern; setting up remedial targets; and designing a sufficiently 'permanent' remedy. Clean-up targets are set as close as possible to natural/'background' levels, or 'acceptable' human health risks such as one additional case of cancer in 10 million.

In other parts of Europe, clean-up criteria have been established. For example, in the Netherlands the Ministry of Environment introduced the concept of A, B and C values (see Table 27.5). These criteria have been adopted by some Länder in Germany.

Table 27.3

Tentative trigger concentrations for selected
inorganic contaminants (ICRCL 59/83)

Contaminants		Planned Uses	Trigger Concentrations mg/kg air-dried soil	
			Threshold	Action
Group A: Contaminants which may pose hazards to health	Arsenic	Domestic gardens, allotments, Parks, playing fields, open space	10 40	* *
	Cadmium	Domestic gardens, allotments, Parks, playing fields, open space	3 15	* *
	Chromium (hexavalent)[1]	Domestic gardens, allotments, Parks, playing fields, open space	25 –	* –
	Chromium (total)	Domestic gardens, allotments, Parks, playing fields, open space	600 1,000	* *
	Lead	Domestic gardens, allotments, Parks, playing fields, open space	500 2,000	* *
	Mercury	Domestic gardens, allotments, Parks, playing fields, open space	1 20	* *
	Selenium	Domestic gardens, allotments, Parks, playing fields, open space	3 6	* *
Group B: Contaminants which are phytotoxic but not normally hazards to health	Boron (water-soluble)[3]	Any uses where plants are to be grown[2,6]	3	*
	Copper[4,5]	Any uses where plants are to be grown[2,6]	130	*
	Nickel[4,5]	Any uses where plants are to be grown[2,6]	70	*
	Zinc[4,5]	Any uses where plants are to be grown[2,6]	300	*

27.28 Soil and Contaminated Land

Notes
(a) This table is invalid if reproduced without the conditions and footnotes.
(b) All values are for concentrations determined on 'spot' samples based on an adequate site investigation carried out prior to development. They do not apply to analysis of averaged, bulked or composited samples, nor to sites which have already been developed. All propose values are tentative.
(c) The lower values in Group A are similar to the limits for metal content of sewage sludge applied to agricultural land; the values in Group B are those above which phytotoxicity is possible.
(d) If all sample values are below the threshold concentrations then the site may be regarded as uncontaminated as far as the hazards from these contaminants are concerned and development may proceed. Above these concentrations remedial action may be needed, especially if the contamination is still continuing. Above the action concentration, remediation action will be required or the form of development will need to be changed.
*   Action concentrations will be specified in the next edition of ICRCL 59/83.
1.   Soluble hexavalent chromium extracted by 0.1 M HCl at 37°C; solution adjusted to pH 1.0 if alkaline substances present.
2.   The soil pH value is assumed to be about 6.5 and should be maintained at this value. If the pH falls, the toxic effects and the uptake of these elements will be increased.
3.   Determined by standard ADAS method (soluble in hot water).
4.   Total concentration (extractable by $HNO_3/HClO_4$).
5.   The phytotoxic effects of copper, nickel and zinc may be additive. The trigger values given here are those applicable to the 'worst case'; phytotoxic effects may occur at these concentrations in acid, sandy soils. In neutral or alkaline soils phytotoxic effects are unlikely at these concentrations.
6.   Grass is more resistant to phytotoxic effects than are other plants and its growth may not be adversely affected at these concentrations.

Table 27.4

Tentative trigger concentrations associated with former coal carbonisation sites (ICRCL 59/83)

Contaminants	Proposed Uses	Trigger Concentrations mg/kg air-dried soil	
		Threshold	Action
Polyaromatic Hydrocarbons[1]	Domestic gardens, allotments, play areas	50	500
	Landscaped areas, buildings, hard cover	1,000	10,000
Phenols	Domestic gardens, allotments	5	200
	Landscaped areas, buildings, hard cover	5	1,000
Free cyanide	Domestic gardens, allotments, landscaped areas	25	500
	Buildings, hard cover	100	500
Complex cyanide	Domestic gardens, allotments	250	1,000
	Landscaped areas	250	5,000
	Buildings, hard cover	250	NL
Thiocyanate[2]	All proposed uses	50	NL
Sulphate	Domestic gardens, allotments, landscaped areas	2,000	10,000
	Buildings[3]	2,000 (note 3)	50,000 (note 3)
	Hard cover	2,000	NL
Sulphide	All proposed uses	250	1,000
Sulphur	All proposed uses	5,000	20,000
Acidity (pH less than)	Domestic gardens, allotments, landscaped areas	pH5	pH3
	Buildings, hard cover	NL	NL

Notes
(a) This table is invalid if reproduced without the conditions and footnotes.

(*b*)   All values are for concentrations determined on 'spot' samples based on an adequate site investigation carried out prior to development. They do not apply to analysis of averaged, bulked or composited samples, nor to sites which have already been developed.

(*c*)   Many of the values are preliminary and will require regular updating. They should not be applied without reference to the current edition of the report 'Problems arising from the development of gasworks and similar sites', HMSO, 1988.

(*d*)   If all sample values are below the threshold concentrations then the site may be regarded as uncontaminated as far as the hazards from these contaminants are concerned and development may proceed. Above these concentrations remedial action may be needed, especially if the contamination is still continuing. Above the action concentration, remediation action will be required or the form of development will need to be changed.

NL   No limit set as the contaminant does not pose a particular hazard for this use.

1.   Used here as a marker for coal tar, for analytical reasons. See 'Problems arising from the redevelopment of gasworks and similar sites' for details of analytical methods.

2.   See also BRE Digest 250: 'Concrete in sulphate-bearing soils and groundwater' [note: this has since been replaced by BRE Digest 363].

3.   Determined by standard ADAS method (soluble in hot water).

Table 27.5

Examples of standards adopted in the Netherlands for soils and groundwater

[Substance]		Concentration in Soil mg/kilogram dry weight			Concentration in Groundwater	
		A	B	C	A	C
Metals	Cr	100	250	800	20	200
	Co	20	50	300	20	200
	Ni	50	100	500	20	200
	Cu	50	100	500	20	200
	Zn	200	500	3,000	50	800
	As	20	30	50	10	100
	Cd	1	5	20	1	10
	Hg	0.5	2	10	0.2	2
	Pb	50	150	600	20	200
Inorganic Pollutants	CN (total free)	1	10	100	5	100
	CN (total complex)	5	50	500	10	200
Aromatic Compounds	Benzene	0.01	0.5	5	0.2	5
	Ethyl benzene	0.05	5	50	0.5	60
	Toluene	0.05	3	30	0.5	50
	Xylene	0.05	5	50	0.5	60
	Phenols	0.02	1	10	0.5	50
	Aromatics (total)	0.1	7	70	1	100
Polycylic Aromatic Compounds (PCAs)	Naphthalene	0.1	5	50	0.2	30
	Anthracene	0.1	10	100	0.1	10
	Phenanthrene	0.1	10	100	0.1	10
	Fluoranthene	0.1	10	100	0.02	5
	Pyrene	0.1	10	100	0.02	5
	Benzo(a)pyrene	0.05	1	10	0.01	1
	Total PCAs	1	20	200	0.2	40
Pesticides	Organic chlorinated (individual)	0.1	0.5	5	0.05	1
	Organic chlorinated (total)	0.1	1	10	0.1	2
	Pesticides (total)	0.1	2	20	0.1	5

Source: VROM, Ministry of Housing, Physical Planning and Environment. Discussion Paper – Soil Quality VROM (The Hague), 1986

The function of the B value is to indicate that remedial action may be required. It is a matter of expert judgement as to whether to take action and then what action to take. In addition to the general land use category other factors which might be taken into account include the quality of the site investigation and the proportion of samples exceeding the trigger value. The function of the Dutch C value is to indicate that clean-up is desirable particularly in relation to sensitive land uses (e.g. housing).

Dutch policy on contaminated land is to clean it up (i.e. treat the soil to meet A type criteria) before permitting its re-use (i.e. cover and containment solutions are not favoured). Note that the Dutch ABC values are under review and revised guidance will be issued shortly.

It is apparent that clean-up policy in the UK is unlikely to follow the Dutch example of a 'very clean' status for all possible future uses. Indeed, even the Dutch are recognising that the ABC values can lead to expensive and sometimes unnecessary clean-up. The cost of such an approach would, it is suggested, far outweigh the benefits and would often merely shift the contamination elsewhere. The aim will be to continue to ensure that the site is remediated to a level of contamination that allows 'fitness for purpose'. UK policy is moving away from the development and application of generic criteria as the sole aid to the decision-making process. Current proposals suggest that site investigation should be sufficiently comprehensive to allow a proper risk assessment, the output of which is then used to define clean-up standards on a site-specific basis. It is the intention that generic guidelines for clean-up and other standards (e.g. drinking water quality etc.) will and should be used in particular cases. In many cases such an approach is likely to involve discussion with the local authority and the National Rivers Authority etc. at the outset of a proposed site clean-up so that agreement can be reached on the standards to be achieved before remediation starts.

27.29 CLEANING UP CONTAMINATED SITES AND GROUNDWATER

Once contamination of a site has been confirmed through site investigation and risk assessment, it may be necessary, depending on the circumstances of the site, to consider undertaking remedial works to clean up the contamination. Guidance is available on currently available remedial technologies in a report prepared by Warren Spring Laboratory (Warren Spring Laboratory). Review of Innovative Contaminated Soil Clean-Up Processes (LR 819 (MR)). HMSO (London), 1992). More detailed practical guidance on factors to be considered in the selection and application of the remedial treatment is available from the CIRIA project.

27.30 Technology options

There are a wide variety of different technology options available for the clean-up of contaminated land and groundwater, some of which are established technologies of proven performance, others which are only now undergoing evaluation and demonstration.

It is not the intention to describe in detail here the wide variety of individual techniques, many of which are proprietary in nature, but rather to examine the principal technology types and their respective technical and financial characteristics.

On this basis, it is possible to identify three main technology types namely:

(*a*)   thermal treatment methods;

(*b*)   physico-chemical methods;

(*c*)   bioremediation.

Each of these general technology classes encompasses a range of specific technologies, each based on different techniques, inputs or processes but involving similar technical principles. Thus, biological methods might rely on naturally occurring or specifically cultivated biological agents and use different handling techniques for the soil or groundwater to be treated (e.g. landbanks or bioreactor). Nutrients may be used to speed up the biodegradation process. The agents used might be proprietary and vary between different companies. Similarly, thermal treatment technologies range from high temperature incineration to low temperature desorption processes, plasma reactors and vapour extraction systems, in mobile or fixed site plant, with varying capacities and energy requirements. Moreover, a treatment technology may use more than one of these general processes (e.g. soil washing and biological treatment of contaminated residues).

27.31 Thermal treatment methods

These use heat to volatise or oxidise organic (and some inorganic) constituents thus effecting their destruction or removal.

A wide variety of techniques are available from direct combustion of the contaminated soils in rotary kilns through to thermal desorption methods in which volatile components of the feedstock are removed from the soil at relatively low temperatures, with only the off-gases undergoing further treatment at high temperature. Basic high temperature, off-site incineration using conventional techniques is considered an established technology both in Europe and the USA for the treatment of organic residues, such as aromatic and aliphatic hydrocarbons, and cyanides.

Disadvantages of high temperature incineration include high energy consumption, the need to provide comprehensive gas cleaning equipment and the potential for the destruction of the life-sustaining, organic fraction of the cleaned soil.

The development of low temperature thermal desorption techniques has aimed to reduce the energy and gas scrubbing requirements of the process, as well as preserving some of the natural organic fraction of the untreated soils.

27.32 Physico-chemical methods

These include a wide variety of treatment methods ranging from the simplest approach of removing the contaminated material from the site and disposing of it under controlled conditions at a licensed disposal facility, to more complex methods of encapsulating the contaminated materials in a glassy (vitrification) or cementitious (solidification) matrix. This category of treatment also includes soil washing and solvent extraction in which the removal of the contaminants is effected using an aqueous or organic extractant and separation processes to remove contamination from the soil matrix, followed by treatment of the solution using physico-chemical or biological methods.

27.33 *Excavation and disposal*

Excavation provides a relatively quick and, in some cases, inexpensive option where the volumes of material involved are not significant. The method also has the advantage of wide applicability to a range of soil and contaminant types. Excavation also overcomes the physical problems, such as instability or poor load-bearing characteristics, often associated with contaminated sites.

The disadvantages of this method include its cost (if extremely toxic or large volumes of material are involved), the environmental impacts associated with the excavation of transport of contaminated materials and the fact that the method does not destroy or treat contaminants, but simply transfers them to another place.

27.34 *Covering/containment*

These methods aim to provide a physical, and in some cases chemical barrier between the contaminated soil and users of the site, or other vulnerable targets (groundwater, fauna, flora, building materials). Hydraulic containment methods may also be used.

The advantages of the method include the avoidance of excavation and the rehabilitation of sites at relatively low cost. The disadvantages of covering or containment include a lack of long term performance data, the need to carry out monitoring to check for failure of the covering/containment systems, the fact that contamination has not been destroyed, only contained, and the possible need for a waste management licence if the contaminated material is redeposited on-site.

27.35 *Stabilisation/solidification*

These methods rely on the use of proprietary reagents to stabilise or immobilise contaminants and thus reduce their availability to, or activity in, the environment. Treatment normally involves mixing treatment agents, e.g. cement, fly ash, proprietary additives to the soil, either by excavating it first or by treating it in-situ by injecting the additives. Stabilisation techniques are particularly applicable to soil with inorganic contamination (e.g. heavy metals).

The advantages of the technique include its relative simplicity and good general applicability to inorganic forms of contamination; the absence of a waste stream requiring further treatment, the potential for re-use of the treated material on-site for reclamation purposes and the relatively low cost (range £20-35/tonne for metal bearing wastes).

However, stabilisation/solidification is less amenable to the treatment of contaminated soils containing a high proportion of organic wastes.

27.36 *Vitrification*

Vitrification makes use of high temperatures and the natural silica content of soils to produce a fused glassy material with good (i.e. low) leachability characteristics. The technique has been used for the treatment of soils contaminated with asbestos and other highly toxic residues.

The technology shares the same basic advantages as incineration, in terms of the effective destruction of contaminants and the potential for re-use on site of the treated materials. However, vitrification is also applicable to the treatment of a wider range of inorganic, as well as organic, forms of contamination. As with incineration, the technology can be energy intensive and requires comprehensive treatment of the off-gases. It is envisaged that clean-up of soil using vitrification is most likely to take place in merchant centralised facilities.

27.37 *Soil washing*

Soil washing technologies rely on the removal of contaminants in aqueous media. In certain types of soil washing processes, use is made of physical mechanisms, such as abrasion, to assist separation of the contaminants. Subsequent treatment of the separated fractions using conventional physico/chemical or biological treatment, is usually required.

The technology is potentially widely applicable, as a pre-treatment method to concentrate contaminants for easier secondary treatment.

Soil washing methods use a dedicated plant to remove the contamination from the soil. They have the advantage that they can be used to treat either organic or inorganic pollution. In some processes, the contaminants are left in the form of solid residue, mixed with fines, which must then be landfilled as a special waste.

Soil washing should therefore be seen as a useful tool in the process of treating soil rather than a complete solution.

27.38 Bioremediation

Biological treatment technologies use the natural biodegradation mechanisms available within biological systems (bacteria, fungi, higher plants) to destroy contaminants to reduce them to less toxic constituents. Both naturally occurring or generically manipulated biological agents can be used.

Biological treatment methods range from the simplest approach utilised, for example, in land farming where minimal assistance is given to the natural degradation process, to the use of advanced bioreactor systems, where a high level of control can be exerted over population size, temperature, oxygen and nutrient status.

The advantages of the method are that, in theory, little or no residual wastes will be generated, and a wide range of biological agents could be developed to deal with most organic contaminants, even recalcitrant substances such as PCBS, which may be difficult or expensive to deal with using alternative systems. Bioremediation also has a potentially valuable role to play in the treatment of large volume/low concentration waste streams where conventional physico-chemical treatments become ineffective or expensive to implement. Biological treatment methods are also considered to be more cost-effective than comparable alternative methods, offering savings in the order of 20–30 per cent.

However, the major disadvantage of such systems is that they can involve much longer treatment periods, of even months or years, depending on the application. Moreover, where advanced reactor systems are used to accelerate the degradation process, the operating requirements necessary to constantly monitor and optimise the process may approach or exceed those of conventional treatment systems.

Bioremediation might be used as the principal treatment technique on a site or combined with other processes. For example, soil washing may be used to extract organic pollutants from the soil, which can then be treated biologically. Alternatively, the same site might be treated by creation of engineered landbanks, using biological reagents to speed up the process and collecting the leachate for biological treatment. The bioreactor could also be used to treat the groundwater beneath the site.

Because it can be used to treat groundwater, leachate or effluents from the other treatment processes, bioremediation is a potentially useful technology.

27.39 Technology developments

Research, development and demonstration activities in the USA, the Netherlands, Germany and Denmark are taking place in the areas of thermal treatment, physico-chemical methods and bioremediation.

However, in most cases the research effort is focused on:

(*a*)   in-situ methods

(*b*)   process requirements

(*c*)   integrated treatment methods.

413

27.40 Soil and Contaminated Land

27.40 *In-situ methods*

To date, the most successful clean-up results have been achieved by excavating soils, or extracting groundwaters, prior to treatment, either on, or off-site. Research efforts and innovative treatments are now directed towards achieving a similar level of performance for clean-up technologies applied in-situ, i.e. without the need to excavate materials prior to treatment. In-situ treatments thus offer the potential to reduce costs (although this cannot be guaranteed) and eliminate the environmental impacts associated with the excavation and handling of contaminated materials.

The successful development of in-situ applications will involve overcoming problems relating to:

(*a*)   the containment of the treatment process only to that area affected by the contamination;

(*b*)   good contact between the treatment reagent (heat source, extractant, biological agent) and the contaminant;

(*c*)   complete recovery of the treatment reagent and any waste residuals.

A number of other techniques have been developed recently, especially in the United States. These include:

(*a*)   vacuum extraction, where organic vapours are extracted from soil using vacuum extraction wells;

(*b*)   chemical oxidation techniques, using chlorine dioxide gas as an oxidising agent to treat soil or groundwater contaminated with organics or cyanide;

(*c*)   freeze separation, which operates on the principle that when water freezes, the crystal structure that forms naturally excludes contaminants from the water molecule matrix. Therefore, if refrigerant is injected into the waste and the ice-crystals are recovered and washed the contaminants can be removed. The process can be applied to groundwater or soil washing solutions to remove a range of contaminants;

(*d*)   an ultraviolet radiation/oxidation technique has been successfully demonstrated. The process uses ultraviolet radiation, ozone (O_3) and hydrogen peroxide (H_2O_2) to destroy toxic organic compounds, especially chlorinated hydrocarbons, in groundwater;

(*e*)   an electro-chemical method to treat heavy metals in the soil has been developed in the Netherlands.

27.41 *Process refinements*

The purpose here is to reduce energy costs and to widen the applicability of the technologies in relation to both contaminants and soil types.

Research and Development activities relate to:

(*a*)   thermal desorption methods, whereby only the volatised contaminants are collected and subjected to high temperature destruction;

(*b*)   the development of proprietary solidification/stabilisation reagents suitable for use with mixed inorganic/organic wastes;

(*c*)   the development of biological systems able to degrade recalcitrant organic species, such as complex chlorinated aromatics.

27.42 *Integrated treatment methods*

The majority of contaminated sites present as complex mixtures of both inorganic and organic contaminants in soil matrices of widely differing origin and physical texture.

Few clean-up technologies are capable of resolving all the problems likely to be present on a typical contaminated site. Consequently, there is a need to develop integrated treatment methods which, by allowing specific technologies to work in combination or in sequences, effectively increase the long term environmental security of the treated site.

Possible examples of integrated methods include the biological treatment of effluents arising from a soil washing plant, or the stabilisation/solidification of inorganic residues remaining in low temperature, heat-treated soils. While few practical examples of such integrated treatment methods exist, this is an area which is likely to receive attention in the future and it is understood that the United States Environmental Protection Agency (USEPA) is currently working to create a joint-industry partnership where such fully integrated demonstration projects will be possible.

27.43 MONITORING AND THE ROLE OF THE NRA

It is evident that the NRA is developing a national policy on contaminated land which is likely to be more stringent than has been the case in the past (NRA, Policy and Practice for the Protection of Groundwater, Bristol, 1992). On a number of sites, the NRA is not only involved in the early stages of the development of remediation plans through consultation with the local planning authority (see 27.7 above) but is also in the process of developing clean-up standards for individual contaminants with respect to the need to protect groundwater quality. Such actions have required the 'developer'/landowner, or his consultant, to undertake much more extensive site investigation work, carry out leaching tests on soils to determine the mobility of pollutants, and undertake a thorough post-treatment validation to ensure compliance with the agreed clean-up standards.

The need to comply with such requirements is clearly adding considerably to the costs of the site investigation and clean-up. In some cases, the NRA have required the developer or site owner to carry out additional remediation works as clean-up progresses.

Groundwater quality monitoring may also be required for a period of at least three years after clean-up and/or development has been completed. This involves the installation of monitoring boreholes and periodic collection and analysis of groundwater samples. The costs of the monitoring programme is normally required to be met by the owner/developer of the site and can be considerable.

Increasingly the NRA is insisting on a programme of groundwater monitoring to run in parallel with the clean-up of a site. It is used to provide information of existing groundwater quality and to ensure that the remediation works do not pollute groundwater due to disturbance of contaminants. For some sites, and as more novel on-site treatments are employed, the requirement for more detailed and extensive groundwater monitoring will also increase.

27.44 CONCLUSION

Although contaminated land is seen as a major environmental problem which will require investigation and assessment, there are technical solutions available to remediate the majority of contamination problems associated with such land. Critical to the successful management of contaminated land, and associated ground and surface waters, is the use of professional expertise.

28   Waste Management

28.1   INTRODUCTION

The law relating to waste management has undergone a thorough revision in recent years. A substantially new legal regime was introduced in the *Environmental Protection Act 1990* (*EPA 1990*), following widespread criticism of the operation of the system established under the provisions of the *Control of Pollution Act 1974* (*COPA 1974*), criticism voiced with particular force by the House of Commons Environment Committee, under the chairmanship of Sir Hugh Rossi.

In addition, the management of waste is an area in which the national law has been (and will continue to be) much influenced by EC law. The following Community initiatives are of particular relevance:

—   the *Framework Directive* of waste – *Council Directive 75/442/EEC*, as amended by *Council Directive 91/156/EEC*;

—   the *Directive* on hazardous waste – *Council Directive 91/689/EEC*;

—   the *Directive* on the supervision and control within the European Community of the transfrontier shipment of hazardous waste – *Council Directive 84/631/EEC*;

—   the draft *Directive* on the landfill of waste and waste incineration; and

—   the Commission's 'Green Paper' on civil liability for environmental damage.

The amended *Framework Directive* seeks to harmonise certain aspects of waste management legislation throughout the Member States. The purpose of doing so is to iron out any inconsistencies in national law which might provide opportunities for producers of waste to take advantage of differences in disposal costs in the various Member States. The *Framework Directive* achieves this end by two principal methods – by establishing Community-wide definitions of significant terms (especially 'waste' and 'disposal') and by laying down the essential elements of a waste management licensing system to be adopted by all Member States.

The *Hazardous Waste Directive* also seeks to establish a harmonised definition of what amounts to hazardous waste, by reference to a complex series of Annexes which address categories of waste, constituents of waste and the properties of such waste. The *Directive* also lays down requirements for a hazardous waste permitting system, for the drawing up by the competent authorities in each Member State of hazardous waste management plans, for the packaging and labelling of hazardous waste, etc.

The *Directive* on transfrontier movement of hazardous wastes introduced a system of consignment notes for international movement of such wastes, in order to provide adequate notification to the competent authorities of Member States concerned that the shipment was proposed. The *Directive* will need to be revised in accordance with the provisions of the Basel Convention on the Control of Transboundary Movements of Hazardous Wastes and their Disposal. A draft Regulation to give effect to the necessary changes in the Community regime was issued by the Commission as long ago as 1990, but there are still differences between Member States as to its acceptability. By the end of 1992, it was still not entirely clear that the Community would ratify the Convention in time for the forthcoming Meeting of the Parties and some Member States (in particular Germany) were becoming restive at the delays involved.

The draft *Directive* on landfill caused a considerable stir in the United Kingdom. The text was drafted on the assumption that, far too often, landfill was being seen by the generators as a first resort rather than a last resort (thus placing an obstacle in the way of achieving the Community aim of maximum reduction and re-use of waste). Furthermore, the draft *Directive* sets out to harmonise the different classes of landfill which can be operated and the technical standards for their operation. It also seeks to achieve the familiar goal of establishing the essential elements of a licensing system which are uniform throughout the Community and to harmonise the regime for closure and aftercare procedures and liabilities. Among the results of the draft *Directive* is a direct threat to the UK system of 'co-disposal', by which special (i.e. hazardous) and non-special wastes may be disposed of together in the same landfill, on a 'dilute-and-disperse' principle. The draft incineration directive seeks to impose strict standards on the operators of waste incinerators.

The Commission's Green Paper on civil liability in the field of the environment followed a mixed reaction from Member States to a draft Directive on civil liability for damage caused by waste. The Green Paper clearly indicated that, for the Commission, civil liability is seen as a facet of a comprehensive environmental policy. Indeed, the Commission seems to regard the fault principle as underpinning regulatory requirements – thus, failure to comply with Community standards is suggested as evidence of fault. While the Commission is not opposed to traditional civil liability (as an essential means of implementing the 'polluter pays' principle), this is seen as an 'imperfect' method of providing compensation. The Commission sees a strong need for strict liability regimes to improve risk management and hints at a policy of introducing Community legislation defining those activities having effect on the environment for which strict liability might be proper. There is also a suggestion that public authorities should be able to act as plaintiffs in environmental civil actions for environmental harm. The Commission is also clearly attracted to what it calls 'joint compensation systems', usually involving an industry levy to provide funds for compensation of victims. It considers that among the benefits of such a system can be included a more rapid response for victims and earlier environmental clean-up, a spreading of the burden around the industry and the availability of additional resources which may enable a higher degree of restoration, while still preserving preventative measures (at least in mutual insurance cases).

28.2   THE PRE-1993 SYSTEM AND ITS SHORTCOMINGS

Until 1 April 1993 the control of waste disposal operations was primarily exercised under the provisions of *COPA 1974*, which imposed on the operators of waste disposal facilities an obligation to obtain a licence (usually known as a 'site licence') for the deposit of 'controlled waste' on any land.

The regime under *COPA 1974* was the subject of severe criticism on a number of grounds.

First, it made no attempt to address the responsibility of the generator for the waste produced and concentrated primarily upon disposal.

Secondly, too many functions were combined in the county councils. As well as being waste planning authorities, they were also waste disposal authorities. In this guise, they both operated their own waste disposal sites themselves and acted as regulatory authorities to ensure that waste disposal sites were properly managed. It was cogently argued (by the House of Commons Environment Committee among others) that this duality of role, as both 'poacher and gamekeeper', tended to produce a significant divergence in operating standards between local authority sites and those in the private sector. Although landfill operators in the private sector formed the view that privately-owned sites were criticised for practices which are everyday occurrences on the waste disposal authority's own sites, there was some evidence that the failure of the authorities to keep their own houses in order may have had some restraining influence upon their readiness to undertake formal enforcement action in respect of shortcomings on private sites.

A third defect of the *COPA 1974* system was that no effective mechanism existed to control entry into the waste disposal market, in that there was no obstacle to persons who were either inadequately qualified, insufficiently financed or who in the past had been guilty of illegal or improper waste disposal practices, from embarking upon or continuing in the waste disposal business.

Fourthly, under the *COPA 1974* system, the holder of a waste disposal licence could at any time surrender that licence to the waste disposal authority and 'walk away' from the site, leaving the authority to deal with whatever aftercare or other remedial works necessary in order to ensure that the site did not become a danger to the environment or to public health or amenity.

28.3   THE NEW REGIME INTRODUCED BY THE ENVIRONMENTAL PROTECTION ACT 1990

Some of the provisions of *Part II* of *EPA 1990* have been brought into force. It was envisaged that the remaining provisions would be brought into force on 1 April 1993 but that did not happen. The delay was caused by the Government's need to ensure that UK law conformed to the emerging EC law. At the time of writing no new date for implementation of *Part II* has been announced.

A new regulatory structure

Waste Regulation Authorities

EPA 1990 ushered in a new era in the administration of waste management in Great Britain. Most of the strategic functions are now discharged by Waste Regulation Authorities (WRAs); English county councils and metropolitan county councils (with the exception of Greater Manchester and Merseyside, where the local WRA will act), Welsh district councils, and Scottish islands or district councils are WRAs, as is the London Waste Regulatory Authority in Greater London. The most important of the WRAs' tasks is the administration of the waste management licensing system (see below), but the authorities also have duties in respect of drawing up plans for the management of waste arising within their areas.

The WRAs also have the responsibility for strategic thinking about waste management in their areas. They are required to prepare a waste disposal plan for the area (based upon an initial assessment of the circumstances), detailing the expected waste arisings in the area (and the amounts of waste arising elsewhere which may be brought into the area for disposal), the methods of disposal which it envisages being employed (and its preferences in this respect), the sites where this disposal will take place and estimated costs. The waste disposal plan should also set out the policy which the WRA has adopted in respect of the granting of waste management licences. In preparing the plan, consultations must take place with the National Rivers Authority, the waste collection authorities and other interested parties.

28.4   *Local Authority Waste Disposal Companies*

In a major departure from pre-1993 practice, local authorities are now prohibited from running waste disposal sites themselves. Sites which were formerly operated by county

28.5 Waste Management

councils must either be sold to the private sector or transferred to a Local Authority Waste Disposal Company (LAWDC) which is at arm's length from the authority itself. By this mechanism, the respective roles of the poacher and the gamekeeper are divorced from one another, leaving the WRA to concentrate on enforcing the regulatory system.

28.5 *Waste Collection Authorities*

The responsibility for collecting waste falls upon district councils in England and Wales (except in London, where the borough councils or their equivalents fulfil this role) and on the islands or district councils in Scotland. They are under an obligation (in almost all cases) to collect domestic refuse and (upon request) commercial waste. (They may also collect industrial waste, but only with the approval of the WRA.)

Collection authorities are not to engage in waste disposal operations. There is an exception, however, in respect of waste which is to be recycled, for it is the collection authority which has responsibility for planning for the recycling of waste in its area.

28.6 *What is waste?*

The statutory definition of waste includes not only effluents, but scrap materials and unwanted surplus substances, as well as substances or articles which are broken, worn out, contaminated or otherwise spoiled. Anything which has been thrown away 'or otherwise treated as if it were waste' is deemed to be waste, in the absence of evidence to the contrary. [*EPA 1990, s 75(2)(3)*]. In practical terms, especially as reuse and recycling become more widespread, what one person regards as waste may appear to another to be raw material. Each of these may take a different view of the character of the material, in commercial terms. At present, however, this is not the legal position. For the purposes of the criminal law, at least, waste is considered from the point of view of the generator, i.e. it remains waste until final disposal – see *Long v Brook [1980] Crim. LR 109*. Disposal may, of course, take the form of refabrication, but the result of that process would be a new material and no longer waste (*R v Rotherham Metropolitan Borough Council, ex p Rankin*) [*1990] JPL 503 DC*.

It should be noted that the *EC Council Directive 75/442/EEC* on waste (*as amended*) provides a Community perspective on what is regarded as waste. Among the categories included in the *Directive* are:

—   off-specification products;

—   products whose date of appropriate use has expired;

—   materials spilled, lost or having suffered 'other mishaps';

—   materials contaminated or soiled as a result of 'planned actions', such as residues from cleaning operations, packing materials, etc.;

—   unusable parts, such as old batteries, spent catalysts, etc.;

—   substances which no longer perform satisfactorily, such as contaminated solvents;

—   residues from industrial or pollution abatement processes;

—   residues from raw materials extraction and processing;

—   adulterated materials;

—   any materials, substances or products whose use has been banned by law;

—   products for which the holder has no further use; and

420

—   contaminated materials, substances and products resulting from remedial action in respect of land.

For regulatory purposes in the UK, *EPA 1990* focuses upon 'controlled waste'. Controlled waste means household, industrial and commercial waste. Household waste is waste from buildings or self-contained parts of buildings used as dwellings, caravans, residential homes and premises forming part either of a university, school or other educational establishment or of a hospital or nursing home. Industrial waste derives from factories (within the meaning of the *Factories Act 1961*), premises used for or in connection with the provision of public transport, with the supply to the public of gas, water, electricity or sewerage services or postal or telecommunications services. Commercial waste means waste which comes from premises which are used wholly or mainly for the purpose of a trade or business or for the purposes of sport, recreation or entertainment (unless the waste is household or industrial waste, waste from a mine or quarry, arrgricultural waste or waste which has been excluded from the category of commercial waste by regulations). [*EPA 1990, s 75(4)–(7)*]. Each of these categories of waste (household, industrial and commercial) has been amplified by the *Controlled Waste Regulations 1992*.

These amplifications mean that each of the categories include some waste which might not immediately be thought of as falling within the category in question. Thus, the following are regarded as *commercial waste*:

—   wastes from offices or showrooms;

—   wastes from hotels;

—   wastes from premises which have a mixed use, but part of which are used for a trade or business;

—   waste from private garages having a floor area of more than 25 square metres or which are not used wholly or mainly for the accommodation of a private motor vehicle;

—   wastes from premises occupied by a club, society or association on which activities are conducted for the benefit of the members;

—   waste from premises occupied by courts, government departments, local authorities, corporate bodies or other persons with statutory functions and chartered corporations;

—   waste from tents pitched elsewhere than on a camp site;

—   waste from a market or fair; and

—   waste collected by a local authority from a place to which the public have access (other than a highway) where the authority has come to an agreement with the land-owner to collect such waste.

Similarly, the following are *industrial waste*:

—   waste from premises (other than a private garage) used for maintaining vehicles, vessels or aircraft;

—   waste from workshops which are not factories within the meaning of the *Factories Act 1961* by reason of the number of people working there or because the activities carried on there are not pursued by way of trade or for gain;

—   waste from dredging operations;

—   waste from a laboratory;

—   spoil and other waste from tunnelling or any other excavation;

—   some sewage and clinical waste;

—   waste arising from aircraft, vehicles and vessels which are not occupied for domestic purposes;

—   waste (other than household waste) which has formed part of any aircraft, vehicle or vessel;

—   waste (other than street-cleaning waste and litter) removed from land on which it has been deposited and any soil with which it has been in contact;

—   leachate from a deposit of waste;

—   poisonous or noxious waste arising from any of the following activities undertaken on premises used for the purposes of a trade or business:

  —   mixing or selling paints;

  —   sign-writing;

  —   laundering or dry cleaning;

  —   developing photographic film or making photographic prints;

  —   selling petrol, diesel fuel, paraffin, kerosene, heating oil or similar substances; or

  —   selling pesticides, herbicides or fungicides;

—   wastes from premises used for breeding, boarding, stabling or exhibiting animals;

—   waste oil (mineral and synthetic), waste solvent or scrap metal (provided that these do not come from dwelling-houses, caravans or residential homes or are otherwise classified by the *Regulations* as household waste;

—   demolition and construction waste (including waste arising from preparatory works);

—   waste imported into Great Britain; and

—   tank-washing and garbage from ships.

28.7   THE DUTY OF CARE

It will be recalled that one of the criticisms which was made of the legal regime of waste under the *COPA 1974* was that it only dealt with the final disposal of waste. This was seen as shutting the stable door after the horse has bolted. More attention should be directed towards integrated waste management, minimisation, reuse, and so on.

EPA 1990 addresses this criticism by imposing, in *section 34*, a general duty of care in respect of waste, not only upon the operators of waste disposal facilities, but on all persons who generate, import, carry, keep or dispose of waste. In other words, it seeks to fasten the duty on every person in the waste management chain. The duty is not really a single duty, but three interconnected duties.

(a)   *To prevent the unlawful disposal of the waste by anybody*
   Note that this does not just mean that the particular person under consideration must take care to see that his or her own immediate dealings with the waste are lawful and that, once satisfied on this account, that person can effectively wash his or her hands of responsibility for what happens to the waste thereafter. The statute is quite clear that the responsibility extends to taking all reasonable steps

to prevent unlawful disposal of the waste by third parties (e.g. waste carriers, disposal contractors, etc.).

(*b*) *To make sure that the waste does not escape from his/her control or that of any other person*
Similarly, this is an extended responsibility. Clearly, it requires the person subject to the duty to ensure that tanks containing liquid waste are sound and effectively bunded, to cover skips with netting or tarpaulins in order to prevent wind-blown litter, etc. The duty also, however, would require that the waste is placed in suitable containers, not only for the period when it is stored on that person's premises, but also for any periods of transport or storage under the custody of other people.

(*c*)　(i)　*Only to transfer the waste to 'authorised persons' . . .*
Authorised persons for this purpose are:

—　the waste collection authority;

—　a properly licensed waste disposal operator – note that, subject to the registration requirement (see below), the generator of waste can transfer the waste either by delivering it to the waste disposal site in his or her own truck or by having the waste disposal company collect it from the plant;

—　a registered waste carrier;

　　(ii)　*. . . and to give the person taking the waste a written description of it which will enable him/her to deal lawfully with the waste (i.e. meet his/her own duty of care)*
This duty involves the introduction by the generator of a standard system of waste documentation (which a prudent generator should have in place anyway!).

This latter duty is of particular importance, when read together with the *Environmental Protection (Duty of Care) Regulations 1992* (*SI 1992 No 2839*). Despite their rather inclusive title, these *Regulations* deal exclusively with the requirements for the *transfer notes* which have become an essential aspect of waste documentation. The *Regulations* require that, when waste is transferred to anyone else, the transferor and the transferee shall make sure that (in addition to the written description mentioned above) the transfer note is completed and signed. The note must include the following details:

(i)　a note identifying the waste and stating whether it is loose or in a container (and, if in a container, what kind);

(ii)　the time and place of transfer;

(iii)　the names and addresses of the parties to the transfer;

(iv)　whether the transferor is the generator (or importer) of the waste;

(v)　if the transfer is for authorised transport purposes, the nature of those purposes;

(vi)　if one of the parties is the holder of a waste disposal/management licence and is to hold, treat or dispose of the waste, the licence number and licensing authority; and

(vii)　if one of the parties is a registered waste carrier, the name of the WRA with which it is registered and the registration number.

Note that *both* parties are under a duty to ensure that these details are provided on the transfer note. So, if the transferor does not tender such a document, the transferee must ask for one to be produced. It will not be sufficient simply to shrug the shoulders and say that one was not tendered. Indeed, it is vital that these requirements are complied with as a basic minimum. In addition, copies of the transfer notes must be kept for two years and the WRA may require production of them.

28.8 What does the duty of care mean in practice?

(a) *Recognise the scale of the problem*

First, it should be recalled that the duty or care extends to all waste which is generated. This is a more extensive class than is sometimes realised. Almost without exception, plant managers will appreciate that process wastes fall within *EPA 1990, s 34*. Thus, raw materials (pure and contaminated), by-products, sludges, residues, etc. will all be included. So, in most cases, will packaging – the few inches of lubricating oil in the bottom of the drum is certainly waste, but so might the drum be also.

But the ambit of the duty is far wider than this. The broad definition of waste (see above) means that office wastes, wastes from the canteen and recreational areas, from the loading bay and the vehicle maintenance areas are also included. Even a site which is entirely occupied for administrative purposes (the group headquarters, for example) will generate a significant quantity of waste packaging, paints, solvents, lubricating oils, inks, adhesives, etc., all of which are subject to the duty.

Note also that, because a decision as to what is waste depends on the attitude of the person disposing of the substance or material, the operation of the duty of care can become quite complex when the person receiving the 'waste' thinks of it as something different, such as a raw material. Consider the case of a company which runs a business which consists of reprocessing waste oils or contaminated solvents with a view to their reuse:

— from the point of view of the generator of the contaminated product, it is a waste and must be subject to the duty of care procedures;

— as a result of the 'once a waste, always a waste' principle, the material should be treated by the processing company as being subject to the duty of care procedures (i.e. the reprocessing represents final diposal); and

— a new duty of care procedure should be applied to the waste from the reprocessing operation.

28.9 *(b)* *Be careful in selecting waste contractors*

It is no longer safe for a plant manager simply to take the view that, once he or she has succeeded in loading the waste onto someone else's lorry and seen it driven out of the gate, he or she can wash his or her hands of the problem. The duty of care requires that due consideration should be given to ensuring that, once the waste is out of sight, it is still going to be handled in an environmentally sound manner, so that there can be no possibility of a later suggestion that, because the waste has been allowed to cause pollution, the plant manager is in breach of the duty. This, in practice, means that care should be taken over the selection of a waste contractor, rather than simply picking a name from the Yellow Pages.

The steps which are necessary to discharge this element of the duty of care will obviously vary from case to case. Clearly, a plant manager wishing to dispose of highly toxic, flammable or other special waste will need to be more demanding than one who is only disposing of material which is wholly inert. In some cases, the plant manager may wish to pay a visit to the disposal site in order to form an impression as to whether waste which is consigned there is going to be dealt with responsibly. Even a person who does not claim to be an expert in waste disposal (but has some management ability) may gain a useful impression just by walking around the site to see if it looks as if it is a well-run operation. He or she should perhaps talk to the site manager and form an impression as to how well this individual knows his or her job. Similarly, he or she may observe whether, for example, the vehicles used are modern, clean, well-maintained, etc. Certainly, enquiries should be made about acceptance procedures, for if the site management does not know what they are receiving, they probably are not going to be able to tell what became of the waste they received. On an allied point, the plant manager should ask what documentation is maintained of waste accepted at the site and should ask to see copies. It would also be prudent (particularly if any dangerous waste is to be consigned) to ask about documentation as to final disposal of waste (e.g. can the site manager pinpoint with reasonable accuracy where on the site individual consignments of dangerous waste will be deposited?). The plant manager should ask whether monitoring of the site is conducted (the site licence will almost certainly require some) and, if so, by whom and what does it amount to?

The plant manager should also consider the size of the contractor's operation, its technical expertise and (not least) its financial capability. There is no harm in asking the WRA whether it is happy with the site and/or the operator. Perhaps one should also enquire as to whether there are any problems with the neighbours, particularly if the site is close to any sensitive receptors (housing, schools, etc.).

Initially, there may be some reluctance on the part of plant managers to make what appear to be instrusive enquiries into whether or not the operator knows its own business, which might not seem to augur well for the quality of a long-term business relationship. This reluctance is misplaced, because such enquiries of this kind are now everyday occurrences for waste disposal contractors. Reputable contractors are anxious to improve the public relations image of the industry and should be glad to co-operate. Hesitation, reluctance or obstruction should ring alarm bells and prompt the plant manager to look elsewhere.

28.10 (c)   Check the paperwork

In practical terms, one result of the imposition of the duty of care is that plant managers should be in a position to prove what has become of their waste and should have taken steps to allocate responsibility for it as between themselves and other actors in the waste management chain.

In this context, oral arrangements with these other actors are fraught with danger. It should be a basic principle to make sure that *all* movements of waste off-site are covered by a written contract. This contract should, among other things:

— specify exactly what the waste being collected consists of;

— deal with the question of title to the waste (who owns it and at what point does ownership pass to the contractor?);

— allocate liability for accidents involving the waste, whether on-site, in transit or at the disposal site;

— pin the contractor down as to adequate frequency of collection (to avoid overfilling of tanks, long-term storage on-site, etc.);

— allocate liability for costs or damage caused by failure to collect, including consequential loss;

— set out the documentation to be employed (e.g. collector to certify that waste has been delivered/disposed of). Some generators will want a little more than the bare legal essentials (see below);

— require the contractor to carry appropriate insurance cover;

— deal with what is to happen if the contractor is taken over by another company or becomes insolvent; and

— provide a right to terminate the contract (without prejudice) in cases of uncorrected breaches (plus an indemnity for any loss which the company has incurred).

28.11 (d)   *Keep own operations and waste management system under constant review*

The growth in popularity of environmental management systems (whether aimed at BS 7750 certification or not) has tended to concentrate managerial minds on the necessity to evaluate all potential exposures to environmental risk and to take steps to counteract them. The introduction of a waste management system is an essential part of this activity. Management should develop a systematic procedure for dealing with waste on-site and should make sure it is *really* comprehensive. Many an otherwise immaculately-run plant is let down by the pile of rusting drums with no labels on a pallet between the factory wall and the railway line! Care should also be taken to establish a clear framework of responsibilities and reporting lines, to ensure that adequate records are kept within the plant of waste arisings and disposals, etc.

It should be appreciated that this review should not be conducted on a 'once-and-for-all' basis, but that there is a constant need to re-evaluate. So, for example, the performance of waste contractors should be reviewed from time to time and a system should exist to programme consideration of waste impacts into changes of production processes, the choice of raw materials or construction projects within the plant. Furthermore, all these matters should be integrated into employee awareness and training programmes, as there is no earthly use in a perfect system which nobody knows how to use.

In addition, plant managers should always be ready for something to go wrong and should have prepared a contingency plan to deal with waste emergencies.

28.12 UNLAWFUL DEPOSIT OF WASTE

Whereas the licensing provisions of *COPA 1974* concentrated on making criminal the unauthorised deposit of controlled waste on land, *EPA 1990* casts its net much wider.

The *Act* indeed provides that it is a criminal offence to deposit controlled waste or knowingly permit or knowingly cause such waste to be deposited on land except in accordance with a valid waste management licence, but it also makes it an offence to 'treat, keep or dispose' of such waste on any land or mobile plant (or knowingly to permit or knowingly to cause such waste to be treated, kept or disposed of) except in accordance with such a licence. [*EPA 1990, s 33(1)(a),(b)*]. It should be noted, however, that these prohibitions do not apply to the disposal of household waste from a dwelling-house which is disposed of within the curtilage by or with the consent of the occupier. [*EPA 1990, s 33(2)*].

There is also a further offence of keeping, treating or disposing of controlled waste in such a manner as is likely to cause pollution of the environment or a threat to human health. [*EPA 1990, s 33(1)*]. This offence is independent of the existence or otherwise of a waste management licence. The *Controlled Waste Regulations 1992* (*SI 1992 No 588*) provide that the subsection does apply in prescribed circumstances where adequate control regimes of other sorts exist to control the disposal of the waste.

This wider ambit of the principal waste offences is accentuated by inclusive definitions of many of the terms used. 'Disposal' of waste includes (but is not limited to) disposal by means of deposit in or on land. Waste is 'treated' when it is subjected to any process, 'including making it reusable or reclaiming substances from it'. [*EPA 1990, s 29(6)*].

The phrase 'knowingly cause or knowingly permit' is a variation on a well-known theme in pollution law in the UK. The equivalent phrase in *COPA 1974* was 'cause or knowingly permit' and the courts have held that, under that *Act*, there was no necessity for the prosecution to prove any mental element to establish the offence of 'causing' pollution – see *Alphacell v Woodward* [*1972*] *2 All ER 475*. The language of *EPA 1990, s 33(1)* would indicate that this is no longer the case and some element of knowledge must be established.

In this context, it should be noted that *EPA 1990* expressly provides that, where controlled waste is carried in and deposited from a motor vehicle, the person who controls or is in a position to control the use of that vehicle shall be treated as knowingly causing the waste to be deposited, regardless of whether or not he or she gave any instructions for this to be done. This new offence is intended to provide an incentive for transport operators to take an interest in what their drivers and other employees do with waste which they may be carrying.

28.13 Exceptions from the licensing requirement

EPA 1990, s 33(4) enables the Secretary of State to provide by regulations exceptions from the requirement to hold a waste management licence before engaging in such kinds of waste operations as may be described in the regulations. The *Act* envisages these exceptions as falling into three categories:

(*a*) deposits which are small enough or of such a temporary nature that they may be excluded;

(*b*) any means of treatment or disposal which are innocuous enough to be excluded; and

(*c*) cases for which adequate controls exist in other legislation.

The Secretary of State has exercised his powers in this regard in the *Collection and Disposal of Waste Regulations 1988* (*SI 1988 No 819*) and the *Disposal of Controlled Waste (Exceptions) Regulations 1991* (*SI 1991 No 508*). These *Regulations* made under *COPA 1974*, set out cases in which waste operations may be conducted without a licence. Among the more significant of these exceptions are:

— the treatment, keeping or disposal of waste in connection with certain processes which are subjected to control under *Part I* of *EPA 1990*; and

— the deposit of waste on the premises on which it is produced, pending its disposal elsewhere.

The penalties on conviction for any of the offences under *EPA s 33* are severe. Before the magistrates, the maximum fine is £20,000 or up to six months imprisonment or both, while on indictment the fine can be unlimited and the maximum prison sentence is two years.

There are some defences. Among these are that the accused took all reasonable precautions and exercised all due diligence to avoid committing the offence. [*EPA 1990, s 33(7)(a)*]. This defence may be more difficult to establish than at first appears. Where the *Environmental Protection (Duty of Care) Regulations 1992* apply, any person to whom waste is transferred (a carrier or waste disposal operator) will have been given a description of the waste and a transfer note. He or she should have spotted any obvious discrepancy between the description of the waste and its actual appearance and should therefore have been put on notice that something was amiss.

28.14   Waste Management

An employee can plead that he or she was acting under the instructions of his or her employer, but in order to be acquitted the accused must show that he or she neither knew nor had reason to suppose that an offence was being committed. So, if any indication is given to the employee that the material is controlled waste, the defence may not be available.

It is also possible to plead that the acts alleged to constitute the offence in question took place in an emergency in order to avoid danger to the public and that, as soon as reasonably practicable afterwards, the WRA was given details of the affair. This defence is also a demanding one to run, as the accused must show that all these elements existed.

28.14 LAWFUL DISPOSAL OF WASTE – PLANNING PERMISSION AND WASTE MANAGEMENT LICENCES

Planning permission

EPA 1990, s 36(2) provides that, before a WRA can grant a waste management licence, it must be satisfied that the operations in respect of which the licence application is made enjoy the benefit of planning consent. Therefore, the applicant must show that there is in existence a grant of planning permission or an established use certificate.

The local planning authority will consult the National Rivers Authority (NRA) about applications relating to waste disposal operations. The NRA will often ask the local planning authority to incorporate into the conditions attached to the permission (or in an associated *section 106* agreement) provisions relating to, for example, leachate or landfill gas monitoring and control schemes.

Any planning consent will invariably be granted subject to a multiplicity of conditions governing various aspects of the operation of the site. It should be remembered that the purpose of the planning law in this context is largely connected with the preservation of amenity of the locality, regulation of traffic, etc. Therefore, the conditions which are attached to the planning permission are likely to relate to matters such as visibility at the point of access to the site, hours of operation, fencing, preservation of trees or hedges or the planting of such vegetation in order to screen the development, etc. Matters which relate specifically to the operation of the site in an environmentally sound manner, in the sense of preventing pollution, are thought to be more suitable for inclusion as conditions attached to the waste management licence.

An important feature of planning consent in modern conditions, however, is that it will contain conditions relating to the restoration, rehabilitation and aftercare of the site. Frequently, these conditions will specify in considerable detail the depth of the final cover of topsoil or other inert material which is to overlay the final layer of waste deposited, the profile which the final surface is to follow and the particular kind of after-use (agricultural land, forestry, etc.) for which the rehabilitation is to make the land fit.

It should also be noted that, unlike a waste management licence (which must be expressly transferred from one person to another, a process which requires the consent of the WRA, a planning permission (except in unusual circumstances) 'runs with the land', i.e. it passes automatically to any purchaser of the property without the need specifically to assign it.

28.15 Waste management licences

Anybody who engages in the treatment, keeping or disposal of controlled waste must have a waste management licence which permits that person to conduct those operations in respect of wastes of that description. This requirement is of broad application. In particular, it does not apply only to operators of final disposal sites, but also waste transfer stations and indeed to manufacturing companies which deal with their own wastes, whether on the production site or at dedicated locations operated by the company. Remember that *all* controlled waste is covered by this requirement and that variants of the licensing requirement apply to mobile waste disposal plant.

EPA 1990, s 35 when in force will require that any person engaged in the treatment, keeping or disposal of controlled waste must have a waste management licence. The licence is granted to the person who is the *occupier* of the land on which these activities are conducted. Therefore, it is not necessarily the freehold owner of the land who holds the waste management licence, but merely a tenant or a licensee. In most cases, however, there should be little difficulty for citizens in identifying the licensee (in cases of emergency or in order to make a complaint), as it is a very frequent condition of waste management licences that there should be displayed at the entry to the site a board bearing the name, address and contact details of the licensee. Until *section 35* is brought fully into force waste management licences will continue to be granted under *COPA 1974.*

The *Act* requires that, if the WRA is of the opinion that the applicant is a 'fit and proper person', it must grant the licence (provided that there is a valid planning permission) unless it is satisfied that the application should be rejected in order to avoid pollution of the environment, harm to human health or serious detriment to the amenities of the locality.

28.16 *Fit and proper persons*

There are three grounds upon which a WRA may consider an applicant not to be a fit and proper person. These are conviction of the applicant or another 'relevant person' of certain environmental offences, lack of technical competence and inadequate financial resources. The WRA may exercise its discretion to overlook convictions and still grant a licence, but it *cannot* ignore the lack of technical or financial resources.

28.17 *Conviction for environmental offences*

Of these three grounds, the first is by far the most complex, and the Department of the Environment has provided guidance to WRAs on the subject. Waste management licences may be held by individuals, partnerships or companies and the rules are different for each of these.

In the case of an individual applicant, the WRA must ask whether the applicant himself or herself has been convicted, but must also enquire as to whether any person has been convicted on such an offence committed in the course of employment by the applicant or in the course of carrying on the business of a partnership which included the applicant as one of the partners, or if an offence has been committed by a company at a time when the applicant was a director, manager, secretary or other similar officer of the company.

If the applicant is a partnership, the WRA must enquire if any of the partners has been convicted of an offence. It must also ask whether any person has been convicted of an offence committed in the course of his or her employment by one of the partners or in the course of carrying on the business of a partnership which included as one of the partners a partner in the applicant partnership, or if an offence has been committed by a company at a time when one of the applicant partners was a director, manager, secretary or other similar officer of the company.

If the applicant is a company, the WRA must ask whether the applicant company itself has been convicted and whether any person has been convicted of an offence committed in the course of his or her employment by the company, or by a person who is a director, manager, secretary or other similar officer of the applicant company, or by another company at a time when a director, manager, secretary or other similar officer of the applicant company held a similar position in that company. (It should be noted that the *Rehabilitation of Offenders Act 1974* only applies to individuals and that companies must declare all their convictions when applying for a waste management licence. The Department of the Environment suggests, however, that it may be proper for a WRA (in deciding whether such a company is a fit and proper person) to have regard to whether the conviction would have been spent in the case of an individual.)

Other matters which the WRA should consider in this context are whether the applicant or any relevant person has multiple convictions; whether offences have been committed by more than one relevant person; whether any of the offences concerned controlled waste or special waste; whether any of the offences caused serious pollution; and what were the penalties imposed on conviction.

28.18 *What are the relevant offences*

'Relevant offences' for the purpose of deciding whether any given postulant is a fit and proper person are likely to include offences under the following enactments:

—   the *Public Health (Scotland) Act 1897*;

—   the *Public Health Act 1936*;

—   the *Control of Pollution Act 1974*;

—   the *Control of Pollution (Amendment) Act 1974*

—   the *Refuse Disposal (Amenity) Act 1978*;

—   the *Control of Pollution (Special Waste) Regulations 1980* (*SI 1980 No 1709*);

—   the *Food and Environmental Protection Act 1985*;

—   the *Transfrontier Shipment of Hazardous Waste Regulations 1988* (*SI 1988 No 1562*);

—   the *Merchant Shipping (Prevention of Pollution by Garbage) Regulations 1988* (*SI 1988 No 2292*);

—   the *Water Act 1989*;

—   the *Environmental Protection Act 1990*; and

—   the *Water Resources Act 1991*.

28.19 *Lack of technical competence*

Various levels of Certificates of Technical Competence in waste management are awarded by the Waste Management Industry Training and Advisory Board (WAMI-TAB). The Department of the Environment, in May 1993 advised WRAs of the levels of qualification expected in respect of the managers of various kinds of waste management facilities.

Thus, the manager of a landfill site receiving biodegradable or special waste or waste which for some other reason requires substantial engineering works to protect the environment should hold a Certificate of Technical Competence in managing landfill sites at level 4. The manager of any other landfill site with a total capacity exceeding 50,000 cubic metres of waste should hold a Certificate of Technical Competence in managing landfill sites at level 3. The manager of a waste treatment plant where special waste is subjected to a chemical or physical process should hold a Certificate of

Technical Competence in managing waste treatment plants at level 4, while the manager of such a plant treating non-special waste need only be certified to level 3. The manager of a transfer station dealing with biodegradable, clinical or special waste must hold a Certificate of Technical Competence in managing waste treatment plants at level 4, while the manager of such a transfer station treating other waste need only be certified to level 3.

28.20 Consideration of the application for a waste management licence – EPA 1990, s 36

The *Act* provides that an application must be made to the local WRA for the area in which the site lies (where the waste operations are taking place at a fixed site) or, in the case of an application for a licence to operate mobile plant, to the WRA for the area in which the operator has its principal place of business.

There is no particular form which an application must follow, although draft regulations prepared by the Department of the Environment would require that it be made in writing. At present, WRAs have developed their own forms and a draft of a new version of the Waste Management Paper dealing with licensing suggests that an application should contain details of:

— the site itself, together with any existing or known prospective development within 250 metres of the boundary;

— the processes to be carried on at the site;

— the infrastructure to be provided;

— boundaries and fencing;

— landscaping and screening;

— waste reception facilities;

— proposed pollution control measures (including leachate and landfill gas management);

— proposals for the restoration of the site (usually required to be undertaken in phases as the parts of the site reach full capacity);

— the technical knowledge and experience of the applicant (or the proposed operator);

— its financial competence; and

— any convictions of the applicant or the operator (or any associated person) for relevant offences.

In practice, the WRA will require the application to be accompanied by additional information. Most importantly, it will require submission of the draft working plan, drawn up by the applicant (or by the proposed operator) to govern the running of the site. Typically, this will consist both of engineering drawings for the site and its infrastructure and a description of the manner in which the operations on the site will be carried out.

Working plans, of course, vary widely, reflecting the particular characteristics of each site. Among the matters which the Department of the Environment expect to see discussed in the working plan for a landfill site are:

— the lay-out of the site and its infrastructure, in terms of site roads, fencing, offices and weighbridges, wheel-washing facilities, plant maintenance areas, etc.;

— the phases in which operations are to be carried out, including the sequence in which various parts of the site are to be used;

— engineering specifications for bunds and liners, drainage systems, etc.;

— details of the design and construction of leachate collection and abstraction systems, estimates of the volumes of leachate expected to be generated, monitoring proposals, removal and treatment systems, etc.;

— landfill gas control systems, including barriers and collection and control systems, monitoring etc.;

— operating hours, staff levels and qualifications, site security, etc.;

— proposals as to which kinds of wastes are to be disposed of or treated in which parts of the site;

— measures proposed for the control of vermin and litter, dust suppression and road cleaning;

— proposed systems for record-keeping and waste documentation;

— monitoring of surface water;

— proposed methods of covering waste in order to avoid the creation of nuisances and the generation of 'perched' leachate between the layers of deposited waste;

— the proposed design, profile and specifications of the final capping cover and the provisions proposed to handle run-off and drainage from it; and

— proposals for the management of the site following its closure, especially with regard to landfill gas and leachate.

Frequently, conditions attached to the waste management licence will require that all operations conducted on the site must be in accordance with the working plan and that any departure from its terms should be approved in writing by the WRA. Conditions also often require that the preliminary works should have been completed to the satisfaction of the WRA before any waste operations are conducted at the application site. Indeed, *EPA 1990* expressly envisages that such conditions may be required. [*EPA 1990, s 35(3)*].

The application must also be accompanied by the appropriate fee. As a response to a widely-held feeling that it was undesirable that the whole burden of the licensing system should be borne by the WRA, *EPA 1990, s 41* provides that the WRA may make charges on applications for waste management licences and Government policy is that these fees should enable the authorities to recover their full costs (including any payments which they may be obliged to make to the NRA in respect of consultations). The amount of the fee varies according to the kind of waste operation which is the subject of the application, the types of waste in respect of which the licence is required and the volumes of wastes involved.

28.21 *Consultations prior to grant of a waste management licence*

EPA 1990 makes it clear that, if the WRA is minded to grant a licence, it must undertake some further consultations before it does so.

The NRA must be consulted in such cases and has a firm policy as to how it will discharge its statutory duty to protect groundwater quality. The NRA will press for the siting of waste disposal sites on non-aquifers (and publishes maps showing the distribution of aquifers and non-aquifers). Furthermore, the NRA will usually oppose the carrying-on of waste operations requiring a waste management licence within defined zones (known as Inner Source Protection Zones) which are immediately adjacent to groundwater sources. In these zones, it is the NRA's view that all waste operations (not just landfill) are potentially damaging and, although each case will be viewed on its merits, there is a presumption that the NRA will object. Similarly, the NRA will object to landfills (although not necessarily to other activities requiring a waste management licence) in Outer Source Protection Zones (areas from the limits of which there is a groundwater travel time of 400 days from a point below the water table to the source). By way of exception, the NRA may not object to landfills which are only to be licensed to receive inert, naturally occurring materials (or possibly, in a proper case, construction or demolition waste). Within the wider catchment area of groundwater sources (and, indeed, even on aquifers), the NRA may not oppose applications for landfills of wastes with a medium or even high pollution potential, provided that adequate engineering measures are taken. What amount to adequate measures will, of course, depend on the locality and the vulnerability of the groundwater, but the NRA will expect that wastes generating large quantities of potentially polluting leachate will be operated on the full containment principle and the NRA will have to be satisfied with whatever scheme is proposed for the collection and disposal of the leachate produced.

Where a proposed landfill would extend to or below the water table in a Source Protection Zone, the NRA will normally oppose the application for a waste management licence, unless adequate engineering measures are taken to counter pollution of the groundwater by leachate, etc. Although normally the NRA considers the retention of an unsaturated zone desirable, exceptions may be made if the site is a full containment site.

In non-aquifers, the NRA will not usually object to landfill on the grounds of groundwater protection (although it may do so if there is a threat to other interests which the NRA is bound to consider, such as surface water quality or flood protection).

The NRA will frequently insist on what it considers to be adequate monitoring and pollution control programmes being incorporated into the licensing process, along with checks on the integrity of any cap, basal or side containment which may be required.

The NRA enjoys a right not shared by other consultees. If the NRA feels that the WRA should not grant a licence which it is minded to grant (or if there is a difference of opinion over conditions to be attached to the licence), either the NRA or the WRA may refer the question to the Secretary of State for a decision.

EPA 1990 also requires that the Health and Safety Executive be consulted by the WRA before it grants a licence and must take account of any representations made by the Executive.

There are also requirements that, before granting a licence for a site which includes a Site of Special Scientific Interest, the proposal must be referred to the relevant nature conservation body for that part of the United Kingdom (for example, English Nature for England, Scottish Natural Heritage, etc.).

These statutory consultees have 21 days to respond unless a longer period is agreed in writing between the consultee and the authority.

In addition to these statutory consultees mentioned expressly in *EPA 1990*, Government guidance suggests that the WRA should also consider whether to consult more widely, involving parish councils and local interest groups, for example.

Furthermore, the WRA must enter all applications for waste management licences on the public registers which it is obliged to maintain under *EPA 1990, s 64*.

28.22   Waste Management

The WRA may either grant or reject the application (although in the latter case there is a right of appeal – see below). Licences are granted to the occupier of the land or to the operator of mobile plant.

Waste management licences, once issued, are not limited in time, but remain in effect indefinitely (unless revoked by the WRA). They may, however, only be surrendered or transferred to another person in the manner provided for in *EPA 1990*.

The WRA has a period of four months from the date upon which it received the application to come to a decision. If it fails to do so within that time, the applicant may treat the failure as a deemed refusal and elect to pursue the matter with the Secretary of State on appeal. The applicant may, however, agree in writing with the WRA to extend the period within which the application may be considered.

28.23 Conditions attached to waste management licences

EPA 1990 requires that waste management licences should be granted subject to such conditions as the WRA may deem appropriate and which relate to:

(a)   the activities authorised by the licence; and

(b)   the precautions to be taken in connection with or in consequence of those activities.

The power conferred on the WRA in respect of the imposition of conditions is very broad. In particular, a condition may be imposed even though compliance would require the holder of the licence to carry out works which he or she is not entitled to do (perhaps because the land on which those works are to be carried out belongs to a neighbouring landowner). In such case, a very unusual provision of the *Act* requires that the third party shall grant to the holder of the licence such rights as may be necessary to enable the condition to be complied with, although it must be said that there does not seem to be any penalty provided for those who fail to accede to this high-handed requirement. [*EPA 1990, s 35(4)*]. It is thought that the most usual circumstance in which the subsection may be relied upon is when additional monitoring boreholes are required on adjacent land.

Conditions are attached to licences relating to operations dealing with controlled wastes, but, where such operations involve wastes other than controlled wastes, those other wastes may also be the subject of conditions on the licence, thus being brought (to this extent, at least) into control.

A typical waste management licence will contain at least a score of conditions. These will govern matters such as:

—   the types of waste which may be accepted at the site;

—   the types of waste the disposal, treatment or storage of which are prohibited at the site;

—   the experience and qualification of the person having supervision or control of the operations carried on at the site and of any other persons working there;

—   the times during which waste may be received at the site and during which operations of any kind can be conducted there;

—   the keeping of records;

—   fencing, gates and other methods of ensuring that the site is secure;

—   covering of loads on vehicles and containers on the site;

— prevention of spillage and litter;

— cleaning of wheels and tracks of vehicles leaving the site;

— the provision and maintenance of equipment on the site;

— bunding and other methods of containment for any liquids (whether waste or not) kept or stored on the site;

— the compaction or covering of wastes in the course of treatment or disposal;

— the monitoring of any watercourses or underground water;

— the monitoring and control of landfill gas generated in the site;

— the control of weeds, pests and vermin;

— the prevention and control of fire;

— restoration, rehabilitation and aftercare of the site. (As in the case of preliminary works, *EPA 1990, s 35(3)* expressly authorised the imposition of conditions relating to the period after waste operations at the site have been completed.)

Note, however, that the draft *Waste Management Licensing Regulations* published by the Department of the Environment will provide that no conditions should be imposed on a waste management licence simply for the purpose of promoting health and safety at work, as this is a matter for the Health and Safety Executive (which will have been consulted as part of the licensing process) and the WRA should not duplicate the functions of the Executive.

Normally, the precise conditions for each waste management licence are a matter for negotiation between the applicant and the WRA, but the *EPA 1990* does provide for the Secretary of State to issue directions to the WRA as to what conditions should be inserted in a licence. It is thought that this power will only be used in exceptional cases. There is also provision for the imposition, by regulations, of other conditions not included on the face of the licence. This power is taken by the Department of the Environment in order to enable it efficiently to give effect to European Community requirements or other international obligations. (Indeed, the draft *Waste Management Licensing Regulations* contain some such conditions, reproducing some of the requirements of *Council Directive 75/439/EEC* on Waste Oils (as amended).)

Conducting waste operations in contravention of the conditions is a criminal offence punishable by severe penalties. In addition, conviction for these offences may result in the accused not being considered a 'fit and proper person' to hold a waste management licence.

28.24 Modification of waste management licences

The terms of a waste management licence will be capable of being modified, either by the WRA on its own initiative or at the application of the holder. The WRA can only exercise this power if it thinks that the modifications involved are desirable and if they do not require the holder to incur unreasonable expense. The WRA is under a duty to modify a licence to the extent that this is necessary to ensure that the waste operations neither cause pollution of the environment or harm to human health nor become seriously detrimental to the amenities of the locality.

In no case can a modification, whether at the instigation of the WRA or the holder, vary conditions imposed by the Secretary of State and the WRA is under a duty to modify any licence in order to reflect such conditions. Furthermore, *EPA 1990* empowers the Secretary of State to direct that licences be modified, but this power will only be used in exceptional circumstances.

The NRA also collaborates with the WRA in reviewing the terms of waste management licences on a five-year cycle (as advised by the Department of the Environment).

The draft *Waste Management Licensing Regulations* contain new requirements as to the disposal of waste oils, the protection of groundwater and the removal of licence conditions which relate only to health and safety matters. The Department (in an accompanying draft Circular) has called upon WRAs to revise licences for which they are the granting authority in order to reflect these new provisions by the end of March 1994.

28.25 Revocation and suspension of waste management licences

EPA 1990, s 38 will provide a mechanism by which the WRA may revoke or temporarily suspend a waste management licence.

Licences may be revoked if:

(*a*)   the holder is convicted of a relevant offence and therefore ceases to be a fit and proper person for licensing purposes. It will be recalled that being a fit and proper person is a *sine qua non* for obtaining a licence in the first place; or

(*b*)   the continuation of the activities by the licence would, in the opinion of the WRA, cause pollution of the environment or be seriously detrimental to the amenities of the locality and that this pollution or harm to amenity cannot be countered by a mere modification of the terms of the licence.

If either of these circumstances exist, the WRA may revoke the licence entirely or revoke only those parts of it relating to the activities in question, leaving the remainder of the licence on foot. This power of partial revocation (but not, apparently, that of total revocation) is also available when the management of the activities authorised by the licence has passed into the hands of persons who are not technically competent to conduct them, with the result that the holder ceases to be a fit and proper person. When a WRA serves a notice revoking a licence, it may specify which provisions of the licence are to continue to bind the holder, notwithstanding the revocation. Thus, revocation is not an entirely 'clean break' and requirements (as to aftercare, for example) may be enforced notwithstanding the termination of the licence.

The WRA may also serve a notice suspending a licence on grounds similar to those justifying revocation. These are if:

(*a*)   the management of the activities authorised by the licence has passed into the hands of persons who are not technically competent to conduct them, with the result that the holder ceases to be a fit and proper person; or

(*b*)   the serious pollution of the environment or serious harm to the amenities of the locality has arisen from, or is about to arise from, the activities authorised by the licence and that this pollution or harm to amenity will continue to occur (or will occur) if those activities are permitted to continue.

Suspending the licence obviously has the effect of making it unlawful, during the period of the suspension, for the holder to carry on any of the licensed activities, but the WRA may, when suspending the licence, require the holder to take such steps as the authority considers necessary in order to deal with the pollution or damage to amenity which has caused the suspension.

Suspension and revocation notices are served on the holder of the licence and they must state clearly the time at which the suspension or revocation is to take effect (and, in the case of suspension notices, the period of its duration or the event on the occurrence of which the suspension will expire).

28.26 Transfers of waste management licences – EPA 1990, s 40

The controls over transfer of waste management licences is a corollary of the *Act*'s insistence that licences only be granted to fit and proper persons.

When *section 40* is brought into force, an application for a transfer should be made to the WRA by the proposed transferor and transferee jointly. The draft *Waste Management Licensing Regulations* list the information which must accompany the application. Much of this information is intended to enable the WRA to determine whether or not the proposed transferee is a fit and proper person to hold a waste management licence. Provided that it is satisfied on this score, the authority must transfer the licence to him or her. There are no other grounds upon which the authority can refuse to do so.

Licences may be transferred even after they have been partially revoked or suspended. Indeed, the passing of the control of waste operations into the hands of someone with insufficient technical competence to qualify as a fit and proper person may well be occasion both for a notice of suspension and an application for a transfer of the licence.

28.27 Surrender of waste management licences and aftercare of landfills

EPA 1990 will introduce a radical change in the procedure for the surrender of waste management licences. Under *COPA 1974* it is possible for the licence holder simply to announce that it is going out of business and to surrender the licence to the waste disposal authority. The fact that the licence may have contained extensive restoration and aftercare obligations, which may require significant expenditure, was no barrier to this sloughing-off of responsibility by the licence holder.

Under *EPA 1990*, where a holder wishes to surrender a waste management licence (other than a licence for the operation of mobile plant, which may be surrendered on payment of any outstanding fees), he or she must make an application in writing to the WRA containing the information set out in *Schedule 2* to the draft *Waste Management Licensing Regulations*. This information includes, in addition to details of the licence holder and the site licence, an estimate of the total quantities of each of the various types of waste dealt with at the site. If the site is a landfill, details must be provided of all engineering works carried out to prevent pollution or harm to human health, including restoration works carried out after tipping was completed. There must also be supplied geological, hydrogeological and hydrological information, including information about the permeability of the surrounding strata to gas and water and about groundwater flows. Monitoring data on the quality of groundwater which could be affected and on landfill gas and leachate production should also be supplied, along with data on the stability of the site. If special waste (see below) has been deposited at the site, the records and plans required by the *Control of Pollution (Special Waste) Regulations 1980* must also be attached. If the site was not a landfill site, the holder must supply only details of the contaminants which are likely to be present on the site, having regard to the activities carried on there (including activities not covered by the licence) and the nature of the wastes dealt with, together with a report which records the analysis of samples taken in sufficient numbers and in the appropriate parts of the site to give a reliable indication of the places where the concentrations of those contaminants are likely to be high. (Details of the sampling methodology should also be supplied.) The holder must also pay the appropriate fee, which will vary depending on the types and amounts of waste dealt with at the site and on whether the site was used for the disposal of waste or merely for keeping or treating waste. The application will be entered on the public register maintained by the WRA.

The WRA is under a positive duty to inspect the land to which the licence relates in order to determine whether the land is in such a condition (as a result of the waste management operations which have been carried on there) as to pose a threat of pollution of the environment or of harm to public health. In carrying out this assessment, the WRA must confine its attention to the question of whether this threat arises from the carrying out of waste operations on the site and is not entitled to refuse to accept a surrender if the land poses a threat for other reasons. On the other hand, all waste operations (including those which occurred in breach of the licence or those which did not require authorisation by the licence) may be considered. The authority has powers to require the licence holder to supply it with such supplementary information as it may require to enable it to make its assessment, which will also appear in the public register.

If the WRA forms the view that the land is unlikely to present such a threat to the environment or human health, it must accept the surrender of the licence, although it may not do so until it has consulted the NRA, which has 21 days (or such longer period as shall be agreed in writing) to consider the application. If this consultation produces a request from the NRA that the surrender should not be accepted, any dispute over the matter should be referred to the Secretary of State and no surrender accepted otherwise than in accordance with his or her decision.

If the surrender is accepted, the WRA will issue to the holder a 'certificate of completion', the effect of which is to complete the surrender of the licence and thereby relieve the former holder of any continuing liability in respect of the licence. Until that certificate is issued, the holder will remain subject to whatever restoration, aftercare and other conditions are imposed by the licence.

If the WRA comes to the view that the condition of the site does present a threat of this nature, it may not accept the surrender of the licence. It should be noted that the WRA has no discretion in this matter. Unless the WRA (and, indeed, the NRA) are entirely satisfied that the site is unlikely to pose difficulties in the future, he or she will remain subject to the requirements of the licence and will not be able to abandon the site with impunity.

Applications to surrender licences which are not disposed of by the WRA within three months are deemed to have been refused, unless an extension of time has been agreed in writing with the applicant.

28.28 Appeals against licensing decisions – EPA 1990, s 43

If an applicant or the holder of a waste management licence is not content with a decision or action of the WRA, he or she may appeal to the Secretary of State. Appeals may be made:

— against the refusal of a waste management licence or against the refusal of an application for a modification in its terms by the holder;

— against the conditions imposed on the licence;

— against a modification of the licence by the WRA;

— against the suspension of the licence;

— against the revocation of the licence;

— against the refusal of an application to surrender the licence; and

— against the refusal of an application to transfer the licence (in which case, the appeal may be made by the unsuccessful transferee).

Appeals should be made in writing to the Secretary of State. The draft *Waste Management Licensing Regulations* require that the appeals should be accompanied by supporting documentation, including a statement of the grounds on which the appeal is made, a copy of the relevant application and correspondence and a statement of whether the appellant wishes the matter to be dealt with at a hearing or by written representations. Either party may ask for a hearing, which may be conducted in private if the inspector appointed by the Secretary of State decides that this is appropriate.

Normally, the decision of the WRA will remain in abeyance until the Secretary of State makes his decision on the appeal, but there are exceptions to this principle. An appeal against the suspension of a licence will not have the effect of lifting the suspension. This is because the power to suspend licences is an emergency power, usually employed only where there is environmental damage or an imminent threat of it. Similarly, the decision of the WRA unilaterally to modify a licence or to revoke it in whole or in part will remain in effect pending the determination of the appeal, in cases where the notice served by the WRA includes a statement that it is of the opinion that the notice is necessary to prevent or minimise the effect of pollution of the environment or a threat to human health. In cases where the decision of the WRA comes into effect and is then overturned on appeal, the appellant may receive compensation from the WRA in respect of any loss suffered as a result.

28.29 Supervision of waste operations – EPA 1990, s 42

The *Act* requires that the WRA must do what is necessary, by inspection or other means, to ensure that the activities which have been authorised by waste management licences granted by it do not cause pollution of the environment or harm to human health and, in particular, that the conditions attached to those licences are complied with.

A draft revision of Waste Management Paper 4 stresses that compliance is primarily a matter for the operator and that quality assurance systems should be required by licence conditions. Nevertheless, regular site inspections should be made by the WRA and these should be more than a mere visual check. They should include a careful examination of the working area and an examination of the monitoring points and site records (e.g. duty of care transfer notes, special waste logs, etc.). Routine inspections at which an overall impression can be gained should be supplemented, at least on larger sites, with more specialised investigations of particular aspects of operations or control, such as monitoring of landfill gas or leachate or of groundwater quality. Special waste records should be checked against other copies of the consignment note on a monthly basis, etc. Complex sites may be suitable candidates for more extensive audits, lasting several days. Inspections on sites licensed to operate outside normal office hours should be conducted on a random basis in the early morning or evening. Regular meetings with the site management should be held in order to provide a channel for feedback to the staff.

In cases of non-compliance with conditions, the WRA may serve a notice requiring compliance within a specified period. If this is not done, the WRA may seek suspension or revocation of the licence.

The WRA has power, if it appears necessary to do so in an emergency, to carry out work on land, equipment or mobile plant and the authority may recover its costs from the holder or (where the licence has been surrendered) former holder of the licence, unless that person can show that there was no emergency requiring such work to be done or that the expenditure or part of it was unnecessary.

If the WRA feels that the waste operations covered by any existing licence are likely to cause water pollution, it must consult the NRA.

28.30 Transport of waste

Registration of waste carriers

Under the provisions of the *Control of Pollution (Amendment) Act 1989*, it is an offence for any person to transport controlled waste in the course of a business or otherwise with a view to profit, unless the carrier is registered with the WRA for the area in which that person has its headquarters. As in the case of the waste management licence, the *Act* contains a requirement that, in order to be registered, the applicant must be a 'fit and proper person'. Similarly, there are provisions (which were the model for similar provisions in *EPA 1990*) that those who have been convicted (or are associated with those who have been convicted) of a range of environmental crimes may not be so regarded.

It should be noted that the *1989 Act* does *not* apply *only* to transport operators and waste contractors. Any person who carries waste 'in the course of a business of his or otherwise with a view to profit' must register. Thus, any company which uses its lorries to move waste from one site to another is, in principle, within the ambit of the *Act*. This rule, however, is subject to some qualifications.

(1)   The *1989 Act* provides that moving waste from one place to another within the same premises (the word is not defined) does not require registration.

(2)   There are a number of exceptions to the requirement for registration. These include, as well as obvious candidates like the various waste authorities established under *EPA 1990*, charities and the person who produced the controlled waste in question (unless it is demolition or construction waste). See *Controlled Waste (Registration of Carriers and Seizure of Vehicles) Regulations 1991 (SI 1991 No 1624)*. Note, however, that a producer of waste is only exempt from registration if it is carrying its own waste. The moment waste produced by any other person (even an associated company) is carried, an offence is committed.

28.31 *Disposal of sludges and slurries*

The spreading on land of certain sludges which are thought to be beneficial from the point of view of fertilising or otherwise conditioning the land is, in some parts of the country, a common practice.

These materials are exempted from the usual system of controls over waste disposal by the *Collection and Disposal of Waste Regulations 1988*. Provided that the wastes do not present an environmental hazard, they may be spread without the necessity for a waste management licence, provided that the WRA is notified in advance of the person making the deposit, the kind of waste and an estimate of the quantities involved and of the location of the deposit and the date on which it is to be made (or the frequency of the deposit, in the case of repeated operations). Regular deposits of similar types of waste can be notified every six months.

Although the *Regulations* require notification to the WRA, they do not expressly stipulate that the NRA should be informed. It is the practice of the NRA to maintain close contact with WRAs in order to keep tabs on this practice and, if the NRA feels that the activity poses a threat to water quality, to ask for the operations to be licensed. In particular, where such operations are proposed in source protection zones and on major or minor aquifers, the NRA will ask the WRA to limit application of wastes which contain 'significant concentrations' of:

—   organohalogen compounds and substance which may form such compounds in the aquatic environment;

—   organophosphorus compounds;

—   organotin compounds;

—   substances which possess carcinogenic, mutagenic or teratogenic properties in or via the aquatic environment;

—   mercury and mercury compounds;

—   cadmium and cadmium compounds;

—   mineral oils and hydrocarbons; and

—   cyanides.

28.32 *Sewage sludge*

The disposal of sewage sludge on agricultural land is governed by the *Sludge (Use in Agriculture) Regulations 1989 (as amended) (SI 1989 No 1263)*. These provide that sludge may not be used on agricultural land unless both it and the soil to which it is to be applied have been tested in accordance with the procedures set out in the *Regulations* (which draw upon and introduce into national law *EC Council Directive 86/278/ EEC*). The *Regulations* also control the amount and rate of permissible application in order to ensure that the concentration in the soil of certain heavy metals (zinc, copper, nickel, chromium, lead and mercury) do not exceed stated levels. No application can take place while any fruit or vegetables are growing or being harvested on the land in question (other than those on fruit trees). Heed must also be taken of the nutrient needs of plants and the quality of surface and groundwater. There are also restrictions on the grazing of animals and the harvesting of forage on the land.

The occupier of the land on the which sludge is spread must provide the producer of the sludge (often the sewerage undertaker) with details of the agricultural land on which it was used, the date and quantities applied and the name of the producer of any other sludge disposed of at the same place and time. There are also record-keeping obligations placed on the producer of the sludge.

The NRA has given notice that it will seek to discourage the dedication of further areas of land to this use.

28.33 *Hazardous waste*

In the United Kingdom, hazardous or dangerous waste is referred to by lawyers as 'special waste' (although some WRAs use the term 'difficult waste' to refer to material which presents certain management difficulties but is not 'special' in this legal sense).

The particular rules relating to special waste are set out in the *Control of Pollution (Special Waste) Regulations 1980*, made under *COPA 1974* but still in force. They will shortly have to be replaced, as an EC Directive to be implemented by the end of 1993 (see below) has adopted a rather different definition of hazardous waste.

'Special waste' means waste which

(a)   consists of or contains the following substances:

—   acids or alkalis;

—   antimony and antimony compounds;

—   arsenic compounds;

—   asbestos (all chemical forms);

—   barium compounds;

—   beryllium and beryllium compounds;

— 　biocides and phytopharmaceutical substances;

— 　boron compounds;

— 　cadmium and cadmium compounds;

— 　copper compounds;

— 　heterocyclic organic compounds containing oxygen, nitrogen or sulphur;

— 　hexavelant chromium compounds;

— 　hydrocarbons and their oxygen, nitrogen or sulphur compounds;

— 　inorganic cyanides;

— 　inorganic halogen-containing compounds;

— 　inorganic sulphur-containing compounds;

— 　laboratory chemicals;

— 　lead compounds;

— 　mercury compounds;

— 　nickel and nickel compounds;

— 　organic halogen compounds, excluding inert polymeric materials;

— 　peroxides, chlorates, perchlorates and azides;

— 　pharmaceutical and veterinary compounds;

— 　phosphorus and its compounds;

— 　selenium and selenium compounds;

— 　silver compounds;

— 　tarry materials from refining and tar residues from distilling;

— 　tellurium and tellurium compounds;

— 　thallium and thallium compounds;

— 　vanadium compounds;

— 　zinc compounds; and

(b)　by reason of the presence of that substance either:

— 　is dangerous to life (see below);

— 　has a flash-point of 21 degrees Celsius or less; or

— 　is a medicinal product available by prescription only.

Materials are 'dangerous to life' if a single dose of not more than 5 cc would be likely to cause death or serious tissue damage if ingested by a child of 20 kilogrammes, or if exposure to it for 15 minutes or less would be likely to cause serious damage to human tissue by inhalation, skin contact or eye contact.

The *Control of Pollution (Special Waste) Regulations 1980* to some extent foreshadow the provisions of the *Environmental Protection (Duty of Care) Regulations*, in that they introduced mandatory documentation for consignments of special waste. A generator of such waste must prepare six copies of a consignment note (or 'trip-ticket'), describing the waste, how it is packed, the process from which it derived and its chemical components. Waste carriers collecting the waste sign the trip-ticket to certify their collection of the waste (returning one copy to the generator who also certifies that he or she had advised the carrier of appropriate precautions to be taken). When the waste arrives at the final disposal site, the operator endorses a note of the delivery on the trip-ticket. In principle, this enables individual consignments to be tracked from generation to disposal.

The trip-tickets are to be kept at each site in a register and the generators and producers are to keep their copies of the notes for not less than two years. Waste disposal operators must keep a record of the location of each deposit of special waste on their site and, when the licence is surrendered, send these records to the WRA.

Note that not every site which is the subject of a waste management licence is authorised to receive special wastes. Deposit of such waste on a site which is not so licensed is a criminal offence. In the past, many UK landfill sites have operated 'co-disposal' of special and non-special wastes, as a form of the 'dilute and disperse' principle so beloved of British waste managers. A draft EC Directive on landfill may not permit this practice to continue. At present, it would permit such activity, but only where it could be demonstrated that 'beneficial interactive processes' would result. Recently, it has been suggested that even this limited exception may not survive into the final form of the Directive.

The *EC Council Directive 91/689/EEC* on hazardous waste contains a package of measures which must be complied with by each Member State before 12 December 1993. These include:

— a requirement that, on every site where hazardous waste is discharged, the waste is properly identified and recorded;

— a requirement that different categories of hazardous waste are not mixed together (and that hazardous and non-hazardous wastes are not mixed) unless this can be done without harm to the environment;

— a requirement that hazardous wastes sites must be 'registered' with the competent authorities;

— a requirement that hazardous wastes be properly packaged and labelled in accordance with Community and international standards during collection, transport and temporary storage; and

— that the competent authorities shall draw up plans for the management of hazardous waste (either as self-standing documents or as part of an overall waste plan).

The *Directive* also contains a very sophisticated set of definitions of hazardous waste. The concept is defined by reference to three Annexes which are rather wider in their ambit than the *Control of Pollution (Special Waste) Regulations 1980*. In addition to a list of 40 categories of wastes which are regarded as hazardous by their very nature, there is a further catalogue of over 50 classes of materials which, if they form a constituent part of any waste, will render that waste hazardous in Community law. In addition, wastes will be hazardous if they display any one or more of 14 characteristics, as defined in a third Annex. These include, explosive, flammable, irritant, toxic, carcinogenic, infectious, tetratomic, mutagenic and ecotoxic wastes.

As a result, the United Kingdom will have to replace the *Regulations* with new provisions to reflect the requirements of the *Directive* in the course of 1993.

28.34 Recycling

The Government has announced ambitious targets for the recycling and re-use of waste and enthusiasm for these methods of waste handling is reflected in *EPA 1990*.

28.35　Waste Management

28.35 *Waste recycling plans*

The principal responsibility for promoting waste recycling is placed firmly with the Waste Collection Authority, which is under a duty to draw up a recycling plan for its area, covering both household and commercial waste. The Department of the Environment has issued guidance to Waste Collection Authorities on how these plans should be compiled (see WASTE MANAGEMENT (28)). Although the guidance stresses the importance of gathering data as to the methods available for sorting and otherwise recovering waste, it also makes it clear that the Waste Collection Authority must consider what steps it should take itself in order to facilitate recycling in the area, for example by considering what provision the authority should make for waste separation and transfer. The plan must also contain assessments of the kinds and volumes of waste for recycling for which the authority is making provision, the plant and equipment which will be required and the scale of costs involved. There must also be some assessment of the economic aspects of the recycling operation, with an estimate of the costs or saving which the Waste Collection Authority looks for from the measures outlined in the plan. The plan must be approved by the Secretary of State. The plan must also be available for inspection by the public.

28.36 *The recycling credit system*

Normally, a Waste Collection Authority is under a duty to deliver all the waste which it collects to the WRA for disposal. [*EPA 1990, s 48(1)*]. There is, however, an exception in respect of household and commercial waste which the Waste Collection Authority proposes to recycle in accordance with the terms of its recycling plan. In order to exercise this power, however, the Waste Collection Authority must, as soon as practicable after it has decided to make arrangements to recycle waste, notify the WRA in writing of this decision. If the WRA has already entered into an arrangement with waste disposal contractors for the handling of household or commercial waste, it may object to the Waste Collection Authority's proposal. Effectively, this acts as a veto and the Waste Collection Authority's duty to deliver the waste (or so much of it as is referred to in the WRA's notice of objection) is reawakened.

29 Water Environment

29.1 This chapter is concerned with legal controls on the use and protection of the water environment – both internal and marine. In addition it deals with the quality of drinking water and the discharge of trade effluent to sewers.

29.2 LEGAL FRAMEWORK FOR WATER RESOURCE MANAGEMENT

In England and Wales the rights of a landowner to use water on or under his land or flowing past it are based on Roman law principles as they have been adapted over the years by our common law system. They are not codified but found in the reports of cases decided by the courts on the subject.

With greater exploitation of water resources, legislation has been enacted to regulate their use. This establishes authorities to manage the resource and gives them guidelines as to how they are to carry out their functions.

The main Acts now providing for control over water supply and quality are the *Water Industry Act 1991* and the *Water Resources Act 1991* (*WRA 1991*). The *Water Industry Act 1991* is concerned with the supply of water to consumers, the quality of that water and disposal of effluent to sewers. The *Water Resources Act 1991* makes provision for environmental matters such as the abstraction of water and the control of discharges to waters.

The *Water Resources Act 1991* also establishes the National Rivers Authority as the principal body controlling the use of water resources; although for a number of important industrial processes its role is secondary to that of HMIP.

29.3 THE NATIONAL RIVERS AUTHORITY

The National Rivers Authority (NRA) was established under *section 1* of the *Water Act 1989* to provide integrated management of river basins and the water environment in England and Wales. It has inherited those functions of the water authorities relating to fisheries, flood protection, pollution control, the management of water resources, navigation and conservation and recreation; these functions now set out in *section 2* of the *Water Resources Act 1991*. The NRA is a corporate body but is not to be regarded as the servant or agent of the Crown or enjoying any of the Crown's immunities or privileges. [*WRA 1991, s 1(5), (6)*].

The membership of the NRA may vary between eight and 15. Two of those members will be appointed by the Minister for Agriculture and the remainder by the Secretary of State. The Secretary will designate one of the members to be the chairman of the Authority.

Regional advisory committees are established under *section 7* of the *Water Resources Act 1991*. These are based on the areas of former water authorities. The members of the committees are appointed by the NRA. A committee must be consulted by the Authority about any proposals it has relating to the general way it will carry out its functions in the region. [*WRA 1991, s 7(1)*]. Meetings of a committee, unlike those of the NRA, are open to the press and public. In Wales a special advisory committee has been established under *WRA 1991, s 6* to advise the Secretary of State about the exercise of the NRA's functions. This is in addition to the regional committee set up under *section 7*.

445

The duties of the NRA in relation to specific functions will be discussed where appropriate. However, it has a general duty under *section 16* of the *Water Resources Act 1991* to exercise its powers to protect the environment. This general duty operates on a sliding scale of protection, so that special sites or species should be protected, it is desirable to protect heritage interests and the effect of operations on natural beauty and amenity should be taken into account. In addition public rights of access to the countryside and heritage features should be considered when planning for the exercise of its functions. The manner in which the NRA should carry out this duty is suggested in the Code of Practice on Conservation, Access and Recreation that has been issued under *section 18(1)* of the *Water Act 1989*.

In exercising any of its statutory powers the NRA must pay particular regard to the water supply and sewerage duties imposed on undertakers by *Parts II–IV* of the *Water Industry Act 1991* that may be affected by the exercise of the power in question. [*WRA 1991, s 15(1)*]. This concerns the duties to maintain an efficient and economical water supply system and to supply wholesome water. If the exercise of the power would adversely affect economical water supply then the NRA must consider that adverse affect but, if it decides that the need to exercise the power is overriding then it may disregard the effect on water undertakers.

The police powers of the NRA involve investigations into possible offences and their prosecution. For these purposes its officers have powers of entry under *section 169* of the *Water Resources Act 1991* and will have various powers to obtain information. Power to instigate proceedings is conferred by *section 4(1)(b)* of the *Water Resources Act 1991*.

29.4   USE OF WATER

Rights to use water

Property rights to use waters are not codified but are set out in decisions of the courts. Occupiers of land adjoining a river (riparian owners/occupiers) have the right to use the water in it as set out in these common law rules.

In *Miner v Gilmore (1859) 12 Moore PC 131* Lord Kingsdown stated (at *p 156*)

> 'By the general law applicable to running streams, every riparian proprietor has a right to what may be called the ordinary use of water flowing past his land; for instance, to the reasonable use of the water for his domestic purposes and for his cattle, and this without regard to the effect which such use may have, in case of a deficiency on a proprietor lower down the stream.'

Thus, if as a result of this 'ordinary' use the water in the stream is exhausted a lower occupier has no redress.

Other uses are regarded as 'extraordinary' and can only be carried out if they do not cause harm to lower occupiers. An 'extraordinary' use here would be for irrigation or a factory. A riparian owner can take the water in a river for such a use but it must be reasonable. It must not harm the rights of others. The water removed must either have no effect on the river or it must be returned to it substantially undiminished in quantity or quality (*Rugby Joint Water Board v Walters [1967] Ch 397*).

Underground waters are of two types – that in a defined channel like an underground stream and water that percolates through the soil. As far as underground rivers are concerned the same rules apply as for those on the surface. Any use of them must be reasonable. A landowner can exploit percolating waters regardless of the effect on others – even if he sinks a well that takes water that would otherwise flow into that of his neighbour. However he cannot pollute the waters.

29.5   **Abstraction and impoundment of water**

The common law rules discussed at 29.4 above are now subject to regulation under *Part II* of the *Water Resources Act 1991*. This establishes a system of licensing. A person entitled to take water at common law can still do so, but subject to a licence from the National Rivers Authority. Licences under these provisions regulate the abstraction of water and its impoundment. It will be an offence under *section 24* of the *Water Resources Act 1991* to abstract water without a licence and under *section 25* to impound it without a licence.

There are various exemptions from the requirement for a licence. One of the most important was that for farmers. Previously they only needed a licence for spray irrigation. Now unless they abstract less than 20 cubic metres of water a day they must have a licence to take the water.

An application for an abstraction licence can only be made by occupiers – including someone negotiating for rights of occupation – of land with access to the waters concerned. [*WRA 1991, s 35*]. The application is made to the NRA in accordance with the provisions of the *Water Resources (Licences) Regulations 1965* (*SI 1965 No 534*). Conditions can be attached to abstraction licences. These may require the water to be returned to the watercourse after use and for records to be kept of the amounts abstracted. Appeals against a licensing decision can be made to the Secretary of State under *WRA 1991, s 43*.

The NRA may not grant a licence if an abstraction under it will prevent the holder of a current licence, or someone abstracting water for domestic or agricultural purposes under *WRA 1991, s 27(6)*, from exercising their rights to the full extent of their entitlement unless the possessor of those rights consents to the new licence. [*WRA 1991, s 39(1)*].

Once granted a licence may be varied at the request of the holder under *WRA 1991, s 51* or on the initiative of the NRA under *section 52*. If the holder objects to the NRA's proposals to vary his licence the matter will be referred to the Secretary of State. If the holder suffers damage as a result of the Secretary of State's decision he may recover compensation from the NRA for his loss. [*WRA 1991, s 61*].

Registers of abstraction licences are held at the regional offices of the National Rivers Authority and must be available for public inspection at all reasonable hours. [*WRA 1991, s 189*].

29.6   **Conservation of river flows**

Over-abstraction can lead to rivers drying up as water is steadily removed from them. To try and remedy this situation the *Water Resources Act 1963* established a method of retaining water in rivers – minimum acceptable river flows (MAFs).

Under *section 21* of the *Water Resources Act 1991*, the National Rivers Authority may submit a draft statement to the Secretary of State for the Environment of its proposals to set up a minimum flow regime for a particular river. There must be extensive consultation with various interests before this is done. The proposed flow will be set by on one hand balancing the need to conserve flows with the interests of those who use the water. The proposed MAF will be approved or rejected by the Secretary of State; possibly after a public inquiry.

In practice the minimum flow regime has never been used. There are too many difficulties in establishing and enforcing a minimum flow. However some Acts authorising abstractions from a river will require that the water flowing over a particular spot should never be less than x million gallons a day so MAFs are possible.

29.7   Water Environment

The National Rivers Authority prefers to rely on alternative methods of conserving flows – introducing additional water to affected rivers, river bed lining or revocation of existing abstraction licences.

The European Community has, in its third action programme on the Environment, considered submitting proposals to deal with over-exploitation of water resources. This was maintained in the fourth programme and survives in the fifth, but so far no proposals have materialised.

29.7   Drought

Initially where there is a shortage of water a water undertaker will make a temporary hosepipe ban for all or part of its area under *section 76* of the *Water Industry Act 1991*. If there has been an exceptional shortage of rain an undertaker or the NRA can ask the Secretary of State for a drought order in accordance with the provisions of *sections 73–80* of the *Water Resources Act 1991*.

29.8   POLLUTION OF WATER

European Community Legislation

The 'Aquatic Environment' Directive

In 1976 the EC Council adopted the *Directive on Pollution caused by certain Dangerous Substances discharged into the Aquatic Environment of the Community* (the *'Aquatic Environment' Directive, 76/464/EEC*). This establishes the framework under which discharges of listed substances into inland surface waters, territorial waters and internal coastal waters are controlled throughout the Community.

List 1 in the *Annex* to the *Directive* sets out a short table of families and groups of substances that are considered especially harmful. Standards are set for particular substances by 'daughter' *Directives*. Two ways of meeting these standards are permitted. They can take the form of limit values which must not be exceeded in a discharge containing the substance. Alternatively an environmental quality objective (EQO) can be set so that the concentration of the substance in the receiving water does not exceed the relevant standard. The UK has adopted the EQO approach.

All discharges that contain a List 1 substance must be authorised. Some 50,000 List 1 substances have been identified. However only 20 or so are the subject of 'daughter' *Directives* so that only discharges containing them require authorisation as List 1 substances for which no standards have been set fall into List 2. Where a new plant discharging a List 1 substance seeks an authorisation it must show that it is using the best technical means available to eliminate pollution from that substance.

List 2 substances are those in List 1 for which no 'daughter' *Directive* has been issued and those which have limited deleterious effects. Member States must establish a programme for the reduction of surface water pollution by these substances. The programmes will set standards for particular substances which should be translated into emission limits in consents for discharges containing them.

29.9   *The Groundwater Directive*

For the purposes of the *EC Directive on the Protection of Groundwater against Pollution Caused by Certain Dangerous Substances* (*80/68/EEC*; OJ EEC 1980 No. L 20/43) 'Groundwater' means all water which is below the surface of the ground in the saturation zone and in direct contact with the ground or sub-soil.

The aim of the *Directive* is to prevent or eliminate pollution of groundwater by the harmful substances specified in Lists I and II of the Annex. These Lists are similar, but not identical, to those in the *Aquatic Environment Directive*. Member States are required to prevent the introduction of substances in List I into groundwater and to limit that of List II substances so as to avoid pollution by them.

No direct discharge of a List I substance may be allowed to groundwater. The *Directive* also requires Member States to take necessary precautions to prevent their indirect introduction and, in particular, to avoid leachate from waste disposal sites reaching groundwaters. The discharge of List II substances may be authorised as long as all technical precautions are taken to prevent pollution.

29.10 *Specific 'substances' Directives*

Specific *Directives*, operating outside the programme of the *Aquatic Environment Directive*, may set standards for certain substances e.g.: The *Directive on Asbestos* (*87/217/EEC*; OJ EEC 1987 No.L 85/40).

29.11 *Specific 'uses' Directives*

Specific *Directives* also set standards for uses of waters such as fisheries, bathing etc. For example, the *EC Directive* concerning the *Quality Required of Surface Water Intended for the Abstraction of Drinking Water in the Member States* (*75/440/EEC*; OJ EEC 1975 No. L 194/26) was adopted to set quality standards for such water and to ensure that it receives proper treatment before distribution.

The *Directive* divides surface waters into three grades: A.1 which only requires simple treatment and disinfection before use; A.2 which requires normal physical treatment such as filtration or chemical treatment; and A.3 which requires extensive treatment. Water below A.3 standard should only be abstracted for drinking in exceptional circumstances. The grade water achieves depends on the concentrations of certain parameters it contains.

The requirements of the *Directive* can be waived in the case of floods or other natural disasters and in certain other circumstances. However, in no case may a waiver lead to a risk to public health.

In England and Wales the classification system of the *Directive* is implemented by the *Surface Waters (Classification) Regulations 1989* (*SI 1989 No 1148*).

A similar regime is established for other directives so that the *'Bathing Waters' Directive* (*76/160/EEC*; OJ EEC 1976 No. L 31/1) is implemented by the *Bathing Waters (Classification) Regulations 1991* (*SI 1991 No 1597*).

29.12 *Specific 'sources' Directives*

Yet other *Directives* will be concerned with specific sources of pollution. For example, the *'Waste Water' Directive* (*91/271 EEC*; OJ EEC 1991 No. L.135/40) establishes standards for the provision of sewerage systems, the treatment of sewage, discharges of trade effluent to sewers, discharges of effluent from treatment works and for the disposal of sewage sludge. In addition *Article 13* of the *Directive* applies its provisions to discharges from specified activities that are considered to have a similar effect on the receiving waters as sewage effluent.

The *'Nitrates' Directive* (*91/676/EEC*; OJ EEC 1991 No. L 375/1) is concerned with pollution caused by nitrates from agricultural sources.

29.13 Water Environment

29.13 Pollution control in England and Wales

For pollution control purposes waters in the territorial sea for three miles from the baseline from which that sea is measured, coastal waters, inland waters – lakes or ponds or rivers and streams above the freshwater limit and ground waters are 'controlled waters'. [*WRA 1991, s 104(1)*]. Maps of freshwater limits are held by the National Rivers Authority. The regime for the management of pollution of controlled waters is administered by the Authority, subject to the direction of the Secretary of State, under the provisions of *Part III* of the *Water Resources Act 1991*.

29.14 *Water quality objectives*

By virtue of *WRA 1991, s 82* controlled waters will be classified according to criteria established by *Regulations* made under that section. A classification may be made in respect of some or all controlled waters or for different classes of them. Two types of classification are provided for. One is concerned with the use to which the waters are put so that in this category the *Surface Waters (Classification) Regulations 1989 (SI 1989 No 1148)* deal with the quality of water abstracted for human consumption. The other is concerned with the substances that are present in, or should be absent from, waters. In this category the *Surface Waters (Dangerous Substances) (Classification) Regulations 1989 (SI 1989 No 2286)* and *1992 (SI 1992 No 337)* classify inland and relevant territorial waters according to their prescribed annual mean concentration of substances for which standards are set under *EC Directives on the Aquatic Environment*.

Once a range of classifications have been established water quality objectives will be set under *WRA 1991, s 83* so that the quality of controlled waters may be maintained and improved. Objectives will be set after a consultation period and, if necessary, a public inquiry. [*WRA 1991, s 213(2)(a)*]. Five years after an objective has been set the NRA may apply for it to be reviewed. The quality objectives for particular waters will be shown on the pollution register.

The Secretary of State and the NRA have a duty to ensure that they exercise the water pollution powers under *WRA 1991* so that quality objectives are, as far as is practicable, achieved at all times. [*WRA 1991, s 84(1)*]. This will mainly be done by setting effluent standards in discharge consents to ensure that particular waters can meet their objective. However it might also require the carrying out of remedial operations under *WRA 1991, s 161*.

29.15 Control of discharges by the NRA

A person commits an offence under *section 85* of the *Water Resources Act 1991* if, amongst other things, he causes or knowingly permits (*Southern Water Authority v Pegrum [1989] 153 JP 581*) any poisonous, noxious or polluting matter or any solid waste matter to enter any controlled waters or discharges trade or sewage effluent into controlled waters – or from land in England and Wales, through a pipe, into the sea beyond the three-mile limit at which the sea ceases to be controlled waters.

He will have a defence under *section 88* if the entry or discharge was made in accordance with a discharge consent granted under the *WRA 1991*, a waste management licence – although such a licence cannot take the place of a discharge consent – a licence to dispose of matter at sea or any other statutory provision or order that expressly confers power to discharge effluent to water. It will also, amongst other things, be a defence that the entry or discharge was made in an emergency in order to avoid danger to health or life.

These offences apply to the discharge of sewage from a sewer or works belonging to a sewerage undertaker. If effluent discharged exceeds consent limits the undertaker will be liable if the breach is due to trade effluent that it was bound to accept into its sewer, while the original discharger will escape liability. [*WRA 1991, s 87(1)–(1c), (3)*, as amended by the *Competition and Service (Utilities) Act 1992, s 46*]. However if the breach was due to an unauthorised discharge or one made contrary to the conditions of a consent the undertaker will not be guilty of an offence. [*WRA 1991, s 87(2)*].

Consents to discharge effluent into controlled waters are usually granted by the NRA under the provisions of *Chapter II of Part III*. However, consents granted before the *WRA 1991* entered into force will still be valid by virtue of the *Water Consolidation (Consequential Provisions) Act 1991*. The Secretary of State will grant the NRA consent for discharges made by it under the provisions of *Chapter II* as modified by the *Control of Pollution (Discharges by the National Rivers Authority) Regulations 1989* (*SI 1989 No 1157*).

Applications for consent must usually be advertised locally and a copy of the application sent to every local authority, including a county council, and water undertaker in whose area the proposed discharge will be made. The NRA must consider any objections it receives about the application and provision is made for the subsequent call-in of an opposed application by the Secretary of State.

If consent is granted the NRA may impose a number of conditions on it as to the manner and place of the discharge, its quality, possibly after pre-treatment, and quantity, provision for sampling and the keeping of records and the transmission of information to the Authority. Different conditions may be imposed for different periods so as to cope with seasonal changes in the flow of the relevant waters or for other reasons.

Appeals against the refusal of an application or the grant of a consent subject to conditions are made to the Secretary of State. The procedure for such appeals is laid down in *regulation 7* of the *Control of Pollution (Consents for Discharges) (Secretary of State Functions) Regulations 1989* (*SI 1989 No 1151*).

Consents must be reviewed from time to time. On such a review the NRA may revoke any particular consent, modify its conditions or impose conditions on a consent that was formerly unconditional. [*WRA 1991, 10 Sch 6*]. However, normally a review should not be made for at least two years after the consent was granted or last reviewed.

The NRA may charge applicants for, or holders of, consents for the exercise of its powers to grant consents. Charges will be recovered under a charges scheme that is available from the Authority.

By virtue of *section 190* of the *Water Resources Act 1991* the NRA is under a duty to maintain pollution registers in accordance with the *Control of Pollution (Registers) Regulations 1989* (*SI 1989 No 1160*). These registers must be available for public inspection free of charge at all reasonable times. The registers will contain information about applications, consents granted and information about samples taken in respect of a particular discharge unless the Secretary of State has issued a certificate under *WRA 1991, 10 Sch 1(7)* that certain information need not be entered in respect of a particular discharge.

Anyone may bring a prosecution for pollution offences. However where prosecution is based on samples the NRA has taken, or arranged to have taken, the procedure in *section 209* of the *Water Resources Act 1991* must have been followed.

29.16 *Control of discharges by HMIP*

The *Environmental Protection Act 1990* introduced a system of INTEGRATED POLLUTION CONTROL (16) for processes prescribed by *Part A* of *Schedule 1* to the *Environmental*

Protection (Prescribed Processes and Substances) Regulations 1991 (SI 1991 No 472) as being regulated by Her Majesty's Inspectorate of Pollution (HMIP). Discharges into the sea, inland waters or groundwaters *[EPA 1990, s 1(11)(a)]* from such processes will be authorised by the Inspectorate and, if so authorised, are outside the regime of *Part III* of the *Water Resources Act 1991*. A Memorandum of Understanding has been agreed between the NRA and HMIP to provide working arrangements for the discharge of responsibilities where both bodies have a role.

Under *section 6* of the *Environmental Protection Act 1990* all prescribed processes will have to be authorised by HMIP within a set period. Applications for authorisations will be made to the Inspectorate. An application must be refused if the Inspectorate consider that the applicant could not carry on the process in accordance with the conditions they propose to include in the authorisation. If a site contains both pre-scribed and non-prescribed processes HMIP will deal with those that are prescribed, the others remaining under the control of the NRA.

The NRA will be consulted about proposed authorisations for discharges to controlled waters, and may recover the costs of dealing with authorisations from the Secretary of State, who in turn, will recover them through fees or charges. *[EPA 1990, s 8(6),(7),(9)]*. If it certifies to HMIP that the proposed discharge would, in its opinion, result in or contribute to the failure of the relevant water to meet any quality objective that applies to it the Inspectorate must refuse authorisation. The NRA may also specify conditions that should be imposed on the authorisation to prevent water pollution and these must be included in the authorisation.

Schedule 5 to the *Environmental Protection (Prescribed Processes and Substances) Regulations 1991* prescribes certain substances whose entry into water – including entry into sewers – are to be controlled. It will be an implied general condition of every authorisation that the operator of the process must use BATNEEC to prevent the release of such substances to water or, if that is not practicable, to reduce such release to a minimum and to render harmless any substances that are so released. The release of any other substance that might cause harm to water should also be rendered harmless. However, if a specific condition relating to a particular substance has already been imposed these implied conditions will not have effect for that substance. *[EPA 1990, s 7(40)]*.

Authorisations once granted may be varied by HMIP in accordance with *section 10* and *Part II* of *Schedule 1* to the *Environmental Protection Act 1990*. The holder of an authorisation may apply to vary its conditions under *section 11*. In both cases there will be consultation about the application. While the NRA does not have power to require refusal of an application under *section 11* it can require HMIP to exercise their powers under *section 10* to vary the conditions of an authorisation in order to prevent pollution of water. *[EPA 1990, s 28(4)]*.

The provisions of *Part I* of the *Environmental Protection Act 1990* are enforced by HMIP. The NRA can prosecute offences under this Part, such as operating without authorisation or in breach of conditions, but should consult HMIP before doing so.

29.17 *Pollution prevention*

A number of provisions in *Chapter III* of *Part III* are intended to prevent pollution arising. Under *section 93* of the *WRA 1991* the Secretary of State may designate an area as a water protection zone in order to prevent or control the entry of poisonous, noxious or polluting matter into controlled waters by prohibiting or restricting the carrying-on in the area of activities that it is felt are likely to result in the pollution of any such waters. Before making such an order any relevant local authority should be consulted. *[WRA 1991, 11 Sch 1(c)]*.

Nitrate sensitive areas are those in which controls are placed on agricultural activities in order to reduce the amount of nitrate leaching from agricultural land to water sources. Such areas will be designated under *section 94* of the *Water Resources Act 1991* by orders made following the procedure in *Schedule 12* to it. Applications for such orders may only be made by the NRA.

Under *section 92* the Secretary of State may make regulations to prohibit a person from having custody or control of any poisonous, noxious or polluting matter, such as oil or silage, unless he has taken prescribed precautions or steps to ensure the matter cannot enter controlled waters. The *Control of Pollution (Silage, Slurry and Agricultural Fuel Oil) Regulations 1991 (SI 1991 No 324)* have been made under this section.

A Code of Good Agricultural Practice has been issued under *section 97* of the *Water Resources Act 1991. [SI 1991 No 2285]*. This sets out what are good practices to avoid pollution. A contravention of the code is not an offence but a prohibition notice can be issued under *section 86* to the farmer as a result of it.

The NRA may make byelaws under *Schedule 25, paragraph 4* to the *Water Resources Act 1991* to prohibit or regulate the washing or cleansing of a specified article in controlled waters and to control the keeping or use of lavatories on specified vessels operating on them.

29.18 *Other offences*

A person will be guilty of an offence under *section 90* of the *Water Resources Act 1991* if, without the consent of the NRA, he removes from any part of the bed of any inland water silt or any other deposit that has accumulated in front of a dam, weir or sluice that holds back the waters, in a way that causes the deposit to be carried away in suspension in the waters. A person who causes or permits vegetation in, or adjacent to, inland waters to be cut or uprooted so that it falls into them or fails to take all reasonable steps to remove it from them will also commit an offence under this section.

Causing or knowingly permitting any matter to enter inland waters that tends to impede their flow and so aggravate pollution is an offence under *section 85(5)*. Matter other than trade or sewage effluent may be discharged from a drain or sewer to controlled waters, or trade or sewage effluent from a building or fixed plant may be discharged onto land or into lakes or ponds that are not 'inland waters' if it does not go into groundwaters. However if the NRA issue a prohibition notice by virtue of *section 86* in respect of such a discharge it will be an offence under *section 85* to continue the discharge or to do anything that contravenes any of the conditions of the prohibition.

Other statutes also create pollution offences. Discharges of oil from a place on land into UK territorial waters or inland waters that are navigable by sea-going ships is an offence under *section 2* of the *Prevention of Oil Pollution Act 1971*. Discharges of liquid radioactive wastes are controlled under the *Radioactive Substances Act 1960* and under the *Water Resources Act 1991*. However a consent under the *Water Resources Act 1991* cannot set conditions as to the radioactive properties of the discharge. *[WRA 1991, s 98; SI 1989 No 1158]*.

It is an offence under *section 4(1)* of the *Salmon and Freshwater Fisheries Act 1975* to put any liquid or solid matter into any waters containing fish to such an extent as to cause the water to be poisonous or injurious to fish. The disposal of diseased animal carcasses is dealt with by *section 35* of the *Animal Health Act 1981*. Controls concerning pesticides are imposed by *Part III* of the *Food and Environment Protection Act 1985* and the *Control of Pesticides Regulations 1986 (SI 1986 No 1510)*; while aerial application of pesticides is regulated under the *Aerial Navigation Order 1989 (SI 1989 No 2004)*.

A polluted pond or watercourse may also be a statutory nuisance under *section 259* of the *Public Health Act 1936*.

29.19 *At common law*

The rights of riparian owners at common law are stated by Lord McNaughton in *John Young & Co v Bankier Distillery Co 1893 AC 691* at *p. 698*. He said:

'The law relating to the rights of riparian proprietors is well settled. A riparian proprietor is entitled to have the water of the stream, on the banks of which his property lies, flow down as it has been accustomed to flow down to his property, subject to the ordinary use of the flowing water by upper proprietors, and to such further use, if any, on their part in connection with their property as may be reasonable under the circumstances. Every riparian proprietor is thus entitled to the water of his stream, in its natural flow, without sensible diminution or increase and without sensible alteration in its character or quality. Any invasion of this right causing actual damage or calculated to found a claim which may ripen into an adverse right entitles the party injured to the intervention of the court.'

A riparian owner, or the holder of fishing rights (other than a mere licence) in polluted waters can bring an action for an injunction and damages, and this he can do without proof of actual damage. Such an action can be in nuisance – *Nicholls v Ely Beet Sugar Factory [1936] Ch 343* – trespass, – *Jones v Llanrwst Urban District Council [1911] 1 Ch 393* – or negligence.

Defences to such an action will include one that the polluter had a prescriptive right to pollute the waters, although this is now doubtful – *Scott-Whitehead v National Coal Board (1987) 53 P & CR 263* – or that the pollution occurred through an 'Act of God', was an inevitable accident or was caused by a trespasser.

An authority may construct works or carry out operations under statutory authority that result in pollution. The most common illustration of this is pollution from sewage treatment works. In such cases the undertaker will generally not be liable unless it has been negligent (*Allen v Gulf Oil Refining Ltd [1981] AC 1001*). The former prohibition on undertakers operating sewage treatment works in such a way as to cause a nuisance has not been continued under the *Water Industry Act 1991*, although there is provision in *section 117(6)* to prohibit a nuisance from adopted sewers. Where a sewerage undertaker is found to be causing a nuisance from its works an injunction may be granted but will be suspended to allow it to carry out works (*Pride of Derby and Derbyshire Angling Association Ltd v British Celanese & Ors [1953] Ch 149*).

29.20 *Anti-pollution operations*

Where it appears to the NRA that any poisonous, noxious or polluting matter is likely to enter, is entering or has entered any controlled waters it may carry out works to remedy the situation under *section 161* of the *Water Resources Act 1991* and recover its reasonable expenses from the person responsible for the problem. This potentially wide-ranging power enables the NRA to take action to deal with potential sources of pollution such as contaminated land or to carry out restoration operations in the wake of a polluting incident.

29.21 DRINKING WATER QUALITY

Standards for drinking water are imposed by the *EC Directive* of *15 July 1980* relating to the quality of water intended for human consumption (*80/778/EEC*; O.J. EEC 1980 No. L. 229/1). This *Directive* is implemented in England and Wales by *sections 67–86* of the *Water Industry Act 1991* and by the *Water Supply (Water Quality) Regulations 1989*. [*SI 1989 No 1147 as amended by SI 1989 No 1384*].

Drinking water quality is supervised by the drinking water inspectorate that is established under *section 86* of the *Water Industry Act 1991* and by district or London borough councils. It is the duty of every such council to take all such steps as they consider appropriate to keep themselves informed about the wholesomeness and sufficiency of both public and private water supplies that are made to premises in their area. [*WIA 1991, s 77(1)*]. Local authorities also have powers to obtain information about water quality and to enter premises to investigate the quality of water supplied to them by virtue of *section 85* of the Act.

Water undertakers must supply water that is wholesome at the time it leaves their pipes [*WIA 1991, s 68(1)*] while private supplies may be required to be wholesome. [*WIA 1991, s 80(1)*]. The wholesomeness of water for domestic drinking, washing or cooking purposes is to be defined in accordance with *regulation 3* of the *Water Supply (Water Quality) Regulations 1989*. *Regulation 3* of and *Tables A* to *E* of *Schedule 2* to the *Regulations* set out a number of parameters for which the concentrations or values set in respect of them must not be exceeded nor must drinking water contain any other matter, whether a parameter or not, at a concentration or value, that, alone or in conjunction with other matter, would be detrimental to public health. The standards set out in the *Schedule* will apply unless the Secretary of State has authorised a relaxation of it in the limited circumstances under which he can relax standards. The undertakers' duty to supply wholesome water is enforceable under *WIA 1991, s 18* by the Secretary of State.

For water quality purposes an undertaker's area is broken down into a number of water quality supply zones within which, according to the undertaker's estimate, not more than 50,000 people live. These zones are the basic units for establishing sampling frequencies, compliance with standards and for giving the public information about water quality in their area. A record of water quality in each zone must be prepared and maintained by the undertaker and these records must be available for free public inspection at all reasonable hours at offices of the undertaker that are normally open to the public. [*SI 1989 No 1147, reg 30(1)*].

It is the duty of every local authority to notify a water undertaker of anything that appears to them to suggest that a supply that it makes for domestic purposes in their area is, has been, or is likely to become, unwholesome or insufficient for the domestic purposes and that this deficiency is, has been, or is likely to lead to a danger to life or health or cause the quality of a source of supply to deteriorate. [*WIA 1991, s 78(1)*]. If the authority consider that the undertaker will not take all the steps necessary to remedy the situation they should inform the Secretary of State about it so that he can take enforcement action.

Fluoride is added to public water supplies through schemes made at the request of a district health authority under the *Water (Fluoridation) Act 1985* (*repealed*) or *sections 87 to 91* of the *Water Industry Act 1991*.

A water undertaker that supplies water unfit for human consumption will be guilty of an offence, although prosecutions for such offences can only be brought by the Secretary of State or the Director of Public Prosecutions. [*WIA 1991, s 54*]. The question of whether water is or is not unfit for human consumption will be one of fact. It must be more than unwholesome, but not necessarily injurious or dangerous to health (*Grieg (David) v Goldfinch* [*1961*] *105 SJ 367*).

The quality of a private water supply – a supply made by a person other than a water undertaker – will be controlled by district or London borough councils. Private water supplies should be as wholesome as public supplies unless relaxations to standards have been made by the Secretary of State or the relevant local authority. Standards for such supplies are set out in the *Private Water Supplies Regulations 1991* (*SI 1991 No 2790*). If an authority has reason to believe that the quality of a private supply is, has been, or is likely to become unwholesome or insufficient for domestic purposes they may serve a remedial notice in respect of it under *WIA 1991, s 80* as supplemented by DoE Circular 20/89. The remedial notice must state why it has been served and the steps the authority consider necessary to remedy the situation. A person served with such a notice may object to it, in which case it will not take effect until confirmed by the Secretary of State. An authority may also require a water undertaker to provide premises they consider have an unwholesome or insufficient supply of water with an alternative supply under the provisions of *section 79* of the *WIA 1991*. Further they can bring statutory nuisance proceedings in respect of a source of a supply that is a nuisance or danger to public health under *section 140* of the *Public Health Act 1936*.

A person supplied with water that causes him injury may bring an action against a water undertaker for breach of statutory duty or nuisance (*Read v Croydon Corporation* [*1938*] *4 All ER 631*). In addition the undertaker or supplier may be strictly liable under *Part 1* of the *Consumer Protection Act 1987* for damage – over £275 in respect of damage to property – caused by defective water supplied by them.

29.22 DISCHARGES INTO SEWERS

Under *section 106(1)* of the *Water Industry Act 1991* (as substituted by the *Competition and Service (Utilities) Act 1992, s 43(2)*)the owner or occupier of any premises has the statutory right to discharge foul or surface water from those premises to a public sewer. However the discharge of certain effluent whose composition, or effluent at a tempera- ature which, would damage the sewers or sewage treatment plant is prohibited under *section 111*.

This right to discharge does not extend to any liquid from a factory, other than domestic sewage or surface or storm water, or to any liquid from a manufacturing process. [*WIA 1991, s 106(2)(a)*]. Instead the owner or occupier of any trade premises – including agricultural or research premises – must have the consent of the sewerage undertaker to discharge any trade effluent from them to the public sewerage system. [*WIA 1991, s 118(1)*]. This is the only means by which trade effluent can be discharged into sewers.

Consents are applied for by what are known as trade effluent notices that are required by virtue of *WIA 1991, s 119*. An undertaker can give its consent to such an application either conditionally or unconditionally or it may refuse the application. [*WIA 1991, s 121(1)*]. The conditions that may be imposed are set out in *WIA 1991, s 121*. Under these provisions the undertaker may specify the sewer or sewers into which the discharge is to be made, its nature and composition, its maximum daily quantity and the highest rate of discharge. The undertaker may also specify the times during which effluent is to be discharged, require pre-treatment of effluent and impose charges and provide for inspection of discharge arrangements.

A condition in a consent may be varied by a direction given under *WIA 1991, s 124(1)*. Unless otherwise agreed no direction can be given within two years of the granting of the consent or of a previous direction. If the undertaker wishes to vary a consent within this period it may do so by virtue of *WIA 1991, ss 125* and *126* but will have to compensate the occupier of the premises for so doing unless the reasons for the variation were unforeseeable at the time the consent was last reviewed.

Where a person is aggrieved by the failure of an undertaker to grant a consent within two months of the date on which application was made, or by its refusal to grant one at all or by a condition attached to it, that person may appeal against the decision, or lack of it, to the Director-General of Water Services. [*WIA 1991, s 122*].

The occupier of trade premises from which trade effluent is discharged without the consent or other authorisation of the undertaker – by an agreement rather than a consent – or in contravention of any condition to which it is subject, will be guilty of an offence under *WIA 1991, s 118(5)* or *121(5)* and liable on summary conviction to a fine not exceeding the statutory maximum or on conviction on indictment to a fine.

Certain discharges of trade effluent, known as 'special category effluent' will need to have a special consent under the regime established by virtue of *sections 120, 123, 127, 130–134* and *138* of the *Water Industry Act 1991*. This regime applies to discharges that either contain prescribed substances, or more than a prescribed quantity of such substances, or to discharges that derive from a stipulated process, or from a process that involves the use of, or of more than the prescribed amount of, a prescribed substance. These substances are those in the 'Red List' and are set out in *Schedule 1* to the *Trade Effluents (Prescribed Processes and Substances) Regulations 1989* (*SI 1989 No 1156 as amended by SI 1990 No 1629* (and see *SI 1992 No 339*)). Discharges of special category effluent are effectively dealt with by HMIP as part of the integrated pollution control system (see 16 INTEGRATED POLLUTION CONTROL).

A register of trade effluent consents, showing applications, consents, variations and other matters must be kept at the relevant sewerage undertaker's offices for public inspection and copying. [*WIA 1991, s 196*]. In addition copies of special category consents must also be kept on that register. The duty to maintain registers is enforceable by the Director-General of Water Services under *section 18* of the *Water Industry Act*.

29.23 PROTECTION OF THE MARINE ENVIRONMENT

Pollution from ships

International rules to protect the sea are provided by the *International Convention for the Prevention of Pollution from Ships 1973* (MARPOL). (Cmnd 5748). The annexes to this *Convention* set out specific regimes for different sources of pollution: *Annex I* being concerned with oil; *Annex II* with noxious liquid substances carried in bulk; *Annex III* with packaged goods; *Annex IV* – which is not yet in force – with sewage; and *Annex V* with garbage.

Reports of incidents involving the actual or probable release of any oil or noxious liquid substance carried in bulk into the sea or any estuary or arm of the sea must be made in the manner provided by Protocol 1 of MARPOL which has been implemented by the *Merchant Shipping (Reporting of Pollution Incidents) Regulations 1987* (*SI 1987 No 586*).

Petroleum-based oils or oily mixtures may only be discharged into the sea from ships to which the *Merchant Shipping (Prevention of Oil Pollution) Regulations 1983* (*SI 1983 No 1398 as amended*) apply if the discharge is made in accordance with the provisions of *regulation 12* or *13*, unless it is the result of damage to the ship or was made to save life or a ship or to control pollution in an approved manner. For these purposes the sea includes any estuary or arm of the sea but discharges of any oil made into waters that are on the landward side of the baselines used to measure the territorial sea and that are navigable by sea-going ships will be offences under *section 2(2A)* of the *Prevention of Oil Pollution Act 1971* rather than under the *Regulations*.

Provision is also made in the *1983 Regulations* for the construction of ships and their equipment in a way to prevent pollution, for an Oil Record Book to be kept so that details of the oil a ship carries and the way it was dealt with can be ascertained. In addition the *Regulations* contain powers to inspect ships, to deny them entry into UK ports or to detain them if they are in breach of the *Regulations* and for the punishment of offences.

The recovery of compensation for loss and damage caused by oil pollution from ships is also governed by international conventions. These are implemented into UK law by the *Merchant Shipping (Oil Pollution) Act 1971* and *Part 1* of the *Merchant Shipping Act 1974*. The *Merchant Shipping (Oil Pollution) Act 1971* makes the owners of a ship carrying persistent oil in bulk strictly liable for any discharge or escape of such oil from his tanker in most circumstances. All oil tankers carrying a cargo of more than 2,000 tons of persistent oil in bulk must be insured to meet any claims under the international convention concerning shipowner's liability. As damages from an oil pollution incident can be high, a fund has been established to allow shipowners to obtain a contribution from the major oil importing companies once the liability exceeds a specified sum. Provision is made for the operation of this fund by *Part 1* of the *Merchant Shipping Act 1974*. Under the *Merchant Shipping (Oil Pollution) Act 1971* the costs of preventive measures can be recovered even if a ship is not carrying a cargo of persistent oil in bulk. Local authorities seeking to take advantage of this provision should consult DoE Circular 29/81. Even if the *Conventions* do not apply, recovery may be possible under the 'industry' agreement known as TOVALOP.

Noxious liquid substances are those that fall into classes A to D of the list of substances contained in *Annex 1* to the *Merchant Shipping (Control of Pollution by Noxious Liquid Substances in Bulk) Regulations 1987 (SI 1987 No 551 as amended)* and any additions to the list. The discharge of these substances into the sea (here all waters navigable by sea-going ships) is controlled with varying degrees of stringency according to the class to which the particular substance discharged belongs. All chemical tankers controlled by the *Regulations* must have a Cargo Record Book and also a Procedures and Arrangements Manual which will set out the way in which the cargo is to be handled and the cargo tanks cleansed.

To enable wastes from oil or chemical tankers to be dealt with without causing pollution, harbour authorities or terminal operators whose harbour or terminal is used by such ships have power to provide, or may be directed by the Secretary of State to provide, adequate reception facilities for residues or mixtures containing residues from their cargo tanks under the *Prevention of Pollution (Reception Facilities) Order 1984 (SI 1984 No 862)*. These wastes should be dealt with in the manner provided for by the *Control of Pollution (Landed Ships' Waste) Regulations 1987 (SI 1987 No 402)*.

The *Merchant Shipping (Dangerous Goods and Marine Pollutants) Regulations 1990 (SI 1990 No 2605)* implement *Annex III* of MARPOL in the UK. They apply to all UK ships and to other ships in UK territorial waters that carry dangerous goods in bulk or packages and marine pollutants in packages. While the *Regulations* are mainly concerned with health and safety, they do require that packages should be marked so that after immersion their contents can still be ascertained and that a stowage plan should be available.

Annex V of MARPOL is implemented in the UK by the *Merchant Shipping (Prevention of Pollution by Garbage) Regulations 1989 (SI 1989 No 2292)* and the *Merchant Shipping (Reception Facilities for Garbage) Regulations 1989 (SI 1989 No 2293)*. Under the *Prevention of Pollution by Garbage Regulations*, no plastics may be disposed of at sea from a ship at all. Most other garbage can be disposed of into the sea from a ship but disposal is banned within three miles of the nearest land and if it is done within twelve miles from that land it must have been ground or comminuted to the required standard.

Civil liability for pollution from ships (other than incidents covered by the *Conventions* or agreements discussed above) can be based on both the common law and admiralty law. At common law a plaintiff will probably have to prove some negligence on the part of those responsible for the ship (*Esso Petroleum v Southport Corporation [1956] AC 218*). Alternatively, an action can be brought *in personam* against the owner or *in rem* against the ship under the Admiralty jurisdiction of the Supreme Court for damage done by a ship where the pollution arose as a consequence of a collision (*The Eschersheim [1976] 1 WLR 339*) and possibly for other incidents of marine pollution caused by a ship.

29.24 Pollution from offshore installations and pipelines

Offshore installations are regulated under the *Mineral Workings (Offshore Installations) Act 1971*. This Act is mainly concerned with health and safety on such installations. Pollution controls are provided for platform drainage by *regulation 30* of the *Prevention of Oil Pollution Regulations 1983 (SI 1983 No 1398)* and for other discharges of oil or oily water in the UK territorial sea by *section 2* of the *Prevention of Oil Pollution Act 1971*; *section 3* dealing with those outside that area. In addition the licence under which the installation is operated will contain a clause to require the licensee to avoid harmful methods of working [*The Petroleum (Production) (Seaward Areas) Regulations 1988 (SI 1988 No 1213) 4 Sch 23*].

Pipelines under the sea must be authorised in accordance with *section 20* of the *Petroleum and Submarine Pipelines Act 1975*. Discharges from them may be an offence under *section 2* or *3* of the *Prevention of Oil Pollution Act 1971*.

The environmental problems that may arise on the abandonment of an installation or pipeline will be dealt with under an abandonment programme that must be approved by the Secretary of State under *Part I* of the *Petroleum Act 1987*.

29.25 Dumping of waste at sea

Dumping of wastes at sea is controlled internationally under the *London Convention* [Cmnd. 6486 & 8555] and, in the North Atlantic, by the *Oslo Convention*. [Cmnd 6228]. These conventions ban the dumping of some wastes and require permits to be issued for those deposits that are allowed.

The deposit of substances or articles within UK waters either in the sea or under the sea-bed from a vehicle, vessel, aircraft or hovercraft, from a marine structure or a container floating in the sea, or from a structure on land whose main purpose is to deposit solids, will normally require a licence under *section 5(a)* of the *Food and Environment Protection Act 1985*. For these purposes 'UK waters' mean UK territorial waters and the waters over designated areas on the UK continental shelf. A number of operations for which a licence is not required are listed in the *Deposits in the Sea (Exemptions) Order 1985 (SI 1985 No 1699)*.

30 Wildlife

30.1 Wildlife protection falls into three general categories:

(a) the protection of individual animals and plants, often referred to as species protection;

(b) the protection of habitat; and

(c) the control of trade in animals and plants.

The oldest controls belong to the first category, though in recent years the law has grown much more sophisticated and many gaps have been filled. Despite this recent legislation on species protection, the habitat protection measures developed since the nineteen forties have become arguably the central mechanism for nature conservation and the number of different types of designated protected area has increased dramatically. The control over trade in animals and plants has changed from being an adjunct in domestic law of the protection of individual animals and plants to a system of control over international trade. This reflects an important shift in wildlife protection law: the international nature of many problems has been appreciated and consequently action has been taken at European Community and at global level to lay down a framework of laws.

30.2 CONSERVATION AGENCIES

History: Nature Conservancy Council

Prior to 1991 nature conservation was the responsibility of the Nature Conservancy Council (NCC), an autonomous central Government body which operated on a Great Britain basis. It acted as the Government's adviser on national and international nature conservation matters, as well as carrying out a number of important operational activities in relation to wildlife and habitat protection. The *Environmental Protection Act 1990* (*EPA 1990*) provided for the NCC's functions to be split between three national bodies, with responsibilities for the separate geographical areas of England, Wales and Scotland respectively.

30.3 The three national nature conservation bodies

In England, the relevant body is the Nature Conservancy Council for England (known by its corporate title of English Nature), which is based in Peterborough.

In Wales nature conservation functions are combined with those relating to amenity and recreation (i.e. the functions that in England are carried out by the Countryside Commission) and are carried out by the Countryside Council for Wales.

In Scotland a similar combination of functions has taken place. The *Environmental Protection Act 1990* originally created the Nature Conservancy Council for Scotland, though this has now been replaced by a body called Scottish Natural Heritage. [*Natural Heritage (Scotland) Act 1991* (*NH(S)A 1991*)].

In this chapter, for ease of explanation all references will be to English Nature, but it may be assumed that the two other national bodies have the same powers unless otherwise stated.

461

30.4 Wildlife

30.4   The three bodies are independent, corporate organisations within central Government. They do not possess Crown immunity. In each case they are funded by grant-in-aid from the Secretary of State and must submit annual reports and accounts to be laid before Parliament. They regulate their own procedures. The members of the councils are appointed by the relevant Secretary of State, as were the three inaugural Chief Officers. Subsequent Chief Officers and all other members of staff are appointed by the council. [*EPA 1990, 6 Sch; NH(S)A 1991, 1 Sch*].

30.5   The functions of the councils for England and Wales are explained in *EPA 1990, s 132*, and of Scottish Natural Heritage in *NH(S)A 1991, s 2*. In each case these include giving advice to the Government on nature conservation matters, disseminating knowledge generally about nature conservation, commissioning or supporting relevant research, acting as statutory consultees in a range of procedures, establishing and managing nature reserves, and carrying out a large number of other operational tasks, particularly in connection with the working of the *Wildlife and Countryside Act 1981*. Scottish Natural Heritage is subject to the extra requirements that anything done in relation to the natural heritage of Scotland is undertaken in a manner which is sustainable, and that in exercising its functions it takes appropriate account of (*inter alia*): the needs of agriculture, fisheries and forestry; the need for social and economic development in any part of Scotland; the interests of owners and occupiers of land; and the interests of local communities. [*NH(S)A 1991, ss 1(1), 3(1)*].

30.6   Joint Nature Conservation Committee

The *Environmental Protection Act 1990* also created a Joint Nature Conservation Committee. This is a Committee of the national councils, and consists of an independent chairman and three members appointed by the Secretary of State, the chairman and one other member appointed by each national council, and the chairman of the English Countryside Commission. In addition, two non-voting members are appointed by the Department of the Environment for Northern Ireland. The Committee receives its finances through the national councils. It regulates its own procedures and must submit annual reports and accounts which must be laid before Parliament. [*EPA 1990, 7 Sch*]. Its functions are set out in *EPA 1990, s 133*, and include the provision of advice to the Government on matters that affect nature conservation in Great Britain as a whole, matters of international importance, and the establishment of common standards throughout Great Britain.

30.7   Voluntary bodies

Although they obviously have few statutory powers, the work of voluntary bodies must be recognised as a valuable supplement to that of public agencies. For example, most prosecutions under the legislation relating to birds is carried out by the Royal Society for the Protection of Birds, and many nationally important nature reserves are managed by voluntary sector bodies such as the National Trust or the county wildlife trusts.

30.8   SPECIES PROTECTION

Common law

At common law wild animals have no rights, and hence no protection, of their own. Unlike domestic animals they are not the subject of absolute ownership: instead, whilst alive, they are in the qualified ownership of the owner on whose land they are. Accordingly, they are unprotected against the landowner, whilst other people interfering with them would only commit a tort against the landowner. Wild plants and vegetation are part of the land itself. Thus, landowners may deal with them as they please. Others who uproot plants commit the crime of theft, though there is an exception for picking flowers, fruit, foliage and fungi. [*Theft Act 1968, s 4(3)*].

30.9 Statutory protections

Statutory protection is far more wide ranging. Wild animals and plants are protected by the *Wildlife and Countryside Act 1981 (WCA 1981)*, *Part I*, mainly by the creation of a large number of criminal offences. Extra protection is given to badgers under the *Protection of Badgers Act 1992* and to seals under the *Conservation of Seals Act 1970*. Many, though not all, of these protections have been developed to implement the requirements of EC and international law, such as *Directive 79/409/EEC* on wild birds and the *Berne* and *Bonn Conventions*. The recently adopted *Directive on Habitats (92/43/EEC)* will necessitate some further amendment of the protections. There is also a wealth of legislation on hunted species: this is not dealt with in this chapter since the protection of the animals concerned is purely incidental.

30.10 *Part I* of the *WCA 1981* deals separately with birds, animals and plants. In many cases the precise extent of the protection afforded depends on whether a bird, animal or plant is included in a Schedule. The Secretary of State has powers to add to or vary these Schedules. [*WCA 1981, s 22*]. There is a specific duty laid upon the Joint Nature Conservation Committee to carry out a quinquennial review of *Schedules 5* and *8*, though its advice is not binding on the Secretary of State. [*WCA 1981, s 24*].

Part I also includes some general enforcement provisions. Wide powers of stop, search and seizure are provided. [*WCA 1981, s 19*]. An attempt to commit an offence is punishable in the same way as the offence itself. [*WCA 1981, s 18*]. The maximum penalty is determined as if a separate offence has been committed in respect of each bird, egg, nest, plant or animal [*WCA 1981, s 21(5)*], and there are provisions on the forfeiture of animals and plants and of equipment used to commit an offence. [*WCA 1981, s 21(6)*]. Provisions on corporate liability for offences are in *section 69*.

30.11 Birds

The basic offences are set out in *section 1*:

(a)   intentionally killing, injuring or taking any wild bird [*WCA 1981, s 1(1)(a)*];

(b)   intentionally taking, damaging or destroying the nest of a wild bird whilst it is in use or being built [*WCA 1981, s 1(1)(b)*];

(c)   intentionally taking or destroying a wild bird's egg [*WCA 1981, s 1(1)(c)*];

(d)   possession of part or whole of a wild bird, live or dead, or of a wild bird's egg [*WCA 1981, s 1(2)*], though there is a defence if it is shown that the bird or egg has not been killed or taken in contravention of the law [*WCA 1981, s 1(3)*]; and

(e)   intentionally disturbing a bird listed in *Schedule 1* whilst it is building a nest, or is in, on, or near a nest containing eggs or young, or intentionally disturbing the dependent young of such a bird. [*WCA 1981, s 1(5)*].

In each case the maximum fine is £1000, although this is raised to £5,000 per bird, egg or nest for birds which are listed in *Schedule 1*. This section does not cover birds which are shown to have been bred in captivity.

30.12 These offences are supplemented by further offences as follows:

(a)   the use of certain cruel or unfair methods of killing or taking wild birds [*WCA 1981, s 5*];

(b)   causing or permitting any other person to commit an offence under *section 5*, a provision which is intended to enable prosecutions to be brought against employers as well as those who actually carry out the prohibited acts [*Wildlife and Countryside (Amendment) Act 1991, s 1*];

(c)   the sale, or offering or advertising for sale, of live wild birds other than those listed in *Schedule 3 Part I* [*WCA 1981, s 6(1)*];

(d)   the sale, or offering or advertising for sale, of eggs of any wild bird [*WCA 1981, s 6(1)*];

(e)   the sale, or offering or advertising for sale, by an unregistered person of dead wild birds not included in *Schedule 3, Part II* or *III* [*WCA 1981, s 6(2)*]; and

(f)   possession of any bird included in *Schedule 4* which has not been ringed or marked in accordance with regulations. [*WCA 1981, s 7*].

30.13   In addition, the Secretary of State may make an order designating an area of special protection for birds (often known as a bird sanctuary). [*WCA 1981, s 3*]. Such an order cannot be made if any owner or occupier of the area, who must be informed of the proposal, objects to it. The order may provide for byelaws which create additional offences relating to birds or to access to the site, though this must not affect the exercise of any rights vested in the owner, lessee or occupier.

30.14   There is a complex set of exceptions and defences to these offences:

(a)   game birds are excluded from all the protections offered by the Act, apart from those relating to prohibited methods of taking or killing birds [*WCA 1981, s 27(1)*];

(b)   outside the defined close season *section 1* does not apply to the wildfowl and quarry species listed in *Schedule 2, Part I* – this close season may be extended by the Secretary of State in the event of bad weather [*WCA 1981, s 2*];

(c)   *section 1* does not generally apply to acts done by owners, occupiers or other authorised persons against the pest species listed in *Schedule 2, Part II* [*WCA 1981, s 2(2)*];

(d)   there are exceptions to *sections 1* and *3* relating to various acts done in pursuance of powers granted by a number of Acts relating to agriculture; killing and taking of injured birds; where an act was the incidental result of a lawful operation and could not reasonably have been avoided; and where it was necessary to prevent the spread of disease, prevent serious damage to livestock or crops, or preserve public health and safety or air safety [*WCA 1981, s 4*];

(e)   *section 16* sets out a lengthy list of situations where a licence may be obtained from the appropriate authority, covering such things as scientific, educational or conservation purposes, ringing, falconry, the protection of public health and the prevention of serious damage to an agricultural activity.

30.15 Animals

Unlike the situation for wild birds, only the wild animals listed in *Schedule 5* are protected by the *WCA 1981*. This list includes all indigenous bats, most reptiles and amphibians, but only a small selection of mammals, fish, butterflies and other animals.

It is an offence intentionally to kill, injure or take any animal listed in *Schedule 5* [*WCA 1981, s 9(1)*], or to have in one's possession or control all or part of such an animal, alive or dead [*WCA 1981, s 9(2)*], or to sell, or offer or advertise for sale, all or part of such an animal, alive or dead. [*WCA 1981, s 9(5)*]. For each of these offences the animal is presumed to be wild unless the contrary is shown. [*WCA 1981, s 9(6)*]. There is a further offence of intentionally damaging, destroying or obstructing the access to any structure or place used for shelter or protection by an animal listed in *Schedule 5*, or disturbing such an animal whilst it is occupying such a structure. [*WCA 1981, s 9(4)*]. In each case the maximum fine is £5,000 per animal affected.

30.16 There are defences and exceptions as follows:

(*a*)   in relation to various acts done in pursuance of powers granted by a number of Acts concerning agriculture [*WCA 1981, s 10(1)*];

(*b*)   killing and taking of injured animals, or where an act was the incidental result of a lawful operation and could not reasonably have been avoided [*WCA 1981, s 10(3)*];

(*c*)   in relation to *section 9(2)*, if it is shown that the animal had not been killed in contravention of the law [*WCA 1981, s 9(3)*];

(*d*)   where an action was necessary to prevent serious damage to livestock, crops, or any other form of property [*WCA 1981, s 10(4)*];

(*e*)   where a licence is obtained from the appropriate authority under *section 16*;

(*f*)   in relation to anything done within a dwelling-house [*WCA 1981, s 10(2)*]: this defence does not apply to any action taken in relation to a bat (except in the living area of the house), unless English Nature is notified in advance. [*WCA 1981, s 10(5)*].

30.17 There are additional offences relating to the use of certain cruel or unfair methods of killing or taking wild animals. *Section 11(1)* lists methods which are outlawed in relation to all animals, whilst *section 11(2)* lists those which are outlawed only for the animals (all mammals) listed in *Schedule 6*. It is also an offence to cause or permit any other person to commit an offence under *section 11*. In each case the maximum fine is £5,000.

30.18 Badgers

Badgers are given enhanced protection under special legislation developed over many years and now consolidated in the *Protection of Badgers Act 1992* (*PBA 1992*). In respect of each offence the maximum fine is £5,000 per badger affected, though in relation to offences under *sections 1(1), 1(3), 2* and *3* a prison term of up to six months may also be imposed. [*PBA 1992, s 12(1)*]. A convicting court may order the destruction or disposal of any dog used in or present at the commission of an offence under *sections 1(1), 2* or *3*, and may disqualify the convicted person from keeping a dog. [*PBA 1992, s 13*].

30.19 The following are offences:

(*a*)   wilfully killing, injuring or taking a badger, or attempting to do these things. [*PBA 1992, s 1(1)*]. Once there is reasonable evidence of the attempted offence, it is up to the defendant to prove that no offence has been committed [*PBA 1992, s 1(2)*];

(*b*)   possession of a dead badger [*PBA 1992, s 1(3)*], though there is a defence if it is shown that the badger had not been killed in contravention of the law [*PBA 1992, s 1(4)*];

(*c*)   cruelly ill-treating a badger, using badger tongs, or digging for a badger. In the last case, once there is reasonable evidence of the offence, it is up to the defendant to prove that no offence has been committed [*PBA 1992, s 2*];

(*d*)   selling, offering for sale, or having possession of a live badger [*PBA 1992, s 4*];

(e)   marking or attaching a marking device to a badger, except under licence. [*PBA 1992, s 5*].

It is also an offence to interfere with a badger sett that displays signs of current use by damaging it, destroying it, obstructing access to it, causing a dog to enter it, or disturbing a badger which is occupying it. [*PBA 1992, s 3*]. This offence may be committed either intentionally or by being reckless as to those consequences.

30.20 There are a number of exceptions and defences:

(a)   killing and taking of injured animals, or unavoidably killing or injuring a badger as the incidental result of a lawful operation [*PBA 1992, s 6*];

(b)   for offences under *sections 1(1)* and *3*, where an action was necessary to prevent serious damage to land, crops, poultry or any other form of property [*PBA 1992, ss 7, 8(1)*];

(c)   where a licence is obtained from the appropriate authority under *section 10* (it should be noted that a licence is still required even where a planning permission is granted if implementation of it would involve an offence under *section 3*);

(d)   interfering with a badger sett by damaging it, obstructing access to it, or disturbing a badger that is occupying it, if the action was the incidental result of a lawful operation and could not reasonably have been avoided [*PBA 1992, s 8(3)*];

(e)   interfering with a badger sett by damaging it, obstructing access to it, or disturbing a badger that is occupying it, in the course of fox-hunting, as long as a number of detailed conditions are satisfied. [*PBA 1992, s 8(4)*].

30.21 Plants

It is an offence for any person other than the owner or occupier of land, or any authorised person, intentionally to uproot any wild plant [*PBA 1992, s 13(i)(b)*]. It is also an offence to pick, uproot or destroy, or to sell or advertise for sale, a wild plant listed in *Schedule 8*. [*PBA 1992, s 13(1)(a)(2)*]. There are defences where an act was the incidental result of a lawful operation and could not reasonably have been avoided [*PBA 1992, s 13(3)*] and where a licence is obtained from the appropriate authority under *section 16*. The maximum penalty for these offences is £2,500.

30.22 Introductions

It is an offence to introduce into the wild any animal which is not ordinarily resident in, or a regular visitor to, Great Britain, or any of the 'undesirable' animals or plants included in *Schedule 9 [WCA 1981, s 14*], unless a licence has been granted by the appropriate authority. There is a defence of due diligence. The maximum penalty is £5,000 on summary conviction and an unlimited fine on conviction on indictment. [*WCA 1981, s 21(4)*].

30.23 HABITAT PROTECTION

Sites of special scientific interest (SSSIs)

SSSIs are given legal protection by the *Wildlife and Countryside Act 1981, s 28. Section 28(1)* states,

'Where [the relevant Nature Conservancy Council] are of the opinion that any area of land is of special interest by reason of any its flora, fauna, or geological or physiographical features, it shall be the duty of the Council to notify that fact –

(*a*)   to the local planning authority in whose area the land is situated;

(*b*)   to every owner and occupier of any of that land; and

(*c*)   to the Secretary of State.'

No criteria have been laid down in the Act as to what constitutes special interest. They have been drawn up over a number of years by English Nature and its predecessors and aim to produce a national series of sites which constitute a representative sample of British habitat types and geological structures. Selection is on scientific grounds and the reference in *section 28* to a duty suggests that any site meeting the criteria should be designated. There are over 5,000 SSSIs in Great Britain, covering over 7 per cent of the land area, with some sites covering many thousands of hectares. Given the inherent flexibility of the criteria, new sites are regularly designated.

30.24 Owners and occupiers must be given three months' notice of the proposed designation. [*WCA 1981, s 28(2)*]. During this period representations may be made to English Nature, which must consider them in deciding whether to confirm or withdraw the designation. The designation will have interim effect. It is a local land charge. [*WCA 1981, s 28(11)*].

In Scotland there is an extra stage. Under the *Natural Heritage (Scotland) Act 1991, s 12*, an advisory committee on SSSIs, appointed by the Secretary of State, is established. If a new designation as an SSSI gives rise to objections that are not withdrawn, the matter must be referred to this committee. In relation to existing SSSIs, if representations are made to Scottish Natural Heritage, the matter must also be referred to the committee. Scottish Natural Heritage must consider the committee's advice before making any decision and must send a copy of the advice to owners and occupiers of the SSSI. [*WCA 1981, s 12(7)*].

30.25 The designation under *section 28(1)(b)* must specify the features which are of special interest and any operations which appear to English Nature likely to damage those features. In *North Uist Fisheries Ltd v Secretary of State for Scotland [1992] SLT 333*, the Court of Session adopted a literal interpretation of the word 'likely' and decided that it required damage to be probable rather than a bare possibility, though it must be added that the test remains a subjective one. In *Sweet v Secretary of State [1989] 1 JEL 245* it was held that 'operations' carries a very wide meaning and may encompass virtually any positive activity, though it would not cover neglect of the site.

30.26 It is a summary criminal offence for an owner or occupier to carry out, without reasonable excuse, a potentially damaging operation on its own land without first notifying English Nature in writing. [*WCA 1981, s 28(5)*]. Unless the operation is carried out with English Nature's written consent, or in accordance with a management agreement, it is also a summary offence not to wait four months after this notification has been given. In both cases the maximum fine is £2,500. [*WCA 1981, s 28(6)*]. The House of Lords decision in *Southern Water Authority v Nature Conservancy Council [1992] 3 All ER 481*, establishes that for the purposes of this section an occupier is someone with a stable relationship with the land: thus a water authority carrying out temporary works on the site could not commit any offence under *section 28*. Provisions on corporate liability for offences are in *section 69*.

30.27 There are two specific defences. One is that the operation was carried out in an emergency and details were notified to English Nature as soon as practicable. [*WCA 1981, s 28(8)(b)*]. The other is that the operation was authorised by a grant of planning permission, though this does not cover one granted by a Development Order. [*WCA 1981, s 28(8)(a)*]. In this second case, English Nature should have been consulted over the application for planning permission by the local planning authority, as required by the *Town and Country Planning (General Development) Order (SI 1988 No 1813), article 18*.

30.28 Wildlife

30.28 There are special duties imposed on bodies in the English water industry. [*Water Resources Act 1991, s 17; Water Industry Act 1991, s 4*]. English Nature must notify relevant bodies in the water industry (the National Rivers Authority, water and sewerage undertakers and internal drainage boards) of SSSIs that may be affected by their activities. These bodies must consult with English Nature over any works they carry out or authorise which appear to them to be likely to damage or prejudice the special interest of the SSSI. For example, the National Rivers Authority must consider the effect that a grant of a discharge consent may have on an SSSI. There is a Code of Practice on Conservation, Access and Recreation, issued in July 1989, which amplifies these duties.

30.29 *Management agreements and SSSIs*

The purpose of the requirement that owners and occupiers notify English Nature of potentially damaging operations is to enable it to negotiate a management agreement with the owner or occupier. This reflects the Government's approach to this area, which is that mandatory controls should be as few as possible and that compliance ought to be achieved by voluntary means.

The ability to make a management agreement over a site is thus a central part of the system of habitat protection. English Nature is empowered to enter into management agreements with owners, lessees and occupiers of SSSIs or adjacent land. [*Countryside Act 1968 (CA 1968), s 15, as amended by EPA 1990, 9 Sch 4*]. They may impose restrictions on the exercise of rights over the land and may provide for the carrying out of such works as are expedient for the agreement. Such agreements are contracts, and restrictive arrangements agreed by landowners will be enforceable against successors in title as restrictive covenants. [*CA 1968, s 15(4)*]. Management agreements will also provide for the paying of monetary compensation to the owner or occupier. Standard rates for compensation have been established in financial guidelines made by Ministers under *WCA 1981, s 50* (published as an Appendix to DoE Circular 4/83). These provide compensation for profits forgone by the owner or occupier, which may be claimed as a lump sum payment or as an annual index-linked payment.

30.30 *Planning permission and SSSIs*

Where a planning application is submitted in relation to land within an SSSI the local planning authority is required by the *Town and Country Planning (General Development) Order (SI 1988 No 1813), article 18*, to consult with English Nature. It need not, however, follow English Nature's advice. This bare legal requirement is supplemented by DoE Circular 27/87, which encourages much wider consultation and sets out Government policy on the importance of nature conservation in planning decisions. A Planning Policy Guidance Note on Nature Conservation, expected in 1993, will replace Circular 27/87 and will include clearer policy advice on the protection of sites, especially those of international importance. It should also be noted that designation as a protected site will often mean that an ENVIRONMENTAL ASSESSMENT (7) is required before development can go ahead.

30.31 **Nature conservation orders**

Under *WCA 1981, s 29*, some marginally stronger powers exist, though they have been used sparingly. The Secretary of State may, after consultation with English Nature, apply a nature conservation order to land for the purpose of securing the survival in Great Britain of any kind of animal or plant or of complying with an international obligation, or for the purpose of conserving flora, fauna or geological or physiographical features of national importance. Owners, occupiers and the local planning authority must be notified of a proposed order and it must be publicised generally. If any objections are made a public inquiry or hearing must be held. The Secretary of State has a discretion whether to confirm the order, or to amend or revoke it, although an order will have interim effect [*WCA 1981, 11 Sch*]. Compensation is payable by English Nature to the owner or occupier of agricultural land for any reduction in value of the land as a result of the order. [*WCA 1981, s 30*]. English Nature has powers to enter land to see if an order should be made, to ascertain whether any offence under *section 29* has been committed, or to assess any compensation under *section 30*. [*WCA 1981, s 51*]. (Scottish Natural Heritage has wider powers to enter land. [*NH(S)A s 7*].)

30.32 It is a criminal offence for any person, without reasonable excuse, to carry out an operation which is specified in the order as likely to damage the special interest of the site. [*WCA 1981, s 29(3)*]. The maximum fine on summary conviction is £5,000, and an unlimited fine may be imposed on conviction on indictment. [*WCA 1981, s 29(8)*]. In addition, a convicting court may make a restoration order requiring the offender to carry out works for the purpose of restoring the land to its former condition. [*WCA 1981, s 31*]. It is a continuing, summary offence to fail to comply with a restoration order. In the event of non-compliance, English Nature has powers to enter land and carry out the specified operations at the expense of the person against whom the order was made.

30.33 No offence is committed where the owner or occupier has given English Nature written notice of the proposed operation and either:

(*a*)   has received the written consent of English Nature;

(*b*)   the operation is in accordance with the terms of a management agreement; or

(*c*)   three months has expired from the date of the written notice. This three-month period may be extended to twelve months if English Nature offers to purchase the interest of the person making the proposal, or offers a management agreement, although if this happens compensation is payable by English Nature for any loss or damage directly attributable to the ban being more than three months. As with SSSIs, it is clear that the major purpose of the restrictions is to give English Nature the opportunity to negotiate a management agreement.

The same two specific defences apply to offences under *section 29* as under *section 28*.

30.34 **National nature reserves**

National nature reserves are defined by the *WCA 1981, s 35*, as areas of national importance which are either:

(*a*)   managed by English Nature under a nature reserve agreement;

(*b*)   held by English Nature and managed as a nature reserve; or

(*c*)   held by an approved body (which includes a number of voluntary bodies) and managed by it as a nature reserve.

A declaration by English Nature that land is a national nature reserve is conclusive. As a matter of practice all national nature reserves are designated as SSSIs.

30.35 This provision supplements the *National Parks and Access to the Countryside Act 1949* (*NPACA 1949*). *NPACA 1949, s 15* defines the purposes of a nature reserve as providing special opportunities for study or research into flora and fauna, or into geological or physiographical features, or for preserving such features which are of special interest. English Nature may buy or lease an appropriate area of land. In addition *section 16* empowers it to enter into a nature reserve agreement with the owner,

30.36 Wildlife

lessee or occupier where it is expedient in the national interest that the land be managed as a nature reserve. It has further powers (which are rarely used) to obtain the land by compulsory purchase if it is unable to conclude an agreement on satisfactory terms [*NPACA 1949, s 17*], or if there is an unremedied breach of such an agreement. [*NPACA 1949, s 18*]. A compulsory purchase order requires the approval of the Secretary of State.

30.36 English Nature is empowered to make byelaws for the protection of a nature reserve. [*NPACA 1949, s 20*]. These may include restrictions on: access to the reserve; the killing, taking or disturbance of living creatures, vegetation or the soil; the deposit of rubbish or litter; and the lighting of fires. Shooting of birds may also be prohibited in areas surrounding or adjoining the reserve, including over the sea. Byelaws may not interfere with vested rights of owners, lessees and occupiers, or with public rights of way (this does not include rights of navigation, see *Evans v Godber [1974] 3 All ER 341*), or with the functions of a statutory undertaker, drainage authority, or certain other bodies. Compensation is payable to any person whose exercise of rights is prevented or hindered by byelaws. [*NPACA 1949, s 20(3)*].

30.37 Local nature reserves

Local authorities are given identical powers to designate and manage areas of local interest as local nature reserves if it is expedient that they should be managed as a nature reserve. [*NPACA 1949, s 21*].

30.38 Marine nature reserves

Owing to the linking of SSSI boundaries to those of local authorities, an SSSI cannot be designated below the low water mark. *WCA 1981, s 36* provides for the designation of marine nature reserves in tidal waters and between high water mark and a line three miles from the baselines established for measuring the territorial sea. They are designated by the Secretary of State, on the application of English Nature, and are managed by English Nature for the purpose of conserving marine flora or fauna or geological or physiographical features of special interest, or providing suitable conditions for study and research into such matters.

30.39 The procedure for making a marine nature reserve is set out in *Schedule 12* and is similar to that for the making of a nature conservation order. The main restrictions within a marine nature reserve are provided by byelaws. These are made by English Nature with the consent of the Secretary of State and may provide for restrictions on: killing, taking, destruction and disturbance of animals and plants; interference with the sea-bed; the deposit of rubbish; and access to the reserve. However, in the last case, byelaws cannot restrict the lawful right of navigation of vessels, except pleasure boats, within the reserve. [*NPACA 1949, s 37*].

30.40 EC Wild Birds Directive

The *Wild Birds Directive (79/409/EEC)* sets out some detailed requirements on the system of species protection that each Member State should have. As a result it had an important role in shaping the *Wildlife and Countryside Act 1981, Part I*. With regard to habitat protection, it imposes a general duty to take measures to maintain a sufficient diversity of habitat for all European bird species. [*Article 3*]. It also imposes a more specific duty to take special measures to protect the habitats of certain listed, rare or vulnerable species and all migratory species. These measures include the designation of special protection areas. [*Article 4*]. In this regard the European Court of Justice has decided in *Commission v Spain [1993]*, unreported, 2 August 1993, that there is a duty to designate any site that fulfils the ornithological criteria laid down in the *Directive*. Steps should be taken to avoid the deterioration of these areas and the disturbance of birds within them. Interpreting *Article 4(4)*, the European Court of Justice has decided that the reduction in area of a designated special protection area was only justified on very restricted grounds, which did not include economic pressures (*Commission v Germany, C57 1989 [1991] ECR 883*). However, the effect of this judgment has been reversed by an amendment to *Article 4(4)* made by the *Habitats Directive (92/43/EEC)*.

Despite evidence that the criteria fit a much larger number of sites, the UK Government has only designated about 70 special protection areas, all of which are also SSSIs. However, it has accepted as a matter of planning policy that all sites meeting the criteria for designation as a special protection area or under the Ramsar Convention should be treated as if they had been so designated.

30.41 EC Habitats Directive

The *Directive on the Conservation of Natural Habitats and of Wild Fauna and Flora (92/43/EEC)* was adopted on 21 May 1992. It aims to contribute towards bio-diversity through the conservation of natural habitats and wild fauna and flora in Europe and will undoubtedly lead to a number of changes in UK law and policy on habitat protection. A particular feature of the *Directive* is that a network of special areas of conservation, entitled Natura 2000, will be established. This will consist of sites hosting the natural habitat types listed in *Annex I* to the *Directive* and habitats of the species listed in *Annex II*. It is aimed at enabling the habitats concerned to be maintained at, or restored to, a favourable conservation status. It will incorporate the special protection areas designated under the *Birds Directive*.

30.42 Member States are required to propose a list of eligible sites to the Commission by May 1995. [*Article 4(1)*]. By May 1998 the Commission is required to establish a draft list of sites of community importance drawn from those lists (though there is an exceptional procedure for other sites to be included). The Commission will then adopt a final list of sites of community importance in the light of the advice of a committee of representatives of the Member States. Once a site is adopted Member States are obliged to designate it as a special area of conservation as soon as possible and within six years at most. [*Article 4(4)*]. For special areas of conservation a Member State is under a duty to establish necessary conservation measures and to take appropriate measures to avoid deterioration of the sites, although it will be possible to allow damage to a site for reasons of overriding public interest, including those of a social or economic nature. [*Article 6*]. Any plan or project likely to have a significant effect on a special area of conservation must be subject to assessment of its implications for the site.

30.43 International conventions

A number of international conventions to which the UK is a party have had an impact on the development of UK wildlife law. The *Ramsar Convention on Wetlands of International Importance Especially as Waterfowl Habitat* was agreed in 1971 and came into force in 1975. It imposes a general duty on all contracting parties to promote the conservation of wetlands and waterfowl, particularly by establishing nature reserves. Contracting parties are under a specific duty to designate at least one site on a list of wetlands of international importance and must carry out planning processes so as to promote the conservation of sites on the list. The UK has designated over 50 sites, all of which are SSSIs and which also gain special protection in planning policy.

30.44 The *Berne Convention on the Conservation of European Wildlife and Natural Habitats*, agreed in 1979, provides both for the conservation of wildlife and wildlife habitats in general and for the special protection of the animal and plant species listed in its Appendices. In particular, it requires that all important breeding and resting sites for the animals listed in *Appendix 2* should be protected. The *Bonn Convention on the Conservation of Migratory Species of Wild Animals*, also agreed in 1979, imposes some more general conservation obligations in relation to migratory species.

30.45 TRADE IN WILDLIFE

The *Washington Convention on International Trade in Endangered Species of Wild Fauna and Flora (CITES)*, agreed in 1973, underpins UK law on the wildlife trade. Its main aims are for a ban on commercial trade in the species listed in *Appendix 1* and for control to be exercised over trade in the species listed in *Appendix 2* so as to prevent it being detrimental to those species. For these purposes a specimen includes a live or dead specimen and whole or part of one. This is to be achieved by a complex system of permits administered by national scientific and management authorities.

The *Convention* is implemented by the *Endangered Species (Import and Export) Act 1976*, though it should be noted that the EC is a party to *CITES* and has passed a number of directly effective *Regulations* implementing it. It is an offence to import or export anything listed in *Schedule 1*, covering animals and birds, or *Schedule 2*, covering plants [*Endangered Species (Import and Export) Act 1976, s 1*], except where appropriate import and export licences have been obtained (in the UK the relevant authority is the DoE). It is also an offence to sell, or advertise for sale, or have in one's possession for the purpose of sale, anything imported contrary to *section 1*, or anything listed in *Schedule 4* and *5. [Endangered Species (Import and Export) Act 1976, s 4]*. In each case the maximum penalty is a fine of £5,000 on summary conviction, or an unlimited fine or imprisonment for up to two years, or both, for conviction on indictment.

Index

Index

Index

Index

Index

Index

Index

Index

Index